VALUATION:
Principles into Practice

VALUATION:
Principles into Practice

(Third Edition)

Edited by

**W. H. REES, B.Sc., (Est. Man.) Lond. F.R.I.C.S.,
(Hon.) F.S.V.A.,**

*Honorary Member of the Rating
Surveyors' Association*

1988

THE ESTATES GAZETTE LIMITED
151 WARDOUR STREET, LONDON W1V 4BN

First Published 1980
Second Edition 1984
Third Edition 1988

ISBN 07282 0107 0

A substantial part of the authors' royalties on the sale of this book have been given to the Royal Institution of Chartered Surveyors' Benevolent Fund

Printed in Great Britain at The Bath Press, Avon

PREFACE TO THE FIRST EDITION

The numbers coming into the surveying profession reading full-time for degrees and diplomas increase year by year. Particularly, in the case of such students, it is desirable that the teaching approach should be to guide their reading rather than to dispense facts in lectures. Students following correspondence courses need to supplement these by further reading. In the subject of Valuations, beyond the intermediate stage, there is comparatively little reading matter available, other than "Modern Methods of Valuation". However, in no way does this book attempt to compete with "Modern Methods of Valuation" which covers principles, law and practice; it is intended to complement the latter. There is said by some to be a gap between the principles of valuation as taught for examinations and practice. The purpose of this book is to provide more reading matter at final year level and to bridge this gap.

The form of the book, as originally intended, was to have been a series of case studies with notes by way of explanation but during the course of preparation it became apparent that some subjects were better covered by text, hence the chapters vary widely in form. There are also wide differences of approach but in this subject there is frequently room for more than one opinion and this is a not unimportant factor of which a student should be aware. In expressing my thanks to the authors I should explain here that their opinions are confined to the chapter each has written. It is also appropriate that I should disclaim all responsibility for the views expressed. The idea of the book was mine and the choice of authors; my intention in that connection was to try to balance those engaged in teaching with those in practice, a coming together of "town and gown" which is perhaps an all too rare occurrence for the good of the valuer's profession.

I decided to draw the line at the end of November 1979 as far as legislation is concerned; thus no account is taken of the Local Government, Planning and Land Bill.

W. H. Rees, B.Sc., F.R.I.C.S.

March 1980

PREFACE TO THIRD EDITION

When it was decided to publish a third edition of this book, the opportunity was taken to extend its scope by adding chapters on "Hotels", "Leisure Properties", "Easements and Wayleaves for Sewers, Pipelines and Electricity" and "Valuations for Insurance Purposes". Again I express my thanks to their authors and to the authors of the chapters in the earlier editions for revising their texts.

The purpose of the book remains as stated in the Preface to the First Edition as do the remarks relating to the opinions of the various authors and the disclaimer as to my own views.

As far as legislation is concerned, the line was first drawn at the end of 1986 but many changes which have occurred since then have been incorporated.

W. H. Rees, B.Sc., F.R.I.C.S.

May 1987

THE AUTHORS

ix

Chapter 1

AGRICULTURAL PROPERTIES

The significant changes since the Second Edition of this book were, firstly, the passing of the Agricultural Holdings Act 1984 (The 1984 Act) and, secondly, the passing of the Agricultural Holdings Act 1986 (The 1986 Act), which came into effect on 18th March 1986. The 1986 Act came as a long overdue consolidating act bringing together in one Act much of the legislation relating to Agricultural Properties. It repeals, amongst several others, the whole of the Agricultural Holdings Act 1948, much of the Agriculture (Miscellaneous Provisions) Act 1976, the whole of the Agricultural Holdings (Notices to Quit) Act 1977 and also the 1984 Act.

Agriculture is now defined in Section 96 of the 1986 Act as well as Section 290 (i) of the Town and Country Planning Act 1971, neither of which includes the breeding or keeping of horses. Nevertheless whilst horses are not within the definition of "livestock" (unless they are kept for the sole purpose of meat production), land used for the grazing of horses can in certain circumstances properly be "agricultural" especially if such grazing is used in conjunction with a trade or business. There is clearly much ambiguity as to when the keeping and/or grazing of horses comes within the definition of agriculture (see Agricultural Tenancies—Law and Practice by C. P. Rodgers for a detailed exposition*).

The procedure for rent reviews is dealt with by Section 12 of the 1986 Act. This re-enacts Section 1 of the 1984 Act which made a fundamental change to the previous well established rent formula in that the old comparable "market rent" basis was qualified by the introduction the "productive capacity of the holding and its related earning capacity". A further point to note is that the rent payable by a Statutory Successor is no longer the "open market rent" but instead as determined by the rent formula within the 1986 Act (see Agricultural Holdings Act 1984—The Practitioners Companion by Donald Troup for a detailed exposition†).

The Agriculture (Maintenance Repair and Insurance of Fixed Equipment) Regulations (Statutory Instrument 1473 of 1973) govern the repairing liabilities of landlord and tenant where there is

---

* Butterworth & Co. Ltd (1985).
† R.I.C.S. Surveyors Publication (1984).

1

no written tenancy agreement or, where there is a written agreement, on the points where the agreement is silent.

Other statutes which affect the values of agricultural properties are Section 10 of the Land Drainage Act 1961 (as amended by Section 21 of the Agriculture (Miscellaneous Provisions) Act 1968). Section 56 and Schedule 15 of the Finance Act 1986 (which replaces Section 68 of the Capital Allowances Act 1968) provides that claims for capital expenditure can be set against income tax but must be written off over 25 years: the benefit of these allowances generally runs with the land on change of ownership; however in respect of agricultural buildings, from 1st April 1986 a taxpayer will be able to claim a balancing adjustment (unlike, for example, Industrial buildings, this adjustment is optional) when an agricultural building is demolished, destroyed or sold within the 25 year period. Tithe (as with Land Tax) is now only of historic interest with the last charge having been made on 1st October 1977 by a double payment of annuities.

Studies, numbered 1–6 inclusive and 11, are based upon a hypothetical farm with the following characteristics:

Size:	100 hectares, including the farmstead of 1 hectare. There are no woods.
Fixed equipment:	Farmhouse, cottage and adequate farm buildings (being partly traditional and partly modern) commensurate with a 100 hectare commercial farm. About three-quarters of the fields are served with mains water.
Soil and Topography:	The ground is level: the whole ploughable and the soil is a good medium to heavy loam.
Farming Policy:	Dairy and Arable. There is a milk quota of 486,000 litres.

Study 1

Valuation of freehold of a tenanted farm

1 (a) Subject to a standard agricultural tenancy
The farm is let on a full annual agricultural tenancy, with standard clauses incorporating S.I. 1473 of 1973. The tenant is in his early 40's and is married with a young family. The current rent, set several years ago, is £8,000 per annum however the landlord's agents have properly served a Notice in accordance with Section 12 of the 1986 Act so that the rent can be increased in just over 12 month's time.

The landlord must now sell the farm and you are asked to advise as to the price to be expected: the tenant is not in a position to purchase. The new rent, to be effective in one year's time, has been agreed by the landlord's and tenant's agents at £11,750 per annum. The owner's drainage rates are £150 per annum.

	£ p.a.	£ p.a.	£
Gross rent receivable		8,000	
Less:			
Repairs 12% (1)	960		
Management 18% (2)	1,440		
Insurance	450 (3)		
Owner's drainage rates	150		
	———	3,000	
Net rent		5,000	
Y.P. 1 year at 2·5% (4)		0·97	
		———	4,850
Reversion to full rental value		11,750	
Less:			
Repairs and Management 30%	3,525		
Insurance & Owner's drainage rates	600		
	———	4,125	
Net reversionary rent		7,625	
Y.P. in perp. 4·25% deferred 1 yr (5)		22·6	
		———	172,325
			£177,175

Expected price to be realised say £175,000 (6)

1 (b) Subject to an agricultural lease
Assuming that the farm was let 5 years ago on a 14-year full repairing and insuring lease with a seven-year rent review. The present rent

is £7,500 per annum and the current rental value is £10,000 per annum.

	£ p.a.	£ p.a.	£
Gross rent receivable		7,500	
Less:			
Management 15% (7)	1,125		
Owner's drainage rates	150		
	——	1,275	
Net rent		6,225	
Y.P. 2 years at 2·5% (4)		1·9	
		——	11,828
Reversion to full rental value		10,000	
Less:			
Management 15%	1,500		
Owner's drainage rates	150		
	——	1,650	
Net reversionary rent		8,350	
(7 year review)			
Y.P. 7 years at 4·5% (5)	5·89		
P.V. £1 in 2 years at			
4·5%	0·92	5·4	
	——	——	45,090
Net reversionary rent at			
end of lease		8,350	
Y.P. in perp. deferred			
9 years at 4·0% (8)		17·6	
		——	146,960
			£203,878

Expected price to be realised say £205,000

Notes

(1) This represents £9·60 per hectare per annum increasing to £14·10 per hectare per annum when the rent is raised. While in theory the volume of landlord's repairs should remain the same, in practice tenants are often more demanding when rents are raised and also, with inflation, costs continue to rise.

(2) This allows for land agents' fees and expenses plus legal and accountancy fees and V.A.T.

(3) This is based upon an insurance cover of £300,000 and includes an allowance for surveyors' and architects' fees plus debris removal.

(4) Low rates are used here as the rent is secured.

(5) Higher rates are used here as the rent has not been secured and there is therefore a higher risk element.

(6) This equates to £1,750 per hectare. Generally institutions are only interested in larger farms and accept lower yields which give rise to higher prices per hectare.

(7) Land agents' expenses are a little less since there will be no repairs to organise.

(8) Slightly lower rates are used here as inflation should make the reversionary rent at the end of the lease more secure.

Study 2

Valuation of freehold with vacant possession

The same physical factors which influence rents also affect vacant possession values, but in this case it is not necessary to assume that the purchaser will be a capable or even a prudent farmer—money is the major criterion—and the valuer's job is to assess what the market will pay, by diligent inspection of the farm itself and comparison with as many relevant transactions as possible. A useful guide to market trends may be found in the monthly returns published by the Ministry of Agriculture Fisheries & Food (in conjunction with the Country Landowners' Association) with more detail in the Farmland Market published by the Estates Gazette. Whereas at the peak of the boom in 1972–73 when most farms or large blocks of bare land in South-East England were fetching upwards of £2,500 per hectare (1), following an unprecedented rise of 150–200% in six months, the market is now much more discriminating. Following a slump in agricultural values in 1974, there has since been a steady increase up until the beginning of 1980 when prices fell back by around 20%; though by 1984 prices had risen back up to their 1979/80 level. However the recent decline in the farming industry has had a marked effect upon land prices and in the last 2 years or so these have fallen back by around 25%. Against this downward trend is a very sharp increase in the value of residential properties which in the South-East have gone up by as much as 50% in the last two years. Thus smaller farms with a good residential content may, despite falling land values, be worth more now than they were 2 years ago.

The farm might now make:

	£	£
100 hectares at £4,250 per ha		425,000
Less: Owner's drainage rates	150	
Y.P. in perp. at 4·0%	25·0	
		3,750
(2, 3 and 4)		£421,250

Notes

(1) Allowing for inflation, based upon the Retail Price Index, this equates in real terms to a current value of about £10,000 per hectare!

(2) The vacant possession value thus equates to about double the value as let. The drop in investment value from an average of two-thirds of vacant possession value in the old days of estate duty with its 45% relief for all agricultural properties may be blamed on the introduction of Capital Transfer Tax in 1974 with relief restricted to occupiers as opposed to landlords: but this disadvantage has been partly reduced by the introduction of 20% C.T.T. relief for let farms in 1981, increased to 30% in 1983. In 1986 C.T.T. became known as Inheritance Tax however the 30% relief for let farms remains.

(3) The balance of capital expenditure claim of £4,500 per annum (based on a net cost of £45,000 about 5 years ago) is available to a purchaser for another 4 years, and may influence the price to a certain degree, particularly for high rate tax payers.

(4) When dealing with such sums it is not possible to value to the last £1,000 (valuation is a matter of opinion and not a precise science) and therefore in this instance the client may be advised that the farm should fetch a sum in the region of £420,000.

Study 3

Valuation of tenant's interest in the freehold

The vast majority of written tenancy agreements contain an absolute prohibition against assignment or subletting, and Section 6 of the 1986 Act now provides for such a clause to be incorporated in agreements when the terms are referred to arbitration. Although in some cases the tenant may only be prohibited from assigning if he fails to obtain the landlord's consent in writing, this means exactly what it says in the case of agricultural tenancies, and there is no question of inferring that such consent should not be unreasonably withheld. The demand for tenancies is such that in the few cases that occur where a tenant is allowed to sell his tenancy to a third party, he can ask a substantial sum for key money, usually included in an overall figure for a lock, stock and barrel sale to include improvements, fixtures, tenant right and other matters which he can only normally claim from his landlord at the end of his tenancy, as well as the whole of his live and dead farming stock. In such cases he is usually successful in obtaining a further hidden premium by stipulating that no deduction be made for any counterclaim for dilapidations whatsoever. Where a tenant cannot assign to a third party, however, he has no marketable interest in the freehold to value, except in the event of compulsory purchase. (See Study 5.)

The situation is completely different if the farm comes on the market for sale in view of the large gap between investment and vacant possession values. If the landlord and tenant are in equal bargaining positions, the latter may be expected to pay about 70% of vacant possession value, but in practice the tenant is more often able to secure his freehold at a relatively small margin over investment value unless it forms part of a larger estate which has a greater value undivided. Alternatively it might pay the landlord to offer a substantial sum in order to sell with possession.

Example of sale to a sitting tenant
Value of farm with vacant possession (see Study 2)   £420,000

Value of farm let on annual tenancy incorporating
S.I. 1473 of 1973 (see Study 1(a))   £175,000

£420,000 and £175,000 represent opposite extremes in this instance. Assuming the tenant has adequate funds and is in the market to purchase the farm, and both parties are in equal bargaining positions, then a figure might be struck at around £300,000. If, however, the landlord has to sell then the tenant may be able to purchase the farm at a figure very much closer to the value as let.

Alternatively, assuming the price is agreed at, say £300,000 but the tenant then finds he cannot afford to service the mortgage, he may agree to surrender part of the farm to enable the landlord to sell with vacant possession. On this 100 ha farm there is a detached block of 20 ha without buildings but which because of its prime position would fetch £3,800 per hectare (1) in the open market.

	£
Value of 20 ha with vacant possession at £3,800 per ha	76,000
Value of remainder of farm; 80 ha with vacant possession (2)	372,000
Value of farm (100 ha) with vacant possession if divided	448,000
Value of farm (100 ha) with vacant possession as a whole	420,000
Increased value as a result of splitting	£28,000

The landlord and tenant agree to share this "profit" equally, in which case the deal could work out as follows:

	£
Price originally agreed for the whole farm	300,000
Add landlord's share of profit by splitting	14,000
Value of landlord's interest on completion	£314,000

This would be made up as:

	£
Value of 20 ha with vacant possession	76,000
Price to be paid by tenant (3)	238,000
	£314,000

The calculations from the tenant's viewpoint are as follows:

	£
Value of whole farm with vacant possession	420,000
Price originally agreed	300,000
Net gain as a result of purchasing the whole farm	£120,000

	£
Value of 80 ha with vacant possession	372,000
Revised price to be paid to landlord	238,000
Net gain as a result of splitting	£134,000

In addition to the increase of £14,000 in his net gain, the average cost of the farm to the tenant will be reduced marginally from £3,000 per ha to £2,975 per ha (£238,000÷80). This should help to compensate for the fact that his profits per hectare are likely to be reduced because most of his annual fixed costs (see Study 4) will be the same on 80 hectares as they were on 100 hectares.

Notes

(1) This compares to £2,400 per ha as its intrinsic value to the whole farm (see note 2 below) and is an example of the difference frequently found in practice between wholesale and retail prices for farms. Often blocks of bare land, without any dwellings or buildings, can fetch as much per hectare, as whole farms and the smaller the area to be sold off, the greater the price per hectare. This is largely attributed to the fact that the market in which there are people with, say, £400,000 is relatively small compared to that with up to, say, £50,000 in which will be included local residents with childrens' ponies and the like, and therefore the competition is that much greater. For example, the odd single hectare may well add £10,000 to the value of a good residential property, without a paddock, and similarly smaller areas will fetch even higher prices per hectare.

(2) The value of the whole farm is £4,200 per ha, however this includes the dwellings and buildings. It is assumed that the "bare land" element values out at £2,400 per ha. This gives a residual value for the 80 ha farm of £372,000 (being £420,000 less 20 ha at £2,400 per ha).

(3) This is the balance which the tenant should pay to reconcile with the landlord's interest.

Study 4

Valuations for rent

The farm is due for a rent review and you are asked to advise as to the rent that the tenant is likely to be able to afford. You know that the tenant has a 90 cow Fresian herd, rears his own replacements and has 40 ha in a spring barley and winter wheat arable rotation. It is assumed that the tenant is of good average capability, and that the farming system is indeed "suitable to the holding".

It would be useful at this stage to quote the rent formula as detailed in Schedule 2 of the 1986 Act.

"1. (1) For the purposes of section 12 of this Act, the rent properly payable in respect of a holding shall be the rent at which the holding might reasonably be expected to be let by a prudent and willing landlord to a prudent and willing tenant, taking into account (. . . . .) all relevant factors, including (in every case) the terms of the tenancy (including those relating to rent), the character and situation of the holding (including the locality in which it is situated), the productive capacity of the holding and its related earning capacity, and the current level of rents for comparable lettings, ..."

In essence the two main methods for the valuer to consider are:–

A. *The current level of rents of comparable holdings*
This may include a field by field valuation, suitably adjusted having regard to the terms of the tenancy agreement, fixed equipment, repairing liabilities and all other relevant factors. The 1986 Act widens the scope of rental evidence to include, lawfully, not only new lettings but also arbitration awards and rents settled by agreement.

B. *The productive capacity and the related earning capacity of the subject holding*
There are clearly a number of difficulties in interpreting the details of this clause, however, for the purpose of this book it will be taken as referring simply to the profit achievable by a competent tenant practising a system of farming suitable to the holding. In dealing with this method the valuer must take into account the inherent fertility of the soil, altitude, topography, stock carrying capacity, fixed equipment and all other relevant factors and then prepare suitable budgets.

4(a) *Rental valuation by use of comparable holdings*
As a starting point the valuer must first carefully read through the tenancy agreement (or if there is no written agreement ascertain the terms of the tenancy) and make a full and proper inspection of the farm. The valuer will then be in a position to compare the subject farm with any other farms of which he has detailed knowledge and to make proper allowances for difference in topography,

fixed equipment and anything else he feels relevant. Finally, the valuer must use his own expertise, and knowledge of the rents being paid in the district in which the farm he is valuing is located, to determine the rent payable.

For this farm a rent of £12,500 per annum (£125 per ha, £50 per acre) has been assessed based upon the evidence of Comparable Holdings.

4(b) Rental valuation using productive capacity
The cropping during a typical year is:

45 ha grass for dairy herd (1)
14 ha grass for dairy replacements (2)
20 ha spring barley
20 ha winter wheat
 1 ha dwellings and farm buildings

100

Gross margins:	£ p.a.	
90 dairy cows at £500 per cow (3)	45,000	
18 in-calf heifers at £250 per heifer	4,500	
20 ha spring barley at £360 per ha (4)	7,200	
20 ha winter wheat at £510 per ha (5)	10,200	
Total gross margin of farm		66,900
Less: Fixed costs:		
Labour (6)	18,000	
Machinery (7)	21,100	
Interest charges (8)	6,000	
Miscellaneous (9)	5,000	
Total fixed costs of farm		50,100
Gross profit per annum before rent		£16,800

A reasonable split of the gross profit is around 55% to the landlord and 45% to the tenant which in this example would give a rent of £9,240 per annum.

4(c) What rent is payable?
It is clearly evident that the rent assessed by the Comparable Holdings and by the Productive Capacity methods can be at substantial variance. At the time of writing the farming industry is going through

a difficult period and this is having a marked effect upon profits which explains the relatively low rent derived from the Productive Capacity method.

The 1986 Act does not specify which method carries the greater "weight", however, in my opinion the evidence of genuine comparables is very strong. Thus it will be up to both the landlord's and the tenant's valuers to argue their respective cases to try to arrive at a settlement. In default of agreement the matter will almost certainly go to arbitration and the arbitrator having listened to all the evidence shall make his award.

For the purpose of this exercise it is assumed that the rent determined is £11,500 per annum.

4(d) The effect of a "tender" on rent

Assume that the same farm is up for letting by tender and a prospective tenant asks your advice as to the rent to tender. He tells you that his farming policy will be as described in Study 4(a).

Anticipated gross profit before rent £16,800.

When dealing with a "tender" rent it must be borne in mind that there will be considerable competition, since, at present, the number of farms on the market to let are exceedingly scarce when compared to the number of prospective tenants. Though there will be no "premium" paid as such, in practice a prospective tenant must be prepared to make only a small profit in the initial years. Assuming the rent is reviewed after three years, the percentage by which a landlord will be able to increase the rent is likely to be low since the initial rent was so high. Care must be taken, however, not to put in a tender that cannot be fully justified by realistic costings.

Despite the strong competition that still exists for new tenancies, in my experience, the current difficulties within the farming industry has meant that prospective tenants are no longer prepared (or able) to bid the excessive rents that until only recently have been tendered but instead are making offers that more closely relate to "sitting tenant" rents. Landlords are also re-adjusting to these changed circumstances and now look in greater depth at the ability and character of applicants and are not so influenced by just the highest tenders: indeed more often landlords are now quoting fixed rents and applicants are judged purely on merit.

The prospective tenant might be advised to tender £13,000 for the farm. This represents about 71% of the gross profit and would only leave the tenant less than £4,000 to pay for rates, and any other contingencies to allow for fluctuations in the market—also for reinvestment; this would be in addition to the £7,000 for his own labour (6).

Notes

(1) Stocking rate assumed to be 2·0 cows per hectare.
(2) Based upon a 20% herd replacement per annum and 1·4 livestock units (heifer, yearling and calf) per cow. This equates to 12·6 ha required. However, for this example it is assumed that 14 ha will be utilised.
(3) Based on 5,400 litres per cow at 15·5 pence per litre.
(4) A yield of 5·0 tonnes per hectare is assumed and at £102 per tonne.
(5) A yield of 7·0 tonnes per hectare is assumed and at £106 per tonne.
(6) A labour force of three is assumed and that earnings, including overtime, will be: dairy cowman £8,000; pre-college student (for 9 months) £3,000 and the tenant's own labour at £7,000.
(7) Assuming repairs, fuel vehicle oil, tax etc. at £115 per hectare and depreciation based on 12% on a capital investment of £80,000.
(8) This is based on the money for the tenant's working capital of £26,000 and the historic cost of the dairy herd (and followers) at £24,000 being financed at 12% interest.
(9) This sum allows for the purchase of materials for property maintenance, insurance, professional fees and general office expenses.

Study 5

Valuations following a compulsory purchase order for a motorway

The basis of valuation for agricultural holdings is largely governed by Section 48 of the Land Compensation Act 1973. Motorway claims are extremely involved and the items of claim can be very diverse. However, the main heads of claim are: compensation for the value of the land taken, severance, injurious affection and disturbance. The examples given do not pretend to be exhaustive, but merely to highlight the more common claims that arise.

Claims for compensation resulting from the acquisition of land for a trunk road, or any other highway improvement, are very similar to that for motorways. However, one important difference is that whereas with motorways the acquiring authority erect and maintain the roadside fence, in all other highway improvement schemes the acquiring authority will usually erect the new roadside fence but the onus of future maintenance and replacement falls upon the claimant. Therefore it is essential that adequate provision is made in a claim to cover such fencing costs (1).

In each of the examples the farm has had 10 ha compulsorily purchased with the result that 5 ha has been severed. The farming policy is the same as detailed in Study 4.

5(a) The Owner-occupier's claim

		£
(a)	Value of land taken:	
	(i) 10 ha compulsorily purchased	
	(ii) 5 ha severed (2)	
	Total 15 ha at £2,400 per ha (3)	36,000
(b)	Injurious affection (4)	25,000
(c)	Temporary disturbance(s) (5)	9,000
(d)	Payment that would normally be made by a purchaser (6)	2,500
	Total of Owner-occupier's claim (7)	£72,500

5(b) The Landlord's claim

		£
(a)	Value of land taken: Total 15 ha (see 5(a) above) at £1,400 per ha (8)	21,000
(b)	Injurious affection (9)	12,000
(c)	Other matters (10)	2,000
	Total of Landlord's claim	£35,000

5(c) The Tenant's claim

(a)	Tenant's interest in the land (11)			500
(b)	Disturbance and other matters not directly based on the value of the land.			
	(i) Loss of profits on 15 ha	2,100	(12)	
	Loss of profits on remaining 85 ha	1,000	(13)	
		3,100		
	Y.P. 30 years at 20% (14)	4·98		15,438
	(ii) Temporary disturbance (5)	7,500		

		B/F	15,938
(iii) Payment that would normally be made by an incoming tenant (6)	2,500		
	———		10,000
			25,938
(c) Deduct 4 years rent at £85 per ha (15)			5,100
			20,838
(d) Add 4 years rent (16)			5,100
Total of Tenant's claim			£25,938

Rider to 5(c)
Another method of calculating the tenant's claim is to take half the difference between the vacant possession value and the investment value, instead of capitalising the profits.

	£
(a) Half the difference between vacant possession and investment values (17)	7,500
(b) Temporary disturbance	7,500
(c) Payment that would normally be made by an incoming tenant	2,500
	17,500
(d) Deduct 4 years' rent	5,100
	12,400
(e) Add 4 years' rent	5,100
Total of tenant's claim	£17,500

In this example there is a clear advantage with the "profits valuation" method and this would be the one adopted in negotiating the tenant's claim.

Notes

(1) An interesting case, highlighting many of the potential claim items is *Cuthbert* v. *Secretary of State for the Environment* (1979) 252 E.G. 921.

(2) This assumes the acquiring authority have accepted the owner's notice under Section 53 of the Land Compensation Act 1973 and will purchase the severed land.

(3) Bare land value taken at £2,400 per ha: see note (1) study 3.

(4) Reduction in the capital value of the remainder of the farm principally as a result of the proximity of the motorway to the farmstead. Another way of assessing this figure is the "before and after" method. For example:

Value of 85 ha farm in no scheme world, say	385,000
Value of 85 ha farm with adjoining motorway	360,000
	£25,000

(5) The claims under this head can be very diverse and include, inter alia, the cost of rearranging field boundaries, water supplies, drainage, electricity supplies, additional cost of carrying out normal farming operations during the construction, removal of stores and fixtures from the acquired land, professional fees and expenses including making a record of state on entry and arranging accommodation works. There could be many others but in this claim it is assumed the items will total £9,000, in respect of the owner-occupier and a little less, say £7,500 in respect of the tenant.

(6) This is in respect of all tenant right and other matters that an incoming tenant or purchaser would normally pay to an outgoing tenant or vendor over and above the agreed purchase price, for example the value of new-sown leys.

(7) Assume no claim for farm loss payment under Section 34 of the Land Compensation Act 1973.

(8) See Study 1(a), note 6: also Study 3 note 1. The value per ha of the bare land will be lower than the value per ha of the whole farm, however the reduction in value will not be as significant as with a vacant possession farm.

(9) The principle is similar to note (4) above. However, the figure could be calculated by capitalizing the reduced rental value and sporting rights of the farm.

(10) This will be largely for professional fees and expenses.

(11) See Study 3-a nominal figure to cover the hope of purchasing one day as sitting tenant. If, however, the tenant had an assignable tenancy then the value of this could be as much as £500 per ha.

(12) Loss of profits on land taken, say 7·5 ha winter wheat and 7·5 ha spring barley. See Study 4(b) but assume this to be average of last 3 years.

	£ per ha	£ per ha
Gross margin on barley	360	
Gross margin on wheat	510	
Average gross margin		435
Less: Rent (allowance made for dwellings, etc.)	85	
Acts of Husbandry	135	
Interest on tenant's capital	35	
Fluctuation risk	40	
		295
Net profit		140
Hectares acquired		15
		£2,100

(13) Largely as a result of increased fixed costs per ha. due to reduction in area. Estimated at £1,000.
(14) Life expectancy of male aged 42 is 30 years. For interest rate see exposition in *Wakerly and another* v. *St. Edmundsbury Borough Council* (1977) 241 E.G. 921, L.T., and (1979) 249 E.G. 639, C.A. (relevant date 1973). However since the relevant date the introduction of possible succession of tenancy under Sections 16–24 of the Agriculture (Miscellaneous Provisions) Act 1976 (the whole of this Act has now been repealed however these provisions are re-enacted within the 1986 Act) may have the effect of slightly reducing the interest rate.
(15) Deducted to avoid double payment—Section 48 (5) Land Compensation Act 1973.
(16) Added separately as this is a tax-free supplemental payment under Section 12 of the Agriculture (Miscellaneous Provisions) Act 1968, as amended by Schedule 14, clause 44 of the 1986 Act.
(17) Vacant possession value per ha (see note 3, above)   £2,400
    Investment value per ha (see note 8, above)   1,400

    The difference   £1,000

Half the difference = £500 per ha multiplied by 15 ha = £7,500.

Study 6

Surface damage claim following the laying of a water main etc.

A local authority has powers under the Public Health Act 1936 to enter, having given reasonable notice of its intention to the owner and occupier, land including farms to lay a water main or a sewer. The Pipelines Act 1962 provides for compulsory powers to lay private pipelines. Under both these Acts there are provisions for paying compensation to owners and occupiers and claims arising are often collectively referred to as "pipe-line claims". Capital payments for "easements" and wayleaves are an entirely separate matter and are dealt with in Chapter 20.

Example of a surface damage claim
Assume that a water authority has laid a 300 mm diameter water main across the farm at an average depth of 2 metres and for which they used a 15 metre working strip which they fenced off. The contractors commenced work in June and left the farm in October of year one. The claim could be as follows:

Part A: Loss of profits
(1) Year one
     (a) Field No. 4: 12·0 ha: grass
          (i) Loss of 2nd hay cut on working

		£	£
strip:			
1·0 ha 3·0 tonnes per ha at £45 per tonne		135·00	
Deduct saving in hay making costs at £50 per ha		50·00	
			85·00
(ii) Loss of second hay cut on severed land (1)			
0·6 ha at net £85 per ha			51·00
(b) Field No. 7: 6·0 ha: spring barley			
(i) Loss of spring barley on working strip:			
0·5 ha at 5·0 tonnes per ha at £102 per tonne		255·0	
Deduct saving in harvesting costs at £44 per ha		22·00	
			233·00

	B/F	369·00
(ii) Increased cost of harvesting rest of field (2) 5·5 ha at £20 per ha		110·00
(c) Field No. 8: 8·0 ha: winter wheat		
(i) Loss of winter wheat on working strip: 0·6 ha at 7·0 tonnes per ha at £106 per tonne	445·20	
Deduct saving in harvesting costs at £48 per ha (3)	28·80	
		416·40
(ii) Increased cost of harvesting rest of field at 7·4 ha at £8 per ha (4)		59·20
(2) Year two and onwards (5)		600·00
	(6)	1,554·60

Part B

(1) Cost of reseeding working strip in field No. 4 1·0 ha at £250 per ha (7)		250·00
(2) Cost of spreading 35 tonnes per ha of farmyard manure over 0·7 ha (8) at £8 per tonne		196·00
(3) Cost of reinstating water supply in field No. 4 (9)		80·00
(4) General inconvenience and disturbance (10)		75·00
Total claim (11)		£2155·60

E. & O.E. (12)

Notes

(1) It is often the case that a corner of a field gets cut off by the fence erected for the working strip, and unless there is alternative access, loss of crops on the severed land will be inevitable.

(2) The fenced off working strip will often result in the splitting of a field into two awkward shapes which will be more costly to work per ha than the field as a single unit.

(3) Harvesting costs are slightly more due to the additional yield of the wheat over the barley, giving rise to, inter alia, higher carting costs.

(4) The division of the field is not as severe as with Field No. 7, and therefore harvesting costs are only marginally increased.

(5) Depending on the type of soil, the area through which the pipe was laid may take up to 5 years (or longer if land drains have been damaged) to recover and give a virtual 100% yield. Therefore an allowance for the reduced yield in future years should be made. This can either be an estimated amount agreed in year one, or else a site inspection with the authority's valuer can be made each year until it is agreed that there is no longer any quantifiable loss. In this example it is assumed that the estimated loss, based upon anticipated future cropping, is calculated and the figure arrived at is £600.

(6) No allowance for loss of straw has been made, since it is assumed that the value of the straw lost will be offset by the cost of baling and carting. It would, however, be quite correct to include the net loss in the value of straw as a separate item, should this be advantageous to the claimant.

(7) This figure takes into account the extra cost of reseeding a long narrow strip over that of an average sized field.

(8) The laying of a "pipeline" will inevitably damage the soil structure along the trenchline and immediate area adjoining it. One way to help restore the soil texture, and thus mitigate a claim for future loss of crops, is to spread a heavy dressing of farmyard manure on the affected area and plough this in when carrying out cultivations for the next crop. Assume: working strip 1,400 metres long and width of affected area 5·0 metres: area to be spread with farmyard manure 0·7 ha.

(9) There are a multitude of claims that could arise on the laying of a "pipeline". Examples are: cattle straying due to contractors leaving field gates open; damage to standing timber; damage to gates, fences, hedges etc.; damage to land drains. In this study it is assumed that the water supply to field No. 4 was damaged during the construction period and had to be reinstated.

(10) This makes an allowance for the time spent by the occupier in having to reorganise his stocking, cropping or harvesting schedules, site inspections and so on.

(11) The valuer should also reserve the right to claim his fees (plus the cost of preparing a record of condition if applicable), and travelling expenses when the claim has been agreed. Also the right to make any further claims for loss of profits etc., arising from future subsidence or damage to land drainage, if attributable to the laying of the "pipeline", should be reserved at this stage.

(12) This stands for "Errors and Omissions Excepted" and should always be added at the foot of a Claim.

Study 7

Valuation of cottages and other dwellings

The same principles of valuation as set out in Chapter 2 of this book apply equally in the country as in the town, but with the passing of the Rent (Agriculture) Act 1976 which deals with the formerly tied agricultural worker's cottage, the position is now even more complex. With the reduction in the number of farm workers since the war, a good proportion of farm cottages as well as those formerly occupied by estate workers are now surplus to requirements. Take the case of a typical three bedroom semi-detached country cottage with all the basic amenities in an attractive situation, which might be sold off in the open market when it comes empty for say £80,000. If occupied, however, the position is completely different, and the value will depend very much on the status of the occupier, as well as his age and family who may be potential successors to his tenancy. If the cottage had become surplus to the farmer's needs some years ago, and he had let it to a tenant who claimed security under the Rent Acts, the value might well be reduced to say £45,000. If the farmer still has an employee in occupation working on the farm, and decides to sell he may well find that his employee prefers to stay on in his old home and that it is not possible to obtain a certificate from the Agricultural Dwelling House Advisory Committee which will enable him to apply to the local authority to rehouse him. In this case an application to the Rent Officer for the Registration of a Fair Rent may be the best answer, and the cottage will fall to be valued on the same lines as an ordinary Rent Act tenancy, except that the prospect of obtaining possession may be slightly less remote for various reasons, including the provision for one statutory successor to the tenancy as opposed to two under the Rent Acts. This might increase the value to say £50,000.

If the same cottage is occupied by persons who for one reason or another cannot claim security of tenure—they might be paying no rent at all or a nominal amount under two-thirds of the rateable value on the appropriate day (1) exclusive of rates and water or they might be service occupiers outside the scope of the Rent (Agriculture) Act—the value should be much closer to the vacant possession price. A purchaser would expect to discount this to allow for the risk and cost of obtaining and enforcing a court order for possession, he should allow upwards of six months to be safe, and with interest on his capital outlay, the value might be of the order of £65,000 or so.

The foregoing remarks all presuppose the fact that the cottage was built prior to the passing of the Town and Country Planning Act 1947 or that there are no enforceable conditions in a subsequent planning permission restricting the occupation to agricultural workers or such like (2). In this event, the market will be considerably restricted: for example, if the cottage only has a garden and no other land, purchasers may be limited to a local farmer or woodland owner or possibly a retired farmer, and the value may be reduced by half or even more as planning authorities are very reluctant to remove such conditions, and only rarely do appeals to the Secretary of State for the Environment succeed (3). Thus the property may prove virtually unsaleable except to someone prepared to take a gamble that he will not be served with an enforcement order for non-compliance by the local authority. On the other hand if the dwelling has sufficient land to justify the purchaser being engaged full time in agriculture or forestry, the discount from full vacant possession value will be less. The value of the cottage referred to above, subject to such a condition, may therefore range from about £50,000 to possibly £70,000 or so, excluding the extra land and any buildings. The valuer must carefully consider all the circumstances and having taken legal advice if necessary on the enforceability of the condition form his opinion as to the saleability of the property.

Notes

(1) The appropriate day is usually the 23rd March, 1965. See Section 25 of the Rent Act 1977.

(2) The usual agricultural occupancy condition which has been imposed by planning authorities since the early 1960's, now reads to the effect: "The occupation of the dwelling shall be limited to a person wholly employed or last employed locally in agriculture as defined in Section 290(1) of the Town and Country Planning Act 1971, or forestry, or a dependent of such person residing with him (but including a widow or widower of such a person)". Some earlier conditions proved to be unenforceable but may still prove a considerable deterrent to purchasers.

(3) It is very rare for a local authority to agree to the removal of an agricultural occupancy condition and those that are lifted are usually as a result of a successful appeal to the Secretary of State: however a very good case has to be presented to stand any chance of success and in most cases appeals are dismissed. Instances where appeals have been successful are, for example,

where most of the farmland has for genuine reasons been sold leaving just the dwelling and a few acres that is no longer a viable unit which has made the dwelling nearly unsaleable and the owner has proved that he has suffered hardship as a result of this.

Study 8

Valuation on woodlands

Although the introduction of Capital Transfer Tax (C.T.T.) in 1974 put a stop to the "death-bed" purchaser (by removing most of the advantages of investment in woodlands to mitigate estate duty, by means of the 45% relief on the land and the non-aggregation of the value of the timber to the value of the estate, thus reducing the rate of duty), nevertheless there are still considerable attractions, particularly to high-rate tax payers. These, inter alia, are firstly there is no Capital Gains Tax payable on timber: (however a profit on the sale of the land itself is liable to C.G.T.): secondly, it is still possible to elect to be taxed under Schedule D and claim to set the cost of establishment (including planting) and maintenance against other income: thirdly, Section 125 of the Capital Transfer Tax Act 1984 provides (subject to certain criteria being met) that the value of growing trees are excluded from the value of an estate on the transfer on death if an election is made within two years of death; however if the growing trees are sold before another death on which no election is made C.T.T. (now Inheritance Tax) becomes chargeable. Furthermore for sales after 26th October 1977 the value chargeable may be reduced by 50% if business property relief would have been granted at the time of death.

The valuation of timber and plantations is the domain of relatively few specialists, and although a timber valuation may be obtained and the prairie or site value of the freehold ascertained having regard to its situation, growing potential and other amenities, the market value of the woodland may well be considerably less than the prairie and timber valuations combined. This is because of the need to obtain a licence from the Forestry Commission for any substantial felling which they must refer to the local planning authority, and felling licences usually stipulate that an equivalent area of woodland be replanted, which at upwards of £1,500 per hectare, depending on fencing, draining and other costs, will bite deeply into the value of the timber. Furthermore some of the timber may not be ready for felling, and its growth rate to maturity will be much lower than the cost of financing the purchase.

8(a) Valuation of a 40 hectare wood for sale
The wood comprises typical oak standards of mixed ages from 50 years to
maturity over an under-storey of overgrown hazel and hornbeam coppice.

	£
Prairie value of freehold, including coppice 40 ha at £600 per ha	24,000
Timber valuation (averaging £3,750 per ha)	150,000
	174,000
Deduct allowance for cost of complying with likely felling licence condition to replant proportion of area, deferment of income (it is most unlikely that a licence to clearfell will be granted) marketing and other expenses, say	84,000
Value of wood for sale (averaging £2,450 per ha)	90,000 (1)

To this may be added the value of any sporting rights if these
are to be included in the sale (see Study 9).

8(b) Valuation of a Commercial Plantation
The valuation of plantations is even more complex than that of
established woodlands. If the estate you have been instructed to
value contains a commercial plantation, you may well seek the assistance of a specialist valuer who will produce the following type
of report which you have to interpret to your client.

Compartment description & Valuation—20 hectares

Cpt.	Area ha	Species	P.Yr	B.H.D.	Top ht.	Vol.	Y.C.	Remarks	Value £
W	5	SP	62	15	11·0	1540	12	Brashed; good vigour first thinning due within next 5 years	6,545
X	5	JL	63	17	14·4	2100	12	Brashed; nice well-grown plantation. Has had first thinning	12,600
Y	6	0	67	—	—	—	—	Poor growth; mainly of amenity value only	3,400
Z	4	DF	73	—	8·5	—	20	Patchy but very good vigour	3,450
	20								£25,995

Estimated value of standing timber, say £26,000

The report may be explained by the following brief notes:

Compartment: Each compartment must have a name, number or letter by which it can be readily identified.

Species: Abbreviations are often used: e.g. SP—Scots Pine; DF—Douglas Fir: JL—Japanese Larch: O—Oak, etc. etc.

Planting Year (P.Yr): This is the year in which the seedling was planted; e.g. P.56 means the trees were planted in the forestry year of 1956 which runs from 1.10.55 to 30.9.56.

Breast Height Diameter: This is the diameter, in centimetres, of a tree at breast height (usually taken at 1·3 metres from the ground). By measuring the B.H.D. of every tree in a sample plot, of say 0·1 hectare, the average B.H.D. of the compartment can be estimated.

The minimum size measured is 10 c.m. In the example compartments Y and Z were below 10 c.m. and therefore no B.H.D. was recorded.

Top Height: This is the average height, in metres, of the 100 trees with the largest B.H.D. per hectare. Though these trees will normally be the dominants they will not necessarily be the tallest.

Volume: This is expressed in cubic metres and is arrived at by knowing the Top Height and B.H.D. of the stand. In the example no volume is shown for compartments Y and Z since their B.H.D.s were less than 10 c.m. and therefore they had no marketable timber volume.

Yield Class: (Y.C.): This is ascertained by knowing both the Top Height and the age of the stand. Very broadly this tells you the rate of growth of the stand and is also a very useful guide in the planning of your thinning cycle and when to take the final crop.

Valuation of plantation:

	£
Value of standing timber	26,000
21 ha of land with good roadways for timber extraction at £750 per ha	15,750
Workshed, sporting etc. say	2,250
Value of plantation	£44,000

Notes

(1) This figure could be arrived at as follows:

			£
Assume a felling licence granted for 60% of timber, i.e. £150,000 × 60%			90,000
Less: Deferment of income for 8 months at 12%		say	7,200
			82,800

		£	
Add: Value of residual timber		£60,000	
But not realisable for say 40 years, therefore: P.V. £1 at 5% 40 years		0·14	8,400
	say		91,200

Deduct:

Replanting costs on, say 14 ha (N.B. though 60% of the timber is to be felled the replanting conditions are unlikely to be 60% of 40 ha) at £1,500 per ha		21,000	
General marketing expenses	say	4,200	
			25,200
			66,000
Add: Prairie value of freehold			24,000
	Value of wood		£90,000

Study 9

Valuation of sporting rights

Whilst the cost of a whole gun in a good syndicate has risen to around £2,000 or more a year as a result of the escalating cost of keepering, rearing pheasants and all other expenses, the market for shooting rights is supported by an increasing demand for a day's or week's sport. A favourably situated estate with a reasonable spread of woodland may thus command a rent of £6 or so per hectare, with extra for a cottage, often with the tenant paying the rates as well. The shooting rights on individual farms with possession are nearly always included in the valuation of the freehold, however, there is no shortage of applicants for "rough shoots" at around £4 per hectare, and deer shooting may bring in another £1 or so a hectare if they are present in adequate numbers. The same applies to fishing rights over all kinds of water, and the value can vary enormously according to the quarry and the location; for example, a well-stocked trout pond might command anything from £50 to £500 per rod per person.

Ten year's purchase is the traditional figure for sporting rights, but as with all investments this can vary both up and down according to the degree of security.

Section 20 of the 1986 Act gives a farm tenant the right to claim compensation from his landlord in respect of damage to his crops by wild animals or birds which he is not entitled to kill himself. Wild animals does not include ground game, such as rabbits and hares, since the tenant is entitled by the Ground Game Act 1880, as amended by the Ground Game (Amendment) Act 1906, to kill all ground game.

Study 10

Other assets of a country estate

Many country estates boast a large house or mansion, the value of which may depend very largely on its suitability, and the availability of planning consent, for other uses. For example, the splitting into a number of flats, maisonettes or houses, or the conversion to some sort of institutional use or even offices. Apart from estate and farm cottages (see Study 7) there may be one or more substantial houses let off which fall to be valued as residential investments (see Chapter 2), unless the rateable value is over £750 (outside Greater London Council area) with the end of the tenancy and vacant possession in sight. Even if not, the most likely purchaser will often be the tenant.

Other assets may include the odd inn, shop and even office, the estate workshop or sawmill, garages and other buildings all of which may find a variety of uses if vacant, subject to planning control. Less tangible items may include minerals, licences for rights of way, encroachments on manorial waste and electricity and telephone wayleaves. Such rentals may command a value of up to ten years' purchase, depending on the degree of security, but in the case of private licences it may well pay to negotiate a capital payment if possible which should have regard to the enhanced value of their property.

Study 11 (1)

Valuation resulting from the transfer of capital

There have been considerable changes in the highly complex provisions for relief on agricultural assets since Capital Transfer Tax (C.T.T.) was first introduced on life-time gifts in March 1974 and transfers on death a year later. The Finance Act 1981 (as amended by the Capital Transfer Tax Act 1984) effectively replaced the full-time working farmer and business property reliefs in respect of transfers of agricultural property made after 9th March 1981.

On 18th March 1986 C.T.T. was re-named as Inheritance Tax (I.T.). This new tax is essentially the same as the former C.T.T. except that tax on a lifetime transfer has been abolished (subject to a tapering scale over 7 years) and a number of other more minor amendments have been introduced. All reliefs and exemptions that applied prior to 18th March 1986 will continue to apply under the new I.T.

Agricultural property relief (see C.T.T. Act 1984, Sections 115/124 and 169) at 50% is now automatically available (within limits) on agricultural land, ancillary woodland, appropriate farm buildings, cottages and houses; also on controlling shares in farming or land-owning companies for farmers who have been farming the land for the previous two years; also for land-owners who have owned the land for the previous seven years and have the right to obtain vacant possession within twelve months of the date of transfer (i.e. the land may be occupied on a grazing licence or the owner may have served a valid Notice to Quit not contested by the tenant). A partner in a farming partnership is treated as occupying the land to the extent of any interest of his in the land (even where the partnership farms under a tenancy from one or more of the partners).

In other cases, such as tenanted farms, relief was made available at 20%, but increased to 30% from 15th March 1983 by the Finance (No. 2) Act 1983, again subject to the seven-year ownership test. There are special provisions for replacement of property, substitute owner/occupiers and special tests in respect of shares in companies.

Relief is confined to the agricultural value of the property only and thus excludes any development value.

Business Property Relief, introduced in 1976, is now covered by Sections 103/114 of the C.T.T. Act 1984. It is available on all business assets including land, buildings, live and dead farming stock and all other assets of a farming enterprise provided (and with only a very few exceptions) the property was owned for a period of two years prior to the date of transfer.

For further details of taxes relating to land ownership and agriculture generally the reader is recommended to "Taxation to Farmers and Landowners" by Oliver Stanley M.A.* and also Smiths Taxation 1986–87†.

Study 11(a)
Assume Inheritance Tax falls to be assessed on the farm on the death of the owner/occupier who satisfies the rules for Agricultural and Business Property Reliefs.

The valuation is as follows:

	£	£
100 ha of freehold farm at £4,200 per ha (2)		420,000
Agricultural Property Relief at 50%	210,000	
Dairy Herd and followers (3)		64,000
Plant and Machinery (4)		50,000
Homegrown and purchased stores, crops and tenant right		16,000
Business Property Relief at 50%	65,000	
Total Value of transfer		550,000
less total amount of reliefs		275,000
		£275,000

Study 11(b)
If, however, the transferor had let the land to a partnership in which he has a share (say 55%), or to a company in which he has a controlling interest, then the valuation is as follows:

	£	£
100 ha freehold tenanted land (5)		175,000
Agricultural Property Relief (6)	71,750	
Transferor's share of partnership assets (7)		71,500

* Butterworth & Co. Ltd. (1981)
† Lofthouse Publications (1986)

		B/F 246,500
Business Property Relief at 50%	35,750	
Total value of transfer		246,500
Less: Total amount of reliefs		107,500
Chargeable transfer		£139,000

Rider to examples above

Assuming that the transferor died with no other assets then the Inheritance Tax payable (year 1986/1987) on the chargeable transfer would be as follows:

11(a) Chargeable transfer £275,000: I.T. £87,400
11(b) Chargeable transfer £139,000: I.T. £23,100

Capital Gains Tax will generally also arise on life-time transfers, however, provided the parties agree and are all U.K. residents for tax purposes, the C.G.T. liability can be postponed until the donee sells the land.

Notes

(1) I should like to record my thanks to Mr G. R. Williams, Chief Taxation Adviser to the C.L.A., who very kindly checked through this Study.
(2) See Study 2.
(3) This is not the historic cost of the livestock but the market value as at the date of death. In this example all the livestock has been valued at £64,000.
(4) Here we must use the current market value which throws up a much lower figure than that used in study 4a (note 7) which was based upon a replacement cost basis.
(5) See Study 1(a).
(6) This will be at 50% in respect of the proportion (55%) which the transferor has a partnership and is "occupying" the land and 30% on the balance being the "let farm" proportion.
   i.e.: £175,000 × 55% at 50% = £48,125
        £175,000 × 45% at 30% = £23,625
(7) Total assets, other than freehold land, £130,000—see 11(a), assuming a 55% share, thus giving £71,500.

Study 12

The insurance of agricultural properties

While insurance premiums are not universally considered to be a necessary expense, it is essential for a landowner to realise the implications of not being fully covered, so that he can then decide to what extent he is prepared to carry the risks himself.

In general terms a landowner requires two types of insurance, firstly against damage to his property, and secondly against injury to other people. Examples of the former are fire, storm, flood, aircraft, explosion and of increasing importance settlement of buildings. The latter can be broadly divided into public liability (e.g. against a claim resulting from a tree falling across a highway and causing an accident, or a chimney pot blowing off and injuring a passer-by) and employers' liability (against an employee being injured on your property in the course of his duties). The owner of our hypothetical 100 ha farm might be covered for £500,000 for public liability and £250,000 for employers' liability. However with the Courts awarding ever-increasing levels of compensation many insurance companies are advocating substantially greater levels of cover.

Before deciding what cover is required to insure a building against fire and similar risks, it is first necessary to assess the full cost of reinstating the building to its original condition, making allowances for debris removal, professional and local authority fees, etc. The most common and simplest method is to measure the external area of the building and multiply by a rate per square metre.

For example a modern detached house of 150 m² in very good condition might cost £450 per m² to build, compared with £400 per m² for a 1930s semi-detached farmworker's cottage of 105 m² in basic order. Again an open-sided steel-framed dutch barn might cost £40 per m² against £85 per m² for a fully-enclosed steel-framed cattle yard.

Alternatively a building might be insured on an "indemnity" basis. Thus in the event of a loss the insured would receive an amount equal to the depreciation of the holding. For example a run-down detached house in one acre might be worth £120,000, however after a total loss the site value of the land with a building plot could be £80,000, and the loss suffered therefore £40,000 which would be the amount paid. Clearly this sum is totally inadequate to rebuild and therefore careful consideration must be given to which type of cover is to be taken; an important factor will be whether or not it is proposed to rebuild in the event of a total loss.

Virtually all fire policies incorporate an "average" clause, under which if the cover proves inadequate the insurers will only pay a proportion of the loss in the event of damage to any part of the building. Thus if a building costing £60,000 to rebuild is only covered for £36,000 (60%), and there is damage costing say £12,000 to repair, then the insurers will only pay 60%, i.e. £7,200 in this instance, and the owner will have to pay the balance out of his own pocket. It is therefore important to arrange adequate cover initially and ensure this is regularly revised. Many companies now operate policies that are index-linked so that the cover is increased automatically each year in line with building costs.

Difficulties can arise over old traditionally constructed farm buildings where the costs of reinstatement of the original timber frame, clad with weatherboarding under a tiled roof, can often be nearly ten times that of a much more convenient modern building, and where an average clause would normally apply in the event of partial loss when cover is restricted to the cost of replacement in modern materials. It is often possible to insure on a "first loss" basis with payment in full up to the agreed cover in return for an increased premium reflecting a proportion of the full declared replacement cost. This would not be appropriate where an owner wishes to reinstate certain buildings to their original condition, or where they are listed as being of special architectural or historical interest, when the local authority has power to enforce full reinstatement in the event of a partial loss.

Further Reading

Chapter 21, "Valuations for Insurance Purposes".
"Property Insurance", a 32 page booklet published by the R.I.C.S. in 1978 is recommended for further reading, together with their Building Cost Information Service annual reports.

© P. J. C. Stone, 1988

Chapter 2

RESIDENTIAL PROPERTIES

The Rent Acts and taxation have in general removed residential property into a category of its own, with a valuation approach entirely different from other types of property. There are two separate and distinct markets, purchase and rental, and there is no direct correlation between them. All valuations must be carried out with an eye on the vacant possession value and, except in the very rarest cases, this is the maximum value which can be put on a property no matter how high or how low a yield this would seem to give.

The Rent Act 1977 (as amended by the Housing Act 1980) is the principal Act giving security of tenure to tenants and limiting the rent payable in respect of residential property, whether furnished or unfurnished (provided the letting comes within the ambit of the Act). There are several types of tenancy under the Act, viz:

(1) Regulated
(2) Secure
(3) Protected Shorthold
(4) Assured

The Rent Act rateable value limits are £1,500 in Metropolitan London and £750 elsewhere, whether furnished or unfurnished so that all but the very best houses and flats are capable of being within either rent control and/or tenants have security of tenure. It is the latter which is destructive of capital value. The legal definition of Fair Rent under the Act is a virtual guarantee that something less than the full open market rental value will be payable. Some lettings within the rateable value limits may still be outside control (e.g. where there is a large degree of service or holiday lettings).

The taxation laws, which allow interest on mortgages of up to £30,000 to be offset against income before tax, militate in favour of the purchaser and against the tenant who cannot claim a tax deduction for his rent. Thus if interest is taken at 10% on a £50,000 house, the after tax cost to a purchaser (assuming a 100% interest only mortgage) with tax at 27% would be £4,190 per annum compared with £5,000 for the tenant (assuming no repayment of capital). If they are prepared to equate their expenditure then the purchaser can pay £5,810 per annum before tax and thus the vacant possession value can be forced up to £58,100 with no

33

detrimental effect on the purchaser when compared to the tenant. In a pure market the tenant would therefore pay no more than £5,000 per annum for a house of up to £58,100 value but the investment value would only be £50,000, giving an instant loss of £8,100. This assumes the position of a standard rate taxpayer. With a top rate taxpayer, the buyer and tenant equate on a house worth £62,000 on the basis of a net payment of £5,000 p.a.

It can be seen from the above that for all property which is saleable with vacant possession to an owner-occupier the valuation approach must be geared to the differential between the vacant and investment values and must thus be principally concerned with marriage values, since, if the aforementioned property was let at £5,000 per annum, a valuation of £50,000 for the investment (using, say, a 10% return) would be illogical where the vacant possession value is £58,100 because the size of the gap between the two figures (i.e. £8,100) is an incentive for the parties to merge their interests and share the profit. In practice, of course, the Fair Rent would be much lower than £5,000 per annum and thus the "gap" would be bigger. In fact a house in London with a vacant possession value of £58,100 would command a Fair Rent of only £1,500 p.a. or thereabouts. Where there is no vacant possession market, entirely different considerations apply.

Properties with vacant possession value to owner-occupiers

It is not possible to set out exact limits to this category because this is a matter which has very much to do with personal taste and at its extremes includes any property capable of being lived in from a sprawling country estate to a dilapidated shack. In practice, the lending policies of the financial institutions tend to limit the compass of the category, although it does vary for different parts of the country.

Whether a property is saleable and the price it will obtain is a matter for local knowledge. An outside valuer must take extreme care when visiting an area of which he has no intimate knowledge; while there are general trends of value the specific will override the general. Accessibility, accommodation, condition and location are the main factors affecting value together with the standard of construction and the quality of the finish.

The majority of the lending societies limit their lending to post-first-world-war purpose-built houses or flats of standard brick construction in good structural condition with pitched tiled or slated roofs. Some will accept flat roofs, or flats provided by conversion, or above shops, but the more the property varies from the standard the more difficult it will be to mortgage, and therefore to sell, and therefore the lower its relative value.

Non-owner-occupier type properties

These generally comprise houses and flats in very poor repair and/or of unsatisfactory design or those too large for single family occupation or in the decaying parts of our towns and cities. Close regard must be had to local authority slum clearance schemes or in Housing Action Areas, as properties within these schemes will clearly not be mortgageable or usually saleable to an owner-occupier.

There should be few properties which cannot be transferred to the owner-occupier category after capital expenditure but there must be a sufficient life expectation (i.e. no redevelopment schemes in the immediate future) and the expenditure must be justified by an adequate increment in value. In many cases these must be considered as development propositions. In other words, a residual valuation approach must be made with allowance made for profit, finance costs, etc.

Properties with vacant possession value to owner-occupiers

Freehold properties let on a regulated unfurnished tenancy at fair rents with single tenancies

Where a property has a recently registered fair rent, there is little or no potential for rent increases unless some improvements which will be reflected in the rental value can be carried out. There is, in fact, little point in carrying out improvements since the investment benefit lies in the potential to vacant possession and not in the rental income.

Study 1

A semi-detached house in a good suburban location with a vacant possession value of £50,000 is let to a regulated tenant at £1,200 p.a. exclusive of rates (just registered)

		£	£
Rent reserved			1,200
Less: Outgoings: repairs	120		
insurance	70		
management	60		
			250

Net income   950
Y.P. in perp. at 7%   14·29
                                            ───────
                                     13,575 say £13,600
                                            ═══════   ═══════

This is the value to an investor on first view. It is of course much
too low for reasons that will follow. The value of £13,600 is the
value to an investor and not to a sitting tenant. Between the investor
and the sitting tenant there is a considerable marriage value notwithstanding the non-open market saleability of the tenant's interest.
The tenant possesses an almost permanent state of irremovability
which has the effect of preventing the real value of the property
being realised.

Study 2

Using the same information as in Study 1:

	£	£
Vacant possession value	50,000	50,000
Investor's value	13,600	
	───────	
Marriage value (MV)	36,400	
Discount to tenant say 50% of MV	×0·5	
	───────	18,200
Price to sitting tenant		£31,800

The investment valuation must now be looked at in detail, as
its yield is considerably below that possibly anticipated for what
appears to be a fairly poor investment, bearing in mind the commercial banks' Minimum Lending Rates. The disadvantages of the
investment are first, that there are landlord's outgoings which might
in some years take a large part, or even all of the income and second,
that the annual rate of growth of the income is limited as it is
not truly related to economic factors. (The new rent is determined
by a Rent Officer or Rent Assessment Committee who can be
influenced by non-economic factors.) The advantages are first, that
the income is secure since its non-payment will give vacant possession (which would be a windfall) and second, that there is a long
term rate of capital growth that far outstrips any other normal
investment.

The following shows the rise in older second-hand (over 40 years old) house values as produced by the Nationwide Building Society for the period 31st December 1970 to 31st December 1985 and the Retail Price Index (all items).

It will be seen that older second-hand houses rose in price over the twelve year period by 717% (an average annual increase of 14·03%) and the retail price index rose by 496% (11·27% per annum). According to the Nationwide Building Society the average price of this older house in Great Britain in the first quarter of 1986 was £36,820 and therefore the average price in the last quarter of 1970 was £5,073 (using the index). On the basis that the average Fair Rent in December 1970 was £250 p.a., the investment value would have been in the region of £3,000 to show a net yield of about 6½%. If vacant possession was obtained and the house sold in March 1986 the growth in value would be from £3,000 to £36,820 which is an increase of 1227% or an average annual increase of 18·19% (compound). If these figures are continued to 1987 values, the yield becomes much greater.

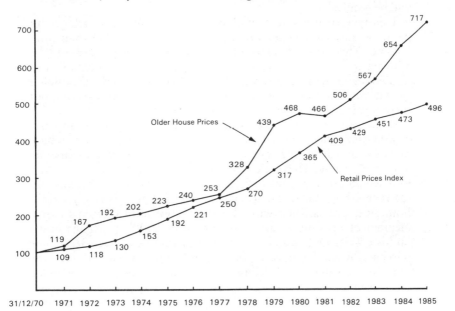

The above analysis excludes the effects of taxation and on a non-tax basis the investment shows a minimum annual yield (including the capital growth) of 25·55% p.a., minimum because there would have been a rent increase in December 1973, December 1976, December 1979, December 1982, December 1984 and December

1986 which would increase the yield in the latter periods. Allowing for capital gains tax of 30%, the capital growth would still have been 550% so that the value of the capital would have almost increased by one and a half times in real terms. It really does not matter when vacant possession is obtained because the final profit will relate to the growth of the vacant possession value and not to the actual purchase price.

This analysis depends on the possibility of obtaining vacant possession in the foreseeable future and this may be frustrated by the law which allows the tenancy to pass twice after the death of the tenants. In the majority of cases, this is more an imaginary possibility than a concrete probability because households are becoming smaller with families not living together and there is the overriding social desire to own rather than to rent a house. However, if there would seem to be little prospect of possession when the particular property is viewed, then the initial yield will have to be revised upwards or, alternatively, the percentage of vacant possession value will be reduced.

This type of investment will be of most interest to a high tax payer because its benefits flow from capital gains rather than from income. Therefore, there is little reason for the property to be allowed to fall into disrepair as any expenditure on repairs will be deductible from the rental income before tax and the higher the tax rate the lower the real cost to the investor of carrying out these repairs.

In addition to the above, there is also the prospect of an early capital gain either from sales to sitting tenants or from the purchase of possession from the tenants. Both of these operations liberate a marriage value. This is clearly shown in Study 2, where the landlord would seem to gain £18,200 from the sale to the tenant and the tenant buys his house for £18,200 less than it is really worth. Both sides are satisfied with the transaction and the tenant or a member of his family can easily obtain a 100% mortgage based on his cost as he has a real equity in the house of over 36%. The purchase by the landlord of the tenant's interest has attracted the unfortunate name of "winkling" as the tenant is seen to be "winkled out" from his shell (house) without proper payment and left with nowhere to go. This emotionalism which has political undertones emanates from the operations of a few unscrupulous owners and should not confuse the financial soundness of the process to both parties. In many cases the house is no longer suited to the tenant because he may have outgrown it or it is now too large or wrongly located. The dearth of houses to rent prevents him from moving and he may have insufficient capital to pay an adequate deposit on a new home; thus additional capital can be supplied by the landlord.

The value shown by Study 1 was said to be too low because it only represents 27·2% of the value with vacant possession. An analysis of recent auctions has shown a value of between 40% and 60%, thereby indicating a value between £20,000 and £30,000 to show net yields between 4·75% and 3·17%.

These low yields are the result of the recent rapid increase in prices with vacant possession which have not been matched by a similar rise in Fair Rents.

It is now very rare to value these properties on a yield basis. It is more usual to go direct to a percentage of capital value with vacant possession. If an investment yield of 4% had been taken in Study 1 (47·5% of VP value) the investment value would have been £23,750 and the sales price to the sitting tenant in Study 2 would have been £36,875 which is a discount of 26·25% from the vacant possession value.

The appropriate yield to apply to the net rent in order to arrive at the pure investment value will depend on the ratio between the net income and the full vacant possession value. It can be as low as 2–3% or as high as 10%. As a rule of thumb, the investment value when let at a recently Registered Rent is 35–50% of the vacant possession value in its existing state.

Freehold properties let on regulated unfurnished tenancies at fair rents with multiple tenancies

During the inter-war period and for a decade or so after the second world war, it was quite common for houses to be let in floors with the bathroom and w.c. shared by the tenants. There was no self-containment between the floors and cooking facilities were provided in the smallest room on each floor. Thus a standard three bedroom semi-detached house would often be occupied as two two-roomed flats each with a kitchen and sharing bathroom, w.c. and gardens. The statistical chance of obtaining full vacant possession is less than for single tenancy houses. There is a market for part possession houses as some owner-occupiers see the let portion as a way of helping to pay for the mortgage but there is, of course, a considerable discount on the full vacant possession value. The extent of the discount is difficult to estimate; it will vary according to location and type of property. This type of property is of considerable appeal to young first-time buyers who can buy at a discount of the full VP value (say 25%) and can benefit from the additional income. The actual discount will depend on the age of the tenants. The property is also of interest to investors who might use the vacant portion to rehouse a tenant from another part possession property which he owns elsewhere.

Study 3

A three storey house with vacant possession of the ground and first floors and the second floor let to a regulated tenant at a rent of £600 p.a. (recently registered). The accommodation comprises 2 rooms and a back addition room on the ground floor, 3 rooms and a back addition containing bathroom and w.c. on the first floor and 3 rooms on the second floor. The second floor tenant uses the bathroom and w.c. on the first floor but the back addition could be extended to provide a bathroom and w.c. for the second floor.

	£	£	£
Vacant possession value ground and first floors if made into self-contained maisonette, say			40,000
Fair rent of improved flat (1)		800	
Less: repairs	80		
insurance	36		
management	40		
	—	156	
		644	
Y.P. in perp. at 5¾% (2) (3)		17·39	
			11,200
			51,200
Less:			
(i) cost of improvement work (6) say	6,000		
(ii) fees on improvement work	600		
(iii) legal and agent's fees	1,200		
(iv) interest on (i) & (ii) (5)	198		
(v) developer's profit say (7)	7,680		
			15,678
Residue being value of the house acquisition costs and interest until sale of improved building			35,522
P.V. £1 6 months at 12%			0·94
Value of house plus acquisition cost of say 2%			33,390
∴ value of house		= 33,390 ÷ 1·02 =	32,735

B/F 32,735

add value of rent receivable during
  improved period (6 months)

		£ p.a.
Fair rent		600
Less: repairs	50	
insurance	36	
management	30	
	—	116
		444
Y.P. 6 months at 10% (4)		0·47

208

32,943

say £33,000

Notes

(1) The tenant's consent to improvements is required, but the courts have power to authorise modernisation works if the tenant does not lose accommodation which he reasonably requires.

(2) Phasing of rent increases has been ignored in this example to simplify the arithmetic and is no longer applicable.

(3) The 5¾% yield reflects the possibility that the tenant might purchase a long leasehold interest in the modernised flat but the price to a sitting tenant would be in accordance with Study 2, assuming a vacant possession value of say £28,000.

(4) The 10% yield reflects the possibility that some rent rebate may be necessary during the course of the works because of disturbance.

(5) Short term finance cost has been taken at 12% averaged over 6 months.

(6) No allowance has been given in this example for improvement grants.

(7) The developer's profit has been taken as 15% of the final estimated entirety value to reflect his risks and to justify the exercise fully.

Study 4

A conventional three bedroom semi-detached house has vacant possession of the ground floor and an "old controlled" (1) tenant in the first floor paying a rent of £100 p.a. exclusive.

	£ p.a.	£ p.a.	£
Vacant possession value			50,000
Rent reserved for first floor—£100,			
but say		600	
Fair rent of ground floor say		600	
		1,200	
Less: repairs	120		
insurance	60		
management	60		
	—	240	
		960	
Y.P. in perp. at 8%		12·5	
Theoretical investment value		12,000	12,000
vacant possession premium			38,000
say half vacant possession premium		19,000	0·5
Value with part possession (2)		£31,000	

Notes

(1) Old controlled tenancies no longer exist by virtue of the Housing Act 1980. These tenancies can now be Registered without any additional formality at a Fair Rent. Some "unconverted" controlled tenancies will be found for many years due to landlord's ignorance or indolence.

(2) This example is one hypothetical method of arriving at a part possession value. There may be an established market in the area which will give a value by comparison. The alternative to a sale with part possession is to wait until full possession is obtained but this will involve a loss of income and a positive expense if there is a void rate provision. Consequently, the part possession value must be dependent on the statistical probability of obtaining vacant possession. This type of property may be difficult to mortgage.

(3) The answer in this example is 62% of vacant possession value. This is a little on the low side if there is a good prospect of vacant possession of the let portion and 75% of vacant possession value could well be paid in such a case. See comment on pages 38 and 39.

Freehold "break-up" valuations

Up to now we have considered single properties with one or more tenants. Many residential investments comprise blocks of purpose-built flats. The valuation of these is a combination of investment analysis as in Study 1 and a development appraisal. In a block of any size a number of flats may become vacant over the course of a year. It is usual to either sell the block unbroken with possession of a number of flats or alternatively to "break the block up"; partially broken blocks are more difficult to sell as the statistical probabilities have been altered by the part disposal and consequently the yield requirement on the balance must be higher. The more vacant flats there are, the greater the potential for general block improvement which will increase the average sales price of the individual flats.

The general considerations already discussed apply to flat break-up as they do to individual units. The flats must be mortgageable and capable of smooth management. There must be an acceptable management structure involving a single company which is responsible for repairs, insurance, services etc., and with which each lessee covenants in respect of payment for a share of the costs: the landlord must similarly covenant in respect of unsold flats. It should be noted that freehold flats are difficult to mortage because of the problems of enforcing positive covenants and therefore a break-up is best effected by the grant of long leases (over 60 years). This may be changed shortly as a Government Commission is considering how the law might be altered to allow the sale of freehold flats. When this happens flat enfranchisement will probably follow. The block should be in good repair before the break-up is commenced because the buying public are (and should be) wary of involving themselves in a large service charge commitment for works which should have been carried out years before. Similarly, sitting tenants would not be too happy for their landlords to escape existing repairing obligations by passing these on to them as buyers. It must be borne in mind that if a sitting tenant buys his flat on a mortgage he will be financially worse off for many years than if he continued renting his flat. The viability and profitability of a break-up scheme will depend on the number of tenant sales.

The sale of the block will be affected by the Landlord and Tenant Act 1987 which, when it is brought into operation, will require an option to be given to the tenants and any sale can be held up for up to seven months. The Act provides that a sale cannot be made to an outside purchaser for less than the block is offered to the tenants.

Study 5

A tenant rents a flat at £1,250 p.a. including £200 p.a. for services. The vacant possession value is £40,000 for a 99 year lease at £25 p.a. The sitting tenant price is £30,000.

		£ p.a.
Present expenditure—	Rent	1,050
	Services	200
Rent fixed for 2 years;		1,250
any increases are phased.		
Proposed expenditure—		
Assuming 100% (interest only) mortgage at 10%		
mortgage interest		3,000
less tax relief at 27%		810
net interest		2,190
services		200
share of repairs and external decorations		130
ground rent		25
building insurance		45
Annual cost		£2,590

Assuming that rent and all costs rise by 10% per annum compound but that interest charges remain constant, it will be about ten years before expenditure is equated, the compensation for this is the immediate capital profit of £10,000 and the added psychological advantages of ownership, although this is not without worry in view of rising service charges.

Study 6

A block of 12 self-contained flats on 3 floors. Three flats are vacant and nine are let to Regulated Tenants at £900 per annum each including £150 for services (just registered). The block is in good repair and the vacant flats are worth £24,000 each, if sold on 99 year leases with £25 per annum ground rents.

Let Flats	£	£	£
9 × £900		8,100	
Less: services—9 × £150	1,350		
repairs at say £50			
per flat	450		
management at say 5%	404		
insurance say	296		
		2,500	
		5,600	
Y.P. in perp. at 7%		14·29	
			80,000
Vacant Flats			
3 × £24,000		72,000	
3 × £25 × 7 Y.P.		525	
		72,525	
Less: (i) legal and agents			
fees 3% on			
realisation	2,175		
Less: (ii) profit at 15%			
on realisation (3)	10,880	13,055	
		59,470	
Less interest for say for			
6 months 12%, say		3,276	
			56,194
			£136,194 (1)

Notes

(1) The average price per flat is £11,350.

(2) Assuming sale of 4 of let flats to sitting tenants at two-thirds of the vacant possession value, the total realisation including the 3 vacant flats is about £136,000 leaving 5 flats at nil cost for profit.

(3) The profit is required in the same way as any wholesaler requires a profit because of the risk of obtaining the estimated prices etc.

The above example may be made more complex by having a variety of tenants at different rents and the need to estimate the relevant Fair Rents. Furnished lettings should be considered separately from unfurnished lettings as the appropriate yield will be different. Potential decrease of rent must be considered together with the cost of putting the block and the individual flats into a saleable state.

Some blocks, because of their location or design, are not capable of being broken up and must be considered as pure investments. If this is the case, then the yield must be much higher because of the absence of the potential to the vacant possession profit. If the state of repair is poor, then the cost of refurbishment and modernisation can be taken as an end allowance together with the financing costs thereon. Many schemes have failed because insufficient allowance has been made for financing the refurbishment expenditure which might be required either to the exterior and common parts or to the interior of flats which are going to be sold off immediately. In order to ensure the viability of a break-up, this expenditure must be recovered from the initial sales or the financing cost must be deducted from the general income, or a combination of both.

It is very unusual to consider a modernisation/break-up without a reasonable percentage of vacancies at the beginning, as in Study 6, since it is very risky to assume that large numbers of sitting tenants will buy; they very often do not have the resources and are too old to obtain a mortgage. It is therefore better to wait until there is a good vacant possession base.

In many developments there are several blocks. A break-up might best be effected by modernising and selling one block at a time. Sitting tenants can be moved by Court Order to suitable alternative accommodation to assist in making individual blocks totally vacant. If a sales campaign to sitting tenants is mounted, then the purchasers should be made aware of the developer's future intensions as to expenditure so that they do not buy cheaply with a "run-down" break-up and then find themselves called upon for further large capital sums to meet their share of the improvement expenditure.

The management of blocks after break-ups have been effected is causing concern and a government commission (the Nugee Committee) have produced a lengthy report.

It is essential that there should be a proper management structure with significant lessee involvement. The Landlord and Tenant Act 1985 sets out rules which must be followed in connection with the levying and collection of service charges and further regulations must be anticipated.

Leasehold properties

The entire analysis so far has been concerned with freehold properties but many residential properties are leasehold. Consequently, the above analysis must be amended to take account of the unexpired term and whether or not a purchaser of the leasehold interest could exercise rights under the Leasehold Reform Act 1967 because, if he can, then the leasehold value is in fact the freehold value less the cost of enfranchisement. Chapter 3 deals in detail with the Leasehold Reform Act 1967 and its subsequent amendments but, of particular concern in the present analysis, is the case of *Bickel* v. *The Duke of Westminster* (1976) 3 All E.R. 801. In that case, the Court of Appeal upheld the lessor's right to refuse consent to assignment of the lease where the assignee would be in a position, after assignment, to enfranchise and where the assignor was not in that position. Some leases are drawn with an assignment clause which only requires registration of the assignment and clearly, in these circumstances, the decision in the Bickel case could not be relevant but where consent is required to the assignment (and this can be refused), then the Bickel decision is totally relevant and, in such a case, the investment nature of the property must continue until the lease expires. The sub-letting clause is equally important because if no consent to sub-letting is required, then, provided the lease has more than 21 years to run, it may be possible to create an enfranchiseable situation by the grant of a sub-lease.

Referring back to the analysis so far, it will be seen that the rate of interest to be adopted in capitalising the income, must depend on the probability of obtaining vacant possession before the end of the lease, bearing in mind the right for the tenancy to pass twice. Where there is a distinct probability that possession will be obtained, then the only difference between the freehold and leasehold house situations is the cost of enfranchisement, assuming that this cannot be prevented, and Study 7 below illustrates an approach in this situation. At the present time, the Leasehold Reform Act only applies to houses, it does not apply to flats and maisonettes. There is no guarantee that this will always be the case. It would be a simple matter to allow enfranchisement by extending leases to 999 years at a peppercorn with a statutory form of full repairing and insuring lease. It may well be that this will be effected by a better system of freehold flats but this will depend on new legislation. When valuing freehold reversions to ground rented long leases, regard must be had to the potential for enfranchisement by the lessee or his successor in title. A view must be taken as to future enfranchisement possibilities.

Study 7

Using the same information as in Study 1, where the vacant possession value freehold is £50,000 and the property is let at £1,200
exclusive but assuming that there is a lease with 60 years unexpired
at £10 p.a. and no consent is required to assign.

	£ p.a.	£ p.a.
Rent reserved		1,200
Less: outgoings		
ground rent	10	
repairs	120	
insurance	70	
management	60	
	——	260
Net income		940
Y.P. 60 years at 8 & 4%		
(Tax at 40%) (2)		11·49
		£10,800 (1)

(compare with freehold value of £13,600).

The validity of the figures in Study 1 were questioned on page
38 where it was shown that the theoretical investment yield of 7%
was too low in view of the percentage of V.P. value that this produced and the valuation was revised to £23,750 which was 47·5%
of V.P. value and which gave an investment yield of 4%. Utilising
the same 4% yield would give a Y.P. of 21·25 which would give
a capital value of £20,000 which is a more realistic answer. However, a lot will depend on the chances of obtaining early vacant
possession or selling to the sitting tenant; as the lease gets shorter
so the cost of the freehold gets greater.

Notes

(1) If vacant possession were obtained immediately and all prices
    remain constant, an assignee could enfranchise in 3 years.
    Assuming the cost of enfranchisement is £250, including all
    costs, then the leasehold vacant possession value should be
    approximately £49,750 which would give the investor a greater
    profit than he would have had, if he had purchased a similar
    freehold but the risks are greater.

(2) There is some inconsistency in taking a dual rate since the justification for the low remunerative rate is the prospect of vacant possession, but because we are dealing with probabilities and not guaranteed events, this might be considered the right approach.

Where there is no probability of obtaining possession or where the freeholder can refuse consent to an assignment (or to a sub-lease capable of being enfranchised) then the investment is one which is badly inflation prone because the rent is limited by statutory control but the outgoings will generally be unlimited which could force at times a negative return. Consequently, the proper rate of interest must be much higher and the only saving grace of the investment is the possibility of a sale back to the freeholder with a view to establishing a marriage value by vacant possession sale of the freehold, should possession ever be obtained. There is also the problem of dilapidations.

Study 7(a)

Using the same information as in Study 7 but assuming a lease with 30 years unexpired.

Net income	£940
Y.P. 30 years at 4 & 4%	
(Tax at 40%)	14·34
	£13,479 say £13,500

Note

(1) Cost of freehold if enfranchised immediately including cost would be about £3,500 but it rises to about £6,500 with 20 years unexpired. If house prices remain constant vacant possession in 10 years will yield a profit of £30,000 (£50,000 − (£13,500 + £6,500)) if the landlord will sell immediately or (£50,000 − (£13,500 + £7,500)) £29,000 if he insists on waiting the three years to allow the resident long lessee to enfranchise.

Study 8

Using the same information as in Study 7, but assume the landlord's consent to assignment can be refused.

	£ p.a.	£ p.a.
Rent reserved		1,200
Less: outgoings:		
ground rent	10	
repairs	120	
insurance	70	
management	60	
	——	260
Net income		940
Y.P. 60 years at 12 & 4%		
(Tax at 40%) (1)		7·87
		9,398
	say	£9,400

Note

(1) The justification for a yield as low as 12% is the probability of vacant possession which will allow negotiations with the landlord for an amalgamation of the two interests.

Study 9

Using the same information as in Study 7, but assuming an unexpired lease of 10 years irrespective of restrictions on assignment,

	£ p.a.	£ p.a.
Rent reserved		1,200
Less: outgoings:		
ground rent	10	
repairs	120	
insurance	70	
management	60	
	——	260
Net income		940
Y.P. 10 years at 15 & 4%		
(Tax at 40%)		3·46
		3,252

	B/F	3,252
Less dilapidations, say		750

£2,502

say £2,500

There must be a general probability that vacant possession will not be obtained before the lease expires. A surrender will often be negotiated in lieu of dilapidations before the end of the lease. If the lease were shorter still (below 3 years), then, even if possession is obtained, no enfranchisement could take place and consequently an even higher yield should be taken although there is a "blackmail value" against the landlord, see Study 9(a) below.

Studies 8 and 9 apply equally to flats as to houses since enfranchisement does not apply. In Study 8, however, the yield would be about 10% although in Study 9 the yield could be increased a little as the vague hope that existed in that case of possession during years 3–10 (to allow a sale where the purchaser could enfranchise before the lease end) would not be of value.

It will therefore be seen that the length of lease is of paramount importance since the longer the lease the greater the prospect of obtaining vacant possession and a market usually exists for leases of all lengths for owner-occupation. Thus, the 10% yield postulated for a leasehold flat with 60 years unexpired reflects the hope of a vacant possession sale but without the benefit of enfranchisement, so that the potential unexpired term is relevant to the value to a greater degree than would be the case with a house. Should legislation change so that flat leaseholders can demand an extended lease (either for 50 years or possibly longer), then the differences between houses and flats would be much less severe and the analysis amended. However, in considering the situation of flats, it has been assumed that "break-ups" are possible and are not prevented by covenants. Where a vacant possession sale to an owner-occupier is not possible at all or only at a very low price (either because it is a house which cannot be enfranchised or it is a flat with too short a lease) there is a second way of looking at its value and that is by considering the effect of a reletting on the landlord.

Study 9(a)

Using the same information as in Study 9 but assuming that vacant possession has been obtained and that £750 p.a. is the rent which would be registered by a Rent Officer,

	£ p.a.	£	£
Value of leasehold interest as an investment			2,500
Value of freehold interest:			
Rent reserved	10		
Y.P. 10 years at 5%	7·72		
		77	
Reversion to Fair Rent	1,200		
Less: outgoings	250		
Net income	950		
Y.P. in perp. deferred 10 years at 7%	7·26		
		6,897	
			6,974
Total of both values			9,474
Value if interests merged			£50,000
∴ Marriage value £40,526			
Splitting this equally, the value of the leasehold interest becomes			£22,763 (1)

Note

(1) Allowance may be made for the costs of sale including interest until sold and for the risk of obtaining the estimated vacant possession price.

The threat of a reletting once possession is obtained could therefore influence the yield on a leasehold flat or house investment and, provided there is a reasonable presumption of possession before the lease end, a lower yield would be appropriate. Hence if in Study 9 the tenant was an octogenarian widow living alone in a flat, the yield might be reduced to as low as 10–11%.

The basic problem with flats and non-enfranchiseable houses is that as the lease gets shorter the vacant possession value gets lower and the prospect of possession before the lease end diminishes. Hence the yield must rise as the term gets shorter.

In Study 10 below, the minimum value of a short lease to an owner-occupier is considered but there is also a special value of a vacant short lease to an investor for rehousing purposes.

Study 9(b)

Using the same information as in Study 1, where the freehold value of the house was £50,000 with possession but only £23,750 if let at £1,200 per annum,

Value of possession (£50,000 – £23,750)   26,250
Maximum price freeholder prepared to pay
for possession, say 50%   0·5
                                            ——— £13,125

If the tenant will not buy or be bought out as in Study 2, the landlord can offer suitable alternative accommodation if he buys the leasehold with vacant possession, shown in Study 9(a) for £13,125 (dilapidations, £500 + tenants removal expenses). The same price would apply no matter how short the lease bought. Thus there is an active buyer other than the freeholder for the short lease with vacant possession.

One of the grounds for obtaining possession against a statutory tenant under the Rent Acts is the offer of suitable alternative accommodation. This is not a mandatory ground and therefore the court has discretion and will only order possession if it considers it reasonable to do so. Assuming that the alternative accommodation is suitable as to size and location (as to size the Local Housing Authority's standards are the best) then reasonableness will turn on the reason for wanting possession, the age of the tenant, the general conduct of the landlord and the nature of the alternative accommodation.

Since Parliament's intension was that this ground for possession should be available the general presumption must be that the courts will grant possession provided the alternative accommodation is generally suitable. However there is no requirement that the alternative accommodation is owned by the same landlord, merely that the tenant must be given security of tenure and that the rent is similar.

Flat leases are a normal market commodity so that the vacant possession value of any lease term can usually be determined fairly accurately by comparison from market transactions. The only problem is one of finance for the vacant property because a mortgage must usually be repaid at least five years before the end of its term. However, the minimum value for a lease should be as shown in Study 10 below.

Study 10

A maisonette has an unexpired term of five years at £20 per annum on full repairing and insuring terms. A fair rent of £750 per annum on internal repairing terms was determined immediately before vacant possession was obtained.

	£ p.a.	£ p.a.	£
Fair rent		750	
Ground rent	20		
Insurance	40		
External repairs	60		
	—	120	
Rent saving		630	
Y.P. 5 years at 8% (1) (3)		3·99	
		—	2,514 (2)
		say	£2,500

Notes

(1) Single rate used as this gives the annual rent saving for the term, discounted to the present day and thus no sinking fund is required.

(2) There will often be security of tenure at the end of the lease by virtue of Part 1 of the Landlord and Tenant Act 1954.

(3) The rate of interest reflects the absence of a rent increase after two years and the net cost after tax relief.

The above must represent a minimum value since in addition a scarcity element may also be added; this would not be an illegal premium under the Rent Acts.

Properties outside the Rent Acts or Restricted Contracts under Section 69 of the Housing Act 1980 and Company Lettings

Where there is no statutory bar to obtaining vacant possession after the lease term, then two valuation approaches would seem to apply. Care must be taken with regard to "company lettings" as many of these may not be bona fide and are merely devices to be outside the Rent Acts, similarly with "holiday lettings" and lettings with services.

Study 11

A semi-detached house with a vacant possession value of £30,000 is part occupied by an owner-occupier and part let, the letting having commenced after the house was bought in 1978. The letting can be furnished or unfurnished.

The lessee will not have security of tenure other than that afforded by the lease or letting agreement and, therefore, the owner can sell with vacant possession. Provided that no substantial term remains on the letting, then the value equals the vacant possession value of £30,000 but he must contract to give full possession. If the property is sold without full possession then the tenancy will establish itself as a regulated one.

If some time remains on the tenancy and the owner-occupier cannot wait until this time expires then the value will be a part possession value as in Study 4.

The benefits of being an owner-occupier pass on death to executors provided they take the appropriate action within the prescribed time, but the right to possession cannot be assigned.

Study 11(a)

A luxury flat with rateable value in central London of £1,750 is let on lease having 5 years unexpired at £6,000 p.a. on full repairing and insuring terms. The full rental value is £10,000 p.a. and the vacant possession value is £220,000.

	£ p.a.	£
Rent reserved	6,000	
Y.P. 5 years at 8½%	3·94	
		23,640
Reversion to vacant possession value	£220,000	
Less:		
(1) (i) cost of sale say 4% 8,800		
(ii) profit say 10% (2) 22,000		
	30,800	
	189,200	
P.V. £1 5 years at 8%	0·68	
		128,656
		£152,296

Notes

(1) No allowance is made for interest between the date of possession and completion of sale as the assumption is made that the flat may be viewed during the last six months of term.

(2) Low rate of profit taken as the present inflationary state of market would indicate a real profit much higher than estimated.

Protected shorthold tenancies

This is a new category of tenancy introduced by the Housing Act 1980. There is a required procedure which must be adhered to and which, if followed, gives the tenant a Regulated Rent but with no security of tenure at the end of the specified period of the letting. In theory, the valuation should be a single one of rent (less outgoings) capitalised for the term with reversion to vacant possession value. The problem is that this type of tenancy is politically suspect since the Labour Party have said that they will abolish them and restore security of tenure. Until there is an all-party agreement to preserve this form of letting, no landlord could be advised to let any property which is saleable at vacant possession prices and no investor should purchase except at a very heavy discount on vacant possession value, unless possession is assured during the life of the current Conservative Government.

Assured tenancies

This is a further new form of tenancy and is one where there is security of tenure but no rent control. The landlord must be of the type specified in the Housing Act 1980 and this rules out the ordinary investor. Again, this is a politically sensitive form of investment but no more will be said here because there will not be any normal market transactions. However the investment value will always be less than the vacant possession value.

Secure tenancies

This applies to Public Sector Property and is governed by Sections 28–61 of the Housing Act 1980 and the Housing Act 1985. Prima facie these tenants now enjoy security of tenure subject to certain exceptions. There is no private property consequences and hence no more will be said of this category.

Non-owner-occupier type properties

In general, there are three types of properties in this category: (i) properties in very poor repair or in areas scheduled for redevelopment; (ii) houses in multi-occupation; (iii) artisan dwellings.

(i) Freehold properties in very poor repair or scheduled for redevelopment

There comes a point in the life of a property when the cost of repair may approach the value of the property in good repair. In such a case, the maximum vacant possession value is the site value less the cost of demolition. In addition, a landlord can be forced to do repairs to the property under the Public Health Acts and the Housing Acts and, in most cases, by a civil action for breach of covenant to repair. Consequently, there will be a capital loss situation in any investment. Local Authorities are now much more active than they have been and are serving notices under Schedule 9 of the Housing Act 1957 requiring major works of repair to be carried out; if the works are not done then they may enter and do the works themselves recovering the costs from the rents. Grants are often available for the work.

Study 12

A terrace house is let to a single tenant at £250 per annum. It has been badly neglected and it will now cost £3,000 to put it into an acceptable state of repair in which condition it will have a fair rental value of £450 per annum. The house is let to a couple who are 45 years old.

	£ p.a.	£ p.a.	£
Fair rent in repair		450	
Less: annual repairs	45		
insurance	23		
management	22		
	——	90	
		360	
Y.P. in perp. at 10%		10	
		——	3,600
Less: Necessary repairs		3,000	
Supervision fees at 10% (1)		300	
		——	3,300
			£300

OR:	£ p.a.	£ p.a.	£
Present fair rent		250	

	B/F		250
Less: outgoings:			
repairs	100		
insurance	22		
management	22		
	———	144	
		106	
Y.P. in perp. at 20% (2)		5	
		———	530
Less: Essential repairs			250
			£280

Notes

(1) The 10% yield reflects the non probability of early possession.
(2) The 20% yield reflects possibilities of notices under the Public Health Acts etc.
(3) This valuation could be affected by the availability of local authority grants and up to 90% of the cost of works could be obtained. If this is the case then the works are worth doing and the value of the property will be considerably increased.

If, because of the disrepair, the tenant does not pay his rent, then possession may be obtained and a profit made but this is a doubtful occurrence as the tenant would be advised to press for the repairs via the local authority.

For property of this type there is always the threat of compulsory purchase as a property which is "unfit for human habitation", with compensation limited to a maximum of cleared site value but subject to a ceiling value equal to the investment value, if this is lower than the site value (see Chapter 9). Regard must always be had in this type of property to the possibility of compulsory purchase. This is an unusual valuation and it assumes that even in good repair the house is not saleable with vacant possession. It would need very little vacant possession value to justify doing the work.

(ii) Houses in multiple occupation

This is a similar category to Studies 3 and 4 but the properties are not of a sufficient quality or of satisfactory design to allow part owner-occupation either by conversion (into all or part self-contained units) or by sharing. Consequently, there may be little logic in leaving part vacant in the hope of full vacant possession (unless this is an early probability) since there is a security risk from squatters and there will be substantial outgoings in the form of repairs, insurance and rates.

This type of property is the poorest possible type of property investment. There is very little prospect of capital profit because there is little or no vacant possession market and consequently there is little option but to relet when a property becomes vacant. This type of property is also politically sensitive since the tenants are usually the poorer members of society who need statutory protection.

Even when there is a vacant possession market for improved properties the probability of obtaining early possession must usually be remote since the pure mathematical chance of this happening is substantially worse than for single tenanted property. This opinion is reinforced by the fact that in the areas where this type of property exists there is a lesser movement towards owner-occupation by the tenants and so voluntary moves are rarer except for local authority and Housing Association rehousing. This type of property usually occurs in Housing Action Areas where the local authority can compel improvements and repairs. Large grants are available but there is still a residual capital liability.

(iii) Artisan dwellings

This is the name given to purpose-built blocks of houses and flats built around the turn of the century by the predecessors of today's Housing Associations, usually charitable trusts. Good examples are those blocks built by the Guinness and Peabody trusts. At the time they were built, these properties were a major advance in "working class' housing then existing: they were often slums before they were even finished.

By today's standards, these artisan blocks are old-fashioned and lack modern amenities. They were built to a very high density with blocks being close together and often five storeys high, without lifts. They often have open landings and staircases. Some of the better blocks can be or have been modernised to acceptable standards so that "break-ups" can be effected. Others, by reason of their design or location, can never be made acceptable owner-occupier type properties although they can be provided with standard amenities. Consequently they provide a purely investment type of property and the yield must reflect a pure income situation. Regard must be given to the state of repair and to the level of outgoings on insurance, services and management. Finally, regard must be had to potential obsolescence, since it is hoped that, in due course, this type of housing will be demolished as not being of a sufficiently high standard in our enlightened age.

Study 12(a)

"Trust Building" comprises an artisan block of sixteen flats on four floors, without a lift. The location is such that there is no potential for vacant possession sales. All flats are let on Regulated Tenancies. Local evidence indicates an increase in Registered Rent levels of 20% including services since March 1985. All rents are exclusive of rates with tenants responsible for internal decorations only. Services are limited to cleaning and lighting of common parts for which £20 p.a. was included in the old Registered Rent. The present cost of the services is £36 per flat. No application has yet been made for new Registrations.

Floor	Flat No.	Registered Rent	Date of Registration	Rent Payable
Ground	1–4	£350 p.a. each	1st March 1985	£350 p.a. each
First	5–8	£350 p.a. each	1st March 1985	£350 p.a. each
Second	9–12	£329 p.a. each	1st March 1985	£329 p.a. each
Third	13–16	£300 p.a. each	1st March 1985	£300 p.a. each

Value as at 1st June 1986	£ p.a.	£ p.a.	£
Rents reserved		5,316	
Less: services—16 × £36	576		
repairs say 16 × £30	480		
insurance say 16 × £15	240		
management at 10%	532		
		1,828	
		3,488	
Y.P. 3 months at 13% (2)		0·23	
			802

			B/F 802
Reversion to New Fair Rents (1)		6,380	
Less: services/repairs/			
insurance	1,296		
management 10%	638		
	———	1,934	
		4,446	
Y.P. in perp. at 15% 6·67⎫		6·50	
P.V. £1—¼ years at 15% 0·97⎭			
			28,899
			29,701
Less: allowance for essential repair			1,600
			28,101
		say,	£28,100

Notes

(1) Assumed modern fair rent £5,316 + 20% = £6,380.
(2) The effective date of registration is the date of registration and the 2 year period runs from this date. The first date on which the higher rent is payable is the first rent day following registration. Hence the above assumes a delay of 3 months from date of application to date of determination. The actual period will depend on local pressures on the Rent Officer service.
(3) Although a different rate has been taken in capitalising the old rent and the new rent, it is not considered that there is any real difference in the security of the new rent, whichever phase is payable.
(4) The high yields reflect the absence of a review procedure to cover the increasing cost of services between registrations.
(5) The valuation set out is the same as in a break-up valuation, only the rates of interest are different to reflect the absence of the capital profit.
(6) In this case the rents payable are the same as the old registered rents but this is not always the case due to landlords' neglect or personal reasons. There may also be some "old controlled" tenancies or tenancies where legal increases have not been effected.

Leaseholds

If a freehold interest in this category of property is one of the poorest investments available, then a leasehold interest must be the worst of all. The discussion contained in Studies 7–10 applies equally here concerning probabilities to possession but there is also the problem of dilapidations. The covenants of the lease must be considered in valuing the lease and if there are the usual forms of repairing covenants then the property may be a liability rather than an asset.

Study 13

The same facts as in Study 12 but in this case, value a lease having 15 years unexpired at £80 per annum on full repairing and insuring terms.

Using the Double Sinking Fund Method*, a.s.f. to recoup the capital value (q) in 15 years at $2\frac{1}{2}\%$ = 0·056q, adjusted for tax at 40% = 0·0932.

	£ p.a.	£ p.a.	£
Rent reserved		5,316	
Less: outgoings	1,828		
ground rent	80		
sinking fund	0·093q		
		1,908 + 0·093q	
Spendable income		3,408 − 0·093q	
Y.P. 3 months at			
17% (1)		0·22	
			750 − 0·02q
Reversion to Fair			
Rent		6,380	
Less: outgoings	1,934		
ground rent	80		
sinking fund	0·093q		
		2,014 + 0·093q	
Y.P. $14\frac{3}{4}$ years			
at 20%	4·66	4,366 − 0·093q	
P.V. £1—$\frac{1}{4}$ year			
at 20%	0·96	4·47	
			19,516 − 0·416q

* For alternative method see p. 151.

Add P.V. £1
3 months
at 17%   0·96
P.V. £1 in 14¾
year at 20%   0·07
            ×q   +0·07q
            ―――――――――――――
        ∴ q =   20,266 − 0·366q
    ∴ capital value =   14,836
Less dilapidation, say (2)   15,000
            ―――――――――――――
                         negative value

Notes

(1) Substantially higher rates of interest are required to reflect the inflation-prone nature of the investment.
(2) A dilapidation provision of this size is not unreasonable if this has to cover such items as repainting, repointing, roof renewal, rewiring etc.

If the property is compulsorily acquired under a slum clearance scheme then the leasehold investor could have a claim against him for the loss to the landlord's reversion, if the property is declared to be unfit for habitation by reason of disrepair.

In many cases, therefore, the leasehold property may be totally unsaleable and the only course of action is to negotiate a surrender to the freeholder (with or without payment from either side) and thus maximise the limited potential of this poor quality property.

Furnished property

This type of property does not really warrant separate treatment as there is no substantial difference today between a furnished or an unfurnished letting since in the majority of cases both types are subject to rent control and the tenants have permanent security of tenure. The maximum value is the vacant possession value but care must be taken in considering whether the rent passing is "fair". Also, allowance must be made for deterioration of furnishings. The prospect of possession will also be influenced in this category by the nature of the tenants and whether he is a temporary resident of this country.

Although in theory there is no difference between furnished and unfurnished lettings, in practice there often is a difference. Many landlords try to find loopholes in the law to allow them to let on a temporary basis. These loopholes are (1) holiday lettings, (2) company lettings, (3) licences, (4) service tenancies.

(1) Holiday lettings can be legitimate, particularly in seaside or tourist areas. In such a case the tenants will not have security of tenure. A letting following a holiday letting will also not be subject to security if Case 13 is followed. However, sham holiday lettings will be caught as the court will look at the intension as opposed to the wording of the agreement.

(2) Companies do not have security of tenure under the Rent Acts although the rents are registerable. However, most company lettings are a sham with its company formed for the precise purpose of taking the tenancy. These lettings have not yet been tested in the courts but the writer considers them to be fraught with danger. What has also not been tested is the relationship between the company and the occupier and whether this could itself create a tenancy.

It is established that a company may have a tenancy of residential property under the Landlord & Tenant Act 1954 for the purposes of its business (e.g. a nurses home). If the premises are not for its business then for what purpose can a company require premises? Hence the sham, as the sole purpose is the housing of an employee or director. Does this therefore lead to a sub-letting with the landlords consent or can it create a licence?

(3) Licences have been considered by the House of Lords in _Street v. Mountford_ [1985] 2 W.L.R. 877 any letting giving exclusive occupation is a lease and the tenant will have security of tenure. Only if there is no exclusive occupation can there be a licence and then it must not be a sham. A letting to husband and wife or man and mistress by way of two separate agreements with neither giving exclusive occupation is a sham, as is one to two cousins simultaneously. A number of licences to a group of friends with each being independently liable only for a given rent and with no licence being dependent on any other is almost certainly valid and will exclude security of tenure.

(4) Service tenancies will succeed in avoiding security of tenure if there is a significant degree of service. One boiled egg a day delivered to the door is unlikely to be sufficient service to qualify, daily cleaning of the room with clean linen regularly provided and breakfast provided will be sufficient.

Where tenants do not have permanent security of tenure

In these cases, vacant possession can be obtained by the landlord although this might be delayed for up to six months. The value is therefore the vacant possession value deferred for the period until it is known that possession will be available less the cost of obtaining possession.

The method of valuation must be the same as for any other residential property except that the rate of interest must be adjusted to take account of the chances that the rent may be increased or decreased (by the Rent Officer), that possession might be recovered by, say, a diplomat (the tenant) being recalled or a foreign tenant's work permit expiring. The rate of interest must also reflect the percentage of the rent attributable to the furniture and the value of the latter. It is essential, in any sale, that the furniture be conveyed with the property.

When advising an owner as to the value of a furnished property for purposes of sale, account should always be taken of the attitude of any prospective purchaser to err on the side of caution. Hence if a tenancy is going to expire within a short period then the vendor should be advised to wait to see if possession will be given up. However, if a valuation for mortgage purposes is being carried out full consideration should be given to the possibility that possession may not be given at the end of the term.

© E. F. Shapiro, 1988

Chapter 3

LEASEHOLD ENFRANCHISEMENT

The Leasehold Reform Act 1967 is a measure to protect certain occupiers of houses holding under long leases at low rents. It was the culmination of argument since the latter part of the last century that although the land in such circumstances may belong in equity to the freeholder the buildings should belong to the leaseholder. Leasehold enfranchisement, or the principle that certain residential leaseholders should be able to expand their interest in premises, was the policy of both major political parties in 1966 but the basis for enfranchisement was the subject of controversy.

The principle of enfranchisement adopted in the 1967 Act is that the tenant either may take a further 50 year term of ground lease at a so called "modern ground rent" subject to review after 25 years or may purchase the landlord's interest. In the latter case the enfranchisement price payable is the value of the landlord's interest subject to the tenant's unexpired term of lease and right to a further 50 years ground lease at a "modern ground rent".

The 1967 Act was amended by Section 82 of the Housing Act 1969 which requires that the additional bid that a tenant might make be excluded from the enfranchisement price. Section 118 of the Housing Act 1974 extended the right to enfranchisement to a further range of interests subject to different rules for assessing prices in the higher rateable value bands. It also made the major amendment that for enfranchisement qualification purposes rateable values may be adjusted to discount the value of any tenants' improvements. The Leasehold Reform Act 1979 closed the loophole in the enfranchisement price provisions of the 1967 Act revealed and confirmed by the House of Lords in *Jones* v. *Wrotham Park Settled Estates and Another* [1979] 1 All E.R. 286.

The Housing Act 1980 made further amendments to the 1967 Act, reducing the 5 years residential occupation requirement to 3 years and correcting and improving the 1974 Act provisions regarding rateable value adjustments. It also included within the protection of the 1967 Act tenancies terminable on death or marriage in order to close an avoidance loophole. It extends transitional relief to tenants paying modern ground rents on lease extensions and introduces a formula approach for those enfranchising against minor superior tenants. Most important however is the provision in Section

67

142 which provides for the referral of valuation disputes in the first instance to leasehold valuation tribunals drawn from rent assessment panels with an appeal right to the Lands Tribunal.

It should be noted that tenants qualifying for enfranchisement do still have the alternative, but less beneficial protection of Part I of the Landlord and Tenant Act 1954. This effectively entitles them to a "Regulated Tenancy" under the Rent Acts at the expiry of the long lease.

Valuations must take account of the effect of enfranchisement rights and are specifically required for the assessment of enfranchisement price or lease extension terms. They must take account of the statutes and the precedents which interact to influence the rights to enfranchisement and the basis and terms for it. There have been about one hundred references to the Lands Tribunal since 1967 on issues under the Act and since 1980 there have been about seventy cases before leasehold valuation tribunals. Many cases have been heard by the courts under these provisions too but the basis for the valuations required is still not always clear.

The principal precedents on enfranchisement terms include; *Kemp* v. *Josephine Trust, Ltd.*, (1970) 217 E.G. 351; *Farr* v. *Millersons Investments, Ltd.*, (1971) 218 E.G. 1177, in which the Lands Tribunal described the generally recognised approaches including three alternative means of calculating the modern ground rent; *Official Custodian for Charities and others* v. *Goldridge* (1973) 227 E.G. 1467, in which the Court of Appeal disapproved of the "adverse differential" approach; *Norfolk* v. *Trinity College, Cambridge* (1976) 238 E.G. 421 and *Lloyd-Jones* v. *Church Commissioners for England* (1981) 261 E.G. 471, the first two cases under the new valuation rules of Section 9 (1A) introduced by the 1974 Act; and the Lands Tribunal case of *Hickman and Others* v. *Phillimore and Others* (1985) 274 E.G. 1261, upheld in the Court of Appeal in *Mosley and Others* v. *Hickman and Others* (1986) 278 E.G. 728, which confirmed that by first extending a lease certain leaseholders could enfranchise more cheaply. While the option of extending the leases of houses in the higher rateable value bands may still in some cases be a cheaper approach to expanding an interest for a tenant, the "Hickman" loophole was closed by section 23 of the Housing and Planning Act 1986. See Study 9 (infra).

The decision in *Pearlman* v. *Keepers and Governors of Harrow School* (1978) 247 E.G. 1173 dealt with tenant's improvements and qualification for enfranchisement under the 1974 Act amendments. On the issue of what is "a house" for enfranchisement purposes a majority decision of the House of Lords in *Tandon* v. *Trustees of Spurgeons Homes* (1982) 263 E.G. 349 held that the tenant of a shop in a parade occupied together with living accommodation above qualified even though the shop part was also a protected business tenancy. The Duke of Westminster has taken a number of cases to the Court of Appeal and one to the House of Lords over the issue of what is a "low rent" in the setting of the qualification provisions of the Act. See Studies 1 and 2 (infra).

The provisions of the Housing Act 1980, which give public sector tenants the right to buy long leases of flats, grants wider rights than those which apply to long leased flats in the private sector which are excluded from the Leasehold Reform provisions. Accordingly there is growing pressure to extend some form of enfranchisement right to private sector flats held on long leases and the possibility of such a legal development in the future should be taken into account in valuations of such premises. The Landlord and Tenant Act 1987 now confers on tenants of flats certain rights to acquire their landlord's reversion.

A proposition was made at 249 E.G. 31 that the Leasehold Reform Act 1967 is contrary to the European Convention on Human Rights as it can allow the expropriation of property unjustly and without fair compensation, other than in the public interest. Following this line of reasoning the principle of the enfranchisement price provisions was questioned by the European Commission on Human Rights and before the European Court of Human Rights at the instigation of the Trustees of the Duke of Westminster. The application was rejected and no breach of the convention was held to have occurred, 8 Chartered Surveyors Weekly 633 and *The Times*, February 22, 1986.

Reference to the Act and Sections of Statute in this Chapter are to the Leasehold Reform Act 1967 unless otherwise stated.

Study 1

Enfranchisement of a long term of lease

This illustrates enfranchisement qualification and price under the Act for an interest in a house held with a long term of lease unexpired.

A terraced house in the Midlands, built 50 years ago, is held on lease with 75 years unexpired term at a rent of £15 p.a. The rateable value of the house was £140 at 23rd March 1965. The present tenant has occupied the house for the last 7 years as assignee of an earlier tenant. An estate of freehold ground rents in the same locality totalling £100 p.a. with reversions in 80 years was recently sold as an investment at auction for £950. An enfranchising tenant on the same estate, with a 78 years unexpired term, recently paid 10·5 Y.P. for his freehold on your advice.

Qualification

There are now four rateable value tests to apply in assessing whether interests qualify to enfranchise; (a) was the rateable value not more than £200 (£400 in Greater London) on 23rd March 1965 or at the commencement of the tenancy or (b) is the rateable value not more than £500 (£1000) in the valuation list on 1st April 1973 or (c) is the rateable value not more than £750 (£1500) on 1st April 1973 and was the tenancy created before 18th February 1966 or (d) if the rateable value in the above cases is greater than the limits given would the figure be within the limits, were any tenant's improvements to be discounted from the rateable value. The rateable value at the appropriate day, in this case 23rd March 1965, was less than £200. The house is held on a long lease of over 21 years at a low rent (1) which was less than 2/3rds of the rateable value at the appropriate day. The premises appear to be within the definition of a house (2) and have been occupied (3) by the enfranchising tenant for at least the last 3 years (4) as his only or main residence. The tenant qualifies to serve notice on the freeholder desiring to have the freehold or an extended lease (5) (6).

If the rateable value was more than £500 (£1000 in Greater London) the question of different assumptions and a payment of marriage value could apply in this case. See *Lowther and Others* v. *Strandberg* and *Same* v. *Silver* (1985) 274 E.G. 53.

Analysis of Comparables

The auction result indicates a market investment yield on these ground rents of 10·5%. The enfranchisement settlement shows a discount rate of 9·5%. From this information a reasonable enfranchisement capitalisation rate is taken as 10%.

Valuation for Enfranchisement Price (7)	£ p.a.	
Ground Rent	15	
Y.P. in perp. (8) at 10% (9)	10	
Enfranchisement price (10) (11)	—	£150

Notes

(1) The full rules on qualification are in Sections 1 to 4 of the 1967 Act as amended by Section 118 and Schedule 8 of the Housing Act 1974 and Section 141 and Schedule 21 of the Housing Act 1980. Section 4 defines a low rent in certain cases

as being less than two thirds of the letting value and in *Manson* v. *The Duke of Westminster and Others* (1980) 259 E.G. 153 the Court of Appeal held that the "letting value" for this purpose should include the annual equivalent of the premium paid. See also *Collin* v. *Duke of Westminster* (1984) 273 E.G. 881 and *Duke of Westminster* v. *Johnson* (1985) 275 E.G. 241 which both involved the issue of "low rent".

(2) A "house" is defined in Section 2 and while it does not include horizontally divided flats themselves it can include a whole house which is converted into flats or part of a building divided vertically as long as there is no part of other premises above or below. See an article at 229 E.G. 1165, *Peck* v. *Anicar Properties Ltd.* (1970) 216 E.G. 1135, *Wolf* v. *Critchley and Carpenter* (1970) 217 E.G. 401, *Baron* v. *Phillips* (1978) 247 E.G. 1079, and *Tandon's* case (supra). In *Cresswell* v. *Duke of Westminster and Others* (1985) 275 E.G. 461 a terraced house with accommodation over a side access passage was held to be within the definition of a house for the purposes of section 2(2).

(3) Section 1 allows enfranchisement rights to tenants "occupying ... as his residence". In *Poland* v. *Earl Codogan* (1980) 256 E.G. 495 the tenant was overseas having, without effect, instructed that the house be let. Later mortgagees took possession for a time. The Court of Appeal held that these were not periods of occupation as his residence. See also *Fowell* v. *Radford and Others* (1970) 21 P&CR 99. In *Duke of Westminster* v. *Oddy* (1984) 270 E.G. 945, a tenant who held the leasehold interest in a house as a bare trustee for a company was held not to be a tenant with rights under the Act even though he occupied the house with his family.

(4) For enfranchisement qualification Section 1 (1)(b) required occupation for the last five years or for periods amounting to five years in the last ten. Schedule 21 (1)(1) of the 1980 Act amends each period of five to three years.

(5) The form of notice to be used by a tenant under the Act is set out in the Leasehold Reform (Notices) Regulations 1967 (S.I. 1967 No 1768).

(6) In *Oliver* v. *Central Estates (Belgravia) Ltd* (1985) 276 E.G. 1358 a house in London had a rateable value of £347 on March 23 1965 but £1,347 on 1st April 1973. The L.V.T. held that the rateable value at the *relevant time* was the 1973 figure and the enfranchisement price fell to be assessed under section 9(1A). In *MacFarquhar and Another* v. *Phillimore and Another* and *Marks* v. *Phillimore and Another* (1986) 279

E.G. 584 the Court of Appeal considered cases where the rateable values of two London houses exceeded £1,500 on 1st April 1973 but subsequent proposals were agreed to reduce these retrospectively. It held that the altered rateable values were the relevant values for the purposes of the 1967 Act and the tenants qualified to enfranchise. The distinction between the relevance of rateable values for qualification purposes and for the purpose of determining the basis for enfranchisement price assessment should be noted. See *Oliver's* case (supra).

(7) The valuation date is the date of the tenant's notice. Sections 9 (1) and 37(1).

(8) The reversion to the modern ground rent in 75 years can be ignored although ones as far distant as 56 years have been valued. See *Gordon* v. *Trustees of Lady Londsborough's Marriage Settlement* (1974) 230 E.G. 509 and *Uziell Hamilton* v. *Hibbert Foy* (1974) 230 E.G. 509. In *Collins and Another* v. *Jones* (1981) 261 E.G. 1001, L.V.T. a leasehold valuation tribunal capitalised a 50 years term of a £5 p.a. ground rent and then the reversion to the modern ground rent deferred 50 years both at 7%. If the rateable value was over £500 and the approach adopted in the *Lowther* case (supra) were to be applied, then the reversion could be sufficiently significant to be included here. In *Cummings* v. *Severn Trent Water Authority* (1986) (unreported W. Midlands L.V.T.) a ground lease with reviews to "current market value", the first in 14½ years and then after a further 30 and 60 years, was dealt with by reverting in perpetuity to a section 15 rent in 14½ years.

(9) The 10% rate follows various Lands Tribunal decisions and in this case is supported by the all important comparables.

(10) See similar decisions in *Jenkins* v. *Bevan-Thomas* (1972) 221 E.G. 640 (10% basis), *Barber* v. *Trustees of Eltham United Charities* (1972) 221 E.G. 1343 (10% basis), *Janering* v. *E.P.C. Ltd., and Nessdale Ltd.*, (1977) 242 E.G. 388 (11% basis), and *Ugrinic* v. *Shipway (Estates) Ltd.*, (1977) 244 E.G. 893 (9% basis). An exception was *Cohen and Another* v. *Metropolitan Property Realisations and Another* (1976) 239 E.G. 666 where 7% was adopted for a 59 year term. In *Yates* v. *Bridgewater Estates Ltd.* (1982) 261 E.G. 1001, L.V.T. a leasehold valuation tribunal valued a £3·62 per annum ground rent receivable for 971 years at £10, a capitalisation rate of interest of 36·2%.

(11) In its decision in *Re Castlebeg Investments (Jersey) Ltd's Appeal* (1985) 275 E.G. 469, the Lands Tribunal accepted the landlord's unchallenged evidence of long term ground rents

selling at 16 years purchase ($6\frac{1}{2}\%$), and more, when linked with an obligation on tenants to insure the premises through the landlord's agency. In *Lynch and Another* v. *Castlebeg Investments (Jersey) Ltd.* the leasehold valuation tribunal capitalised insurance commission separately at 15% (referred to in C.S.W. Vol. 2 No. 2—9th July 1987). In *Divis* v. *Middleton and Another* (1983) 268 E.G. 157, a ground rent with fixed rent increases in twenty three, fifty six and to full value in eighty nine years was capitalised at 7%.

Study 2
A 50 years lease extension

This further considers enfranchisement qualification together with the assessment of a modern ground rent on a 50 year lease extension to a house held with a short term unexpired. Extensions are rare in practice, as they may not give the tenant such a good deal, but they have to be assumed in enfranchisement cases where a tenant wishes to buy the freehold of a house with a rateable value of less than £500 (£1,000 in London) under Section 9 (1). It would appear that a tenant taking a 50 year extension and falling in the £500 to £750 rateable value band (£1,000 to £1,500 in London) would also qualify to take that extension at a modern ground rent under Section 15 and not on the assumptions to be adopted for assessing enfranchisement price under Section 9 (1A). For such lessees extension may be more beneficial. See Article at 268 E.G. 876,978 and further in Studies 7, 8 and 9.

A 98 year old house in London is held with one year unexpired term of lease at a rent of £25 p.a. The rateable value of the house at 23rd March 1965 was £380 and at 1st April 1973 was £980. The lessee has held the interest for the last 10 years during which time he has used the ground floor as his main residence for the 6 years when he was not abroad. A small area of the ground floor has been sublet as a betting office and the upper floors have been sublet as unfurnished flats. Both sublettings contravene the headlease covenants. The house is a "Listed Building" with an indeterminate but reasonable future life. The adjacent houses do not qualify to enfranchise but the plot might have some redevelopment potential. The plot area is 800 square metres and evidence shows that the house if improved might sell for £50,000 feehold with vacant possession. Sites in this area are worth about 40% of the freehold vacant possession value of such houses.

Qualification

The house is within the £400 London rateable value limit at 23rd March 1965, the "appropriate day", and the low rent level. It has been occupied as a main residence for more than 3 out of the last 10 years. Although the house has been used for other purposes it may still qualify for enfranchisement. (1)

Assessment of Modern Ground Rent for Extended Lease (2)

Standing House Approach: (3)	£	£ p.a.
Entirety value (4) (5)	50,000	
Site value at say 40% (6)	20,000	
Section 15 rent at 7% (7)	0·07	
	———	1,400
Less: factor to reflect possible repossession rights say 10% (8)		140
		———
Section 15 modern ground rent (9)(10), reviewable after 25 years		£1,260 p.a.

Notes

(1) See the Court of Appeal cases *Harris* v. *Swick Securities* (1969) 211 E.G. 1121 and *Lake* v. *Bennett and Another* (1969) 213 E.G. 633. In *Baron* v. *Phillips* (*supra*) the subletting of the ground floor shop part led to the loss of enfranchisement rights. In *Tandon* v. *Trustees of Spurgeons Homes* (*supra*) a shop in a parade with a flat above occupied by the retailer was held to be a house. In *Methuen-Campbell* v. *Walters* (1978) 247 E.G. 899 the Court of Appeal held that the enfranchisement right did not extend to 1·6 acres of paddock demised with the premises. See also *Gaidowski* v. *Gonville and Caius College, Cambridge* (1975) 238 E.G. 259.

(2) Where a tenant requires an extended lease the new rent is fixed not earlier than 12 months before the original term date and the tenant bears all costs. Section 15 (2)(b). For a case relating to the determination of the rent for an extended lease see *Burford Estate and Property Co Ltd* v. *Creasey* (1985) 277 E.G. 73, L.V.T. In this case the tribunal rejected a tenant's claim that acceptance by the landlord of the old ground rent for four years of the extended lease implied agreement of the old rent figure as the revised section 15 rent for the first 25 years of the new lease.

(3) The "standing house" approach is one of the three generally accepted ways of arriving at the Section 15 modern ground rent and stems from *Kemp* v. *Josephine Trust, Ltd.* (1970)

217 E.G. 351 but the Lands Tribunal has heavily criticised it in *Miller* v. *St. John Baptists College, Oxford* (1977) 243 E.G. 535 and in *Embling* v. *Wells and Campden Charity's Trustees* (1978) 247 E.G. 909. It has now stated that the approach should only be used where there is no relevant evidence of a market in residential development land. About 30% of the cases referred to the Lands Tribunal and 41% of those heard by leasehold valuation tribunals have led to determinations using the standing house approach.

(4) Entirety value has become a way of expressing the full freehold vacant possession value. There may not be evidence on the basis required by the Act but there should normally be evidence to support the entirety value. See *Carthew and Others* v. *Estates Governors of Alleyn's College of God's Gift* (1974) 231 E.G. 809.

(5) As the modern ground rent is to be the ... "letting value of the site for the uses ... of the existing tenancy, other than uses which by the terms of the new tenancy are not permitted ...". (Section 15 (2)(a)) there may be some argument here as to the basis for the entirety value. See *Lake* v. *Bennett* (1971) 219 E.G. 945, where the best entirety value for the house was the value as two maisonettes, the most profitable use permitted by the lease. In *Kingdon* v. *Bartholomew* (1971) 221 E.G. 48 the basis for entirety value was taken to be mixed commercial and residential use. In *Barrable* v. *Westminster City Council* (1984) 271 E.G. 1273, the entirety value was taken at the higher value as if the house was converted into three flats, even though it was used as a single dwelling at the date of enfranchisement.

(6) The approach may be acceptable where the house is likely to remain standing for the foreseeable future. This figure was adopted in *Carthew*'s case (supra) but the percentage accepted will depend on locality, building costs, site attributes, evidence etc. In decided cases the figure has ranged between 15% and 40% of entirety value and the percentage to be adopted depends very much on location. In the Kensington and Hampstead areas of London, for example, 40% has often been applied. In North and East London figures of 27·5% to 30% have been used while in South Wales, the Midlands and the North figures of between 20% and 30% are more usual. In the *Embling* case (supra) the Lands Tribunal was critical of the valuers' arbitrary approach to the percentage for site value.

(7) This percentage will depend on the evidence available but decisions by the Lands Tribunal have ranged between 6% and

8% but of late 7% seems to have become the generally accepted
figure. In virtually all the leasehold valuation tribunal determinations since 1980 a rate of 7% has been applied in this part
of the valuation.

(8) Section 17 reserves to the landlord the future right to possession
for redevelopment where a tenant takes an extended lease.
In *Carthew*'s case (supra) it was accepted that the possibility
of repossession might reduce any potential rental bid under
Section 15.

(9) Section 15 Modern Ground Rents calculated as percentages
of "fair rents" were held to be inappropriate in *Carthew*'s
case (supra).

(10) An alternative method might be the "new for old approach".
See Study 5.

Study 3

Enfranchisement price with a short lease unexpired

This study examines the possible enfranchisement price on the
facts assumed in Study 2 as the tenant in that case must look at
the alternative merits of buying the freehold rather than taking
the 50 years lease extension. The approach adopted takes account
of the reversion to the full value of the house and premises
after the assumed 50 years extension has expired. This follows
the decision of the Lands Tribunal in *Haresign* v. *St John the
Baptist's College, Oxford* (1980) 255 E.G. 711, but whether
such a reversion is built in to the valuation will depend on the
significance of it and the strength of evidence to justify such an
approach. As the rateable value at the relevant time is not more
than £1,000 the price will be under the assumptions required by
Section 9(1).

Valuation for Enfranchisement Price Assessment

Term		£ p.a.	£
Rent receivable		25	
Y.P. 1 year at 7% (1)		0·935	
			23
Reversion to Section 15 rent figure adopted as assessed in Study 2		1,260	
Y.P. 50 years at 7%	13·8		
P.V. of £1 in 1 year at 7%	0·935		
		12·90	
			16,254

Reversion to standing house
    value (2) in 51 years   50,000
P.V. £1 in 51 years at 7%   0·032
                                               ———————   1,600

Enfranchisement price of the
    freehold interest   17,877

                                                     say £17,850

Notes

(1) Although 7% has been adopted in virtually all L.V.T. determinations since 1980, in *Haresign*'s Case (supra) 6% was adopted in discounting a term rent for 3 years and the reversion to the Section 15 rent. 7% was adopted only for the reversion to the standing house at the end of the notional lease extension. However in the case of *Lowther and Others* v. *Strandberg and Others* (1985) 275 E.G. 53, the Lands Tribunal approved the adoption of 9% throughout the valuation. The figure finally adopted will depend on the relative strength of any supporting evidence.

(2) In *Haresign*'s Case (supra) it was argued successfully that, as the residue of the contractural term was so short, the three stage basis of taking into account the landlords reversion to freehold possession at the end of the lease extension was sufficiently material to be included. See also for example *Lowther's* case, (supra). In *Ball* v. *Johnson* (1973) 226 E.G. 473 a reversion to a development site after the fifty years lease extension was allowed for where the house had additional land with it not likely to remain as garden indefinitely.

(3) Dependable evidence is often difficult to obtain. In *Letorbury Properties* v. *Ivens* (1983) 265 E.G. 51, L.V.T. the sale of a freeholder's interest at auction a few days after the enfranchisement notice was held to be the most dependable market evidence.

Study 4

Enfranchisement against two superior interests and alternative approaches to Section 15 rent

This illustrates the approach to assessing enfranchisement price for a house held with a short term of lease but with two superior interests against which to enfranchise. The house has a limited life but the freeholder intends to impose covenants on the freehold which will restrict the use and value of the premises.

The house is on a 0·2 h.a. site and is held with 5 years unexpired term of sublease at £10 p.a. from the head-leaseholder who holds an 8 years unexpired term from the freeholder at a rent of £5 p.a. The occupying sub-leaseholder qualifies to enfranchise and has recently served valid notices to acquire both superior interests. It has been agreed that the freeholder will impose covenants in the conveyance to the effect that not more than one house be erected on the site, that any new design and layout be within certain constraints, and that there be various domestic limitations. The existing house, after much needed improvements, would have an entirety value of £20,000. Comparable sites have sold for £7·50 per square metre for flat development, planning permission for which is readily forthcoming in the neighbourhood. Large single house plots with planning permission but subject to restrictive covenants such as those to be imposed are worth about £42,000 per ha.

Valuations for Enfranchisement Price Assessment (1)

Section 15 Modern Ground Rent (2)

	£	£ p.a.
Cleared site approach:		
0·2 ha. restricted use value (3)		
0·2 × £42,000 site value	8,400	
Section 15 rent at 6%	0·06	
		504
Or		
Standing house approach:	£	
Entirety value	20,000	
Site value at 25% (4)	0·25	
	5,000	
Section 15 rent at 6%	0·06	
		300

Assume that the cleared site approach is the most suitable in this case. (5)

Section 15 Modern Ground Rent	£504 p.a.

Enfranchisement Price of the Freehold Interest

Term	£ p.a.	£
Rent receivable	5	
Y.P. 8 years at 6%	6·2	
		31

	B/F		31
Reversion to Section 15 rent	504		
Y.P. in perp. (6) at 7% deferred 8 years	8·3		
	——	4,183	
		4,214	
Enfranchisement price of freeholder's interest	say	£4,200	

Enfranchisement Price of the Head lessee's Interest

Term	£ p.a.		£
Rent receivable	10		
Rent payable	5		
Net income	5		
Y.P. for 5 years at 7 & 4% (Tax at 40%)	2·6 (7)		
	——		13
Reversion to Section 15 rent	504		
Rent payable	5		
Net income	499		
Y.P. 3 years at 8 & 4% (Tax at 40%)	1·6		
P.V. £1 in 5 years at 8%	0·68	1·1	
	——	——	549
			562
Enfranchisement price of the head lessee's interest (8) (9) (10)			
		say	£560

Notes

(1) Provisions on enfranchisement by subtenants are in Section 5 (4) and Schedule 1. The "Reversioner", in this case the free-holder, acts for all the superior interests in dividing up the total enfranchisement price. See *The Goldsmiths' Company* v. *Guardian Assurance Co. Ltd., and Syrett* (1970) 216 E.G. 595, *Hameed* v. *Hussain and Others* (1977) 242 E.G. 1063, *Nash* v. *Central Estates (Belgravia) Ltd* (1978) 249 E.G. 1286, *Burton* v. *Kolup Investments Ltd* (1978) 251 E.G. 1290, *Mortiboys* v. *Dennis Fell Companies* (1984) (unreported W. Midlands L.V.T.) and *Pilgrim* v. *Central Estates (Belgravia) Ltd* (1986) 278 E.G. 1373.

(2) In *Farr* v. *Millersons Investments Ltd* (1971) 218 E.G. 1177 it was suggested that the valuer should use one main approach to the Section 15 site value and one of the other accepted approaches as a check. As the life of the property is unsure, the so called "new for old approach" may have been appropriate here. See Study 5.

(3) Section 10 deals with the restrictions which may be imposed on the freehold title and in the event of dispute these matters may be referred to a leasehold valuation tribunal and an appeal to the Lands Tribunal. Restrictions on the freehold title to be conveyed may reduce the enfranchisement price but the rights to be assumed in assessing the Section 15 rent must be borne in mind. See *Buckley* v. *S.R.L. Investments Ltd.*, and *Cator and Robinson*, (1979) 214 E.G. 1057, *Peck* v. *Hornsey* (1970) 216 E.G. 943, *Hutton* v. *Girdlers* (1971) 219 E.G. 175, *Grime* v. *Robinson* (1972) 224 E.G. 815 and *Barrable* v. *Westminster City Council* (1984) 271 E.G. 1273 for examples of covenants being imposed on the freehold titles conveyed. See note (5) to Study 2 (supra).

(4) This percentage is assumed but would have to be justified. See note (6) to Study 2 (supra).

(5) See the Lands Tribunal's decision in *Farr*'s case (supra).

(6) The effect of the notional 25 year rent review and the reversion after 50 years may be ignored in the calculation. See *Farr*'s case (supra) but see also *Haresign*'s case (supra).

(7) This interest is valued on a conventional dual rate tax adjusted basis as it is a short leasehold interest. Although differential risk rates are applied to the term and reversion in this Study, in more recent tribunal decisions the same rate has been applied to both the term and the reversion. Wholly net of tax valuations were rejected in *Perrin* v. *Ashdale Land and Property Co. Ltd* (1971) 218 E.G. 573. The tax rate is negotiable.

(8) Marriage of the headleasehold and freehold interests prior to enfranchisement can put up the total enfranchisement price a little in this sort of case.

(9) The House of Lords in *Jones* v. *Wrotham Park Settled Estates and Another* [1979] 1 All E.R. 286 confirmed the validity of a freeholder creating an intermediary headlease which increased the total costs of enfranchisement from £300 to £4,000. This loophole was closed by the Leasehold Reform Act 1979 which requires that the enfranchisement price cannot be artificially increased by transactions involving the creation of new intermediary or similar interests or the alteration in the terms of the lease after 15th February 1979.

(10) In this case had the head leaseholder a profit rent of not more than £5 per annum and a reversion of not more than one month the enfranchisement price would be on a formula basis as set out in Schedule 21 (6) of the Housing Act 1980. The formula is:

$$\text{Price (P)} = \frac{\text{Profit Rent (R)}}{2\frac{1}{2} \text{ Consols Yield (Y)}} - \frac{R}{Y(1-Y)^n}$$

and it capitalises the term profit rent at the current $2\frac{1}{2}\%$ Consols yield. The formula counts any part of a year as a whole year. There is no appeal to a leasehold valuation tribunal on the enfranchisement price in such cases. See *Afzal* v. *Cressingham Properties Ltd* (1981) (unreported W. Midlands L.V.T.).

Study 5

Enfranchisement price, comparables and the adverse differential issue

This considers further the methods of arriving at site value in the "normal" enfranchisement hypothesis of Section 9 (1) of the Act and examines the now generally discredited concept of the "adverse differential". It also looks at the role of enfranchisement settlements as evidence and the use of other risk rate approaches.

A large residential estate is the subject of much enfranchisement and most of the houses are held on ground leases expiring shortly at rents of £15 p.a. each. The landlord's valuers have settled several enfranchisement claims at figures of about £4,600 for 5 year unexpired terms. The frontage, depth and amenity of the plots vary although the plot areas are all very similar. The landlord's valuers have established a comprehensive approach to site values on the estate and have developed techniques to adjust prices to allow for minor differences between the plots.

The study considers enfranchisement price from both the landlord's and the tenant's point of view in order to draw out various matters which might be the subject of negotiation. The interest concerned qualifies for enfranchisement within the less than £500 (£1,000 in Greater London) rateable value bands and the price falls to be assessed under the assumptions of Section 9 (1). The lease has an unexpired term of 5 years at £15 p.a. The house has a limited life and the plot has a frontage of 10 metres, a depth of 40 metres and an area of 400 square metres.

Enfranchisement price using arguments to the landlord's advantage

Term

	£ p.a.	£
Rent receivable	15	
Y.P. 5 years at 6% (1)	4·2	63

Reversion to Section 15 rent
Cleared site approach: (2)
10 metres frontage at landlord's
  adjusted rate per metre frontage for
  plots of 400 square metres, 10 metres
  at £450 (3)   £4,500
Adjustments to site value; (4)
  i) for better location/amenity + 15%   £675
  ii) 10 metres deeper than average plot
      + 10%   £450

Site value	say	£5,625
Section 15 rent at 6%		0·06

Section 15 rent		338
Y.P. in perp. at 6% deferred 5 years (5) (6)	12·5	4,225

                                                                        £4,288

Landlord's view of enfranchisement price   say   £4,300 (7)

Notes

(1) The rate of 6% or 7% was generally adopted for the term follow-
    ing *Farr*'s case (supra) and the lower rate favours the landlord.
(2) The "Cleared Site" approach is used as the house has a limited life.
(3) A similarly scheduled approach to site values on a large estate
    was used by landlord's valuers in *Siggs and Others* v. *Royal
    Arsenal Cooperative Society Ltd* (1971) 220 E.G. 39. The Lands
    Tribunal was noncommital but accepted the approach in that case.
(4) These adjustments are given solely by way of illustration and
    could only be used in practice with clear and careful justification.
(5) The Section 15 rent has been recapitalised at the same 6%.
    This follows *Official Custodian for Charities and the Trustees
    of St. Pancras Church Lands* v. *Goldridge* (1973) 227 E.G.
    1467 in which the Court of Appeal disapproved of the "adverse
    differential". This differential was earlier adopted by the Lands

Tribunal to take account of Section 82 of the Housing Act 1969 and it's exclusion of the tenant's bid for the freehold in assessing enfranchisement price. See *Farr*'s case (supra) and many subsequent cases where site values were decapitalised at about 6% and then recapitalised at 8% giving an adverse differential of 2%. In *Grainger* v. *Gunter Estate Trustees* (1977) 246 E.G. 55 an attempt to use a larger adverse differential was rejected by the Lands Tribunal. In *Wilkes* v. *Larkcroft Properties Ltd* (1983) 268 E.G. 903, the Court of Appeal held that evidence of "en bloc" sales of ground rents did not justify a claim that the adverse differential should be applied as a matter of law. The Court also explored the nature of evidence required to support a decision by the Tribunal.

(6) In the *Siggs* case (supra) it was held that the large estate landlord might bid for leaseholds as they came onto the market in order to reap marriage value. This enabled the larger estate to argue against the "adverse differential" and apply one common rate in arriving at the Section 15 rent reflecting the "marriage by sale incentive". The Court of Appeal disapproved of this argument in the *Goldridge* case (supra).

(7) Enfranchisement settlements should be adjusted before use as evidence to reflect the "Delaforce effect". This is the extra amount a tenant might be willing to pay in a negotiated settlement to avoid the worry, risk and costs of litigation. See *Delaforce* v. *Evans* (1970) 215 E.G. 315 and *Ugrinic*'s case (supra). In this Study settlements are given at about £4,600 and it therefore might be argued that there has been a £300 "Delaforce effect" allowance in this price. In *Wilkes*'s case (supra) the Court of Appeal held that the Lands Tribunal did not err in declining to make a deduction for the *Delaforce effect*.

Enfranchisement price using arguments to the tenant's advantage

	£ p.a.	£
Term Rent payable	15	
Y.P. 5 years at 8% (1)	4	
	——	60

Reversion to Section 15 rent		
New for old approach: (2)	£	
Sale price of new house on site	20,000	
less: building costs	16,500	
	——	
Section 15 site value	3,500	

OR

Sale price of new house on site	20,000	
Site value at 20%	0·2	
	———	
Section 15 site value	4,000	
Adopt lower	3,500	
	———	
Section 15 rent at 8%	0·08	280
Y.P. in perp. at 10% (3) deferred 5 years	6·2	
		———
		1,736
Tenant's view of enfranchisement price		£1,796
		———
		say £1,800

Notes

(1) The tenant might argue for 8% or higher if interest rates are high. In *Patten* v. *Wenrose Investments Ltd* (1976) 241 E.G. 396 8% was accepted at all stages of the valuation and in *Lowther*'s case (supra) 9% was adopted throughout for houses in Holland Park, London.

(2) The "new for old" approach is an alternative where the house has a limited but indeterminate future life. See *Gajewski* v. *Anderton and Kershaw* (1971) 217 E.G. 885 and *Farr*'s case (supra). The figures here are assumed and would need to be supported with evidence.

(3) Although the Court of Appeal disapproved of the adverse differential in the *Goldridge* case (supra) there have been cases before the Lands Tribunal since when it has been accepted. The Court of Appeal left the matter open if the concept could be justified with evidence and reason. See *Lead* v. *J. & L. Estates Ltd* (1976) 236 E.G. 819 and *Perry* v. *Barry Marson Ltd* (1976) 238 E.G. 793.

Possible form of valuation for a negotiated settlement in this Study

	£ p.a.	£
Term Rent reserved	15	
Y.P. 5 years at 7% (1)	4·1	
	———	
		62

Reversion to Section 15 rent. Site			
value say	£4,500		
Section 15 rent at 7% (1)	0·07	315	
Y.P. in perp. at 7% deferred 5 years		10·19	3,210
Enfranchisement price (2)			£3,272
		say	£3,300

Notes

(1) For the settlement figure calculation a rate of 7% has been adopted but this would of course need to be supported by dependable market evidence derived from consistent analysis of market transactions and settlements. See *Custins* v. *Hearts of Oak* (1969) 209 E.G. 239.

(2) No reversion to the "standing house" after 55 years has been included as was in *Haresign*'s case (supra) as the house has been stated as having a very limited future life and such an approach would be inconsistent with the cleared site and new for old approaches adopted.

Study 6

Rateable value adjustment for qualification

This examines further qualification for enfranchisement or extension under the amendments of Section 118 and Schedule 8 of the Housing Act 1974 as amended by Section 141 and Schedule 21 of the Housing Act 1980. There are matters under these amendments which have not yet been tested in reported cases.

A bungalow outside London is held on the residue of a long lease with 10 years unexpired term at a ground rent of £12 p.a. The premises had a rateable value of £300 at the 23rd March 1965, one of £805 at the 1st April 1973 and has a Gross External Area (GEA or "Reduced Covered Area") of 225 m². The present occupier purchased the premises in 1970 and at once built an extension with a GEA of 25 m². The previous owner had installed central heating and erected a double garage in 1968. The value of the bungalow now, freehold and with vacant possession, would be £65,000 but without the tenant's improvements would be only £45,000. Apart from the apparent rateable values the tenant is assumed to be otherwise qualified under the Act.

Qualification for enfranchisement

The tenant did not qualify under the original 1967 rateable value limit and at first sight does not qualify under the amendments of the Housing Act 1974 as the rateable value is over £750. The tenant may however use Section 1 (4A) of the Act, contained in Schedule 21 of the Housing Act 1980, which enables a tenant who is otherwise qualified to claim a reduction (1) in the notional rateable value for enfranchisement purposes to exclude the annual value of any tenants' (2) improvements (3) (4).

Adjustment to the rateable value under Section 1 (4A) of the Act and Schedule 8 of the Housing Act 1974

			£
Rateable value at 1.4.1973	(5)	£805	
Gross value at 1.4.1973		£1,000	
Analysis of gross value	225 m² @ £3·67		825
	Central heating		80
	Double garage		95
	Gross value		£1,000
Assessment without tenants' improvements (exclude 25 m² extension)	200 m² @ £3·67		734
	No central heating		—
	No garage		—
	Gross value		734
less statutory deductions			151
Adjusted rateable value without tenants' improvements. (5) (6)			£583

Therefore the lessee will qualify to enfranchise but the enfranchisement price will be under the additional Section 9 (1A) introduced in 1974 as the rateable value is over £500. (7) (8)

Notes

(1) The tenant first serves a notice on the landlord requiring him to agree to the nature of the improvements to be discounted and proposing a figure for the reduced rateable value. The form of notice is set out in Schedule 8 of the Housing Act 1974

and the tenant must specify the improvements and works concerned. The tenant must bear the reasonable costs of the landlord's investigations of the works of improvement claimed on
any notices after the 21st December 1979. (See Schedule 21
(8) of the Housing Act 1980.)

Failing agreement between the parties the County Court may
determine the extent and nature of the improvements to be taken
into account and the valuation officer may be required to determine the reduced rateable value excluding the value of the
improvements.

(2) The provisions regarding the adjustment of rateable value apply
to the improvements of both the current and any previous
tenants. (Schedule 8 (1)(1) of the Housing Act 1974.)

(3) The time scale for the procedures under schedule 8 is generally
mandatory and a tenant may only make a single application
under them for that reason. See *Pollock* v. *Brook Shepherd*
(1982), 266 E.G. 214. In *Arielli* v. *Duke of Westminster* (1984)
269 E.G. 535, the Court of Appeal overruled a County Court
decision to refuse an extension of time to originate an application to the Court under schedule 8. In *Johnston* v. *Duke of
Westminster* (1984) 272 E.G. 661 a twelve day extension of
the time to refer the matter to the court was held to be within
the Judge's discretion.

(4) Improvements in this context include works amounting to structural alteration, extension or addition, for example a garage.
Whether the construction of a replacement house is an improvement is not clear but the Court of Appeal in *Pearlman* v. *Keepers
and Governors of Harrow School* (1978) 247 E.G. 1173 decided
that the installation of central heating in this context was an
improvement.

(5) There is some uncertainty as to the date by reference to which
rateable values are to be considered and adjusted. See article
at 266 E.G. 187 and *Pollock*'s case (supra).

(6) An alternative approach to the adjustment of rateable value
based on a factor with the unimproved capital value over the
improved capital value was illustrated in an earlier edition of
this chapter. The rating approach here is however one more
likely to be adopted by the Valuation Officer where the landlord
and tenant cannot agree to the appropriate reduction.

(7) There is no appeal against a valuation officer's certificate of
adjusted rateable value. In *R.* v. *Valuation Officer for Westminster and District, ex parte Rendall* (1986) 278 E.G. 1090 a tenant
argued that the valuation officer's certified adjusted rateable
value was incorrect, it being more than £1,500, and sought

judicial review. This was dismissed by the High Court and the Court of Appeal.

(8) As the rateable value after adjustment is over £500 the enfranchisement price must be assessed under the assumptions in Section 9 (1A) of the Act, contained in Section 118 (4) of the Housing Act 1974.

Study 7

Enfranchisement price where the rateable value is over £500 (£1,000 in London)—the "Norfolk" approach

This illustrates the assessment of enfranchisement price under the provisions of Section 9 (1A) which do not assume a modern ground rent for the notional fifty years lease extension and do not preclude any marriage value from a tenant's bid. Using the facts adopted in Study 6 and with the rateable value reduced to £583 the tenant now qualifies to enfranchise but at a price to be assessed under the less favourable assumptions introduced by Section 118 of the Housing Act 1974 and interpreted by the Lands Tribunal in *Norfolk* and *Lloyd-Jones (supra)*. See also pages 90 and 91.

Enfranchisement Price Assessment

Valuation of Lessor's Interest excluding marriage value (1)

Term	£ p.a.	£ p.a.	£
Rent receivable		12	
Y.P. 10 years at 7%		7	84
Reversion to a protected tenancy under the Landlord and Tenant Act 1954 (2)			
Assume "Fair Rent" 10% of the unimproved (3) standing house value (4) of £45,000	4,500		
Less: outgoings say 15%	675		
		3,825	
Y.P. in perpetuity at 12% (4) deferred 10 yrs		2·7	
			10,328
Value of lessor's interest excluding marriage value			10,412
(see note 5 for an alternative approach)			say £10,500

Valuation of the Lessee's interest excluding marriage value

Term	£ p.a.	£
Annual value of house say 10% on the full freehold vacant possession value (4) of £65,000	6,500	
Less: Rent payable	12	
Profit rent	6,488	
Y.P. 10 years at 12% (4) & 4% (tax 40%) (6)	3·9	
		£25,303

Value of lessee's interest excluding marriage value   say £25,300
(No value has been put on the reversionary right)

Apportionment of marriage value to arrive at enfranchisement price (7)

1. Value of lessor's interest exclusive of marriage value   £10,500
2. Assessment of lessor's share of marriage value
   - a) Freehold vacant possession value   £65,000
     less lessee's improvements   £20,000

          £45,000
   - b) Value of lessor's interest exclusive of marriage value   £10,500
   - c) Value of lessee's interest exclusive of marriage value £25,300
     less value to the lessee of his improvements (8)   £7,400

          £17,900
   - d) Total value of free-hold and leasehold interests unmarried b + c   £28,400
   - e) Gain on the marriage of the interests ignoring the lessee's improvements   £16,600

	B/F	£16,600	
f) Lessor's share of the gain	say 50% (9)	0·5	
			£8,300
3. Enfranchisement price			£18,800

Notes

(1) The study follows the apportionment of marriage value basis used by the Lands Tribunal in *Norfolk* v. *Trinity College, Cambridge* (1976) 238 E.G. 421. The principle confirmed in that case was that Section 118 (4) of the Housing Act 1974 (the new Section 9 (1A) of the 1967 Act) does not exclude the extra value of the "tenant's bid" where the enfranchisement price is assessed under the Section 118 provisions. The price therefore includes any extra amount that a tenant might pay for the value increase arising on the marriage of the freehold and leasehold interests.

(2) The principle now in Section 9 (1A) (b) is that instead of reverting to a "modern ground rent" enfranchising tenants revert in the enfranchisement hypothesis to a protected tenancy under the Landlord and Tenant Act 1954 which will be at a "fair rent".

(3) The valuation must ignore the value of any tenant's improvements. It seems that the word improvement here has a wider meaning than for the rateable value reduction provisions in Schedule 8 of the 1974 Act.

(4) The assumptions here are illustrative only and clearly will be open to negotiation. In *Lloyd-Jones* v. *Church Commissioners for England* (1981) 261 E.G. 471, the second reported case under the different valuation assumptions introduced by the 1974 Act, it was held that such an approach was inappropriate in London as it was almost unknown for tenants of particular types of house to continue in occupation at a fair rent. Tenants, it was stated, normally surrender and renew leases or purchase the freehold. In *Lowther and Others* v. *Strandberg and Others* (1985) 275 E.G. 53, the effect of the tenant's bid on a Holland Park, London W14 estate was considered and the *Lloyd-Jones* approach was adopted even though the reversion was not for 81 years. A discount rate of 9% was adopted throughout the valuation.

(5) In the *Lloyd-Jones* case (supra) the Lands Tribunal accepted the strong settlement evidence of the landlord's valuers and dismissed, as being out of touch with reality, the tenant's view of the reversion to a fair rent. The approach adopted for the landlord's reversion was to simply deduct 10% from the freehold vacant possession value to reflect the risk of a tenant claiming a tenancy under Part I of the Landlord and Tenant Act 1954.

The *Lloyd-Jones* case approach to the value of the landlord's interest excluding marriage value would be:

Term as before			£84
Reversion to unimproved vacant possession value	£45,000		
less for risk of tenant claiming a tenancy under Part I of the Landlord and Tenant Act 1954 10%	£4,500		
	£40,500		
× P.V. of £1 in 10 yrs 7%		0·5	£20,250
			£20,334

In this Study the enfranchisement price would be little different but in the *Lloyd-Jones* case it increased the enfranchisement price by £68,000.

(6) The lessee's term has been valued on a conventional dual rate tax adjusted basis. No value has been placed on the lessee's right to a further protected tenancy although there would certainly be a loss in value to the lessor.

(7) This is the apportionment approach used in *Norfolk*'s case (supra).

(8) This has been found by taking an annual value of £750 for the improvements and capitalising it on a dual rate tax adjusted basis for the lessee's term unexpired.

(9) The percentage applied in the *Norfolk* case (supra).

Study 8

Further rateable value adjustments as a means of reducing enfranchisement price

This study considers the effect of obtaining a further reduction in the rateable value to below the £500 (£1,000) figure in order to enable enfranchisement price to be assessed under Section 9 (1) which is more favourable to the tenant.

The facts are as in Studies 6 and 7 except that on detailed survey of the house and premises it becomes apparent that part of the bungalow dates from 1900 and part from 1922. The GEA of the premises as originally constructed in 1900 can be shown to be 160 m². The value of the premises without these further improvements would be £35,000.

Qualification for enfranchisement

Adjustment to the rateable value under Section 1 (4A) and 9 (1B) of the Act

Gross value at 1.4.1973 (as before)	£1,000
Gross value without tenant's improvements	
160 m² @ £3·67	£587
No central heating	—
No double garage	—
Gross value	£587
less statutory deductions	£126
Adjusted rateable value without tenant's improvements (1)	£461

The tenant qualifies to enfranchise but as the rateable value is less than £500 the enfranchisement price will be assessed under the normal Section 9 (1) assumptions of the 1967 Act.

Enfranchisement price assessment (2)

Term	£ p.a.	£
Rent reserved	12	
Y.P. 10 years at 7%	7	
	——	84
Reversion to Section 15 rent		
Standing house approach; (3)		
Entirety value	£65,000	
Site value at 25%	£16,250	
Section 15 rent at 7%	0·07	
	—— 1,138	
Y.P. in perp. at 7% deferred 10 years	7·3	
	——	8,307

Enfranchisement price (4)   £8,391

This compares with £19,500 in Study 7 (5)   say £8,400

Notes

(1) In the leasehold valuation tribunal case of *Effra Investments Ltd* v. *Stergios* (1982) 264 E.G. 449, L.V.T. a house in London had been converted into flats taking the rateable value over £1,000. Although the tribunal gave the tenant time to take action to reduce the rateable value under Schedule 8 of the Housing Act 1974 he did not do so and the tribunal fixed a high enfranchisement price under the provisions of Section 9 (1A), closely following the principles of the *Norfolk* decision.

(2) In this case the value of any tenant's bid which might include a marriage value component is excluded by Section 82 of the Housing Act 1969.

(3) This approach was considered more fully in Studies 3 and 4.

(4) It can be seen from this enfranchisement price that it may well be in the lessee's interest to try and ensure that the rateable value is reduced to a level which brings the enfranchisement price within the 1967 Act rules and excludes the marriage value component and the resulting higher enfranchisement prices adopted under Section 9 (1A) in the *Lloyd-Jones* and *Norfolk* cases (supra).

(5) The enfranchisement price assumptions for premises in the £500 to £750 (£1,000–£1,500 in London) rateable value bands are those of Section 9 (1A). If a tenant in that band of value served a notice to take an extended lease instead, he would be entitled to such at a modern ground rent for 50 years notwithstanding the rateable value level. Subject to the repossession rights of Section 17 (see Study 10) he might avoid having to pay the marriage value element yet would still obtain a very valuable interest. See article at 268 E.G. 876, 978 and Study 9 (infra).

Study 9

Houses in the higher rateable value bands: extending a lease as an alternative to, or prior to, buying a freehold

The Lands Tribunal in *Hickman and Others* v. *Phillimore and Others* (1985) 274 E.G. 1261, confirmed by the Court of Appeal in *Mosley and Others* v. *Hickman and Others* (1986) 278 E.G. 728, determined that a tenant of a house in the higher rateable value band, who had first extended the lease for fifty years at a section 15 rent, could enfranchise at a price reflecting that extended lease. Section 23 of the Housing and Planning Act 1986 has since amended Section 9 (1A) of the Act to require that no rights to an extension be assumed and that if a lease has been extended it is to be assumed to terminate at the original term date. The alternative of lease extension was also examined at 268 E.G. 876,978 where it was shown in some cases to be potentially better value for a tenant than enfranchising under the assumptions of section 9 (1A). This alternative is still available to otherwise qualified tenants in the higher rateable value band who wish to expand their interest under the Act but without any capital outlay.

Ths study assumes a house in London with a 1st April 1973 rateable value of £1,300 held on a ground lease with ten years to run. The ground rent is £50 per annum and the tenant is assumed to qualify under the provisions of the Leasehold Reform Act as amended. The house is agreed as having an unencumbered freehold value of £100,000 at the relevant date.

Lease extension
The tenant of the house can claim under section 14 to have an extended lease of a further fifty years in addition to the present term and such a lease would be in substitution for the existing one. This new lease would be for sixty years, the first ten years term at the existing rent and the further fifty years at the section 15 rent. The section 15 rent would not be fixed until the last year of the original lease, in this case in nine years time. The new lease would normally provide for a rent review, in this case in thirty five years time, section 15 (2). The tenant will still have the right to serve a notice to have the freehold upto the time when the original lease would have expired, in this case during the next ten years, section 16 (1)(a). Such an arrangement would ensure that the tenant retains a quite valuable interest at quite a modest cost, in present value terms, without having to borrow any capital. However the nature of the section 15 rent could mean that the interest is less marketable than it would be freehold.

Valuation of the tenant's interest after extension
Term of existing lease
Full annual value say 10% on £100,000   £10,000 pa
less ground rent   £50
                                                    ─────────

Profit rent	£9,950	
Y.P. 10 years at 10% & 4% tax 40% (1)	4·187	
		£41,660
Reversion to section 15 rent and extended term (2)		
Full annual value as before	£10,000	
Section 15 rent based on site value		
as 30% of the entirety of £100,000		
Section 15 rent at 9% of £30,000	£2,700(3)	
Profit rent	£7,300	
Y.P. 50 (4) years at 10% & 4% (tax 40%)		
deferred 10 years at 10%	3·476	£25,375
Total value of tenant's extended interest		£67,035
	say	£67,000

Notes

(1) All the component figures would need justification by reference to market evidence.

(2) While the extended lease will in due course become a wasting asset it might appeal to a tenant who only wishes to remain in occupation and has no intention or wish to realise the best financial return from a sale of the house.

(3) Extension of the lease would limit the cost of remaining in occupation to the present value of the liability to pay the Section 15 rent. This would be about £10,500 today but this should be compared with the present value of the interest obtained and the cost of an outright purchase of the freehold (supra).

(4) It must be remembered that a tenant who has taken an extended lease can be the subject of proceedings for possession for redevelopment under Section 17, subject to the compensation right for the value of the extended lease (see Study 10).

(continued on page 98)

Enfranchisement price if notice to have the freehold is served after the lease has been extended

(The application of this approach is now limited by the effect of Section 23 of the Housing and Planning Act 1986.)

If the leaseholder were to serve notice to have the freehold after the lease was extended, but before the 7th November 1986, the enfranchisement price might be assessed "on the assumption that the vendor was selling ... subject to the tenancy". The tenancy now existing is the extended one at a section 15 "modern ground rent", not the type of tenancy normally to be assumed under Section 9 (1A) for houses in the higher rateable value band. The tenant is not however excluded from the notional market in which the freehold is being sold and a marriage value bid may be included in an enfranchisement price calculation.

Enfranchisement price calculation (5)

Assessment of the enfranchisement price following an earlier application for and grant of a 50-year lease extension at a modern ground rent under Section 14, with the notice to have the freehold served before 6th November 1986, the "Hickman approach" prior to the 1986 Act restriction on its application

Valuation of lessor's interest excluding prospect of marriage value

Term			
Rent receivable	£50		
Y.P. 10 years @ 9% (6)	6·418		£321
Reversion to 50 years' lease extension			
To modern ground rent under Section 15 site value, say 30% of entirety value			
30% of £100,000	£30,000		
Section 15 rent at 9% (7)	£2,700		
Y.P. 50 years @ 9%	10·962		
deferred 10 years @ 9%	0·422	4·626	£12,490
Reversion to entirety value	£100,000		
deferred for 60 years @ 9%	0·00568	£568	£13,379

Lessor's share of marriage value (8)			
Estimated value of unencumbered freehold interest		£100,000	
Less			
(i) value of lessor's interest excluding prospect of marriage	£13,379		
(ii) value of lessee's interest excluding prospect of marriage, say	£65,000	£78,379	
Gain on marriage		£21,621	
50% to the lessor			£10,811
Enfranchisement price			£24,190
			Say £24,000

Lessee's value excluding marriage value (as used in (ii) above)			
Term Profit rent for 10 years	£9,950		
Y.P. 10 years 10% 4% SF (tax 40%)	4·187	£41,660	
Reversion to decreased profit rent for 50 years with section 15 rent of £2,700, say			
Profit rent	£7,300		
Y.P. 50 years 10% 4% (tax 40%) deferred 10 years at 10%	3·476	£25,375	£65,035

Say £67,000

Enfranchisement price if a notice to have the freehold was served without the lease having first been extended or if section 23 of the 1986 Act applies

Assessment of enfranchisement price on the basis generally adopted for houses in the higher rateable value band following the Lloyd-Jones *decision.* No earlier extension of the lease is assumed.

Valuation of lessor's interest excluding prospect of marriage value.

Term			
Rent receivable	£50		
Y.P. 10 years 9%	6·418	£321	
Reversion			
Estimated value of unencumbered freehold interest	£100,000		
Less for risk of tenant claiming a tenancy under Part I of LTA 1954, say 10%	£10,000		
	£90,000		
P.V. of £1 in 10 years @ 9%	0·422	£37,980	£38,301
Lessor's share of marriage value Estimated value of unencumbered freehold interest		£100,000	
Less			
(i) value of lessor's interest excluding prospect of marriage	£38,301		
(ii) value of lessee's interest excluding prospect of marriage (£9,950 profit rent for 10 years—see the lessee's term at top of page 95)	£41,660		
		£79,961	
Gain on marriage		£20,039	
50% to the lessor			£10,020
Enfranchisement price (9)			£48,321

Say £49,325

Notes (continued from page 95)

(5) No valuations were published in the *Hickman* decision but the approach adopted here may well be similar.

(6) Although 9% has been adopted in this study, and was in the *Lowther* case, the appropriate discount rate will depend on the reliability of the supporting evidence of the parties.

(7) Although the house is in the higher rateable value band the lease has been extended for 50 years at a Section 15 rent and the Section 9 (1A) assumption of an extended lease at a rack rent for the building is overruled by the terms of the extended lease, given that the notice to have the freehold was served before Section 23 of the Housing and Planning Act 1986 became effective.

(8) The *Norfolk* and *Lloyd Jones* approach to the marriage value bid has been used here.

(9) It can be seen that on the figures assumed here the price for the freehold after the tenant has first extended the lease is less than half that of a direct purchase of the freehold. The tenant's professional fees and costs for this route to enfranchisement would be higher than on a direct purchase of the freehold but could be well worthwhile.

Study 10

Premises with redevelopment potential and the repossession rights under Section 17

This examines the assessment of enfranchisement price where the house and premises have development potential. The problem is how to take account of the landlord's rights to repossession for redevelopment under Section 17 of the Act. The principles have not been tested before the Lands Tribunal or the Courts, probably because of the fact that the gains available through marriage via enfranchisement are sufficient to ease successful negotiations.

A large obsolete house on a 0·7 ha plot is held with 6 years unexpired term at a ground rent of £25 p.a. The house had a rateable value of £195 at 23rd March 1965 and the tenant qualifies to enfranchise. The value of the plot with planning permission for the best feasible redevelopment would be £90,000 freehold with vacant possession. The value of the site restricted to use for one dwelling would be £11,000 and the entirety value of the house improved would be £30,000, both figures being freehold with vacant possession. The lessors are willing to sell the freehold interest without restrictions on redevelopment on the title and have accepted the lessees' notice of enfranchisement. The lessee requires a valuation of his current interest as he is now proposing to sell to a developer.

Valuation of the Lessee's Interest for Sale (1) *taking account of the landlord's redevelopment rights under section* 17 (2)

Costs of Enfranchisement	£ p.a.	£	£
Term			
Rent payable	25		
Y.P. 6 years at 7%	4·8		120
Reversion to full redevelopment value		90,000	
less Section 17 + Schedule 2			
compensation			
The value to the lessee of a 50 year			
lease at a Section 15 modern ground			
rent. (2)			
Annual value of house say (3)	3,000		
less Section 15 rent based on			
7% of £11,000	770		
Notional annual profit rent	2,230		
Y.P. for 50 years at 10 & 4%			
(tax 40%)	9·0		
Schedule 2 compensation in 6 years			
time (3)		20,070	
Value of reversion less compensation		69,930	
P.V. £1 in 6 years at 10% (4)		0·56	
Present value of lessor's reversionary			
rights under the enfranchisement			
hypothesis			39,161
Total enfranchisement price (5)			39,281
add landlord's and tenant's			
enfranchisement costs (6)		say	1,000
Total enfranchisement costs (7)			40,281
		say	£41,250

Full development value of the site (as
given)   £90,000
Less costs of enfranchisement   £40,250

Value of lessee's interest for sale (8)   £49,750

Notes

(1) A lessee may assign his lease with the enfranchisement rights
    as soon as a valid notice of enfranchisement has been served.
    Section 5.
(2) Section 17 reserves to the landlord of a dwelling, where the
    lessee has taken an extended lease under the Act, the right to
    repossession for redevelopment. Here it is assumed in assessing
    enfranchisement price that a tenant has an extended lease it
    would appear logical to incorporate in the valuation the notional
    right of the landlord to repossession. This right is available not
    earlier than one year prior to the original term date and the
    landlord must compensate the tenant under Schedule 2 for a
    50 year lease at a Section 15 modern ground rent.
(3) The basis for and approach to these figures is open to consider-
    able argument and negotiation.
(4) The deferment allows for the notion that the lessor cannot
    obtain possession until the end of the term when he will then
    have to pay the lessee compensation under Schedule 2.
(5) If the rateable value was over £500 (£1,000 in London), so
    that the enfranchisement price fell to be assessed under the
    Norfolk v. *Cambridge* and *Lloyd Jones'* approaches, (supra)
    the marriage value component might add further to the enfran-
    chisement price and reduce the value of the lessee's interest,
    even though the assumptions under Section 9 (1A) preclude
    the notional right to repossession under Section 17 and assume
    a reversion to a fair rent rather than a modern ground rent.
    A tenant of a house on a site with significant redevelopment
    potential might first extend the lease to take advantage of the
    lease extension approach (supra) if the premises was in the
    higher rateable value band. The landlord could however argue
    for allowance for the section 17 right, as in this study, and
    also for marriage value in assessing a price for the freehold
    under the Act following a subsequent claim to have the freehold.
(6) The tenant is responsible for the landlord's reasonable legal
    and valuation costs incurred in connection with the enfranchise-
    ment. Section 9 (4).

(7) No cases have been referred to the Lands Tribunal or the Courts on the points covered in this study. The Lands Tribunal briefly considered a related Section 17 matter in *Cottingham Mundy v. Dover Borough Council* (1971) 220 E.G. 817.

(8) If the lessee assigned his interest before agreement as to the enfranchisement price, negotiations might subsequently delay development. Therefore the full redevelopment value of the site might be deferred for a suitable period to allow for agreement.

A valuation of the lessee's interest in this case but ignoring the Section 17 redevelopment rights gives a very different answer. The total enfranchisement costs on a cleared site approach under Section 9 (1) would be about £7,500 giving a value to the lessee's interest of about £82,500. It can therefore be seen that the Section 17 approach is very much a landlord's view.

Further Reading

Aldridge, T. M. Leasehold Law, Oyez Longman.

Aldridge, T. M. Rent Control and Leasehold Enfranchisement, Oyez.

Barnes, D. M. W. The Leasehold Reform Act 1967, Butterworths.

Hague, N. T. Leasehold Enfranchisement, Sweet and Maxwell.

Hubbard, C. C. and D. W. Williams, Handbook of Leasehold Reform, Sweet and Maxwell.

Wellings, V. G. Woodfall's Landlord and Tenant, Sweet and Maxwell.

© C. C. Hubbard, 1988

Chapter 4

THE LANDLORD AND TENANT ACTS
(as they apply to business tenancies)

Note. References in this chapter to sections of the 1954 Act are shown in the same type as the text, e.g. Section 25: references to sections of the 1927 Act are shown in italics, e.g. *Section 3.*

The Landlord and Tenant Act 1954 Pt II (as amended by the Law of Property Act 1969) together with the Landlord and Tenant Act 1927, gives security of tenure to tenants of business premises together with a right to possible compensation at the end of their tenancies. This security is afforded by:

(a) automatic continuance of the tenancy notwithstanding expiry of the term at common law (Section 24);
(b) compelling a landlord who desires possession to establish one or more of the grounds listed in Section 30;
(c) giving the tenant a right to apply for a new tenancy by a Section 26 request or on a counter-notice to a Section 25 notice to terminate.

Conditions for security of tenure to apply

Before these rights accrue, the tenancy must be one to which the 1954 Act applies, such conditions being outlined in Section 23 (1) which provides "... applies to any tenancy where the property comprised in the tenancy is or includes premises which are occupied by the tenant and are so occupied for the purposes of a business carried out by him or for those and other purposes". In practice, therefore, firstly there must be a tenancy so that licences are excluded. In *Street* v. *Mountford* [1985] 1 E.G.L.R. 128 the House of Lords held that where residential accommodation is granted for a term at a rent with exclusive possession the grant is a tenancy. Whilst this decision relates to occupation of residential accommodation it is submitted that it is just as applicable to business premises.

Secondly, the premises must be occupied by the tenant for the purposes of a business. Usually, this will not give rise to any problems, as occupation by an agent, for instance a manager, will suffice, as in *Cafeteria (Keighley) Ltd* v. *Harrison* (1956) 168 E.G.

668. It has been suggested, in *Bagettes* v. *G. P. Estates Co. Ltd* (1960) 167 E.G. 249, that a tenant who occupies premises for the sole purpose of subletting parts of the building is outside the scope of the 1954 Act so that the right to renew does not ennure in favour of a tenant who has totally sublet. See *Narcissi* v. *Wolfe* [1960] Ch. 10. In *Linden* v. *Secretary of State for Social Services* (1985) 277 E.G. 543 flats which were occupied by persons employed by a district health authority which, in turn, was exercising the functions on behalf of the Secretary of State were held to be occupied for the purposes of a government department. An interesting decision was reached in *Cristina* v. *Seear* [1985] 2 E.G.L.R. 128 where the business premises were occupied by a company of which the tenant owned all the shares. The tenants contended that the company was a mere vehicle or *alter ego* through which the business was carried on by them. The Court of Appeal held they were not entitled to apply for a new tenancy.

Finally, "business" is defined in Section 23 (2) as including "a trade, profession or employment and includes any activity carried on by a body of persons, whether corporate or incorporate". This has been held to include the activities of a tennis club and the storage of goods in a lock-up garage (see *Bell* v. *Alfred Franks & Bartlett Co. Ltd* [1980] 1 All E.R. 356). The term will obviously include such premises as shops and offices. However, it should be noted that if a tenant carries on a business in breach of a prohibition in the lease, the protection of the 1954 Act does not apply to the premises unless the landlord has consented to, or acquiesced in, the breach; Section 23 (4). (See also *Groveside Properties Ltd* v. *Westminister Medical School* (1983) 267 E.G. 593).

Excluded tenancies

If the tenancy comes within Section 43 of the 1954 Act it will not be subject to the security of tenure provisions. In general, the Act does not apply to (i) agricultural holdings, but may apply to a field used for horse riding lessons (*Wetherall* v. *Smith* (1980) 256 E.G. 163); (ii) mining leases; (iii) licensed premises; (iv) service tenancies; (v) short leases which, with certain exceptions, are for terms not exceeding six months; (vi) extended leases as there is no right to renew an extended tenancy granted under Section 16 (1) of the Leasehold Reform Act 1967; (vii) tenancies at will (*Manfield* v. *Botchin* [1970] 2 Q.B. 612); (viii) tenancies granted by exempt bodies; Sections 57–59 of the 1954 Act.

Automatic continuance under Section 24

Under Section 24 a tenancy to which the Act applies cannot come to an end save in the manner provided by the Act so that if the procedure laid down in Sections 25 and 26 are not strictly adhered to, the tenancy continues in force indefinitely. Section 24 provides that a tenancy to which the Act applies shall not come to an end unless terminated in accordance with the provisions of the Act and the tenant under such a tenancy may apply to the court for a new tenancy,

(a) if the landlord has given notice under Section 25 to terminate the tenancy, or,
(b) if the tenant has made a request for a new tenancy under Section 26.

This section also expressly reserves several common law methods of terminating a business tenancy; for instance, a tenant can surrender his lease provided that the instrument of his surrender was not executed nor any agreement to surrender concluded, before the tenant had been in occupation for one month. The right to forfeit the tenancy or any superior tenancy is also provided for as well as the ability of the tenant to serve a notice to quit; Section 24 (2). It may be, however, that the tenancy ceases to be one to which the Act applies and should this happen during a Section 24 continuance, then the landlord may terminate by giving between 3 and 6 months notice (Section 24 (3)(a)). In *Aireps Ltd* v. *City of Bradford Metropolitan Council* [1985] 2 E.G.L.R. 143 the 1954 Act did not apply as the premises for which a new tenancy was sought no longer existed.

Termination of business tenancy

The renewal or termination procedure may be commenced either by the landlord serving a Section 25 notice to terminate, or the tenant serving a Section 26 request for a new tenancy. A schematic diagram of the operation of the 1954 Act is contained in Diagram 1, page 106.

(a) Section 25 notice
    Such a notice must be in the prescribed form and must be given by the "competent" landlord (see Landlord and Tenant Act 1954 (Notices) Regulations 1983 S.I. 1983 No. 133). The "competent" landlord is the first superior landlord having an interest that will not come to an end within 14 months by effluxion of time (Section 44). Such a notice must state the date on which the current tenancy will come to an end and such a date must

Diagram 1.
Landlord and Tenant Act 1954 Pt II: Procedure for Termination-Renewal.

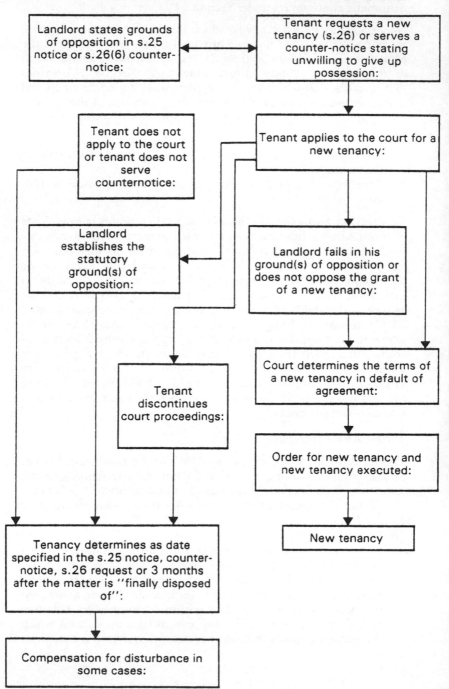

Landlord states grounds of opposition in s.25 notice or s.26(6) counter-notice:	Tenant requests a new tenancy (s.26) or serves a counter-notice stating unwilling to give up possession:

Tenant does not apply to the court or tenant does not serve counternotice:

Tenant applies to the court for a new tenancy:

Landlord establishes the statutory ground(s) of opposition:

Landlord fails in his ground(s) of opposition or does not oppose the grant of a new tenancy:

Tenant discontinues court proceedings:

Court determines the terms of a new tenancy in default of agreement:

Order for new tenancy and new tenancy executed:

Tenancy determines as date specified in the s.25 notice, counter-notice, s.26 request or 3 months after the matter is "finally disposed of":

New tenancy

Compensation for disturbance in some cases:

Note: At any of these stages (before a court order) the parties may agree a renewal by agreement.

not be earlier than the date on which the tenancy would expire either by notice to quit (periodic tenancy) or by effluxion of time (fixed term tenancy).

The Section 25 notice must be given not more than 12 months and not less than 6 months before the termination date specified in the notice (Section 25 (2)). In computing the date of service of the Section 25 notice or a tenant's counter-notice the general rule is that only one day of the notice period is excluded and not both the date of service and the date of expiry (*Hogg Bullimore & Co.* v. *Co-operative Insurance Society Ltd* (1984) 50 P. & C.R. 105). Further the notice must require the tenant, within two months after the giving of the notice, to notify the landlord in writing whether or not at the date of termination he will be willing to give up possession. The notice must also contain a statement as to whether the landlord would oppose an application to the court for the grant of a new tenancy and, if so, on which of the grounds in Section 30 he would do so.

If a 21 year lease contained a break clause giving the landlord an option to terminate the lease every 7 years, what would be the effect of Section 25 on the provisions in the lease? In *Weinbergs Weatherproofs* v. *Radcliffe Paper Mill Co.* [1957] 3 All E.R. 663, it was stated that the service of an ordinary break clause notice would not satisfy Section 25 but may enable a Section 25 notice to be served thereafter, while in *Scholl Manufacturing Co. Ltd* v. *Clifton (Slim-line) Ltd* [1966] 3 All E.R. 66, it was held that a single notice may, in certain circumstances, operate both the break clause and satisfy Section 25.

It should be noted that the provisions of Section 25 (3) and (4) (the "not earlier than" provision) do not apply where the tenancy has already expired or been terminated at common law and is continuing under Section 24 (*Lewis* v. *M.T.C. (Cars) Ltd* (1975) 29 P. & C.R. 495). In such an example, the notice under Section 25 can be given at any time to expire not more than 12 nor less than 6 months later than the date on which it is given.

(b) Section 26 request

For a tenant's Section 26 request to be valid, the tenant's current tenancy must have been granted for either a term of years certain exceeding one year or a term of years certain and thereafter from year to year. However, a request cannot be made after the landlord has served a Section 25 notice. Such a request gives the tenant the right to apply for a new tenancy within two months (Sections 26 (6) and 30 (1)). Should the landlord fail to reply, he will lose his right to oppose a new tenancy.

Application to the Court

Where a Section 25 notice or a Section 26 request has been served, the tenant can apply to the court for a new tenancy. Sections 24 (1) and 29 (1), provide that where the application is consequent upon a Section 25 notice the tenant must have notified the landlord in writing within two months that he was unwilling to give up possession. Such application to the court must be made not less than two months and not more than four months after the Section 25 or Section 26 requirements have been complied with (Section 29 (3)). In computing the two and four months' time limit for the tenant's application to the court for a new tenancy the corresponding date rule should be applied, see *E. J. Riley Investments Ltd* v. *Eurostile Ltd* [1985] 2 E.G.L.R. 124.

It is of the utmost importance to note that recourse to the court to determine the terms of the new tenancy is only to be made where there is disagreement. Section 28 provides that where the landlord and tenant agree to the grant of a further tenancy of the holding, the current tenancy will continue until that date but will not be a tenancy to which the 1954 Act applies. To satisfy Section 28 the agreement must be in writing and there must be agreement on all the material terms, see *Derby & Co. Ltd* v. *I.T.C. Pension Trust Ltd* (1977) 245 E.G. 569. In *R. J. Stratton Ltd* v. *Wallis Tomlin & Co. Ltd* (1985) 277 E.G. 409 an "agreement" for the purposes of Section 28 was held to be a binding contractual arrangement enforceable by the parties at law. Application to the count within the strict time limits is essential to protect the tenant's interest.

Landlord's grounds of opposition

Whether the landlord states his opposition in his own Section 25 notice or in his counter-notice to the tenant's Section 26 request he will have to confine himself to the seven grounds outlined in Section 30 (1) paras (a) to (g) which are as follows:

(a) Failure to repair: In order to be able to rely on this ground the landlord must prove that the state of repair of the holding is such that the tenant should not be granted a new tenancy. There is a discretion in the court as to the degree of disrepair, see *Lyons* v. *Central Commercial Properties Ltd* [1958] 1 W.L.R. 869. In *Eichner* v. *Midland Bank Executor and Trustee Co. Ltd* (1970) 216 E.G. 169 the court was of the opinion that it was entitled to consider the whole of the tenant's conduct in relation to his obligations and was not limited to the landlord's grounds.

(b) Persistent delay in paying rent: It is clear from *Horowitz* v. *Ferrand* [1956] C.L.Y. 4843 that the arrears of rent do not have to be sustained, but if the reason for the delay no longer applies, the landlord may not succeed under this ground (see also *Hopcutt* v. *Carver* (1969) 209 E.G. 1069).

(c) Breaches of other obligations: This ground includes substantial breaches of the tenant's obligations under the current tenancy or any other reason connected with the tenant's use or management of the holding. In ground (a), (b) and (c) the whole of the tenant's conduct may be considered (see *Eichner* (*supra*)).

(d) Alternative accommodation offered: Where the landlord offers alternative accommodation to the tenant such accommodation must be provided or secured by the landlord. The terms of the alternative accommodation must be reasonable having regard to the current tenancy and be suitable to the tenant's requirements enabling him to preserve goodwill.

(e) Better return if let or sold as larger unit: Where the competent landlord is a superior landlord (and not the immediate one) and the tenancy in question is a subtenancy the landlord may oppose a new tenancy on the ground that by letting all the premises contained in the head lease together more rent could be obtained.

(f) Intention to demolish or reconstruct: This ground will apply where the landlord establishes that on the termination of the current tenancy he intends to demolish or reconstruct the premises comprised in the holding (or a substantial part of it) or to carry out substantial work of construction that he could not reasonably do so without obtaining possession. In *Betty's Cafes* v. *Phillips Furnishing Stores* [1959] A.C. 20, it was held that the landlord must have this intention at the date of the proceedings and he will fail if major obstacles still lie ahead of him (e.g. no planning permission obtained). Further, in *Fisher* v. *Taylors Furnishing Stores* [1956] 2 Q.B. 78, it was stated that the motive for effecting the work was immaterial.

The type or amount of work needed to satisfy ground (f) is a question of fact and degree. In *Houseleys Ltd* v. *Bloomer-Holt Ltd* [1966] 2 All E.R. 966, the court held that demolishing a garage and wall was sufficient. Demolition without reconstruction is also sufficient. In *Botterill* v. *Bedfordshire County Council* (1985) 273 E.G. 1217 the Court of Appeal held that infilling by removal of topsoil, depositing waste and replacing the topsoil was not reconstruction within Section 30 (1) (f). Under Section 31A the tenant may still be able to obtain a new tenancy if he agrees to the inclusion in the new tenancy of terms giving

the landlord sufficient access to undertake the work or that
he is willing to accept a tenancy of a smaller part of the holding.
In *Mularczyk* v. *Azralnove Investments Ltd* [1985] 2 E.G.L.R.
141 the Court of Appeal rejected the contention that the works
proposed could be undertaken under the provisions of Section
31A (1) (a) because the landlord could not reasonably carry
out the works without obtaining possession of the holding and
without interfering for a substantial time or to a substantial
extent with the business user of the land. Further, the tenant
may be able to show that the current tenancy contains an access
clause and the work falls within the terms of that clause (see
Heath v. *Drown* [1973] A.C. 498).

(g) Intention to occupy himself: The landlord can establish this
ground where he proves that on the termination of the current
tenancy he intends to occupy the holding for the purpose or
partly for the purposes, of a business to be carried on by him
there, or as his residence. In Re *Crowhurst Park, Sims-Hilditch* v.
Simmons (1974) 28 P. & C.R. 14 it was held that the requirement
of para. (g) was satisfied where the landlord intended to use the
premises for partnership purposes. In *Westminster City Council*
v. *British Waterways Board* [1984] 3 W.L.R. 1047, it was held
that a tenant council could not protect its occupation by intimating
its refusal of planning permission to the landlord waterboard.

Some problems occur in practice regarding the intention to
occupy where the landlord concerned is a company forming
a group of companies. In such a case, Section 42 (3) provides
that the intention is to be construed as including intended occupation by any member of the group for the purposes of a business
to be carried on by that member. Finally, it should be noted
that the court must be satisfied that the landlord has a sufficient
intention and it will enquire into the matter as under para. (f)
(see *Gregson* v. *Cyril Lord Ltd* (1963) 184 E.G. 789). In *Euro-
parks (Midlands) Ltd* v. *Town Centre Securities plc* (1985) 274
E.G. 289 the Court of Appeal accepted the following as showing
a firm and settled intention on the part of the landlords (i)
minutes of board meetings; (ii) evidence of quotations received
from the supplier of equipment; and (iii) an affidavit from the
landlords' property director.

Terms of a new tenancy granted by the Court

Section 32–35 provide guidance to the court when it is called upon
to determine any of the terms of a new tenancy. Given a successful
application by the tenants, the court is bound to order the grant

of a new tenancy (Section 29). As a general rule, the following limits will apply insofar as the parties have failed to agree.

Property to be comprised in new tenancy (Section 32)

As a general rule, the new tenancy must comprise the premises as they stood at the date of the order, except that where the landlord has sought to oppose a new tenancy on ground (f) the court may grant a tenancy of part of the holding under Section 31A.

Duration of a new tenancy (Section 33)

The length of the new tenancy shall be as agreed between the landlord and tenant or, if decided by the court, it shall not exceed 14 years. It is clear that the duration of the old lease is a relevant factor as in *Betty's Cafes (supra)* where a 14 year term was ordered but was reduced to a 5 year term by the Court of Appeal so that the court will rarely grant a term longer than the original lease. Where the landlord fails to establish any of the grounds (d) to (g) but persuades the court that he is likely to be able to satisfy the grounds in the near future, the court may order a short term lease (see *Upsons Ltd* v. *E. Robins* [1956] 1 Q.B. 131).

In view of the comments concerning the interrelationship of Section 25 and a break clause it is significant to note that the court can insert a break clause into a new tenancy (see *McCombie* v. *Grand Junction Canal Co. Ltd* (1962) 182 E.G. 369. An interesting example of this power took place in *Adams* v. *Green* (1978) 247 E.G. 49 where the landlord owned a block of 12 shops in one of which the tenant asked for a new lease. The landlord wished to have a break clause inserted which would enable him to determine the lease after giving notice. The Court of Appeal granted a 14 year lease with a break clause included. In *CBS (UK) Ltd* v. *London Scottish Properties Ltd* [1985] 2 E.G.L.R. 125 the court stated that whilst it was perfectly fair and proper for the landlord to seek to maximise the value of his investment the court has to decide what is reasonable in the circumstances and the matter ought to be decided with fairness and justice. As the tenants were in the process of moving to a new location the court granted a 12 months term whilst the landlord had argued for a 14 year term. (Contrast with the decision in *Charles Follett Ltd* v. *Cabtell Investment Co. Ltd* (1986) 280 E.G. 639.)

Rent under new tenancy (Section 34)

Such rent is to be determined by the court having regard to the terms of the tenancy (other than those relating to rent) at which the holding might reasonably be expected to be let on the open market by a willing lessor there being disregarded:

(a) any effect on rent of the fact that the tenant has or his predecessors in title have been in occupation of the holding,

(b) any goodwill attached to the holding by reason of the carrying on thereat of the business of the tenant (whether by him or by a predecessor of his in that business),

(c) any effect on rent of an improvement to which this paragraph applies,

(d) in the case of a holding comprising licensed premises; any addition to its value attributable to the licence, if it appears to the court that having regard to the terms of the current tenancy and any other relevant circumstances the benefit of the licence belongs to the tenant.

The working of Section 34 needs some explanation as it touches on other areas of landlord and tenant law concerning, for example, rent review. It is clear that the terms of the lease may have a direct bearing on the rent. The point was emphasised in *Charles Clements (London) Ltd* v. *Rank City Wall* (1978) 246 E.G. 739 where the court rejected an attempt by the landlord, as a means of raising the rent, to force on the tenant a relaxation of a covenant limiting user which would have been of no benefit to the tenant. But what "tenant" must the court have in mind? Section 34 directs the court to the "willing lessor". The answer to the meaning of this phrase was given in *F. R. Evans (Leeds) Ltd* v. *English Electric Co. Ltd* (1977) 245 E.G. 657 where Donaldson, J. was of the opinion "the willing lessee is an abstraction—a hypothetical person ... He will take account of similar factors but he too will be unaffected by liquidity problems, governmental or other pressures." On the other hand, it is suggested that the open market rent may be affected by the profitability of the tenant's particular business. Whatever the position on profitability, the amount of the previous rent is not a factor for determination of the new rent. Further, Section 34 (3) allows the insertion of a rent review clause.

Other terms of the new tenancy (Section 35)

It is in determining the new rent and other terms of the new tenancy that the courts have faced problems in recent years. This problem was highlighted in *O'May* v. *City of London Real Property Co. Ltd* (1982) 261 E.G. 1185 where the lease was of office premises for a term of five years. Under the lease the landlord was responsible for maintenance and repairs. When the lease expired, the landlord agreed to offer the tenants a new lease but wished to change it into a "clear lease" by which responsibility for maintenance and repairs was to be on the tenants. An additional service charge was to be levied in return for which the tenants would be compensated by a reduction in the proposed new rent. The tenants applied to the court for a new tenancy. At first instance, Goulding, J., enunciated four tests in deciding whether a particular landlord's proposals were justified:

(i) Has the party demanding a variation of the terms of the current tenancy shown a reason for doing so?
(ii) If the party demanding the change is successful, will the party resisting it in principle be adequately compensated by the consequential adjustment of open market rent under Section 34?
(iii) Will the proposed change materially impair the tenant's security in carrying on his business or profession?
(iv) Taking all relevant matters into account is the proposal, in the court's opinion, fair and reasonable as between the parties?

The House of Lords agreed with the first three tests, but stated that the fourth test of discretion should be applied in each of the preceding stages. It thus seems that, to justify a change in any of the other terms in a lease, the landlord will have to satisfy the tests laid down in the *O'May* case (see also *Gold* v. *Brighton Corporation* [1956] 1 W.L.R. 1291).

Contracting out of the 1954 Act

Agreements which attempt to exclude the tenant's right to renew his tenancy are void unless they are authorised by the court (Section 38 (1)). Under Section 38 (4) the court may, on the joint application of both parties, authorise an agreement excluding the right to renew a tenancy to which the 1954 Act applies. In *Cardiothoracic Institute* v. *Shrewdcrest Ltd* [1986] 1 W.L.R. 368 there were successive extensions of a tenancy agreement negotiated subject to a condition that the extension should be the subject of a tenancy agreement approved under Section 38 (4). In such circumstances it was held that it was clearly intended by the parties that until the approval of the county court was obtained there was no legally binding tenancy agreement between them. Following *Allnatt London Properties Ltd* v. *Newton* (1983) 265 E.G. 601, "offer to surrender back" clauses infringe Section 38.

Rent reviews and business tenancies

The problem of the implementation of a rent review clause may occur in a business tenancy at two stages, namely, at any time during the currency of the lease and/or on renewal. In most cases, the rent review or reviews will take place during the currency of the lease and will require careful consideration. Draftsmen now recognise that there are several essential matters that must be stipulated in such a clause, namely:

1. Stipulations as to time in the service of notices.
2. Interval of rent review.
3. Formula and machinery for determining the new rent.
4. Provisions in event of disagreement.

1. Service of notices

It is frequently the case that the rent review procedure is activated by the service of a "trigger" notice which commences the rent review process. In most cases, the notice will be served by the landlord on the tenant and the main problem that has arisen in this area is whether a failure to keep strictly to the timetable set in the rent review clause will result in the landlord losing his rights to a reviewed rent. In *United Scientific Holdings Ltd* v. *Burnley Corporation* [1977] 2 All E.R. 62, the House of Lords laid down the general rule that time was not of the essence in the service of notices in a rent review process, but stated that there could be exceptions to this general rule. It is possible to make time of the essence by stating expressly in the lease that it should be so, but time can also be made of the essence where there is an interrelationship between the rent review clause and some other clause in the lease. Such was the case in *Al Saloom* v. *Shirley James Travel* (1981) 259 E.G. 420 where an underlease contained both a break clause and a rent review clause. The last date on which the landlord could serve the rent review notice was the same as that on which the tenant could give notice exercising his option to determine the underlease. In these circumstances, it was held that the presence of the break clause has the effect of making time of the essence. Where the lease provides for a period between service of the rent review notice and exercising the break clause, so as to allow the tenant to determine whether he wishes to continue in occupation, the service of the rent review notice will be of the essence (see *Coventry City Council* v. *Hepworth* (1983) 265 E.G. 265). In *United Scientific* (*supra*) it was suggested that extreme delay in the service of a trigger notice may have a prejudicial effect on the landlord's cause. The question of what constitutes unreasonable delay has arisen on several occasions. In *H. West* v. *Brech* (1982) 261 E.G. 156 a delay of 18 months was not sufficient to affect the landlord's rights (see also *Accuba* v. *Allied Shoe Repairs* [1975] 1 W.L.R. 1559 where also 18 months delay was insufficient and contrast with *Telegraph Properties (Securities)* v. *Courtaulds* (1980) 257 E.G. 1153 where a six year delay was fatal to the landlord's action). More recently in *Amherst* v. *James Walker (Goldsmith and Silversmith) Ltd* (1983) 267 E.G. 163 Oliver, L. J. commented:

> "But I know of no ground for saying that mere delay, however lengthy, destroys the contractual right. It may put the other party in a position, where, by taking the proper steps, he may become entitled to treat himself as discharged from his obligation: but that does not occur automatically and from the mere passage of time..."

In *United Scientific (supra)* the House of Lords recognised that a contra-indication may make time of the essence for the service of a rent review trigger-notice. What amounts to a contra-indication is the subject of dispute. In *Henry Smith's Charity Trustees* v. *A.W.A.D.A. Trading and Promotion Services Ltd* (1983) 269 E.G. 729 the clause contained an elaborate time schedule and provided that the rent stated by the landlord be deemed to be the rent of the tenant's counter-notice was not served in time. The Court of Appeal held that where the parties had not only set out a timetable but had provided what was to happen in the absence of strict compliance with that timetable the general rule was rebutted. The Court of Appeal reached a different conclusion in the interpretation of a "deeming" provision in *Mecca Leisure Ltd* v. *Renown Investments (Holdings) Ltd* (1984) 271 E.G. 989. In *Greenhaven Securities Ltd* v. *Compton* (1985) 275 E.G. 628 the rent review clause provided that if the parties had not, within a 15 month time limit, agreed on an arbitrator or made an application for the appointment of an arbitrator the new rent should be a sum equal to the old rent. Goulding J distinguished the decision in *Mecca* and held that the default provision constituted a contra-indication. The opposite view was taken in *Taylor Woodrow Property Co. Ltd* v. *Lonrho Textiles Ltd* (1985) 275 E.G. 632 where the court noted that in *Henry Smith's* the deeming provisions were two-way whilst in *Mecca* they were one-way. In *Taylor Woodrow* the deeming provision was one-way so that time was not of the essence in the service of the counter-notice.

2. Interval of rent review

It is clearly important for the interval of rent review to be expressly stated so that, for example, on a 21 year lease the rent review clause may become operative in the 7th and 14th years. Where it is not so, the rent review clause runs the risk of being inoperable. In *Brown* v. *Gould* [1972] Ch. 53 the option for a new lease was for a term of 21 years "at a rent to be fixed, having regard to the market value of the premises at the time of exercising the option". The court held that if no machinery was stated for working out the formula, the court will determine the matter itself. A liberal approach to the construction of an option to purchase was adopted in *Sudbrook Trading Estate Ltd* v. *Eggleton* (1983) 265 E.G. 215.

3. Formula and machinery

The formula and machinery has, of necessity, a direct relationship with the interval of rent review. Valuers are faced with enough problems on rent review without the clause adding to those problems by failing to define the rental on review. Such was the case in *Beer* v. *Bowden* [1981] 1 All E.R. 1070 where the clause provided only that the rent should be the fair market rent for the premises. In the particular circumstances of the case the Court of Appeal stated that the rent should be the fair market rent for the premises. See also *Thomas Bates and Sons Ltd* v. *Wyndhams Lingerie Ltd* [1981] 1 All E.R. 1077 where a term was implied that the rent was to be that which is "reasonable as between the parties". By way of contrast, in *King* v. *King* (1980) 255 E.G. 1205 the court refused to look at the defective rent review clause from a reasonableness viewpoint.

Some novel provisions on rent are being considered by draftsmen seeking to increase the landlord's benefit as a *Bovis Group Pension Fund Ltd* v. *G.C. Flooring and Furnishing Ltd* (1983) 266 E.G. 1005 where the clause provided for the new rent to be assessed by reference to the rent that could be obtained if the premises were let for office purposes and the court stated that it was to be assumed that the building had planning permission for office use notwithstanding that no such permission had, in fact, been granted. Similarly, in *Pugh* v. *Smiths Industries* (1982) 264 E.G. 823 it was held that the rent review should be on a literal construction of the lease where the formula provided that the presence of the review clause should be disregarded in calculating the new rent (see also *Lister Locks Ltd* v. *T.E.I. Pension Trust Ltd* (1982) 264 E.G. 827). The converse situation applied in *GREA Real Property Investments Ltd* v. *Williams* (1979) 250 E.G. 651 where it was decided that the effect of improvements on a rent review of premises in shell-form only had to be disregarded. If no such improvements disregard clause is present, the tenant will have to pay increased rent on his own improvements (contrast with the situation on a lease renewed under

Section 34 of the 1954 Act). If a strict user clause is present in the lease, this may also have a dampening effect on the new rental level as in *Plinth Property Investments* v. *Mott, Hay and Anderson* (1978) 249 E.G. 1167. See also *Law Land Co. Ltd* v. *Consumers' Association Ltd* (1980) 255 E.G. 617. The factors contained in the hypothetical lease for the purpose of the determination of the revised rent may pose problems for the valuer. In *National Westminster Bank plc* v. *Arthur Young McClelland Moores & Co.* (1984) 273 E.G. 402 the court held that in that particular lease the fair market rent had to be ascertained on the assumption that there was no rent revision clause contained in the hypothetical terms which the arbitrator had to apply . A similar conclusion was reached (at first instance) in *Equity & Law Life Assurance Society plc* v. *Bodfield Ltd* (1985) 276 E.G. 1157. Different conclusions from these two cases were reached in *Datastream International Ltd* v. *Oakeep Ltd* (1985) 277 E.G. 66 and *M.F.I. Properties Ltd* v. *B.I.C.C. Group Pension Trust Ltd* (1986) 277 E.G. 862. In *British Gas Corporation* v. *Universities Superannuation Scheme Ltd* (1986) 277 E.G. 980 Browne-Wilkinson V.C. said that the correct approach in these circumstances was as follows:

"(a) words in a rent exclusion provision which require *all* provisions as to rent to be disregarded produced a result so manifestly contrary to commercial common sense that they cannot be given literal effect;

 (b) other clear words which require the rent review provision (as opposed to all provisions as to rent) to be disregarded must be given effect to, however wayward the result; and

 (c) subject to (b), in the absence of special circumstances it is proper to give effect to the underlying commercial purpose of a rent review clause and to construe the words so as to give effect to that purpose by requiring future rent reviews to be taken into account in fixing the open market rental under the hypothetical letting."

These were stressed as being only "guidelines" by the Court of Appeal in the *Equity and Law Life* case [1987] 1 E.G.L.B. 124.

4. Disagreement

A well drafted rent review clause should always provide for a procedure in event of disagreement between the landlord and tenant on the new rental level. It should be made clear whether reference to an arbitrator or independent expert is desired. (In this context, reference can usefully be made to the RICS/Law Society Model Forms of Rent Review Clause (1985) Edition and the ISVA Recommended

Rent Review Clauses). In most cases, if the parties cannot agree on whom should be appointed, the President of the Royal Institution of Chartered Surveyors is the person most frequently requested to appoint someone. Alternatively, an application may be made to the Lands Tribunal to determine disputes.

Compensation

If a tenant has to leave business premises because the landlord successfully objects to one of the three grounds in Section 30 (1)(e), (f) or (g), he may claim compensation from the landlord. The compensation which the tenant receives is equal to either 3 times the rateable value or 6 times the rateable value of the premises, as provided by Section 37 (2) and (3) and the Landlord and Tenant Act 1954 (Appropriate Multiplier) Order 1984 S.I. 1984 No. 1932. Where the tenant has been in occupation for 14 years, the higher rate is payable. The Landlord and Tenant Act 1954 (Appropriate Multiplier) Regulations 1981 S.I. 1981 No. 69 gave rise to some dispute as to when the date for assessing compensation for these premises actually arose. Since *Cardshops* v. *John Lewis Properties* (1982) 263 E.G. 791 and *International Military Services Ltd* v. *Capital and Counties plc* (1982) 261 E.G. 778, it is now clear that it is the date when the tenant actually quits the premises.

Compensation for improvements

The Landlord and Tenant Act 1927 as amended by the Landlord and Tenant Act 1954 Part III provides that on quitting a holding at the termination of the lease, a business tenant (Section 17) may, in certain cases, claim compensation from the landlord for improvements carried out by the tenant or his predecessor in title (Section 1).

In order to qualify for compensation, the tenant must follow the statutory procedure strictly. Prior notice of the proposed work must be served on the landlord giving an opportunity for him to object, or to elect to undertake the work in consideration of a reasonable increase of rent, or such rent as the court determines (Section 3 (1)). If the landlord objects, and no agreement is reached, the tenant may apply to the court for a certificate that the work is a proper improvement. This will be granted if the work adds to the letting value of the holding, is reasonable to its character, and does not reduce the value of any other nearby property belonging to the landlord. Where no notice of objection is served, or a court certificate is obtained, the tenant may proceed with the work. A further certificate of completion must be obtained from the landlord or the court (Section 3 (6)). Any increased rent under a renewed lease should not include the value of improvements carried out by the tenant or his predecessors in the business within the previous 21 years (Section 34 Landlord and Tenant Act 1954, as amended).

The tenant's claim for compensation must be made within the appropriate time limits (Section 47). The amount is the lesser of the net addition to the value of the holding resulting directly from the work or the reasonable cost of carrying out the work at the termination date less an allowance for obsolescence (Section 1 (1)). As the basis of the compensation is the value of the improvements to the landlord, the amount may be reduced if the landlord intends to alter or change the use of the premises, and no compensation is payable if the premises are to be demolished (Section 1 (2)). If disputed, the amount may be determined by the court (Section 1 (3)).

© Delyth W. Williams, 1988

Chapter 5

INDUSTRIAL PROPERTIES

Introduction

An industrial property valuer requires an all round grasp of the activities and needs of users both in the United Kingdom and overseas if he is to carry out his tasks to standards of maximum efficiency. This is because there is an element of specialisation in the majority of industrial buildings and, nowadays increasingly, in warehouses as well. At one extreme the property element is merely an envelope or package for specialised plant. On the other hand, a degree of flexibility is always desirable and there is an element of compromise applicable to industrial premises generally which does not apply to the same extent to other types of property. Such matters as location for a particular use, obsolescence, labour availability and communications are particularly relevant.

Scope

The valuation of industrial property can in very broad terms be considered as coming under one of three headings:

(i)   The valuation of factories and warehouses as such, for what might be called the usual purposes. This includes sale with vacant possession and the assessment of rental value for letting—which might be in the market with vacant possession or at a special figure to reflect an inter company arrangement. In addition, of course, industrial premises will require valuation in connection with their replacement value for insurance purposes, rating and for other statutory purposes.

(ii) Often valuation is required for financial reasons for the balance sheet or, for example, in connection with take overs or the defence of companies therefrom. All these valuations to an extent reflect the "going concern" element of valuation in connection with the land and buildings of the particular undertaking which is now referred to as "depreciated replacement cost".

(iii) The valuation of specialised premises and of plant and machinery. This particularly arises with specialist properties, often adopted for a special process, when the plant is to a greater

121

or lesser extent synonymous with the buildings themselves. With a tendency for industrial premises to be built to house a particular process the importance of this type of valuation may increase.

As a field for valuation, industrial property undoubtedly comprises the greatest range of size compared with shops and offices, ranging from small workshops in a shed or single room of perhaps 150 sq ft to vast complexes containing over a million sq ft on a site of some hundreds of acres. At the one extreme might be a room on the upper floor of an old building where only one or two people work, perhaps concerned with the rag trade and having as machinery only a sewing machine while at the other end of the range might be one of the major chemical companies. In practice one has to consider fully automated warehouses as well as traditional industrial operations, one would hesitate to call them processes, which have not changed for centuries and are really part of our heritage as examples of living industrial archaeology. They are tending to disappear and then reappear in an updated form.

Types of industry

The government recognises 27 main groups of industries in its Standard Industrial Classification and these "Main Order Headings" (MOH's) are further broken down into varying numbers of Minimum List Headings. Generally these industries can be broken down into four basic groups:

(i) Primary Industries—MOH's 1 & 2 which are concerned with extracting material direct from the land or the sea and do not involve any processing or fabrication of a finished product. Mining and quarrying come within this category.

(ii) Secondary Industries—MOH's 3 to 19 inclusive. This includes the vast bulk of manufacturing industries from food and drinks through chemical and mechanical engineering to paper printing and publishing.

(iii) Tertiary Industries—MOH's 20 to 27 inclusive which provide services and are basically orientated towards the retail market. Such industries as construction, leisure and transport and communication are included in this group.

(iv) Quaternary Industries—these are undifferentiated in the main industry group but include such activities as research establishments which are concerned with the provision of information and expertise.

While these classifications indicate the fields which have to be covered the limitations of them for some practical purposes must be recognised. For example MOH XIV— Vehicles— includes bicycles as well as space satellites.

Industrial decline

1986, being Industry Year, it is encouraging to see that after a period of decline, and sometimes great rupture, industrial production is once again increasing and with this, hopefully the scope for the industrial valuer. In the past one has seen great changes in the economy and that which is increasing presently, the tertiary sector, which comprises services of various kinds. The total output of industries as measured by the Gross Domestic Product of which 30·4% was contributed in 1974 by the manufacturing sector, had shrunk to 24·4% in 1984 while the contribution of the primary sector, largely through North Sea Oil, had increased from 7·2% to 13·4%.

The importance of location

It is necessary, in the valuation of industrial premises, to understand the locational need of different types of industry both for manufacturing and for distribution. Clearly primary industries have to be located at the source of raw materials—coal can only be extracted from a coalfield. On the other hand the locational requirement of secondary industries, which form the vast majority of those which a valuer will be called on to consider, are much more complex. Some are mainly located with reference to the markets which they serve, such as bakeries, while others are strongly tied to their raw materials, such as brickworks. The majority are intermediate between these extremes including vehicle manufacturing and ship-building.

The tertiary or service-industries, are necessarily, almost always located where the appropriate services are required, at the market. So far as the electricity industry is concerned for example, the existence of a national grid very much increases the location options. Warehouses, on the other hand, used in connection with the distributive trades, need to be precisely located with regard to the market they serve. Quaternary industries are very often market-orientated and usually, as for example with computer operations, need to be located where suitable skilled labour is available, since basically information, which is what they deal in, can easily be transmitted from place to place.

Having therefore outlined the broad spectrum of industry and understood some of the locational functions which are so important to any assessment of value, it would be useful to consider the principal factors which are important for any particular location to be chosen. Clearly it is irrelevant what the quality of the factory is if certain factors are missing thus making operations uneconomic. Consider a typical factory; it has many inputs and these are processed to become throughputs. These inputs and subsequent outputs must be moved through the transport network. Very broadly, inputs plus their transport costs have to be balanced with sales, and this difference between cost and revenue produces profit which, is of course, essential in order to purchase or rent properties.

In all but the smallest employer's enterprise, the availability of labour, be it skilled or unskilled, working on production or manufacture or in a warehouse, is generally the most important factor affecting demand for industrial premises. The choice of location for large, labour-intensive enterprises is really very limited indeed in the United Kingdom even allowing for comparatively high unemployment figures. This is because of the variety of skills needed, the requirement of technology for access to such centres as universities and a general shortage of suitable sites not only for the factory but for housing both for executives and workers.

Perhaps equally important in assessing value are communications. Clearly labour must be able to get to work but what is really important is access to raw materials—inputs—and to markets. Improvement of the motorway network with corresponding reductions in the use of relatively inflexible railway communications may have made this factor less important than it was. However docks are still important for some industries, particularly those which may be export-orientated, and airports are more and more vital especially where premises are likely to be of interest to overseas companies looking for a foothold in the United Kingdom. However, it is interesting to note that government proposals regarding the employment of dockers in warehouses within a particular distance of a port have had a depressing effect on values in several areas. As a basic rule, the cost of handling goods, loading and unloading, is more important than the cost of petrol.

For many industries the provision of services is of fundamental importance. Some processes demand gas which is not always easily available, while others need very adequate supplies of water. If sewage disposal is difficult this can often make industrial premises expensive, particularly if occupiers have to install their own treatment plants.

Before examining the effect of legislation on industrial valuation the effect of environment needs examination. Almost whatever industrial or storage operation is set up in a residential area, it will give rise to a greater or lesser volume of complaints from time to time because of noise, vehicles using residential roads, etc. Considerable inconvenience to operations can be caused by local residents complaining to their local councillors, and the problems confronting the user of a non-conforming industrial use in a residential area are much greater than those of an office or a shop. This applies to the greatest extent to large enterprises such as nuclear power stations which have great environmental impact.

Statutory regulations

Naturally factories and warehouses are subject to the normal planning legislation. One has to cope with the provisions of the Factories Acts and regulations enforcing clean air, noise and so on. The Industrial Development Certificate scheme under which the Department of Industry had powers effectively to direct large industrial units to specific parts of the country by refusing consent for their development elsewhere has now been abolished. But the stick of control was supplemented by the carrot of grants to industry in specific areas of high unemployment. Regulations change from time to time. The effect of grants is to reduce the cost of providing a factory to the level where the equivalent rent is very much lower than that at which it is economic for the private sector to provide warehouse accommodation for letting. This factor tends to distort the market in certain areas. Again such schemes as enterprise zones can be a direct discouragement to private sector property investment because of their repressive effect on rental values through rate relief.

Building characteristics

Most, if not all, the premises which are concerned with primary industries are to a greater or lesser extent built for a specific purpose and have a degree of specialisation which makes them unsuitable for other occupiers. In addition their location often presents a further disability. While this often applies to secondary industries the trend is for modern industrial premises to have maximum flexibility. This is illustrated by the initial planning consent for many industrial estates being for warehousing purposes and consent for industrial use, which much more often than not involves no adaptation, is obtained for specific occupiers as necessary. General purpose buildings not only have a higher value, relative to cost, in the open market and are almost always preferred by occupiers who do not need a high degree of specialised construction. So called "High Tech" buildings are in demand by certain occupiers generally where development work is done and flexibility as between offices and high class industrial accommodation is required. These are generally built to a high standard, often air conditioned and sometimes on two storeys. Externally they can often be identified by bright coloured plastic sheets and large areas of glazing, while, theoretically offering greater flexibility in use, often the reverse is true. Rents are often double those of new "shed" type premises, theoretically somewhere between industrial rents and office rents. In seeking premises there are certain characteristics which occupiers look for and the most important are as follows:

Flexibility. Modern conditions require an ability to change production flows and general arrangements within buildings so as to be able to vary techniques from time to time. This needs to take place on all three dimensions. Accordingly premises require reasonable eaves height and the usual practice is to require about eighteen feet. This enables lorries to enter the building if need be and for storage racking to be erected to a reasonable height which is also suitable for the use of fork lift trucks. As a rule manufacturing concerns do not require so much height but the general rule in modern premises is to maintain an overall constant height. This flexibility implies clear floor space and adequate goods entrance. However within the last few years there has been increasing recognition of the comparatively low cost of industrial buildings compared, in many cases, with the very expensive plant and equipment which goes into them. This is leading to a re-examination of the desirability of a return towards more specialised buildings.

Construction. It is important that buildings have good floor loading capability and as a rule these days 500 lbs/sq ft is an absolute minimum. A span of about sixty feet seems quite adequate for most users who also require adequate insulation and natural light, partly to ensure good working conditions and partly to economise in fuel costs.

Services. Industry, in particular, needs adequate supplies of water, gas and electricity. Some processes need a particular abundance of one or more of these services and, particularly in the case of water which can be expensive, this factor can have an important effect on location. In addition drainage can be a problem if a lot of effluent is produced from a process, however if it is noxious in any way this has to be treated before entering a public sewer or a watercourse. In a building itself it is necessary to ensure that the services are reflected in such matters as adequate toilets but also in terms of high pressure air, gas and other things needed within the works.

Office accommodation. Almost all industrial concerns need some office space in every building and it is necessary, in valuation, to ensure that the amount available is reasonable. Factories with too large a proportion of offices do not command, as a rule, any premium in the market, indeed often the reverse. As a very general rule, an average proportion of office space in a factory would be 10% of the whole. In this connection also it is usual to have a separate entrance and separate toilet facilities for the offices.

Site requirements. Apart from the basic locational factors which have already been considered there is a great need for the industrial building itself to have good access. This involves good roads to the premises and the ability to get into it from several directions if it is of reasonable size so that the loading and unloading can easily be carried out. Adequate car parking is generally an essential and adequate space for possible future expansion is often an important factor.

In practice the valuer will find that many older buildings which do not offer the flexibility and facilities indicated above are quite adequate for their uses. However such obsolescent buildings have a limited future under modern conditions. Not only are maintenance costs high and it is sometimes difficult to comply with modern statutory conditions, but their financing is often a problem. Investing institutions still very much favour the modern, general purpose building so that those which are not up to date are not only expensive to run but also tend to be expensive to own. Regard needs to be had as to whether the cleared site would have more value than the site plus buildings.

Industrial processes and plant and machinery

As indicated above not only are there an enormous number of different industrial processes but these themselves are often tied up with detailed locational requirements such as the need for pure water or a particular quality of labour force. Clearly to value such a range of operations often requires highly specialised skills and a knowledge that goes beyond the expertise needed to value land and buildings. At any particular time a plant & machinery valuer may not be able to value a particular plant, especially if it is of an unusual or specialised type. However the training of such a valuer will have included an understanding of how to rapidly assimilate the nature of a specific process and, by enquiry and research, to establish inherent obsolescence, which is an important factor in such valuations. Almost always much of the associated plant and equipment in a factory is common to many others. This applies, for example, very much to the chemical industry where a complex looking process may appear to represent an insoluble conundrum. On detailed examination however this will break down into a series of pipes, pumps, condenser tanks, filtration plants and so on leaving only a few unfamiliar items which need to be researched.

Clearly anyone who holds himself out to be an industrial valuer must have the ability to recognise what he sees in all the major branches of industry. He must have at his fingertips records giving the present day cost of all the plant he is likely to come across and know where to obtain such information about unusual items. Although it is an essential in every valuation, an ability to properly describe the plant which has been converted is necessary.

Often it is necessary to decide which items of plant and machinery are to be included with the land and buildings, particularly if two different valuers are concerned with the separate components. Plant which is generally considered part of the building includes electricity, gas and other services where they are not part of the process, heating installations (though free-standing hot air blowers are often a tenant's property), air-conditioning and ventilation. Such items as crane gantries, which would usually pass with a building on sale or letting, but are really fitted in order to help with a specific process, may need special consideration.

Financial valuations

General purpose buildings can usually be valued for market purpose by the usual method of capitalising the rent passing or rental value at the proper rate of return for the appropriate periods and making any appropriate adjustments. However specialised buildings, which may only be of use for one process or those, for example, which are very large and would not command an alternative market in a particular area present special problems. It is the valuation of such industrial assets in order to establish their true worth to the business that has always been the basis of industrial valuer's work since the discipline was first established.

With the introduction of inflation accounting concepts the valuer is increasingly engaged in up-dating the asset side of the balance sheet. This enables correct present day values to be substituted for the existing values which may well have been calculated on the basis of historic cost. Fixed assets naturally include land, buildings, plant, equipment and transport as opposed to current assets which relate to work in progress, stock in trade (though both may be dealt with by a valuer), debtors, stocks, etc.

Such valuations in the past have often been dealt with on a going concern basis, but the need for definitions in the accountancy profession has led to a tightening up of the old concept, which in any case gave rise to many problems, and the issue by the Royal Institution of Chartered Surveyors of its "Guidance Notes on the Valuation of Assets".

The basic concept is that of establishing, either for specialised buildings or plant, a depreciated replacement cost. Depreciation is defined as the measure of wearing out, consumption, or other loss of value of a fixed asset whether arising from use, effluxion of time or obsolescence through technology and market changes. In order to establish the future economic useful life of buildings it is necessary to consider depreciation under two heads:

Depreciation as such. This is the judgement of the valuer as to the physical obsolescence of the premises or plant bearing in mind such factors as the age, present condition and cost of both maintenance and repair required at the date of valuation and in the future.

Functional obsolescence. This involves a consideration of the suitability of the premises or plant for their present use and their likely efficiency if continued in that use or used for some other purpose of the business if it appeared possible. In assessing functional obsolescence the valuer will have to consider the relative efficiency of the process the buildings are constructed to contain compared with a modern plant and the likely efficient use of the plant.

In simple terms the industrial valuer is seeking to quantify for the balance sheet in money terms at today's value the proportion of the total worth of a concern which is contained within the fixed assets which he is valuing. In such an appraisal regard must be had to the fact that the concern must have adequate profitability.

In considering his approach to the valuation of an industrial property the valuer must give very careful attention to the buildings and to the plant depending upon his precise instructions. The ascertainment of rental value, whether for an existing or a proposed building is no different from the process which is used for a shop or an office. However the need for specialised buildings in industry requires special skills. The advent of inflation accounting and, so far as *plant* is concerned, the fluctuating value of the pound, has presented special problems. The solutions to these difficulties are becoming apparent but in the meantime it is essential that valuers ensure they contribute to the development of their own expertise and the future of the industrial valuers' skills. Such expertise now needs to embrace an understanding of alternative uses for industrial undertakings and their associated land holdings. The concent of "employment land" is becoming increasingly important. As undertakings, particularly large ones which have been major local employers. This is reflected in starter unit developments which substitute for the former industrial employers as well as leisure activities, particularly appropriate to quarries for example and such other uses as shopping centres.

Industrial Estates

Although much industry is purpose built on sites owned by the respective undertaking the majority of factories and warehouses are located on industrial estates. These are normally built where they can provide the facilities in terms of location for a wide range of occupiers. In areas where private finance is difficult to obtain, promotion is often under the aegis of the central government (e.g. English Industrial Estates) or local authorities. Additionally statutory undertakings such as British Steel are very active in promoting new industrial users where, for example, large steelworks have had to be closed down.

Such estates are becoming in some cases more specialised and such terms as high technology development, science park and so on are being increasingly banded about. However from the view point of the valuer provided he understands what is intended and what is actually going on, he will continue, as always, to provide the right answer.

Study 1

This indicates a typical approach to a valuation on an open market basis.

A freehold factory standing on a site of 4 ha has the following accommodation: 6,000 square metres of modern single story factory buildings: 6,000 square metres of old multi-storey accommodation partly used for production but mainly for storage: 6,000 square metres of offices: caretaker's house: 1 of the 4 ha of land is held for expansion, has no planning consent except for its current use as a sports field.

	£ p.a.	£
6,000 square metres of modern factory at £15 per square metre	90,000	
Y.P. in perp. at 8%	12·5	
		1,125,000
6,000 square metres of multi-storey mixed uses at £2·5 per square metre	15,000	
Y.P. in perp. at 12%	8	
		120,000
6,000 square metres of modern offices at £25 × 50% to allow for premises being over officed	75,000	
Y.P. in perp. at 6%	16·6	
		1,245,000
Caretaker's house, say,		5,000
1 ha of "white land" at £10,000		10,000
		2,505,000
	say	£2,500,000

Study 1(a)

This indicated the difference between a valuation on an open market basis (Study 1 above) and a valuation on a depreciated replacement cost basis. The same facts are assumed.

	£	£
6,000 square metres of modern factory, as above		1,125,000
6,000 square metres of multi-storey mixed uses (assume well adapted to the business)		
Cost of construction at £150 per square metre	900,000	
Less: depreciation and obsolescence say 60%	540,000	
		360,000

	£	£
6,000 square metres of modern offices (essential to the business) Cost of construction at £300 per square metre		1,800,000
Caretaker's house		
At cost	20,000	
Less: depreciation at 25%	5,000	
		15,000
Land held for expansion		50,000
		£3,350,000
	say	£3,300,000

Comparison of depreciated replacement value with profit.

Value of undertaking on depreciated replacement cost	£3,300,000
Plus value of plant and machinery, say	£1,500,000
	£4,800,000

The profits = Percentage return × capital invested (depreciated replacement cost plus working capital)

If this equation produces a return reasonably compatible to that obtainable in the particular industry then the valuation can be considered satisfactory. If, however, it is markedly different, then the valuation may need adjustment.

Study 2

This illustrates an approach to the valuation of an industrial development site.

A freehold site of approximately 0·3 ha has a detailed planning permission of an industrial building of 1,700 square metres including a 20% office content. The site has good access to trunk roads and is situated on an established industrial estate. Land in the area was selling for £310,000·00 per ha about six months ago.

The recent sale evidence is the preferred guide, provided that allowance is made for changes in the market. Assuming there are no significant changes then the value would be in the order of £93,000. In certain areas freehold industrial land is not often found in the market and could attract an overbid from potential owner-occupiers who would be prepared to develop the site themselves.

An alternative approach on a residual basis could be used for appraisal purposes by a developer.

Gross development value

Income

	£ p.a.
1,700 m² say 1,600 m² net a £35 m² (allowing for office content)	£56,000
YP in perp. at 8½%	11·76
	658,560
Less: sale costs at say 3%	19,750
Value of completed development:	638,800

Building Costs:

	£	
1,700 m² at £220 m²	374,000	
Architects', Surveyors' fees at 10%	37,400	
Finance at 13% for 6 mths	26,741	
Commission on letting at 10%	5,600	
Marketing	5,000	
Legal Costs	3,000	
Contingencies	15,000	
Developer's risk & profit at 15% on building costs say,	68,000	
		534,741
Residue		£104,000

Site finance, 13% for 1 year
Legal costs on acquisition at 3% of site value

Hence: $\dfrac{104,000}{1·16} = £89,700$

The developer can, therefore, afford to pay up to, say £90,000 for the site, which accords closely to the recent market evidence.

If however the scheme had been for a Hi-Tech* development located within London or the Home Counties then the land and development value could have been derived as follows:

1,700 m² say 1600 m² net at £80 m²		128,000
YP in perp @ 7·25%		13·79
		1,765,517
less sale costs at say 3%		52,965
Value of completed development		1,712,550
Building Costs		
1700 m² at £450 m²	765,000	
Architects and Surveyors fees at 10%	76,500	
Finance at 13% for 6 months	54,700	
Commission on letting at 15%	19,200	
Marketing	20,000	
Legal costs	5,000	
Contingencies	40,000	
Developers Risk and Profit 15%	140,400	
		1,120,800
Residue		£591,750

Site finance 13% for 1 yr

Legal costs on acquisition at 3% of site value

Hence: $\dfrac{£591,750}{1·16} = £510,130$

This equates to £1,700,000 per hectare or approximately £700,000 per acre.

* (Class B1. The Town & Country Planning (Use Classes) Order, 1987 (S.I. 1987 No. 764. See also Circular 13/87).)

© J. E. CULLIS
D. J. SIMMS, 1988

Chapter 6

OFFICES

Office buildings are invariably valued by the investment method, which is the determination of the present value of the right to receive, and liability (if any) to pay a future sum or a series of future sums by discounting them at a compound rate determined by direct comparison with yield obtained on the other investments, i.e. it is the determination of the value of an interest by the capitalisation of rental income. There are various ways of carrying out any valuation and the important methods are the:

      (a) Hardcore method
      (b) Term and reversion method
      (c) Equivalent yield method

Hardcore method

This method is based on the assumption that the term rent or rent immediately payable, i.e. the "hardcore" rent is relatively secure throughout the life of the investment and can therefore be capitalised for the whole term at a lower rate than the "marginal" rent (i.e. the additional income after the rent has been reviewed).

Term and reversion method

This method is based on capitalising the net rent received for the appropriate period until the rental income has been increased to open market rent and then capitalising the open market rent for the remainder of the term. The initial rent being capitalised at a lower rate, as it is more secure, than later rent.

Equivalent yield method

This method uses a single remunerative rate which when applied to rent currently receivable and also to rent receivable upon reversion produces the same capital value as is obtained by the application of the initial and reversionary yields to those rents. It is the weighted average yield of an investment representing the "overall" rate of return.

    It is also essential to calculate the "initial yield" once the valuation has been completed since at the present time (1987) the institutional

Valuation: Principles into Practice

investors would not be prepared to accept an initial yield below 2% however good the ultimate investment may be.

The attention of all surveyors carrying out any valuation is drawn to the Guidance Notes on the Valuation of Assets issued by the Royal Institution of Chartered Surveyors.

The methodical assembly of all the information required is of paramount importance to ensure that no relevant factors are over-looked. How this is done is illustrated in this chapter by considering the valuation of various interests in an office building. The following are introductory matters.

The freeholder (A) in the study, built on the site an office building which was completed and let in 1939 to a tenant whose lease expired in 1964. He then relet the building to tenant (B) for a term of 75 years. B has subsequently underleased the building to various occupying tenants. A valuation is required as at 1987 of the following interests in the building.

the freehold;
the head leasehold;
the freehold in possession, i.e. the value to the freeholder if he was entitled to receive the rack rents receivable by the head lessee.

The building is assumed to be in a first class location in the West End of London. The accommodation comprises a basement used as storage and offices on the ground and six upper floors. The floors were leased in open space, and these areas formed the basis for the apportionment of service charges (see later). Tenants have installed their own internal partitioning. The building is centrally heated by two gas fired boilers which were renewed two years ago and this system is in good working order. The upper floors are served by three lifts, all of which have been renewed within the last two years. The sixth floor of the building was constructed three years ago by J. Limited, the occupational tenants, at their own expense.

The first essential in valuing any office building is to read the various leases and to prepare a synopsis of the relevant details.

The leases

The head lease: The freehold is owned by A who has leased to B on the following terms:

Offices

Term: 75 years from 1968.
Initial rent: £40,000 p.a. exclusive of all outgoings.

Rent reviews: At the end of the 25th (1993) and 50th (2018) years.

Basis of rent review: £40,000 p.a. plus ⅜th of the annual rack rental value (1) of the building at the date of review in excess of £64,000 p.a. subject to such figure being not less than the rent being paid at the date of review. The rent on review is to be assessed having regard to the terms of the head lease and on the assumption that the building is vacant and available for letting in accordance with market practice at the date of review (2).

Insurance: The tenant is required to insure against all risks at full replacement cost and for 3 years loss of rent.

Repairs: The tenant is required to carry out all repairs and decorations internally and externally and to maintain all plant and equipment (e.g. lifts and central heating installations) in sound working order.

Notes

(1) It is customary to estimate the rental value at the date of review on the basis of rental values current at the date of valuation and this will need to be done in order to arrive at the amount of the head rent on review.

(2) On this basis it must be assumed that the building is let to its best advantage. It could be assumed to be let as a whole or by floors or by parts of floors. Some head leases put restrictions on how a building may be let, i.e. no more than one tenant per floor or no more than a given number of tenants in the building as a whole. It is also assumed that if current market practice is to let on the basis of 5 year rent reviews the tenant will let on that basis.

The underleases: The synopsis of the underleases is best prepared in schedule form as shown on page 139. Although it may be purported that all sub-lettings are in accordance with a standard form of underlease, all leases should be perused as variations from the standard are frequently to be found. As the building has been let to a number of tenants their superior landlord B will endeavour to recover from them a proportion of the cost of the outgoings he has to bear. These will be recovered by "service charges" but the liability for payment by individual occupiers may not be identical in all cases. The method of apportioning service charges should also be noted. It is usual in the case of office buildings to base the apportionment on the ratio of the floor area occupied by a particular tenant to the total area of the building and therefore it is important to note the definition of floor area (if any) in the underleases. Many leases which intend to recover 100% of the cost of services provided when a building is fully let, do not in fact do so. Where in respect of any tenancy the landlord does not recover the whole of the apportioned service charge a deduction from rent will have to be made in respect of the amount of service charge which is irrecoverable. It is advisable on this schedule to record the area of each sub-letting, the floor on which it is situated, the specific use and the estimated rental value on reversion.

Notes on Schedule I (see page 139)

(1) Companies C, D, E and F are all substantial public companies. G Limited is a public property development company which has lately been in financial difficulty and its covenant value is doubtful. H are a firm of apparently successful solicitors and the two senior partners are guarantors under the terms of the lease. J Limited is a foreign based oil exploration company and for the last two years they have disclosed substantial losses in their annual accounts.

(2) The lease to G Limited is subject to upward only rent reviews and the rent from this floor which was negotiated 6 years ago is now considered to be in excess of the current market rent by about 25%. There may therefore be no increase in rent on review in 1990.

(3) This floor was constructed by J Limited at their own expense in 1983. There is no provision in the lease requiring them to construct this floor and whilst it is provided in the lease that on review improvements carried out at the expense of the tenant are to be ignored in assessing the rent, due to an oversight the tenant has failed to serve the required notice on the landlord under Section 3 (1) of the Landlord and Tenant Act 1927.

(4) The rents payable under these leases are fixed until the expiration of the terms in 2018 (32 years) and the tenants do not contribute towards the cost of lifts or heating. Owing to likely further inflation the head lessee will receive a steadily declining income on this account.

Cost of services

The head lessee B is responsible for all outgoings and these need to be carefully analysed in order to calculate the landlord's residual

Schedule I

Schedule of underleases

Tenant (1)	Floor	Use	Floor area in square metres	Rent paid £ p.a.	Service charge	Rent review/ end of lease	Estimated reversionary value £ p.a.
C Limited	Basement	Storage	371	1,000 (4)	No provision for re-covery of the cost of heating or lifts	End of Lease 2018 No rent reviews	15,953
D Limited	Ground	Offices	492	2,500 (4)	No provision for re-covery of the cost of heating or lifts	End of Lease 2018 No rent reviews	47,724
E Limited	First	Offices	492	33,500	Full recovery	Rent reviews 1988 and 1993 End of Lease 1998	47,724
F Limited	Second	Offices	492	38,000	Full recovery	Rent reviews 1989, 1994 and 1999 End of Lease 2004	47,724
G Limited	Third	Offices	492	60,000 (2)	Full recovery	Rent reviews 1990 and 1995 End of Lease 2000	47,724
H & Co.	Fourth	Offices	492	33,500	Full recovery	Rent review 1988 End of Lease 1993	47,724
J Limited	Fifth	Offices	492	33,500	Full recovery	Rent reviews 1988 and 1993 End of Lease 1998	47,724
J Limited	Sixth (3)	Offices	232	Nil (Tenant Improve-ments)	Full recovery	End of Lease 1998	22,504

liability in those cases where the apportioned cost is not fully recoverable from the underlessees. A detailed analysis of the service charge is shown in Schedule II. It will be noted that there is no provision for the recovery of any sum in respect of the renewal of plant or equipment. Where this is the case a deduction will need to be made at the end of the valuation to allow for obsolescence where renewal is imminent. The landlord has however renewed the boilers and lifts recently so that no deduction is required in this case. The cost of services varies from building to building and where actual figures are not available estimates must be built up by pricing the individual services supplied.

Schedule II

Schedule of items included in the service charge and analysis of the actual cost per square metre of providing these services

Item	Cost per square metre
Staff wages	£1·38
Rent for caretaker's flat	22p
Cleaning of common parts	45p
Electricity	41p
Central heating of building (1)	£1·50
Heating maintenance contract (1)	47p
Building and third party insurance	96p
General maintenance	£2·37
Lift maintenance (1)	32p
Gardening	3p
Managing agent's fee (2)	£1·02
Auditor's fee	6p
Total cost of the provision of services per square metre	£9·19

Notes on Schedule II

(1) Cost of lifts and central heating: It is necessary to calculate these separately in respect of the basement and ground floor as they are not recoverable from the underlessees.

Central heating	£1·50
Heating maintenance contract	0·47
Lift maintenance	0·32
	£2·29

Area in square metres

Basement   371
Ground floor   492
               ———

863 at £2·29 per square metre = £1,976

(2) Managing agents fees based on 12½% of the total cost of services and not on a percentage of rent.

Reversionary rental values

Where parts of the building are let at rents which do not reflect current rental values these will have to be estimated. Such rents on reversion should be calculated at current rental values and not, on the estimated rental value at the date of review on the assumption that there will be an increase due to inflation. The best comparables for this purpose will be recent lettings or sub-lettings which have taken place in the building itself. As a check on their validity recent lettings in comparable buildings in the vicinity should be examined. Schedule III illustrates the methods used in the devaluation of comparables. More comparables would be required in practice. From a consideration of the devalued comparables the valuer will determine his basic current market valuation rates per square metre. This determination will be based not entirely on mathematical calculations but also on the valuer's judgement based on experience. In the example he has decided on £43 per square metre for the basement storage and £97 per square metre for the office floors.

Notes of Schedule III (see page 142)

(1) F. Ltd (see Schedule I) have retained 218 square metres of office accommodation for their own use. In order to provide access to the office suite let to K. Ltd and to their own accommodation, a common access passage has been partitioned off from the area originally leased by F. Ltd. This has an area of 88 square metres.

   As the basis for valuation is the total internal floor area for each floor exclusive of lavatories, lift lobbies and staircases, the net rent per square metre of the sub-let portion needs adjustment to allow for a proportionate share of the internal corridor as follows:

$$\frac{\text{Rent of sub-letting}}{\text{Net area of sub-letting}} = \frac{£22,000}{186\,\text{sq m}} = £118\cdot27 \text{ per square metre}$$

Schedule III

Schedule of comparables

Address	Tenant	Floor	Area in square metres	Service charge	Date of letting	Rent paid £ p.a.	Adjustment	Adjusted rent per square metre £ p.a.
The Subject Property	K. Ltd. (1)	Part 2nd	186 (1)	Full	Letting just agreed. Lease to 1999. Rent reviews 1989 & 1995	22,000 (118·27 per square metre)	See Note 1	97·12
The Subject Property	L. Ltd (2)	Basement	371	No provision for the recovery of the cost of heating or lifts	Lease just agreed for 5 years	16,800 (2) (45·28 per square metre)	For Service Charge See Note 2	42·99
A similar property	M. Ltd (3)	4th floor	550	Full	Agreed 1 year ago. Lease for 20 years to 2005. Rent reviews 5 yearly	56,375 (102·50 per square metre)	See Note 3	96·00

Adjustment:

$$\frac{\text{Total net area of occupied parts}}{\text{Total area of sub-letting}} \times £118{\cdot}27$$

$$\frac{186 \text{ square metres} + 218 \text{ square metres}}{492} \times £118{\cdot}27 = £97{\cdot}12$$
$$\text{per sq m}$$

(2) C. Ltd (see Schedule I) have let the entire basement area at a rack rent but otherwise on the same terms on which they themselves hold it. This rent therefore reflects the fact that the tenant has no liability to reimburse the landlord with a proportion of the cost of heating or providing lifts. An adjustment to the rent will have to be made to take this into account. Rent £16,800 less £850 (irrecoverable cost of heating and lifts) = £15,950 (£42·99 per square metre).

(3) This floor has been partitioned by the landlord to provide individual offices. It is estimated that the partitioning adds approximately £6·50 per square metre to the value of this accommodation. In the case of the subject property no partitioning has been provided by the landlord and therefore this must be deducted for the purpose of comparison.

Inspection of the building

The collection of data may take some time but having put the work in hand an inspection of the building should now be made. It is not proposed to go into detail on matters to be noted on inspection but the following are the principal ones:

Location—general and particular.
General description, construction and condition of the building.
Services: e.g. lifts, central heating and public services available.
Degree of obsolescence of building and services with particular reference to renewals for which the head lessee may be liable.
Floor areas should be checked against plans if available otherwise a survey will be necessary. In the measurement of any building this should be in accordance with the Code of Measuring Practice issued by the Royal Institution of Chartered Surveyors and the Incorporated Society of Valuers and Auctioneers, e.g. for offices it is the net internal area that is required.

Enquiries of public authorities

Information should be obtained on town planning consents any established use rights and Building Regulation consents. Local authority development plans should be inspected to see whether any developments are projected in the vicinity and the highway authority should be consulted on road proposals as either of these matters might affect the potential value of the property.

Assessment of the rental data (Schedule IV, page 145)

Having collected all the relevant data it is necessary to analyse and co-ordinate it. Since the valuation will be arrived at by capitalisation of net income the reversionary rental values of all underleases will need to be calculated and thereby the increased income at each rent review is ascertained. This has been summarised in Schedule IV to give the total rents receivable by the head lessee at each rent review year based on current rental values. From these totals will be deducted the head rent and any irrecoverable service charges. The head rent falls to be reviewed in 1993 and is calculated as follows:

Calculation to determine rent to be paid on review under head lease

Rack rental value of building

	Area in square metres	Rent per square metre £ p.a.	Rent £ p.a.
Basement storage	371		(2)
Ground/fifth floor offices	2,951	97	286,344
Totals	3,323 (1)		£302,297 (2)
Rack rental value	£302,297		
Less	64,000		
	£238,297		

Revised head lease rent $= \frac{5}{8} \times 508 \times £238,297 + 40,000$
$$= £188,935$$

Notes

(1) The sixth floor is excluded from the calculation as this is a tenant's improvement which the lease provides is not to be taken into account for rent review purposes.

Schedule IV

Schedule showing the present and future net income at current rental values receivable by the head lessee

	1986/87 1 £ p.a.	1988 2 £ p.a.	1989/1992 3 £ p.a.	1993 4 £ p.a.
Basement (1)	1,000	1,000	1,000	1,000
Ground floor (1)	2,500	2,500	2,500	2,500
First floor	33,500	47,724	47,724	47,724
Second floor	38,000	38,000	47,724	47,724
Third floor	60,000	60,000	60,000	60,000
Fourth floor	33,500	47,724	47,724	47,724
Fifth floor	33,500	47,725	47,724	47,724
Sixth floor (1)	—	—	—	—
Total rents receivable	202,000	244,672	254,396	254,396
Less: irrecoverable service charge	1,976	1,976	1,976	1,976
Total net rents receivable	200,024	242,696	252,420	252,420
Less: rent received for 3rd floor in excess of rental value	12,276	12,276	12,276	12,276
	187,748	230,420	240,144	240,144
Less: head lease rent	40,000	40,000	40,000	188,935
Net rents receivable	£147,748 p.a.	£190,420 p.a.	£200,144 p.a.	£51,209 p.a.

(2) The rent review is based on rack rental value and not rent received.

A further deduction to arrive at net income has been made in respect of that part of the income arising from the rent of the 3rd floor which is in excess of current rental value. This unsecured income will be valued separately.

For more information on rent see Chapter 15, Lease Renewals and Rent Reviews of Commercial Property.

Note on Schedule IV (page 145)

(1) The reversionary income in respect of the basement, ground and 6th floors have been ignored because they are so long deferred. In the case of the basement and ground floor the under-lease still has 32 years unexpired whilst in the case of the 6th floor, despite the fact that no notice has been served under the Landlord and Tenant Act 1927, the tenant will still have the benefit of these improvements if a new lease is granted by virtue of the Law of Property Act 1969.

In order to comprehend this information it is advantageous to illustrate the income pattern in graph form. From this it is easy to appreciate that the head lessee suffers a substantial reduction in income in 1993 when the head rent is reviewed (see p. 148).

Two factors affecting the capitalisation rate at which income is valued are the frequency of rent review and the quality of the covenant of the tenant. It is therefore advisable to analyse the rental data to illustrate the position. This has been done in Schedule V.

Schedule V

Analysis of existing and future rental income from the property

Analysis of rent received by frequency of review

	£ p.a.	%
Rent received at present subject to 5 yearly reviews	198,500	98·3
Rent fixed for 32 years	3,500	1·7
	£202,000 p.a.	100%

Analysis of rental value of property by frequency of rent reviews

	£ p.a.	%
Rental value of parts subject to 5 year reviews	238,620	73·5
Rental value of part where rent fixed for 32 years	63,677	19·6
Rental value of tenants' improvements	22,504	6·9
	£324,801 p.a.	100%

Analysis of rent received from underlessees according to covenant value of tenants

	£ p.a.	%
Major public companies	75,000	37·1
Public company in financial difficulties	60,000	29·7
Private partnership	33,500	16·6
Foreign based company	33,500	16·6
	£202,000 p.a.	100%

The capitalisation rates to be applied will be ascertained by analysis of market transactions. It is important that transactions are analysed on the same methods as are adopted for the valuations. Office property is but one form of investment which is competing for investment funds and its performance must be measured against other investments in terms of current yield, rental and capital growth. Other sources of investment whose current performance can be readily ascertained from the *Financial Times* are fixed interest investments such as Government Stock, Debentures and also Equities. Yields are constantly varying thus affecting the popularity of particular types of investment, so that any valuer must keep himself up-to-date with the investment market in general. Valuation is however not an exact science: it is the valuer's personal interpretation of the market in relation to the particular property being valued which is important. It has been assumed in the valuations which follow that the current yield obtainable on prime freehold office investments is of the order of 5%. "Prime" is not easy to define but in simple terms it means a well built modern building, fully let at reasonable current market rents, subject to 5 year rent reviews and to tenants

CURRENT & FUTURE INCOME PROJECTION

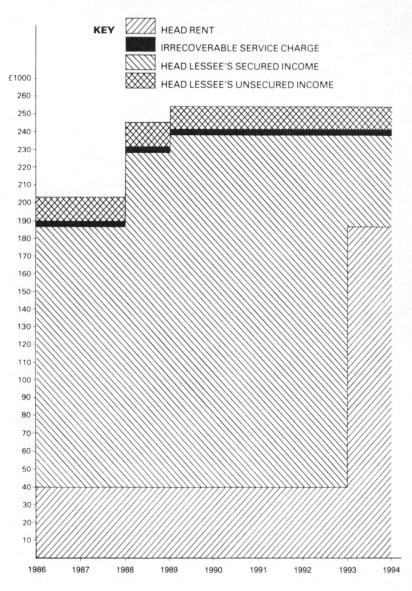

KEY

- HEAD RENT
- IRRECOVERABLE SERVICE CHARGE
- HEAD LESSEE'S SECURED INCOME
- HEAD LESSEE'S UNSECURED INCOME

whose covenant is sound. Yields adopted for the valuation take into account the variations in the property being valued from the prime freehold investment. Adjustments to the yield will need to be made in respect of age, location, quality of building and frequency of rent reviews. Although it is customary to adopt values current at the date of valuation in estimating reversionary values, the extent to which a property is a hedge against inflation will depend on the frequency of rent reviews. Corresponding yields for different frequencies of rent review at varying growth rates are to be found in Donaldson's Investment Tables.*

Valuation of the freehold interest subject to the head lease

	£ p.a.	£
Present income	40,000	
Y.P. in perp. at 10·5% (1)	9·5	
		380,000
Increase in rental income received in 1993	149,000	
Y.P. in perp. at 12·5% deferred 7 years (2)	3·5	
		521,500
Value of freehold subject to the head lease		901,500
Less purchasers costs 2½% (3)		22,538
		£878,962
	say	£879,000

Notes

(1) This part of the income is fixed for the full term of the head lease so it has been valued in perpetuity. Assuming that long dated gilts are showing a return of 13% this investment though long dated has the advantage that (a) there is an ultimate reversion to a central London freehold, (b) there is a substantial "marriage value" (see below) and so justifies a yield of somewhat less than long dated gilts.

(2) The estimated additional income receivable in 7 years is fixed for 25 years. The reversion to full market value is so long deferred, so uncertain and the building will be 100 years old at the end of the lease that it has been ignored and the reversion-

* Donaldsons Investment Tables are available from Donaldsons, London, SW1Y 6PE.

ary income receivable in 1989 has been valued in perpetuity. The increase income is also less secure than the basic ground rent because it is dependent on rental values in 7 years time hence the yield has been adjusted to 12½%.

(3) Purchaser's costs in aquiring the interest being valued are deducted so as to give the actual rate of return to the investor based on his total capital outlay which will include costs of acquisition. The costs comprise 1% stamp duty on purchase, 1% agents fees and ½% legal fees. The percentage deducted needs to be altered as changes occur, i.e. stamp duty on purchase reduced from 2% to 1% in 1985.

An examination of Schedule IV and the Graph will show that the income receivable by the head lessee falls into three parts. Due to the substantial increase in head rent in 1993 only approximately £51,000 (referred to below as "Minimum Income") is secured for the full term of the head lease after deducting the non-recoverable service charge and the excess of rent payable over rental value for the 3rd floor (Schedule I Note (2)). Of this income £3,500 p.a. (approx. 7%) is not reviewable until 2018 (32 years hence) but the balance is subject to 5 year rent reviews. Nevertheless, the head rent payable on review in 1993 represents about 78% of estimated net rent receivable at that date after deducting the excess rent of the third floor and the non-recoverable service charge expenditure.

The second part of the income is that received only until the head lease rent review in 1993 (referred to in the valuation as "Excess income received before review in 1993"). This income is only receivable for 7 years and its capital value must therefore be amortised over the 7 year term. This type of income pattern is unattractive to an institutional investor who favours a steady income growth over a period whereas in this case the income received from the property falls substantially in 7 years time. Consequently whilst this income is reasonably well secured a relatively high rate of interest namely 10% is used.

Finally there is the excess income over rental value in respect of the third floor payable by a tenant whose covenant is doubtful. This income has therefore been valued at a high rate (20%) and amortised over the remainder of the term using the taxed sinking fund rate.

Valuation of head lessee's interest

(a) *Minimum Income* (see Schedule IV column 4)

	£ p.a.	£
(i) *Years 1986/93*		
Net rent (1)	51,209	
Y.P. 7 years at 8½% &		
4% (tax at 40%) (1)	3·38	
		173,086

(ii) *Years 1993/2043*

Net rent (2)		51,209	
Y.P. 50 years at 9% &			
4% (tax at 40%)	9·909		
P.V. £1 in 7 yrs at 9%	0·55	5·45	
		———	279,089
			———
			£452,175

Notes

(1) For sinking funds tax at 40p in the £ is the usual rate adopted by valuers but some valuers use 35p in the £ to reflect rate of corporation tax.

(2) Although the net income is the same as in the first 7 years it is now "top slice" income subject to the payment of a head rent of about 78% of the total income.

(b) *Excess income received before review in 1993*

	£ p.a.	£
Years 1986/87		
Net rent	96,539	
Y.P. 2 years at 10%	1·73	
	———	167,012
Year 1988		
Net rent	139,211 (1)	
Y.P. 1 year at 10%	0·90	
P.V. £1 in 2 years at 10%	0·83	
	—— 0·75	
	———	104,408
Years 1989/92		
Net rent	148,935 (1)	
Y.P. 4 years at 10%	3·17	
P.V. £1 in 3 years at 10%	0·75	
	—— 2·38	
	———	354,465
		———
		£625,885

"Pannell fraction"*: (2)

$$\frac{\text{Y.P. 7 years at 10\% \& 4\% (Tax at 40\%)}}{\text{Y.P. 7 years at 10\%}} = \frac{3 \cdot 21}{4 \cdot 87} = 0 \cdot 66$$

$$0 \cdot 66 \times 610,238 = £402,757$$

* See Chartered Surveyor Vol 100 February 1968, page 402. For alternative method, see page 62 *supra*.

(c) *Rent received in excess of rental value for third floor*

	£ p.a.	£
Rent	12,276	
Y.P. 14 years at 15% & 4%		
(Tax at 40%)	4·33	
		53,155

Total value of head lessee's interest

	£
(a)	452,175
(b)	402,757
(c)	53,155
Total value	908,087
Less purchasers costs 2½%	22,702
	£885,385
	say £885,000

Notes

(1) All rents have been reviewed to current rental values by 1993 except for the basement and ground floor. As these are not reviewable for 32 years the value on reversion is negligible.

(2) This is the adjustment to allow for amortisation over 7 years.

Valuation of freehold interest in possession (i.e. subject to the occupation leases)

The figures of net income have been extracted from Schedule IV.

		£ p.a.	£
Current rental income 1987		187,748	
Y.P. 2 years at 6%		1·83	
			343,578
Reversion in 1988 to		230,420	
Y.P. 1 year at 6½%	0·94		
P.V. £1 in 2 years at 6½%	0·88		
		0·83	
			191,248
Reversion in 1989		240,144 (1)	
Y.P. in perp. deferred 3 years at 6½%		12·74	
			3,059,434
			3,594,260

Excess rental income received for third floor

Rent	12,276	
Y.P. 14 years at 15% & 4% (2)	4·33	
(Tax at 40%)		53,155
		3,647,415
Less purchasers costs 2½%		91,185
		£3,556,230
	say	£3,556,000

Notes

(1) The rental value of 5th floor tenant's improvement has been ignored since the tenant has the benefit of these improvements for another 12 years under his existing lease and for the term of any subsequent lease or 21 years whichever is longer (Law of Property Act 1969), similarly the rental value of the basement and ground floor has been ignored as these are subject to leases without review for an unexpired term of 32 years.

(2) Although this is in the nature of short leasehold interest it is unlikely to be of interest to a gross fund who above all want a secure income and consequently it has been valued using a tax adjusted table.

The freehold subject to the head lease is not an attractive purchase for an institution because of the infrequency of the rent reviews. Equally, the head leasehold interest is unattractive because of the sharp fall in income in 7 years time. The valuation of the freehold subject to the occupation leases illustrates the considerable increase in value by amalgamating the freehold and head leasehold interests. The difference between the value of the freehold in possession and the value of combined freehold and leasehold interests valued separately is known as the "marriage value".

	£	£
Value of freehold in possession		3,556,000
Value of freehold subject to head lease	879,000	
Value of head lessee's interest	885,000	
		1,764,000
Marriage value		£1,792,000

It would be usual that, at some stage, either the freeholder or the head lessee will endeavour to effect an amalgamation by buying out the other at a price equivalent to the value of his own interest together with somewhere around 50% of the marriage value. The final outcome depending on negotiating skills of the parties concerned.

© A. A. Taylor, 1988

Chapter 7

SHOPS

The valuation of shops for non-statutory purposes is affected to only a limited extent by legislation, the principal enactments being Part II of the Landlord & Tenant Act 1954 (as amended by the Law of Property Act 1969), Part I of the Landlord & Tenant Act 1927 and the Offices, Shops & Railway Premises Act 1963. Reference may also need to be made to the Town & Country Planning (Use Classes) Order 1987.

The wide variation in types of shops, ranging from the isolated "round the corner" shop to the departmental store of 40,000 square metres occupying an island site in a premier shopping position in a major city probably provides the valuer with a greater test of his expertise than is generally encountered in the valuation of other types of commercial property.

With few exceptions shops, whether freehold or leasehold, owner-occupied or held for investment, are normally valued on an "investment" basis, i.e. by the capitalisation of rents and rental values, and it is the assessment of rental value to which the valuer has initially to apply his mind.

Rental value

Situation
In arriving at rental value the situation of the shop concerned is of paramount importance. Where the shop is located in an established shopping centre the pattern of trading will usually be readily ascertainable from inspection and from commercially produced street plans which are available for the major centres giving the names of all the traders. Shop valuers commonly identify the section of a street which commands the maximum rental value as the "100% position" and from analysis of rentals elsewhere in the street are able to describe the less valuable sections in percentage terms, i.e. the "90% position", "75% position" etc.

Where there are long continuous parades of shops the points at which rental values change may be difficult to identify and may in fact be constantly moving. Where parades are interrupted by side roads or by non-retail frontages such "breaks" often become the divisions between sections of different rental values.

155

The level of rents achieved in the "100% position" will largely depend on the size and importance of the centre concerned and the rental value in the peak position in one town may be several times greater than the rental value for a similar sized unit in the peak position in a smaller town even though the occupier of both units is the same multiple shop company.

In practice the identification of the rental value pattern has become increasingly difficult in recent years. There has been a great deal of development activity in the shopping field and in some cases existing shopping centres have been entirely renewed. In other cases new centres have been built adjacent to existing centres and have caused a radical distortion of the previous trading pattern. In the latter cases inspection alone may not be sufficient to identify those positions which have increased or decreased in value and discussions with traders and such aids as pedestrian counts may be necessary. Where completely new centres are being built the previous level of rentals may no longer be appropriate and in the case, for example, of New Towns there may be no previous history of rental values at all. In such cases the valuer may have to advise on the initial rental values and to call on his knowledge of other comparable centres coupled with an economic survey to estimate the catchment area likely to be served by the centre and the income groups and spending habits of the potential shoppers.

Known future developments may have to be taken into account. For instance, a proposed multi-storey car park in a centre badly provided with parking facilities may have the effect of increasing the value of shops close to the cark park, possibly at the expense of shops previously of higher value.

Identification of trends can be important. Carnaby Street, W.1., and Camden Passage, N.1., are examples of small London streets which have changed in value dramtically in recent years because they have become centres for the sale of trendy clothes and antiques respectively. Similarly the change to "speciality" shopping in South Molton Street W.1. produced a rapid escalation in rental values. Even established shopping streets such as Kings Road, Chelsea, can undergo changes which produce a greater than average variation in rental values over a short period. It should be borne in mind that changes in rental value brought about by special demand might be short-term changes only and could be quickly reversed. Local, regional and national trends can vary considerably both in rate and in direction and it is this irregular movement of rental values which makes it impossible to construct indices which can be used for valuation purposes.

In a limited number of cases development costs may be a factor in determining rental values. This could happen, for instance, where a new development takes place in an elderly shopping centre or where an entirely new centre is built. It should be emphasised, however, that a rent calculated to give an adequate return on the landlord's development costs will still have to stand the test of profitability in the eyes of potential tenants.

All potential tenants will first make an estimate of the turnover likely to be achieved in the shop in question and from the "mark up" (i.e. the amount by which the sale price exceeds the cost) appropriate to their particular merchandise they will then calculate the rent they can afford. The process is not wholly objective and a wish to be represented in a particular location or the prospect of above average turnover growth can be among factors which override purely actuarial considerations. Rents related directly to turnover are common in the USA but there are relatively few cases in the United Kingdom—the shopping centres at Eldon Square, Newcastle-upon-Tyne and The Ridings, Wakefield being two of the major examples.

Size and type

The traditional shopping street in the smaller towns often started life as a series of terraces of houses which were progressively converted into shops and this origin accounts for the limited size of many of the shops in the older centres, as a typical 19th century terraced house frequently had external dimensions of about 5·5 metres by 12 metres. The tendency in recent years has been for tenants to require larger shops and a major shopping centre will now contain a number of large shops of, say, 15 metres by 60 metres. It will be necessary for the valuer to know the level of demand for the various sizes of shops as otherwise interpretation of rental evidence can be misleading. For instance, demand for small "boutique-type" shops in a particular location may produce rental values which cannot be safely applied to larger shops, even by zoning or other discounting methods. Similarly, a special demand for large units may produce evidence of rental values which show overall rates per square metre as high, if not higher, than those of smaller units. The special demand might only exist, however, for a limited time. The kind of problem which often faces a valuer is the valuation of the property of, say, an old established draper who has occupied very large ground floor premises in a good position in a multiple shopping street for many years. If it is known that one or more of the major space users at present occupying badly-planned premises in an inferior position are in the market for better premises the rent which the valuer estimates might be received may be in excess of rentals previously achieved. Conversely, if all the major space users are already locally represented in adequate premises the valuer might decide that there would be no demand for the unit as a whole and arrive at his rental value by dividing the property into viable units, and making allowance for the cost of conversion in his capital value.

Merchandise display is an important factor in retailing and a major retail company can spend as much on finishing and fitting a shop as on the cost of the structure. Consequently the internal design has to be taken into account in assessing rental value and irregular shape, low ceiling heights, badly sited staircases, differences in floor levels, intrusive stanchions and beams etc., can adversely affect value.

Parking restrictions are making off-street loading facilities increasingly important and lack of rear loading facilities can make shops in heavily restricted areas unlettable for certain trades, i.e. supermarkets where large and frequent deliveries are necessary.

Although it has been customary for corner shops with display windows on the return frontage to be regarded as having a greater value than non-corner units, the difference in value is largely a matter of judgement in the particular circumstances. In some cases any additional value could be completely offset by the cost of the increased length of shop front; a corner unit at the junction between a primary and a good secondary shopping street would normally be expected to command a higher rental than a similar unit without a return frontage.

The majority of retailers require staff or stockroom facilities within their shop units either at the rear of the shop, in the basement or on an upper floor. The analysis of rents of lock-up shops, shops with basements and shops with basements and/or upper floors in a shopping centre will usually provide the valuer with a guide to the value of the ancillary accommodation but experience is necessary when building up a composite value, e.g. of a shop with a basement and first floor, when rental evidence is not available of directly comparable properties. Attempts are sometimes made to value basements and upper floors on the basis of a proportion of the value of the ground floor. In practice, however, the market is usually too erratic for any viable analysis of this nature to be made and it cannot be over-emphasised that this type of mathematical analysis plays virtually no part in the process by which a tenant arrives at his estimate of the rent he thinks he can afford to pay. The shop valuer should guard against the tendency to substitute theory for experience in cases where direct evidence is not available.

It is customary in the case of existing shop units to calculate floor areas on a net basis, i.e. excluding lavatories, staircases, lifts, landings, escalators, plant rooms etc. In new developments, however, where shops are being let in "shell" form (i.e. with no wall or ceiling finishings and where the tenants are to install lavatories etc.) it is not uncommon for letting areas to be quoted on a "gross internal" basis. The definitions of gross internal area and net internal area given in the Code of Measuring Practice issued jointly by The Royal Institution of Chartered Surveyors and The Incorporated Society of Valuers and Auctioneers should be followed in all cases.

Although zoning of ground floors plays an essential part in rating valuations and in the preparation of valuations for Lands Tribunal or court cases it should be borne in mind that in the open market the zoning system has to be adapted to suit the facts and should not be used on a pre-conceived basis. Ideally, the depth and number of zones should be arrived at by analysis of known rentals, but the frequent absence of open market lettings has resulted in a tendency for the adoption of "standard" Zone A depths. Over-reliance on standard depths, particularly when used in conjunction with the analysis of secondary evidence, such as rent review settlements, can produce misleading results. Mathematical precision is not a feature of the valuation of shops for open market rental purposes and even between skilled valuers the margin of opinion may be surprisingly wide because of the imperfections in the market. In times of considerable activity and rising values a difference of 10% is not exceptional; differences of nearer 20% may occur, however, when transactions are limited and values erratic.

For zoning purposes some valuers, instead of halving back through each zone in terms of value, do a similar exercise in terms of Zone A ("ITZA") i.e. the area for each zone is progressively halved so that the Zone A rental figure can then be applied to the total of the adjusted areas. This can facilitate comparison but to avoid confusion with the actual floor areas it is essential that where the ITZA approach is adopted this is clearly stated.

Study 1

A rental valuation is required for lease renewal purposes. The shop has a frontage of 6·5 metres, a depth of 22·5 metres and a net internal area of 133·1 square metres.

Evidence is available of the following current transactions:

Shop 1: Lease renewed at £30,000 p.a. Similar position. Frontage 6·5 metres, depth 15 metres. Net internal area 90·5 square metres. (£331·5 per square metre overall)

Shop 2: New letting at £44,000 p.a. Better position. Frontage
   7·2 metres, depth 25·1 metres. Net internal area 173·6
   square metres. (£253.5 per square metre overall)
Shop 3: New letting at £37,200 p.a. Similar size and position
   but better property. Net internal area 129·2 square
   metres. (£288 per square metre overall).
Shop 4: Lease renewed 6 months ago at £34,000 p.a. Identical
   to the subject unit. (£255·5 per square metre overall)

The average sized unit in this location is about 6·5 metres by
20 metres and the subject property and shops 3 and 4 fall into
this category. It is reasonable to assume, therefore, that the overall
rate for a standard unit will fall between the slightly older letting
of shop 4 and the current letting of the more attractive shop 3.
   The resulting valuation could, therefore, be:

Ground floor: 133.1 square metres at £266   £35,405 p.a.
                                        say £35,400 p.a.

Shops 1 and 2, although not directly comparable, support the
valuation when size and position are taken into account.

Study 2

As for Study 1, but the valuation is for the High Court hearing
to determine the rent for the new lease. Analysis of the rentals of
the four comparables shows that by adopting two 7·5 metre zones
and a remainder and "halving back" a reasonably consistent Zone
A figure can be deduced:

	Area in square metres	£	£
Shop 1: Ground floor:			
Zone A	46·3	439	20,325
Zone B	44·2	439/2	9,680
No reminder			—
	90·5		£30,005 p.a.
		say	£30,000 p.a.

Shop 2: Ground floor:

Zone A	52·5	459	24,097
Zone B	52.5	459/2	12,022
Remainder	68·6	459/4	7,889
	173·6		£44,008 p.a.
		say	£44,000 p.a.

Shop 3: Ground floor:

Zone A	50·1	466	23,347
Zone B	39·8	466/2	9,273
Remainder	39·3	466/4	4,559
	129·2		£37,179 p.a.
		say	£37,200 p.a.

Shop 4: Ground floor:

Zone A	48·2	421	20,292
Zone B	45·1	421/2	9,471
Remainder	40·2	422/4	4,221
	133·5		£33,984 p.a.
		say	£34,000 p.a.

Shop 2 is in a better position than the subject property and should have a higher Zone A value; Shop 3 is a better shop and will also have a higher Zone A value. Shop 4 gives a good indication of the rental value 6 months ago but is now low. The analysis suggests a Zone A value of £445 per square metre for the subject property and this is supported by Shop 1.

Valuation	Area in square metres	£	£
Ground floor:			
Zone A	47·2	445	21.004
Zone B	43·6	445/2	9,679
Remainder	42·3	445/4	4,695
	131·1		£35,378 p.a.
		say	£35,400 p.a.

Note

It has been assumed that the lease terms are similar in each case. In practice adjustments may have to be made, e.g. for differing repairing liabilities to produce comparable rents. The analysis will also include any basements or other floors included in the leases.

Supermarkets, which are mainly associated with the grocery trade, have in recent years developed on separate lines from normal shops. The tendency has been for size requirements to increase, with great importance being placed on the proximity of car parking facilities. In new centres supermarkets with a total area of at least 3,000 square metres are not uncommon. The relationship between gross area and sales area varies between retailers but ancillary space (storage, preparation etc.) equivalent to about 30%—40% of the ground floor sales area will usually be required. Initially, most supermarkets were planned on ground floor level only. Second generation supermarkets often included first floor sales areas, but the present trend is a reversal to ground floor sales areas only. Early supermarkets were predominantly food-based, but latter developments contained an increased range of merchandise such as hardware, clothing and furniture. Changes in operational requirements tend to be relatively rapid and it is important that the valuer should be aware of current developments.

Normal rental valuation practice for purpose-built supermarkets is to apply a single rate per square metre to the total net internal area or alternatively to apply a rate to the sales area only where there is a constant relationship between sales and ancillary space. It is becoming increasingly common, however, for supermarket operators to work in terms of gross internal area. Whichever basis is used for valuation purposes it is obviously essential that the same approach should be used for analysis and synthesis.

Purpose-built supermarkets, particularly the larger ones, have become a specialised category of shop properties as their size and location have made comparison with normal shop properties increasingly difficult. It is now generally accepted that, in the absence of evidence of rental values of similar sized units in the same location, comparison may have to be made with the rentals of supermarkets in other locations.

Departmental stores present particular problems as their number is limited and there is rarely any direct evidence of comparable transactions available. The majority of the older stores are owner-occupied, the tenure being either freehold or long leasehold and where stores do change hands it is more often than not as part of a transaction involving the sale of the owning company. Some rental evidence is found from sale and leaseback transactions and rack-rented stores are occasionally found in new shopping centres although in the latter the tendency is for the store operator to ground-lease a site in the scheme and to carry out his own development.

Attempts are sometimes made to relate the value of the ground floor of a store to the value of the ground floors of the adjacent shops. Where, however, the maximum depth of shop units for which rentals are known is 25 metres and the depth of an adjoining store is 60 metres, any projections of value are incapable of support and are likely to be highly unreliable.

It should be appreciated that whereas the proprietor of a normal sized retail shop will usually stock merchandise which is both limited in range and chosen as far as possible to produce the maximum profit margin, a departmental store will usually offer a very wide range of merchandise with varying profit margins and may even operate some sections at a loss in order to be able to offer a full service. As a general rule the smaller and faster moving lines are sold on the ground floor and the larger and slower moving lines, such as furniture, on the upper floors or in the basement. In practice, an analysis of turnover by departments can show that, in terms of profitability, the basement and first floors of a multi-floor store are worth more in relation to the value of the ground floor than would be the case if a similar analysis was made of the turnover of a conventional shop. The analysis will also probably show, however, that the value of the floors above first floor level despite service by lifts and escalators falls much more rapidly than would be indicated by the analysis of normal sized shop properties, and that fourth and fifth floors, if used for retailing, may have a minimal or even a nil value in profitability terms.

The extent to which profitability should be taken into account is a matter of experience but it is common for store operators to think of rent in terms either as a percentage of overall turnover or as an overall rate per square metre. In arriving at his final answer the valuer might have to use a combination of a conventional floor-by-floor valuation, an estimation of rent as a proportion of turnover and an estimate of the alternative use value of the premises. The alternative use value may be of little consequence in the case of a modern, purpose designed store but may produce the only viable valuation in the case of an old, out-of-position store. The alternative use value is sometimes referred to as the "break up" value where the only practical alternative is the division of the ground and other floors into smaller units with appropriate provision being made for the costs of conversion.

It has been customary for floor areas to be divided between "public" and "non public" space with different values being applied; this distinction is less common with modern, purpose-built stores, the floor areas of which are usually calculated on a gross internal basis.

Study 3

A valuation is required for rent review purposes of a department store on the fringe of a good multiple shopping position. The store was purpose-built in 1925 but has been modernised and is adequately served by lifts and escalators. Turnover is currently about £8,700,000 per annum and has kept pace with the general pattern of retail trading. The lease provides that for the purpose of the rent reviews the renatl value shall be that of a department store.

The store comprises ground floor, basement and four upper floors; the ground floor has a frontage of 30 metres and a depth of 60 metres. The largest shops in the adjoining parades are about 7 metres by 25 metres with ground floor rental values of £50,000 per annum. Knowledge of other stores suggests that for a store of this type, age and location an efficient operator could pay a rental in the region of 5% of turnover.

Valuation	Net internal area in square metres	£	£
4th floor:			
Public (restaurant)	462	20	9,240
Non-public (staff & admin.)	524	12	6,288
3rd floor:			
Public (sales)	780	30	23,440
Non-public (stock) (2)	198	18	3,564
2nd floor:			
Public (sales)	1,183	44	52,052
Non-public (stock)	145	26	3,770
1st floor:			
Public (sales)	1,105	60	66,300
Non-public (stock)	192	40	7,680
Ground floor:			
Public (sales)	1,210 (3)	140	169,400
Non-public (loading and despatch)	143	40	5,720

Basement:

Public (sales)	527	50	26,350
Non-public (stock)	614	30	18,420
	7,083		392,184

(overall £55.34 m²)   say £392,000 p.a. (1)

Notes

(1) The rental value of £392,000 per annum is about 4½% of the turnover which provides a rough check on the valuer's figures.

(2) For the purpose of this study it is assumed that the public and non-public areas throughout the building are not interchangeable without substantial expenditure.

(3) In view of the size of the ground floor it is considered that no useful comparison can be made with other shops in the vicinity.

(4) The definition of rental value in the lease precludes any consideration of value for alternative uses.

Superstores are of comparatively recent origin in the United Kingdom and vary from isolated "green fields" stores unsupported by other shops to stores designed as the hub of new shopping centres. Wide variations in design can be found ranging from buildings of warehouse-type construction to fully fitted departmental stores. Overall size is, however, likely to be in excess of 3,000 square metres and extensive parking facilities are required (in the case of very large superstores it is not unusual for over 1,000 car parking spaces to be provided). Superstores are generally valued at an overall rate on the gross internal area and comparisons may need to be made on a regional or even a national basis.

Lease terms

Where a shop is valued subject to a lease, the terms of the lease will have to be taken into account in the valuation. There has been an increasing tendency in recent years for landlords to seek to pass the responsibility for all outgoings to the tenant and first lettings of modern properties frequently provide for the tenant to be responsible for rates, insurance and all repairs. In the case of entire properties the tenant will usually be required to undertake all repairs; lettings of parts properties can require the tenant to pay a rateable proportion of the expenditure incurred by the landlord in repairing the property. Many leases of parts of older properties still provide for the tenant to be responsible for internal repairs only and where such leases are renewed the provisions of the Landlord & Tenant Act 1954 make it diffciult for the landlord to succeed in widening the repairing covenant (*O'May* v. *City of London Real Property Co. Ltd* (1982) 261 E.G. 1185).

Leases of shopping centres frequently provide for the payment of an annually reviewable charge by the tenant to cover all outgoings, including normal services, special sevices such as security staff and the maintenance of large areas of common parts such as service roads. The charge is usually related to floor areas but is sometimes linked to rateable values. In covered centres with air conditioning and heating the service charges can be high and in some centres it is possible that the level of service charges may adversely affect rental value when the shops' rents are due for review.

The frequency of rent reviews is a factor which has a major effect on the value of properties subject to existing leases. The current fashion is for rents to be reviewed at 5 year intervals although in the period immediately prior to the collapse of the property market in 1973/1974 intervals of 3 years were sometimes achieved.

Rental valuations may have to be made, however, of properties which are the subject of leases which were granted in the early days of rent reviews with intervals of 14 or 21 years and possibly even longer. The assessment of the rental to be paid at the review dates can cause difficulties as there is likely to be no evidence of new lettings with a review frequently longer than, say, 5 years and very little information as to settlements in similar cases. It is generally assumed that a tenant would pay a higher rent for a lease with a term of, say, 14 years without review than for a lease with reviews at 5 or 7 yearly intervals. Because of the lack of evidence, calculations are sometimes made which are intended to show the rent which a tenant could afford to pay for the longer term and which are largely dependent on assumptions as to the likely rate of increase in rental values. It is debatable whether assumptions as to future rates of inflation or future rental values should ever be employed by valuers concerned with the assessment of open market values but the biggest objection to such wholly hypothetical calculations is that it is very unlikely in practice that a tenant could be found who would be prepared to commit himself to a rent greatly in excess of the normal open market rental value in the hope of enjoying a substantial profit in the later part of the review period, particularly when he would be competing with other retailers on a reduced margin of profit in the early part of the period. In the relatively few cases where settlements are known and are capable of analysis the agreed rental is usually within the upper limit of normal valuation tolerances.

Leases which provide for payment of a rent based on a percentage of turnover are sometimes encountered, mainly in fairly modern shopping centres. The most common form of percentage rent clause provides for the payment of a base rent and for the payment of an additional rent based on turnover. Where there is a base rent there is usually also a base turnover, e.g. the lease might stipulate a rental of £15,000 p.a., plus an additional rental of 7% of the turnover in excess of £215,000 p.a. The base rent is often related to the base turnover as in the example and may be subject to review at periodic intervals. The additional rent is usually calculated annually on audited accounts. The valuer may be called upon to assess both the initial base rent and the rent at the review dates and this calls for a knowledge of the relative profitability of different trades as the percentage of turnover may vary from trade to trade. It may be necessary to vary the percentage on different parts of the turnover of a particular retailer, e.g. in the case of a confectioner and tobacconist the percentage on the turnover of cigarettes and tobacco, a large proportion of the price of which is duty, will be less than the percentage of turnover on sweets and chocolates. Considerable experience is necessary when valuing properties subject to leases which contain percentage rent clauses as it is not uncommon to find that the turnover of similar shops let to similar trades varies widely—this can happen for instance with ladieswear shops which tend to cater for particular age or fashion groups.

It sometimes happens that a shopping centre may contain shops let at normal rack rental leases and shops let on percentage leases and there may be discrepancies in the relative rental levels. Experience is required on the part of the valuer in deciding which basis provides the true rental value. There is as yet little or no indication as to the attitude of the Courts to percentage rents when leases are renewed under the provisions of the Landlord & Tenant Act 1954.

User clauses in shop leases vary between fairly open users and users limited to a particular trade and can have a considerable bearing on rental value. It can be argued that a limitation to a specific trade will always restrict the potential market and will, therefore, adversely affect rental value. In practice the effect will be least where there is likely to be sufficient demand from other traders in the specified trade to generate the full open market rental value. Where the specified trade is one which has gone "down market" or for which there is likely to be little demand if the shop was offered in the open market with the same restriction the adverse effect can be considerable. In the case of shopping centres, however, it is usually found that the "monopoly" effect of any user retrictions counter-balances what might otherwise have been the adverse effect on rent of the restrictions.

Study 4

The leases of three similar shops in the same parade are due for renewal and rental valuations are required by the landlord. Since the leases were granted 14 years ago the position has improved considerably and Marks & Spencer and W. H. Smith have opened new stores in the adjoining block. Originally there was a mixture of private traders and small multiples but recent lettings and assignments have been to major multiple companies. Evidence suggests that the open market rental value of each of the three shops is £25,000 per annum.

Shop 1: let to a chemist, with no user restriction in the lease.

Shop 2: let to a greengrocer and the lease contains an absolute prohibition against change of use. Although the tenant operates three other shops and trades efficiently the maximum rental which he could afford to pay for this branch is £20,000 per annum and the latter figure is supported by audited accounts.

Shop 3: let to an ironmonger with a restriction against assigning or subletting to any trade already represented in the parade.

Valuations

Shop 1 is straightforward and a valuation of £25,000 per annum can be reported.

Shop 2 presents the valuer with a problem. The tenant's trade is one which in recent years has been unable to compete with the profit margins achieved by other trades except in secondary positions. If the greengrocer decides to seek a renewal of his lease he will argue that the restriction adversely affects rental value and in the event of court proceedings will probably succeed in having the restriction continued in the new lease (*Charles Clements (London)* v. *Rank City Wall Limited* (1978) 246 E.G. 739). Evidence of the effect of such a restriction is unlikely to be available in which case the valuer will probably advise that the landlord may have to be prepared to accept a rental of £20,000 per annum (tenants' accounts are not, however, generally admissible as evidence of rental value— *W. J. Barton Ltd.* v. *Long Acre Securities Ltd* [1982] 1 W.L.R. 398).

Shop 3. If there are a number of trades not represented in the parade the valuer may take the view that the restriction does not affect the rental value and report a figure of £25,000 per annum. If, however, most of the potential uses are already present the valuer may have to advise that some reduction may be necessary but not of the same magnitude as that of Shop 2.

In the case of new shopping centres in good locations where all the units are marketed simultaneously there is generally little or no variation between the rentals achieved for units of similar sizes and in similar positions, regardless of whether or not there are user restrictions in the leases. In such cases there are grounds for arguing that a similar result should be achieved when reviewing rents or renewing leases. Provided there is not an excess of the less profitable users the latter's semi-monopoly status mitigates the effect of the user restriction. In small local parades restrictions can enhance the value of individual units.

By their nature shops are more likely to have alterations and improvements made to them than other types of commercial properties. The shop valuer must always, therefore, take steps when dealing with properties subject to leases to identify alterations which have been made by the tenant or his predecessor and which could rank as improvements for the purposes of Section 34 of the Landlord & Tenant Act 1954. Where qualifying improvements have been made and the purpose of the valuation is to advise the landlord or the tenant as to the rental value for renewal of the lease, the property has in effect to be valued as if the improvement had not been carried out. Where an improvement was made during the currency of the expiring lease and regardless of the length of that lease and of the date of the improvement, the effect on rent of the improvement is to be disregarded for the duration of the subsequent lease (the duration being at the discretion of the court with a maximum of 14 years). Where an improvement was made during a previous lease and more than 21 years prior to the expiry of the current lease the tenant loses the right to have the improvement disregarded.

Study 5

A 35 year lease is approaching expiry and the tenant requires a rental valuation preparatory to negotiating a new tenancy. The building comprises a shop with two upper floors. Present floor areas are: ground floor 97 square metres; first floor 92 square metres; second floor 78 square metres. 25 years ago the tenant, at his own expense, extended the ground and first floors at the rear, the net additional area on each floor being 11 square metres. He also removed the original staircase between the ground and first floors and replaced it with a new staircase in the extension. The original staircase occupied an area of 5 square metres on the ground floor and 3 square metres on the first floor. Current rental values are: ground floor £250 per square metre: first floor £45 per square metre; second floor £30 per square metre.

Valuation	Area in square metres	£	£
Second floor	78	30	2,340
First floor	78 (92–11–3)	45	3,510
Ground floor	81 (97–11–5)	250	20,250
			£26,100

say £26,000 p.a.

Notes

(1) For the purpose of the study it has been assumed that the same rate per square metre can be applied to the area of the original and of the extended ground floor; in practice a higher rate may be applicable to the former.

(2) The tenant is entitled to the benefit of his improvement during the currency of the new tenancy up to a maximum term of 14 years.

It is sometimes suggested that the value in the unimproved state should be increased to reflect an element of potential, possibly by ascribing a notional ground rental value to the area occupied by the improvement but it is comparatively unusual for improvement potential to be reflected in the rental value of normal types of shops.

It should be appreciated that the provisions of Section 34 of the Landlord & Tenant Act 1954 do not apply to rent reviews. It is common practice for wording either identical or similar to that of Section 34 to be incorporated in rent review clauses but in the absence of such wording improvements carried out by the tenant need not be disregarded when assessing rental value for review purposes (*Ponsford* v. *HMS Aerosols Limited* (1978) 247 E.G. 1171).

Where a rent review clause is silent on the subject of improvements an anomaly can arise in that the tenant may have to pay the full rental value for the shop in its improved state at the rent review date(s) but on termination of the lease may be entitled to a new lease at a rental disregarding the improvements.

The question of whether or not a shopfront is an improvement sometimes arises. In the case of a shop in a multiple shopping position it is customary for the major retailers to have their individual and distinctive shop fronts. The existence of a shop front in these situations is, therefore, likely to be of little interest to potential tenants, who would immediately remove the shop front and replace it with one of their own pattern, which would be unlikely to qualify as an improvement. A modern shop front in a secondary shopping street which could be used by any of a number of private traders could in some circumstances add to the rental value of the shop and be properly regarded as an improvement.

Where a shop is let in shell form and the lease is not granted in consideration of the tenant completing the fitting out, the works if extensive may qualify as improvements, and can cause problems for the valuer as at the end of the lease (or at the review date(s)); there could well be no evidence of the rental value of shops let in shell form. (*G.R.E.A. Real Property Investment Ltd.* v. *Williams* (1979) 250 E.G. 651.)

Although the volume of new legislation has been relatively low in recent years the interpretation of leases has been a major source of litigation and it is essential that the valuer should be aware of current court decisions, particularly in respect of repair, user, alienation, improvements and rent reviews.

Capital value

The rate of interest at which the rents and rental values of shops is to be capitalised can vary considerably over a relatively short period and will depend on the demand for shop investments at the time of the valuation. Where a property is let the demand will be primarily from the investment market and the interest rate will be derived from experience and from the analysis of transactions involving similar properties. In the case of vacant shops there may be competition from potential occupiers and the valuer will need to identify situations where the investment or the occupational market is in the ascendancy in any particular case.

The primary factors which decide the yields likely to be acceptable to investors are the location, age and condition of the shop, the calibre of the tenant, the tenure and the terms of the lease and the likely future rate of growth of rental values. The lowest yields occur when there is an optimum combination of these factors.

Location is important and the majority of investors favour shops situated in centres where there is an established and stable pattern of trading and where a majority of the traders are well known retail companies. As location deteriorates yields rise disproportionately and different classes of investors may be involved. Traditionally, the highest rents and lowest yields and consequently the highest capital values were to be found in the cities and the larger towns. More recently, however, declining populations, competition from out-of-town centres, congestion and lack of car parking have adversely affected rental growth in some of the large conurbations and the lowest yields are now likely to be found in good market towns.

Maximum security of income is usually associated with the financial standing of the tenant and shops let to major retailers with large numbers of branches provide the highest level of demand and the lowest yields. Since the larger multiple retailers have branches in centres of widely differing size and importance the particular combination has to be taken into account in assessing value.

A feature of the shop property market is the considerable variation in the type and age of the properties concerned. Shops can range from units in newly erected shopping centres to converted period buildings and yields may have to be adjusted accordingly. Although the repairing liability imposed on the tenant by the lease may make a lack of routine repairs of little concern, the presence of more serious defects can adversely affect the likely yield.

Investors pay the highest prices for properties where the outgoings and liabilities of the landlord are at a minimum and where the rental income is at a maximum. The lowest yields are obtained from the properties let for optimum terms (currently 20 or 25 years) for normal sized shop units at full open market rentals and on modern leases which provide for rent review at frequent intervals and for the tenant to be responsible for all repairs and outgoings. Frequency of rent review has varied in the past but in recent years has stabilised at 5 year intervals, although shorter intervals are sometimes encountered.

Chapter 8

TAXATION

(Throughout this chapter Finance Act is abbreviated F.A.).

This chapter deals with the computation of tax on a sum or gain of a capital nature arising out of land. Such an amount will be treated for tax purposes as either capital or income and taxed in one or more of the following ways. First, as a chargeable gain under capital gains tax or, in the case of a company, corporation tax on a fraction of the gain. Secondly, as the value transferred under a chargeable capital transfer made on or within 7 years of death and subject to inheritance tax. Thirdly, as the profit or gain from a trade or adventure in the nature of trade and taxed as income under Case I of Schedule D. Fourthly, as a gain of a capital nature arising out of the disposal or development of land and taxed as income under Case VI of Schedule D. Fifthly, as a premium on a short lease and taxed as rental income under Schedule A.

The separate taxation of development value or gain has now been abolished and, although outstanding cases of development land tax and even development gains tax are still found in practice, these taxes are not dealt with in this chapter.

The computation of the amount subject to tax involves both calculation and valuation. In some cases the taxable amount is found by calculation only, e.g. the profit from a trade in land; in others, the taxable amount can only be found by a combined process of calculation and valuation, e.g. the computation of the chargeable gain under capital gains tax. This chapter is concerned only with the second group of computations and deals with capital gains tax and inheritance tax. The object is to explain the valuations and computations necessary to produce the amount of gain or value assessable to tax. Calculations showing the amount of tax payable have been omitted.

The statutory provisions governing valuations for taxation are summarised under each of the taxes, but they have a common base, "open market value". This is defined in similar terms for both taxes and has received a judicial interpretation which may be generally applied. It is summarised as follows.

A sale in the open market assumes a seller who is a free agent, not anxious to sell without reserve, but one who would only sell

173

at the best possible price that is obtainable. It assumes a purchaser with a knowledge of the condition and situation of the property and all surrounding circumstances. The market is open and includes every possible purchaser, including a special purchaser who would bid more because the property has a special value to him. A special purchaser would not necessarily need to make only one bid more than the general price to secure the property but may be forced to bid higher by speculators hoping to buy and sell to him at a higher price. The price which a property is expected to fetch in the open market is found by reference to the expectations of properly qualified persons who have fully informed themselves of all relevant information about the property, its capabilities, the demand for it and the likely purchasers (*IRC* v. *Clay & Buchanan* [1914] 3 K.B. 466; *Glass* v. *IRC* [1915] S.C. 449; *Raja Vyricherla Narayana Gajapatiragu* v. *The Revenue Divisional Officer, Vizagapatam* [1939] A.C. 304; *Lynall* v. *IRC* [1972] A.C. 680).

The open market is not a purely hypothetical market, exempt from restrictions imposed by law, but the actual market and any restrictions on either seller or purchaser may be taken into account (*Priestman Collieries* v. *Northern District Valuation Board* [1950] 2 K.B. 398). Market value may be assessed on the assumption that the property is divided into separate units and each unit is sold at the best price which a purchaser might reasonably be expected to pay. This assumption may be made irrespective of whether it would or would not have been actually possible to put the property on the market in this manner or realise the open market price at that time (*Duke of Buccleuch* v. *IRC* [1967] A.C. 506; *Earl of Ellesmere* v. *CIR* [1918] 2 K.B. 735).

A valuation may take into account any inherent possibilities or prospects attaching to the property at the date of valuation, e.g. hope value for future development or the possibility that a lease might be surrendered. Where the valuation is actually made after the valuation date, however, it would appear that it may not take into account events which occurred subsequent to that date and which showed how those possibilities or prospects in fact turned out, e.g. the grant of planning permission or the surrender of the lease. The valuation must reflect those events as possibilities and not as the certainties they have become by the time the valuation is made (*Gaze* v. *Holden* (1967) 266 E.G. 998).

Where a freehold property is let to a company controlled by the freeholder, the interest is to be valued as subject to that tenancy and not as if it were an unencumbered freehold (*Henderson* v. *Karmel's Executors* [1984] S.T.C. 572).

Capital Gains Tax

The FA 1965 introduced capital gains tax (C.G.T.) in respect of chargeable gains accruing to a person on the disposal or assumed disposal of assets after 6th April 1965. The statute law on C.G.T. is now contained in the C.G.T. Act 1979 as amended by subsequent Finance Acts. C.G.T. is payable by individuals, trustees and partnerships; companies pay corporation tax on their chargeable gains.

From 1965 to the introduction of betterment levy in 1967, C.G.T. stood alone, but, between 1967 and 1970, it was restricted to a tax on increases in current use value. The abolition of betterment levy on 22nd July 1970 restored C.G.T. to its former position as the sole tax on capital gains, but it again suffered restrictions in scope on two further occasions. First, on 17th December 1973 when the so-called development gains tax (DGT) was introduced to tax as income that part of the chargeable gain termed a development gain. Secondly, on 1st August 1976 when development land tax (DLT) generally replaced DGT while C.G.T. continued to tax increases in current use value. DLT has been abolished for disposals after 19th March 1985 and C.G.T. is once again the sole tax on capital gains.

A gain of a capital nature arising out of the disposal of land, which is not specifically exempt, will not automatically suffer C.G.T. Two hurdles must first be overcome. First, the disposal must not be a trading disposal or an adventure in the nature of trade. If it is then it will not be subject to C.G.T., but the profit or gain will be taxed as trading income under Case I of Schedule D. Secondly, the disposal must not fall within the anti-avoidance provisions in Section 488 of the Income and Corporation Taxes Act 1970. This is a widely drawn section designed to tax as income under Case VI of Schedule D a gain of a capital nature arising out of the disposal of land which was acquired, held as stock or developed, with the objective of realising a gain.

C.G.T. applies to the disposal or assumed disposal of land. The term "disposal" is not defined but includes a sale, assignment, gift, grant of a lease at a premium, grant of an option, receipt of a capital sum, settlement of land on trustees and the demolition or destruction of a building.

In general terms, a C.G.T. computation has one, two or three stages depending on the circumstances of the particular disposal. First, the total gain is calculated by deducting from the disposal consideration certain allowable expenditure, e.g. cost of acquisition, improvements, incidental costs of disposal. Secondly, and where the property was acquired before 6th April 1965, part of the total gain is apportioned to the period after that date. Thirdly, a deduction is made for inflation occurring after 31st March 1982.

A C.G.T. computation may require the incorporation of values, depending on the circumstances of ownership and disposal. Various valuations may be required. Those most usually needed are market value at the date of disposal (e.g. where there is a gift or disposal otherwise than by way of a bargain at arm's length) (Study 1), market value at 6th April 1965 (e.g. where land is sold at a price above current use value (Study 3) or material development has been carried out after 17th December 1973 or an election has, or might be, made to calculate the gain by reference to market value at that date (Study 1)) and market value at 31st March 1982 for the purpose of calculating the indexation allowance (Studies 1–7). Other valuations that may be required include: the value of the interest retained following a part disposal (for incorporation in the part disposal fraction) (Study 4), current use value at the date of disposal (where it is not immediately apparent whether the disposal consideration included development value) (Study 3), the capital value of a rentcharge or income (where the consideration for the disposal comprised or included such an annual sum), and the notional premium for the gratuitous variation or waiver of lease terms.

The statutory definition of "market value" for C.G.T. purposes is contained in Section 150 C.G.T. Act 1979. It is the price which the property might reasonably be expected to fetch on a sale in the open market, no reduction being made for the assumption that the whole of the property holding has been placed on the market at one and the same time. Where a valuation is made on a disposal, the date of that disposal is the date of the contract and not the conveyance, or, in the case of a conditional contract, the date when the condition is satisfied (Section 27 C.G.T. Act 1979).

Where a property is subject to any interest or right by way of security it shall be assumed, both on acquisition and disposal, that the property is not subject to such security (Section 23(3) C.G.T. Act 1979). In certain circumstances, where a person making a disposal retains a contingent liability, no allowance for this is made in the valuation. If the liability subsequently becomes enforceable then a retrospective adjustment in the assessment is made (Section 41 C.G.T. Act 1979).

Study 1

This Study sets out the basic framework of a C.G.T. computation where the property disposed of was acquired *before* 6th April 1965.

It also illustrates the relief for a disposal at undervalue.

A purchased the freehold interest in a commercial building in June 1960 for £10,000. His incidental costs of acquisition were £300. In June 1964 he spent £200 on improvements. On 6th April 1965 the property was let on a full repairing and insuring lease, with 5 years unexpired, at a rent of £750 p.a. exclusive. The rack rental value was £1,100 p.a.

In December 1969 A spent £750 in legal costs successfully defending his title to the property. On 31st March 1982 the property was let on a full repairing and insuring lease, with 3 years unexpired, at a rent of £1,500 p.a. exclusive. The rack rental value was £2,500 p.a.

In February 1986 A transferred the freehold to his son for a consideration of £20,000. The incidental costs of disposal were £600. At the date of disposal the property was let on a full repairing and insuring lease, with 12 years unexpired, at a rent of £3,000 p.a. exclusive with 5 yearly rent reviews; the next review was in 4 years time. The rack rental value was £3,500 p.a.

All references are to C.G.T. Act 1979, except where indicated otherwise.

This transaction is between connected persons (Section 63 (2)): it is, therefore, otherwise than by way of a bargain at arm's length and market value must be substituted for the actual consideration (Sections 29A and 62 (2)).

(i) *Market value at disposal (Section 150)*

	£ p.a.	£
Rent on lease	3,000	
Y.P. 4 years at 7%	3·4	
		10,200
Rack rental value	3,500	
Y.P. perp. deferred 4 years at 7%	10·9	
		38,150
		£48,350
	say	£48,500

(ii) *Market value at 31st March 1982 (Section 150 and Section 68 F.A. 1985)*

	£ p.a.	£
Rent on lease	1,500	
"Y.P. 3 years at 7½%	2·6	
		3,900

Rack rental value   2,500
Y.P. perp. deferred 3 years at 7½%   10·8
                                                               ————
                                                                           27,000
                                                                         ————————
                                                                           £30,900
                                                                         ————————

                                                               say   £31,000
                                                                         ════════

(iii) *Market value at 6th April 1965 (Section 150 and para. 12*
      Schedule 5)

                                                       £ p.a.   £
Rent on lease   750
Y.P. 5 years at 6%   4·2
                                                       ————
                                                                      3,150
Rack rental value   1,100
Y.P. perp. deferred 5 years at 6%   12·4
                                                       ————
                                                                     13,640
                                                                   ————————
                                                                    £16,790
                                                                   ————————

                                                       say   £16,750
                                                                   ════════

C.G.T. Computation
Straightline growth (time apportionment) (para 11 Schedule 5) (1)
Overall Gain
The first step is to calculate the total or overall gain.

                                                        £   £
 (i) Deemed consideration for disposal
     (market value)   48,500
(ii) *Less:* allowable expenditure:
     consideration for acquisition
     plus incidental costs (Section 32 (1) (a))   10,300
     enhancement expenditure (Section
     32 (1) (b))   200
     legal costs defending title
     (Section 32 (1) (b))   750
                                                      ——————
     Relevant allowable expenditure   11,250
     incidental costs of disposal   600
     (Section 32 (1) (c)) (2)   ——————   11,850
     Unindexed gain (Section 86 (2) (a)   ————————
     F.A. 1982 as amended)   36,650

(iii) *Less:* indexation allowance (Sections 86, 87 and Schedule 13 F.A. 1982 as amended by Section 68 and Schedule 19 FA 1985):

   (a) by reference to relevant allowable expenditure   11,250

      multiplied by

$$\frac{RD - RI}{RI} \text{ where}$$

RD = retail price index (RPI) for month in which disposal occurs = 381·1

RI = retail price index (RPI) for March 1982 = 313·4

$$\frac{RD - RI}{RI} = \frac{381 \cdot 1 - 313 \cdot 4}{313 \cdot 4} = \qquad 0 \cdot 216$$

                         2,430

    or

   (b) by reference to market value at 31st March 1982 (3)   31,000

      multiplied by $\dfrac{RD - RI}{RI}$ (above)   0·216

                         6,696

   (b) is higher   6,696

Overall gain   £29,954

Apportionment of overall gain

The overall gain is apportioned proportionately to the items of allowable expenditure under section 32 (1) (a) and (b) (para. 11 Schedule 5):

                                                 £

  (i) Consideration for acquisition plus incidental costs

$$\frac{10,300}{11,250} \times £29,954 = E\,(O) = \qquad 27,424$$

(ii) Enhancement expenditure

$$\frac{200}{11,250} \times £29,954 = \text{E (1)} = \qquad\qquad 533$$

(iii) Legal costs defending title

$$\frac{750}{11,250} \times £29,954 = \text{E (2)} = \qquad\qquad 1,997$$

Overall gain   £29,954

Chargeable gain
The proportion of each of the above items of expenditure relating to the period after 6th April 1965 is now calculated. The chargeable gain is the sum of the above items each multiplied by the fraction

$$\frac{T}{P + T}$$

where P = the period from the date of acquisition, or date when the expenditure was incurred or reflected in the property, to 6th April 1965; and T = the period from 6th April 1965 to the date of disposal (para. 11 Schedule 5).

£

(i) Consideration for acquisition plus incidental costs

$$£27,424 \text{ (E(O))} \times \frac{250}{58 + 250} \text{ months} = \qquad 22,260$$

(ii) Enhancement expenditure

$$£533 \text{ (E(1))} \times \frac{250}{10 + 250} \text{ months} = \qquad 512$$

(iii) Legal costs defending title

$$£1,997 \text{ (E(2))} \times \frac{250}{0 + 250} \text{ months} = \qquad 1,997$$

Chargeable gain (subject to relief—see below)   £24,769

Assumed acquisition at 6th April 1965 (para. 12 Schedule 5)
A may elect to have his gain calculated on the assumption that
he sold and immediately reacquired his freehold interest at market
value on 6th April 1965:

		£	£
(i)	Deemed consideration for disposal (market value)		48,500
(ii)	*Less:* allowable expenditure: consideration for assumed acquisition (market value at 6th April 1965) (Section 32 (1)(a))(4)	16,750	
	legal costs defending title (Section 32 (1)(c))	750	
	Relevant allowable expenditure incidental costs of disposal (Section 32 (1)(c))	17,500 600	18,100
	Unindexed gain (Section 86 (2)(a) F.A. 1982 as amended)		30,400

(iii) *Less:* indexation allowance (Sections 86, 87 and Schedule 13 F.A. 1982 as amended by Section 68 and Schedule 19 F.A. 1985):

		£
(a)	by reference to relevant allowable expenditure	17,500
	multiplied by $\dfrac{RD - RI}{RI}$ (above)	0·216
		3,780

or

		£
(b)	by reference to market value at 31st March 1982	31,000
	multiplied by $\dfrac{RD - RI}{RI}$ (above)	0·216
		6,696

(b) is higher   6,696

Chargeable gain (subject to relief—see below)   £23,704

This is smaller than the straightline gain and, provided A is confident that he can agree a 1965 value of about £16,750 with the district valuer, he should elect to use this alternative method of calculating the chargeable gain.

Relief (Section 79 F.A. 1980 as amended)
There is general relief for gifts and A's chargeable gain will be reduced to £1,900 (calculated as follows), provided *both* A and his son claim this relief:

	£	£	£
Chargeable gain (subject to relief)			23,704
Less: held-over gain		23,704	
reduced by excess of actual			
consideration received by A	20,000		
over total allowable			
expenditure	18,100	1,900	21,804
		Chargeable gain	£1,900

The son's acquisition cost will be reduced to £26,696 (i.e. £48,500 market value less £21,804 held-over gain).
The chargeable gain is subject to C.G.T.

Notes

(1) The deemed consideration for disposal is not in excess of current use value and no material development has been carried out: therefore, either the straightline growth (time apportionment) or assumed sale and reacquisition at 6th April 1965 method of calculating the gain may be used (paras. 11 and 12 Schedule 5).

(2) Actual costs of disposal must be used (Section 32 (4)).
(3) This is a disposal after 6th April 1985 of an asset held on 31st March 1982; the indexation allowance may, therefore, be calculated by reference to an assumed sale and reacquisition on that latter date. A claim for this alternative basis must be made within two years of the end of the year of assessment or accounting period in which the disposal occurred (Section 68 and Schedule 19 F.A. 1985). This alternative method of calculating the indexation allowance is not, of course, available where the property was acquired after 31st March 1982.
(4) On an assumed sale and reacquisition it is not to be assumed that incidental costs were incurred (Section 32 (4)).

Study 2

This Study sets out the basic framework of a C.G.T. computation where the property disposed of was acquired *after* 6th April 1965.

In March 1982 A purchased the freehold interest in a shop for £200,000. This was also the open market value. The incidental costs of purchase were £7,500. In June 1985 he spent £10,000 on improvements and sold the property in March 1986 for £300,000. His incidental costs of sale were £5,500.

All references are to the C.G.T. Act 1979, except where indicated otherwise.

C.G.T. Computation

	£	£
(i) Consideration for disposal		300,000
(ii) *Less:* allowable expenditure: consideration for acquisition plus incidental costs (Section 32 (1)(a))	207,500	
enhancement expenditure (Section 32 (1)(b))	10,000	
Relevant allowable expenditure	217,500	
incidental costs of disposal (Section 32 (1)(c))	5,500	223,000
Unindexed gain (Section 86 (2)(a) F.A. 1982 as amended)		77,000

(iii) *Less:* indexation allowance (Sections 86,
87 and Schedule 13 F.A. 1982 as
amended by Section 68 and Schedule 19
F.A. 1985):
(a) by reference to relevant allowable
expenditure: consideration for
acquisition plus incidental costs,
£207,500 multiplied by

$$\frac{RD - RI}{RI} \text{ where}$$

RD = RPI for month in which
disposal occurs = 381·6

RI = RPI for March 1982 = 313·4

$$\frac{RD - RI}{RI} = \frac{381·6 - 313·4}{313·4} = 0·218$$

£207,500 × 0·218   45,235

enhancement expenditure,
£10,000 multiplied by

$$\frac{RD - RI}{RI} \text{ where}$$

RD = RPI for month in which
disposal occurs = 381·6
RI = RPI for month in which
expenditure occurred
= 376·4 (1)

$$\frac{RD - RI}{RI} = \frac{381·6 - 376·4}{376·4} = 0·014$$

£10,000 × 0·014   140
                                                  ‾‾‾‾‾‾
                                                  45,375
                                                  ‾‾‾‾‾‾

or

(b) by reference to market value at 31st
   March 1982:
   market value at 31st March 1982,
   £200,000
   multiplied by

$$\frac{RD - RI}{RI} \text{ (above)} = 0.218$$

   £200,000 × 0·218   43,600

   enhancement expenditure, £10,000
   multiplied by

$$\frac{RD - RI}{RI} \text{ (above)} = 0.014$$

   £10,000 × 0·014   140
                                                      ———
                                                      43,740
                                                      ———

(a) is higher   45,375
                                                                  ———

                              Chargeable gain   £31,625
                                                =======

Note

(1) Where expenditure is incurred *after* 31st March 1982 the RPI
    for the month in which that expenditure is incurred is used
    in place of the RPI for March 1982.

Study 3

This Study illustrates the C.G.T. computation where land acquired
before 6th April 1965 is sold at a price in excess of current use
value. It also illustrates roll-over relief on the disposal of business
assets.

In 1964 A purchased for £7,500 the freehold interest in a site
of 0·364 ha with planning permission for industrial development.
His incidental costs of acquisition were £300. He commenced building works in June 1965 and in the following December he completed
the construction of a factory of 1,440 sq m at a total cost of £65,000.
He occupied the factory for the manufacture of ball bearings until
February 1986 when he sold it for £250,000, incurring incidental
costs of disposal of £7,000. A reinvested £200,000 in the purchase
of another factory to carry on his business.

All references are to C.G.T. Act 1979, except where indicated otherwise.

(i) *Current use value at disposal (Section 150 and Part I Schedule 3 F.A. 1974 as applied by para. 9 (5)(c) Schedule 5)*
"Current use value" (C.U.V.) is defined as market value calculated on the assumption that it is, and would continue to be, unlawful to carry out any development of the land, other than development authorised by planning permission and started after 17th December 1973 and before the valuation date.

"Material development" is the making of any change in the state, nature or use of land other than the minor works and uses listed in paras. 7 and 8 Schedule 3 F.A. 1974.

	£
(a) Rental value, 1,440 sq m at £17·50 say	25,250
Y.P. perp. at 12%	8·3
	£209,575
	say £210,000

or

(b) Site with assumed planning permission to demolish existing factory and build a new factory with a cubic content of up to 110% of existing factory (para. 7 (1)(b) Schedule 3 F.A. 1974)

	£
0·364 ha at £625,000 per ha	227,500
less cost of demolition	10,000
	£217,500

Both valuations are less than the sale price: the disposal was, therefore, at a price in excess of C.U.V. (para. 9 (1)(b) Schedule 5).

(ii) *Market value at 31st March 1982 (Section 150 and Section 68 F.A. 1985)*

	£
Rental value, 1,440 sq m at £16 say	23,000 p.a.
Y.P. perp. at 10%	10
	£230,000

(iii) *Market value at 6th April 1965 (Section 150 and para. 12 Schedule 5)*

Site with planning permission for the
construction of a factory of 1,440 sq m:

		£
0·364 ha at £35,000 per ha		12,740
	say	£12,750

C.G.T. Computation

This disposal was at a price in excess of C.U.V.: the chargeable gain must, therefore, be calculated by reference to either the market value at 6th April 1965, or the cost of acquisition, whichever produces the smaller gain or loss. Time apportionment is not available (para. 9 Schedule 5).

By reference to market value at 6th April 1965 (para. 9(2) Schedule 5)

	£	£
(i) Consideration for disposal		250,000
(ii) *Less:* allowable expenditure:		
consideration for assumed acquisition		
(market value at 6th April 1965) (Section		
32 (1)(a))	12,750	
enhancement expenditure		
(Section 32 (1)(b))	65,000	
Relevant allowable expenditure	77,750	
incidental costs of disposal		
(Section 32 (1)(c))	7,000	
		84,750
Unindexed gain		
(Section 86 (2)(a) F.A. 1982		
as amended)		165,250
(iii) *Less:* indexation allowance (Sections 86,		
87 and Schedule 13 F.A. 1982 as		
amended by Section 68 and Schedule 19		
F.A. 1985):		

(a) by reference to relevant
    allowance expenditure (above)   77,750
    multiplied by

$$\frac{RD - RI}{RI} \text{ where}$$

RD = RPI for month in which
     disposal occurs = 381·1

RI = RPI for March 1982
    = 313·4

$$\frac{RD - RI}{RI} = \frac{381·1 - 313·4}{313·4} = \qquad 0·216$$

                                                          _____
                                                          16,794
                                                          _____

or

(b) by reference to market value
    at 31st March 1982   230,000
    multiplied by

$$\frac{RD - RI}{RI} \text{ (above)} \qquad\qquad 0·216$$

                                                          _____
                                                          49,680
                                                          _____

(b) is higher   49,680
                                                                    _____

            Chargeable gain (subject to relief—see below) £115,570
                                                                    ======

By reference to cost of acquisition (para. 9(4) Schedule 5)

	£	£
(i) Consideration for disposal		250,000
(ii) *Less:* allowable expenditure: consideration for acquisition plus incidental costs (Section 32 (1)(a))	7,800	
enhancement expenditure (Section 32 (1)(b))	65,000	
Relevant allowable expenditure	72,800	

incidental costs of disposal
(Section 32 (1)(c))   7,000   79,800

Unindexed gain (Section 86 (2)(a)
F.A. 1982 as amended)   170,200

(iii) *Less:* indexation allowance (Sections 86,
87 and Schedule 13 F.A. 1982 as
amended by Section 68 and Schedule 19
F.A. 1985):

(a) by reference to relevant allowable
expenditure   72,800
multiplied by

$$\frac{RD - RI}{RI} \text{ (above)}$$ 0·216

15,725

or

(b) by reference to market value at
31st March 1982   230,000
multiplied by

$$\frac{RD - RI}{RI} \text{ (above)}$$ 0·216

49,680

(b) is higher   49,680

Chargeable gain (subject to relief—see below)   £120,520

The chargeable gain calculated by reference to market value at 6th
April 1965 (£115,570) is smaller and is, therefore, automatically
used. No election is necessary (para. 9(4) Schedule 5).

Roll-over relief (Sections 115–121 as amended)
A disposed of a qualifying asset (his factory) used exclusively for
the purposes of a trade, and spent most of the proceeds on the
purchase of new premises for the continuance of his business. He
may, therefore, and provided the amount reinvested (£200,000)

exceeds the chargeable gain (£115,570), elect to defer his C.G.T. liability by deducting part of his chargeable gain from the acquisition cost of the replacement factory.

	£	£
Chargeable gain eligible for relief		115,570
Less: deduction for amount of proceeds of sale not reinvested:		
chargeable gain	115,570	
less: amount not reinvested (£250,000–£200,000)	50,000	
Rolled-over gain		65,570
Chargeable gain		£50,000

The acquisition cost of A's replacement factory will be reduced to £134,430 (i.e. £200,000 purchase price less £65,570 rolled-over gain). The chargeable gain of £50,000 is subject to C.G.T.

Notes

(1) Where part only of the overall gain is a chargeable gain (e.g. where the gain is time apportioned) and part only of the proceeds of sale is reinvested, the following adjustments are made. First, the part of the proceeds not reinvested is reduced to the proportion that the chargeable gain bears to the overall gain when calculating the amount of the chargeable gain which cannot be deferred. Secondly, the balance of the chargeable gain is then deducted from the acquisition cost of the replacement property (Section 116).

(2) The roll-over relief available to A does not alter the acquisition cost to the purchaser of A's factory nor the sale proceeds to the vendor of the new factory purchased by A (Sections 115(1) and 116(1)).

Study 4

This Study illustrates the C.G.T. computation where there is a part disposal of a freehold interest by the grant of a short lease at a premium. It also illustrates the relationship between C.G.T. and income tax Schedule A.

A purchased the freehold interest in a commercial building in 1966 for £15,000. His incidental costs of acquisition were £300.

In 1970 he spent £1,000 on improvements. On 31st March 1982 the building was let on a full repairing and insuring lease with 3¾ years unexpired at a rent of £2,000 p.a. exclusive. The rack rental value was £2,250 p.a.

In January 1986 A granted a full repairing and insuring lease for 15 years at a fixed rent of £500 p.a. exclusive and a premium of £25,000. The rack rental value was £2,500 p.a. His incidental costs of this part disposal were £500.

All references are to C.G.T. Act 1979, except where indicated otherwise.

(i) *Market value at 31st March 1982 (Section 150 and Section 68 F.A. 1985)*

	£ p.a.	£
Rent on lease	2,000	
Y.P. 3¾ years at 8%	3·1	
		6,200
Rack rental value	2,250	
Y.P. perp. deferred 3¾ years at 8%	9·4	21,150
		£27,350
	say	£27,500

(ii) *Market value of the property undisposed of after part disposal (Section 35 (2)(b) and para. 2(2) Schedule 3)*

	£ p.a.	£
Rent on lease	500	
Y.P. 15 years at 15% (1)	5·8	
		2,900
Rack rental value	2,500	
Y.P. perp. deferred 15 years at 7½%	4·6	11,500
		£14,400
	say	£14,500

This amount is B in the part disposal fraction $\dfrac{A}{A+B}$ (see below).

C.G.T. Computation

Apportionment of premium (para. 5 (1) Schedule 3 and Section 80 Income and Corporation Taxes Act 1970)
The premium on a lease of less than 50 years is subject to C.G.T. and income tax Schedule A. The part of the premium subject to C.G.T. is calculated as follows:

		£	£
(i)	Total premium		25,000
(ii)	*Less:* part taxed as income under Schedule A:		
	total premium	25,000	
	deduct 1/50th for each year of term other than 1st:		
	14/50 × £25,000	7,000	
			18,000
	Part of premium treated as consideration for C.G.T. part disposal		£7,000

Chargeable gain
The grant of a lease at a premium is a part disposal of the landlord's interest (para. 2 (1) Schedule 3).

		£	£
(i)	Consideration for part disposal (premium)		7,000
(ii)	*Less:* allowable expenditure: consideration for acquisition plus incidental costs (Section 32 (1)(a))	15,300	
	enhancement expenditure (Section 32 (1)(b))	1,000	
		16,300	

apportioned to the part disposal by the fraction (Section 35)

$$\frac{A}{A + B} \text{ where}$$

A = consideration for part disposal
= £7,000 in numerator but £25,000 in denominator (para. 5 (1) Schedule 3)

B = market value of property
   undisposed of = £14,500

$$\frac{A}{A+B} = \frac{7,000}{25,000 + 14,500} = \qquad 0{\cdot}18$$

Relevant allowable expenditure	2,934	
incidental costs of disposal		
(Section 32 (1)(c)	500	
		3,434

Unindexed gain (Section 86 (2)(a)
F.A. 1982 as amended)   3,566

(iii) *Less:* indexation allowance (Sections 86,
87 and Schedule 13 F.A. 1982 as
amended by Section 68 and Schedule 19
F.A. 1985):
(a) by reference to relevant
   allowable expenditure   2,934
   multiplied by

$$\frac{RD - RI}{RI} \text{ where}$$

RD = RPI for month in which
        disposal occurs = 379·7
RI = RPI for March 1982 = 313·4

$$\frac{RD - RI}{RI} = \frac{379{\cdot}7 - 313{\cdot}4}{313{\cdot}4} = \qquad 0{\cdot}211$$

                                                           619

or

(b) by reference to market value
   at 31st March 1982   27,500
   apportioned to the part disposal
   by fraction

$$\frac{A}{A+B} \text{ (above)} \qquad 0{\cdot}18$$

                                                          4,950

multiplied by

$\dfrac{RD - RI}{RI}$ (above)   0·211

                                                              ⎯⎯⎯
                                                              1,044
                                                              ⎯⎯⎯

(b) is higher   1,044
                                                              ⎯⎯⎯

                                        Chargeable gain   £2,522
                                                        ⎯⎯⎯⎯⎯⎯

The chargeable gain is subject to C.G.T (but is likely to fall within the annual exemption limit). The part of the premium not taxed under C.G.T. (£18,000) is taxed as income under Schedule A.

Note

(1) High capitalisation rate used to reflect the fact that a fixed rent for 15 years would be unattractive to a prospective purchaser.

Study 5

This Study illustrates the C.G.T. liability arising on the disposal of a short lease for a premium.

In December 1970 A took an assignment of the headlease of a shop which had 45 years unexpired at a fixed rent of £100 p.a. exclusive. He paid a premium of £20,000 and incurred incidental costs of £500.

A spent £10,000 on improvements to the property in March 1974. He sub-let the property on a full repairing and insuring lease for 10 years from 25th March 1982 at a rent of £9,000 p.a. exclusive, with a rent review at the fifth year.

In January 1986 A disposed of his headlease for £80,000. His incidental costs were £1,500.

All references are to C.G.T. Act 1979, except where indicated otherwise.

(i) *Market value at 31st March 1982 (Section 150 and Section 68 F.A. 1985)*

	£
Rent receivable	9,000 p.a.
Less: rent payable	100 p.a.
Profit rent	8,900 p.a.

Y.P. 33¾ years at 9 and 4% (taxed at 40%)   8·8

                                                                    £78,320

                                                      say   £78,000

C.G.T. Computation

		£	£
(i)	Consideration for disposal		80,000

(ii) *Less:* allowable expenditure (1):
consideration for acquisition plus
incidental costs (Section 32 (1)(a)),
£20,500 reduced by amount written off
(para. 1 Schedule 3)

$$= £20,500 \times \frac{P(1) - P(3)}{P(1)}$$

where

P(1) = % derived from Table for duration
        of lease at acquisition (45 years)
        = 98·059

P(3) = % derived from Table for duration
        of lease at disposal (29 years 9
        months)
        = 87·054

amount written off:

$$£20,500 \times \frac{98·059 - 87·054}{98·059} \quad (0·11)$$

£20,500 × 0·11 = £2,255

reduced amount = £20,500 − £2,255 =   18,245
enhancement expenditure (Section
32 (1)(b)), £10,000 reduced by amount
written off (para. 1 Schedule 3)

$$= £10,000 \times \frac{P(2) - P(3)}{P(2)}$$

where

P(2) = % derived from Table for duration
        of lease when expenditure first
        reflected in the lease (41 years 9
        months)
        = 94·456

P(3) = % derived from Table for duration
of lease at disposal (29 years 9
months)
= 87·054
amount written off:

$$£10,000 \times \frac{94 \cdot 456 - 87 \cdot 054}{94 \cdot 456} \ (0 \cdot 1)$$

£10,000 × 0·1 = £1,000

reduced amount = £10,000 − £1,000 =   9,000
                                           ────────

Relevant allowable expenditure   27,245
incidental costs of disposal
(Section 32 (1)(c))   1,500
                                           ────────   28,745
                                                            ────────

Unindexed gain (Section 86
2(a) F.A. 1982 as amended)   51,255

(iii) *Less:* indexation allowance (Sections 86,
       87 and Schedule 13 F.A. 1982 as
       amended by Section 68 and Schedule 19
       F.A. 1985):

(a) by reference to relevant
     allowable expenditure   27,245
     multiplied by

$$\frac{RD - RI}{RI}$$

where

RD = RPI for month in which
        disposal occurs = 379·7
RI = RPI for March 1982 = 313·4

$$\frac{RD - RI}{RI} = \frac{379 \cdot 7 - 313 \cdot 4}{313 \cdot 4} =$$ 0·211
                                                            ────────

                                                             5,749
                                                            ────────

or
(b) by reference to market value
    at 31st March 1982   78,000

    multiplied by

$$\frac{RD - RI}{RI} \text{ (above)} \qquad 0{\cdot}211$$

                                 16,458

(b) is higher   16,458

                    Chargeable gain   £34,797

Note

(1) A lease is treated as a wasting asset when the duration is less than 50 years at the relevant time, i.e. at acquisition or disposal (para. 1 (1) Schedule 3). The allowable expenditure in respect of such a lease is written off over the duration on a reducing basis (as opposed to the straightline basis in Study 1) in accordance with the Table in para. 1 Schedule 3.

Study 6

This Study illustrates the C.G.T. computation where there is a part disposal of a leasehold interest by the grant of a sublease at a premium out of a headlease with less than 50 years unexpired.

In June 1975 Z granted to A a full repairing and insuring lease of a shop for 25 years at a fixed rent of £100 p.a. exclusive and a premium of £7,500. A's incidental costs were £250.

In December 1978 A let the property on a full repairing and insuring lease for 7 years at a fixed rent of £2,500 p.a. exclusive. In March 1982 the rack rental value was £3,000 p.a.

On the expiration of this lease in December 1985 the tenant vacated the premises and A let them to B on a full repairing and insuring lease for 10 years at a fixed rent of £250 p.a. exclusive and a premium of £25,000. His incidental costs were £750.

All references are to C.G.T. Act 1979, except where indicated otherwise.

(i) *Market value at 31st March 1982 (Section 150 and Section 68 F.A. 1985)*

	£ p.a.	£
Rent receivable	2,500	
Less: rent payable	100	

Profit rent		2,400	
Y.P. 18¼ years at 10 & 4%			
(taxed at 40%)		6·2	
			14,880
Rack rental value		3,000	
Less: rent receivable		2,500	
Additional profit rent		500	
Y.P. 14½ years at 10 & 4%			
(taxed at 40%)	10·7		
P.V. of £1 in 3¾ years			
at 10%	0·7	7·5	3,750
			£18,630
		say	£18,500

(ii) *Notional premium on sublease to B if rent under sublease*
(£250 p.a.) had been same as rent under headlease (£100 p.a.)
(para. 4 (2)(b) Schedule 3)

	£ p.a.	£
Premium under sublease		25,000
Add: additional premium if rent under		
sublease reduced to rent under headlease:		
Rent under sublease	250	
deduct: rent under headlease	100	
	150	
Y.P. 10 years at 12 & 4% (taxed		
at 40%)	3·9	
		585
		£25,585
	say	£25,500

C.G.T. Computation

	£	£
(i) Consideration for part disposal		
(premium)		25,000
(ii) *Less:* allowable expenditure:		
consideration for acquisition plus		

incidental costs (Section 32 (1)(a)) 7,750
apportioned to part disposal by fraction
(para. 4 (1) & (2)(b) Schedule 3) (1)

$$\frac{P(1) - P(3)}{P(2)}$$

where

P(1) = % derived from Table for duration
　　　of headlease at grant of sublease
　　　(14 years 6 months)
　　　= 60·294

P(2) = % derived from Table for term of
　　　headlease at grant of that lease (25
　　　years)
　　　= 81·1

P(3) = % derived from Table for duration
　　　of headlease at termination of
　　　sublease (4 years 6 months)
　　　= 24·352

$$\frac{P(1) - P(3)}{P(2)} = \frac{60 \cdot 294 - 24 \cdot 352}{81 \cdot 100} = \qquad 0 \cdot 443$$

　　　　　　　　　　　　　　　　　　　3,433

Less: for reduction in premium on
sublease due to increased rent over
headrent (para. 4 (2)(b) Schedule 3):

$$\frac{\text{premium paid on sublease}}{\text{notional premium on sublease}} = \frac{25,000}{25,500} = \qquad 0 \cdot 98$$

Relevant allowable expenditure 3,364
incidental costs of part disposal
(Section 32 (1)(c)) 750
　　　　　　　　　　　　　　　　　　　　　　　　4,114

　　　　　　　　　　　　　　　　　Gain 20,886

(iii) *Less:* part of premium taxed under
　　　Schedule A (para. 5 (1) Schedule 3 and
　　　Section 80 Income & Corporation Taxes
　　　Act 1970):
　　　Premium 25,000
　　　deduct 1/50th for each year of term other
　　　than 1st: $9/50 \times £25,000$ 4,500

20,500

Less: allowance for premium paid on
grant of headlease (Section 83 (1) & (4)
Income & Corporation Taxes Act 1970)
(2) amount chargeable on Z at grant of
headlease:
£7,500 − (24/50 × £7,500) = £3,900

multiplied by

$$\frac{\text{duration of sublease to B at grant}}{\text{duration of headlease to A at grant}} = 10/25$$

allowance 10/25 × £3,900   1,560
                                                                                ——— 18,940
                                                                                ————

Unindexed gain (Section 86 (2)(a) F.A.
1982 as amended)   1,946

(iv) *Less:* indexation allowance (Section 86,
87 and Schedule 13 F.A. 1982 as
amended by Section 68 and Schedule 19
F.A. 1985):
(a) by reference to relevant allowable
    expenditure   3,364

    multiplied by

$$\frac{RD - RI}{RI} \text{ where}$$

    RD = RPI for month in which
         disposal occurs = 378·9
    RI = RPI for March 1982 = 313·4

$$\frac{RD - RI}{RI} = \frac{378·9 - 313·4}{313·4} =$$ 0·209

                                                                                ———
                                                                                703
                                                                                ———

or

(b) by reference to market value at
    31st March 1982   18,500
    apportioned to part disposal

by fraction

$$\frac{P(1) - P(3)}{P(2)} \text{ (above)} \qquad\qquad 0 \cdot 443$$

$$\overline{8,195}$$

multiplied by

$$\frac{RD - RI}{RI} \text{ (above)} \qquad\qquad 0 \cdot 209$$

$$\overline{1,713}$$

   (b) is higher   1,713

Chargeable gain £233

The chargeable gain is subject to C.G.T. (but is likely to fall within the annual exemption limit). Part of the premium (£18,940) is taxed as income under Schedule A.

Notes

(1) The normal part disposal fraction (see Study 3) does not apply where the part disposal is the grant of a sublease out of a lease with less than 50 years unexpired (para. 4 (1) & (2) Schedule 3).

(2) Part of the premium paid by A to Z (£7,500) on the grant of the headlease is set-off against the Schedule A liability arising out of the premium of £25,000 paid by B to A on the grant of the sublease (Section 83 (1) & (4) Income & Corporation Taxes Act 1970).

Inheritance Tax

The F.A. 1975 abolished estate duty and introduced a new tax, capital transfer tax (C.T.T.). Subject to certain exceptions, this applied to gifts and other gratuitous transfers of property (actual or deemed) made during a person's lifetime after 26th March 1974 and the deemed transfer on death after 12th March 1975. Substantial alterations were made to C.T.T. by the F.A. 1976, with further amendments in successive Finance Acts and their consolidation in the C.T.T. Act 1984.

Under the F.A. 1986 C.T.T. was renamed inheritance tax (I.T.) and largely restricted in scope to transfers of property after 17th March 1986 on or within 7 years of death. Lifetime gifts made more than 7 years before the donor's death are (with certain exceptions) now outside I.T. Thus, in broad terms, the former estate duty has been resurrected within the framework of C.T.T, and named I.T. The majority of the provisions of C.T.T. continue in force as part of the new tax and the C.T.T. Act 1984 is renamed the Inheritance Tax Act 1984. It will be referred to by this new title throughout this part of this chapter. All references to C.T.T. in previous Acts and documents are now treated as references to I.T.

I.T., like C.T.T., is based on the "chargeable transfer". This is broadly a disposition whereby the transferor's estate is reduced in value, unless it is excluded because it is not intended to confer a gratuitous benefit and it is or might be an arm's length transaction between unconnected persons.

Thus, a gift, a transfer at undervalue or overvalue, or the creation of a settlement are chargeable transfers; on death, a person is assumed to have made a chargeable transfer immediately before his death of all his remaining estate; the gratuitous use of assets by another is treated as a disposition whereby the lender's estate is reduced in value.

The F.A. 1986, however, in changing C.T.T. to I.T., introduced the "potentially exempt transfer". This is a transfer of property (e.g. a gift) made between individuals or into an accumulation and maintenance trust or trust for the disabled. If the transferor lives for at least 7 years after the date of transfer it is exempt from I.T. Thus, I.T. is largely restricted to the transfer of property on or within 7 years of death. Other lifetime gifts are exempt from I.T. (with minor exceptions) but will continue to be subject to C.G.T.

I.T. is the sole tax on death (after 17th March 1986), as was its predecessor (C.T.T.) between 12th March 1975 and 17th March 1986. C.G.T. ceased to apply to disposals on death after 30th March 1971.

I.T. is chargeable on the same basis as C.T.T., namely the loss to the transferor by his gifts or other transfers, as they occur throughout each 7 year period (previously 10) on a cumulative basis at progressively higher rates of tax, provided that the transfer is not an exempt transfer, e.g. a gift made more than 7 years before the donor's death. On death the deceased is deemed to have made a last chargeable transfer of all his remaining property. His death may also trigger a tax liability on potentially exempt transfers made within the previous 7 years. There is now only one table of tax rates for I.T. This is the higher scale for deaths formerly applicable under C.T.T., indexed to reflect the increase in the retail price index in the year to December 1985. The tax payable is tapered where a potentially exempt transfer is caught by the transferor's death within 7 years, but the transfer was made between 3 and 7 years before death. Furthermore, the previous relief under C.T.T. whereby the additional tax payable on a lifetime gift made within 3 years of death could be calculated on the basis of market value at death, if lower than the value at the date of gift, is carried into I.T. with the extension of the 3 year period to 7 years.

Where tax is charged on a *chargeable* lifetime transfer it is levied at one half of the scale rates and, if the transferor dies within 7 years, the additional tax is calculated as at the date of death. Examples of chargeable lifetime transfers are: gifts made to or by a company, gifts with reservation (i.e. where the donor retains rights in the subject-matter of the gift) and transfers into a trust other than an accumulation and maintenance trust or for the disabled.

Questions of valuation arise whenever a chargeable transfer is made or deemed to have been made. On such a transfer a valuation will be required of the loss to the transferor's estate. This loss will usually be the value of the property transferred, plus the I.T. payable thereon, and therefore a valuation of the transferred property only will be required. In some cases, however, the loss to the transferor will exceed the value of the property transferred due to the consequent depreciation in value of the transferor's retained estate and any related property. Here, valuations will be required of the whole of the transferor's estate both before and after the disposal. Indeed, a strict application of the valuation provisions of I.T. requires that *every* chargeable transfer needs valuations of the *whole* of the transferor's estate both before and after the transfer. This poses innumerable valuation problems, particularly where the estate is large or varied: questions of "lotting" and yields before and after the transfer could be fertile ground for argument. In practice, and particularly where the property transferred forms a clearly separate unit, it seems to be readily agreed that the value of the property transferred will also represent the loss to the transferor's estate for I.T. purposes.

The basic I.T. valuation provision is the definition of "market value" in Section 160 of the I.T. Act 1984. The value of property for I.T. purposes is defined as the price which the property might reasonably be expected to fetch if sold in the open market; no reduction in price is to be assumed on the ground that the whole of the property is placed on the market at one and the same time. In determining the value of a person's estate his liabilities are to be taken into account, provided they were imposed by law (e.g.

rates) or incurred for consideration (e.g. a mortgage) (Section 5 (3) and (5) I.T. Act 1984), but a liability in respect of which there is a right of reimbursement is taken into account only to the extent that reimbursement cannot reasonably be expected to be obtained (Section 162 (1) I.T. Act 1984). A liability is valued at the time of the chargeable event and, if it is a future liability, it may be discounted (Section 162 (2) I.T. Act 1984). A liability which is an encumbrance on a particular property shall, so far as possible, be taken to reduce the value of that property (Section 162 (4) I.T. Act 1984). Most importantly, the transferor's I.T. liability on the chargeable transfer under consideration, but not generally his other tax liabilities thereon, is to be taken into account when valuing his estate immediately after the transfer (Section 5 (4) I.T. Act 1984). Thus, the net value transferred must be grossed up by the amount of tax in order to arrive at the value transferred. This amount then takes its place in the aggregate of chargeable transfers during each 7 year period. This grossing up process does not apply where the tax is paid by the transferee or on the deemed transfer on death.

Where the right to dispose of any property has been excluded or restricted then, on the next transfer, that exclusion etc. shall be ignored unless consideration was given for it. If the contract imposing the exclusion etc. was a chargeable transfer then allowance must be made for the part of the value transferred attributable to the exclusion or restriction (Section 163 I.T. Act 1984).

Special rules apply to the deemed transfer on death. For example, any change in the value of all or part of the deceased's estate due to his death shall be taken into account in the valuation as if it had occurred before death. Reasonable funeral expenses may be deducted in computing the value of the deceased's estate (Sections 171 and 172 I.T. Act 1984). The F.A. 1986 introduced special provisions, similar to those under the former estate duty, concerning the treatment of certain debts and encumbrances when valuing a deceased's estate (Section 103 and para. 13 Schedule 19).

Special reliefs apply in respect of business property, agricultural property and woodlands, necessitating special valuation rules. Those relating to business property and agricultural land are illustrated in Study 7 below. In the case of commercial woodlands transferred on death, and provided certain conditions are satisfied and an election for relief is made, the land is valued disregarding the value of trees and underwood. If the timber is subsequently transferred before the next death, with or without the land, a further I.T. liability may arise and will be calculated having regard to the tax position which existed at the date of the prior death (Sections 125 and 126 (1) I.T. Act 1984; see also Section 127 (2) I.T. Act

1984: relief where the woodlands are business property at the date of death).

Study 7

This Study sets out the I.T. computation where a potentially exempt transfer (a lifetime gift) becomes subject to tax by the death of the donor within 7 years of the transfer. It also deals with agricultural and business reliefs and the relationship between I.T. and C.G.T. on gifts.

In September 1970 A purchased the freehold interest in a farm for £65,000. His incidental costs of purchase were £2,000. The farm has a total area of 91·13 ha and comprises a farmhouse (occupied by the farm manager), two cottages (occupied by farmworkers), farm buildings and 90·13 ha of arable and pasture. The farm was operated by A as a business. On 25th March 1986 A made a gift of his freehold to his son. His legal costs were £3,500. The property was unencumbered at the date of transfer. In 1987 A's son applied for planning permission for housing development on 1·13 ha. This was refused and an appeal to the Secretary of State for the Environment was unsuccessful. A died on 10th April 1988. A's death within 7 years of his gift to his son renders this transfer subject to I.T.

(i) *Value transferred at date of gift (I.T.)*
This is the market value of the farm at the date of gift, before the reduction for agricultural relief and as if no tax were chargeable on it (Sections 116 (1) and (7) and 160 I.T. Act 1984).

	£
Farmhouse (2)	25,000
2 cottages, 2 at £9,000 (2)	18,000
Arable and pasture, including farm buildings, 89 ha at £4,500	400,500
Land with "hope value" for housing development, 1·13 ha at £9,500	10,735
	£454,235
	say £454,250

(ii) *Agricultural value at date of gift (I.T.)*
This is the value on the assumption that the property is subject to a perpetual covenant prohibiting its use otherwise than as agricultural property (Section 115 (2) and (3) I.T. Act 1984).

	£
Farmhouse	25,000
2 cottages, 2 at £9,000	18,000
Arable and pasture, including farm buildings,	
90·13 ha at £4,500	405,585
	£448,585
say	£448,500

(iii) *Value transferred at date of death (I.T.)*
This is the market value of the farm at the date of death (Section 160 I.T. Act 1984).

	£
Farmhouse (2)	30,000
2 cottages, 2 at £9,750 (2)	19,500
Arable and pasture, including farm buildings,	
90·13 ha at £4,600	414,598
	£464,098
say	£464,000

This is also the agricultural value at the date of death.

(iv) *Market value at 31st March 1982 (C.G.T.) (Section 150 C.G.T. Act 1979 and Section 68 F.A. 1985)*

	£
Farmhouse (2)	26,000
2 cottages, 2 at £10,000 (2)	20,000
Arable and pasture, including farm buildings,	
90·13 ha at £4,850	437,130
	£483,130
say	£483,000

(v) *Market value at date of gift (C.G.T.) (Section 150 C.G.T. Act 1979)*

	£
Farmhouse (2)	29,000
2 cottages, 2 at £11,000 (2)	22,000

Arable and pasture, including farm buildings,
   89 ha at £4,500   400,500
Land with "hope value" for housing development
   1·13 ha at £9,500   10,735

                                        £462,235

                          say   £462,250

I.T. and C.G.T. Computations

I.T. Computation

The agricultural value is eligible for agricultural relief; the amount of the value transferred in excess of agricultural value is eligible for business relief. The value transferred at the date of gift (on which I.T. is payable) is:

	£	£
(a) Value of agricultural property (Section 115 (3) I.T. Act 1984)	448,500	
Less: agricultural relief, 50% (Section 116 (2) I.T. Act 1984)	224,250	
		224,250
(b) Value of relevant business property: Value transferred	454,250	
Less: value of agricultural property	448,500	
Value of relevant business property (Section 105 I.T. Act 1984)	5,750	
Less: business relief, 30% (Section 104 I.T. Act 1984)	1,725	
		4,025

Value transferred   £228,275
                         plus I.T.
             payable thereon

The reduced value transferred at the date of death would have been:

                                          £

Value of agricultural property (market value)
   (Section 115 (3) I.T. Act 1984)   464,000
Less: agricultural relief, 50%

(Section 116 (2) I.T. Act 1984)   232,000

Value transferred   £232,000

This is higher than the reduced value transferred at the date of gift (£228,275) and, therefore, *no* claim should be made to use the alternative value at death (Section 131 I.T. Act 1984 as amended by Section 101 (1)(e) and para. 23 Schedule 19 F.A. 1986).

C.G.T. Computation

	£	£
(i) Deemed consideration for disposal (market value)		462,250
(ii) *Less:* allowable expenditure: consideration for acquisition plus incidental costs (Section 32 (1)(a) C.G.T. Act 1979)	67,000	
incidental costs of disposal (Section 32 (1)(c) C.G.T. Act 1979)	3,500	
		70,500
Unindexed gain (Section 86 (2)(a) F.A. 1982 as amended)		391,750
(iii) *Less:* indexation allowance (Sections 86, 87 and Schedule 13 F.A. 1982 as amended by Section 68 and Schedule 9 F.A. 1985):		
(a) by reference to relevant allowable expenditure: consideration for acquisition plus incidental costs multiplied by	67,000	

$$\frac{RD - RI}{RI} \text{ where}$$

RD = RPI for month in which disposal occurs = 381·6
RI = RPI for March 1982 = 313·4

$$\frac{RD - RI}{RI} = \frac{381 \cdot 6 - 313 \cdot 4}{313 \cdot 4} =$$

0·218

14,606

or

(b) by reference to market value
at 31st March 1982   483,000
multiplied by

$$\frac{RD - RI}{RI} \text{ (above)} = \qquad\qquad 0{\cdot}218$$

                                            105,294

(b) is higher   105,294

                    Chargeable gain (subject to relief) 286,456

(iv) *Less:* relief for gift (Section 79 F.A. 1980
as amended):
held-over gain   286,456
no consideration for gift, therefore no
deduction for excess consideration over
total allowable expenditure   nil
                                            ———   286,456

                              Chargeable gain   nil

A's son's consideration is reduced to £175,794 (i.e. £462,250 market value less £286,456 held-over gain). On the subsequent disposal of the land by A's son the I.T. payable on the gift to him will be deducted from the chargeable gain on this disposal, but not so as to produce a loss (Section 79 (5) F.A. 1980 and Section 101 (2) F.A. 1986).

Notes

(1) It has been assumed that the necessary conditions for agricultural relief and business relief can be satisfied, and that the limitations on both reliefs will not be exceeded by this transfer. It has also been assumed that A did not have any unused exemptions or reliefs that would otherwise be used to reduce the value transferred.

(2) When valuing for I.T. farm cottages occupied by persons employed solely for agricultural purposes, no account is to be taken of any value attributable to the fact that the cottages might be suitable for persons not so employed. Thus, any value as a second home to a city-dweller is to be disregarded. This restriction does not apply to market value for C.G.T. purposes

and, accordingly, the values of the farmhouse and cottages have been increased to reflect this additional value.

(3) The incidental costs of making a gift are to be left out of account in the I.T. computation if borne by the donor; if borne by the donee they are to be deducted from the value transferred (Section 164 I.T. Act 1984).

© P. H. Clarke, 1988

Chapter 9

COMPULSORY PURCHASE

The following abbreviations are used in this chapter:

L.C.A. 1845	Lands Clauses (Consolidation) Acts 1845
L.C.A. 1961	Land Compensation Act 1961
C.P.A. 1965	Compulsory Purchase Act 1965
T. & C.P. 1971	Town & Country Planning Act 1971
L.C.A. 1973	Land Compensation Act 1973
C.G.T.A. 1979	Capital Gains Tax Act 1979
A.L.A. 1981	Acquisition of Land Act 1981
H.A. 1985	Housing Act 1985

The Lands Clauses (Consolidation) Acts 1845 were a code designed to regulate the procedure, compensation and any other disputed matters likely to arise between owners and acquiring authorities. The provisions of the Acts have since been incorporated in enabling powers of compulsory purchase although certain sections may be specifically excluded by the terms of some enabling Acts. The Acts and their interpretation by the Courts form the basis of the existing law of compensation on compulsory purchase.

The A.L.A. 1981, previously the Acquisition of Land (Authorisation Procedure) Act 1946, lays down a detailed procedure for making and confirmation of a compulsory purchase order applicable to acquisitions by local authorities and the Minister of Transport and incorporates the 1845 Acts, dealing with the acquisition itself except for certain sections thought to be outdated. Thus Section 92 relating to acquisition of part only is modified to include a "material detriment" provision. The Compulsory Purchase Act 1965 re-enacts the 1845 Acts thus amended.

The statutory basis of compensation under the 1845 Acts was the value to the owner, but the Acquisition of Land (Assessment of Compensation) Act 1919 provided modifications to that basis. The "six rules" of that Act were re-enacted in Section 5 Land Compensation Act 1961 and the Act made applicable to all cases of compulsory acquisition. The L.C.A. 1973 dealt with many deficiencies in the compensation provisions. Thus nearly all acquisitions will now involve the rules of the 1965 Act, the procedure of the 1981 Act and the compensation provisions of the 1961 and 1973 Acts.

211

When Notice to Treat has been received, the "Special Act" must always be considered. There may be special provisions as to taking part only or the right to acquire easements or special compensation provisions, such as the right to acquire at site value only.

The valuation effect of the service of notice to treat

When a notice to treat has been served, the owner may be forced to sell and the acquiring authority to purchase the land in question after the statutory time limit of 6 weeks for withdrawal of a Notice to Treat on receipt of a claim or, in the absence of a valid claim, 6 weeks after the decision of the Lands Tribunal (S.31. L.C.A. 1961). In the absence of agreement, the Lands Tribunal can determine the price to be paid. In the case of absent owners the Acquiring Authority pays money (on a certificate of valuation issued by the Lands Tribunal) into Court and gets title to the property. Thus if an owner accepts the compulsory purchase order there are advantages in the service of a notice to treat. However, this will not fix the date for valuation and the owner should continue to insure, maintain and protect the property from vandalism (see *Lewars* v. *G.L.C.*—L.T. Ref/104/1980). Disturbance claims can, in some circumstances, now relate to losses before notice to treat—see *Prasad & Anr.* v. *Wolverhampton B.C.* (1983) 265 E.G. 1073, C.A. Compensation can only be claimed in respect of such interests in the land as existed at the date of the notice to treat and the acquiring authority's total burden cannot be increased by the creation of fresh interests after that date if done with the object of increasing the compensation. *Mercer* v. *Liverpool Railway* [1904] A.C. 461. Thus the grant of a lease to a limited company to give them a compensatable interest and a claim for disturbance may well have to be disregarded. There have been many cases dealing with such occupational difficulties see e.g. *Smith, Stone and Knight Ltd* v. *Birmingham Corporation* [1939] 4 All E.R. 116 where it was held that a subsidiary company without a lease operated as the servant of a parent company owning the premises. In a 1976 Court of Appeal decision, *D.H.N. Food Transport (in liquidation)* v. *Tower Hamlets London Borough Council* (1976) 32 P. & C.R. 240, C.A., three companies, having no real separate identity, were treated as one and were able to claim compensation accordingly. However, the House of Lords in *Woolfson* v. *Strathclyde Regional Council* (1978) 248 E.G. 777 concluded that the strict view should prevail and the "corporate veil" was not to be pierced.

The importance of the issue has to some extent been removed by Sections 37 and 47 L.C.A. 1973.

The rule against increasing the burden to an acquiring authority also applies to events before notice to treat as the A.L.A. 1981 directs the Tribunal to disregard the effect of any work done or interest created if it is satisfied that it was not reasonably necessary and was only done with the object of increasing compensation.

The date of valuation on compulsory acquisition

As a result of the case of *Birmingham Corporation* v. *West Midlands Baptist (Trust) Association (Inc.)* (1968) 19 P. & C.R. 9, C.A. the date of valuation is:

for *Rule 2 cases.* The earlier of the date on which the valuation is made (i.e. the date of the negotiations) or the date on which the acquiring authority took possession. *Courage Ltd.* v. *Kingswood District Council* (1978) 247 E.G. 307 was concerned whether a council had actually taken possession after service of a notice of entry under Section 11 (1) C.P.A. 1965.

For *Rule 5 cases.* The earliest of the date on which the valuation is made, the date on which the work on the new premises could reasonably have been expected to start, and the date of possession.

The Bwllfa principle is important in considering what weight, if any, may be attached to evidence or events after the date of valuation. (*Bwllfa and Merthyr Dare Steam Collieries Ltd* v. *Pontypridd Waterworks Co* [1903] AC 426. As Lord Macnaghten said in that case, "Why should the arbitrator listen to conjecture on a matter which has become an accomplished fact? With the light before him, why should he shut his eyes and grope in the dark?" See also *Bolton Metropolitan Borough Council* v. *Waterworth & Another* [1982] J.P.L. 33, C.A.

Capital Gains Tax—SS 110, 111, 111A and 111B, C.G.T.A. 1979 S.83 Finance Act 1982

If land is disposed of under a compulsory purchase procedure, or in the face of a threat thereof, the total compensation can be apportioned for tax purposes between its constituent parts. Compensation for loss of profits or stock and re-imbursement of removal expenses are assessable under Case I or II of Schedule D. (Statement of Practice SP8/79.) Compensation for the land itself will be subject to capital gains tax and any amount apportioned as injurious affection or severance compensation is treated as a part disposal of the land retained for capital gains tax (*Stoke-on-Trent Council* v. *Wood Mitchell & Co. Ltd* [1980] 1 W.L.R. 254.

For disposals after 6th April 1982, a landowner who realises a capital gain on the disposal of land to an authority having compulsory purchase powers may be able to claim "roll-over" relief if he applies the proceeds of the disposal in the acquisition of "new land" which meets certain conditions. He must, however, not have advertised the land for sale or taken any other steps to make known to the authority, or others, that he was willing to sell the land.

Compensation where depreciation in value is occasioned by the scheme but where no land is taken

Compensation under Section 10 C.P.A. 1965

Prior to the L.C.A. 1973 the only legislation dealing with this was Section 10 C.P.A. 1965. (Section 68 L.C.A. 1845.) The effect of this section was clarified by the four rules in *Metropolitan Board of Works* v. *McCarthy* (1874) L.R. 7 H.L. 243. To obtain compensation depreciation in the value of land has to be caused by the lawful execution of the works which would have been actionable but for the statutory powers to proceed with the works. The McCarthy rules were considered in the House of Lords in the case of *Argyle Motors (Birkenhead)* v. *Birkenhead Corporation* [1974] 1 All E.R. 201, H.L., where it was confirmed that the claimants were not entitled under S. 10 for damages for loss of profit. Section 10 rights still apply but the scope for compensation in different circumstances has been greatly increased by Part I L.C.A. 1973. An example of a recent case under Section 10 C.P.A. 1965 is *Wilson's Brewery Ltd* v. *West Yorkshire Metropolitan County Council* (1978) 244 E.G. 811. This was a claim for injurious affection for the loss of support for a gable end wall by the demolition of an adjoining property.

Flanagan v. *Stoke-on-Trent City Council* (L.T. Ref/68/1980) concerned a corner general store. Its situation was drastically altered by road construction works whereby the owner was deprived of the easy access previously enjoyed, although vehicular and pedestrian access were still available. It was held that compensation could be claimed under S.10. (Contrast this decision with *Jolliffe* v. *Exeter Corporation* [1967] W.L.R. 993.) The Tribunal also held, in *Flanagan*, that S.10 compensation could include damage arising through negligence.

Study 1

(Note: to save repetition no mention is made of surveyors' fees and legal costs and interest on the agreed consideration where appropriate, in this and all subsequent Studies in this chapter.)

The land A B C D has been compulsorily acquired and a primary school is being built close to Blackacre. A restrictive covenant in favour of Blackacre limits the use of the site to agricultural use. A vehicular right of way to Greenacre crosses its nothern part and will be extinguished as the land is essential for inclusion in the primary school site.

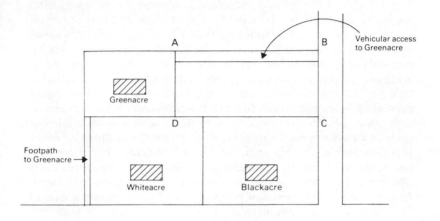

Claim for freeholder of Greenacre under Section 10 C.P.A. 1965

	£
Before value: value with both vehicular and footpath access	60,000
Less: After value: footpath access adjoining Whiteacre only	50,000
Claim for depreciation	£10,000

Claim for freeholder of Blackacre under Section 10 C.P.A. 1965

	£
Before value: open market value with the benefit of the restrictive covenant	80,000
Less: After value: value with a primary school adjoining	75,000
Claim for depreciation	£5,000

The owner of Whiteacre has no claim under Section 10 C.P.A. 1965. N.B. the possibility of a claim under Part 1 L.C.A. 1973 should be considered in each case as explained below.

Compensation under Part I L.C.A. 1973

Part I L.C.A. 1973 greatly increased the scope for compensation for injurious affection where no land was taken by providing that, in addition to any rights under Section 10 C.P.A. 1965, compensation is payable for depreciation by the use of certain public works, particularly highways, caused by the physical factors specified in Section 1 (2)—noise, vibration, smell, fumes, smoke and artificial lighting and the discharge on to the land of any solid or liquid substance. Section 2 sets out interests which qualify for compensation, an owner or owner occupier in the case of a residential property, an owner occupier of a farm, or an owner occupier of other premises with a rateable value of £2,250 or below. For these purposes, an owner can be a leaseholder with not less than three years unexpired. In *Essex County Council* v. *Essex Incorporated Church Union* (1963) it was held that properties exempt from rating cannot be said to have an annual value greater or less than the sum prescribed and thus do not qualify for compensation under Part I.

This case is also important in connection with the right to serve Blight notices. Section 3 as amended by s. 112 of the Local Government, Planning & Land Act 1980 deals with the submission of claims. Section 4 (1) specifies that compensation will be based on prices current on the first day of the claim period, which is 12 months after the works began to be used. Account is to be taken of the use of the works at that date and of any intensification that could then have reasonably been expected—see *Hickmott* v. *Dorset County Council* (1977) 243 E.G. 671, CA. The Court of Appeal upheld the Lands Tribunal's decision that there was no depreciation in value although it considered that the Member had gone too far in incorporating in his decision his own site experiments. See also *Streak and Streak* v. *Royal County of Berkshire* (1976) 32 P. & C.R. 435 where the physical factors arising from a new scheme added little to an already adverse locality. In *Barb* v. *Secretary of State for Transport* (1977) (L.T. REF/47/1977) and *Rigby* v. *Same*, two cases heard together, the Tribunal awarded depreciation of 7½% of the value of the properties with the motorway but without the physical factors in respect of houses 620 metres and 730 metres respectively from a motorway. Complementary to this reference, the Lands Tribunal in *Barb* v. *Hayes* (V.O.) (L.T. LVC/754/1976) and *Rigby* v. *Same* allowed similar depreciation to the gross values for rating purposes. *Shepherd* v. *Lancashire County Council* (1976)

33 P. & C.R. 296 concerned a council tip: the Tribunal found that the property had been depreciated by the works but this was due to the proximity of the tip and not the use and the claim therefore failed. The Tribunal accepted however that depreciation need not be permanent to be compensatable.

Study 2

"Fairview" is a house on the edge of a town which had open country at the rear. Some 2 ha of this land immediately behind the house has been purchased by the local council from a farmer for a refuse disposal plant which is in use. There are two cranes and an incinerator in use for some six hours a day and a large metal press. About 50 vehicles a day use the road alongside "Fairview" to obtain access to the rear. The value of the house has been depreciated by the loss of privacy and view and also by the operations in the area.

Compensation is limited to the "physical factors" in Section 1 (2) and will not cover loss of view or privacy. A before and after approach can be adopted as below:

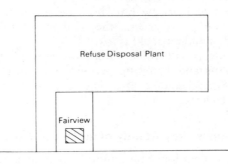

Before value

	£
Open market value assuming that the works are in existence but without the "physical factors" (to confine compensation due to use)	80,000

Less: After value

Open market value allowing for the "physical factors"	70,000
Claim for depreciation on account of the use of the works	£10,000

This approach seems to be called for by the wording of Section 1 and was adopted in the Barb & Rigby cases referred to above and also in *Arkell* v. *Department of Transport* (1983) 267 E.G. 855, although Lord Denning in the Court of Appeal in Hickmott (above) said: "If the traffic after the alteration is such as to cause a depreciation in the value of the house from what it would otherwise have been without the alteration, this is ground for compensation". In *Maile & Brock (executors)* v. *West Sussex County Council* (1984) 270 E.G. 653, neither valuers used the Arkell approach and the Tribunal decided that a more realistic view was to value the property in a 'no scheme world' (as used in *Davies* v. *Bexley LBC* (L.T. Ref/227/1982) and award a percentage of that value as the depreciation due to physical factors. The tribunal felt that it was possible for a skilled valuer to undertake such an exercise.

Had the land been taken for a modern sewerage disposal works capable of operating without noise or smell, but nevertheless the market value of the house was reduced by £5,000 because of public prejudice against its close proximity, a claim under Part 1 L.C.A. 1973 would fail as the depreciation would not be caused by the physical factors specified in Section 1 (2).

If any part of Fairview had been taken, even a small part of the garden to improve access, then compensation would not have been limited as under Part I L.C.A. 1973.

Section 5 deals with the assumptions as to planning permission on the relevant land. Planning permission is not to be assumed for other than 8th Schedule rights. Thus depreciation to development value is not covered.

Compensation where part only of the land is taken

The first consideration where notice to treat is served in respect of part of a property is whether Section 8 (1) C.P.A. 1965 or Section 53 L.C.A. 1973 apply and whether they should be invoked by serving a counter notice to take the whole property. Section 8 (1) applies if (a) the notice to treat is in respect of part of a house, building or manufactory or of part of a park or garden belonging to a house and (b) the part cannot be taken without material detriment to the house, building or manufactory or, in the case of a park or garden, without materially affecting the amenity or convenience of the house. *Rafenseft Properties* v. *London Borough of Hillingdon* (1968) 20 P. & C.R. 483 clarifies the tests for material detriment. This concerned the taking the rear access, garage and garden of Old Bank House, High Street, Uxbridge, said to be the cradle of Barclay's Bank. The Tribunal concluded that the taking of the rear portion clearly transformed the property into something quite different from what it was before, the change being wholly for the bad.

In considering material detriment, Section 58 L.C.A. 1973 applies; regard shall be had not only to severance but to the use of the whole of the works. Section 8 (2) applies to land not in a town or built upon and deals with circumstances under which an owner can require the authority to acquire severed land of less than half an acre. Section 8 (3) contains provisions whereby the acquiring authority may require the owner to sell severed land if the owner requires certain accommodation works. Section 53 L.C.A. 1973 applies where notice to treat is served in respect of part of a farm where the remainder can neither be farmed efficiently by itself nor with other "relevant land".

If it has been agreed that part only will be acquired the first step is to consider whether or not accommodation works will be carried out by the acquiring authority. Although the authority does not have to carry out accommodation works, it invariably does so because:

(i) it will reduce the amount of compensation payable as the works will be reflected in the after value of the retained land and
(ii) the works can almost certainly be carried out by the same contractors who carry out the remainder of the work. The cost of such works is normally added to the remainder of the compensation payable for the purpose of calculating the fee to be paid to the claimant's surveyor.

Statutory basis of compensation where part only is taken

Section 7 C.P.A. 1965. If part only is taken, the owner is entitled, not only to the value of the land to be purchased, but also for damage sustained as a result of severance, or otherwise injuriously affecting other land previously held with it. *Cowper Essex* v. *Acton Local Board* [1889] 14 App. Cas. 153 clarifies the meaning of "held with". Section 44 L.C.A. 1973 provides that compensation for injurious affection is to be assessed in relation to depreciation arising from the whole of the works and not just that arising from the land previously held with the land retained. Compensation is restricted to injury likely to arise from the proper exercise of statutory powers. Thus injuries caused by unauthorised acts cannot give rise to compensation but to an action for damages, or possibly an injunction.

Section 7 L.C.A. 1961 applies the principle of set-off where the person entitled to the relevant interest is also entitled in the same capacity to an interest in other contiguous or adjacent land which increases in value due to the scheme as defined in the 1st Schedule of L.C.A. 1961. Thus, in *John* v. *Rhymney* (1964) 192 E.G. 309 the acquisition of land for a reservoir enhanced the value of retained housing land and set-off applied. Section 222 Highways Act 1959 provides special set-off provisions in the case of acquisitions for widening a highway not limited to contiguous or adjacent land.

Betterment of the retained land can exceed the value of the land taken, resulting in only nominal compensation. This applied in both *Grosvenor Motor Co. Ltd* v. *Chester Corporation* (1963) 14 P. & C.R. 478 and *Cotswold Trailer Parks* v. *Secretary of State for the Environment* (1972) 27 P. & C.R. 219. Section 8 L.C.A. 1961 applies where such contiguous or adjacent land is subsequently compulsorily acquired. Section 278 (4) Public Health Act 1936 provides for set-off where sewers are constructed or water mains laid.

Study 3

A is the freeholder of a large stone house standing in grounds of about 1½ ha situated on the eastern outskirts of an industrial town. Permission to develop the whole for housing purposes has been refused on several occasions over the past 10 years on the grounds that any further extension of the town in the direction proposed would be inappropriate. The planning position, however, has recently been changed as a by-pass on the eastern side of the town has been approved which will entail the acquisition of an area of your client's land 15 metres wide for the whole of its width of 80 metres. The proposed road will be elevated along this section and will be, at its nearest, some 85 metres from the house. In these changed circumstances planning permission would be forthcoming for residential development on the remainder of the land.

The following preliminary matters have to be considered: Section 8 C.P.A. 1965 and Section 58 L.C.A. 1973. A decision must first be reached as to whether to accept a notice to treat in respect of part only or whether to serve a counter-notice to take the whole. If served, a counter-notice would probably be upheld. However, on the assumption that the owner wishes to remain and is prepared to sell part only, the first step must be to agree the accommodation works which will be carried out by the acquiring authority. When agreed, a claim for compensation can then be prepared. This will comprise:

Value of land taken *plus* injurious affection to land retained (Section 7 C.P.A. 1965 and Section 44 L.C.A. 1973) *less* set-off for betterment of land retained (Section 7 L.C.A. 1961).

In addition a disturbance claim could be made if consistent with the basis of claim. (The same applies to injurious affection.)

A before less an after value gives a composite total for compensation but this must be broken down into its constituent parts to comply with Section 4 L.C.A. 1961 dealing with submission of claims with possible effect on costs. This before and after approach was criticised by the Lands Tribunal in the case of *Abbey Homesteads Group* v. *Secretary of State for Transport* (1982) 263 E.G. 983 in favour of valuing the land taken and severance and injurious affection to the retained land separately. This concerned compensation for a strip of land for a road through land having residential development potential and meant that the land taken had to be valued as a strip only (see also *Hoveringham Gravels Ltd* v. *Chiltern District Council* (1978) 35 P. & C.R. 295, C.A.)

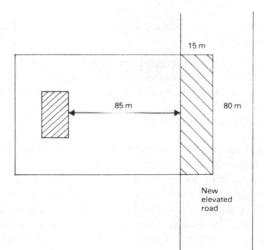

Assessment of compensation

Before value £ £

Value of house and 1½ ha garden land
   prior to the scheme for the ring road;
   no reasonable prospect of planning
   permission 70,000

After value

Either value of house with garden of
1,200 square metres less in extent having regard to the construction and use
of the motorway and also to any works
of mitigation carried out by the acquiring authority under Part II L.C.A. 1973
and to agreed accommodation works,
say,   60,000

or 1·38 ha housing land at say, £300,000
per ha, less cost of demolition, say,   410,000

It will be profitable to develop the retained land after the scheme;
the value, therefore, is £410,000.

The betterment due to the scheme exceeds the value of the land
taken and compensation will be nominal.

Notes

(1) Where land is taken, there can be no claim under Part I L.C.A.
1973, Section 8 (2).

(2) A certificate of appropriate alternative development under Section 17 L.C.A. 1961 could have been applied for but only in
respect of the land taken. A certificate specifying no alternative
use apart from the acquiring authority's scheme was assumed
for the purpose of the above.

Acquisition of part of a property subject to a lease— apportionment of the rent payable

If a part only of a property held on lease is taken, it will first be
necessary to apportion the lease rent as to a rent for the part taken
and the part retained. Only the latter will continue to be payable
under the lease. The Lands Tribunal have power to apportion in
the absence of agreement. Compensation to both freeholder and
leaseholder for land taken may then be arrived at on the basis of
"before" less "after" values.

Study 4

A shop has a net frontage and depth of 6 metres and 20 metres.
There is also a private forecourt of 3 metres deep and two floors
of living accommodation set back from the road above the shop.
It is held on lease having 5 years unexpired at a net rental of £1,400

per annum. The private forecourt and the front 3 metres of the shop are to be acquired for road widening but the upper part will not be affected. Accommodation works to re-instate the shop front have been agreed. Comparables would indicate a present net full rental value of £100 per square metre for a zone A of 6 metres deep on the basis of two 6 metre zones and a remainder and "halving back". (This relates to shops without forecourts.)

Estimated full rental value "before"

	£
Zone A 6 metres × 6 metres × £100	3,600
Zone B 6 metres × 6 metres × £50	1,800
Zone C 6 metres × 8 metres × £25	1,200
Forecourt, say,	300
Upper part	1,100
Full net rental value	£8,000

Estimated full rental value "after"
(effectively loss of Zone C and forecourt)

	£
Zone A 6 metres × 6 metres × £100	3,600
Zone B 6 metres × 6 metres × £50	1,800
Zone C 6 metres × 5 metres × £25	750
Upper part	1,100
Full net rental value	£7,250

Apportionment of rent of £1,400 per annum.

		£
Part retained $\dfrac{7,250}{8,000} \times 1,400$	say	1,270
Part taken $\dfrac{750}{8,000} \times 1,400$	say	130
		£1,400

Assessment of compensation

Freeholder's claim

Before value

	£	£	£
Net income	1,400		
Y.P. 5 years 7%	4·1		
		5,740	
Reversion to full net rental value	8,000		
Y.P. perp. deferred 5 years 8%	8·5		
		68,000	
			73,740
Less: After value	1,270		
Y.P. 5 years 7%	4·1		
		5,207	
Reversion to	7,250		
Y.P. perp. deferred 5 years 8%	8·5		
		61,625	
			66,832
			£6,908

Leaseholder's claim

Before

	£	£
Net full rental value	8,000	
Less rent payable	1,400	
Profit rent	6,600	
Y.P. 5 years 9 and 4% (tax at 40%)	2·5	
		16,500
Less: After value		
Net full rental value	7,250	
Less rent payable	1,270	
Profit rent	5,980	
Y.P. 5 years 9 and 4% (tax at 40%)	2·5	
		14,950
Claim for leaseholder		£1,550

Compensation for disturbance for, at the minimum, temporary disruption to trade during the carrying out of the accommodation works, will also be claimable.

Compensation for land taken

Section 5 L.C.A. 1961 contains the "six rules" which relate to the six sub sections. The following notes refer to detailed points on each of these sub-sections.

Rule 1 Home Loss payments (Sections 29 to 33 L.C.A. 1973) and Farm Loss payments (Section 34 to 36 L.C.A. 1973) may now be payable, however.

Rule 2 (as clarified by *I.R.C.* v. *Clay* [1914] 3 K.B. 466). Rule 2 excludes any special value to the owner which is not reflected in market value but the actual owner may be considered a bidder in the market. It allows for potentialities and "hope" value in so far as they would be reflected in market value and would include an unexpended balance of established development value if it could be obtained on a planning refusal. In *Ali* v. *Southwark L.B.C.* (1977) 246 E.G. 663 the fact that the tenants were close friends of the claimant landlord and there was an understanding that they would vacate if he wished to re-occupy was decided by the Tribunal to be of no relevance and compensation was awarded on an investment value approach.

Compensation would nevertheless be based on vacant possession value if the occupier was a licencee—*John David* v. *London Borough of Lewisham* (1977) 243 E.G. 608. Section 50 L.C.A. 1973 prescribes that no abatement in vacant possession value may be made on account of the rehousing of an owner-occupier. In the case of *Sullivan* v. *Broxtowe B.C.* (L.T. REF/205/1984) it was held that the claimant was entitled to take into account the possibility of obtaining a home improvement grant in assessing his claim for compensation.

In *Stokes* v. *Cambridge Corporation* (1961) 13 P. & C.R. 77, followed in *Challinor* v. *Stone Rural District Council* (1972) 27 P. & C.R. 244 and *Haron Development Co. Ltd* v. *West Sussex* (1974) C.C. 230 E.G. 515, an allowance of one third of the development value was made for the cost of acquiring land to gain access to developable backland without existing access, if it was the key.

The deduction of one third is not sacrosanct as in the circumstances of *B. & H. Oberman* v. *Arun District Council* (L.T. REF/3/1976), 50% was deducted as the cost of securing access in the open market. The Court of Appeal in *Abbey Homesteads (Developments) Ltd* v. *Northamptonshire County Council & Another* (1986) 278 E.G. 1249 decided that land subject to a Section

52 agreement under the T. & C.P. 1971 reserving it for school purposes was thus subject to a permanent restrictive covenant running with the land.

Rule 3. There are two limbs to Rule 3, one of which is not contentious and concerns disregarding any special value to the acquiring authority. The other was designed to cover the circumstances in *I.R.C.* v. *Clay* [1914] 3 K.B. 466 and exclude special purchaser value in other cases. However, "purpose" in Rule 3 refers to a physical purpose and does not extend to excluding marriage value between legal interests—*Lambe* v. *Secretary of State for War* [1955] 2 Q.B. 612. *Mountview Estates Ltd* v. *London Borough of Enfield* (1968) 20 P. & C.R. 729 illustrated the Tribunal's approach to the value of a leasehold interest in a deemed cleared site to the freeholder. *Honisett* v. *Rother District Council* (1979) 249 E.G. 847, C.A. concerned compensation for a leasehold interest in a development site where the freehold title was difficult to establish and the question was whether he would be in the market. See also *Trocette Property Co.* v. *Greater London Council* (1974) 28 P. & C.R. 408.

Recent cases appear to restrict severely the effect of the second limb of Rule 3. Thus, *Barstow* v. *Rothwell Urban District Council* (1971) 22 P. & C.R. 942 should be referred to and also *Rathgar Property Co. Ltd* v. *Haringey London Borough* (1978) 248 E.G. 693 and *Blandrent Investment Developments Ltd* v. *British Gas Corporation* (1979) 252 E.G. 267, H.L. In *Dicconson Holdings Ltd* v. *St. Helens Metropolitan Borough* (1979) 249 E.G. 1075, the Tribunal held that Rule 3 applied only to an actual identifiable living person who for his own special purposes, such as a pressing need to expand his factory or nursing home on adjoining land, has made an actual inflated bid, thereby forcing up the price.

J. D. Britton & Son v. *Hillingdon London Borough Council* (1977) 245 E.G. 317 involved the acquisition of a small area of land separating a development site from a road. The planning consent for development of the backland provided for access from another road but passed through a house in a conservation area. The access across the subject land would be shorter and the gain to the developer would be £10,000. The claimant's £7,500 was reduced by the Tribunal to £2,500. Rule 3 was not raised despite the appearance of two distinguished counsel. In *Chapman Lowry & Puttick* v. *Chichester District Council* (L.T. REF/177/1982), the facts were similar although the subject land was the only possible access and the alternative figures were £200 or £25,000. It was agreed by both parties that the reference land had a special suitability as access to the rear land but the Tribunal held that the acquiring authorities needs were not peculiar to itself and that the reference land was the key unlocking the development value in whoever's hands the rear land happened to be. Compensation was therefore awarded of £25,000.

Rule 4. In connection with *Section 5 (4)*, if building operations or a change of use have taken place without planning permission, the four year rule in Section 87 T. & C.P. 1971 should be considered and also the possibility of planning consent being assumed under Sections 14–17 L.C.A. 1961.

Rule 5. With regard to *Section 5 (5)*, the case of *Zoar Independent Church Trustees* v. *Rochester Corporation* [1975] Q.B. 246 seemed to extend the scope of Rule 5. It clarified the meaning of "devoted to a purpose" and "bona fide intention to re-instate". Rule 5 has been held to apply to a theatre in Kidderminster although the Tribunal thought the position might have been different had the theatre been in London. *Harrison & Hetherington Ltd.* v. *Cumbria County Council* (1985) concerned a livestock market at Botchergate, Carlisle. It was held by the House of Lords that a latent demand was not a general demand within the meaning of Rule 5 and only manifested itself in the rare event of market premises being offered for sale. Rule 5 was therefore applicable.

Wilkinson & Others v. *Middlesbrough Borough Council* (1982) 261 E.G. 673, C.A. concerned the acquisition of premises occupied by veterinary surgeons' multi-principal practice. The Court of Appeal held that Rule 5 did not apply as the claimants had not discharged the burden of proof of establishing that there was no general demand or market for property for carrying on veterinary surgeons practices. The date for valuation is the earliest of the date of possession, date of valuation or the date when redevelopment might reasonably have commenced—see *Birmingham Corporation* v. *West Midlands Baptist (Trust) Association (Inc.)* (1968) 19 P. & C.R. 9, C.A. A further point in this case is to be found in the judgment of Sachs L.J. that no deduction should be made for the age of the building. Compensation under Rule 5 could alternatively cover the cost of acquiring another building and converting it. If the Rule 2 basis exceeds the Rule 5 figure, the owner will, of course, claim the former.

Rule 6. Under *Section 5 (6)* disturbance claims must always be consistent with the basis of value under Rule 2—see *Horn* v. *Sunderland Corporation* [1942] 2 K.G. 26. Thus an owner will compare compensation on an existing use basis together with a disturbance claim, with compensation based on redevelopment value only and will choose that which is the more favourable to him. His different tax position in each case must be borne in mind and the requirements to obtain 'rollover' relief from capital gains tax in each circumstance.

Leasehold Reform Act 1967

If a valid notice to enfranchise is served before a notice to treat, the notice to enfranchise shall "cease to have effect" but the compulsory purchase compensation will have regard to it (Section 5 (6)(b)). If, however, the notice to treat precedes a notice to enfranchise, Section 5 (6)(a) states that the latter notice will be of no effect. For the effect on valuations of this, see *Boaks* v. *Greater London Council* (1978) R.V.R. 17. *Sharif* v. *Birmingham City Council* (1979) 249 E.G. 147 was the case of a purchase of a leasehold interest with the benefit of a valid notice to enfranchise; the award was on the basis of the freehold value less the enfranchisement price and surveyor's and legal fees. No end deduction for contingency costs and time and trouble was made.

Assumptions as to planning permission

The following assumptions may be made in ascertaining the value of the relevant interest and the owner will choose that which is most valuable to him.

Section 14 (2) L.C.A. 1961—any planning permission actually in force at the date of notice to treat.

Section 14 (3) permits the payment of "hope" value if the evidence is that the market would allow it. Any development value would probably be heavily discounted in most cases if merely based on hope.

Section 15 (1)—permission such as would permit development in accordance with the proposals of the acquiring authority (but consider the relevance, if any, of Section 5 Rule 3). There are no qualifying rules as to its likelihood in a no scheme world and permission is to be assumed—see *Myers* v. *Milton Keynes Development Corporation* [1974] 1 W.L.R. 696.

Section 15 (3) and (4)—permission is to be assumed for both Part 1 and Part 2, 8th Schedule T. & C.P.A. 1971 development unless compensation under Part 2 has become payable. Any development allowed by the G.D.O. ("permitted development") may be taken into account and this may well exceed Part II 8th Schedule rights. Thus the new limits for extension in the G.D.O. is 25% for industrial and warehouse properties, subject to an extension not in excess of 1,000 m^2 (S.I. 1985/1011).

Section 16 (2) permission is to be assumed for development for which planning permission might reasonably be expected to be granted for the zoned use in the Development Plan. The Court of Appeal in *Provincial Properties Ltd.* v. *Caterham and Warlingham U.D.C.* [1972] 1 Q.B. 453 decided that the test of reasonableness could entail a planning permission being completely disregarded for the zoned use if that permission would not, in fact, have been granted.

Sections 16 (4) and (5). In Comprehensive Development Areas or Action Areas the planned range of users in the area has to be considered and then there must be determined that which might have been appropriate had there been no such defined area and the Development Plan had not contained any proposals for the area.

It must further be assumed that no development or redevelopment had taken place in the area in accordance with the Plan and none of the land was proposed to be acquired for public purposes. The intention is to ascertain what consents would have been likely in the no-scheme world.

Schedule 7 of the T. & C.P.A. 1971 deals with the application of the planning assumptions under Section 16 L.C.A. 1961 in the context of structure plans and local plans under Part II of the 1971 Act.

Section 15 (5) states that regard should be had to any certificate of appropriate alternative development and any conditions specified therein.

Section 17; a certificate of appropriate alternative development may be applied for where the relevant land is not in a C.D.A., an action area, or in an area shown in the development plan as allocated primarily for a use which is of a residential, commercial or industrial character.

Section 17 (5) deals with conditions in such certificates.

In *Eardisland Investments* v. *Birmingham Corporation* (1970) 22 P. & C.R. 213 it was decided that a Tree Preservation Order acts independently of the development plan and need not be mentioned in a certificate.

Section 47 Community Land Act 1975 amends Section 17 and the revised section is now set out in the 9th Schedule of the 1975 Act. Acquiring authorities may now apply for a negative certificate, the applicants must give reasons for a positive certificate and "might have been expected to be granted" is substituted by "would have been granted" in Section 17 (4).

It should be noted that the costs of obtaining a positive certificate on appeal are not recoverable as the purpose was said to be to increase the value and not simply to ascertain it—see *Hull and Humber Investment Co. Ltd.* v. *Kingston-upon-Hull Corporation* [1965] 2 Q.B. 145. A certificate may sometimes be granted, perhaps for land in a green belt, for "institutional use in large grounds". For valuation problems in these and similar circumstances see *Lamb's Exors.* v. *Cheshire County Council* (1970) 217 E.G. 607.

The situation thus far is that for the purposes of assessment of market value, the planning assumptions referred to above may be taken into account and the owner will select that which is most favourable to him. In assessing market value, there are certain valuation rules to be considered.

Under Section 9 L.C.A. 1961 any depreciation in value of the land acquired by reason of designation or other indication of intention to acquire compulsorily is to be disregarded, e.g., comparables of sales within the "scheme" may well be ignored—see *Jelson* v. *Blaby District Council* (1977) 243 E.G. 47, C.A. where reduction in value stemmed from past "indication" of likely acquisition and also *Trocette Property Co.* v. *Greater London Council* (1974) 28 P. & C.R. 408.

The Pointe Gourde principle and Section 6 and First Schedule L.C.A. 1961 cause particular difficulties.

Pointe Gourde principle (Pointe Gourde Quarrying and Transport Co. v. *Sub-intendent of Crown Lands* [1947] A.C. 565.

"It is well settled that compensation on compulsory purchase of land cannot include an increase in value which is entirely due to the scheme underlying the acquisition". This also applies to diminution in value—see *Salop County Council* v. *Craddock* (1969) 213 E.G. 633, C.A. and *St. Pier* v. *Lambeth Borough Council* (1976) 237 E.G. 887. "Scheme" for the purposes of Pointe Gourde may differ from the scheme as defined in the 1st Schedule L.C.A. 1961— see *Bird* v. *Wakefield Metropolitan District Council* (1978) 248 E.G. 499.

Section 6 and 1st Schedule L.C.A. 1961.

Any increase or decrease in the value of the land taken is to be ignored in so far as it is due to development or prospective development under the scheme except in so far as it would have occurred in the absence of the scheme.

The 1st Schedule sets out four cases:
Case 1. Normal C.P.O. cases
Case 2. Comprehensive Development Areas and Action Areas.
Case 3. New Towns
Case 4. Town Development Act 1952 cases

The Local Government Planning & Land Act 1980 added a further case:

Case 4A. Urban Development Areas.

In each case the schedule sets out the development which is to be taken as part of the scheme, the effect on value of which is to be disregarded, except in so far as it would have taken place but for the scheme.

Section 6 and 1st Schedule have not superceded the "Pointe Gourde" principle. They act both independently and in conjunction with each other—see *Camrose (Viscount)* v. *Basingstoke Corporation* (1966) 64 LGR 337 C.A. In this case, the "relevant land" exclusion referred to in the 1st Schedule comprised a substantial part of the scheme and the claimants argued that betterment on this land could therefore be included. The Pointe Gourde principle was invoked to defeat this contention. In *Myers* v. *Milton Keynes Development Corporation* [1974] 1 W.L.R. 696, land was taken for a New Town providing for it to be developed for residential purposes in 10 years time. The effect on value of the New Town Scheme had to be disregarded when compensation was assessed but deferred planning permission for houses in accordance with Sections 15 and 16 L.C.A. 1961 had to be taken into account. Pointe Gourde does not require any assumed permission to be disregarded, only value due to the scheme which gives rise to it (but for the New Town scheme, permission would not have been forthcoming). It was also pointed out that Section 15 (1) contains no qualifying words as in Section 16 (2)(b) and consent for the acquiring authority's proposals must therefore be assumed.

In *Halliwell and Halliwell* v. *Skelmersdale Development Corporation* (1965) 16 P. & C.R. 305, both valuers substituted for what had actually happened what they thought would have taken place in the "no scheme world". It was said that this was wrong and that the valuation rule was "rebus sic stantibus". What has to be ignored is the effect on value, not the development itself. This rather tenuous difference illustrates the legal and valuation difficulties involved in discounting betterment.

Study 5 To illustrate planning assumptions

A freehold site (0·15 ha) of a factory built in 1890 but demolished after a fire eight years ago is to be acquired for housing purposes, for which purpose it is allocated in the Development Plan at a density of 200 persons per ha. It has been occupied for the past 5 years by a car breaker. The present rent is £1,000 p.a. (exclusive) on a yearly tenancy, the rent having been fixed two years ago. The present full net rental value is £1,350 p.a. Temporary planning permission for this use expires in three years time. The net annual value for rating is £708.

Claim for freeholder

The following matters have to be considered:

Section 5 (2) L.C.A. 1961—open market value.

Section 14 (3) L.C.A. 1961—it must not be assumed that planning consent would automatically be refused for uses other than industrial or residential which, in this case, are to be assumed under Section 15 (3) and (4) and Section 16 (1). When a consent cannot be assumed, a refusal is not to be presumed. If therefore further permission might be obtained for car breaking but for the compulsory acquisition, this may be taken into account. The figures show, in any case, that this would produce a lower capital value.

Section 15 (3) and (4) L.C.A. 1961. Assume Part I, 8th Schedule, T. & C.P.A. 1971 (subject to 18th Schedule)—the right to rebuild factory plus 10% as the building demolished was an "original" building.

Section 16 (1). Residential development at a density of 200 persons per ha.

Valuations based on the following planning assumptions are allowable, the claimant being able to use whichever gives the highest value:

(a) Car breaking income for 3 years with reversion to the higher of either industrial or residential value (no Landlord and Tenant Act 1954 compensation to car breaker as he would serve a tenant's notice to quit if he could not use the site)

or

(b) Car breaking income for, say, 1 year to allow time for possession after a landlord's notice to quit with similar reversions but less compensation to tenant under Landlord and Tenant Act 1954.

Valuations required:

(a) Site of 0·15 ha with planning consent to re-instate the original building plus 10% cube subject to 10% gross floor space addition not being exceeded. A residual valuation might well be required as comparables would allow for full permitted plot ratio and more economic design and layout for new factories. Say, value for Section 15 (3) and (4) purposes   £60,000

(b) Site of 0·15 ha with planning consent for housing purposes at a density of 200 persons per ha. Gross site area, say, 0·18 ha = 36 persons, say, 36 rooms at £1,500 per room (based on comparables)   £54,000

Industrial site value is higher and therefore housing development can be ignored for valuation purposes. The question is whether possession would be sought as soon as possible for industrial purposes or whether it would be more profitable to enjoy the car breaking income for the full remaining 3 years and then secure possession.

Value if possession sought for redevelopment by service of a notice to quit at the first opportunity

	£	£
	1,000	
Y.P. 1 year at 11%	0·9	
(allow one year to	———	900
secure possession)		
Reversion to industrial		
site value	60,000	
Less: compensation to		
tenant 3×N.A.V.	2,124	
	———	
	57,876	
P.V. 1 year at 8%	0·93	
(unsecured ground rent rate)	———	53,823
		———
		£54,723
		say £55,000

Value if car breaking income allowed to continue for full 3 years

		£	£
		1,000	
Y.P. 1 year at 11%		0·9	
		———	900
Reversion to full rental			
value for car breaking		1,350	
Y.P. 2 years at 13%	1·67		
P.V. 1 year at 13%	0·88	1·47	
		———	1,984
Reversion to site value		60,000	
P.V. £1 3 years at 8%		0·79	
		———	47,400
			———
			50,284
			say £50,300

The compensation to the freeholder is therefore £55,000. The yearly tenant is not entitled to receive a notice to treat. If notice of entry

234 *Valuation: Principles into Practice*

is served and possession taken, compensation will be assessed under Section 20 C.P.A. 1965 and Section 47 L.C.A. 1973. From the above figures, it appears that, in the absence of the scheme, the landlord could have been expected to secure possession as soon as possible for redevelopment. This may limit compensation for disturbance under Section 47 L.C.A. 1973 (see page 250).

Study 6 Purchase notice and planning assumptions in a C.D.A. (Action Area)

Your client owns the unencumbered freehold interest in the remains of a factory built in 1932, which was destroyed by fire last year. The factory had a net useable floor space of 1,400 m², the site area being 800 m².

The site, within a C.D.A., is shown on the C.D.A. map as the site for a future primary school. For this reason planning permission for the rebuilding of the factory was refused and the refusal upheld on appeal, although the proposal for the school cannot be implemented for many years. What action can your client now take and what are the financial consequences?

The following preliminary matters have to be considered:

Section 180 (1) Town and Country Planning Act 1971

The conditions for the service of a purchase notice after refusal of planning permission are satisfied as the land has become incapable of reasonably beneficial use in its existing state as clarified by Section 180 (2). This means that the value after the planning refusal can only be compared with 8th Schedule value not taking into account "new" development.

As the factory was built before 1st July 1948 valuable 8th Schedule rights exist to rebuild.

See paragraphs 4–6 of Circular 26/69 dealing with relevant factors in ascertaining whether there is a reasonably beneficial use.

Section 181 (2) Town and Country Planning Act 1971

Date of deemed notice to treat.

Basis for valuation
Section 5 (2) L.C.A. 1961. Open market value.
Date of valuation. *Birmingham Corporation* v. *West Midlands Baptist (Trust) Association (Inc.)* (1968) 19 P. & C.R. 9, C.A.
Planning Assumptions. Section 15 (3) L.C.A. 1961. 8th Schedule subject to 18th Schedule T. & C.P. 1971.

The right to rebuild plus 10% cubic content subject to gross floor space not being exceeded by more than 10%.

Section 16 (4) L.C.A. 1961. As the land is in a C.D.A. one has to consider the planned range of users and decide which would have been appropriate in the hypothetical circumstances envisaged by the section. Assume residential as the area was primarily residential in the pre-scheme world.

The Section 17 Certificate procedure is not applicable in C.D.A.'s

The effect on value of Section 6 and 1st Schedule L.C.A. 1961 must also be considered.

Summary

What is required is the higher of the value for either industrial or residential purposes disregarding any increase or decrease in value due to development or potential development in accordance with the C.D.A. except in so far as development would have taken place in the "no scheme" world.

Valuation

Factory site value
Value of a factory site of 800 square metres with planning permission to re-erect the previous building + 10% (if considered economic). The value may be enhanced by the existence of useable remains or depreciated by the necessity to remove them. This would be reflected in reduced or increased costs in a residual valuation. Say £45,000 as industrial site value.

Comparable industrial land transactions must be treated with caution as the plot ratio and other planning requirements may be substantially different.

Residential site value
Net site area 800 square metres, including half the surrounding roads say, 900 square metres. 900 square metres at a density of 200 persons per ha.

Accommodation for 18 persons
occupancy ratio say 1:1
18 rooms

	£
18 rooms at £1,500 per room*	27,000
Less: demolition say	1,000
	£26,000

* Assuming this is the most convenient comparison unit in this instance.

Compensation therefore is £45,000 on industrial site value basis.

Study 7 Equivalent re-instatement basis

A non-conformist chapel with a small congregation of about 30 is some 200 years old, in poor structural condition, and is sited in a shopping street. The adjoining shops are old and the area is allocated for residential purposes but with shopping frontage to the shopping street in the approved local plan.

The chapel occupies a site of 12 metres frontage and 20 metres depth and is to be compulsorily acquired as part of a residential redevelopment scheme. The chapel site is to be used for shopping, each shop to have one floor for storage above. Notice to treat was served three years ago. Some two and a half years ago a less valuable privately owned site in a residential area was suggested for re-instatement but the trustees have only recently decided to go ahead with its purchase at a cost of £30,000. The Planning Authority has made a condition in the grant of planning permission for the new chapel that a car park be provided.

Either Section 5 (2) L.C.A. 1961. Open market value of building (or site value less demolition costs) having regard to planning consents.

Planning assumptions Section 14 (3). Consent to use the building for storage purposes probably available in the absence of compulsory purchase.

Section 15 (1) and Section 16 (2) shopping site value less cost of demolition.

Or Section 5 (5) L.C.A. 1961. Cost of equivalent re-instatement. Date of valuation—date when valuation being made or date when redevelopment could reasonably have commenced. This could be a matter of dispute due to trustee's delay in arriving at a decision. The question arises as to whether the cost of the car park may be included in the equivalent reinstatment basis. If the Chapel Trustees wished to provide a car park and there had been no such facilities with the original chapel and the planning authority were not insisting on the provision, the cost of providing it could not be included as equivalent reinstatement.

Valuation
(a) Site value for shopping
    Residual valuation may be required. For a good example of a residual valuation, see *St. Pier* v. *Lambeth Borough Council* (1977) 4 C.L. 37 where a higher plot ratio in the "no scheme world" was the basis taken by the Lands Tribunal.

	£
Say, however, site value	71,000
Less: cost of demolition	1,000
	£70,000

(b) Storage income from building
200 square metres at

	£
£15 per square metre	3,000
Y.P. perp., say,	9
	£27,000

(c) *Rule 5 Compensation*

	£
(a) *Purchase of alternative site* Purchase price, legal costs and other disbursements of conveyance, surveyors' fees and interest on these items	32,000
(b) *Cost of new equivalent building* Cost, architects' and quantity surveyors' fees and interest on these items	87,500
(c) *Site works,* costs fees and interest	2,125
(d) *Removals and other disturbance items*	1,750
(e) Cost of providing car park	5,000
	£128,375

The Rule 5 basis will therefore be adopted. Compensation will be say £128,500 subject to the following.

Note: In *Roman Catholic Diocese of Hexham and Newcastle, Trustees of* v. *Sunderland County Borough Council* (1964) 186 E.G. 369, the cost of essential repairs to the existing hall, and fees were deducted from the compensation payable—see, however, the comments by Sachs, L.J. on the reasons against making deductions for age in *Birmingham Corporation* v. *West Midlands Baptist (Trust) Association (Inc.)* (1968) 19 P. & C.R. 9, C.A.

Study 8 Acquisition of back land and houses to provide access

A compulsory purchase order is to be made for school purposes on the land shown hatched on the plan. This is allocated for educational use on the development plan and comprises:

Reference No. 1. Freehold back land at present unused with an access 2 metres wide to Woodlands Road.

Reference No. 2. A freehold house subject to a regulated tenancy and worth £11,000 as an investment in the open market.

Reference No. 3. A freehold owner-occupied house worth £40,000 in the open market with vacant possession.

All the houses have frontages to Woodlands Road of 7 metres, those marked X on the plan being owner-occupied. The remainder are let to regulated tenants.

Compensation for Reference No. 1
As the land is not allocated for residential, commercial or industrial use in the plan, it may be prudent to apply for a Certificate of Appropriate Alternative Development under Section 17 L.C.A. 1961.

Assume that the certificate specifies residential use by the erection of 40 three-roomed flats subject to an access of a minimum of 14 metres to Woodlands Road being provided.

	£
40 flats at £10,000 per flat plot value	400,000
Less cost of procuring an access in the open market. No-one here possess the "key" to the development as any two houses would probably suffice, particularly two adjoining owner-occupied houses. It is assumed that the freehold of Reference No. 2 could be purchased for £15,000 and Reference No. 3 for £50,000. It is further assumed that the tenant in the former would vacate for £5,000, a total of £71,000, including £1,000 for demolition and clearance costs. Say, however, £75,000 to allow a reasonable margin	75,000
Open market value of the back land	£325,000

N.B. if one owner possessed the "key" to the development, the approach in *Stokes* v. *Cambridge Corporation* (1961) 13 P. & C.R. 77 would be adopted.

Compensation for Reference No. 2
Assume that Section 5, Rule (3) does not now operate in these circumstances to exclude the special value of References Nos. 2 and 3 to provide access to the back land.

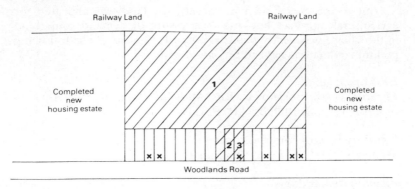

Freeholder

	£
Freehold special purchaser value Section 5 (2) L.C.A. 1961	15,000

Tenant

Possible Home Loss payment to the tenant together with a disturbance claim under Section 37 L.C.A. 1973 Compensation for Reference No. 3

Freeholder

	£
Freehold house with vacant possession to special purchaser (Section 50 L.C.A. 1973 precludes an abatement in compensation if the owner is rehoused by the acquiring authority)	50,000

Disturbance claim under Section 5 (6) L.C.A. 1961 inconsistent as development value included in purchase price. Possible Home Loss Payment under Sections 29 and 30 L.C.A. 1973

However, if Rule (3) does apply (see page 226), the compensation would be £11,000 and £40,000 together with respective compensation for disturbance.

Study 9 Acquisition for new town purposes

An owner-occupied farm of 150 ha is in an area recently designated as the site of a new town. It is on the edge of a village about 4 km from an existing motorway. The village has a railway station on the main line to London. When acquired, 135 ha of the farm will be used for housing, 12 ha for a school and 3 ha for road purposes.

Prior to the New Town proposals, the land was allocated for agricultural purposes but due to pressure of demand some land in the village was yearly being released for housing. The following preliminary matters have to be considered.

Date of valuation
Birmingham Corporation v. *West Midlands Baptist (Trust) Association (Inc.)* (1968) 19 P. & C.R. 9, C.A.

Statutory basis of compensation
Section 5 (2) L.C.A. 1961. Open market value.

Planning assumptions
Section 14 (3) L.C.A. 1961. If the market would pay more than agricultural value, then that may be taken into account: it would be a matter of evidence.

Section 15 (1) L.C.A. 1961. Acquiring authority's use (housing on 135 ha in this case).

Section 16 (2) L.C.A. 1961. Plan allocated use, as for the intended use in this case.

Section 15 (5) L.C.A. 1961. Section 17 Certificate of appropriate alternative development on the 15 ha not allocated for housing— likely to be residential also if not required for school or road purposes.

Effect of Section 6 and 1st Schedule, L.C.A. 1961
Case 3. Disregard any increase in value due to development or prospective development of the new town on the value of the land taken which would not have taken place but for the new town scheme.

Summary
It is necessary to value 150 ha with planning permission for housing in the "no scheme world" reflecting the rate of natural growth without any artificial influx due to the scheme, remembering that planning permission without demand does not create value. *Camrose (Viscount)* v. *Basingstoke Corporation* (1966) 64 L.G.R. 337, C.A.

The basic problem here is to assess what the demand for this land with planning permission would have been in the "no-scheme" world. Suppose that it is agreed that there would have been a demand for 5 ha per annum for 5 years but that thereafter any further demand would have been unlikely. If residential value, based on comparables, is £120,000 ha then the total sale price of the housing land over the next 5 years will be £3m.

This must be deferred for the average time for receipts—$2\frac{1}{2}$ years.

	£	£
Total proceeds from sale of housing land	£3m	
P.V. £1 $2\frac{1}{2}$ years at 12%, say	0·75	
	———	2,250,000

(12% reflects the risk of the estimated demand not being achieved.)

(An alternative approach giving the same result would be to capitalise the yearly income, £600,000 p.a. by the Y.P. 5 years at 12%)

Add: Agricultural income from the 25 ha also for an average period of $2\frac{1}{2}$ years.

25 ha at say £100 (net)	2,500	
Y.P. $2\frac{1}{2}$ years at 5% per ha. p.a.	2·29	
	———	5,724
Balance of 125 ha		
125 ha at £10,000 ha reflecting some "hope value"		1,250,000
		—————
		£3,505,724

say £3·5 million

N.B. If it is unlikely, in practice, that there would be a demand for any of the land, albeit with planning consent, in the "no scheme" world, then only a small amount in respect of hope value over agricultural value would be justified.

Land subject to agricultural tenancies

In valuing either the freehold interest subject to a tenancy or compensation to tenants of agricultural holdings dispossessed by an acquiring authority, the issue of whether possession could be obtained under Section 24 (2)(b) of the Agricultural Holdings Act 1948 on the grounds that planning permission has been given for a non-agricultural purpose is important. The acquiring authority's scheme is normally such a ground and in *Rugby Joint Water Board* v. *Foottit* [1972] 2 W.L.R. 757 and *Minister of Transport* v. *Pettit* (1968) 20 P. & C.R. 344 it was held that the interests had to be valued allowing for possession which increased the freeholder's compensation at the expense of the tenant. Section 48 L.C.A. 1973 now provides, in effect, that possession shall only be considered if it would have been obtainable apart from the authority's scheme. It is necessary to determine how long the occupancy might have continued but for the compulsory purchase. The Lands Tribunal's approach to the uncertainties involved in valuing, in effect, a life expectancy of profit, was illustrated in *Wakerley* v. *St. Edmundsbury Borough Council* (1977) 251 E.G. 921. The rights to succession on death under the Agricultural (Miscellaneous Provisions) Act 1976, must now be considered although S.2 of the Agricultural Holdings Act 1984 abolished succession rights in respect of agricultural tenancies granted on or after that Act and S.3 amended the 1976 Act provisions relating to statutory succession in cases not covered by S.2. S.1. contains new provisions for the determination of the rent of an agricultural holding.

Disturbance

There is no statutory provision which expressly gives a right to disturbance on dispossession of the owner. Under the L.C.A. 1845 compensation was based on "value to the owner". One element of this was the loss he would suffer as a result of being dispossessed. The 1919 Act (now Section 5 (2) L.C.A. 1961) altered the basis of valuation for the land taken to open market value, but Section 5 (6) specifically leaves unaffected the right which the owner would previously have had to a disturbance claim.

The general rule is that any loss suffered by a dispossessed owner which flows from acquisition is compensatable provided that (a) it is not too remote, and (b) it is the natural and reasonable consequence of dispossession—see *Harvey* v. *Crawley Development Corporation* (1957) 55 L.G.R. 104, C.A.

An owner cannot obtain more than his losses and the principle of *Horn* v. *Sunderland Corporation* [1941] 2 K.B. 26 must always be considered. A disturbance claim must be consistent with the basis of valuation of the land taken and thus an owner cannot claim redevelopment value for land taken plus disturbance to an existing business.

Prasad & Anr v. *Wolverhampton B.C.* (1983) 265 E.G. 1073 C.A., concerned a person who, when threatened with inevitable displacement from land because of compulsory acquisition acted reasonably in moving to other accommodation before notice to treat. It was held that he was displaced in consequence of the acquisition of the land and entitled to a disturbance payment.

There is also a duty to mitigate losses as far as possible; a claimant must take all reasonable steps to minimise his losses so that his claim is for no more than the direct, reasonable and natural consequence of expulsion. Disputes on this often relate to whether other premises should have been taken. Thus in the following cases the claimant did not take other premises and the acquiring authorities fought total extinguishment claims:

Jones v. *Edmonton* (1957) 8 P. & C.R. 86
Alternative accommodation offered by the local authority on a leasehold basis was rejected by the claimant. It was held that the claimant is entitled to consider who his new landlord may be and what sort of control the landlord would exercise.

Rowley v. *Southampton Corporation* (1959) 10 P. & C.R. 172
Alternative premises were rejected as the rent was too high for the claimant. The Tribunal held that it was for the dispossessed owner, not the acquiring authority to decide what he can afford to pay for new accommodation.

Bede Distributors Ltd v. *Newcastle-upon-Tyne Corporation* (1973) 26 P. & C.R. 298
It was held that although it would be unreasonable for a viable company with financial backing to go into voluntary liquidation and incur a far greater loss than would be sustained by moving into alternative premises, a claimant is justified in winding up his business where he lacks the financial liquidity to undertake removal.

Freeman, Hardy and Willis v. *Bradford Corporation* (1966) 203 E.G. 1099 also *Ind Coope (London)* v. *Enfield London Borough Council* (1977) 245 E.G. 942.
Other premises were available but the claimants made a business decision not to move. It was held that where the decision of the claimant to close down is made reasonably and in good faith, it is to be accepted.

Knott Mill Carpets v. *Stretford B.C.* (1973) 26 P. & C.R. 129, L.T.
The claimant was held justified in not moving where the increase in turnover in the new area would be unlikely to be sufficient to pay the greatly increased rent there.

Bailey v. *Derby Corporation* (1965) 1 All E.R. 443
The claimant, a builder, did not take alternative premises as he was too ill to move. The Court of Appeal supported the Tribunal and held that there was sufficient evidence to show that the ill-health was not due to the acquisition but was coincidental. It was therefore

'an extraneous and independent matter which must be put on one side'.

Hall v. *Horsham District Council* (1976) 241 E.G. 695
The claimant's failure to proceed with the relocation, coupled with his general conduct, was fatal to the claim for total extinguishment.

Section 46 L.C.A. 1973 deals with persons over the age of 60 who are displaced from trade or business premises and who may now elect for a total extinguishment basis.

The amount of a claim should be the actual loss suffered by the owner and would include, e.g. actual costs of removals and "Crawley costs" (see *Harvey* v. *Crawley Corporation* on page 246). Every forseeable loss or expense which is likely to result from dispossession should be claimed, provided that it is the direct, natural and reasonable consequence of being dispossessed. Once there is a binding contract to purchase, it is too late to claim further items, even though they would have been properly payable.

In *Palatine Graphic Arts Co* v. *Liverpool City Council* [1986] Q.B. 335, C.A., the claimant qualified for a 22% regional development grant in respect of certain disturbance items. The Court of Appeal held that the grant need not be deducted to arrive at the claimant's loss as it was not related to compulsory purchase.

Basis of compensation for disturbance

The acquisition may lead to the total extinguishment of a business, partial permanent loss of profits or only temporary disruption to trade, but what has to be considered is the loss to the owner. Thus where the business depended upon the personality of the owner and there was no saleable goodwill, the claimant was entitled to claim on the basis of the loss to himself.

Total extinguishment claims

The main items of claim will be for the value of the land taken and a claim for total loss of profits. In the case of industrial properties there may also be a claim for loss on forced sale of plant and machinery. It will be necessary for the owner to dispose of such items and his claim will be as follows:

> *Open market value* of the plant and machinery (assuming
> willing seller and buyer)
> *Less:*   *Forced sale value* (possibly only scrap value)
> *Equals:* *Loss on forced sale* (payable by the acquiring authority).

Tamplins Brewery v. *Brighton County Borough Council* (1971) 22 P. & C.R. 746 illustrated a different approach. This was a removal case and dealt with the proper method of ascertaining loss where new plant and machinery were installed in alternative premises even though the old plant and machinery had a useful life. It was held that compensation should be based upon the cost of the new plant and machinery less the scrap value of the old and less also the value of the new plant and machinery at the date when the old plant and machinery would have reached the end of its life. Saving in handling costs had also to be deducted.

Loss on forced sale of fixtures and fittings is normally arrived at by taking a percentage of their value in situ and loss on forced sale of stock, by taking a percentage of its cost.

No list of items claimable can possibly be comprehensive as any reasonable loss or expense is compensatable. Thus in *Widden* v. *Royal Borough of Kensington and Chelsea* (1970) 213 E.G. 1442 the following were properly claimable:

Redundancy payments and interest on a loan raised to pay them.
Cost of cancellation of specific contracts.
Holiday pay due on the termination of employment.
Wages to staff to clear up after close-down.
Advertising expenses in abortive search for new premises.
A percentage of "bad debts" as these would be more difficult to recover once the business was wound up.

Removal cases
As any reasonable loss suffered by the owners is compensatable, no comprehensive list of items under this heading can be made but the following may well be involved:

Removal costs including the cost of dismantling, adaptation and re-installing of plant and machinery or of fixtures and fittings and loss on forced sale of those items which cannot be taken. A claim may extend to extra temporary supervision after re-installation of machinery. Minor items would include notifications of new address, reprinting stationery and telephone removal.

In *Succamore* v. *Newham London Borough* (1977) 245 E.G. 404 removal 31 miles away was held to be reasonable and properly compensatable although other premises were available within a shorter distance.

Duplicated expenditure. These claims arise from the necessity to operate two premises for an overlap period. A claim would extend to double rent, rates and additional wages, heating, lighting and telephone. If the new premises are not rented, but purchased, then loss of interest on capital would be included. The claim should run until the date of completion of purchase or if earlier the date the acquiring authority take possession as they will pay interest on the purchase price from that date and the claimant should have no financial liability in respect of the property after the Acquiring Authority has taken possession.

Repairs and cost of adapting new premises. The purchase price or lease terms of new premises should have had regard to disrepair, and thus expenditure on repairs would not be recoverable. As far as adaptations are concerned, the expenditure would be recoverable in so far as it does not increase the value of the new premises—see *M. and B. Precision Engineers Ltd* v. *London Borough of Ealing* (1972) 225 E.G. 1186 and *Smith* v. *Birmingham City Council* (1974) 14 R.V.R. 511.

Cost of new premises and increased overheads. A higher price for alternative accommodation will not normally be compensatable as the owner will be presumed to have obtained value for money, but in *Metropolitan and District Railway Co.* v. *Burrow* (1884), The Times, 22 Nov. H.L. and *Mogridge (W.J.) (Bristol 1937)* v. *Bristol Corporation* (1956) 8 P. & C.R. 78 circumstances arose where increased overheads were allowed. The decisions in *Greenberg* v. *Grimsby Corporation* (1961) 12 P. & C.R. 212 concerning a new shop and *J. Bibby & Sons Ltd* v. *Merseyside County Council* (1979) 251 E.G. 757 dealing with new and larger replacement offices, applied the principle that greater efficiency of the new premises should be set off against increased financial liabilities.

In *Service Welding* v. *Tyne and Wear County Council* (1979) 250 E.G. 1291 C.A. bank interest and loan charges to build an alternative factory were held not compensatable as the claimants had obtained "value for money".

Additional distribution costs were capitalised at 7 Y.P. rather than a normal lower Y.P. applicable for the valuation of goodwill in *West Suffolk County Council* v. *Rought (W)* (1955) 5 P. & C.R. 215.

Reasonable fees incurred in obtaining new premises of a comparable kind were allowed in *Harvey* v. *Crawley Development Corporation* (1957) 55 L.G.R. 104, C.A. A claim may extend to reasonable abortive expenditure in seeking alternative accommodation, the costs of terminating a mortgage and taking out a new one, travelling expenses, and loss of earnings during time reasonably spent in searching. However, Denning, L.J. in the Harvey case said of an investor, "if he chooses to buy another house as an investment, he would not get the solicitors' costs on the purchase. These costs would be the result of his own choice of investment and not the result of the compulsory purchase". Interest on a bridging loan for a new property would be a proper item and also financial losses involved in having to terminate a low interest fixed rate mortgage and taking a new one at a higher rate. Moving might necessitate the purchase of new school uniforms, which would be payable. However, claims must be reasonable. Thus in *Mogridge (W.J.) (Bristol 1937)* v. *Bristol Corporation* (1956) 9 P. & C.R. 78 costs of drawings and preparation of quantities were disallowed as approximate estimates would have been sufficient to arrive at a decision.

Goodwill

On compulsory purchase any goodwill is not purchased by the acquiring authority but the owner is compensated for what he will lose by being displaced. Thus the issue is always to decide how much, if any, of the existing trade will be transferred. If none, then the minimum compensation will be the market value of the goodwill as, but for the acquisition, such a sum could have been obtained as part of the consideration on sale of the business. "Loss to the owner" might conceivably be a higher figure as for example in the case of a small one man business.

The value of goodwill is usually measured by calculating an average Adjusted Net Profit and applying a Y.P. The last 3 years average profits from the actual accounts are usually considered but any year which is affected by the scheme should be disregarded, e.g. if profits have been reduced by nearby clearance. A higher Y.P. than normal will be adopted if the profits show a rising trend as past profits are only a guide as to what future profits might have been. Conversely, falling profits justify a lower Y.P. than would be normal.

The following adjustments to the profit from the accounts must be considered.

Adjustment for rent

If a claimant is the freeholder the full rental value must be deducted. If he is a leaseholder, the profit rent must be deducted (arrived at by adding back the rent paid and deducting the full rental value). It was decided in *Widden & Co. Ltd* v. *Royal Borough of Kensington and Chelsea* (1970) 213 E.G. 1442 that an increase in rent to full rental value could not merely be passed on by way of increased charges and the profit rent had to be deducted.

Deduction for interest on capital employed in the business (other than land and buildings)

This will comprise plant and machinery, stock, fixtures and fittings, and vehicles etc. and also cash in hand and in a bank current account.

This was traditionally taken at 5% but see *Reed Employment Ltd* v. *London Transport Executive* (1978) 246 E.G. 233 where

10% was taken although the claimants stated that their financial arrangements were such that the money was borrowed interest free. See also *Handley* v. *London Borough of Greenwich* (1970) 21 P. & C.R. 645 where 10% was taken and *Bostock Chater & Sons* v. *Chelmsford Corporation* (1973) 26 P. & C.R. 321 where 8½% was adopted.

Proprietor's remuneration in the case of a one-man business
Following *Perezic* v. *Bristol Corporation* (1955) P. & C.R. 237 it is now clear that no deduction need be made for the value of an owner's own services in such cases.

Deductions might have to be made for the value of a wife's services in the business if nothing or insufficient appears in the accounts, but this was not done in *Zarraga* v. *Newcastle-upon-Tyne Corporation* (1968) 19 P. & C.R. 609.

As far as companies are concerned a proper amount should appear for the value of the work of each director—see *Shulman (J.) (Tailors)* v. *Greater London Council* (1966) 17 P. & C.R. 244. If, however, the company is virtually one man, his salary might be dealt with in the same way as proprietor's remuneration in the case of a one-man business—see *Lewis's Executors and the Palladium Cinema (Brighton)* v. *Brighton Corporation* (1956) 6 P. & C.R. 318.

Deduction from profits of a branch of a proportion of head office expenses
It is necessary to deduct from the branch profits the saving of head office expenses (if any) due to the closure—see *Reed Employment Ltd* v. *London Transport Executive* (1978) 246 E.G. 233.

Compensation for loss of goodwill

In the case of total extinguishment, the minimum that a claimant will lose will be the market value of the goodwill.

A Y.P. which should be based on market evidence is applied to the adjusted net profit as previously determined. However, the Lands Tribunal in *W. Clibbett* v. *Avon County Council* (1976)—237 E.G. 271—drew attention to the lack of market transactions adduced as evidence and claims are often made on the basis of previous Tribunal awards. The Y.P.s adopted vary up to four or so and appear to be gradually increasing.

It must be emphasised that compensation is for goodwill that will not be transferred. A milkman with a shop and also a milkround might well retain the latter on moving even if all goodwill attached to the shop is lost.

In *Neubert* v. *Greater London Council* [1969] R.V.R. 263, the conventional compulsory purchase "analytical" approach of valuing the land taken and goodwill separately was challenged and on the evidence the Tribunal preferred the "lock, stock and barrel" approach of the claimant's business transfer agent. This was that the market would pay 2¼ Y.P. of the adjusted net profit, the latter figure being arrived at without any deduction for director's services. This approach does not seem to have been advocated in later cases.

In *Widden and Co. Ltd* v. *Royal Borough of Kensington and Chelsea* (1970) 213 E.G. 1442, 3½ Y.P. was awarded in respect of a business of car repairs, spraying and sales.

Handley v. *London Borough of Greenwich* (1970) 21 P. & C.R. 645, concerned a substantial and well established car business. The Tribunal expressed the view that 1 to 1½ Y.P. was only appropriate to small businesses in clearance areas. Compensation was awarded on the basis of 3 Y.P. being the correct figure had the business been totally extinguished.

W. Clibbett v. *Avon County Council* (1975) 237 E.G. 271 (an engineering business) was a case where the Tribunal adopted a "robust" approach similar to that used by the courts in assessing general damages as there was a lack of any evidence other than the ipse dixit of each of the valuers. This approach was followed in *Tragett* v. *Surrey Heath Borough Council* (1975) 237 E.G. 423 concerning a sports shop. *Roy* v. *Westminster City Council* (1975) 31 P. & C.R. 458 concerned a national health service doctor's practice which legally was not a marketable asset. Compensation was nevertheless awarded on the basis of the loss to the owner. 3 Y.P. was awarded for loss of goodwill of a long established family cafe business in *Viazzani* v. *Afan Borough Council* (1976) (L.T. REF/150–1/1975). In *Ind Coope (London)* v. *Enfield London Borough Council* (1977) 245 E.G. 942 4½ Y.P. was awarded for brewer's loss of wholesale profits under a tie in respect of an off-licence subject to a tied tenancy. The Tribunal felt that tied trade had more security than a free one or than any other retail business and also decided that an off-licence should be treated no differently from any other shop.

Tax deduction on temporary loss of profits and certain expenses

Following *West Suffolk County Council* v. *Rought (W.)* (1955) 5 P. & C.R. 215, it became necessary to deduct tax on compensation for temporary loss of profits as it was held that such compensation would be tax free to the claimant. This was subsequently extended to certain expenses which were admissible deductions from profits for tax purposes. This position held until reversed by *Bostock, Chater & Sons* v. *Chelmsford Corporation* (1973) 26 P. & C.R. 321. It was explained that since the Finance Act 1965, capital gains tax was levied on the basis that the consideration for disposal included any compensation for temporary loss of profits. As such, compensation was therefore taxable in the hands of the claimant and it was inappropriate to make any tax deduction from the compensation otherwise payable.

Furthermore, under S.110/111 C.G.T.A. 1979, an Inspector of Taxes is empowered to apportion the compensation as between capital and revenue, the effect being to free the compensation for temporary loss of profits of its capital nature and enable it to be treated as a trading receipt. An Inland Revenue statement of practice (8/79) endorses this new treatment and deals similarly with loss on trading stock, removal expenses and interest. There is thus no case now for the deduction of tax in respect of temporary loss of profits or removal expenses. See also, *Hobbs (Quarries)* v. *Somerset County Council* (1975) 30 P. & C.R. 286 which concerned compensation resulting from a Discontinuance Order.

Short tenancies

The right of a lessee to a new lease of business premises under Part II, Landlord and Tenant Act 1954 is reflected in the Y.P. for loss of goodwill. However, yearly tenants or less are not entitled to a notice to treat and may be dealt with either by purchase of the superior interest and service of a notice to quit or by notice of entry and the taking of possession when compensation is assessed under Section 20 C.P.A. 1965. Until the L.C.A. 1973, Section 39 (1) Landlord and Tenant Act 1954 provided that rights under Part II of the Act to a new tenancy had to be disregarded in assessing compensation under Section 20. Section 47 L.C.A. 1973 repeals Section 39 (1) so that compensation will now reflect any right to continue in occupation.

Sections 37 and 38 L.C.A. 1973 as amended by Schedule 13 paragraph 39 H.A. 1974 apply to persons without compensatable interests. Disturbance payments must now be made to such persons assessed under Section 38, comprising expenses in removing and in the case of a business, disturbance having regard to the period the business might have continued. Section 37 (4) restricts compensation to either Section 38 compensation or Landlord and Tenant Act 1954 compensation, but not both.

Compensation paid to a tenant under Section 37 Landlord and Tenant Act 1954 is not liable to capital gains tax *Drummond*

(Inspector of Taxes) v. *(Austin) Brown,* [1986] Ch. 52 neither is compensation for disturbance under Section 34 (1) Agricultural Holdings Act 1948 *Davis (Inspector of Taxes)* v. *Powell* [1977] 1. W.L.R. 258.

Study 10 Factory in a Comprehensive Development Area or Action Area

A C.D.A. contains predominantly old warehouse and industrial buildings interspersed with two storey Victorian cottages. A C.P.O. has been made in respect of the whole area under Section 112 of the T. &. C.P.A. 1971, the planned range of users in the C.D.A. map being shops, public buildings, offices, warehouses and flats.

You are acting for both the freeholder and the lessee of an old factory of 500 square metres net sited within the C.D.A. and allocated for use as a pedestrian precinct. The factory is subject to a lease now having 9½ years unexpired at a rent of £5,500 p.a. on tenant's internal repairing terms. The current net full rental value is £7,500 p.a. Notices to treat were served on the owners of both interests two years ago and possession of the leasehold interest was taken six months ago after the tenant had moved to a new factory nearer the outskirts of the town. This factory has an area of 400 square metres net and the rent is £10,000 p.a. on full repairing and insuring terms.

The following matters have to be considered:

Section 5 (2) L.C.A. 1961. Open market value.

Section 15 (1). Development such as would permit the acquiring authority's proposals but development value approach precludes disturbance (*Horn* v. *Sunderland* [1941] 2 K.B. 26).

Section 15 (3). Existing use value and a proper disturbance claim.

Section 16 (4). Consider which of the planned range of users would have been appropriate in the circumstances of Section 16 (5). Probably factory or warehouse.

Section 6 (1). Disregard any increase or decrease in value in the circumstances of the second case in the first column of Schedule 1 as is attributable to development in column 2, subject to the qualifications of Section 6 (1)(a) and (b).

N.B. The Section 17 certificate procedure does not apply in C.D.As.

Conclusion. Valuations on the basis of the existing factory value including 8th Schedule rights together with a proper disturbance claim will be the most profitable approach. The value in the "no scheme world" will be taken ignoring any increase in value of the factory due to redevelopment in the area as it is considered that but for the "scheme" no private developer would have been active.

Freeholder's interface

Date of valuation = date when valuation being made.

	£	£	£
Rent reserved		5,500	
Less external and structural			
repairs, say,	500		
insurance (based on			
reinstatement costs)	250		
management (5% of rent			
passing)	275		
	——	1,025	
Net income		4,475	
Y.P. 8 years at 11%		5·15	23,046
Reversion to full			
rental value		7,500	
Y.P. perp. deferred 8 years			
at 13% (freehold full rental			
value rate)		2·89	
		——	21,675
			44,721
		say	£44,750

Leaseholder's interest

Date of valuation = date of possession, 6 months ago but assume values have not materially changed since then.

		£
F.R.V. net		7,500
Add External and ⎤ as in		
structural repairs, ⎬ freehold	500	
Insurance ⎦ valuation	250	
Management	375	
		1,125
		——
Full Rental Value		
(internal repairing lease)		8,625

	B/F	8,625
Less Rent payable		5,500
Profit rent		3,125
Y.P. 8½ years at 15% & 4%		
(Tax at 40%)		3·12
Compensation for land taken		£9,750

Disturbance claim

Basis of claim—the actual loss suffered by the leaseholder.
(It is assumed that the additional rent at the new premises is not compensatable in view of increased business efficiency). Removals of plant and machinery, fixtures and fittings and stock and loss on forced sale of anything not taken. Insurances against loss during the move. Duplicated expenditure, rent, rates, heating and lighting etc. from the date of renting the new accommodation until the date of possession by the acquiring authority. "Crawley" costs, legal and surveyor's fees in renting the new premises and director's time and expenses in the search.

Capitalised yearly increased distribution costs.

Permanent loss of profits if the level of production will be lower in the new premises as a result of the reduced floor area.

Temporary loss of profits as a result of disruption of the business.

Study 11 Leasehold disturbance claim involving adjustment of accounts

A shop with a residential upper part on two floors is to be acquired compulsorily for public open space purposes. The property has been occupied for 10 years by the lessee who lives in the upper part and carries on a small grocery business from the shop. The rent payable for the whole is £500 p.a. exclusive on an internal repairing lease having 10 years unexpired without review. The full rental value of the property is £3,000 p.a. net of which £2,200 is attributable to the shop. The rateable value of the whole is £1,150.

The accounts show that the outgoings for the upper part have been deducted as well as the rent of £500 for the whole premises. Other relevant details are as follows:

The net profit after deducting mortgage interest of £400, repairs, £160, and rates of £920 is £7,000. The figures for repairs and rates relate to the whole structure. No deduction appears for the owner's or his wife's services. She works about 10 hours a week in the shop and he is virtually full time. There are no suitable alternative shop premises available and the acquiring authority agree that this is a total extinguishment case.

Prepare a claim for compensation for the lessee.

Leasehold claim on existing use value plus disturbance basis Section 5 (2) and (6) L.C.A. 1961.

Land taken

	£
Full rental value of whole premises (net)	3,000
Add: Landlords outgoings (external repairs, insurance and management) say,	300
Full rental value, internal repairing lease terms	3,300
Less: Rent payable under lease on the same basis	500
Profit rent	2,800
Y.P. 10 years 12% & 4% (Tax at 40%)	3·86
	£10,808
Value of land taken, say	£10,800

Disturbance claim

The accounts include outgoings for the residential upper part. The profit for the shop is isolated by adding back all rates and internal repairs and deducting figures applicable to the shop only.

	£	£
Unadjusted net profit		7,000
Add back		
Mortgage interest	400	
Rent payable (the full rental value of the shop will be deducted	500	
Internal repairs	160	
Rates	920	
		1,980
Profit if no deductions for rent, rates or repairs		8,980
	£	£
Less		
Apportioned rates for $\dfrac{2,200}{3,000} \times £920$ shop	680	

		B/F 680	8,980
Full rental value of the shop on internal repairing terms	£ 2,420		
Add tenant's internal repairs on shop	80	2,500	3,180
			5,800
Less interest on tenant's capital 10% of £2,500			250
			£5,550
No deduction made for proprietor's remuneration but say £20 per week for wife (however, see *Zarraga v.Newcastle-upon-Tyne Corporation* (1968) 19 P. & C.R. 609)			1,040
			£4,510
Y.P. based on comparables (back street shop), say,			2
Compensation for total loss of goodwill			9,020
Loss on forced sale of tenant's fixtures and fittings, say, 80% of £500			400
Loss on forced sale of stock, say, 50% of £1,500			750
Abortive costs of seeking alternative premises, say			200

Home Loss Payment for residential upper part. It is necessary to apportion the total rateable value of £1,150:

The rateable value of the upper part is:

$$\frac{800}{3,000} \times £1,150 = £307 \times 3 \qquad\qquad 921$$

"Crawley" costs and removals for the upper part, say	100
Total disturbance claim	11,391
Value of land taken (above)	10,800
	£22,191
Total claim say	£22,200

Study 12 A total extinguishment claim in a Blight Notice case

You have been asked to advise a client, a grocer. He is now 70 years old and wishes to retire but his efforts to sell his business have been frustrated as the property is allocated as a future library site, a proposal which is to be implemented in about ten years time. His shop and upper part are in a poor trading position. He has a lease having 9 years unexpired at £1,000 per annum exclusive on a tenant's internal repairing lease. The rateable value is £1,600 and the present full net rental value is £2,350 per annum.

He has been trading as a grocer for the past 10 years and his net profits for the last 3 years were:

> £10,500
> £12,000
> £11,200 (most recent)

Both he and his wife work in the business but no figure for remuneration appears in the accounts for either of them. The wages of a part time help and delivery boy have been deducted in the accounts.

The following preliminary matters have to be considered:

Sections 192–208 T. & C.P. Act 1971. Provisions enabling an owner-occupier affected by planning proposals to require purchase of his interest (Part V L.C.A. 1973 extends the clases of "blighted" land.)

Section 17 L.C.A. 1961. A certificate of appropriate alternative development could be applied for, but a claim on existing use value and disturbance basis is likely to be the most favourable.

Section 46 L.C.A. 1973. As the person carrying on the trade or business has attained the age of 60, compensation for disturbance may, at the option of the owner, be assessed on the assumption that it is not reasonably practicable to carry on the trade or business elsewhere.

Section 29 (5) L.C.A. 1973. No home loss payment may be made where a blight notice is served.

Open market value of leasehold interest

	£	£
Full rental value of whole premises, net	2,350	
Add: Landlord's external repairs, insurance and management	350	
Full rental value (internal repairing lease basis)	2,700	
Less: Rent payable on the same basis	1,000	
Profit rent	1,700	

	B/F	1,700	
Y.P. 9 years at 10% & 4% (Tax at 40p.)		3·88	
Value of land taken			6,596

Disturbance claim for shop part

Average unadjusted net profit	11,233	
Assuming that the rent of £1,000 p.a. for the whole but rates and repairs for the shop alone have been allowed in the accounts, it is necessary to make an adjustment for rental value		
Add back: rent paid	1,000	
	12,233	
Deduct full rental value of shop only on tenant's internal repairing lease, say	2,000	
Profit after making a deduction for the full rental value of the shop	10,233	

Less: Interest on tenant's capital

10% of £3,000	£300		
Wife's wages: say £40 per week (but see *Zarraga* v. *Newcastle-upon-Tyne Corp.* (1968) 19 P. & C.R. 609)	2,080	2,380	
		7,853	
Y.P. for total extinguishment based on comparables for this type of business		3	23,559
Loss on forced sale of fixtures and fittings say 80% of £500			400
Loss on forced sale of stock, say 30% of £2,000(mainly tinned food which could be disposed of easily)			600
Claim for land taken and disturbance claim on a total extinguishment basis (but excluding items below)			£31,155

Disturbance claim for the residential upper part.
"Crawley" costs based on actual and reasonable costs incurred.
Removal costs (including telephone) and expenses incidental thereto similarly assessed.
Depreciation of fixtures and fittings due to removal.

Note If the claimant's wife had been an employee he would have had to make her redundant and a redundancy payment would have been a valid item of disturbance claim.

Acquisition of unfit houses ("pink" properties) under Park IX Housing Act 1985—clearance areas—sections 289 to 298

Added lands ("grey") and badly arranged buildings ("pink hatched yellow") are excluded from consideration as compensation is, in general terms, on the normal statutory basis.

The following legislation is relevant in addition to that which applies generally on compulsory acquisition:

Section 585 in Part XVII H.A. 1985 Value as a site cleared of buildings and available for redevelopment in accordance with the bye-laws and planning assumptions of the L.C.A. 1961. N.B. The necessity to obtain building regulation consent might well nullify the assumed 8th Schedule rights.

Section 6 and 1st Schedule L.C.A. 1961. In *Davy* v. *Leeds Corporation* (1965) 16 P. & C.R. 244, the question was whether the effects of the demolition of other property in the area had to be excluded from the valuation by virtue of Section 6 ("no scheme world"). Although not normally so, clearance is development for the purposes of Section 6 (Section 6 (3)(b)) and as there was no prospect of the land being cleared other than by the corporation, the claimant could only claim the value of his sites cleared for development but with the surroundings still encumbered with buildings. This important decision might well mean that marriage value with an adjoining property will be difficult to achieve in such slum clearance cases.

Section 586 and Schedule 23 H.A. 1985. Well maintained payments are available in respect of wholly or partially well maintained houses, but not if the ceiling value applies or if an owner-occupier's supplement is payable. The Housing (Payments for well maintained houses) Order, 1982 increased the multiplier for a full payment to 14 after 6th July 1982.

The ceiling value L.C.A. 1961, paragraph 1 (2) 2nd Schedule, is the value assuming that none of the provisions of the 1985 Act as to compulsory purchase at site value apply. If the land has a high site value a reversion to site value after a number of years should be considered to see if it increases the ceiling valuation as possession for redevelopment might be obtained by vacation, amendment of the Rent Acts, or other action under Part IX of the Housing Act 1985, such as Demolition or Closing Orders—see *Foster* v. *Birmingham Corporation* (1961) 12 P. & C.R. 291 and *Budgen* v. *Birmingham Corporation* (1964) 189 E.G. 263.

Section 587 and Schedule 24 H.A. 1985. An owner-occupier supplement, if payable, will bring compensation up to full compulsory purchase value, including disturbance. At the relevant date and throughout the qualifying period the house must have been wholly or partly occupied by the owner or a member of his family as a private dwelling—see *Laundon* v. *Hartlepool Borough Council* (1977) 244 E.G. 885 and *Panchal* v. *Preston Borough Council* (1978) (L.T. REF/53/1978) about the effect of periods of vacancy.

Schedule 24 Part I para 2 deals with circumstances where a house was purchased within two years of the relevant date but where the supplement may nevertheless be payable.

If only part of a house is owner-occupied the supplement nevertheless applies to the whole. The owner will obtain in total open market value with part possession—see *Khan* v. *Birmingham City Council* (1978) (L.T. REF/127/1977) and *Babij* v. *Metropolitan Borough of Rochdale* (1976) 33 P. & C.R. 119 (*Hunter* v. *Manchester City Council* [1975] Q.B. 877 distinguished).

Schedule 24 Part II applies the supplement to a business part of a house which is unfit. The full compulsory purchase value would include compensation for disturbance including loss of goodwill.

The case of *R. G. Leigh* v. *Wigan Metropolitan Borough Council* (1976) (L.T. REF/206/1976) is useful in setting out the provisions relating to these supplements.

Section 37 (2)(b) L.C.A. 1973 applies Disturbance Payments assessed under Section 38 to cases where compensation for the interest is subject to site value provisions and no owner-occupier's supplement is payable.

Study 13 Compulsory acquisition claims in respect of freehold and leasehold interests in a terrace of unfit houses in a northern industrial town

Two adjoining similar individually owned freehold two-storey cottages are let as follows, a third being owner-occupied.

No. 13—let unfurnished at a recently agreed regulated rent of £12·00 per week (exclusive).

No. 15—The freehold is subject to a ground lease having 5 years unexpired at £10 p.a. The house is let on similar terms to No. 13.

In each of these lettings the tenants are responsible for internal decorative repairs only.

No. 17—also similar, is owner-occupied by the freeholder, who has lived there for six years.

All the cottages have been represented as unfit for human

habitation and a "well-maintained" payment will only be payable in respect of No. 13. The land is zoned for industrial purposes. Each cottage site measures 5 metres (frontage) × 18 metres. The rateable value of each is £102 and the rate poundage, including water rate is £1 in the £1. The freehold vacant possession value of each is about £12,000.

The following matters have to be considered:

Section 585 H.A. 1985. Site value.
Section 5 (2) L.C.A. 1961. Open market value.
Section 15 (3) L.C.A. 1961. Planning permission to be assumed for 8th Schedule rights.
Section 16 (2) L.C.A. 1961. Reasonable planning permission having regard to zoned use.
Paragraph 1 (2) 2nd Schedule L.C.A. 1961. Ceiling value.
Section 587 and Schedule 24 H.A. 1985. Owner-occupier supplement in respect of No. 17.
Section 586 and Schedule 23 H.A. 1985. Well-maintained payment for No. 13.
Sections 29 and 30 L.C.A. 1973. Home Loss Payments to those residential occupiers, freeholders, lessees or tenants who qualify.
Section 37 L.C.A. 1973. Disturbance Payments for those without compensatable interests; in this case the tenants of Nos. 13 and 15 who will not be entitled to a notice to treat but will be rehoused by the acquiring authority.

Freeholder's claim for No. 13

	£
Site value	
Industrial value 90 square metres at £10 per square metre (site for small workshop) if planning permission would have been reasonable for a small site	900
or residential value for	
rebuilding the small house if building regulations consent would be obtained, say	600
Site value therefore £900	900
Plus: Well maintained allowance 14 × £102	1,428
	£2,328

Ceiling value i.e. valuation assuming that it was not   £
being acquired on a site value basis.
Gross income   624
Less: Repairs   80
          Insurance   25
          Management   62
                                                         ____

                                                                               167
                                                                              ____

                                                                               457
Y.P. perp. at 12·5% (from conventional analysis
of sales of poorer houses subject to regulated tenancies)   8
                                                                              ____

                                                                            £3,656
                                                                            ====

Alternatively, comparables might indicate that houses of this type
sell for 6 Y.P. of the gross income, say, £3,700 or alternatively
30% of the freehold vacant possession value, about £3,600.

Compensation to freeholder: as site value plus well-maintained
payment is the lesser, the ceiling value does not apply and compensation is £2,328.

Compensation to tenant: Home Loss Payment if he qualifies under
the five year occupation rule, Section 29 (2) L.C.A. 1973 and a
disturbance claim.

Freeholder's claim for No. 15

The head lessee cannot enfranchise as he is not in occupation. It
is also assumed that he would not be in the market to purchase
the freehold interest and marriage value is therefore excluded.

Site value
                                                             £   £
Rent receivable   10
Y.P. 5 years 8%   4   40
                                                           ____

Reversion to site value   900
P.V. £1 5 years 8½%
(unsecured freehold ground rent rate)   0·66
                                                           ____
                                                                       594
                                                                      ____

                                                                      £634
                                                                      ====

Ceiling value

Rent receivable	10	
Y.P. 5 years 8%	4	
		40
Reversion to net income from		
regulated tenancy—as No. 13	457	
Y.P. perp. deferred 5 years at 12½%	4·5	
		2,056
		£2,096

Compensation to freeholder £634.

Leasehold interest in No. 15

Site value

As the ground lease has only 5 years unexpired it is worthless except to the freeholder to marry the interests. Following the valuation approach in *Mountview Estates Ltd* v. *London Borough of Enfield* (1968) 20 P. & C.R. 729, and assuming the freeholder would be in the market to purchase, the value of the lease may be arrived at as follows:

Freehold unencumbered site value	900	
Less: Value of freehold subject to		
lease—as above	634	
Total gain to freeholder by		
"marriage"	266	
Less: Costs of marrying interests and profit, say	156	
	£110	

	£	£
Ceiling value		
Net Income	457	
Less: Ground rent	10	
Profit rent	447	
Y.P. 5 years at 15% & 4%		
(Tax at 40%)	2·18	
		974
Less: Outstanding dilapidations under full repairing		
and insuring lease, say		374
		£600

(This does not allow for the possible purchase by the tenant who might buy the head lease with a view to enfranchisement.)

Compensation to a leaseholder £110.
Occupying tenant's claim—as for No. 13.

Freeholder's claim for No. 17

As the freeholder purchased 6 years ago, he is entitled to an owner-occupier's supplement to bring compensation up to full compulsory purchase value, including a disturbance claim under Section 5 (6) L.C.A. 1961, and to a Home Loss payment.

	£	£
Site value		900
But add: Supplemental compensation—the difference between full compulsory purchase value and site value		
Full value as house	12,000	
Less: Site value	900	
	11,100	
Proper disturbance claim, say	400	
		11,500
		12,400
Add: Home loss payment Section 30 (1)(b) L.C.A. 1973:— 3 × R.V. = 3 × £102		306
Total compensation		£12,706

© R. E. Clark, 1988

Chapter 10

COMPENSATION FOR PLANNING RESTRICTIONS

(All references in this Chapter are to the Town and Country Planning Act 1971, unless otherwise stated.)

The General Development Order 1977 and amendments to it

Before considering whether or not to make a planning application, the practitioner should remember that not all activities require the approval of the local planning authority. Section 22 sets out the definition of development, but then goes on to list several things which are specifically stated not to constitute development at all. Furthermore, planning permission for much development is already granted by virtue of the General Development Orders (G.D.O.s) 1977 to 1985(b). Schedule 1 to the 1977 Order (as amended) contains 30 classes of permitted development.

The Order of 1977 has been amended six times, by the following General Development (Amendment) Orders:

   (i) S.I. 1980, No. 1946.
  (ii) S.I. 1981, No. 245.
 (iii) S.I. 1981, (No. 2 Order), No. 1569.
 (iv) S.I. 1983, No. 1615.
  (v) S.I. 1985, No. 1011.
 (vi) S.I. 1985 (No. 2 Order), No. 1981.

These Orders may be cited collectively as The Town and Country Planning General Development Orders 1977 to 1985(b).

Furthermore, the Town & Country Planning (National Parks, Areas of Outstanding Natural Beauty and Conservation Areas etc.) Special Development Order 1985, (S.I. 1985 No. 1012), as amended by the Special Development (Amendment) Order 1986 (S.I. 1986 No. 8), overrides some of the provisions of the General Development (Amendment) Orders in specified areas such as National Parks. As a generalisation, the Special Development Orders restrict the extent of some of the permitted development to what it had been before the G.D.O. of 1977 was amended, but this is done without removing any of the additional restrictions imposed on the original G.D.O. by the subsequent Amendment Orders.

265

The Special Development (Amendment) Order of 1985 (No. 1982) has been revoked.

The best advice that can be given is that the relevant Orders themselves should be referred to on each occasion that they have to be used as there are now too many variations for any rule of thumb to be relied upon with any safety.

The 1980 amendments (S.I. 1946) are largely to do with procedures.

The first amendments of 1981 (S.I. 245) include changes to some of the classes of permitted development contained within Schedule 1 of the G.D.O. itself—in particular Classes I, III and VIII. The current provisions, taking account of all the amendments to these three classes, are outlined at the end of this section of the Chapter.

Where land is situated in a National Park, Area of Outstanding Natural Beauty (AONB), conservation area or an area specified under Section 41(3) of the Wildlife and Countryside Act 1981, the provisions are different. Here the Town and Country Planning (National Parks, Areas of Outstanding Natural Beauty and Conservation Areas etc.) Special Development Order 1985 (S.I. No. 1012), as amended by the 1986 Amendment Order (S.I. No. 8) applies, and strikes out some, but not all, of the amendments made to Schedule 1 of the G.D.O. by the Amendment Order of 1981 (S.I. No. 245). The consequence is that in conservation areas etc., the increases in permitted development contained within S.I. 245 do not apply. Instead, the limits remain those of the 1977 G.D.O., except that the additional restrictions imposed by S.I. 245 do continue to apply in these areas, as elsewhere.

The second amendment order of 1981 (S.I. No. 1569) prescribes the information which must be kept in, and the manner of keeping, registers of enforcement and stop notices. The duty to maintain such registers is imposed on local planning authorities by the Local Government and Planning (Amendment) Act 1981.

The 1983 amendments (S.I. 1615) impose conditions upon permitted development so as to bar its subsequent use for purposes which would involve the presence of a notifiable quantity of a hazardous substance within the meaning of the Notification of Installations Handling Hazardous Substances Regulations 1982. There are exceptions affecting existing users (who may have to notify the Health and Safety Executive), and the inspection, repair or renewal of existing pipelines. There are special exemptions for gas undertakers but Class XVIII.D has been amended to require that notice be given to the local planning authority before a notifiable pipeline (as defined by s. 65 of the Pipelines Act 1962) is laid. Part IV and Schedule 7 of the Housing and Planning Act 1986 have made further changes regarding hazardous substances. New sections have been added to the 1971 Act (namely Sections 1A, 1B, 58B—58N, 101B.) and several of the existing sections have been amended or added to. Compensation provisions are included and these are dealt with later in this Chapter.

The first of the two amendment orders made in 1985 (S.I. 1011) deals with development by telecommunications operators and introduces two new classes of permitted development for their benefit (Classes XXIV and XXV), both of which are modified so far as land affected by the Town and Country Planning (National Parks, Areas of Outstanding Natural Beauty and Conservation Areas, etc.) Special Development Order 1985 S.I. No. 1012 (as amended by S.I. 1986 No. 8) is concerned. S.I. 1011 also replaces Class XVIII.I. with new text appropriate to the work of the Post Office following the separation of Post Office and Telecommunications activities, and makes minor amendments to the Acts of 1971 and 1984 to the same end.

The second amendment order introduced in 1985 (S.I. No. 1981) makes various changes, including amendments affecting Article 4 Directions and the introduction of five new classes of permitted development. The new Classes are:

Class XXVI	Mineral exploration activities.
Class XXVII	Removal of minerals in certain cases.
Class XXVIII	Extensions to existing warehouses. This is similar to the provisions of Class VIII, which permits certain extensions to industrial buildings.
	The maximum permitted increase is 25% of the gross volume or 1,000 square metres aggregate floor space, but 10% and 500 square metres if located in a conservation or other area affected by the Special Development Order 1985 (S.I. No. 1012) as amended by S.I. 1986 No. 8. There are other conditions—see the G.D.O. as amended.
Class XXIX	The provision of small buildings and machinery in amusement parks and on seaside piers.
Class XXX	Development by the Historic Buildings and Monuments Commission.

Other changes made by this amendment order affect the following Classes of permitted development:

Class I	Satellite antenna for dwellinghouses.
Class VI	Mineral extraction and waste tipping on agricultural land is restricted. Minerals may not be exported, nor waste imported.

Class VIII	Relaxation of limits on extensions for industrial purposes.
Class XVIII	Certain developments by the Civil Aviation Authority.
Class XVIII.E	Relaxation of limits on extensions to buildings on the operational land of electricity undertakings.
Class XXVI.2	Introduces speedier provisions for making an Article 4 Direction in connection with mineral exploration.
Class XXVII.2	As XXVI above, but for mineral extraction.

In conclusion, the current position as regards Classes I, III and VIII.(iv) is as follows:

Class I: Development within the curtilage of a dwellinghouse
I.1 The enlargement, improvement or other alteration of a dwelling house:

(a) All terraced houses (including end-of-terrace).
     All dwellings within conservation areas, national parks and areas of outstanding natural beauty etc., whether terraced or not:
>   Maximum increase: the greater of 50 cubic metres or 10%, subject to a maximum of 115 cubic metres.

(b) Other dwellings:
>   Maximum increase: the greater of 70 cubic metres or 15%, subject to a maximum of 115 cubic metres.

(c) Garages and coachhouses:
  i. These count as enlargements of the dwelling itself (Class I.1) if they are sited within 5 metres of any part of the latter, or within a conservation area, national park, AONB etc.
  ii. Otherwise they come within Class I.3 and do not count as enlargements of the dwelling but as ancillary buildings.

(d) Stables and loose-boxes:
>   These always count as enlargements of the dwelling.

I.2. The construction of a porch outside any external door.
I.2A The installation of a satellite antenna on, or within the curtilage of, a dwelling.
The maximum dimension of the antenna is 90 cm in any direction and it must not rise above the highest part of the roof. If the Special Development Orders (S.I.s 1012 and 8) apply, the antenna may not project in front of the forwardmost part of a wall which fronts a highway.

I.3. The erection or alteration of any building or enclosure within the curtilege of a dwelling house for a purpose incidental to the enjoyment of the latter, including the keeping of livestock. This consent excludes the provision of additional dwellings, stables, loose-boxes or satellite antenna.

I.4. The provision of hardstanding for vehicles.

I.5. The siting of an oil storage tank of up to 3,500 litres for domestic heating purposes.

Notes

(1) A commonly imposed condition is that the permitted develop-ment shall not extend beyond the forwardmost part of any wall of the original dwellinghouse which fronts a highway. An L-shaped building may present two walls to the same highway. It was held in *North West Leicestershire District Council* v. *Secretary of State for the Environment* [1982], J.P.L. 777, that development which stood in the recess behind the forwardmost of the two walls, but in front of the rearmost, did not breach this condition.

(2) A variety of additional conditions are imposed governing maxi-mum heights, siting, proximity to boundaries and site coverage. Generally, not more than 50% of a site may be built upon.

Class III: Changes of Use

Light and general industrial buildings may be used as wholesale warehouses or repositories (and *vice versa*) subject to a floorspace limitation of 235 square metres. This is not affected by the Special Development Orders (S.I.s 1012 and 8).

Class VIII: Development for industrial purposes

The permitted increase in the cubic content of extensions or alter-ations to buildings is raised from 10% to 25% and in the aggregate floorspace from 500 to 1,000 square metres, but the Special Deve-lopment Order of 1985 (S.I. 1012) retains the old limits for buildings within conservation areas etc. The rule that no part of the building shall, as a result of the development, be within 5 metres of the boundary, always applies.

Note that Class XXVIII gives a similar consent for warehouse buildings.

In conclusion it should be noted that at the time of writing, the Government has published draft, consultative, proposals for the amendment and, it is understood, simplification of the General Development Order. The draft does not affect conservation areas,

National Parks, areas of outstanding natural beauty, nor the Norfolk Broads, for which separate proposals will be published later.

The significance of Schedule 8 development: Existing Use Value and Permitted Development Value

There are many instances where the measure of compensation is the difference between the value of the claimant's interest as valued before and after the imposition of an adverse planning decision, adverse meaning a decision which diminishes the value of the interest.

In order to assess the amount of the loss, the statutes specify certain assumptions which are to be made as to the availability of planning consent, the value of these consents forming part of the value of the claimant's interest subject to the adverse decision. This is the "after", or depreciated, value. The "before" value is usually easier to determine, and is frequently the value of the interest had the planning decision been favourable. The approach might, for example, be to say "the depreciation in value is equal to the value of the interest with planning permission less its value subject to the refusal but assuming consent for. . . ."

Frequently, the "after" value includes an assumed planning consent for any of the development specified in Schedule 8, and sometimes this development is made subject to the conditons set out in Schedule 18. These Schedules are discussed below, see Studies 1–5.

There are, also, many occasions where the measure of compensation is the difference between permitted development value and existing use value, particularly when a purchase notice is served by the claimant but the Secretary of State gives a direction as to the availability of some other planning permission (if sought). Existing Use Value (E.U.V.) and Permitted Development Value (P.D.V.) are defined in Section 187 (5). Permitted Development Value is the value of the claimant's interest on the assumption that planning permission would be granted solely in accordance with the Secretary of State's direction, and that not other consents would be forthcoming. Existing Use Value is defined as the value of the interest with the benefit of permission for development listed in the 3rd Schedule of the Town and Country Planning Act 1947 but with the addition of paragraph 13 of Schedule 8 to the 1971 Act.

It is important not to confuse the concept of Permitted Development Value used for compensation calculations with the classes of permitted development contained within Schedule 1 of the General Development Order, and equally important to avoid confusion between these classes and the development described in Schedule 8.

Another source of confusion is that a distinction has to be made between cases where there has been an actual refusal of planning consent for Schedule 8 development and those where there has not.

Compensation following a refusal of planning permission, or its grant subject to conditions

Section 22 defines development and lists six categories of activity which, not being development, require no planning permission save in the case of listed buildings. The word "development" is used in this Chapter with the same meaning as in Section 22.

The General Development Order 1977 (as amended) grants planning consent for several categories of development. There is some overlapping between these and the development listed in Schedule 8. The latter does not, however, grant planning permission for anything—it merely specifies development for which consent is to be assumed for valuation purposes.

Any development will either fit within the descriptions of Schedule 8 or it will not. If it does not fit, it is called "New Development". Development which does fall within the Schedule will fit into either Part I or Part II. The first step is, therfore, to settle whether a refusal relates to New Development, or to Schedule 8 Part I, or to Schedule 8 Part II, since the valuation rules are different for each.

The development described within Schedule 8 Part I involves the rebuilding of any building, or the sub-division of a single dwellinghouse into two or more dwellings. This is something of an over-simplification, and the Schedule itself should be referred to. So far as rebuilding is concerned, the replacement must be a replacement and not a wholly new creature bearing little resemblance to what went before, although new construction methods and some internal re-arrangement—such as the omission of some internal walls—could perhaps be claimed as falling within Part I.

The rebuilding work may incorporate an enlargement of up to the greater of 1/10th of the gross volume or 1,750 cubic feet in the case of dwellings, or 1/10th of the gross volume in any other case, so far as Schedule 8 is concerned. In some instances, however, Schedule 18 will also apply, and this changes the size of the allowable increase. The effects of Schedule 18 are complex, and are dealt with later in the Chapter, see page 277. It should be noted, however, that Schedule 18 does not always apply: it has no application, for example, to the calculation of compensation for compulsory purchase under the Land Compensation Act 1961 (which, amongst other allowances, assumes planning consent for the whole of Schedule 8.) The limitations of Schedule 18 would not, therefore, apply to cases where the service of a purchase or blight notice was the appropriate remedy.

The descriptions of development contained within Schedule 8 Part II run to six paragraphs (paragraphs 3–8). The following is but an approximate resumé:

3. The enlargement, improvement or other alteration of a building, provided the gross volume is not increased by more than the greater of 1/10th or 1,750 cubic feet in the case of a dwellinghouse, or 1/10th in any other case. These allowances may be altered in cases to which Schedule 18 also applies.
4. Executing building or other operations on agricultural or forestry land in connection with that use, but excluding work to dwellings, or buildings used for market gardens, nurseries, timber yards or otherwise not connected with general farming or silviculture.
5. The winning and working of minerals, for agricultural purposes, on land held with farmland. This includes works to any associated buildings.
6. The use of a building falling within a general class specified in the Town and Country Planning (Use Classes for Third Schedule Purposes) Order 1948 (S.I. 1948 No. 955), for any other purpose within the same general class.
7. Where a building or land is used for more than one purpose, an increase in the extent of one use by up to not more than 1/10th of the gross volume or 1/10th of the land area used for that purpose. The increase is measured by reference to the volume (or area) already used for the purpose which is to be expanded, not by reference to the whole.
8. The continuing deposit of mineral waste or refuse in connection with existing mineral workings on a site already used for this purpose.

Development within Schedule 8 is generally to be included as part of the "existing use value" (E.U.V.). Section 278 determines when Schedule 18 is to be applied to Schedule 8 Part 1 paragraph 1 (rebuilding), or Part II paragraph 3 (enlargement, alteration or other improvement). Schedule 8 is modified for buildings erected after the 1st July 1948 (see Section 278 (2)), and the rules are different again when Section 187 (5) has to be applied (see Section 278 (3)). Section 187 (5) defines "existing use value" and "permitted development value" (P.D.V.). Section 187 becomes applicable where a purchase notice is served.

The relevance and application of Schedule 18 to Schedule 8 is complicated and is made more so because the former is of no relevance in certain types of compensation claim. Each case must be looked at individually and any attempt to apply a rule of thumb would be unwise. Basically, Schedule 8 specifies development which is included within the concept of E.U.V. and so is present both in valuations for compulsory purchase and in the calculation of the depreciation in the value of an interest following some adverse planning decision.

In fact Schedule 8 development is of relevance to three distinct categories of compensation claim. First, planning permission for it may be assumed when calculating the E.U.V. of an interest for compulsory purchase (see Chapter 9), in which case the additional limitations of Schedule 18 are to be ignored. Second, planning consent for it is to be assumed when calculating the depreciated value of an interest following certain planning decisions. It is impossible to generalise about the contents of this second category, but Studies 6 onward provide some clear examples. Note that, as with the first category, Schedule 18 is to be ignored. The third category is where planning consent for development within Schedule 8 itself has been refused: see Studies 1–5 in this Chapter. If compensation has been paid following the specific refusal of development coming within Schedule 8, consent for that development cannot later be assumed for the purposes of either of the first two categories mentioned above.

Refusal lying within Schedule 8 Part I

This does not rank directly for compensation, but Section 180 allows the owner to serve a purchase notice.

Study 1

In this case the land is rendered incapable of reasonably beneficial use.

A small freehold factory, built in 1930 and occupied by the freeholder, has been burned down. The Local Planning Authority has refused consent for its rebuilding as the site lies on the line of a proposed by-pass. The owner's purchase notice, served on the District Council under Section 180, has been accepted by the Highway Authority under Section 181.

The site measures 18 metres frontage by 45 metres deep, the building had been of 600 square metres gross floor space and 2,200 cubic metres. Industrial land is worth £270,000 per ha.

Assess the purchase price to be paid.

Site value assuming planning permission for a factory of 2,420 cubic metres (1)

E.U.V. 810 square metres at £27 per square metre
industrial site value (2)   £21,870

Purchase price = Value of site £21,870

Notes

(1) Distinguish between Sections 180 (2), 278 (1), and Section 187 (5). When considering "beneficial use" in purchase notice cases any development which is either New Development or in excess of the limitations imposed by Schedule 18 must be disregarded, and when calculating depreciation in value, Section 278 (1) makes Schedule 18 apply to Schedule 8 (1) and (3). See Note (5) below.

However, when calculating E.U.V. for cases under Section 187 (2) Schedule 8 of the 1971 Act is not to be assumed to apply but Schedule 3 of the 1947 Act together with Schedule 8 (13) of the 1971 Act. This definition of E.U.V. is in Section 187 (5). Since Section 278 does not apply, neither does Schedule 18.

(2) The land value should be found from the analysis of sales of comparable sites, reduced to some appropriate unit of comparison, and taking into account differences between sites. Only if such evidence is scant should a residual approach be used, working from the value of the completed development. It must be remembered that any valuations of comparable sites will have taken account of the plot ratios applicable to those sites, whereas all that can be claimed for the subject land is the right to rebuild the old factory plus 10%. The effect that such a restriction will have must be reflected in the valuation.

(3) The purchase notice having been accepted, the valuation is as for compulsory purchase. See Chapter 9.

(4) The loss of the building itself ought to be an insurance matter.

(5) Paragraph 1 of Schedule 8 deals with an owner's "right" to rebuild, which is not the same as putting up a different type of structure by way of improvement—this latter would be New Development. A distinction must be made between "original" and "non-original' buildings. An original building is the first building put up on the site and a non-original building is a replacement structure put up after 1st July 1948.

If rebuilding an original building (whether it is a pre-July 1948 structure or one first erected after that date) consent for the replacement to include an enlargement of not more than 10% gross volume and 10% gross floor space may be assumed.

If rebuilding a non-original building that was erected after 1st July 1948, consent may be assumed for the reconstruction to incorporate an extension of 10% gross volume but with no increase in the gross floor space—this seems to mean literally that the roof may be raised, which might be worthwhile if rebuilding certain types of storage buildings.

Should it ever come about that the replacement building has itself to be replaced it is the measurements of the old original building that remain relevant. (Schedule 8 paragraph 13.)

Study 2

This illustrates the calculation to be made when some worthwhile planning consent is available. In these circumstances the owner retains the site whilst receiving compensation for its loss in value.

The same factory as in Study 1, but in this case placed in a residential area. Planning permission for its reconstruction has been refused on the ground that a factory is a non-conforming and unacceptable user.

The owner's purchase notice has been sent to the Secretary of State under Section 181 (1)(c), and he has directed, under Section 183 (3), that planning permission for three houses shall be granted if applied for.

Industrial land is worth £270,000 per ha and residential building plots are worth £5,500 each.

Assess the compensation to be paid.

	£
Existing Use Value (E.U.V.) (1)	
Industrial site, 810 square metres at £27 per square metre site value	
Assume consent for factory of 2,420 cubic metres	21,870
Less:	
Permitted Development Value (P.D.V.) (2)	
3 residential building plots at £5,500	16,500
Compensation (3), under Section 187 (2)	£5,370

Notes

(1) The E.U.V. is calculated on the same assumptions as in Study 1.
(2) The P.D.V. is calculated on the assumption that no consent would be given other than in accordance with the Secretary of State's direction. See Section 187 (5).
(3) The claimant need not be the freeholder. See the definition of "owner" in Section 290.

Study 3

This shows the position where a pre-1948 structure which has already been replaced once after July 1948 has again to be rebuilt.

In this case the 1930 factory was of 2,200 cubic metres (600 square metres) gross, but it was replaced in 1950 with a similar structure of 2,420 cubic metres (660 square metres) designed to support overhead gantry-cranes. The planning policy of the 1950s has since been reversed and the area is now zoned for residential use. Two years ago the replacement factory was burned down and planning consent for rebuilding was refused. The subsequent history is the same as in Study 2.

The site is of 810 square metres, but you have no comparable evidence to determine industrial site value. Residential site value is £2,500 per plot, and permission for three houses would be forthcoming.

Existing Use Value (1)
   Gross development value (G.D.V.)
      660 square metres gross, say 630
      square metres net at £25 p.a. per
      square metre (full rental value)

	£ p.a.	£
Net income	15,750	
Y.P. perp at 10%	10	
		157,500
Less:	£	
Costs of development		
Construction 660 square metres		
at £145 per square metre, say	95,700	
Site clearance, say	4,000	
	99,700	
Professional fees at 10%	9,970	
	109,670	

Interest on £54,835, 1 year at 12%	6,580	
Legal and Agents' fees at 3% of G.D.V.	4,725	
Developer's profit at 15% of G.D.V.	23,625	
		144,600
		12,900
P.V. £1 in 1 year at 12%		·8929
E.U.V., *Industrial site value*, say		11,518
Less: Permitted Development Value		
P.D.V., 3 building plots at £2,500		7,500
Compensation equal to depreciation		£4,018

Notes

(1) E.U.V. and P.D.V. are as defined in Section 187 (5).

E.U.V. takes account of development within the Third Schedule of the 1947 Act subject to the proviso of paragraph 13 of Schedule 8 of the 1971 Act which makes the 1930 building, and not the 1950 replacement, the "original building".

See Note (5) to Study 1 and page 278 for an explanation of "original building".

(2) Avoid confusion between Section 187 (5) and Section 278 (1). The latter deals with cases where one must assume planning permission for Schedule 8 development, and it makes Schedule 18 apply to Schedule 8 (1) and (3).

In the above Study, the planning permission derives from the Third Schedule of the 1947 Act and not from Schedule 8 at all, so Section 278 does not apply.

(3) If the factory had been erected for the first time after July 1948 it would still be permitted to assume the 10% increase when calculating E.U.V. since Section 187 (5) makes no distinction between buildings first erected before or after July 1948.

See Note (1) on page 279.

Refusal lying within Schedule 8 Part II

Section 169 refers to compensation for the refusal of Schedule 8 Part II development. Section 278 lays down the assumptions to be made as to planning permission where an interest has to be valued on the assumption that consent for Schedule 8 development is available.

The first distinction to be made when considering the value of rights lying within Schedule 8 Part II, is between "original" and "non-original" buildings. These are defined in Schedule 8 Part III. Generally speaking an original building is the first building on the site, and a non-original building is a replacement structure put up after 1st July 1948. The second distinction has only to be made if dealing with an original building, and is between pre- and post-1st July 1948 construction.

There are, therefore, three categories: pre-July 1948 original, post-July 1948 original, and non-original (erected after July 1948). Each one of these three has its own rules governing the size of enlargement for the purposes of Schedule 8 Part II paras (3) and (7).

Work within Paragraph (3) (Enlargement of the building)
For pre-July 1948 original buildings see Schedules 8 and 18 (1), which limit the extension to an increase of 10% in gross cube and gross floor area. (1,750 cubic feet for a house if this will give more.)

For post-July 1948 original buildings see Sections 169 and 278, in particular see Section 169 (6). No increase in volume may be assumed although Schedule 18 (1) still applies and allows a 10% increase in gross floor space. This could probably only be relevant if planning consent was refused for a mezzanine floor since it is unlikely ever to be worth considering reducing a roof height in order to use the volume to cover a 10% increase in floor area.

For post-1948 non-original buildings, no increase in either volume or area may be assumed.

Work within Paragraph (7) (Extension of a use)
For pre-July 1948 buildings, the extension of the use must not exceed 10% of the gross volume in that use on 1st July 1948 or on the date the use began if this is later.

For post-July 1948 buildings, paragraph (7) does not apply at all, regardless of whether the building is original or not—see Section 169 (6)(b).

For land, the extension of the use is not to be more than 10% of the area used for the same purpose on 1st July 1948 or on the date the use began. It is possible to interpret the final "so used on that day" in Paragraph (7) to mean the 1st July 1948 only, in which case a use starting after July 1948 would not be covered (i.e. no right to extend it could be assumed).

Notes

(1) With the exception of the mezzanine floor, mentioned above, there is no compensation for the refusal of consent to extend a post-1948 structure under Part II of Schedule 8 (because of Sections 169 and 278), but you may assume the right to do so when valuing following the refusal of planning permission for Part I of Schedule 8, because Section 187 (5) makes no distinction between buildings first erected before or after 1st July 1948.

(2) In some cases there is an overlap between Schedule 8 and the classes of permitted development contained in Schedule 1 of the General Development Order (G.D.O.) 1977 (as amended). Where there is an overlap, planning consent being given by the Order, there can be no question of a claim arising for a refusal except as explained in Note (3) below.

    When considering the amount of any overlap, each case must be considered individually. Sometimes the G.D.O. gives more than is specified in Schedule 8, sometimes it gives less, and sometimes nothing at all—offices, for example, are not mentioned in the G.D.O.

(3) Where a planning consent derives from an Order, such as the G.D.O. 1977, but a Direction requires that specific consent be obtained; then, if that consent is refused, compensation is as under Section 164 (Revocation of planning permission). Any claim for compensation must be made within 12 months of the date on which the Direction takes effect. (Town and Country Planning (Compensation) Act 1985, Section 1 (1), amending s. 164.) See headnote to Study 10, below.

(4) If a purchase notice is served following the refusal of planning permission for development coming within Schedule 8 Part II, no compensation can be recovered under Section 169. This is merely to avoid double payment since the purchase price will follow the ordinary compulsory purchase rules including E.U.V. assuming planning permission for the whole of Schedule 8.

(5) If flats are involved, Section 1 (2) of the Town and Country Planning (Compensation) Act 1985 places restrictions on the ability to claim compensation following the refusal of planning permission for development falling within paragraph 3 of Schedule 8. No compensation will be recoverable if the application sought either to increase the number of flats within the building or to increase the size of any flat by more than 1/10th of its own cubic content.

This Section is intended to prevent any recurrence of the situation which arose in *Camden L.B.C.* v. *Peaktop Properties (Hampstead) Ltd* (1983) 127 S.J. 579. In this case the claimant was able, at the second attempt, to frame an application for the extension of a block of flats in a way which satisfied the conditions attached to paragraph 3 of Schedule 8, and those imposed by Schedule 18, such that a 1/10th increase in the volume of the block would have contained additional, new, flats. The local planning authority eventually granted consent rather than face a compensation claim of about £400,000, although the proposal was not acceptable in planning terms.

Section 1 (2) of the 1985 Act amends Section 169 of the 1971 Act and distinguishes between buildings which contain "two or more separate dwellings divided horizontally from each other or from some other part of the building" and other buildings. Paragraph 3 of Schedule 8 no longer extends to the enlargement of the former if this would result in the provision of more flats, or in a greater than 1/10th increase in the cubic content of any individual flat.

(6) One further lesson to be learned from the *Peaktop* case is that if the enlargement applied for exceeds the 1/10th allowance, the excess—however slight—is fatal to the claim. In *Peaktop*, the first application failed in the Court of Appeal because, whilst the proposal was within the 10% volume rule of Schedule 8, it exceeded the 10% floorspace rule of Schedule 18 by 1·49%. This caused Section 169 (3)(c) to defeat the entire claim and not just the 1·49% excess, the whole of the proposed development being ranked as New Development as a consequence of there being an excess over and above what is envisaged by Schedules 8 and 18. A failure for this cause may be tiresome, but an applicant is always free to submit a further application which does comply with the rules.

Study 4

This concerns an original building erected before July 1948. Planning consent for an enlargement has been refused. (A case within Schedule 8 (3).)

The building is a lock-up shop which the owner sought to enlarge by building a store room at the back. The shop measures 5·5 metres by 14 metres deep and has a content of 293 cubic metres. The store would have measured 7·7 square metres and 29 cubic metres, both measured externally.

Assess the compensation.

Value had consent been given (1)

	£ p.a.	£
77 square metres gross,		
65·5 square metres net		
Net full rental value, say	6,000	
Plus full rental value of store, say	250	
Net full rental value if enlarged	6,250	
Y.P. in perp. at 7%	14·3	
	say	89,375
Less: cost of building store, including fees		1,200
Value with planning permission		88,175
Less: Value subject to the refusal of consent (2)	£ p.a.	
65·5 square metres net, without store		
Net full rental value	6,000	
Y.P. in perp. at 7%	14·3	
		85,800
Compensation = depreciation =		£2,375

Notes

(1) Refer to the General Development Order 1977 as amended, Schedule 1 of which lists 30 classes of permitted development. There is, in some cases, an overlap between Schedule 8 Part II and the G.D.O.
(2) It is arguable that without the store the full rental value of the shop and/or the yield would be different. Whether or not this is so depends upon the circumstances of the case.
(3) A purchase notice could be served if the refusal of consent rendered the building incapable of reasonably beneficial use. In practice, the refusal of a small extension is unlikely to have such a marked effect.
(4) See Section 169 (2) for the planning assumptions to be made when assessing the depreciation following the refusal of consent for Schedule 8 Part II development.
(5) See Study 10 for a case involving the refusal of consent for permitted development.

Study 5

This illustrates a case coming within Schedule 8 (7), the refusal of planning permission to extend one use within a multi-use building.

A pre-war factory is now used in parts. The areas used and their full net rental values are as follows:

		Net full rental value
Use	% of the whole	£s per square metre p.a.
Warehousing	50	15
Cash and carry shopping	30	45
Offices	20	30

The building has only one floor and measures 32 metres by 41 metres. It is 5 metres high.

The owners applied for permission to increase the area used for shopping by extending it into some of the warehouse accommodation. The shopping space would have been increased by 35 square metres. Permission was refused.

There are two questions which must be answered when assessing the claim for compensation.

First, would the extension have been within the limits imposed by the Schedules? (Schedules 8 and 18.)

Present cubic content (Schedule 8 (9))	6,560 cubic metres
Present gross floor space (Schedule 18 (4))	1,312 cubic metres
Proposed increase in shopping use	35 square metres
Volume previously so used, 30% of 6,560 cubic metres	= 1,968 cubic metres

Gross floor space previously so used for

shopping	30% of 1,312 square metres	= 393·6 square metres
office	20% of 1,312 square metres	= 262·4 square metres
warehouse	50% of 1,312 square metres	= 656 square metres

A claim can be made since the proposed increase was within 10% of both the volume and area previously used for shopping. The building is an original building and was in existence before the appointed day (1st July 1948).

Second, what is the amount of the compensation?

Value had consent been given

	£ p.a.	£
Office, 262·4 square metres gross		
Say 223 square metres net at £30 per square metre	6,690	
Shopping (enlarged) 428·6 square metres gross		
Say 364 square metres net at £45 per square metre	16,380	
Warehouse (reduced) 621 square metres gross		
Say 527 square metres net at £15 per square metre	7,905	
Net income	30,975	
Y.P. in perp. at 8½% (1)	11·8	
		365,505

	£ p.a.	£
Less: Value subject to refusal (2)		
Office, as above	6,690	
Shopping 393·6 square metres gross		
Say 335 square metres net at £45 per square metre	15,075	
Warehouse 656 square metres gross		
Say 558 square metres net at £15 per square metre	8,370	
Net income	30,135	
Y.P. in perp. at 8½%	11·8	
		355,593
Compensation = depreciation =		£9,912

Notes

(1) If the building was let in parts to tenants of appreciably different reliability, it would be appropriate to value the three elements of the net income at different yields.

(2) See Section 169 (2) for the planning assumptions to be made.

Refusal of development not coming within Schedule 8

Development other than that described in Schedule 8 is "new development". Compensation for such a refusal, or for a conditional approval, is governed by Part VII of the Act. No compensation is available unless there is an unexpended balance of established development value (U.X.B.) attached to the land and a "qualifying interest" which is depreciated by the decision. Compensation will be the lesser of the U.X.B. and the depreciation in the value of the interest. See Sections 134 and 146.

For the valuation rules see Sections 152, 153 and 163.

For the derivation, reduction, apportionment, extinguishment, and repayment of the U.X.B., and other matters, see Sections 135–145, 158–162, and Schedules 15–17.

The availability of certain alternative consents can preclude a claim (Section 148), as can some reasons for refusal or certain conditions attached to a consent (Section 147).

Study 6

This illustrates a simple case where consent for new development is refused but the land continues to have some beneficial use.

A freehold paddock on the outskirts of a village, used for keeping horses, has a U.X.B. of £300. Planning consent for two houses was recently refused on the ground that the paddock lies beyond the natural boundary of the village. The paddock is at present worth £6,500 but would fetch £16,000 with the planning consent.

How much compensation should the freeholder receive?

Value had the consent been granted

	£
Two building plots at £8,000	16,000
Less: Value subject to the refusal (1)	
Existing use value	6,500
Depreciation	£9,500

Compensation = lesser of depreciation and U.X.B. = U.X.B. = £300

Notes

(1) See Sections 152, 153, and 163 for the valuation rules.
(2) If the refusal had been for any of the reasons specified in Section 147 then the freeholder would be unable to claim.

(3) Claims are sent to the Local Planning Authority for transmission to the Secretary of State. See Sections 154–157, 38–39, and 148.
(4) If, after any planning decision, the land is left without reasonably beneficial use, the owner may serve a purchase notice under Part IX of the Act, regardless of whether there is a U.X.B. or not.

Study 7

This illustrates the point made in Note (4) to Study 6 above, with the additional complication that the Secretary of State promises the grant of an alternative consent instead of confirming the purchase notice.

The law is contained in Sections 180–187.

No. 7 is an old, dilapidated, detached cottage adjoining some shops but protruding beyond the rear line of the pavement. The owner has repeatedly tried to sell it in its present condition but has been unable to do so as the council is threatening to make a demolition order.

No. 10, a comparable cottage, was renovated by its owner at a cost of £18,000 and later sold for £34,000, but it was never in so serious a state of disrepair as No. 7. Further down the road a vacant building plot with consent for a small house fetched £6,000 at a recent auction.

The owner of No. 7 sought planning consent to renovate the cottage in a way which would have involved making material changes to its external appearance, but permission was refused for a variety of reasons including that the site might one day be wanted by the council to give access to back-land. The owner therefore served a purchase notice on the district council under Section 180. The council refused to accept it and the Secretary of State has now directed that consent should be given for a modern house set back to the building line.

Assess the amount of compensation to which the owner is entitled.

Existing Use Value (1)

	£
Value with the right to rebuild and/or extend cottage by up to 1/10th its cubic content. (2) Say	36,750
Less costs of renovation and extension (3)	22,500
E.U.V. with benefit of the 1947 Act's Third Schedule rights	£14,250

B/F   £14,250

Less Permitted Development Value (1)

	£	
Single vacant building plot, value based on comparable	6,000	
Less cost of demolition and clearance net of salvage	1,300	
Permitted Development Value	——	£4,700
Compensation = depreciation =		£9,550

Notes

(1) See Section 187 (5) for the definitions of E.U.V. and P.D.V. E.U.V. = E.U.V. in accordance with the Third Schedule of the 1947 Act subject to paragraph 13 of the 8th Schedule of the 1971 Act.

(2) Value based on the sale price of No. 10 with an allowance for the increase in size allowed to No. 7.

(3) In practice these should be accurately costed, and detailed.

(4) In the case described the owner must claim his compensation from the local planning authority. See Section 187 (2)–(5).

(5) Had the Secretary of State confirmed the purchase notice then the ordinary compulsory purchase valuation rules would apply and the owner would receive £14,250 for his property. See Chapter 9.

Compensation for the revocation or modification of a planning consent

Sections 45–46 deal with the powers available to a local planning authority, Sections 164–168 with the compensation, and Sections 187–188 have relevance if, as a result of the authority's Section 45 order, a purchase notice is served.

Where consent derives from an order such as the General Development Order 1977, but a Direction requires that specific consent be obtained, then if that consent is refused (or granted subject to conditions) compensation is available under Section 164 and not as outlined in the first part of this chapter. See page 291 for a fuller discussion of this.

Section 178 applies to most cases which come within Part VIII of the Act. Part VIII deals with compensation for adverse planning decisions other than those restricting New Development.

The claimant need only be a "person interested in the land". It is a nice point whether—for compensation purposes under Section 164—there is any difference between a person "having an interest in land", one "being entitled to an interest in land", and one who is "interested in the land". The last is the form of words used in Section 164: see *Pennine Raceway Ltd* v. *Kirklees Metropolitan Council* (1982) 263 E.G. 721, C.A. In this case the owner of a licence, who had an enforceable right against the freeholder, was able to claim compensation. A prospective purchaser who owned an enforceable option to purchase would be entitled to claim. A contractor employed by a person entitled to claim may have to proceed against the latter for damages for breach of contract rather than against the planning authority concerned, but in this event the damages would be added to the compensation claim itself as being "loss or damage which is directly attributable to the order" and so it is perhaps at least arguable that the contractor might claim to be "interested in the land".

Special rules for the assessment of compensation may apply in the case of mineral workings which are the subject of a revocation or modification order, see Sections 164A and 178A–178C which were introduced by the Town and Country Planning (Minerals) Act 1981. These provisions are dealt with later in this Chapter.

Study 8

This illustrates a straightforward case where planning permission is revoked before the land is sold.

The owner of a house and orchard employed a surveyor to obtain planning consent for a house on part of the orchard plot and to sell that land with the benefit of the consent.

The surveyor obtained outline planning permission and received a genuine and fair offer of £7,000 for the plot, but before this could be accepted the consent was revoked and the offer withdrawn. The surveyor charged £60 for obtaining the consent and £200 in connection with the attempted sale.

Prepare the freeholder's claim.

1. *Depreciation* in value because of the revocation of consent. (1)

	£
Value of land with permission for one house	7,000
Less: Value subject to Section 45 Order (2) Say	2,500
Depreciation	£4,500

2. *Abortive expenditure* £

Cost of obtaining consent	60
Agent's fee for the attempted sale	200
Total claim	£4,760

Plus: Professional fees for preparing the claim.

Notes

(1) See Section 164 for heads of claim.

(2) The value subject to the Order is to be calculated on the assumption that consent would be given for 8th Schedule development. This is the only consent to be assumed, but the value of any actual planning permission still available would be brought into the valuation here.

See *A. H. Burlin* v. *Manchester City Council* (L.T. Ref/68/1975) and Section 164 (4).

(3) Note that any compensation received for the depreciation in the value of an interest is registered as a compensation notice and may be repayable on the grant of a subsequent planning permission. See Sections 166–168.

(4) The cost of all professional fees for plans and obtaining planning consents are recoverable under Section 164 (2) even though these may precede the grant of the planning consent.

See *Burlin* v. *Manchester* (above) and earlier cases, in particular *Holmes* v. *Bradfield R.D.C.* [1949] 2 K.B.1.

(5) Had the owner of the plot, instead of attempting to sell the land, set about having the house built for his own use, then upon revocation he would be entitled to claim such direct losses as compensation to a builder for breach of contract, in addition to the depreciation in the value of his interest.

(6) Losses claimed, including depreciation and/or loss of profits, need not themselves have arisen on the site that is the subject of the revocation or modification order provided they were directly caused by the order. The test is that the loss must not be too remote: there must be causation. See *Cawoods Aggregates (South Eastern) Ltd* v. *Southwark L.B.* (L.T. REF/222/1980):— "... there seems to me to be nothing in Section 164 of the 1971 Act which limits loss to the land which is the subject of a revocation order."

(7) The question of tax is ignored in all the examples which follow, but at the time of writing the position seems to be that the compensation should be paid gross of tax and the tax accounted for to the Inland Revenue by the claimant.

See *Loromah Estates Ltd* v. *Haringey L.B.* (1978) 248 E.G. 877. In this case, among other things, the claimant sought extra compensation to reflect a liability to pay Development Land Tax. This liability arose for the first time in the period between the confirmation of a revocation order (May 1973) and the payment of the compensation (1978)—the appointed day for the Development Land Tax Act 1976 being the 1st August 1976.

If the compensation had been paid before August 1976 D.L.T. would not have been payable. This part of the claim was dismissed on the ground that the liability for D.L.T. was a consequence of the passing of the D.L.T. Act and not a consequence of the revocation order—in other words the loss was too remote. It is more important to note that the local planning authority paid compensation in accordance with the valuation and not that sum minus the new tax liability.

The reader is referred to an article by P. H. Clarke, "The Taxation of Compensation", in the Journal of Planning Law, August 1976.

Study 9

This shows the calculation of a claim for a developer who has started work but whose planning permission is modified before the development is complete. Loss of profit is taken into account.

A developer bought 1 ha of land with outline consent for 28 houses some years ago for £185,000. He later obtained full approval and started work. An estate road was built, a sewer laid and construction started on 10 houses. The local planning authority, responding to intense local pressure, revoked the consent on 0·25 ha where no work had been done. The district council has offered to buy this part of the site for £3,000 to add to the village green, otherwise the land must remain undeveloped as amenity land.

Prepare the freeholder's claim.

Valuation before revocation order

		£
G.D.V. 0·25 ha with consent for 7 houses (1)		630,000
7 at £90,000		
Less:		
Costs of development:	£	
Construction, 7 houses at £54,000	378,000	
Site works, sewer, road etc., say	24,000	
	402,000	
Architect and quantity surveyors' fees	40,200	
	442,200	
Interest on £221,100		
2 years at 11%	51,317	

Legal and agent's fees at 3% of G.D.V.	18,900	
Developer's risk and profit, 5% of G.D.V. (2)	31,500	
		543,917
		£86,083
P.V. £1 in 2 years at 11%		0·8116
		£69,865
Value before order, say		
Less: Value subject to the order		3,000
Direct loss		£66,865

Plus:

Abortive expenditure. See Note (3).
Professional fees in connection with plans. Note (4).
Professional fees in connection with the preparation of the claim.

Notes

(1) The 0·25 ha could be valued either as here or by valuing the 1 ha in its totality both before and after the order. A problem could arise if there is some abortive expenditure to identify as care must be taken to avoid double counting. See Note (2), Study 11.

(2) The compensation under Section 164 is to be full compensation for loss or damage. Subject to the rules against remoteness and double-counting, this can include profits provided these are reasonably close at hand and certain. Generally the development value of the land will reflect the possibility of profit from a purchaser's point of view.

For cases in which lost profit was discussed and/or formed a direct element in the compensation see:

Burlin v. *Manchester* (page 288)
Hobbs (Quarries) Ltd. v. *Somerset C.C.* (1975) 234 E.G. 829
Excel (Markets) Ltd v. *Gravesend B.C.* (1968) 207 E.G. 1061
Bollans v. *Surrey County Council* (L.T. Ref/222/1967)
Cawoods Aggregates (South Eastern) Ltd v. *Southwark L.B.* (L.T. Ref/222/1980)

In Study 9 it is assumed that the profits are close at hand and this is allowed for by deducting only 5% developer's risk instead of the 15% used elsewhere.

(3) The sewer laid on the 0·75 ha part of the site may now be larger than is strictly necessary. Whether or not this extra cost could be recovered is arguable. It could probably be if none of the developer's proft came into the compensation, but since the profit on the 0·25 ha could only be made by providing the services, and as that profit has been included in the compensation, then it is not thought reasonable also to claim for the excess capacity in the services. See Section 164 (3).

(4) If the 0·25 ha is no longer capable of agricultural or other beneficial use, the service of a purchase notice would be in order.

Compensation for the refusal of permitted development

Section 1 (1) of the Town and Country Planning (Compensation) Act 1985 amends Section 165 of the 1971 Act to impose a 12-month time limit for claiming compensation following the revocation or modification of a planning consent originally granted by a development order.

A planning authority may, with the consent of the Secretary of State, make a direction under Article 4 of the General Development Order 1977 to strike out some, or all, classes of permitted development. The direction may be applicable to an entire district or to a single property. Similar powers may be attached to Special Development Orders. The effect of such a direction is to remove the relevant consents so far as those whose properties are affected are concerned, so requiring them to seek specific planning consent. If that consent is not forthcoming, or is granted subject to adverse conditions, the applicant has been disadvantaged by comparison with those whose properties do not come within the scope of the direction. The disadvantaged person may, therefore, claim for compensation under the auspices of a Section 164 (modification or revocation of planning consent), the basis of which is as shown in Studies 8–11. This basis is available regardless of whether the consent "lost" was for New Development or Schedule 8 Development, the Development order having originated a consent which has effectively been revoked or interfered with.

The 1985 Act states that compensation under these circumstances will only be forthcoming if the application for specific consent was made within 12 months of the date upon which the Direction came into operation. This time limit applies to all applications made after 9th May 1985. If the Direction took effect before this date, then the applicant had until 8th May 1986 to submit the planning application for specific consent and (if refused) become eligible for compensation. Applications for consent made out of time remain valid as planning applications, but cannot secure compensation if consent is refused.

Study 10

The refusal of consent for permitted development. See Section 165.

A farmer wished to erect a new dairy unit. The building would have come within Class VI of the General Development Order 1977 but a Direction under Article 4 of the Order made it necessary to obtain the specific consent of the local planning authority. Consent was refused. The farmer's surveyor had sought full planning and building regulation approvals and had spent some time discussing the project with the Ministry of Agriculture. The fees incurred so far are £450.

To what compensation is the farmer entitled?

	£
Value had consent been given (1)	
Value of farm without new dairy	125,000
Plus: value of dairy net of constructions costs (2)	4,000
	£129,000
Less: Value subject to refusal (3)	
but assuming consent for the whole of the 8th Schedule (4)	£129,000
Depreciation	Nil
Plus: Professional fees incurred at any time (5)	450
Compensation under Section 164. See Note (6)	£450

Plus professional fees in connection with the preparation of the claim.

Notes

(1) See Section 165.
(2) It is assumed that the new dairy would add £4,000 to the value of the farm after deducting the costs of construction, net of any grant received.
(3) See Section 164 (4).
(4) See Schedule 8 paragraph 4.

(5) See Section 164 (2).
(6) So far as compensation under Section 164 is concerned, compensation for depreciation could only be for that part of the permitted development which exceeded the tolerances of Schedule 8.

 The farmer has however, been refused consent for development within Part 2 of Schedule 8 and so may claim for the depreciation in the value of his interest under Section 169.

The claim under Section 169 would be:

	£
Value with consent	129,000
Less value subject to refusal	125,000
Compensation under Section 169 = Depreciation =	£4,000

 The total claim would amount to £4,450, plus the costs of preparing the claim.
(7) If for any reason a claim under Part 2 of Schedule 8 could not be made there would be no compensation on that score, in which case (on the above figures) only the £450 plus valuation fees would be recoverable, despite the fact that the total loss was £4,450. An example might be the refusal of consent to enlarge a dwelling erected after 1st July 1948.
(8) The case of *J. Jones* v. *Metropolitan Borough of Stockport* (L.T. Ref/140/1981 V. G. Wellings, Q.C.), is one in which an Article 4 Direction struck out Class VI permitted development: building operations for agricultural purposes on agricultural land. This case dealt with the resumption of an abandoned agricultural use: held—planning consent not required by virtue of Section 22 (2)(e). It also dealt with the question of whether Class VI permitted development could apply if the agricultural use was merely prospective since an intending purchaser would be aware of the Class VI rights when deciding how to use the land: Held—the use must be current, not prospective. This defeated the claim. Finally it dealt with the issue of whether an intensive pig unit was an agricultural building. Agriculture as defined includes the keeping and breeding of livestock, and the Secretary of State has indicated that the old view—which was that the livestock must depend upon the land itself for their support—is wrong (see Journal of Planning Law 1982 p. 127.): Held—the erection of an industrial piggery comes within Class VI and the refusal of specific planning consent

following an Article 4 Direction has, for compensation purposes, the same effect as a revocation order.*

Compensation where a Purchase Notice is served following the making of a Revocation Order

Study 11

The revocation of planning permission, the land being rendered incapable of reasonably beneficial use.

The owner of a piece of scrubland sought planning permission for one house. This was granted, but before offering the land for sale the owner, in the hope of receiving a better price, spent £750 on demolishing a derelict shed and partly laying a drain. The consent was, however, revoked before this work was completed.

Comparable unimproved building plots are worth £5000. The owner paid £60 to the agent who obtained the consent. Deprived of its consent the land is worthless save perhaps as a car park to serve the local parish hall.

A purchase notice has been served on the local council and ac-cepted. The purchase price is agreed at £500.

Prepare the owner's compensation claim.

Compensation under Section 164 (1). (See Note 1)

	£
Value with consent for one house (2)	
Unimproved site value, say	5,000
Less: value subject to the Revocation Order (3)	500
Depreciation	4,500
Plus: compensation under	
Section 164 (2), fees	60
Section 164(3), expenditure on work rendered abortive	750
To be received from the local planning authority	£5,310

Compensation under Section 188 (1). (See Note 4)

	£
Purchase price (4)	500
Less: if compensation is paid for expenditure on abortive work, the value of that work (5), say	200

* REF/140/1981 was over-ruled by the Court of Appeal in December 1983: REF/159/1979 (*Joan Jones* v. *Metropolitan Borough of Stockport*) (R. C. Walmsley, C.B., FRICS) was upheld in the same judgment. See (1984) 269 E.G. 408.

To be received from the district council   £300
_____

Total claim   £5,610
plus the costs of preparing the claim   ══════

Notes

(1) See Sections 164, 187, 188.
(2) This is unimproved site value. The use of the improved site value here would lead to double counting if the cost of the works (£750) was also claimed. The work would not be abortive if it raised the site value from unimproved to improved value.

In practice, evidence of value based on comparables would have to be carefully scrutinised to distinguish between improved and unimproved sites.

It would be open to the claimant to opt for whichever calculation gave the better compensation. The choice here is between unimproved site value plus abortive expenditure on one hand and improved site value only on the other. While it might be expected that when completed the site works would add more than their cost to the value of the site, it is more likely that in a partially completed state the cost incurred would exceed the value added.

Section 164 (1)(a) is ambiguous. Is it the work or the expenditure that is abortive?
(3) See Section 164 (4). In addition to any real planning permission in hand, planning consent for Schedule 8 development (and only Schedule 8) may be assumed. In this Study the assumption of consent for Schedule 8 does not help. The existing use value is established at £500.
(4) The valuation for acquisition under a purchase notice follows the ordinary compulsory purchase rules, modified as directed by the 1971 Act. For the law start with Section 188, which makes Section 187 applicable. Refer, therefore, to Section 187 (4), and thence to Sections 178–179.

See Chapter 9 for details of compulsory purchase valuations.
(5) Section 187 (1) requires that where compensation is paid for expenditure on work under Section 164, the compensation on acquisition is to be reduced by the value of the works in respect of which compensation was paid under Section 164. Section 164 pays compensation based on the expenditure, whereas Section 187 deducts the value of the works. There is no reason to suppose that cost and value are equal. The reader is reminded

that the purpose of compensation is to compensate, giving neither more nor less than the amount of the loss.

Whether fees paid for under Section 164 (2) are to be deducted from the purchase price is not clear from Section 187 (1).

The key question may be whether the "value with consent" used in the calculation of depreciation under Section 164 takes account of the value of the work, for if it does it may be possible to argue that the work was not abortive. In many cases, however, it is likely that the cost of preliminary work will not be met by an increase in value. Carelessness here in the preparation of the claim could leave the claimant out of pocket when the total received is compared to the apparent intention of Section 164, which is to pay full compensation. Perhaps the intention of Section 187 (1) is merely to avoid double payment.

Compensation for discontinuance orders, including those requiring some reduction in the intensity of a use

Section 51 authorises the making of a discontinuance order, Sections 170 and 178 deal with the compensation, and Section 189 with the possibility of serving a purchase notice.

Note that if a purchase notice is served and compensation is paid on acquisition under Sections 189 and 187 (2), then no compensation can be claimed under Section 170—see Section 189 (4). This is not the same as for a purchase notice following a revocation order.

Special rules for the assessment of compensation may apply in the case of mineral workings which are the subject of a discontinuance order. See Sections 170A, 170B and 178A–178C which were introduced by the Town and Country Planning (Minerals) Act 1981. These provisions are dealt with later in this Chapter.

Study 12

In which a discontinuance order requires a reduction in the intensity of use and thereby depreciates the value of both freehold and leasehold interests.

(continued on page 298)

Freeholder's claim

Valuation of freehold interest prior to the order

	£ p.a.	£	£
Net income	30,000		
Y.P. 5 years at 10½% (1)	3·7		
		111,000	
Reversion to full net rental value	55,000		
Y.P. perp. at 11% deferred 5 years	5·4		
		297,000	
			408,000

Less: Value of freehold interest after Order (2)

	£ p.a.	£	
Net income	30,000		
Y.P. 5 years at 10½%	3·7		
		111,000	
Reversion to full net rental value	47,000		
Y.P. perp. at 11% deferred 5 years	5·4		
		253,800	
			364,800

Freeholder's total compensation claim	= £43,200

Plus professional charges for preparing the claim.

Tenant's claim

Value of leasehold interest prior to order

	£ p.a.	£
Rent received, full rental value	55,000	
Less: rent paid	30,000	
Net profit rent	25,000	
Y.P. 5 years at 13% and 4%		
(Tax at 40%)	2·285	
		57,125

Thereafter Landlord & Tenant Act lease
  Value before the order

Less: Value of leasehold interest after order

	£ p.a.	
Rent received, full rental value	47,000	
Less: rent paid	30,000	
Net profit rent	17,000	
Y.P. 5 years at 13% and 4%		
(Tax at 40%)	2·285	

Thereafter Landlord & Tenant Act lease		
Value after order		38,845
Depreciation		18,280
Plus:		
Loss of profit (3)	35,750	
Y.P. say	3	
		107,250
Costs of complying with the order, alteration to plant		52,500
Tenant's total compensation claim		£178,030

Plus professional charges for preparing the claim.

The tenant and the freeholder of a factory near a residential area have been served with a Section 51 Order requiring a reduction in the factory's working from 24 to 15 hours per day. The tenant is willing to comply but the loss of night production will necessitate alterations to some of the plant at a cost of £52,500, and profits will fall by 25% from their present average of £143,000 p.a. before tax.

The tenant holds on a lease having 5 years to run at a net rent of £30,000 p.a. The current net full rental value is £55,000 but with reduced operating time this will fall to £47,000 p.a.

On the assumption that the order is confirmed, set out the compensation claims for freeholder and tenant.

Note: As with revocation orders, the question of tax on compensation is ignored. See Note (6), Study 8.

The claims are set out on page 297.

Notes

(1) A lower rate is used here because the income is secure.
(2) If as a result of the order the investment was sufficiently changed to justify a change in the yields, used this should be done. The term here is still secure, although secured on a reduced profit rent.
(3) Any other losses that the claimant could show would also be recoverable. An example might be interest on the excess capacity of plant and machinery now used less intensively.

Study 13

In which a discontinuance order extinguishes a use, requires work to be done and grants planning permission for some alternative development on the site.

A coal yard adjoining a residential area and in use for many years is operated by the freeholder. Part of the work done in the yard includes the mechanical grading and bagging of coal.

A discontinuance order has been confirmed requiring the cessation of the business on the site and the removal of the old machinery and stacks of coal. The order also gives planning permission for four houses on the land.

In its present use the site is worth £20,000. If cleared for housing it is worth £15,000. A suitable alternative site for the business could be bought for £27,000. This site is two miles away.

Prepare the freeholder's compensation claim.

Depreciation (1)

	£	£
Value prior to the order	20,000	
Less: Value subject to the order (2)	15,000	
Depreciation	5,000	5,000

Cost of complying with the order (3)	£	£
Demolition of buildings etc.	3,000	
Removal of fuel stocks	500	
	3,500	3,500
		8,500

Less salvage value received (4)		
Hardcore etc. from demolition of buldings		400
		8,100

Plus disturbance (1)

(a) Loss on forced sale of plant and machinery (5)	£	
Value to incoming tenant	3,000	
Less: scrap value	450	
		2,550

(b) Other losses, including temporary and/or permanent loss of profit, any reasonable increase in distribution costs (capitalised) duplicated expenditure, "Crawley" costs, etc. (6)

Say	6,000
Total compensation claim	**£16,650**

Plus professional charges incurred because of the order.

Notes

(1) See Section 170 (2).
(2) Cleared site value with planning permission for seven houses.
(3) See Section 170 (3).
(4) See Section 170 (4). Note that the salvage is to be deducted from the total claim and not just from the costs of compliance.
(5) See Chapter 9 for details of disturbance claims.
   So far as the plant and machinery is concerned, the loss is the difference between the scrap value achieved and what would

have been paid for it by an entrepreneur coming in to operate the business on the site. It has been assumed that it would not be economic to remove the machinery to the new site. A claimant must always minimise his loss.

(6) For these items of claim, only an indication of some likely ones has been given and a spot figure assumed. It is important to avoid double counting. The cost of removing the coal stocks, required by the order, has already been claimed. Any other removal expenses, however, could be claimed here.

It is also important to exclude items which are not allowable. The £7,000 difference in site values between the two coal yards would not, for instance, be recoverable. The reason for this is that the claimant will be deemed to have received value for money in the purchase of the new yard—it is up to him if he buys a better one.

(7) See *K. & B. Metals Ltd.* v. *Birmingham City Council* (1976) 240 E.G. 876 regarding compensation for activities between the making and the confirmation of the order. A Section 51 order does not take effect until confirmed.

(8) For a further example of a valuation following a Section 51 order, in which one use was extinguished and an alternative consent given, see *Raddy* v. *Cornwall County Council* (1967) 230 E.G. 976 (or "Valuer's Casebook" (R. W. Westbrook), Vol. 2 p. 65.)

Compensation where a Purchase Notice is served following the making of a Discontinuance Order

Study 14

In which a use is extinguished and the land is rendered incapable of reasonably beneficial use.

0·25 ha of land on the edge of a heathland nature reserve has been used since before 1964 as a dump for scrap metal (see Note 1), a dealer paying the freeholder the full rental value of £200 p.a. for the use of the land.

A discontinuance order requiring the cessation of the use and the removal of the scrap has been confirmed. No alternative consent has been given. Neither the freeholder nor the dealer have other land in the vicinity. As bare heathland the site is worth £300.

Prepare the freeholder's claim.

Existing use value, open storage (4)

	£ p.a.	£
Net income	200	
Y.P. in perp. at 14%	7·2	
		1,440

Purchase price if Section 189 Purchase Notice is upheld = £1,440
(2) plus professional fees.

Notes

(1) The use is established regardless of whether planning permission was obtained or not. See Section 94. If a limited consent had been granted the effect of the limitation would have to be taken into account.

(2) The freeholder has the choice of whether to claim under Section 170 or to serve a purchase notice under Section 189. The latter would seem the better choice. This would preclude a claim by him under Section 170 but the scrap dealer's rights to claim under Section 170 would not be affected. Note the words "of that order" in Section 189 (4).

(3) The scrap dealer may claim under Section 170 regardless of whether his interest is sufficient for him to satisfy Section 189 or not.

(4) The valuation rules under Section 189 are those of the Land Compensation Act 1961, Sections 5, 14–16 etc.

One of the values thereby allowed is Existing Use Value, plus disturbance if applicable.

In this Study a "Nil" Section 17 Certificate of Appropriate Alternative Development is assumed to have been given. See Chapter 9.

(5) If the freeholder had been running the business on the site he would have the same choice between Section 170 and Section 189. If he chose the latter he could not recover the cost of complying with the order but would sell as if his interest was being compulsorily acquired. The disturbance compensation would depend upon the availability or otherwise of alternative accommodation. The value of the site as a scrap dump would form part of the total compensation.

Compensation for restrictions concerning listed buildings

The relevant sections of the 1971 Act have been amended by Sections 1 and 4–7 of the Town and Country Amenities Act 1974, and by Section 90 and Schedule 15 of the Local Government Planning and Land Act 1980.

In the 1971 Act, Sections 54–58 deal with listing and protection, Sections 96–101 with enforcement, Sections 171–173 with compensation, and Section 190 (with Sections 180 and 188) with purchase notices. Section 278, Schedules 11 and 19, and the Town and Country Planning (Listed Buildings and Buildings in Conservation Areas) Regulations 1977 (S.I. 1977: 228) are also relevant.

If a building is listed, Section 55 requires that specific consent be obtained for any work of demolition, alteration or extension which would affect its character as a building of special architectural or historic interest. This is all embracing and wider than the definition of development contained in Section 22. It means that specific consent must be obtained even if the proposed work fits within Section 22 (2)(a), or if consent might already appear to have been given by Schedule 1 of the General Development Order 1977.

The surveyor who has to deal with compensation for the refusal of listed building consent for work coming within the remit of Schedule 1 of the General Development Order (as amended) should note that, for dwellings, the limits of permitted development differ for all terraced houses and for all dwellings within national parks, areas of outstanding natural beauty and conservation areas on the one hand and for non-terraced houses elsewhere on the other. The rules do not distinguish between listed and unlisted buildings as such, so a listed building standing within a national park, for example, will be subject to slightly different rules from one that is outside the park.

NOTE. Section 40 and Part 1 of Schedule 9 of the Housing and Planning Act 1986 make further changes to the law governing listed buildings but these do not affect the established compensation provisions.

Compensation for the refusal of listed building consent, or its grant subject to conditions.

See Section 171, which is only concerned with the alteration or extension of a listed building and not with demolition.

The point to watch is that, to give rise to a compensation claim, the adverse decision must concern either permitted development or work that is not development at all. Development is defined in Section 22. Work over and above these two groups comes within the normal compensation code—see the earlier parts of this Chapter.

Study 15

The refusal of listed building consent.

Elm Cottage, a listed building, is one of several detached and semi-detached cottages surrounding a village green. The village is a conservation area. The owner applied for permission to extend the cottage by building on an extra bedroom and bathroom at the back, and to erect a garage. The cottage is small and the new work would add £15,000 to its present value of £45,000. The extension as planned measured 5 metres × 6 metres × 2·75 metres high (gross), and the garage 5·2 metres × 2·2 metres × 2·7 metres.

Planning permission has been refused in order to protect an important view of the church and to preserve the character of the cottage. The Secretary of State has upheld the decision.

To what compensation is the owner entitled?

Value had consent been given (1)

		£
Value as at present		45,000
Plus: value of extension and garage		15,000
Value when work completed		60,000
Less:	£	
Costs of work:		
Extension, say	9,000	
Garage, say	2,250	
	11,250	
Architect's fee 12½%	1,400	
		say 12,650
Value with consent		47,350
Less: Value subject to refusal (2)		45,000
Compensation = depreciation =		£2,350

Notes

(1) See Section 171 (1)(a). Both the extension and the garage come within Class I of Schedule 1 of the General Development Order 1977—(permitted development). Their total volume is less than 115 cubic metres gross and it is assumed that all the other requirements of Class I are complied with.

(2) Section 171 (3) specifies the assumptions to be made. Compensation is to be the depreciation in the value of the interest in the land. See Note (4) below.

(3) The General Development (Amendment) Order 1981 (S.I. No. 245) increases the measure of permitted development for dwelling houses (other than terraced ones) although the absolute maximum remains at 115 cubic metres.

The Town & Country Planning (National Parks etc.) Special Development Order 1985 (S.I. No. 1012) as amended by the 1986 Order (S.I. No. 8) retains the old limits for dwellings within conservation areas (and elsewhere). It does not specifically mention listed buildings, the amount of permitted development for which will differ depending upon location. If the permitted development differs, so may the amount of compensation following the refusal of listed building consent. The new rules do not apply to any terraced houses.

Elm Cottage is subject to the old (1977) rules not because it is listed but because it stands within a conservation area.

(4) If the Secretary of State had, when refusing the listed building consent, undertaken to grant consent for some other works to the building, then those other works would have to be brought into the reckoning when preparing the compensation claim for the refusal. (Sections 171 (3)(b).)

Compensation for the revocation or modification of listed building consent

See Section 172. The provisions are similar to those of Section 164 except that there is no equivalent to Section 164 (4). The listed building consent may originally have been for more or less than the categories of Section 171 (1)(a), which latter, if revoked, must be included in the compensation.

Study 16

The modification of listed building consent.

The facts are the same as in Study 15 but in this case consent was initially given for both the extension and the garage, then modified to allow only the construction of the garage.

Value with the original listed building consent

	£
Calculated as in Study 15	47,350
Less: Value subject to the modified consent	

	£	£
Value of cottage at present		45,000
Plus:		
Value of garage, say		3,500
Value when garage built		48,500
Less:		
Cost of garage	2,250	
Architect's fee	280	
		2,530
		45,970
Depreciation (1)		1,380
Plus:		
Compensation for abortive fees (2)		1,120
Compensation for abortive work (3)		Nil
Total claim		£2,500

Plus professional fees for preparing the claim.

Notes

(1) See Section 172 (1)(b).
(2) See Section 172 (2).
(3) See Section 172 (3) and Section 172 (1)(a). There is no claim under this head in the present case.

Study 17

The modification of listed building consent for New Development.

Planning permission was obtained for the division of a listed building into three houses and for the construction of three garages. The conversion work involved changes to the facade of the building and the consent was modified to allow only the internal division of the building into two units with a common front door.

Prepare the freeholder's claim for compensation.

Value with the original listed building consent (1)

		£
3 houses at say £40,000		120,000
	£	
Less:		
Costs of conversion	48,000	
Cost of 3 garages	6,300	
Architect's fees	5,430	
	59,730	59,730
Value		£60,270

Less Value with consent as modified (2)

		£
2 houses at say £50,000		100,000
	£	
Less:		
Costs of conversion	40,000	
Cost of 3 garages	6,300	
Architect's fees	4,630	
	50,930	50,930
Value		£49,070

Depreciation = £60,270 − £49,070 = £11,200   £11,200

Plus: £
professional fees rendered abortive,
calculated by apportionment of the fees
actually incurred
Abortive element, say   900

Total claim   £12,100

Plus professional fees for preparing the claim.

Notes

(1) It is irrelevant whether the consent permitting New Development is a listed building consent or otherwise. In either case a planning consent has been revoked or modified and the consequential loss is recoverable.

Compare Section 164 (1) and Section 172 (1).

(2) Note that there is no mention of Schedule 8 in Section 172.
(3) The modification would involve further work by the architect, but not all his preliminary work would be wasted. Compensation is due for the extra fees involved if this is the true measure of the cost of the modification to the owner.

Compensation for the imposition of a building preservation notice

See Section 173. The rules for calculating any compensation differ depending on whether the building preservation notice results in the building becoming listed or not.

If the building is subsequently listed, compensation is paid as for any other listed building and in accordance with Section 171. Section 173 (2) prohibits the payment of compensation under Section 171 until the building is listed but does not prevent a claim being made in advance of listing.

If the building is not subsequently listed, compensation is payable for direct loss or damage. This would include compensation paid by the claimant for breach of contract. See Section 173 (3) and (4).

Study 18

In which a building preservation notice is imposed and the building is subsequently listed.

The owner of an old but inconveniently planned house obtained approval under the Building Regulations for extensive internal alterations at an estimated cost of £5,000. He served with a building preservation notice forbidding any alteration, and the building has since been listed under Section 54. If altered the value of the house would rise by £6,000 from its present £32,000. It is clear that no internal alterations will be allowed.

Prepare the owner's claim for compensation.

	£
Value had consent been given (1)	38,000
Less: cost of alteration	5,000
	33,000
Less: Value subject to refusal (2)	32,000
Compensation = depreciation =	£1,000

Notes

(1) The depreciation is calculated in accordance with Section 171. Internal alterations do not constitute development—see Section 22.
(2) See Section 171 (3).

Study 19

In which a building preservation notice is imposed but the building is not subsequently listed.

The facts are as in Study 18 but by the time the building preservation notice ceases to have effect the builder's estimate has risen by 14% and house values have fallen by 3%.

Compensation will be the additional cost of the work, £700. (14% of £5,000).

Notes

(1) The fall in house values is in no way attributable to the imposition of the building preservation notice. Section 173 (3) awards compensation for any loss or damage directly attributable to the effect of the notice.
(2) If the alterations reduced the running costs of the building, then the additional costs incurred as a result of the enforced postponement would come within Section 173 (3) provided they were not too remote.

Purchase notices in connection with listed buildings

See Section 190 and Schedule 19. The valuation rules are similar to other purchase notice cases—see Studies 11 and 14. In particular see Section 190 (2), Schedule 19 paragraph 4, and Section 116. Sections 180 and 188 are also relevant.

If a purchase notice takes effect, no compensation may be claimed under Section 171—see Section 171 (4).

Compensation derived from tree preservation orders

Amendments have been made to the 1971 Act by Sections 8–12 of the Town and Country Amenities Act 1974, and by Section 90 and Schedule 15 of the Local Government, Planning and Land Act, 1980.

In the 1971 Act, Sections 59–62 deal with protection, Sections 102–103 with enforcement, and Sections 174–175 with compensation. Section 191 allows the service of a purchase notice, but see Section 184.

The Town and Country Amenities Act 1974 imposes a tree preservation order on all trees in a conservation area, amends the penalties, and gives grants for historic gardens.

The Local Government, Planning and Land Act 1980 makes local planning authorities solely responsible for confirming tree preservation orders, and ends the Secretary of State's responsibility for this.

The relevant Regulations are the Town and Country Planning (Tree Preservation Order) Regulations 1969 (S.I. 1969: 17) as amended by the T. & C.P. (T.P.O.) (Amendment) and (Trees in Conservation Areas) (Exempted Cases) Regulations 1975 (S.I. 1975: 148), and by the T. & C.P. (T.P.O.) (Amendment) Regulation 1981 (S.I. 1981: No. 14).

Compensation under Section 174

Where a tree preservation order is in force compensation for loss or damage caused by the refusal of consent (or by the imposition of conditions attached to a consent) may become payable, but subject to any exceptions or conditions specified in the order.

The measure of the compensation is the loss or damage caused by the adverse decision. Its calculation by means of a "before and after" valuation would be reasonable.

See *Bollans* v. *Surrey County Council*, 1967 (REF/222/1967). In it the Lands Tribunal discussed several important issues and concluded:

1. Damage or expenditure consequential on a refusal under a tree preservation order is analogous to loss or damage directly attributable to a revocation of planning permission.
2. That loss of profit *may* be too remote if the use for the profitable purpose had still to be started at the time of the revocation or order.
3. That it would not be double counting to allow a claim which included both the value of the tree as timber and the profit from its subsequent disposal if the claimant operated both the growing and retailing businesses from which those profits came.

Study 20

In which consent is refused for the conversion of woodland, the subject of a tree preservation order, to pasture.

The freeholder of a farm sought consent for the felling of 6 acres of woodland, the subject of a tree preservation order made under section 60, in order to convert the land to pasture. A Ministry grant would be forthcoming. The local planning authority has refused consent. The land would be worth £2,000 per acre as pasture or £500 per acre as woodland, inclusive of the value of the trees. Compensation is payable under section 174.

Value had consent been given (1)

	£	£
6 acres pasture at £2,000		12,000
P.V. £1 for 3 years at 4% (2)		0·8889
		10,667
Less: cost of reclamation	2,700	
P.V. £1 for 1 year at 4% (3)	0·962	
	2,597	
Less: proceeds from sale of trees	1,400	
	1,197	1,197
Value with consent for reclamation		9,470
Less value subject to refusal of consent 6 acres woodland at £500		3,000
Depreciation in value		6,470
Plus consequential losses and disturbance Value of any grant towards cost of reclamation (4), say	810	
P.V. £1 for 1 year at 4% (5)	0·962	
	770	770
Total claim		£7,240

Plus professional fees for preparing the claim.

Notes

(1) See *Bell* v. *Canterbury City Council* (1986), 279 E.G. 767, for a case in which many of the principles are discussed, and on which this Study is based.

(2) The deferral reflects the time which must elapse following grubbing out before the pasture is fully established.
(3) The Lands Tribunal considered that the reclamation costs should be deferred for 1 year in Bell's case, but did not defer the sale of timber. The report does not discuss the reasoning, but presumably the timber would be sold in advance of reclamation.
(4) The cost of reclamation used (£2,700) is the full cost. If a grant towards the cost of the work is likely to be forthcoming—for example from the Ministry of Agriculture, Fisheries and Food—then its amount should be brought into the calculation, either as here or by using the net-of-grant cost of reclamation in the earlier part of the valuation.
(5) The Tribunal did not show deferral of grant for 1 year in Bell's case, adding it directly as a consequential loss, perhaps because the grant figures were not disputed. It would, however, seem consistent to discount this for the same period as the reclamation costs since the grant would not be paid until the work had been carried out. Failure to discount would result in different final totals between the two approaches.

Compensation under Section 175

Where a local planning authority directs that land cleared in the course of forestry operations be replanted, and the Forestry Commission decides not to make a cash advance under Section 4 of the Forestry Act 1974 because the direction frustrates the use of the land for commercial forestry, then compensation is payable for any loss or damage due to the direction to replant.

Purchase notices under Section 191

Where a tree preservation order is in force and a refusal of consent concerning the trees renders the land incapable of reasonably beneficial use, a purchase notice may be served. Sections 180–183, 186 and 187 are applicable.

Tree felling does not seem to come within the definition of development in Section 22. When considering whether land has beneficial use, Section 180 (2) requires that the prospect of New Development be disregarded and that the limitations of Schedule 18 be observed. Once it has been established that following the refusal of consent the land has become incapable of reasonably beneficial use, the normal compulsory purchase code applies.

Purchase Notices are considered later in this Chapter.

Study 21

In which a parcel of land is rendered incapable of reasonably beneficial use in its existing state by the imposition of a tree preservation order.

A freehold site within the confines of a village's residential area contains sufficient gnarled pine trees to prevent its use. The trees are attractive and are the subject of a tree preservation order. Consent for felling has been refused.

The general form of development surrounding the site is of good class housing, some set amongst trees and some with trees along the plot boundaries only.

If limited felling had been allowed it would have been reasonable to expect planning permission for four houses on the site. If all but the boundary trees were removed then eight houses could be fitted onto the site. The plot values would be £8,000 and £5,000 respectively, both based on comparable but cleared sites.

Advise the freeholder and assess the compensation. The following preliminary question arises: *Has the land been rendered incapable of reasonably beneficial use by the decision?* Yes. It could, if cleared, have been used—perhaps for horticulture or planted as an orchard without carrying out any New Development. A purchase notice could therefore be served.

Compensation

Assessment follows the normal compulsory purchase rules. See Sections 14–17 of the Land Compensation Act 1961 for the planning assumptions to be made. These are discussed in Chapter 9. If planning permission for residential development could have been expected the claimant will receive residential site value.

The claim would be calculated on the site value disclosed by the planning assumptions with the tree preservation order being disregarded. If consent could be expected only for houses set amongst trees the price would be £32,000 (4 plots worth £8,000), but £40,000 if it would be reasonable to expect consent for housing with a boundary screen of trees (8 plots worth £5000).

Notes

(1) See *Eardisland Investments Ltd* v. *Birmingham Corporation* (1967) 214 E.G. 1579.

In this case a purchase notice was served and accepted following the imposition of a tree preservation order and the refusal of planning permission for residential development.

One issue was whether the order should be ignored because it wa not referred to the Section 17 Certificate. The claimant argued that the certificate was tantamount to an unrestricted planning permission for residential development, whilst the corporation maintained that a tree preservation order (T.P.O.) stood on its own as an established statutory encumbrance on the land which a prospective purchaser could find out about. (A T.P.O. is a registered land charge.)

The Tribunal held that a Section 17 Certificate cannot be deemed to be more definite than an outline planning permission, even if it can be said to go as far as that, whereas a tree preservation order acts independently of any development plan.

The Tribunal identified two chief factors controlling the density of development, and thereby market value. These were the density of the surrounding development and the tree preservation order itself.

"... conformity with the surrounding development was the most that could be expected. The Planning Officer said that 10 houses per acre could be so arranged as to leave a substantial number of trees, particularly where they were growing around the boundaries. I consider this to be a reasonable measure of development density to which the market would be attracted, and on which I should therefore base the value for compensation."

The Tribunal then decreed a lump sum figure—an open market value having regard to the density of development that could have been reasonably expected, based on 10 houses to the acre.

The inference of the report seems to be that the tree preservation order (at least in this case) made no material difference to the density of development that might be expected having regard to the development plan and with a Section 17 Certificate substituted for the private open space shown. The report is not as clear as one would wish. What does seem clear is that the valuation might be undertaken in two stages, first the calculation of the site value subject to the normal planning expectations but as if the tree preservation order did not exist, and then the calculation of the value subject to the restrictions of the order. The difference between these two figures would be the loss attributable to the order. The unencumbered site value would, of course, have regard to the development plan. This would leave the valuer with the figure for depreciation because of the order—which might be recoverable under Section 174 (depending upon the wording of the order)—and a value on which to base a claim for compensation if a purchase notice should be the appropriate remedy.

Compensation for restrictions on advertising

Regulations are made under Section 63, as amended by Section 45 of the Housing and Planning Act 1986. Section 64 gives certain planning permissions, Section 109 deals with enforcement, Section 176 with compensation for advertisements in place before 1st August 1948, and Section 191 with purchase notices.

The regulations are the Town and Country Planning (Control of Advertisements) Regulations 1984, S.I. 1984: 421.

Schedule 16 of the Local Government Act 1972 as amended by Schedule 15 (15) of the Local Government Planning and Land Act 1980 may have some relevance to the definition of areas of special control.

Compensation for the removal or alteration of an advertisement is different for advertisements for which express consent was obtained on the one hand, and those in existence before 1st August 1948 on the other.

There is no compensation for the outright refusal of planning permission for advertisements.

Study 22

The modification of an express consent.

An owner obtained express consent for the display of an illuminated advertising hoarding on the gable wall of his shop. The hoarding had nothing to do with advertising his own business and would have brought in a revenue of £500 p.a. net. Before its construction was completed the planning permission was modified by the withdrawal of the consent for lighting. The advertisers insisted upon a £150 reduction in the charges. The owner had spent £75 in obtaining the consent and the electric lighting had been partly installed at the time of the modification order.

Prepare the owner's compensation claim.

Direct loss or damage (1)

	£ p.a.	£
Reduction in revenue	150	
Y.P. 5 years at 12% (2) (3)	3·6	
		540
Plus cost of abortive work		
Abortive electrical work and its		
subsequent removal (4)		80
Compensation claim		£620

Plus professional charges for preparing the claim.

Notes

(1) See Regulation 25 for heads of claim.
(2) See Regulation 20. Consent cannot be granted for longer than 5 years. I assume that the first payment is close at hand.
(3) Whether dual rte tables should be used here depend upon whether the valuer regards the income as terminable or not. The fact that the local planning authority cannot grant permission for more than five years does not mean that it must thereafter refuse consent.
(4) Although the revocation cannot affect so much of the work as has been done (Regulation 24 (3)), it would be unreasonable to expect the owner to retain a partly completed and useless installation.

Study 23

The discontinuance of a deemed consent for an advertising station in use before 1st August 1948.

A discontinuance notice under Regulation 16 required the removal of a large advertisement hoarding erected on land belonging to a factory near a busy road junction. The hoarding was put up before August 1948.

Assess the compensation.

Compensation (1)
The reasonable cost of complying with the notice, say   £125

Notes

(1) The right to compensation is given by Section 176. If the hoarding had been erected after 1st August 1948 there would be no right to compensation in the absence of express consent for its erection.

Compensation for stop notices

Section 90 deals with the power of a local planning authority to serve a stop notice and Section 177 with a claimant's right to compensation. The Town and Country Planning (Amendment) Act 1977 provides a new version of Section 90 and amends Section 177.

Note that compensation is only recoverable in certain, specified, circumstances. See Section 177 (2) as amended.

Study 24

Compensation for a stop notice attached to an enforcement notice which is quashed on appeal.

A householder enlarged his house to the full extent permitted by Class I paragraph 1 of the General Development Order 1977 (as amended). Some time later, and without planning permission, he contracted with a local builder for the erection of a brick-built carpentry workshop. This was partly constructed when an enforcement notice, coupled with a stop notice, was served on him. He appealed against the former under Section 88 (1)(b) on the ground that the workshop came within paragraph 3 of Class I. Two years later he won his appeal but the cost of the work had risen from the original £2,200 to £3,500. In addition he spent £100 protecting the part-built structure.

Assess his compensation.

Direct loss or damage (1)	£
Increase in the cost of construction	1,300
Expenditure on protective work	100
Compensation	£1,400

Notes

(1) Section 177 (1) specifies that compensation is for "any loss or damage directly attributable to the prohibition ...". Section 177 (2) specifically includes payments in respect of breaches of contract caused by the obligation to comply with the stop notice as compensatable.

(2) It is arguable that interest should be claimed for the loss of any money spent on the work prior to the stop notice, since this has effectively been tied up without either interest or use for the length of time taken by the appeal.

(3) See *Robert Barnes & Co Ltd* v. *Malvern Hills District Council* (1985) 1 E.G.L.R. 189 for a case which raised a number of head of claim, including interest charges. Interest on the purchase of the affected site was allowed. A claim for interest on

the postponed receipt of development profits was disallowed because the claimant failed to show that the profits were any less than they would have been without the stop notice. It was the claimant's failure to establish the extent of the loss, not the concept of claiming interest, which was defective. A claim for interest on the amount of the award from the date on which building work resumed until the date of the Tribunal's decision was rejected both because it was inappropriate under the circumstances of the case and because Section 179 (stop notice) compensation cases could not be treated differently from those under Section 164 (the revocation or modification of planning consent) as both come within Part VIII of the Act. It has already been etablished so far as Section 164 cases are concerned that the Tribunal does not have the power to award such interest.

(4) See *J. Sample* (*Warkworth*) *Ltd v. Alnwick District Council* (1984) 271 E.G. 204 for a review of the question of remoteness of loss. The meaning of "directly attributable" is not qualified by the concept of "reasonable forseeability".

(5) The costs of the appeal against the enforcement notice are not recoverable since that notice does not stem from the stop notice but precedes it. See *Barnes* v. *Malvern*, and *Sample* v. *Alnwick*, above.

(6) See *Knibb and Knibb* v. *National Coal Board* (1984) 273 E.G. 307 for a review of the authorities on the question of interest.

(7) There is no prescribed form for a claim under Section 177, but the claimant's letter must, if it is to count as a claim, make it clear that a claim is being made, not that one will be made at some future date. Neither the amount of compensation nor other details need be given at this stage. See *Texas Homecare Ltd* v. *Lewes District Council* [1986] 1 E.G.L.R. 205.

Compensation for the closure of a highway to vehicles

Section 212 empowers a local planning authority to apply to the Secretary of State for an order banning vehicles from a highway (other than a principal or trunk road) so as to improve the amenity of the area. If this is done the status of the highway is reduced to that of bridleway or footpath, as happens when a street is turned into a pedestrian precinct.

Section 212 (3) allows for exceptions to the ban, in terms of vehicle type, particular persons or time of day.

Section 212 (5) deals with compensation for anyone having an interest in land which has lawful access to the highway. Sections 178–179 also apply.

The measure of compensation is the depreciation in the value of the interest directly attributable to the order, plus any other direct loss or damage. This would include the costs of making the claim.

Interest on the amount of the award is not recoverable. See *Saleem* v. *City of Bradford Metropolitan Council* (1984) 271 E.G. 119 in which it was ruled that the principle which precludes interest on the award in revocation order cases would also apply to claims under Section 212.

A simple "before and after" valuation would determine the depreciation. Direct loss or damage could include increased operating costs, loss of profits (if any), and so on. If, however, the scheme improved the amenity of the area, any claim for losses would need careful preparation. There appears to be no provision for set-off, nor for the repayment of compensation if the scheme is subsequently done away with.

Compensation for the preservation of ancient monuments

The Ancient Monuments and Archaeological Areas Act 1979 is the relevant statute. It has been considerably amended by the National Heritage Act 1983. The 1979 Act deals with the protection of ancient monuments, guardianship agreements, the acquisition of monuments (including by compulsory purchase) adjoining land and easements, and with compensation.

A compensation claim may arise in one of three ways
1. *Compensation following the refusal of scheduled monument consent or its grant subject to conditions.* See Section 7 of the 1979 Act.

   To give rise to a claim the loss must stem from the refusal of scheduled monument consent for work within one of three categories:
   (a) Work in connection with development for which express planning permission was given (not by way of a G.D.O.) prior to the scheduling of the monument. This permission must itself be effective when the scheduled monument consent is applied for. A permission that had time-expired would not do.
   (b) Work which is not development at all (see Section 22 of the 1971 Act) or which is permitted development under a General Development Order. Even so, no compensation is payable if the work would result in even partial destruction

    or demolition of the monument unless that work is incidental to agricultural or forestry use (Section 7 (2) and (4)).

(c) Work that is necessary for the continuation of the existing use(s) to which the monument was being put immediately before the application for scheduled monument consent. Such use(s) must not be in breach of any legal restrictions.

Note that where an express planning consent is frustrated by the refusal of scheduled monument consent (or its grant subject to conditions), compensation is not recoverable if the planning consent was granted after the monument was scheduled. A planning authority may of course, refuse planning consent in order to protect a monument.

So far as compensation is concerned, the link between monument protection and planning control is akin to that between listed building consent and planning permission in general. In *Hoveringham Gravels Ltd* v. *The Secretary of State for the Environment* (1975) 235 E.G. 217, it was held that the value of the claimant's interest had been damaged chiefly by the failure to obtain planning permission to work minerals rather than by the imposition of a preservation order which merely frustrated agricultural permitted development under the G.D.O. The compensation was, therefore, severely limited. This position has now been reinforced, in that compensation is not payable if the implementation of a planning permission is frustrated by the refusal of scheduled monument consent, if that planning permission was granted after the monument was scheduled.

The measure of any compensation claim under Section 7 is the amount of expenditure or other loss or damage suffered by a person having an interest in all or part of the monument. It will include the depreciation in the value of the interest—a "before and after" valuation in accordance with the rules of Section 5 of the Land Compensation Act 1961, for which see Chapter 9, and professional fees.

Section 8 of the 1979 Act deals with the recovery of compensation if consent is subseuently granted.

2. *Compensation following the cessation of authorisation of works affecting a scheduled monument following the modification or revocation of scheduled monument consent.*

Section 9 of the 1979 Act deals with such cases, the compensation being for expenditure on works rendered abortive because further work has ceased to be authorised, and for any other loss or damage directly due to this cessation, including the depreciation in the value of an interest in the land. The claimant must have an interest in all or part of the monument. The entitlement to compensation is based on Sections 164 and 165 of the 1971 Act (revocation orders). Professional fees would be recoverable.

3. *Compensation for damage caused by the exercise of certain of the powers contained within the 1979 Act.*

A claim may be made if the exercise of the powers contained within Sections 6, 26, 38, 39, 40 and 43 results in damage to land or to any chattels thereon.

Compensation in connection with hazardous substances

Section 58H, introduced into the 1971 Act by the Housing and Planning Act, 1986, empowers a hazardous substances authority to revoke or modify a hazardous substances consent in any of several specified circumstances or if, having regard to any material consideration, it appears expedient to do so. If this last method is used, compensation becomes payable under Section 170, just as if a discontinuance order had been made under Section 51, but with the hazardous substances authority standing in place of the local planning authority. See Section 58H(3) and (8).

Section 58J states that a hazardous substances consent enures for the benefit of the land to which it relates unless the terms of the consent provide otherwise. Such consent is, however, automatically revoked if there is a change in the person in control of part of the land, unless prior application is made by him to the hazardous substances authority for the continuation of that consent after the change. If such an application is made, the authority—in addition to agreeing to the change—has the right to modify or revoke the consent, but if it does other than agree then it must pay to the person who was in control of the hole of the land before the change, compensation for any loss or damage sustained by him which is directly attributable to the modification or revocation of the consent. If the person who is in control of the land omits to apply, in advance, for the hazardous substances consent to continue after the change of control, then no compensation will be payable for the automatic revocation of consent which will follow that change of control.

Compensation for restrictions on mineral workings
(See also Chapter 11, pages 342–347.)

The Town and Country Planning (Minerals) Act 1981 introduced a number of new sections into the 1971 Act, notably Sections 164A, 170A and B, 178A, B and C. These provisions came into effect on the 17th September, 1982, and enable a minerals planning authority to invoke the compensation provisions now contained in the

Town and Country Planning (Compensation for Restrictions on Mineral Workings) Regulations 1985 (S.I. 1985 No. 698). These provisions substantially modify the compensation code applicable to "mineral orders" in revocation, modification and discontinuance order cases, with the result that the compensation payable is reduced. Section 164A deals with revocation and modification, Sections 170A and 170B with discontinuance.

The Town and Country Planning (Minerals) Act 1981 also introduced new Sections 51A—51F into the 1971 Act. These are to do with prohibition, suspension and supplementary suspension orders (the first of which prohibits a resumption of the working or winning of minerals).

Minerals planning authorities may only invoke these provisions after prior consultation with, among others, those interested in the land or its minerals. The consultations must include both the making of, and the terms of, the order. The rules for this are to be found in the new sections mentioned above.

These changes to the normal compensation provisions are designed to ensure that mineral operators pay more towards the costs of environmental restoration.

Compensation for statutory undertakers

Sections 237—240 provide for compensation to be paid to statutory undertakers on a special basis under a variety of circumstances which include the refusal, conditional grant, revocation or modification of planning permission on operational land, the imposition of a requirement to remove or re-site apparatus, the extinguishment of a right of way, and compulsory purchase. Not all planning refusals are compensatable. The valuation rules are set out in Section 238.

Compensation for losses under the Wildlife and Countryside Act 1981

Section 29 of this Act provides protection for areas of special scientific interest, and Section 30 (2) states that if the value of the interest in the land is less than it would have been had the Order not been made, the amount of the compensation shall be equal to the difference between the two values.

Compensation for planning blight

The law is to be found in Sections 192–207 of the 1971 Act and in Sections 68–82 of the Land Compensation Act 1973. The claimant must serve a Blight Notice but authorities are empowered to serve counter notices which are frequently upheld because although the property is adversely affected by planning or other provisions (e.g. by a housing programme), they are not blighted within the statutory provisions. Once the claimant has got a valid blight notice established the valuation rules are as if the relevant compulsory purchase procedure had arrived at the notice to treat stage. Note, however, that no home loss payment will be available. The reader should refer to Chapter 9.

Purchase notices and "reasonably beneficial use"

Section 180 enables an owner to serve a purchase notice on the district council, if following either the refusal of planning permission or its grant subject to conditions, his land is "rendered incapable of reasonably beneficial use in its existing state".

The refusal of consent does not have to reduce the value of the land, indeed an outright refusal can never do this since planning permission need never be sought merely to continue what is already lawfully established. (An exception is if planning permission was originally given for a limited time and that time has expired. Apart from this one case the only way in which a lawful or established use can be upset is by the service of a discontinuance order.) It follows, therefore, that since the refusal of consent cannot reduce value, neither can the refusal itself render the land incapable of reasonably beneficial use. The worst that a refusal can do is to prevent an owner putting his land to some more advantageous use.

So far as entitling an owner to serve a purchase notice is concerned, it must be because events other than the planning refusal have so upset the status quo that the current use has ceased to be of reasonable benefit; thus forcing the owner to seek permission to crry out some form of development. If this permission is refused, or is granted subject to conditions, so that the owner is pinned down and unable to shift to a beneficial use, then he may serve a purchase notice. This in effect says to the council, "If you like my property so much the way it is, then buy it from me or find someone else to do so, for it is useless to me." However, a purchase notice is not intended to provide a remedy merely because an owner is refused permission to release development value. It is to deal with the case where an owner is trapped with land that has become incapable of reasonably beneficial use.

It has, by some, been considered a nice point as to whether or not a purchase notice could be used to help an owner whose land has always been useless. That it may be so used was decided in the case of *Purbeck District Council* v. *The Secretary of State for the Environment and Another* (1982), 263 E.G. 258, where it was held that all that is necessary is to look at the situation as it has become following the refusal of planning consent, there being no need to look at the history of the land or to be concerned with what had brought about the present situation: Section 180 (1) refers only to the land's existing state. This applies even if it is the owner's or occupier's activities which have rendered the land useless: there is nothing in the legislation which states that the cause has to be involuntary. It should, however, also be noted that in this case the Secretary of State's decision to uphold the purchase notice was quoshed because the occupier, the claimant's tenant, had rendered the land useless by persistent defiance of conditions attached to a planning consent despite the Council's best efforts to force compliance. It was held that a claimant should not be allowed to take advantage of his own wrongdoing to foist the land on an unwilling local authority, and that Section 180 (1) excludes situations where the land has become incapable of reasonably beneficial use because of (in planning terms) unlawful activities on the land: "It would be monstrous if a local planning authority were not entitled to say 'We should not have to buy because the reason the land is incapable of reasonably beneficial use is because conditions we imposed in giving planning permission were not complied with'." A breach of planning control is unlawful: see *L.T.S.S. Print and Supply Services Ltd* v. *Hackney London Borough* (1976) Q.B. 663, C.A.

This decision follows that in *Adams and Wade Ltd* v. *The Minister of Housing and Local Government and Another* (1965) 18 P.&C.R. 60, page 67: "The purpose of the Section is to enable an owner whose use of his land has been frustrated by a planning refusal, to require the local authority to take the land off his hands. the reference to beneficial use must therefore be a reference to a use which can benefit the owner (or prospective owner) and the fact that the land in its existing state confers no benefit or value upon the public at large would be no bar to the service of a purchase notice."

If part of a parcel of land is rendered incapable of reasonably beneficial use, but part is not, the owner can only oblige the authority concerned to purchase the part which is not capable of such use. See the Court of Appeal decision in *Wain and Others* v. *The Secretary of State for the Environment and Others* (1982) 262 E.G. 1085.

When deciding whether land is capable of reasonably beneficial use, Section 180 (2) says that no account is to be taken of New Development and that the limitations of Schedule 18 are to be observed. The implication is that you assume planning consent for

Schedule 8 development subject to Schedule 18, but for nothing more. Section 22 (2) specifies some activities which are not development at all. Schedule 18 is here of relevance when considering whether there is reasonably beneficial use. If there is not, the purchase price will be in accordance with the rules of the Land Compensation Act 1961 and Schedule 18 will cease to be relevant to Schedule 8. See Studies 1, 11, 14 and 20.

In summary, when deciding whether a purchase notice can be served, the existing use must be looked at. If the land has become of no reasonable benefit, and if it cannot be made beneficial without carrying out development which requires planning permission, then a purchase notice can be served following a planning refusal. It is essential to realise that "incapable of reasonably beneficial use" is not just another way of saying "less valuable", nor even "less useful". So far as agricultural land is concerned, it will be incapable of reasonably beneficial use if its size, shape or location is such that farming is not practicable and any other use requires development and, hence, planning consent.

It is wrong to say that a purchase notice can only be served once permission for Schedule 8 development has been refused. One can be served whenever land is left incapable of reasonably beneficial use, including after the refusal of Schedule 8 development. Once a purchase notice has been served and accepted, the valuation rules are those of the Land Compensation Act 1961. The planning assumptions to be made are those of Sections 14–17 of that Act. See Chapter 9.

There are two distinct stages to be thought about. The first is whether the land has been rendered incapable of reasonably beneficial use, and here one ignores the possibility of carrying out New Development. Once that stage has been passed, and a valid purchase notice resorted to, one moves on to the second stage, which is to prepare the valuation for the purchase. At this stage one takes account of the planning assumptions, by virtue of which it may be that the purchase price paid by the acquiring authority will include the value of New Development.

The following is a summary of paragraphs 4–6 of Circular 26/69 which relate to reasonably beneficial use.

1. The question in each case is whether the land in its existing stage, and taking account of operations and uses for which planning permission or listed building consent are not needed, is incapable of reasonably beneficial use.
2. No account shall be taken of:
   (a) Any prospective use which would involve carrying out New Development.

   (b) Works for which listed building consent would be needed, unless such consent has been promised by the local planning authority or the Secretary of State.
   (c) A use which would be beneficial to someone other than the owner or prospective purchaser of the land.
3. Relevant factors when considering the land's capacity for use:
   (a) The physical state of the land.
   (b) Its size, shape and surroundings.
   (c) The general pattern of uses in the area.
   (d) A use of relatively low value may be beneficial if such a use is common for similar land in the vicinity.
   (e) It may be possible to render a small piece of land capable of reasonably beneficial use by using it in conjunction with some larger parcel—provided, in most cases, that the latter is owned by the owner or prospective purchaser of the small piece.
4. Valuation evidence:
   (a) Profit from the land may be a useful test, but to point to an absence of profit is not conclusive evidence that the land has no beneficial use. The notion of reasonably beneficial use is not specifically identifiable with profit.
   (b) When considering whether land has become incapable of reasonably beneficial use a relevant test—in appropriate cases—is to consider the difference between the annual value of the land in its existing stte and the annual value if Schedule 8/18 development is undertaken.
   (c) A purchase notice is not intended as a remedy merely because an owner is unable to realise the full development value of his land—the prospect of New Development is to be disregarded. Compensation for the loss of New Development value as such is possible but is limited to the amount of the U.X.B.
5. "Land cannot be rendered capable of reasonably beneficial use by carrying out development for which planning permission has been granted or promised." Section 180 (1)(c).

   Such permission or promise must have been given before the service of the purchase notice. If neither permission nor promise has been given, but the local planning authority thinks that some type of development not sought in the application ought to be allowed and that this would render the land capable of reasonably beneficial use, it (the authority) should ask the Secretary of State to direct under Section 183 (3) that such a permission would be granted if asked for. Where such a direction is made, the Secretary of State will not confirm the purchase notice.

The following cases are of particular relevance:

R. v. *M.H.L.G. ex parte Chichester R.D.C.* [1960] 2 All E.R. 407.

General Estates Co Ltd v. *M.H.L.G.* (1965) 194 E.G. 201.

Trocette Property Co. Ltd v. *Greater London Council and London Borough of Southwark* (1974) 226 E.G. 1011.

R. E. H. Hayward, 1988

Chapter 11

MINERALS

It is normally possible to view the subject matter of a valuation be it land or buildings and thus to assess the various factors affecting value. Minerals, however, are hidden from view beneath the earth's surface and before a valuation is made tests must be carried out to ascertain the quantity and quality of the mineral which is present. It is beyond the scope of this chapter to pursue the extent and different types of tests that are involved.

For the minerals to be of value it must be possible to extract them and, having done so, to process them to bring them into a fit state for marketing. Thus the mining engineering problems and their solutions will affect the value of the minerals.

Also the mineral must be marketable. Whether this is possible or not often depends on the economics of extraction and processing and the cost of transporting the mineral to the market.

The valuer must understand the concepts involved in these three processes, weighing the various factors to arrive at an overall view of the risk involved.

Surface mineral extraction has been described as a use of land insofar as an existing use must give way to the use for mineral extraction. Usually this existing use can not be resumed when mineral extraction ceases. The extraction of the minerals necessarily destroys the use of the land for that purpose as the mineral extraction proceeds until finally no minerals remain and the land must be put to some other use or restored to its original use.

Minerals represent a commodity that can be sold rather than an asset from which an income can be derived. The shorter the period of extraction the more true this is. The valuation of minerals takes this into account either by treating the income from mining leases as a capital payment by instalments whereby when the minerals are exhausted they will have been paid for, or by providing for a sinking fund, which will replace the initial capital invested when the income from mineral extraction ceases.

Mining leases usually provide for three kinds of rent.

1. A surface rent in respect of surface occupied. This can vary in the case of surface mineral extraction according to the extent of land occupied.

2. A royalty rent which is payable for each tonne (or some other measure) of mineral extracted and sold.
3. A minimum rent which is payable regardless of the quantity of minerals extracted. (Sometimes called a certain rent or dead rent.)

Usually the royalties merge with the minimum rent. That is no payment is made for the initial tonnage each year up to a figure equivalent to the minimum rent. Thus the sum of the royalty rent and the minimum rent will be equal to the total tonnage at the royalty rate.

Where the royalties are less than the minimum rent the difference between the two is known as the shortworkings and it is often provided in a lease that shortworkings should be recouped (i.e. deducted) from subsequent overworkings. The overworkings are the excess of royalties over the minimum rent and occasionally payments of minimum rent can be made out of accrued overworkings.

On page 329 is a typical table that can be used to calculate the amount due to a mineral royalty owner:

Finally, one of the most important functions of a valuer is to advise on value taking account of legislation which affects landed property; similarly the mineral valuer must be aware of any special legislation affecting minerals. Below is a list of the more important legislation which must be considered in a mineral valuation:

Railway Clauses Consolidation Act 1845
Waterworks Clauses Act 1847
Public Health Act 1875 (Support of Sewers) Amendment Act 1883
Mines (Working Facilities and Support) Act 1923
Water Act 1945
Finance Act 1970 (Taxation of Mineral Royalties)
Income Tax Act 1970 (Mineral Depletion Allowances)
The Mineral Workings Acts 1951 and 1971 (Ironstone Restoration Fund)
The Coal Industry Act 1975

Study 1

The freeholder of an area of land containing limestone has been approached by the lessee who wishes to purchase the freehold interest. The lessee is the operator of a quarry which is capable of producing 400,000 tonnes per annum and has proven reserves of 5 million tonnes with possible further reserves of 3 million tonnes. The expected output over the next four years will be 150,000, 200,000,

Year	Minimum rent	Amount of royalties	Shortworkings in year	Overworkings in year	Shortworkings recouped in year	Total shortworkings to date	Overworkings set off in year	Total overworkings to date	Amount due
1	2,000	1,000	1,000	—	—	2,000	—	—	2,000
2	2,000	2,000	—	—	—	3,000	—	—	2,000
3	2,000	4,000	—	2,000	—	3,000	—	—	2,000
4	2,000	5,000	—	3,000	2,000	1,000	—	2,000	4,000
5	2,000	5,000	—	3,000	1,000	—	—	5,000	5,000
6	2,000	6,000	—	4,000	—	—	—	9,000	6,000
7	2,000	1,000	1,000	—	—	—	1,000	8,000	2,000

250,000, and 350,000 tonnes respectively, building up to full production by the fifth year. Approximately two hectares of surface land are occupied for the purpose of processing limestone.

The terms of the lease are:

Total area included in lease	50 ha
Rent for surface land occupied	£70 per ha p.a.
Minimum rent	£20,000 p.a.
Average clause & shortworkings clause	
Royalties: first 200,000 tonnes p.a.	12p/tonne
remainder	10p/tonne

Term 25 years unexpired with no break clause
Restoration: area to be restored to agricultural use or a fine of £2,000 per ha in lieu of restoration.

If there are shortworkings to date of £21,000 advise the lessor of his freehold interest value in the 50 ha.

Life of quarry

		tonnes
		tonnes
Proven reserves		5,000,000
Less next 4 years workings	150,000	
	200,000	
	250,000	
	350,000	
	———	950,000
Reserves when full production commences		4,050,000
Divided by annual output		400,000
		10·125 years remaining
Possible reserves		3,000,000
Divided by annual output		400,000
		7·5 years remaining

Royalty values

		£	£
Year 1	150,000 at 12p		18,000
Year 2	200,000 at 12p		24,000
Year 3	200,000 at 12p	24,000	
	50,000 at 10p	5,000	29,000
Year 4	200,000 at 12p	24,000	
	150,000 at 10p	15,000	39,000
Years 5–21	200,000 at 12p	24,000	
	200,000 at 10p	20,000	44,000
Year 22	200,000 at 12p	24,000	
	50,000 at 10p	5,000	29,000
			(1)

(1)

Recoupment

Year	Royalty value £	Minimum rent £	Short workings £	Over workings £	Shorts to date £	Amount due £	
1	18,000	20,000	2,000	—	23,000	20,000	
2	24,000	20,000	—	4,000	19,000	20,000	
3	29,000	20,000	—	9,000	10,000	20,000	
4	39,000	20,000	—	19,000	—	29,000	(2)
5	44,000	20,000	—	24,000	—	44,000	
6	44,000	20,000	—	24,000	—	44,000	
21	44,000	20,000	—	24,000	—	44,000	
22	29,000	20,000	—	9,000	—	29,000	
23	—	20,000	20,000	—	20,000	20,000	
24	—	20,000	20,000	—	40,000	20,000	
25	—	20,000	20,000	—	60,000	20,000	

Lessor's interest

	£ p.a.	£	
Minimum rent	20,000		
Y.P. 22 years at 12 & 2½% (Tax at 40%)	5·63	112,600	(3)
add minimum rent years 23–25	20,000		
Y.P. 3 years at 15 & 2½% (Tax at 40%)	1·45		
P.V. £1 in 22 years at 15%	0·05	0·07	1,400	(4)
Royalties			(5)
add			
Years 4–22	4,000		
Y.P. 18 years at 14 & 2½% (Tax at 40%)	4·66		
P.V. £1 in 3 years at 14%	0·67	3·12	12,480	(6)
Year 4	5,000		
Y.P. 1 year at 15 & 2½% (Tax at 40%)	0·55		
P.V. £1 in 3 years at 15%	0·66	0·36	1,800	(7)
Years 5–21	20,000		
Y.P. 16 years at 16 & 2½% (Tax 40%)	4·06		
P.V. £1 in 4 years at 16%	0·55	2·23	44,600	(8)
Year 22	5,000		
Y.P. 1 year at 16 & 2½% (Tax at 40%)	0·55		
P.V. £1 in 20 years at 16%	0·05	0·02	100	
add rent for land occupied 2 ha at £70	140		
Y.P. 25 years at 6%	12·78	1,789	(9)
add reversion of lease area to agric.			
50 ha at £60 per ha p.a.	3,000		
Y.P. on perp. deferred 25 years at 6%	3·88	11,640	
add fine 50 ha at £2,000	100,000		
P.V. £1 in 25 years at 12%	0·06	6,000	(10)
Deduct cost of restoration			

50 ha at say £4,000	200,000		
P.V. £1 in 25 years at 10%	0·09	18,000	(11)
Total		174,409	

Capital value say £174,400.

Notes

(1)
	tonnes
Proved reserves	4,050,000
Possible reserves	3,000,000
	7,050,000
less 17 years working at 400,000 p.a.	6,800,000
Final year	250,000

(2) Amount due being minimum rent plus difference between excess workings and shortworkings to date.
i.e. £20,000 plus (£19,000 minus £10,000)

(3) Minimum rent considered at risk rate of 12% as it is less than 50% of expected income *and* assured.

(4) The quarry will not be working during this period therefore the minimum rent is not so secure.

(5) The minimum rent will be paid whether the quarry is producing or not, but royalties are paid on output which from the lessor's point of view is not so secure as the minimum rent therefore the royalties are given a higher risk rate.

(6) Similarly the royalties on the first 200,000 tonnes at 12p per tonne are more certain than those at 10p.

(7) The remainder after deduction of minimum rent and the part of the royalty included above. The risk is not so high as the following years but higher than the first 200,000 tonnes of output.

(8) The royalties over and above the first 200,000 tonnes.

(9) Single rate as land is not a wasting asset and can be returned to agricultural use.

(10) If the operator has the choice he would opt to pay a fine rather than restore because of the cost. The risk can be compared to that for the minimum rent.

(11) The lessor would restore to agricultural land.

Study 2 (see also Study 21 on page 380)

Sandylands Farm is beside a major road some 25 km from Bigtown. It is some 100 ha in extent and it has been proved that a deposit of sand and gravel 7 metres thick underlies an average of 2·5 metres of overburden. The sand and gravel contains approximately 75% sand, 25% gravel. The farm is owned by Sandyland Quarrying Co. freehold.

Concrete Aggregates Ltd have a quarry which they hold under a lease which commenced on 1st April two years after the valuation list was made for a term of 21 years, certain rent £1,000 p.a., royalty 23p/tonne. The sand and gravel at the quarry is 7 metres thick with overburden 2 metres thick and is contaminated by clay inclusions which cause processing difficulties.

XYZ Quarrying Co. have a sand and gravel quarry which is situated 40 km from Bigtown and is reached by narrow twisting roads and country lanes. The sand and gravel is of good quality some 6 metres thick underlying 7 metres of overburden. It is not known whether the quarry is held freehold or under lease but it is known that the output averages 20,000 tonnes per annum and the valuation list shows an assessment of £34,000 net annual value: £18,000 rateable value.

Sandyland Quarrying Co. have just completed the erection of a sand and gravel processing plant and intend to open a new quarry. On the assumption that the annual output will be 225,000 tonnes what is the probable rating assessment?

Analysis of information

Concrete Aggregates Ltd

Lease details accord with statutory definition of Net Annual Value.

	per tonne	
Royalty payable	23p	(1)
Adjust for increase in value between date of valuation list and lease—2 years	−4p	(2)
	19p	
Adjust for non-disability—clay inclusions	+1p	(3)
Equivalent royalty for "tone of list"	20p	(4)

XYZ Quarrying Co.

Figure in list £34,000 net annual value: £18,000 rateable value (5)

M.V. + B.P.V. = Net annual value

Where M.V. = royalty value × output

B.P.V. = value of buildings and plant

and $\frac{1}{2}$ M.V. + B.P.V. = rateable value   (5)

Subtracting $\frac{1}{2}$M.V. = net annual value − rateable value

Substituting $\frac{1}{2}$M.V. = £16,000

So   M.V. = £32,000

But output is 200,000 tonnes so royalty value is

£32,000 divided by 200,000 = 16p per tonne

But adjust for distance from market   10%

   and adverse overburden ratio   10%

Equivalent "tone of list" royalty = 20p per tonne.

Valuation of Sandylands quarry

Equivalent "tone of list" royalty is 20p per tonne.

   As there are no disabilities the royalty value of Sandylands Farm quarry is taken as 20p per tonne.

Buildings, plant and machinery   (6)

	Area in square metres	Rate per square metre £	£	£
Buildings:				
Store	21·7	25	540	
Workshops	70·4	30	2,100	
Pumphouse	13·0	20	260	
Messroom	33·0	25	825	
Office	12·6	30	380	
Weigh office	22·1	35	775	
Switchhouse	4·0	30	120	
Switchhouse	22·0	30	660	
Oil store	6·3	20	125	
Switchhouse	7·5	30	225	
Cabin	2·0	20	40	
				6,050
Plant:				
Feed hopper and foundations 25 tonne capacity			1,100	
Conveyor structure and supports 23 metres run			470	
Supports for washer			475	
Conveyor structure and supports 63 metres run			945	

ditto 85 metres run	850		
ditto 51 metres run	945		
Catwalk 36 metres run	360		
Support for pump	280		
Hoppers—8 in number each 70 tonne capacity	11,200		
Supports for crusher	250		
Sand separator tower	3,000		
Feed hopper capacity 12 tonne	240		
Conveyor structure and support 45 metres run	795		
Hoppers—3 in number each 70 tonne capacity	4,200		
Supports for pipeline 2 at £15	30		
Pumps 2	500		
Pit for weighbridge	500		
Electrical equipment	1,500		
		27,640	
Total effective capital value		33,690	
at 5% net annual value			£1,684

Valuation

		£	
Net annual value of right to extract mineral 225,000 tonnes at 20p	(a)	45,000	(1)
Buildings, plant and machinery		1,684	
Net annual value		46,684	
Less 50% of (a) per Article 4 of Mines and Quarries (Valuation) Order, 1971		22,500	(5)
Rateable value		£24,184	

Notes

(1) The rent for the purpose of arriving at the statutory definition of net annual value is, for the purpose of mineral producing hereditaments, taken to be the royalty value of the mineral multiplied by the appropriate annual output.

(2) Assuming that the valuation at the date of the proposal would result in a higher value because of inflation.
(3) The analysis aims to arrive at the rent which would be payable in respect of a comparative hereditament without disabilities. It is, therefore, necessary to add back any allowances which would have been made because of actual disabilities—in this case for the additional cost of separating the clay from the sand and gravel.
(4) The royalty value which would have been payable for a quarry free of disabilities which equates with the rating hypothesis for truly comparable hereditaments.
(5) By virtue of Article 4 of the Mines and Quarries (Valuation) Order, 1971 that part of the net annual value of a mineral producing hereditament which is attributable to the occupation of land for the purpose of winning, working, crushing, grading of minerals is to be reduced by half to arrive at the rateable value for that part. This reduction is applied to the royalties as they are payments for those purposes but it is not applied to that part of the net annual value relating to buildings, plant and machinery for the obverse reason.
(6) Buildings, plant and machinery situated on mines and quarries are valued using the "contractor's test" method of valuation.

Study 3

A mineral operator owns an area of land with the underlying gypsum some 80 ha in extent. Approximately 16·5 ha have been worked out by surface extraction methods and 4 ha are used for processing the gypsum, leaving 59·5 ha to be worked.

The gypsum is 4·5 metres thick and it is anticipated that 5 ha of land will be excavated each year.

A motorway is to be constructed over the unworked portion of land and a Compulsory Purchase Order has been made in respect of 5 ha of land. What is the owner's claim for compensation?

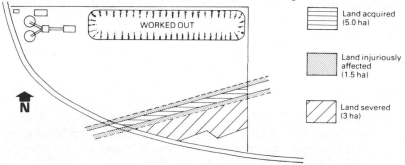

WORKED OUT

N

Land acquired (5.0 ha)

Land injuriously affected (1.5 ha)

Land severed (3 ha)

Land acquired

	£ p.a.	£	£
Area 5·0 ha			
5·0 ha at £5,000			25,000 (1)
Injurious affection			
1·5 ha at £5,000		(2)	
Less agricultural value 1·5 at £2,000		3,000	4,500 (3)
Severance			
Area 3·0 ha			
3·0 ha at £5,000		15,000	(4)
Less agricultural value 3·0 at £2,000		6,000	9,000 (3)
			(5)
Disturbance			
Annual value of plant	45,000		
Y.P., 2 years at 16 & 2½% (Tax at 40%)	1·02	45,900	
Break up value at closure	30,000		
P.V. £1 in 2 years at 16%	0·7		
Gain because of disturbance (£30,000–£21,000)	21,000	9,000	
		36,900	
P.V. £1 in 10 years at 16%		0·2	7,380
Total claim			£45,880

Notes

(1) Comparable transactions have been analysed and adjustments made for differences between them and the land being considered. A figure of £5,000 per hectare is indicated, including the minerals.

(2) The motorway must be supported on either side which means that a strip of minerals either side can not be worked. These minerals are not acquired but their value is injuriously affected by the acquisition to the extent that it is totally eliminated.

(3) On the south side of the motorway the land injuriously affected and the land severed (see note 4) will continue to be used for agricultural purposes. The loss suffered, therefore, for those portions is the mineral value less the agricultural value.

(4) The piece of land to the south of the motorway. Neither the planning authority nor the economics of extraction will permit the working of this small area in isolation and there are no

prospects of it being worked with other adjacent land. The cost of providing a bridge over the motorway is in excess of £25,000.

(5) The loss of 9·5 ha of land means that the processing plant will reach the end of its useful life two years earlier than it would have done but for the motorway. That is, at the end of the tenth year instead of at the end of the twelfth. The acquisition is, therefore, the direct cause of the loss of the annual value of the plant for that period. However, the break up value of the plant will be realised two years earlier so the actual loss suffered will be reduced by the difference between the two. The loss will be deferred ten years which is the life of the reserves remaining to be worked after the acquisition.

Compulsory purchase and compensation under the "mining codes"

The Railway Clauses Consolidation Act 1845 Sections 77–85 known as the "mining code" introduced a code of practice regulating the right of support of railways from the underlying minerals.

Briefly, the code requires a mine owner, who can be the owner, lessee or occupier of the minerals, to serve a "notice of approach" to a railway company when any workings reach forty yards distance from any railway, buildings or works and if the railway company requires the minerals to remain unworked to support the railway then they must serve a "counter notice" requiring support and pay compensation to the mine owner for the minerals unworked. The amount of compensation is the loss suffered by the owner by virtue of leaving the minerals unworked plus any additional expense incurred.

Similar "mining codes" are incorporated in other enactments such as the Waterworks Clauses Act 1948, Public Health Act 1875 (Support of Sewers), Amendment Act 1883, Public Health Act 1936 and Water Act 1945. There is statutory provision for the "mining code" to apply to land and buildings that are included in compulsory purchase orders.

The "mining code" was amended by Part II of the Mines (Working Facilities and Support) Act 1923, so far as it applies to railways, providing for the mine owner to serve the "notice of approach" and determines an area of protection, being the width of the protected works plus a distance of forty yards or half the depth of the seam whichever is the greater. The area of protection is divided into an inner area and outer area, the inner area being the width of the protected works plus forty yards, the remainder being the outer area. The compensation is to be assessed separately for the mine owner and the royalty owner and is specified at a rate per tonne for the whole area and payable at 100% for the inner area and $33\frac{1}{3}$% for the outer area.

It should be noted, however, that if the mine owner has a right to work and withdraw support then all the minerals are deemed to be within the inner area.

Study 4

Mining code

A railway company wishes to obtain a pillar of support for a length of track with associated buildings and has served a "counter notice" to a "notice of approach" served under the Mines (Working Facilities and Support) Act 1923 by the lessee of a seam of fluorspar. The lessee is a substantial operator making a net profit of £5 per tonne. The relevant terms of the lease are—royalty 25p per tonne; minimum rent £2,000 per annum; there is an average clause; prior to the acquisition of the land by the railway company there was a right to work the fluorspar but not to let down the surface.

The buildings to be supported measure 50 metres by 50 metres and are located in a built-up area. The fluorspar workings are at a depth of 100 metres and it has been agreed that the loss of minerals over the next 4 years will be as follows:

Next year: 1,000 tonnes within the inner area and
             2,400 tonnes within the outer area of the proposed pillar of support

Year 2:   1,200 tonnes within the inner area and
             2,700 tonnes within the outer area

Year 3:   1,700 tonnes with the inner area and
             3,000 tonnes within the outer area

Year 4:   1,500 tonnes within the inner area and
             2,550 tonnes within the outer area of the proposed pillar of support

In addition, it has been agreed that there will be 24,000 tonnes of unworkable fluorspar which would have been worked over a period of 3 years after the minerals in the proposed pillar of support had been extracted.

It will also be necessary to spend £20,000 on extra precautionary underground works to support surrounding property which would otherwise suffer damage from the premature cessation of working.

Advise both the freeholder and the operator of the fluorspar of their claims for compensation from the railway company for the proposed sterilization of the fluorspar.

Lessee's claim

	£	£	
1,000 at £5	5,000		(1)
2,400 at £1·67	4,000		(2)
	9,000		
P.V. £1 1 year at 15%	0·869	7,821	(3)
Add Year 2			
1,200 at £5	6,000		(1)
2,700 at £1·67	4,500		(2)
	10,500		
P.V. £1 2 years at 15%	0·756	7,938	(3)
Add Year 3			
1,700 at £5	8,500		(1)
3,000 at £1·67	5,000		(2)
	13,500		
P.V. £1 3 years at 15%	0·657	8,869	(3)
Add Year 4			
1,500 at £5	7,500		(1)
2,550 at £1·67	4,250		(2)
	11,750		
P.V. £1 4 years at 15%	0·572	6,721	(3)
Add Remainder			
8,000 at £5	40,000 p.a.		(4)
Y.P. 3 years at 15%	2·283		(5)
P.V. £1 4 years at 15%	0·572 1·13	52,235	
Compensation for minerals		83,584	

Plus

Cost of extra work incurred to prevent damage to property on perimeter of proposed pillar	20,000	(6)

Plus

Expense incurred by interruption to present workings and extra development work, say	5,000	(7)
Total claim	£101,549	

Freeholder's claim

	£	£	
Year 1			
1,000 at £0·25	250		(1)
2,400 at £0·25 / 3	200		(2)
	450		
P.V. £1 1 year at 14%	0·877	395	(8)
Add Year 2			
1,200 at £0·25	300		(1)
2,700 at £0·25 / 3	225		(2)
	525		
P.V. £1 2 year at 14%	0·769	404	(8)
Add			
1,700 at £0 25	125		(1)
3,000 at £0·25 / 3	250		(2)
	675		
P.V. £1 3 years at 14%	0·675	456	(8)
Add			
1,500 at £0·25	375		(1)
2,550 at £0·25 / 3	212		(2)
	587		
P.V. £1 4 year at 14%	0·592	347	(8)
Add			
8,000 at £0·25		2,000 p.a.	(4)
Y.P. 3 years at 14%	2·322		(5)
P.V. £1 5 years at 14%	0·519 1·205	2,410	(8)
Total claim		£4,012	

Notes

(1) The inner area at full value.
(2) The outer area at ⅓rd value.
(3) The compensation is for loss of profit and not for loss of return on an investment and therefore there is no sinking fund element required to recoup investment capital.

(4) 24,000 tonnes over 3 years represents an annual tonnage of 8,000.
(5) As in (3) above, income equal over 3 years therefore Y.P. single rate.
(6) The cost will be incurred immediately.
(7) Additional compensation under the "Mining Code".
(8) The risk is not as high for the royalty owner, he would receive a minimum rent irrespective of whether the minerals were worked or not.

Study 5

Discounted cash flow

On the basis that the operator wishes to purchase the minerals in Study 1. Assuming that the *net* profit will be 15p per tonne, the operator requires his capital to earn 14%, the estimated cost of restoration will be £4,000 per hectare and part of the restoration will take place after 10 years.

Year	Net cash flow £	Discounting factor at 14%	Discounted cash flow £	
1	+ 22,500	0·877	+ 19,732	
2	+ 30,000	0·769	+ 23,070	
3	+ 37,500	0·675	+ 25,312	
4	+ 52,500	0·592	+ 31,080	
5–21	+ 60,000			
	6·373			(1)
	+382,380	0·592	+226,369	(2)
22	+ 37,500	0·056	+ 2,100	
10	−100,000	0·270	− 27,000	(3)
23	−100,000	0·049	− 4,900	(3)
23	+ 50,000	0·049	+ 2,450	(4)

The company can afford to offer £298,213 for the interest in the minerals and earn 14% interest on their capital, but the capital will be written off at the end of the project as there has not been any payment into a sinking fund. The figure of £174,409 in Study 1 represents the value to the royalty owner whereas £298,213 represent the maximum that the operator can offer in order to earn 14% on his capital.

Notes

(1) Y.P. for 17 years single rate tables in preference to using P.V. of £1 tables for 17 years.
(2) Discounted to the start of the 5th year, therefore, P.V. £1 in 4 years.
(3) Assuming 25 hectares restored.
(4) Capital value of reversion to agriculture i.e. from Study 1:

Rental value	£3,000 p.a.	
Y.P. in perp. at 6%	16·66	£50,000

Compensation for mineral planning decisions

Consequent to the Town and Country Planning (Minerals) Act 1981 and the Town and Country Planning (Compensation for Restrictions on Mineral Workings) Regulations 1985 there is a special planning regime which applies only to mineral working.

Part of this regime provides for:

(a) the extension of the provisions of Section 5 of the Town and Country Planning Act 1971 enabling orders for the discontinuance of any use of land to include the discontinuance of development consisting of the winning and working minerals;
(b) the making of orders requiring steps to be taken for the protection of the environment where the winning and working of minerals has been temporarily suspended (suspension orders); and
(c) the making of orders prohibiting the resumption of working and requiring removal of plant and machinery, alleviating injury to amenity, requiring compliance with planning conditions, and requiring restoration where the winning and working of minerals has permanently ceased (prohibition orders).

Suspension and prohibition orders

The provisions in respect of suspension and prohibition orders are now embodies in Section 51A and Section 51B of the Town and Country Planning Act 1971.

Discontinuance, modification and revocation orders

The provisions for discontinuance, modification and revocation orders are contained in Section 45 and Section 51 of the Act of 1971. As in the case of suspension and prohibition orders the Town and Country Planning (Compensation for Restrictions on Mineral Working) Regulations 1985 modifies the Act of 1971 provisions for compensation consequent to the making of discontinuance, modification and revocation orders as they apply to minerals. The special mineral compensation provisions apply only where the requirements set out in Section 170B and Section 164A are satisfied.

In the case of a discontinuance order compensation, the special mineral compensation applies where the following requirements are satisfied:

(a) Where the order imposes conditions on the continuance of the use of land for the winning and working of minerals or requires that buildings, plant or machinery used for the winning and working of minerals be altered or removed.
(b) The development consisting of the winning and working of minerals began more than five years before the date of the order.
(c) The order does not impose any restriction on the winning and working of minerals or modify or replace any such restriction already imposed.
(d) Where the minerals planning authority carries out special consultations about the making and terms of the order.
(e) It is more than five years since the last order was made.

The meaning of "impose ... imposed" in (c) above is defined in Section 178C as being any provision:

(a) as the expiration of the period before which development consisting of the winning and working of minerals was to begin;
(b) as to the size of the area to be used for the winning and working of minerals;
(c) as to the depth to which operations for the winning and working of minerals were to extend;
(d) as to the rate at which any particular mineral was to be extracted;
(e) as to the period at the expiration of which the winning and working of minerals was to cease; or
(f) as to the total quantity of minerals to be extracted.

Where the special compensation provisions apply the ordinary Section 170 compensation is reduced by deducting from it the appropriate portion of £5,000.

Where the person making a claim is the only person with an interest in the site then the appropriate portion is 100%. That is the whole of the £5,000 is deducted from the valuation. Where more than one person has an interest in the site the deduction is arrived at according to the formula:

$$£5,000 \times \frac{p}{t}$$

where t is the total value of the site and p is the value of the claimant's interest in the site.

Compensation where a discontinuance, modification or revocation order is made

First of all the compensation payable in the ordinery case is assessed.

The regulations apply where the conditions set out above are satisfied. The special compensation provisions in the regulations have the effect of reducing the ordinary compensation payable under Section 170 or Section 164 as the case may, by deducting from it the greater of the sum of £2,500 or £X provided that the deduction shall not be more than the appropriate proportion (see above) of £100,000, and there:

$$X = AV \times RP \times S2 \times \frac{10}{100}$$

Annual value
AV is the annual value as calculated in accordance with Schedule 1 of the regulations by reference to the net annual value and the rateable value of the rating hereditament which the site comprises, or forms part of. It is possible to separate that part of the net annual value which applies to the winning, working, grading, washing, grinding and crushing of minerals. This is done by taking the difference between the net annual and the rateable values (as shown in the valuation list) and multiplying it by two. This is the annual value (AV).

Indexation of the annual value
The formula includes an element of indexation to bring the values in the valuation list, which was prepared in 1973, to present day

values. The RP in the formula is the figure arrived at by multiplying the retail price index for the month in which the order took effect by 0·0108225 rounded off to two decimal places.

Capitalisation of annual value
The annual value is capitalised having regard to the reserves of minerals unworked and the annual rate of extraction—that is the estimated life of the site. Schedule 2 contains a table showing the estimated life and the multiplier. Section 2 in the formula is the appropriate multiplier for the estimated life.

The estimated life is found by dividing the quantity of minerals left unworked in the site by the annual rate of extraction.

Study 6

A minerals planning authority has made an order modifying a planning permission for the extraction of sand and gravel. The order imposes a new condition requiring the construction of a new quarry entrance with associated landscaping treatment. The cost of the additional work is £50,000, the valuation list shows an entry in respect of the quarry at £35,000 NAV £20,000 RV, and there are 1,200,000 tonnes of sand and gravel remaining to be worked and the annual rate of output is 230,000 t.p.a. The retail price index is 381·2.

Compensation

	£	£	
Expenditure on abortive work		5,000	
Additional work due to order:			
Landscaping	20,000		
Change in access road	30,000		
	———	50,000	(1)
Ceiling			
Annual value			
(NAV £35,000 − RV £20,000) × 2	30,000		(2)
Index RPI × ·0108225 =			
381·2 × ·0108225	=	4·13	
Multiplier			
Quantity of mineral unworked			
1,200,000 t			
Annual rate of extraction 230,000 t			
Estimated life 1,200,000/230,000	=	5·22 yrs	
Multiplier	=	3·3 ———	(3)
		55,000	

	B/F 55,000	
Deduction		
$30,000 \times 4{\cdot}13 \times 3{\cdot}3 \times {\cdot}10$	40,887	(4)
Compensation payable	£9,113	

Notes

(1) See Chapter 10 Compensation for Planning Restrictions.
(2) See Town and Country Planning (Compensation for Restrictions on Mineral Working) Regulations 1985, Sechedule 1, paras 4, 5, and 6.
(3) See Town and Country Planning (Compensation for Restrictions on Mineral Working) Regulations 1985, Schedule.
(4) See Town and Country Planning (Compensation for Restrictions on Mineral Working) Regulations 1985, Reg. 6.

Chapter 12

RATING

When I came to the revision of this chapter for the third edition of the book I considered the current state of rating as a local tax, and also sought the opinions of practitioners, as well as academic colleagues who use the book for their students. The concensus that emerged was that any revision of worked examples would be premature. The reasons were that the 1973 Valuation List is still in force and will remain so until the proposed re-valuation of non-domestic property comes into force in 1990; that the examples in the chapter are to demonstrate methods rather than to reflect current values and that rating of dwellings was still in limbo due to political vacillation. So, with all the foregoing in mind I decided to leave the chapter much as before.

The aim of all methods of assessing property to rates is to find the annual rental value of the property; it is the occupier of the property who is rated (except in very rare cases, see Part IV of the General Rate Act 1967) and the measure of value of that occupation is the annual rent. This annual rent is subject to certain conditions depending on whether the property is to be assessed to Gross Value (G.V.) or Net Annual Value (N.A.V.).

Gross value is defined in Section 19 of the General Rate Act 1967 (G.R.A. 1967) and briefly is the annual rent the property would command in its existing state with the landlord carrying out repairs and the tenant paying all other outgoings. Net annual value is also defined in Section 19 of G.R.A. 1967 as the annual rent with the tenant carrying out all repairs and paying all outgoings.

Since it but rarely happens that property is let on exactly these terms actual market rents have to be adjusted to bring them into line with the appropriate statutory definition.

The date at which properties are valued is that at which the current Valuation List came into force; at the time of writing this is 1 April 1973. In practical terms however values usually reflect market rents current in the year before the coming into force of the list. For properties brought into assessment after the date of the list and those altered after that date, Section 20 of G.R.A. 1967 provides that they shall be valued on the "tone of the list", that is, by reference to the level of values appearing in the current Valuation List.

To decide which class of property is valued to G.V. and which to N.A.V. it is necessary to consult Section 19 of G.R.A. 1967 but the following guide may be of help.

Assessed to G.V.
Dwellings of all types; shops; offices; warehouses; schools; licensed premises; cinemas public buildings.

Assessed to N.A.V.
Factories; mineral properties; some petrol filling stations; sporting rights; some caravan sites.

The solecism of saying "Gross Annual Value" should be avoided south of the Scottish border; there is no such thing in English rating practice. Similarly "Gross Rateable Value" does not exist.

There are only three methods of valuing property for rating although there are other methods, usually formulae, for special properties which are not valuations but which nevertheless produce assessments. The three methods of valuation are:

Rental comparison by which market rents after adjustment by various means to comply with G.V. or N.A.V. terms as appropriate, are then analysed to produce a price per unit, usually a unit of area and that unit price applied pro rata to all other properties of the same sort judged by the valuer to be comparable to those from which the rental evidence was taken. If however there are no directly comparable properties it may be necessary to take the nearest available rental comparisons and by valuation skill adjust the pattern of values indicated by the rental evidence to allow for the differences. The rental comparison method is the best since it relies entirely upon market transactions. In the absence of these, one of the two other methods of valuation may have to be relied on. The vast majority of rateable property is valued by rental comparison or methods derived from it.

Contractors method in which it is assumed that the imaginary tenant in the absence of a suitable property to rent has bought land and thereon built the property to be rated, with his own or borrowed capital. This method of valuation takes the depreciated replacement cost of the existing building, adds to it the current value of the site and derives G.V. or N.A.V. by applying a percentage to the final total capital sum. In current practice a figure of either 6% or 5% respectively is not infrequently used.

Profits or accounts method. Certain properties cannot be valued by the contractors method in the absence of rental evidence and it may be apt to look at the accounts of the business carried on in the property so as to deduce from the profits of that business the amount that could be paid as rent and hence G.V. or N.A.V. Usually some form of monopoly or quasi-monopoly exists in such properties. The method entails taking the gross receipts of the business and deducting from them working expenses, leaving an amount known as the "divisible balance". From this is taken a sum called the "tenant's share" to give remuneration to the imaginary tenant for running the business, and the amount left after this deduction is the amount which the business can afford to pay in rent and rates for the occupation of the property. The rental figure is calculated from the amount left for rent and rates by a simple algebraic formula.

It should be noted that these three methods of valuation are not interchangeable. Over 95% of all properties are assessed by rental comparison and one cannot in rating law and practice seek to use either the contractors or the profits method merely because rental comparison is difficult to apply. Only in the total absence of valid rents is it correct to use one of the other methods.

The following are case studies and notes upon the methods of valuation of most of the types of property assessed to rates in England and Wales: the law and practices described apply neither to Scotland nor Ulster where law and practice, though similar, in each country has significant differences.

Typical rental valuations are shown in Case Studies Nos. 4, 5, 6, 7, 8, 9, 10 and 18, Contractors Method valuations in Case Studies Nos. 15, 16, 17, 22 and 23 and typical Profits valuations shown in Case Studies Nos. 11, 13, 19, 20, 24 and 25. All values are at approximately 1973 levels, since at the time of writing the 1973 Valuation List is still in force.

Dwellings

These form by far the largest class of property valued for rating; about 80% of the total in England and Wales, and present considerable difficulties for two main reasons. The first is that there is now and has been for many years almost no valid rental evidence, since all statutorily controlled rents are inadmissible and the second is that dwellings present a considerable array of sizes and types and occur in a wide variety of locations. The last time at which a substantial body of rental evidence was available for dwellings was the revaluation of 1956 which so far as dwellings were concerned was based upon rents current in 1939. These rents were analysed to a price per square foot either to reduced covered area (R.C.A.) found by taking the external dimensions of the house for each storey and totalling the areas this obtained, or to effective floor area (E.F.A.) found by taking the internal area of each room within the house. The results of these analyses after careful adjustment were applied to all comparable houses and additions were made for extras such as garages, central heating, and like matters. The value of these extras could often be deduced from rental evidence but in some cases had to be decided empirically.

Because of the absence of value rental evidence the revaluations of 1963 and 1973 so far as houses were concerned were achieved by applying "factors" or, in plain English, multipliers, to the assessments appearing in the previous list so that almost all rating assessments of dwellings can be traced back to the Valuation List of 1956 and hence to a rental pattern that emerged in 1939.

Study 1

Houses assessed for the 1973 valuation list

1. Detached house of good quality	£
R.C.A. 112 square metres at £4·50	504
Garage (brick/tile)	25
Full central heating	25
	554
Gross value, say	£555

2. Semi-detached house; average quality	
R.C.A. 93 square metres at £4	372
Pre-cast concrete garage	20
	392
Gross value, say	£390

3. Detached bungalow; average quality	
R.C.A. 83·6 square metres at £5	418
Central heating (part)	20
Garage (pre-cast concrete)	20
Garage (asbestos)	18
	476
Gross value, say	£475

4. Terraced house pre 1918 brick/slate construction
   R.C.A. 74·3 square metres at £2·50   186
   Add for conversion of 3rd
      bedroom to bathroom/w.c.   14
   ____
                                                200
   ____
   Gross value   £200
   ====

Caution is needed in applying this approach to very large houses and those in rural areas; the automatic application of a unit price/R.C.A. derived from small and medium sized houses to large ones, wherever situated, can result in absurd assessments emerging. Problems may also arise in assessing local authority houses although usually the basis used for privately owned and occupied houses can quite easily be used; it may sometimes be apt to make a deduction for "council house stigma" depending upon the circumstances.

The considerable problem of valuing large old and sometimes valuable rural houses remains. Frequently these are best valued on a "spot" basis based upon the valuer's skill and judgement and looking carefully at other assessments especially those of large houses in the outer suburbs of nearby towns, if such comparisons are available. Problems may also arise in the value of redundant upper floors.

Study 2

Detached house in rural area
   Late Victorian house; brick/tile construction; grounds and gardens of ca. 1 ha; all main services and full central heating

	£
R.C.A. 230 square metres, say	500
Garages (2)	45
Loose box and tack room	40
Stores	10
Greenhouses etc.	15
	610
Gross value, say	£600

Study 3

An alternative approach to the house in Study 2

	£
E.F.A. of ground and first floors	
150 square metres	300
Third floor, say	150
Central heating	75
Garages (2)	50
Outbuildings	30
	605
Gross value, say	£600

Large mansions and "stately homes" present yet other problems, not least of these being that the actual occupier may be the only possible tenant both in the rating hypothesis and in reality. The whole property may be used on a semi-commercial basis for visitors and only in part as a dwelling and if there are other attractions such as a safari park or like matters it may be that a valuation of the whole concern upon a profits basis will be appropriate. It should not be overlooked in making the assessment that the occupier who is also the owner might be only too glad to pay rent upon gross value terms since this would relieve him of an onerous repairing liability, and so his hypothetical bid should be considered.

Flats

Many of the same considerations that apply to house valuation apply to the valuation of flats; there are however some valid modern rents available and this class of property is usually valued by direct rental comparison. Care needs to be taken because of the wide differences in value between the extremes of the market; compare for example a luxury flat in the best part of a town with a poorly converted third floor in a decayed Victorian tenement house; yet both are flats. Again the process of adjustment and analysis of actual rents and valuation by applying a unit price, usually to E.F.A., is carried out. A complication is that rents for flats in a purpose built block (and sometimes elsewhere) may include items for landlords services, e.g. portering, heating and lighting of common parts, provision of lifts and sometimes central heating and hot water to the actual flats. The cost of these items less an amount for those items covered by Section 23 of G.R.A. 1967 is deducted from the gross rent. The items mentioned in Section 23 are cost of repairs etc. of the common parts, maintenance and insurance of the common parts and any profit made by the landlord on the provision of services.

Study 4

The assessment of flats in a modern purpose built block of 30 similar flats; each flat is 36 square metres E.F.A. Tenants are liable for rates and internal repairs; landlord liable for external repairs, cleaning, lighting and heating common parts, porters; lifts; central heating and hot water to each flat. The rent for each flat agreed one year ago is £525 p.a.

	£
Gross rents for block	15,750
Deduct for landlords services (1)	2,850
	12,900
Add for internal repairs to each flat say £25 p.a. (2)	750
Aggregate G.V.	13,650
Apportion between 30 similar flats	30
Gross value of each flat	£455

Analysis of G.V.   £12·6 per square metre E.F.A.

Notes

(1) This item is net of Section 23 items; see notes above.
(2) An adjustment to rents for repairing liability is often made by taking 10% for all repairs and 5% for internal repairs. This can lead to anomalies particularly when as sometimes happens the same rent passes for different size flats in the same block. A more accurate way is to assess each repairing liability according to the circumstances of each case.

Study 5

Valuation of an individual flat in a similar block but with flats of varying sizes.

	£
Gross rent for flat 45 square metres	665
Deduct for landlord's services (1)	119
	546
Add for internal repairs (2)	32
	578
Rent in G.V. terms	578
Gross value, say	£570

Analysis of G.V.   £12·6 per square metre E.F.A.

Notes

(1) This item is net of Section 23 items; the amount for each flat is found by dividing the gross amount for the block by the total E.F.A. of all the flats and applying the resultant figure per square metre to each flat.

(2) See note at (2) above.

Offices

Wide variations in type and location exist but all are valued by the normal method of rental comparison after adjusting market rents to G.V. terms as set out for flats; in the valuation of large modern offices many similar considerations apply as for flats especially in the adjustment for repairing liability, landlords services and the effects of Section 23 of G.R.A. 1967. A further point needing careful attention is the effect of the decision of the Lands Tribunal in the case of *British Bakeries* v. *Gudgion (V.O.) & Croydon L.B.C.* (1969) R.A. 465 in which it was held that demountable internal partitioning in a modern office block was rateable as plant. In letting such blocks either as one unit or floor by floor it is usual for the floors to be let without partitions, the tenants thereafter installing partitions to suit their own needs. The value of this partitioning, if it is considered to be rateable, must be reflected in the rent and hence in the G.V.; usually this can be done by increasing the unit price or by taking a percentage of the depreciated replacement cost of the partitions and adding this to the rent.

Study 6

Analysis and valuation of a suite of offices on 1st and 2nd floors above a bank in the High Street of a country town let to solicitors four years ago at £800 p.a., tenant doing internal repairs. E.F.A.; 1st floor 47 square metres; 2nd floor 45 square metres. Rents have risen by 10% in the last 4 years. No landlord's services.

Analysis

	£
Rent passing	800
Add for internal repairs (1)	50
Add for rental increase since lease was granted	80
Rent in G.V. terms	£930 p.a.

Either £930 p.a. for 92 square metres = £10·1 per square metre
Or 1st floor 47 square metres × 1 = 47·00
  2nd floor 45 square metres × $\frac{3}{4}$ = 33·75

  80·75

$$\frac{£930}{80·75} = £11·51 \text{ per square metre 1st floor}$$

£8·63 per square metre 2nd floor (i.e. $\frac{3}{4}$ of £11·51)

The second method of analysis should only be used if there is clear evidence that 2nd floors are achieving lower rents than otherwise comparable 1st floors and the ratio of 1:$\frac{3}{4}$ must in fact be obtained from such evidence.

Assessment

		£
First floor E.F.A. 47 square metres at £11·5		541
Second floor 45 square metres at £8·5		383
		924
Gross value, say		£925

Note

(1) A percentage addition for repairing liability would not be apt here; estimate annual expenditure at costs current at the date of valuation instead.

Study 7

Valuation of a large city centre office block "Meltown House" with 10 floors each of 500 square metres; lifts; central heating; 20 car parking spaces; owner occupied.

Rental evidence: "Station House"; a similar office block in a similar location. Eight floors each of 465 square metres; lifts; central heating; no car parking. Let 2 years ago with no internal partitions; there has been no marked increase in office rents since then.

G. and 1st floors: 20 year lease; reviews at 5 yearly intervals. Rent £20,000 p.a.; tenant doing internal repairs; separate service charge reviewed annually, currently £1,000 p.a.

2nd to 6th floors inclusive: each let separately on leases as above; rent for each floor £11,000 p.a.; current service charge per floor £500 p.a.

7th and 8th floors: let as one unit on lease as above; rent £13,000 p.a.; current service charge £1,000 p.a.

In all the above leases landlord provides lifts, portering, cleaning, heating and lighting of common parts and makes service charges as specified; these are reviewed annually.

Analysis of rents of "Station House"

		£ p.a.
G. and 1st floors lease rent		20,000
Add for internal repairs		1,000
	service charge	1,000
		22,000
Deduct proportion of service charge relating to common parts (1)		800
Rent in Gross Value terms 930 square metres at		£21,200

= £22·8 per square metre

		£ p.a.
2nd–6th floors lease rent per floor		11,000
Add for internal repairs		500　(2)
	service charge	500
		12,000

Deduct part of service charge as above	400
Rent in Gross Value terms 465 square metres at	£11,600

$= £24·95$ per square metre

7th and 8th floors lease rent	23,000
Add for internal repairs	1,000 (2)
service charge	1,000
	25,000
Deduct part of service charge	800
Rent in Gross Value terms 930 square metres at	£24,200

$= £26·00$ per square metre (4)

Notes

(1) This is in compliance with Section 23 G.R.A. 1967.
(2) It will be seen that the same repairing charge has been applied to each floor irrespective of the percentage it forms of the lease rent thus according with fact.
(3) In all the above leases it has been assumed that each occupier has minimal partitioning which is not included in the lease rents.
(4) It is not uncommon to find the top floors of an office building commanding higher rents than lower floors and especially the ground floor.

Valuation of "Meltown House" using rental evidence taken from the analysis of lettings at "Station House".

		£
Ground floor	500 square metres at £23	11,500
1st floor	500 square metres at £24	12,000
2nd–9th floor inc.	4,000 square metres at £25	100,000
10th floor	500 square metres at £26	13,000
		136,500

Add for partitioning installed at cost of £50,000 at 6%	3,000
20 car parking spaces at £50 (2)	1,000
	140,500
Gross value, say	£140,000

Notes

(1) It is assumed that there is clear evidence of demand for office blocks of such size and hence no quantity allowance is appropriate.

(2) This figure should be obtained from other lettings; if however the rental evidence comes from office blocks which include car parking this facility will have been allowed for in the rents and hence no further addition should be made.

Shops

Many variations exist but all shops can be valued by rental comparison. In order to facilitate comparison between shops of different sizes and frontages in the same street or precinct the method known as zoning has been used for many years. This is only a convenient way of analysing rents and synthesising valuations; it also helps to provide uniformity of assessment if in fact the rental evidence supports this. Zoning is based upon the premise that the front part of a shop is more valuable than the rear and although the values must diminish gradually from front to rear, for convenience the shops are divided into a number of bands or zones. Usually the depth of the zones is decided empirically but having some regard to the depth of the shallowest shop in the street. Whatever depth of zone is decided on should be maintained consistently throughout the whole street both in analysis and valuation. As before, rental evidence is converted to G.V. terms and the rent attributable to ancillaries such as upper parts, staff rooms etc. stripped from the rent leaving only the rent of the retail part of the premises. This sometimes presents difficulty especially if there is no evidence as to the rental value of these upper parts etc. and in such case empirical judgements may have to be made. The denuded rent of the retail shop is then analysed on the basis that the front zone "A" is worth the highest price per square metre, the next zone "B" is worth one half of the price per square metre of Zone A and the next zone

"C" is worth one quarter of the price per square metre of Zone A. Thus all shop rents if analysed on this basis can be expressed in terms of a price per Zone A. The whole process is known as "halving back".

Study 8

The following shops (illustrated in the diagram) are to be valued for rating in the High Street—the best shopping position—in a prosperous country town. There are similar shops opposite and on either side of those to be valued.

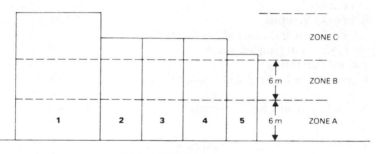

Shop 1: Frontage (F) 12·5 metres; Depth (D) 18·5 metres; 1st floor 12·5 metres × 18·5 metres.

Let one year ago on 20 year lease full repairing and insuring terms; 5 year reviews; developer's finish; £3,000 p.a. to national multiple.

Shop 2: F 6 metres; D 15 metres; 1st floor 6 metres × 15 metres.

Shop only, let one year ago on the same terms as Shop 1 to national multiple at £1,000 p.a. but on 25 year lease.

1st floor let as offices 10 years full repairing and insuring lease £270 p.a. one year ago.

Shops 3 and 4: Each F 6 metres; D 15 metres; 1st floor 6 metres × 15 metres.

Each shop and upper part owner-occupied by substantial local traders.

Shop 5: F 4·5 metres; D 12·5 metres.

Let one year ago on 20 year full repairing and insuring lease £1,275 p.a. 5 year reviews; fully fitted and with modern shop front.

1st floor, 4·5 metres × 2·5 metres, let as offices 7 year full repairing and insuring lease £170 p.a. one year ago.

Analysis of rents

	£
Shop 1	
Lease rent	3,000
Add for tenant's repairing liability	300
Annual equivalent of shop front and fittings by tenant at cost £5,000	

$$\frac{5,000}{\text{Y.P. 20 years 10 \& 4\%}} \quad \frac{5,000}{6} = \qquad 833$$

	£
(Tax at 40%)	—
Rent in G.V. terms	4,133
(1) Deduct rental value of 1st floor; the evidence of Shops 2 and 5 suggest that this is	
£3 per square metre × 231 square metres	693
Rent of shop only in G.V. terms	£3,440

Zone A 12·5 metres × 6 metres = 75 square metres × 1   = 75·0
Zone B 12·5 metres × 6 metres = 75 square metres × ½   = 37·5
Zone C 12·5 metres × 6·5 metres = 81·5 square metres × ¼ = 20·3

Shop area in Zone A terms (I.T.Z.A.)   132·8 sq m

Lease rent in G.V. terms

$$\frac{£3,440}{132·8} = £25·9 \text{ per square metre in Zone A terms}$$

	£
Shop 2	
Lease rent	1,000
Add for tenant's repairing liability	100
Annual equivalent of shop front and fitting by tenant at cost £1,000	

$$\frac{1,000}{\text{Y.P. 25 years 10 and } 2\frac{1}{2}\%} \quad \text{(Tax at 40\%)}$$

$$= \frac{1,000}{6·7} \qquad\qquad 150$$

	£
Rent in G.V. terms	£1,250

Zone A 6 metres × 6 metres = 36 square metres × 1 = 36
Zone B 6 metres × 6 metres = 36 square metres × $\frac{1}{2}$ = 18
Zone C 6 metres × 3 metres = 18 square metres × $\frac{1}{4}$ = 4·5

Shop area in Zone A terms   58·5 sq m

Lease rent in G.V. terms $\dfrac{£1,250}{58·5} =$

£21·4 per square metre in Zone A terms

Lease rent of 1st floor   270
Add for repairs   30

Rent in G.V. terms   £300

6 metres × 15 metres = 90 square metres = £3·3 per square metre

Shop 5   £
Lease rent (2)   1,275
Add for tenant's repairing liability   130

Rent in G.V. terms   £1,405

Zone A 6 metres × 4·5 metres   = 27 square metres × 1 = 27
Zone B 6·5 metres × 4·5 metres = 30 square metres × $\frac{1}{2}$ = 15 (3)

                                             42 sq m

Lease rent in G.V. terms $\dfrac{£1,405}{42} =$

£33·4 per square metre in Zone A terms (I.T.Z.A.)

Lease rent of 1st floor   170
Add for repairs   20

Rent in G.V. terms   £190

4·5 metres × 12·5 metres = 56·25 square metres =£3·3 per square metre.

Notes

(1) In order to arrive at this conclusion the rents of Shops 2 and 5 would have to be analysed first with their separately let first floors and the results applied to the analysis of Shop 1.
(2) This lease rent is for a fully fitted shop and so no addition need be made for the annual equivalent of fittings as was done for Shops 1 and 2.
(3) For convenience, the tiny area of Zone C is added to Zone B.

Valuation   From the analysis of shop rents the following valuations might be made.

Shop 1

	Square metres	£	£
Zone A	75	25	1,875
Zone B	75	12·50	938
Zone C	81·25	6·25	508
1st floor	231	3	693
			4,014
Gross value, say			£4,000

Shop 2

	Square metres	£	£
Zone A	36	26	936
Zone B	36	13	468
Zone C	18	6·50	117
			1,521
Gross value, say			£1,520

First floor separately assessed as offices.

Shop 3 and 4

	Square metres	£	£
Zone A	36	26	936
Zone B	36	13	468
Zone C	18	6·50	117
1st floor	90	3	270
			1,791

Gross value for each of Shops 3 and 4, say   £1,800

Shop 5

Zone A	27	26	702
Zone B	30	13	390
			1,092

Gross value, say   £1,100

First floor separately assessed as offices.

The methods outlined above is adequate for smaller shops although care needs to be taken in applying zoning too rigidly; if this is done sometimes odd results may appear. There is also the problem that over the last 20 years shops have been built in increasing sizes and the large supermarkets and other walk-round stores such as Marks & Spencer have become common. Normal zoning methods of valuation for such shops do not seem appropriate and various attempts have been made to deal with the assessment of these shops by other means, usually variations on the traditional zoning method. At present no wholly satisfactory method has emerged. The Lands Tribunal in the cases of *Trevail* v. *C. & A. Modes*; *Trevail* v. *Marks & Spencer* (1967) 13 R.R.C. 194 and *Marks & Spencer and Cambridge City Council* v. *Allsop* [1969] R.A. 274 has given limited support to the zoning principle and the method of halving back for large stores; the problem is largely that of the absence of rents from big shops and the difficulty of using rents taken from small ones. This also raises the question of allowances for quantity in the size of the "take". Again the Lands Tribunal has given limited approval to an allowance for quantity but has said in the case of *Woolworth (F. W.) & Co.* v. *Christopher and Lincoln City Council* [1972] J.P.L. 508 that ratepayers who contend for a quantity allowance must prove that it should be given.

Factories and warehouses

Industrial premises, i.e. factories and works are valued to N.A.V. and warehouses and storage premises are valued to G.V. But normal modern factories and warehouses are often structurally and locationally similar and each is valued by rental comparison; there are usually enough rents for an accurate estimate of value to be made. Care should be taken in analysing rents since factories, assessed as they are to N.A.V., do not need rents from full repairing and insuring leases adjusted for repairs; similar full repairing and insuring lease rents of warehouses must be adjusted for repairs since these properties are valued to G.V.

Some large industrial premises such as oil refineries, chemical or steel works comprise large amounts of plant and machinery, all or most of which is rateable. It is beyond the scope of this chapter to deal with the assessments of such properties; rateable plant and machinery is however dealt with in a later section of this chapter.

Study 9

Three factories on a small industrial estate are illustrated below.

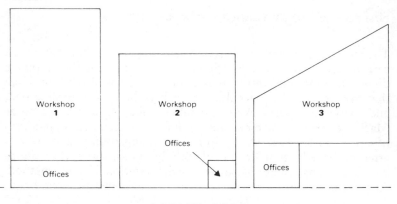

ESTATE ROAD

Factory 1: modern building; steel frame; brick walls; double skin asbestos roof on light steel trusses; offices plastered out; oil-fired central heating to offices; workshop heated by "Colt" heaters. Headroom to workshop 5 metres.

Let on 7 year lease one year ago full repairing and insuring terms £20,000 p.a.

Workshop 1,579 square metres; Offices 279 square metres.

Factory 2: structurally similar to Factory 1; let 2 years ago on 20 year full repairing and insuring lease £17,500 p.a. 5 year upward only reviews.

Workshop 1,812 square metres; Offices 84 square metres.

Factory 3: built about 30 years ago; steel frame, single skin brick walls; single skin asbestos roof on light steel truss; no central heating in offices; coke stoves in workshop; headroom to workshop 3·6 metres.

Vacant and to let.

Workshop 1,254 square metres; Offices 232 square metres.

Analysis

Factory 1

Lease rent in N.A.V. terms total floor area

$$\frac{£20,000}{1,858 \text{ square metres}} = £10·76 \text{ per square metre}$$

Factory 2

Lease rent in N.A.V. terms total floor area

$$\frac{£17,500}{1,896 \text{ square metres}} = £9·23 \text{ per square metre}$$

An alternative approach might be

Factory 1

Offices, 279 square metres × 1	=	279
Workshop, 1,579 square metres × ¾	=	1,184
		1,463
Lease rent in N.A.V. terms		£20,000
		1,463

Offices, £13·6 per square metre
Workshop, £10·25 per square metre

Factory 2

Offices, 84 square metres × 1	=	84
Workshop, 1,812 square metres × ¾	=	1,359
		1,443

Lease rent in N.A.V. terms	£17,500
	1,443

Offices, £12·12 per square metre
Workshop, £9·10 per square metre

It will be seen in the second method of analysis that the same principles and methods have been used as for zoning shops but on the evidence there is no justification for saying that the workshop space is worthy only ¾ of the office space and in the examples given the first method of analysis to be preferred since it follows market rents more closely.

Valuation

Factory 1	£
1,858 square metres at £10	18,580
or	
Offices, 279 square metres at £12·75	3,557
Workshop, 1,579 square metres at £9·50	15,000
	18,557
Net annual value	£18,500

Factory 2	
1,896 square metres at £10	18,960
or	
Offices, 84 square metres at £12·75	1,071
Workshop, 1,812 square metres at £9·50	17,214
Net annual value	£18,285

Factory 3	
1,486 square metres at £8·60	12,779
or	
Offices, 232 square metres at £11	2,552
Workshop, 1,254 square metres at £8	10,032
	12,584
Net annual value	£12,750

In valuing Factory 3 the unit prices have been reduced because of the high potential cost of repairs to the hypothetical tenant who will occupy on N.A.V. terms, and the poor layout and structure. In the analysis of rents of factories some valuers ignore the presence of such items as toilets, central heating and boiler rooms and similarly do not include them in the valuation; others analyse them and do include them in the valuation; what must be avoided is analysis on one basis and valuation on the other, e.g. using rental evidence that includes for central heating etc. and then adding a further sum for it. Factory car parks are another item to be dealt with in a similar way. The analysis and valuations set out in Study 9 are valid for small and medium sized factories and warehouses largely homogeneous in size, structure and location but in valuing larger premises built over a long time span considerable variation in unit prices is necessary to give effect to the differences in structure, age and general suitability for modern industrial methods. These factors test the best skills of the most experienced valuers. Study 10 is a valuation of a very large works with buildings of varying age and quality. No direct rental evidence is likely to be available for such a property and therefore critical valuation decisions as to the unit price of each part of the premises compared one with another, have to be made. These prices may have to be deduced from other works of similar size and it may be necessary to look over a whole region to find comparable properties.

Study 10

Valuation of large factory for the motor industry built piecemeal over the last 30 years and well maintained.

	E.F. area square metres	Unit price £ per square metre	Rental value £
Office block			
Ground floor	1,039	6·46	6,712
1st floor	975	6·46	6,299
2nd floor	1,074	5·65	6,068
3rd floor	145	4·84	702
Main factory			
Part A height 4·3 metres	43,157	3·23	139,397

Part B height 9·0 metres	15,005	3·77	56,569
Part C height 9·0 metres	1,170	4·04	4,727
(C is a new building)			
Research shops	3,089	4·04	12,480
Boiler houses	584	4·48	2,616
Ancillary buildings	1,880	4·04	7,595

Plant and machinery
Depreciated replacement
  cost £150,000 at 5%   7,500

Car parks   71,860   0·12   8,623

                                      £259,288

Net annual value, say   £260,000

Note

(1) For the avoidance of doubt it should be noted that only effective floor areas are valued which accounts for the variations floor by floor in the office block, i.e. toilets, passages etc. have been omitted.

It must also be mentioned that there are some very special factories or works which have been built purposely to house one type of industrial process. These will almost certainly not be readily lettable on the market, there will be few or no rental comparisons and recourse will have to be made to valuation by the contractors method. Steel works, and chemical works such as the I.C.I. plant at Billingham on Teesside as well as oil refineries and similar properties are of this class.

Warehouses

Warehouses are valued to G.V. by rental comparison using similar methods as outlined for factories. An important point to note in the value is the working height of the building; most modern goods handling is done by fork-lift truck, stacking goods on wooden pallets. Normally a maximum of 6 pallets each approximately 1·2 metres high can be stacked thus making a maximum working height 7·6 metres and warehouses below this height must have lower unit prices ascribed to them since they do not offer the same storage capacity for the same floor area as a more lofty building.

Licensed premises (See also Chapter 17)

These fall broadly into two categories, normal public houses selling beers, wines and spirits, and hotels and inns, which in addition to liquor sales, which may be only a small part of the trade done, offer accommodation for guests. Each type is valued by a variation on the profits method since it is but rarely that there are enough rents passing to form a basis of assessment.

Public houses are usually valued by a direct profits approach; it is assumed following case law that rental bids in the rating context may be made not only by potential private tenants but also by breweries and in the latter case it is also necessary to take into account the profits that would be made by the brewery in supplying liquor to a "tied" house; these would be greater than those the brewery would make by selling to non-tied houses in competition with other breweries. A proportion of these higher "tied" profits are assumed to be in the nature of rent. The profits on sales are expressed as a price per barrel of beers and per gallon of wines and spirits. Details of all such trade, but not of the level of profits are obtainable by the Valuation Officer of the Inland Revenue by means of statutory rent returns, following the case of *Watney Mann* v. *Langley* (V.O.) (1963) 10 R.R.C. 176. Profit per unit of liquor sale has to be estimated by the valuer.

Study 11

"Red Lion", a typical tied house in centre of a market town; owned freehold by a brewery and let to a tied tenant. Average annual trade: 150 barrels draught beer; 75 barrels bottled beer; 90 gallons wines and spirits. Tied rent £150 p.a.

Brewers profit

	£
150 barrels draught beer at £10	1,500
75 barrels bottled beer at £28	2,100
90 barrels wines/spirits at £2	180
Total brewers wholesale profit	3,780
Tied rent	150
Total brewers income	3,930
Brewers share, say 60% (1)	2,358
Brewers rental bid	1,572
Gross value, say	£1,575

Notes

(1) The brewers share is akin to the tenants share in a normal profits valuation.

(2) Today many breweries run houses by appointing a salaried manager and not a tied tenant and in such case it may be appropriate to omit the tied rent from the calculation.

In practice many skilled licensed property valuers produce rating valuations at a direct price per unit of sales without the calculations set out in Study 11. A typical example of this approach might be:

Study 12

"Red Lion" P.H. as for Study 11 but run by a salaried manager

	£
150 barrels draught beer at £4	600
75 barrels bottled beer at £12	900
90 gallons wines and spirits at £1	90
	1,590
Gross value, say	£1,575

Hotels (See also Chapter 18)

Hotels are usually valued by the profits method whoever is the likely occupier. A typical example might be:

Study 13

A good class country hotel with excellent all the year round trade; full on-licence. Three years trading accounts are available from which the following figures emerge:

	£
Gross profit	
1. Catering and letting bedrooms	35,000
2. Liquor sales	20,000
	55,000
Working expenses	41,250
Net trading profit	13,750

Less interest on tenant's
capital (1)   £
Chattels   30,000
Stock   7,500
Cash   2,500
                              _____
                             40,000   at 10%   4,000
                                                           _____

Divisible balance   9,750
Tenant's share (2)   4,500
                                                           _____

Rent and rates   5,250
Less general and water rates
    at 50p in £ on R.V. £3,500   1,750
                                                           _____

R.V.   £3,500
                                                           ======

G.V.   £4,234
                                                           ======

Notes

(1) In the rating hypothesis the tenant has to provide these items
    from his own capital and therefore is entitled out of the business
    to interest on the use of that capital.
(2) This is the amount that the tenant would require from the busi-
    ness to remunerate him for running it; it is normally in addition
    to a managers salary.

It is sometimes possible to value hotels and similar premises such
as boarding houses, particularly in towns where there is a number
of this type of property, by direct rental comparison. One unit of
comparison often used is the "reduced bedroom" based upon the
concept that double rooms are worth more than single rooms and
their values fluctuate as functions of their relative positions within
the hotel. Matters such as sea views, nearness to lifts or the converse
are also taken into account.

Study 14

An average quality seaside hotel in a large town with evidence of
market rents of hotels and boarding houses.

Accommodation:
  Ground floor: lounge; 2 bars (full on-licence); dining room.
  1st floor: 10 double; 3 single rooms; all with sea views.
  2nd floor: as for 1st floor.
  3rd floor: 2 double rooms with no sea views; 2 staff bedrooms.

Rental evidence from other premises shows a price per "reduced bedroom" between £350 for the best to £150 for the poorest.

Valuation

1st floor	10 double rooms at 100% =	10
	3 single rooms at 75% =	2·25
2nd floor	10 double rooms at 75% =	7·5
	3 single rooms at 50% =	1·5
3rd floor	2 double rooms at 50% =	1·0
	Staff rooms at	nil
		22·25

Say price per reduced bedroom deduced from rents £250 × 22·25 =	£5,625
Gross value, say	£5,600

Schools

Schools which are owned or occupied by Local Education Authorities are assessed by reference to regulations made by the Secretary of State for Education and Science under Section 30 of G.R.A. 1967 and are assessed to G.V. In practical terms the regulations are a species of formula which effectively forms a contractors method assessment and are to be agreed with the Local Education Authorities by virtue of Sub-section 3 of Section 30 G.R.A. 1967.

Some private schools of the type found in large converted houses may best be valued by rental comparison with similar premises which are the subject of lettings in similar situations, e.g. offices.

Public schools and purpose-built independent schools may have to be valued by the contractors method. If the buildings are reasonably modern no great problems may emerge; if however the buildings are old structurally and functionally obsolescent but yet of great historic and architectural merit, then very careful thought has to be given to the initial estimation of costs and land values, and the allowances for all age and obsolescence factors. It is not possible in a chapter such as this, if indeed anywhere, to lay down rules. A valuer confronted with such an exercise can do no better than read the evidence and the judgements in the cases referred to below, on pages 376 and 377 in Study 17.

Public buildings

These include town halls, local authority sports buildings, crematoria, and large educational properties such as polytechnics, universities, training colleges and the like. In a few cases, especially of offices occupied by local authorities, there may be rental evidence available but most of this class of property will have to be valued by the contractors method. The problems are those of deciding the initial cost of the building and then the deductions for the various factors affecting obsolescence.

Study 15

Modern sports complex owned/occupied by a District Council; a purpose-built steel framed brick and glass structure with flat roof, containing heated swimming pool, 4 squash courts, gymnasium and badminton courts, changing rooms, toilets, cafeteria and offices. 2 ha of land with 3 soccer and 2 rugby pitches and adequate surfaced car parking. Built one year ago at a total cost of £700,000, including all site works and fees.

	£
Estimated present day building cost including all fees	775,000
Site	
2 ha including site works of drainage fencing levelling and grading	50,000
Car parks	10,000
Total costs = Effective capital value	835,000
Estimated rental value = G.V. at 4½%	£37,575

Study 16

A modern crematorium built by a District Council; at the time of valuation there are some 2,750 cremations annually but the premises has a full working capacity of some 7,500 cremations annually; thus some of the facilities provided are surplus to requirements.

	£
Estimated present day building cost of crematorium	135,000
Cremators (furnaces) (1)	25,000

Site works	10,500
Land	5,000
	175,500
Deduct for surplus accommodation, say 40% (2)	70,200
Effective capital value	105,300
N.A.V. at 3¾%	3,948
N.A.V. = R.V., say	£4,000

Notes

(1) Such items are rateable as plant even though they do not occur in industrial premises, as here.
(2) This item is estimated, inter alia, by reference to the ratio between actual use and potential cremation capacity.

Study 17

A leading modern case is *Eton College* v. *Lane (V.O.) and Eton Urban District Council* [1971] J.P.L. 577 and this study is based upon the valuation approved by the Lands Tribunal in that case. Eton College comprises buildings that are old, of great intrinsic merit and interest but which are less than ideal for use as a large boarding school.

Buildings		£
Estimated replacement costs		4,600,000
Less allowances for age and obsolescence factors say 63%		2,898,000
Effective capital value		1,702,000
Site of buildings	£	
22·67 ha at £17,910 per ha (1)	406,000	
Less 63%	256,000	
		150,000
E.C.V. of land and buildings		1,852,000

Playing fields
80 ha at £1,063 per ha   85,000

Total E.C.V.   1,937,000
_____

G.V. at 3½% (1)   67.795
Deduct end allowance say 10%   6,780
_____

                                                   61,015
_____

G.V. say   £61,000
_____

Note

(1) These figures were taken from those adopted by the Lands Tribunal in the cases of *Downing College, Cambridge University* v. *Allsop* (*V.O.*) (1968) R.A. 603.

Cinemas

These are usually valued by a direct profits method by taking a percentage of the gross receipts, which are readily calculated from known facts, i.e. the prices of admission and the number of seats in the house. What has to be estimated or obtained is the number of "full houses" in each week. Sometimes a skilled and experienced valuer can make a direct assessment at a price per seat of capacity by comparison with other assessments.

Study 18

A modern cinema with 750 seats; average admission charge is £1·00 per seat and there are 4½ full houses per week throughout the year.

	£
Box office receipts per full house £750 × 4½	3,375
	52
Estimated annual box office receipts	175,500
Receipts from sundries; ice-cream, tobacco and sweets etc.	1,500
	177,000

G.V. at 6%   £10,620

G.V., say   £10,600

Petrol filling stations and garages (See also Chapter 14)

These properties in the valuation context are somewhat akin to licensed premises in that they not only enjoy a quasi-monopoly to sell vital fluids but are often owned and let on tied tenancies. Rental evidence of filling stations seems but rarely to be on the basis of a full arms-length open market rent and therefore it is usually necessary to value them by a direct profits method based upon the "throughput" or sales of petrol, derv and other fuels. A figure per 1,000 gallons of fuels sold is deduced from the profits as being the market rental element in respect of the forecourt, pumps, sales kiosks and all items above ground connected with the sale of petrol etc. If in addition there are ancillary buildings for the sale or repair of vehicles these are valued in the normal way at a unit price by the rental comparison method; usually rental evidence can be found from other similar workshops and like properties in the locality.

The key to all such valuations is the price per 1,000 gallons for sales of petrol and oils and this is best estimated from a calculation based upon the retailers gross profit; the actual sales figure can normally be obtained from the operator. It should be noted that as one would expect the rental price per 1,000 gallons increases with the volume of sales.

Study 19

A filling station and garage on a busy trunk road just outside a large town; the filling station stays open from 0600 to 2200 hours each day of the year (1).

Petrol sales
  2 × 2,000 gallon tanks
  2 × 1,500 gallon tanks
  serving 4 pumps

                                                    £

  Annual sales 400,000 gallons at £20
    per 1,000 gallons   8,000

Buildings
  Repair workshop, 186 square metres at £3   558

Lubrication bay, 45 square metres at £1·25	56
Office, 30 square metres at £4	120
Petrol sales kiosk included in "throughput" figure	—

Rateable plant

4 brick/concrete pits to house tanks (2), say	750
Compressor, say	20
	9,504
G.V., say	£9,500

Study 20

A small filling station serving a rural village only; open from 0700 to 1800 daily but closed Sundays and Bank Holidays (1).

Petrol sales	£
2×500 gallon tanks serving 2 pumps	
Annual sales 25,000 gallons at £10	
per 1,000 gallons	250

Buildings	
Workshop, 40 square metres at £2	80
Petrol sales kiosk included in "throughput" figure	—
Rateable plant	
1 brick/concrete pit for tanks (2), say	100
	430
G.V., say	£430

Notes

(1) It is sometimes claimed that since filling stations are able to remain open at the decision of the operator there should be variations in the levels of assessment based upon potential rather than actual throughput between those with short and those with longer periods of opening. It is submitted that rebus sic stantibus it is correct to take actual throughput based on actual opening

hours in each case since both profits and rents would surely follow the pattern shown by these factors.

(2) Following the decision in the case of *Shell-Mex & B.P.* v. *Holyoak* (*V.O.*) [1959] 1 W.L.R. 188 in which the House of Lords decided that a petrol storage tank was not rateable although the brick and concrete pit built to contain it, was in fact rateable.

Mineral properties (See also Chapter 11)

The main properties likely to be encountered in this category are quarries and gravel pits. Coal mines in the U.K. are almost all vested in the National Coal Board and then fall to be valued by a formula under powers set out in Section 35 of G.R.A. 1967. Mineral properties are valued to N.A.V. by reference to the royalty paid, or estimated by the valuer as likely to be paid for the mineral extracted annually; to this sum is added a figure for the rateable plant and buildings on the property. By virtue of the Mines & Quarries (Valuation) Order 1971, only one half of the annual royalty figure is to be regarded as a rent for rating purposes and the Order relates to the royalty only for that part of a mineral hereditament used for the purpose of winning, working, grading, washing, grinding and crushing of minerals and thus not for rent or royalty paid for extra land.

Study 21

A gravel pit having a maximum annual output of 75,000 tonnes and plant adequate to deal with that output. Current royalties in the district vary between 30p and 50p per tonne dependent upon ease of working and the proximity of the various pits to the nearby large town where most of the aggregate produced is used.

Gravel output	£
75,000 tonnes for 12 months 1 Jan–31 Dec (1)	
at 45p per tonne	33,750
less 50% to comply with 1971 Order	16,875
	16,875
Washing and grading plant	
Effective capital value based on depreciated	
replacement cost £100,000 at 5%	5,000

Buildings
Offices, messroom etc.

19 square metres at £2	40
	21,915
N.A.V., say	£21,900

Notes

(1) The output will vary from one year to another so the valuation officer will require a return of output to be completed by the operator showing actual output between 1 Jan and 31 Dec in any one year. The Valuation Officer then makes a proposal to come into force before 31st March in the following year to keep the assessment of the mineral property up-to-date.

(2) It sometimes occurs that the plant at a pit is too large for the output and in such cases it is right that the figure ascribed in the valuation to the N.A.V. of plants should be reduced proportionately in the ratio of the actual to the potential output.

(3) See also Chapter 11, page 332, Study 2.

Holiday camps and caravan sites

Holiday camps, in the almost total absence of reliable rental evidence, are usually valued by the contractors method. In view of the similarity between such properties and the larger holiday caravan parks it may be that a profits method valuation ought also to be considered. Considerable difficulties are sometimes claimed as arising in the estimation of the actual income and expenditure for holiday camps because they are owned by large companies; but licensed premises, also owned by large companies, have successfully been assessed by the profits method for many years.

Holiday caravan sites fall into two classes; those in which the actual caravans are not rateable and those in which they are. The test of rateability follows the decision of the Court of Appeal in the case of *Field Place Caravan Park* v. *Harding* (V.O.) [1966] 2 Q.B. 484; broadly a caravan permanently established in one location or on a permanent pitch in a caravan site for twelve months or more may be in the rateable occupation of its occupier together with the pitch on which the caravan stands, even if the occupier is not the owner of that pitch. Where the caravans on a site are not rateable the whole site is valued by the profits method excluding the value of the caravans but including in the gross receipts the rents paid by the caravan owners to the site operator for their pitches. If, however, the caravans are rateable and the site has an area of more than 400 square yards the Valuation Officer may at his sole discretion elect to value the site and the caravans as one unit in the occupation of the site operator, notwithstanding the fact that he may not own the caravans; in these circumstances again a profits method may be used. The Rating (Caravan Sites) Act 1976 sets out the law on the inclusion of vans in the assessment of leisure caravan sites; it should be noted that this Act does not apply to residential caravans nor their sites.

Study 22

A medium sized seaside holiday camp with a steel framed block built central building containing dining hall and kitchen, and an entertainments complex of dance hall, bars, lounge, and reception/admin. offices. There are four blocks of chalets built of block with felted roofs; a heated covered swimming pool; 2 ha of grassed playing field. All buildings have main services. The roads are tarmac and there is a surfaced car park for 200 cars. Total site area 5 ha.

	£
Central buildings, 1,322 square metres at £180	237,960
Chalet blocks, 1,240 square metres at £100	124,000
Swimming pool and filtration plant	30,000
Roads, main services and car park	50,000
Land, 5 ha at £12,000	60,000
Effective capital value	£501,960
6% of E.C.V. =	£30,118
G.V., say	£30,000

This valuation assumes that the property is modern in construction and layout; it may be however, that it is not. Study 23 is an example of a similar holiday camp built piecemeal over a number of years and poorly maintained.

Study 23

A similar camp to Study 22 but first built in 1930 with subsequent additions, the last in 1965. The chalets have been modernised by

the addition of internal toilet facilities since their erection in 1950.
The layout of the camp is inconvenient.

	£	£
Central buildings as before	237,960	
Less say 15% depreciation	35,694	
		202,266
Chalets as before	124,000	
Less 10% depreciation	12,400	
		111,600
Swimming pool (built 1973) as before		30,000
Roads etc.		50,000
Land		60,000
		453,066
Less depreciation for poor layout 2½%		11,346
Effective capital value		442,520
6% of E.C.V.		26,551
G.V., say		£26,500

Study 24

A small holiday caravan site of 100 pitches; the vans are not considered rateable and so do not form part of the assessment. There
is a small shop let on a licence, a licensed club run by the site
operator and a one-way tarmac camp road. There are two brick/tile
toilet blocks. The site operator sells caravans on the site and also
operates a holiday booking service from the site office for the van
owners to let their vans when they do not wish to occupy them;
he makes a charge for this service.

	£	£
Gross receipts		
Pitch rents	6,000	
Shop rent	750	
Commission on van sales, hire purchase fees and van lettings	2,000	
Club bar net profit	2,000	
		10,750

Outgoings

Wages and National Insurance	1,500	
Repairs	150	
Insurances	150	
Transport	100	
Bank charges	150	
Heat and light	200	
Printing, 'phones, postage	300	
Advertising	500	
Sundries	300	
	——	3,350
Divisible balance		7,400
Tenant's share, say		3,000
Rent plus rates		4,400
Rates at 50p in £ on R.V. £2,933		1,466
R.V. = N.A.V.		£2,934
N.A.V., say		£3,000

Study 25

A similar site to Study 24 except that all the caravans are rateable and the valuation officer has decided to include them in the assessment.

	£	£
Gross receipts		
Rents of 100 vans and pitches	12,000	
Rent of shop, letting commission etc. as before	4,750	
	——	16,750
Outgoings, as before		3,350
Divisible balance		13,400
Tenant's share, say		4,000
Rent plus rates		9,400
Rates at 50p in £ on R.V. £6,267		3,133
R.V. = N.A.V.		£6,267
N.A.V., say		£6,300

Plant and machinery

It is first necessary to decide which items of plant are rateable; under Section 19 of G.R.A. 1967, for any property not valued by the profits method, plant is rateable if it is of a type specified in the Plant & Machinery (Rating) Order 1960 as amended by the Plant & Machinery (Rating) (Amendment) Order 1974. It should be noted that premises do not have to be industrial in use or occupation to contain rateable plant; such items can and do occur in any type of building. In properties valued by the profits method plant must be fixed to the hereditament to be rateable.

The Plant and Machinery Order divides rateable plant into five classes which briefly are:

Class 1A   Power plant
Class 1B   Service plant e g central heating
Class 2   Passenger lifts
Class 3   Railways and tramways
Class 4   Plant in the nature of a building or structure
Class 5   Pipelines

(These were added to the Order by the Pipelines Act 1962.)

Having decided that the plant is rateable it is valued by the contractors method by taking the current replacement cost, reducing it by an appropriate amount for depreciation and then applying a percentage to obtain G.V. or N.A.V. as appropriate. It should be noted that some items of plant such as central heating equipment, lifts and electrical power supply fitments are almost always included in the unit price of the property both in analysis and valuation and no further addition need be made in these circumstances. Many items of plant are very specialised and unless the valuer has a great deal of experience in such matters it may be advisable to seek the assistance of an engineer. Also in applying a suitable rate of depreciation it may be unwise to take account of the rates used by accountants for taxation purposes; in many cases these will be quite misleading in deciding the life of the plant and hence its depreciation factor.

© M. J. Rayner, 1988

Chapter 13

DEVELOPMENT PROPERTIES

When it was said that "there is no such thing as absolute value in this world. You can only estimate what a thing is worth to *you*" the author might well have been referring to the appraisal of properties for development or redevelopment. What is an apparently simple and straightforward valuation task is arguably the most susceptible to error, and one, moreover, which is heavily reliant upon individual judgement. Because of the sensitivity to fluctuation by the internal elements within a development scheme, the results of an appraisal or viability study can never be wholly accurate, but merely reflect informed professional opinion. Nevertheless, despite the speed of legislative change, the vagaries of political policy and the volatility of an erring economy, there remains a need to underpin entrepreneurial flair with some degree of analytical rigour.

   Probably the most important part of the valuation process when considering development properties is the appraisal of all the determining factors which underlie and condition the various components of the valuation itself. Rental income or capital value, costs of construction and other development charges, initial yield and thus capitalisation rate, building contract period and the total time taken to complete and dispose of the project, and the cost of finance and method of funding the scheme are all dependent upon a number of critical surveys and investigations. Some of these can be listed briefly as follows:

(i) *Planning Policy*: reference should be made to any approved statutory development plans, relevant planning and development briefs, design guides, zoning designations, density standards, user constraints, conservation policies, highway proposals and general attitude towards planning gain agreements.

(ii) *Planning History*: inquiries in respect of past and present planning decisions relating to the site in question and to surrounding properties should be made. It also pays to have some regard to the personalities and politics involved in local planning issues, and be aware of the influence of various interest groups and amenity societies.

(iii) *Statutory Undertakers*: in addition to any discussions held with the local planning authority it will usually be necessary to consult with certain statutory undertakers to ensure the availability of such services and facilities as gas, water, sewerage, drainage, electricity, telephones and transport.

(iv) *Market Analysis*: it should almost go without saying that research into prevailing market conditions is a prerequisite to valuation and will normally take account of such matters as capital values, rental levels, past rental growth, achieved yields, vacancy rates, outstanding planning permissions, developments in the course of construction, cleared sites and other opportunities, comparable transactions, rates and some conception of future trends.

(v) *Locality*: special consideration would be given to the immediate vicinity of the site to be valued, in particular, the general environment, communications, transport, labour, local access, services, facilities and adjoining premises.

(vi) *The Site*: a thorough and comprehensive survey of the site is, of course, essential, and will cover aspects like ownership, acquisition, boundaries, area, topography, landscape, stability, access, layout, buildings, services, archaeological remains and any other physical factors likely to affect development potential.

A development valuation or viability study can basically be undertaken for a number of different purposes which include:

(i) calculating the likely value of land for development or redevelopment where acceptable profit margins and development costs can be estimated;
(ii) assessing the probable level of profit which may result from development where the costs of land and construction are known;
(iii) establishing a cost ceiling for construction where minimum acceptable profit and land values are known.

A combination of these calculations can be conducted to explore alternative levels of acceptable costs and returns but all valuations for development purposes require an agreed or anticipated level of income or capital value with which to work.

Several methods of assessing viability can be employed, with the appropriate choice of technique largely resting upon the individual circumstances and objectives of the developer concerned. The principal method used is that of *capital profit*, by which total development costs are deducted from gross development value and a residual profit is established. An alternative approach is the estimation of the *yield* produced by a development scheme. This can be a simple comparison of the anticipated initial income expressed as a percentage of the likely development costs; or it can be a more refined relationship between estimated income allowing for rental growth and the attainment of a specified yield by a selected target date. A further method, more commonly employed abroad, is that of *loan repayment* whereby the period it takes to repay a fixed interest loan is used as a comparative test of viability between alternative projects. In conjunction with all these methods of appraisal it is possible to use a *discounted cash flow* approach towards analysis so as to explore more closely the effects through time. It is also becoming normal practice to use two or more techniques of appraisal both as supplementary checks and in order to avoid any inherent anomalies. Whatever the result of the appraisal it is nonetheless essential that the *opportunity cost* of the prospective development should be identified in respect of alternative areas of enterprise. Although the completed building becomes an investment property, development appraisal is essentially concerned with gauging viability; it does not produce valuations for either investment or sale.

The foundation of all valuations for development purposes is the *residual method*. This produces a capital sum representing either profit or land value, depending upon the situation, which may be applied in reaching a particular development decision. It should be recognised that the Lands Tribunal are extremely sceptical about adopting the residual approach as a primary method of valuation in the context of their jurisdiction because of the variability of the constituent factors. A small adjustment in a certain item can disproportionately affect the final residual value, and consequently the technique is open to manipulation in the interests of a particular case. Nevertheless, where a potential development scheme is being appraised to assess its viability, and open market transactions are taking place, it is a common, if not usual, method of valuation being related to a specific site, a known developer, unique negotiations, and established conditions of finance, design, management and disposition. It is also appropriate where no readily comparable transactions are available or where the scale of the scheme is such as would be likely to affect the local market.

It should be appreciated that all rents and costs quoted in the following studies are for illustrative purposes.

Study 1

The purpose of this Study is to set out a conventional format for preparing a simple residual valuation to find a land value and, in doing so, to identify the basic components in a scheme of development and illustrate a method of treatment.

A prospective developer finds it necessary to ascertain how much he can afford to offer for a small prime suburban site in London which has planning permission for 2,000 square metres of offices producing 1,600 square metres of lettable floorspace. The projected development period is expected to be 24 months and the building contract period 12 months. Six months have been allowed before building works start to take account of detailed design, estimation and tendering. Six months following practical completion have been allowed for any possible letting voids which may occur. Finance can be arranged at 12%, comparable schemes have recently yielded 5½%, rentals of around £85 per square metre net of all outgoings have currently been achieved on similar properties, and a developer's profit of 15% on capital value is required. Construction costs have been estimated at £550 per square metre. A development valuation to assess the residual value of land can be conducted as follows:

Valuation

	£	£
A. *Capital Value after Development*		
Anticipated net rental income (1)	136,000	
Y.P. in perp. at 5½% (2)	18·18	
Estimated gross development value		2,472,480
B. *Development Costs*		
(i) Building costs (3)		
2,000 square metres gross floor area at £550 per square metre	1,100,000	
(ii) Building finance (4)		
Interest on building costs 12% × 18 months × ½	101,913	
(iii) Professional fees (5)		
12½% on building costs	137,500	
(iv) Interest on fees (6)		
12% × 18 months × ⅔	16,985	
(v) Promotion and marketing (7)		
Estimated budget (including interest)	25,000	
(vi) Contingency (8)		
5% on costs (including interest)	69,070	
(vii) Agents fees (9)		
Letting at 10% on initial rent	13,600	
Sale at 3% on capital value	74,174	
(viii) Developers profit (10)		
15% on capital value	370,872	
(ix) Total development costs		1,909,114

C. Residual Land Value (11)

  (i) Sum available for land, acquisition and interest   563,366
 (ii) Let x = land value
(iii) Finance on land (12)
    12% × 24 months = $0.254\,x$
(iv) Acquisition costs (13)
    0.04 at 12% × 24 months = $0.05\,x$
 (v) $1.304\,x = £563,366, \therefore x =$ 432,029
(vi) Residual land value now (14)   Say £430,000

Notes

(1) Rental income is assessed by reference to net internal areas, sometimes known as net lettable or net usable areas, and even effective floor area. In this particular scheme the gross to net floor area relationship, called the "efficiency ratio", is 80%, which is an average figure for small new office buildings.

(2) The initial yield used to find the rate at which the rental income is capitalised to calculate the Gross Development Value is market derived. It is selected either by reference to other similar transactions or by negotiated agreement with a financial institution willing to enter into a forward purchase commitment. The rate will vary according to the nature of any funding arrangement and the exact needs of the long-term investor involved.

(3) Building costs are normally calculated by reference to the gross internal area of a building and based upon an analysis of the principal elements such as foundations, basement, superstructure, services, external envelope, internal division and finishes. The reasoning behind this is that it allows for a general comparison derived from other schemes without being too specific about varying external finishes. At this stage in a development appraisal it is quite usual to use slightly adjusted figures applied to gross external measurements because detailed plans have not yet been prepared and only schematic drawings are available.

(4) To facilitate preliminary appraisal in the absence of an actual building contract it is normally assumed that the regular payments made to the contractor are equal throughout the contract period. As a developer will only borrow funds as liabilities occur it is reasonable at this stage to calculate the cost of building finance in an approximate way to reflect cash flow. This can be done in a number of ways. The full rate of interest

can be applied for the entire construction period and half the result taken as the finance charge, as here; or half the rate of interest can be applied for the funding period; or the full rate can be applied to half the period; or a percentage figure other than 50% can be applied to the full rate for the whole period if an obviously irregular cash flow or compounding is likely. In practice, the phasing and breakdown of costs typically follows an "S" shaped curve showing a gradual build-up of expenditure normally reaching a peak after about 60% of the contract has elapsed, with something of a tailing-off towards the end. The profile of the curve varies between sectors. In this study the building costs are funded for the 12 month construction period and for the possible subsequent 6 month letting void. Strictly speaking the total costs should be compounded at the full rate of 12% for the final 6 months rather than being halved to reflect cash flow or a higher percentage than 50% adopted.

(5) Professional fees can vary considerably depending upon the nature of the work, the size of the scheme and the problems encountered. While they are normally made in accordance with the relevant professional scales conventionally observed within the building industry, the more complex the project the higher the level of fees or, alternatively, the larger the scheme the more likely a negotiated fee arrangement below $12\frac{1}{2}$% can be agreed between the parties. In very broad terms these fees may be broken down among the various contributing professions so that the architect usually receives about 6% on construction cost, the quantity surveyor $2\frac{1}{2}$%, the consulting engineer $2\frac{1}{2}$% and other specialist engineering services a further $2\frac{1}{2}$%.

(6) Payments to professionals are usually made at prescribed points in the process such as upon the receipt of contract documents and then at various stages during construction until completion. It has been shown, however, that an acceptable measure of the cost of financing these payments can be taken at between $\frac{2}{3}$ and $\frac{3}{4}$ of the full rate of interest over the construction period. Frequently, however, professional fees are added to building cost and finance charges calculated together.

(7) The amount of the budget allowed for promotion and marketing can vary considerably depending upon the nature and location of the project concerned. Because marketing needs differ so widely between developments it is unwise to adopt a simple percentage of cost or value. Rather, a figure related to the probable costs of promoting the individual development must be estimated.

(8) Although the developer's profit margin makes some allowance for risk, and many would argue that there should be no provision for miscalculation, a contingency sum of about 5% on building cost is advisable.

(9) Again the level of letting fees is frequently negotiable and may be reduced where either a sole agent is appointed or a regularly retained agent employed. In the residential sector a figure of between 2% and 3% of sale price is used. Where two agents are jointly instructed, as frequently happens in the commercial sector, fees are often taken at around 15% of initial rent. The sale fee assumes that the developer will sell on the development to an investor and though negotiable is, usually pitched at around 3% to 4% of the agreed price or at this stage the gross development value.

(10) Developer's profit reflects the required return for enterprise, organisation, overheads and risk. Where the value of land is known it is commonly expressed as a percentage of total capital expenditure, and may be anything between 15% and 25%. When deriving a residual land value, however, and total development cost is uncertain, it is frequently pitched at a slightly lower percentage of capital value—between 10% and 20%. Experience shows that there is a very rough relationship between say 20% on cost and 15% on value among different schemes.

(11) The method described in the Study for calculating the residual value of the land is theoretically correct. In practice, however, some valuers still apply the relevant Present Value of £1 to the sum available for land, acquisition and interest. While unsound, the result is little different.

(12) The cost of financing the land is "rolled-up" and calculated over the whole development period because all acquisition costs usually occur at the moment of purchase and recoupment does not commence until some form of disposition.

(13) Acquisition costs are taken at an average of 4% comprising typically estate agents fees of about 2% on the cost of land, conveyancing costs of around 1% and stamp duty of 1%.

(14) In this way £430,000 is available to purchase the land. Any price in excess of this sum erodes the developer's profit and *vice versa.*

(15) Throughout this, and all subsequent studies, it should be recognised that in practice a valuer will frequently rely upon direct comparable evidence to assess development value. If similar land has recently been sold for the same purpose in the locality, and a general level of £*x* per square metre, per hectare or

per plot can reasonably be established, then the residual method should be checked against market comparables.

Study 2

This study shows how development profit can be assessed when the value of land is known or can be assumed.

A vacant and partially derelict deconsecrated church building in the centre of a large provincial town is being offered for sale at £1 million. A local property development company are interested in converting the building into a small speciality shopping centre on two floors. The reconstructed building will be approximately 3,000 square metres gross in size providing about 2,000 square metres of net lettable floorspace divided into 18 units of between 50 and 250 square metres. Rental income is predicted to average out at around £120 per square metre. An investment return of $6\frac{1}{2}\%$ is sought. Building costs are estimated at £400 per square metre. Bridging finance is available at 14% and the development will probably take 18 months to complete and let. The development company are anxious to know what will be the likely level of profit.

Valuation

		£	£
A.	**Gross Development Value**		
(i)	Estimated rental income at £120 per square metre on 2,000 metres	240,000	
(ii)	Y.P. in perp. at $6\frac{1}{2}\%$	15·38	
(iii)	Gross development value		3,691,200
B.	**Development Costs**		
(i)	Building costs at £400 per square metre on 3,000 metres (1)	1,200,000	
(ii)	Professional fees at 15% (2)	180,000	
(iii)	Contingencies at 5% on (i) and (ii) (3)	69,000	
(iv)	Promotion, say	25,000	
(v)	Finance on (i) to (iv) at 14% for 18 months × 0·65 (4)	208,087	
(vi)	Letting fees at 10% of rent	24,000	
(vii)	Sale fee at 3% of GDV	110,736	
(viii)	Land cost	1,000,000	
(ix)	Acquisition at 4%	40,000	
(x)	Finance on land and acquisition at 14% for 18 months	225,875	
(xi)	Total development costs		3,082,698

C. *Development Profit*

(i) Residual value in 18 months	608,502
(ii) P.V. of £1 in 18 months at 14%	0·822
Value now	500,189

(iii) Profit on cost in 18 months

$$\frac{608,502 \times 100}{3,082,698} = 19\cdot7\%$$

Profit on cost now (5)

$$\frac{500,189 \times 100}{3,082,698} = 16\cdot2\%$$

(iv) Profit on value in 18 months

$$\frac{608,502 \times 100}{3,691,200} = 16\cdot5\%$$

Profit on value now

$$\frac{500,189 \times 100}{3,691,200} = 13\cdot5\%$$

(v) Return on cost

$$\frac{240,000 \times 100}{3,082,698} = 7\cdot8\%$$

Notes

(1) Building costs are more difficult to estimate accurately for reconstruction or renovation work.
(2) Professional fees are slightly higher than normal due to the special and complex nature of the project and the need for additional structural engineering advice.
(3) A reasonable contingency budget is essential in work of this kind.
(4) A proportion of 65% rather than the usual 50% approximation has been allowed to take account of the front loading of fees and the rolling up of the entire debt charge during the period of letting voids following completion.
(5) In theory it is correct to discount the residual profit upon completion and sale to a present value now. In practice this is not always done. Both the profits on cost and value in 18 months and those expressed as a return now are presented. The difference between them will obviously depend upon the length of

the development period and the finance rate used for discounting.

Study 3

To show that the residual method can be modified to take account of phased development projects.

Consider the freehold interest in a cleared site which has planning approval for the construction of 90 detached houses. It is thought probable that any prospective purchaser would develop the site in three phases, each of 30 houses. The total development period is estimated at three years with separate contract periods of twelve months for each of the three phases. The sale price of the houses is set at £100,000 each. Construction costs are estimated at £45,000 a house, and the cost of site works and the provision of services is assessed at an average of £5,000 per house plot. Finance is available at 14% per annum and a developer's profit of 10% on gross development is considered likely to be sought.

A phased residual valuation can be conducted as follows:

Valuation

Phase 1	£	£
A. *Sale Price of House*		100,000
B. *Development Cost*		
Building costs	45,000	
Site works and services	5,000	
Professional fees at 10%	5,000	
Advertising, say	1,000	
Finance on £56,000 at 14% for 12 months		
$\times \frac{1}{2}$	3,920	
Disposal fees at 3% of sale price	3,000	
Developers profit at 10% of sale price	10,000	
Total development costs		72,920
Balance per plot		27,080
C. *Site Value Phase 1*		
Numbers of plots		30
Amount available in 12 months		812,400

Let site value $= 1\cdot000\,x$
Acquisition costs $= 0\cdot040\,x$
Finance at 14% on $1\cdot04\,x$ for 1 yr $= 0\cdot146\,x$

$$1\cdot186\,x$$

$1 \cdot 186\, x = 812{,}400$
$\therefore x \quad = 684{,}992$

Site value of Phase 1, say		685,000

D. Site Value of Phase 2

Site value Phase 1	685,000	
P.V. of £1 in 1 yr. at 14%	0·877	
		600,700

E. Site Value of Phase 3

Site value Phase 1	685,000	
P.V. of £1 in 2 yrs at 14%	0·769	
		526,800

F. Value of Entire Site	**£1,812,500**

Notes

(1) It can be seen that the value of each phase is in the order of £685,000 if development on all three phases started immediately. Allowance has been made, however, for the cost to the developer of holding Phase 2 for a further 12 months and Phase 3 for a further 24 months. Even if the three phases were sold separately to different developers it is assumed that the local demand for new housing would not hold up sufficiently to permit consecutive development of all 90 houses within the first year. An alternative calculation with adjusted selling prices to reflect increased supply could with advantage be performed.

(2) Although the method suggested above is an improvement to a global residual it still gives only a broad indication of value. A detailed discounted cash flow analysis would provide a much better approximation of value.

Study 4

This study demonstrates that the phased residual valuation can be taken a stage further so as to produce a residual cashflow valuation. Consider a 10 hectare site on a motorway location some 12 miles west of London. It has planning permission for "high technology" industrial development and a site coverage of around 30% is envisaged. Rents of £45 per square metre are forecast and a major financial institution has shown interest in buying the scheme once completed if it can show an initial yield of 7%. The total development period will be about 3 years, but it is considered possible to develop and let the equivalent of one hectare every 3 months starting in month 9. Construction costs are estimated at £250 per square metre and short-term finance can be arranged at 14%. The site is on offer for £4 million. A residual cashflow valuation to take account of the effects of expenditure and revenue during the development period and show the likely level of profit can be performed as follows (see Table on p. 399):

Preliminaries
   (i) 10 hectares = 100,000 square metres.
  (ii) Site coverage at 30% = 30,000 square metres gross.
 (iii) Less 5% = 28,500 square metres net lettable floorspace.
  (iv) Building costs of £7,500,000 averaged at £625,000 a quarter.
   (v) Promotion costs of £250,000 spread over the first 2½ years at an average of £25,000 a quarter.
  (vi) Professional fees taken at 10% of building costs and paid at an average rate of £62,500 a quarter.
 (vii) Letting fees taken at 10% of initial annual rents and paid as quarterly rents are received.
(viii) Sale fee of £549,423, being 3% of gross development value payable upon completion and sale.
  (ix) Rental income at 10% of the total quarterly rent roll to commence in month 9 and grow by a further 10% each quarter until month 36 when the full quarterly rent roll of £320,625 is reached.
   (x) Gross development value of £18,314,100 calculated by capitalising rental income of £1,282,500 a year by 14·28 Years Purchase and received in 3 years time.
  (xi) Annual interest of 14% to be taken at 3·3% a quarter.
 (xii) All cashflow figures rounded to the nearest thousand.

		£	£
A. *Gross Development Value*			18,314,000
B. *Land and Construction Costs*			
Land		4,160,000	
Building		7,500,000	
Promotion		250,000	
Fees		1,423,000	
Interest		3,142,000	
Total		————	16,475,000
Less			
Revenue during development		1,760,000	
C. *Total Development Costs*			14,715,000
D. *Development Profit*			
(i) Development profit in 3 years			3,599,000

Residual Cashflow ('000's)

Timescale		Cash Outflows				Cash Inflows		Cumulative cashflow	Interest at 14% p.a.
Year	Month	Land	Building	Promotion	Fees	Rent	Sale		
	0	(4,160)		(25)				(4,185)	
	3		(625)	(25)	(62)			(4,897)	(138)
	6		(625)	(25)	(62)			(5,609)	(166)
	9		(625)	(25)	(75)	32		(6,302)	(191)
1	0		(625)	(25)	(75)	64		(6,963)	(214)
1	3		(625)	(25)	(75)	96		(7,592)	(237)
1	6		(625)	(25)	(75)	128		(8,189)	(258)
1	9		(625)	(25)	(75)	160		(8,754)	(279)
2	0		(625)	(25)	(75)	192		(9,287)	(298)
2	3		(625)	(25)	(75)	224		(9,788)	(316)
2	6		(625)		(75)	256		(10,235)	(333)
2	9		(625)		(75)	288		(10,644)	(349)
3	0		(625)		(75)	320		(11,024)	(363)
					(549)		18,314	6,741	
TOTAL		(4,160)	(7,500)	(250)	(1,423)	1,760	18,314	6,741	(3,142)

(ii) P.V. of £1 in 3 years at 14%   0·675
Development profit now   2,429,325
(iii) Profit on cost in 3 years =

$$\frac{3,599,000 \times 100}{14,715,000} = 24 \cdot 4\%$$

Profit on cost now

$$\frac{2,429,325 \times 100}{14,715,000} = 16 \cdot 5\%$$

(iv) Profit on value in 3 years

$$\frac{3,599,000 \times 100}{18,314,000} = 19 \cdot 6\%$$

Profit on value now

$$\frac{2,429,325 \times 100}{18,314,000} = 13 \cdot 3\%$$

(v) Return on cost

$$\frac{1,282,500 \times 100}{14,715,000} = 8 \cdot 7\%$$

Study 5

This compares the conventional residual method of valuation with a discounted cash flow analysis in order to demonstrate the need to be more conscious of the effects of time and the incidence of costs and revenue in the valuation of development properties.

A local property development company have been offered a prime corner site on the high street of a prosperous provincial town for £1 million and are anxious to establish the probable viability for development with a view to disposing of it to an institution once fully completed and occupied. The site is currently used as a builder's yard with some vacant and near derelict shops and has a high street frontage of 120 metres and a depth of 45 metres. It lies within an area zoned for shops and offices with an overall plot ratio of 1·5:1 and a general height restriction of three storeys. Preliminary discussions indicate that the usual parking standards of one space to every 200 square metres of office floorspace and five to every 100 square metres retail floorspace could be relaxed if 30 spaces are provided on-site and a Section 52 agreement under the Town and Country Planning Act 1971 is entered into whereby a further 50 spaces are funded by the developer in a nearby local authority car park to be constructed in one or two year's time. A condition limiting a substantial proportion of any office floorspace to local firms will almost certainly be imposed on a planning permission. All ground floor development must be retail and rear access to shops is considered essential. A small supermarket of approximately 1,000 square metres is thought likely to attract support and, because the local planning authority are concerned that some form of suitable development takes place as soon as possible, negotiations should be relatively straightforward with permission probably granted in three months.

The quantity surveyor retained by the company has supplied the following information:

(a) A 6 metre grid to be used throughout with 5 metres ceiling heights for retail space and 3 metres ceiling height for offices.
(b) Building costs for shops to be taken at £300 per square metre excluding fitting out and shop fronts and equally phased over 9 months. Standard shop units to be 6 metres × 24 metres.
(c) Building costs for offices to be taken at £600 per square metre for letting, including lifts and central heating, and equally phased over 15 months.
(d) Demolition and site preparation to be allowed for at £10 per square metre across the entire site.
(e) All payments to be made 3 months in arrears.

The property development company's knowledge of the area indicates rental levels of £100 per square metre p.a. for supermarket space, an average of £20,000 p.a. or approximately £140 per square metre p.a. for a standard shop unit and £65 per square metre p.a. for offices. Given 3 months to obtain planning permission and prepare the site and 9 months to construct the shops, it is envisaged that a further 3 months should be time enough to allow for a successful letting campaign and sufficiently complete the superstructure of the building so that the shops could be let at the end of 15 months. In view of the probable local user condition the letting climate of the offices is slightly more uncertain, and it is considered appropriate to allow a full 6 months following completion before they are fully let and disposition to an institution can be effected. Professional fees to the architect and quantity surveyor have been negotiated so that £40,000 is paid as a lump-sum following planning permission and the remainder calculated subsequently at 10% of building cost on a 3 monthly basis. Short-term finance has been arranged with a merchant bank at 12½%.

It is well reported that institutions are interested in schemes of this nature, scale and location but seek yields of between 6% and 7%. It is therefore necessary to establish whether a yield can be accomplished which provides for this and also additionally allows for the developer's risk.

SITE LAYOUT

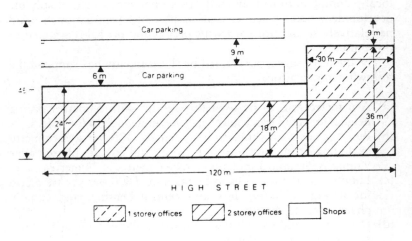

HIGH   STREET

1 storey offices   2 storey offices   Shops

Preliminaries	*Square metres*
(a) *Site*	
Site area = 5,400 square metres	
Plot ratio = 1·5:1	
Therefore gross permitted commercial floorspace	= 8,100
(b) *Shops*	
Supermarket 30 metres × 36 metres	= 1,080
Standard units 90 metres × 24 metres less 2 ground floor office entrances 3 metres × 12 metres	= 2,088
Total gross retail floorspace	= 3,168
(c) *Offices*	
(Gross permitted commercial floorspace— gross retail floorspace) 8,100 square metres − 3,168 square metres	= 4,932
Taking account of 6 metre grid constraint: 2 storey above shops 120 metres × 18 metres	= 4,320

Development Properties 403

Single storey extension above supermarket
18 metres × 24 metres   =   432
Add—2 ground floor entrances
3 metres × 12 metres   =   72

Total gross office floorspace   = 4,824

(*d*) *Gross areas to net*

	Gross	Deduction	Net square metres
Supermarket	1,080 square metres	10%	972
Standard units	2,088 square metres	15%	1,775
Offices	4,824 square metres	20%	3,859

(*e*) *Income*   £ p.a.

Supermarket
972 square metres at £100 per square metre p.a. =   97,200
Standard units
1,775 square metres at £140 per square metre
     p.a. =   248,500
Offices
3,859 square metres at £65 per square metre p.a.=   250,835

     £596,535

Conventional Residual

	£	£
A. *Capital Value after Development*		
(i) Estimated net rental income	596,535	
(ii) Y.P. in perp. at 6½%	15·38	
(iii) Gross development value		9,174,708
B. *Development Costs*		
(i) Building costs		
Shops—3,168 square metres at £300 per square metre	950,400	
Offices—4,824 square metres at £600 per square metre	2,894,400	
Site preparation	108,000	
External works	142,000	
Total	4,094,800	
(ii) Professional fees		
Arch and Q.S. by negotiation	449,480	

(iii) Contingencies
       5% on (i)   204,740
(iv) Finance on building
       12% × 24 months × $\frac{1}{2}$ on (i) + (ii) + (iii)   604,075
 (v) Agents' fees
       Letting fees 15% on initial rent   89,480
       Sale fees at 3% on G.D.V.   275,241
(vi) Land costs
       Land   1,000,000
       Acquisition   40,000
       Finance at 12% for 24 months   264,576
(vii) Total development costs   7,022,392
                                                                     ──────────

C. *Residual Capital Value*
  (i) Capital value in 24 months time   2,152,316
 (ii) P.V. of £1 in 2 yrs at 12%   0·797
                                                                     ──────────
(iii) Net present value (Developer's Profit)   £1,715,396

D. *Profit*
  (i) Profit on G.D.V. $\dfrac{1,715,396 \times 100}{9,174,708} = 18\cdot7\%$

 (ii) Profit on cost $\dfrac{1,715,396 \times 100}{7,022,392} = 24\cdot4\%$

(iii) Development yield $\dfrac{596,535 \times 100}{7,022,392} = 8\cdot5\%$

Development Profit (see Table A, p. 406)
  (i) Net Present Value £1,800,567 (The sum of N.P.V.s—see Table A,
       p. 406)

 (ii) Profit on value $\dfrac{1,800,567 \times 100}{9,174,708} = 19\cdot6\%$ (see Table A, col. 8)

(iii) Profit on cost $\dfrac{1,800,567 \times 100}{6,414,704 + 184,102} = 27\cdot3\%$
                                                        (see Table A, cols. 7 & 8)

(iv) Yield on development $\dfrac{596,535 \times 100}{6,414,704 + 184,102} = 9\cdot0\%$
                                                        (see Table A, cols. 7 & 8)

It can, therefore, be seen that an oversimple conventional approach produces a lower residual capital value representing a commensurately lower development profit and return. Using the same data, a more detailed examination of the incidence of respective cash flows (Table A, p. 406) reveals what would be an even more attractive scheme. It should be recognised that such a discounted cash flow analysis will always produce more accurate results, but that inevitably schemes with front-heavy capital investment and delayed revenue streams will perform adversely when compared with a conventional residual appraisal, and schemes with early revenue flows and relatively steady expenditure will naturally improve.

An alternative approach towards the analysis of a cash flow produced by a capital project over time is the computation of the internal rate of return. Instead of calculating the present value of a scheme at a chosen discount rate, the rate at which future cash flows are reduced to a present value of zero is ascertained. The criterion usually applied under this method is that a project should be deemed acceptable if it produces an internal rate of return greater than the minimum return required on capital. In addition to which a suitable margin for profit will be sought.

The internal rate of return is found by applying trial rates of discount to the cash flow. Although this is most easily done by iterative computer program it can also be performed manually by conducting two trial discounts at rates of interest (6% and 10% here) either side of the probable yield. The internal rate of return can then be interpolated either by formula or by graphical estimation.

Formula Calculation of IRR (see Table B, p. 406)

$$\text{IRR} = 6\% + \frac{628}{1{,}074} \times 4\% \text{ per quarter } (1{,}074 = 628 + 446)$$

$$= 6\% + 2{\cdot}34\% \text{ per quarter}$$
$$= 8{\cdot}34\% \text{ per quarter}$$

Effective annual rate $= (1{\cdot}0834)^4 - 1$
$$= 0{\cdot}377$$
$$= 37{\cdot}7\% \text{ per annum}$$

Graphical Estimation of IRR (see p. 407)

While the internal rate of return or yield method avoids the arbitrary or subjective selection of a discount rate, it can obviate the

(continued on page 407)

Table A—Discounted Cash Flow Analysis

Item / Quarter	0	1	2	3	4	5	6	7	8
Land cost	(1,000,000)								
Acquisition costs	(40,000)								
Site preparation		(108,000)							
Building costs:									
Shops		(316,800)	(316,800)	(316,800)					
Offices		(578,880)	(578,880)	(578,880)	(578,880)	(578,880)			
Other				(14,000)	(14,000)	(114,000)			
Arch. and Q.S. fees		(140,368)	(89,568)	(90,968)	(59,288)	(69,288)			
Contingency		(50,184)	(44,784)	(45,484)	(29,644)	(34,644)			
Agency and legal fees						(51,855)			(312,866)
Shop income						86,425	86,425	86,425	
Sale proceeds									9,174,708
Cash flow	(1,040,000)	(1,194,232)	(1,030,122)	(1,046,132)	(681,812)	(762,242)	86,425	86,425	8,861,842
P.V. of £1 at 2·87%	1·0	0·972	0·945	0·919	0·893	0·868	0·844	0·820	0·797
N.P.V.	(1,040,000)	(1,160,793)	(973,465)	(961,395)	(608,858)	(661,626)	72,948	70,868	7,062,888
Cumulative costs	(1,040,000)	(2,234,232)	(3,294,202)	(4,405,313)	(5,183,533)	(6,074,974)	(6,141,024)	(6,233,327)	2,447,138
Quarterly interest		(29,848)	(64,979)	(96,408)	(129,199)	(152,475)	(178,728)	(181,377)	(184,102)
Cumulative costs at end each quarter	(2,264,080)		(3,359,181)	(4,501,721)	(5,312,732)	(6,227,449)	(6,319,752)	(6,414,704)	2,263,036

N.B. The figures in the last 3 lines do NOT form part of the Discounted Cash Flow.

Table B—Internal Rate of Return

	0	1	2	3	4	5	6	7	8
Cash flow (£000's)	(1,040)	(1,194)	(1,030)	(1,046)	(682)	(762)	86	86	8,862
P.V. at 6% p.qtr.	1·0	0·943	0·89	0·84	0·79	0·75	0·70	0·67	0·63
N.P.V.	(1,040)	(1,126)	(917)	(879)	(539)	(569)	61	58	5,583
Total N.P.V.									628

	0	1	2	3	4	5	6	7	8
Cash flow (£000's)	(1,040)	(1,194)	(1,030)	(1,046)	(682)	(762)	86	86	8,862
P.V. at 10% p.qtr.	1	0·91	0·83	0·75	0·68	0·62	0·56	0·51	0·47
N.P.V.	(1,040)	(1,087)	(855)	(785)	(464)	(472)	48	44	4,165
Total N.P.V.									(446)

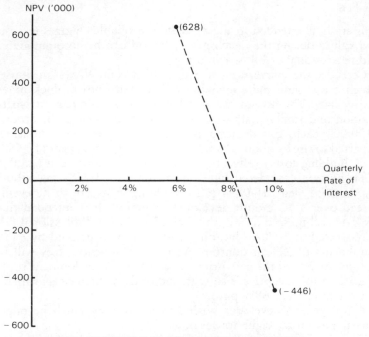

GRAPHICAL ESTIMATION OF INTERNAL RATE OF RETURN

need to anticipate alternative costs of funding; it allows a greater margin for risk in making comparison with finance costs and gives sensible answers for accept/reject decisions when used against the opportunity cost of capital. It is, however, not so good for ranking projects which are mutually exclusive, and it can pose problems where projects have unconventional cash flows, such as large negative payments following a series of positive payments. The method sometimes produces multiple yields, for example, the cash flow series $-1,000 + 2,500 - 1,575$ has internal rates of return of 5% and 50%; some cash flows have no internal rate of return. It is affected by the volume of capital expended and the time period for investment, and is said to present certain reinvestment problems regarding positive cash flows.

Although all projects having an internal rate of return exceeding the cost of capital must also have a positive net present value it is generally agreed that the net present value method tends to give better results—and, moreover, the market uses it.

Study 6

This study is intended to illustrate how probable changes in costs and values during the development period can be accommodated within a residual cashflow valuation.

Consider the conversion of a terrace of eight Victorian houses which are vacant and somewhat dilapidated, into a block of 24 luxury flats. The houses are situated in a desirable part of North London and similar flats to those planned are selling for around £100,000 each, but demand is such that prices are confidently expected to rise by about 1% per month over the next year (12·68% p.a.). Building costs to effect the conversion are estimated at £25,000 a flat but are considered likely to increase by 1·25% per month for the next year (16·08% p.a.). Building costs are to be evenly spread over a 12 month development period. It is intended that six flats will be sold in months 9 to 12 inclusive. Professional fees are assessed at 10% of building costs, and will be paid by equal instalments of 2½% a quarter. Agents and solicitors fees will be charged at 2% of the sale price of each flat. A development profit of 25% of the sale price is sought, and bridging finance is available at 1% a month (12·68% p.a.).

A prospective developer wishes to know how much he might have to pay for the eight houses now.

Preliminaries
Receipts
Month 9 sees six flats sold at £100,000 each × 1·0937 = £656,220
Month 10 sees six flats sold at £100,000 each × 1·1046 = £662,760
Month 11 sees six flats sold at £100,000 each × 1·1157 = £669,420
Month 12 sees six flats sold at £100,000 each × 1·1268 = £676,080

Building Costs + Fees + Profits
Total costs are 24 flats at £25,000 = £600,000
Average of £50,000 a month
Increase by 1·25% per month

	£
1	50,625
2	51,258
3	51,899 + 10% fees
4	52,548
5	53,205
6	53,870 + 10% fees
7	54,543
8	55,225
9	55,915 + 10% fees + 2% fees + 25% profit
10	56,614 + 2% fees + 25% profit
11	57,322 + 2% fees + 25% profit
12	58,038 + 10% fees + 2% fees + 25% profit

It is assumed that surpluses in the latter few months will be reinvested at the same rate of interest. The resulting residual represents an absolute maximum bid.

Valuation

Month	Receipts	Costs	Net cashflow	Capital outstanding	Interest
1		(50,625)	(50,625)	(50,625)	(506)
2		(51,258)	(51,258)	(102,389)	(1,024)
3		(67,277)	(67,277)	(170,690)	(1,707)
4		(52,548)	(52,548)	(224,945)	(2,249)
5		(53,205)	(53,205)	(280,399)	(2,804)
6		(69,832)	(69,832)	(353,035)	(3,530)
7		(54,543)	(54,543)	(411,108)	(4,111)
8		(55,225)	(55,225)	(470,444)	(4,704)
9	656,220	(249,662)	406,558	(68,509)	(686)
10	662,760	(235,559)	427,201	357,925	3,579
11	669,420	(238,065)	431,355	792,859	7,929
12	676,080	(257,777)	418,303	1,219,091	

Sum available in 12 months =   £1,219,091

Let the value of the houses = $1 \cdot 0000 x$
Acquisition costs at 4% = $0 \cdot 0400 x$
Finance at 12·68% on 1·04x = $0 \cdot 1319 x$

$$\therefore 1 \cdot 1719 x = 1,219,091$$
$$\therefore x = 1,040,269$$

The developer might offer *£1 million* for the eight houses.

Study 7

This study shows how it is possible to explore the effect of changing levels of performance during the development period among such factors as yield, cost, rent, finance and time. To begin with, a simple sensitivity analysis known as a Mini-Max Evaluation is demonstrated, then the sensitivity of a scheme is tested by the Extinguishment of Profit Method and finally the individual components are measured by the Percentage Change Method.

Consider the position of a developer who has paid £400,000 for a plot of land which has planning permission to build a discount cash and carry warehouse of 4,000 square metres gross. Rents of around £45 per square metre overall have been quoted in the vicinity. Initial yields in the region of 7½% are reported for similar properties. Construction costs are estimated at £300 per square metre. Finance can be arranged at about 12% per annum and the development is considered to take approximately 18 months to complete and let.

I. Median or Realistic Valuation

	£	£
A. Gross Development Value		
(i) Rental income at £45 per square metre on 4,000 square metres	180,000	
(ii) Y.P. in perp. at 7½%	13·33	
(iii) Gross development value		2,399,400
B. Development Costs		
(i) Building costs at £300 per square metre on 4,000 square metres	1,200,000	
(ii) Professional fees at 10% of (i)	120,000	
(iii) Finance at 12% for 18 months × ½	122,296	
(iv) Letting at 10% of rent	18,000	
(v) Land	400,000	
(vi) Acquisition at 4%	16,000	
(vii) Finance at 12% for 18 months	77,083	
(viii) Total development costs		£1,953,379
C. Development Profit		
(i) Sum available in 18 months		446,021
(ii) P.V. of £1 in 18 months at 12%		0·844
Profit now		376,442

(iii) Profit on cost $\dfrac{376,442 \times 100}{1,953,379} = 19 \cdot 3\%$

(iv) Return on cost $\dfrac{180,000 \times 100}{1,953,379} = 9 \cdot 2\%$

II. *Maximum or Optimistic Valuation*
Rents predicted at £50 per square metre
Initial yield taken at 7%
Building costs estimated at £275 per square metre
Finance at 10% per annum
Development period and letting 15 months

A. Gross Development Value	£	£
(i) Rental income at £50 per square metre	200,000	
(ii) Y.P. in perp. at 7%	14·28	
(iii) Gross development value		2,856,000

B. Development Costs		
(i) Building costs at £275 per square metre	1,100,000	
(ii) Professional fees at 10%	110,000	
(iii) Financc at 10% for 15 months × ½	76,548	
(iv) Letting at 10% of rent	20,000	
(v) Land	400,000	
(vi) Acquisition	16,000	
(vii) Finance at 10% for 15 months	52,634	
(viii) Total development costs		1,775,182

C. Development Profit		
(i) Sum available in 18 months		1,080,818
(ii) P.V. of £1 in 15 months at 10%		0·888
Profit		959,766

(iii) Profit on cost $\dfrac{959,766 \times 100}{1,775,182} = 54\%$

(iv) Return on cost $\dfrac{200,000 \times 100}{1,775,182} = 11 \cdot 3\%$

III. *Minimum or Pessimistic Valuation*
Rents down to £40 per square metre

Initial yield up to 8%
Building costs up to £325 per square metre
Finance at 14% per annum
Development period 21 months

A. *Gross Development Value*   £   £
  (i) Rental income at £40 per square metre 160,000
  (ii) Y.P. in perp. at 8%   12·5
  (iii) Gross development value   2,000,000

B. *Development Costs*
  (i) Building costs at £325 per square
    metre   1,300,000
  (ii) Professional fees at 10%   130,000
  (iii) Finance at 14% for 21 months × ½   184,269
  (iv) Letting at 10% of rent   16,000
  (v) Land   400,000
  (vi) Acquisition   16,000
  (vii) Finance at 14% for 21 months   107,211
  (viii) Total development costs   2,153,480

C. *Development Profit*
A loss of   (£153,480)

Note

It can, therefore, be seen that changes to the various components of rent, yield, cost, finance and time can have dramatic effects upon the profitability of a scheme when acting in concert.

Extinguishment of Profit

Another way of testing the sensitivity of individual components is to gauge the degree to which one factor changing independently can extinguish development profit. Given the same circumstances as those above rough calculations show that the various components have to change as follows:

Rent from £45 to £37 per square metre
= Nil profit = 17·8% change
Yield from 7·5% to 9·2%
= Nil profit = 22·7% change
Building costs from £300 to £400 per square metre
= Nil profit = 33·3% change

Finance from 12% to about 36%
= Nil profit = 300% change
Time from 18 months to about 45 months
= Nil profit = 250% change

Note

(1) Thus, the scheme can be seen as relatively sensitive to changes in rent and yield, and, to a lesser extent, building costs. It is hardly sensitive at all, however, to independent changes in the rate of interest charged on bridging finance or the time taken to complete the development.
(2) In reality, of course, these changes would not necessarily take place independently. More likely would be a combination of adjustments, possibly in different directions.

Percentage Change

Yet a third approach to testing sensitivity is by subjecting the individual components to a percentage change and assessing the extent to which the level of profit is affected.

Rent   10%   increase = 29·5%   profit on cost
                      decrease = 9·0%   profit on cost
Yield   10%   increase = 9·9%   profit on cost
                      decrease = 30·8%   profit on cost
Building costs 10%   increase = 12·1%   profit on cost
                      decrease = 27·5%   profit on cost
Finance   10%   increase = 18·2%   profit on cost
                      decrease = 20·4%   profit on cost
Time   10%   increase = 18·4%   profit on cost
                      decrease = 20·2%   profit on cost

Notes

(1) Naturally, the same sensitivities emerge, but at the very least a prospective developer is directed towards those aspects of the scheme which merit the closest attention in respect of optimising profit.
(2) Although the way in which these tests are presented here might appear somewhat simplistic, the advent of computer programs permitting detailed and different adjustments to be made to all the various components enables a development valuer to explore a wide range of possible outcomes according to the information available in a comparatively short time and at little additional cost.

Further Reading

Baum, A. and Mackmin, D. *The Income Approach To Property Valuation* (2nd Edition) RKP, 1981.

Darlow, C. (ed) *Valuation and Development Appraisal* Estates Gazette, 1982.

Jolly B. *Development Properties and Techniques in Residual Valuation* CALUS, 1979.

Chapter 14

GARAGES AND PETROL STATIONS

This chapter deals with the valuation of motor-trade properties, garages, petrol service stations and petrol filling stations. Such premises are occupied or owned for the purposes of trade and they fall into two categories; namely those which sell sufficient petrol to be of interest to oil companies and to petrol distributors—for which there is, at the time of writing, a keen market—and those which are simply of interest to the garage trade. Such being the case, while the process of valuation normally involves arriving first at a rental value and then at a capital value, the direct investment approach is not appropriate and the method normally used is based partly on profits analysis with the introduction of a weighting element for special value elements. In fact petrol stations are rarely bought simply for investment purposes, but if they are then they usually command comparatively low prices in relation to income because of their specialised nature, the common lack of an alternative use and for other reasons that will become apparent to the reader of this chapter. Investors, institutional or otherwise, with no direct connection with the garage and petrol station business, might well expect to see yields of between 12% and 16%, although in the best cases they might accept yields nearer 10%, but at this rate the property would either have to have a valuable alternative use or be a prime station likely to survive and not likely to be affected by new competition.

Normally valuations are carried out in connection with purchases or sales, lettings and rent reviews and the parties involved are either oil companies or petrol distributors on the one hand, or motor-traders, dealers and garage operators generally on the other hand. Speaking generally, the motor trade is suffering from over-capacity and the returns on capital employed are often too low. The number of petrol stations has fallen and will continue to fall, high volume stations replacing smaller stations by redevelopment or otherwise. Old stations are being reconstructed, at costs averaging £250,000 to £300,000, with large shops and good forecourts. It is on record that in this way petrol sales volumes have been as much as doubled and the major oil companies are now looking for sites selling at least one million gallons a year. Dealers' profits are enhanced by shop sales and by such additions as car wash facilities. There is a tendency to separate car sales, repairs and servicing from the petrol selling function. When petrol filling stations and service stations or simply forecourts are purchased or leased by oil companies, it is to secure a tied outlet for their fuels, but oil companies do not enter the market when the petrol sales potential is too low to make acquisition for throughput worthwhile. In these latter circumstances the market is restricted to dealers who, as tenants or as owners, normally make solus agreements with oil companies for the sale of particular brands of petrol. Oil companies having purchased, have a number of options open to them: they either operate their stations through wholly owned subsidiaries, or by licensee operation or tenant operation.

The valuer should always consider the possibility of redevelopment for other uses. Garages and petrol stations in urban areas are often found to be on sites with considerable development value for other purposes. The valuer should also think in terms of obsolescence because garage premises are often badly laid out, showrooms are sometimes too small or, more often, too large, workshops are frequently badly arranged and parking space is often grossly inadequate.

The basis of valuation

As is the case with the valuation of hotels, public houses, restaurants, cinemas and theatres, a close knowledge of the trade carried out on the premises is a necessary concomitant of this type of work, so a general description follows.

Oil companies do not purchase for investment but to obtain an outlet. Their petrol profits arise from the refining and wholesaling process—and to some extent from rents from tied outlets—whereas dealers' profits arise from retailing. The concept of a tied rent and a free rent must be understood. The free rent is the rent which an oil company is prepared to pay and is the total of the tied rent that it can expect to receive from its dealer plus an overbid, or special value element, which in fact is met out of refining and wholesaling margins. The dealer pays his rent out of his retailing profits, whereas the oil company can and does add to the rent received from the dealer a proportion of its own earnings. In practice oil companies will be found in most cases to purchase rather than lease their outlets.

It must be borne in mind that this special aspect of property valuation involves projections in an imperfect, uncertain and even somewhat subjective market; this in the sense that where substantial petrol throughputs are involved, the oil companies, retailing groups and petrol distributors are virtually the only buyers and, further-more, their interest varies from month to month because of market-ing or budgeting factors rather than for property investment reasons. There is a limited number of possible purchasers and they are not all in the market at the same time and neither are they necessarily in the market at the same place. In the circumstances consistency will be found to be lacking and it is probably more true to say in this case than most that the value of the property is what it will fetch.

The valuer must be cautious in terms of analysis and synthesis when dealing with individual transactions because it is occasionally the case that excessively high prices are paid for large volume outlets. The oil companies usually operate within budget parameters and the availability of funds as well as marketing needs conditions offers. It is of vital importance that he should consider all factors likely to affect petrol sales and the trade generally such as possible road diversions and variation in traffic volume, the possibility of new stations being established, of old stations being enlarged and improved and of stations being closed. Valuable information can usually be obtained from the planning and highway authorities.

Directly comparable evidence is of great assistance but it is not often available and valuations may well have to be constructed from first principles. To be useful, comparables must be directly analo-gous and, by way of example, if in search of such evidence the valuer analyses the sales at say ten stations on a busy 30 mile stretch of road with little variation in traffic volume, he will nevertheless find great variations in sales due to such things as comparative acces-sibility, visibility, lay-out, dealer operation standards and of course pricing policy, and it is after all from throughput and the consequent profit that forecourt rent derives. Competitive pricing is vital but standards of operation are equally so and, surprising though it is, a good dealer might possibly sell twice as much petrol as a bad dealer at a given station.

It must be made clear that stations on other routes are no more directly comparable than would be rental evidence taken from shops in positions other than the one a valuation relates to, although it is of course true that there is a general pattern of values and it is this pattern that the specialist valuer must build up in his mind in the course of practice. With particular reference to forecourts, there is a clear indication that oil companies apply specific rates per gallon on a sliding scale adjusted for throughput when buying or leasing.

A paucity of evidence in lease renewal arbitrations and in new tenancy cases under the Landlord and Tenant Act 1954 can sometimes be removed by applying for an order for the discovery of documents, and such an order can usually be obtained if the rental valuation depends on evidence of profits, as is so often the case with petrol filling stations where throughput profit is a vital element in determining the rental value of the forecourt. Discovery might include valuation reports and would normally exclude "without prejudice" correspondence, but it does mean that it should usually be possible to obtain evidence of the volume of petrol sales. The case of *Harewood Hotels Limited* v. *Harris* [1958] 1 W.L.R. 108 is relevant: in this case the trading accounts of an hotel were admitted in settling a rent on the renewal of a lease. Therefore if proceedings are pending it is sometimes possible for a lessor to persuade a lessee to produce records of petrol sales.

Oil companies are in competition with each other and they are also in competition to some extent with petrol importers who buy the finished product at spot prices on the Rotterdam market and are able to take advantage of shifts in prices. This competitive situation maintains the value of higher volume stations. There is an excess refinery capacity in Europe at present and the surplus product is sold on the Rotterdam market at "on barge" prices which fluctuate greatly. This fuel tends to be used to supply smaller stations which are therefore somewhat at risk in terms of price.

The development of the petrol business

Petrol is one of several products manufactured from crude oil, diesel fuel, commonly called Derv, being another, but the products include fuel oil, lubricants, kerosene, naphta and so on. The proportions of different products produced during the refining process are in the first instance determined by the type of oil but the proportion of petrol to other products can be increased greatly by a further processing method known as catalytic cracking.

Petrol was first imported from the U.S.A. and marketed in Britain at the turn of the century and at that time it was sold in sealed two-gallon cans. After the first war, private motoring and commercial road transport developed quickly and there was a consequent increase in the number of petrol retailers. In 1920 hand-operated petrol pumps came into use in conjunction with underground storage tanks of about 500 gallons capacity and premises where petrol had been sold in cans then became pump sites. By 1938 there were over 35,000 outlets with an average throughput of 24,000 gallons per annum and there was only about a fifth of today's traffic on the roads. After the first war Shell and Esso controlled the market but between the wars various other suppliers established themselves.

There was a rapid growth in demand and the establishment of re-fineries in the U.K. quickly followed.

The Petroleum Board, which controlled petroleum distribution and prices during the last war, was dissolved in 1948 and Anglo-American (Esso) introduced the tied garage or solus trading system from the U.S.A. Considerable capital investment by oil companies was needed for the construction of refineries and it was therefore particularly necessary for the companies to secure assured outlets for their products. When petrol rationing ended, Esso, followed by Shell-Mex and B.P. and then by others, started to acquire outlets to secure ties and within a very short period all the leading suppliers had introduced similar arrangements, so that by 1953 eight out of ten stations were subject to exclusive supply arrangements of one sort or another. There were by then five supplying groups, namely Shell-Mex, B.P. and National Benzole; Anglo American (Esso) and Cleveland; Regent; Vacuum (Mobil) and Fina (Petrofina) and they controlled virtually the whole market. These companies invested heavily in the improvement of existing petrol stations and the development of new stations, either directly or through their dealers. The then existing system would not have been adequate to cope with the increased demand and the oil companies provided the basis and finance for change; indeed at the beginning of this period many petrol stations had no forecourts and were simply prepared to sell petrol, over the pavement as it were, as an adjunct of their garage and repair business.

At the end of the last war there were about 30,000 stations still in existence, mostly of poor quality, and the number of stations hardly altered over the next twenty years, although average sales per station doubled more or less in line with the increase in motor traffic. For some years prices were fairly stable, but Jet entered the market in 1958 and began to cut prices, to be followed by others.

In 1975 there were some 31,000 stations in existence selling an average of about 143,000 gallons per annum, but during the years to the end of 1985 this figure fell steadily to 21,000 stations selling an average of 275,000 gallons per annum. Thus by 1985 total sales had risen by about 30% over a decade and the number of stations had fallen by more than 30% during the same period, so as the result of a process of rationalization encouraged by market pressures there are now fewer and bigger stations selling more petrol and the companies' share of the market has increased. In the process some smaller stations have been enlarged but many have gone out of use, particularly those in country districts on roads with low traffic volumes or where better stations have been established in the vicinity. During the period referred to petrol consumption has risen by over 11% but increased car ownership has been followed by a slight fall in consumption per car.

At the present time petrol quality is governed by British Standard BS4040 and the minimum rating for 4 star petrol is 97 RON [research octane number] but a limited number of U.K. companies market 98 RON grade petrol which is more suitable for high performance cars and this is a marketing factor, although perhaps not as significant as pricing policies.

Distribution and supply

At the time of writing, of the 21,140 petrol outlets existing in the U.K. some 6,642, or 31%, are company owned, these being largely the high volume stations. About 39% of the total are self-service operations. The major distributors are Shell, Esso and B.P. who between them operate nearly 50% of the stations in the U.K., followed by Texaco, Jet, Burmah, Mobil and Fina who share about 25% of the market and are in their turn followed by Pace, Total, Ultramar, Anglo, Elf, I.C.I., Gulf and various small companies who make up the rest of the market. Shell and Esso compete as market leaders. Oil companies have by now sold off the majority of their small stations, that is to say stations with throughputs of under about 500,000 gallons per annum—usually subject to a covenant preventing continued petrol sales, so they tend to become car-sales sites or repair garages.

Petrol is normally transported from the refinery by sea, road, rail or pipeline to storage depots from which it is delivered by road tanker to retailers. The petrol importers distribute from leased bulk storage. The major companies supply petrol throughout large parts of the U.K. but the smaller companies supply in defined areas and there are reciprocal supply and storage arrangements between different companies.

In general terms there are five types of retail petrol outlets:
1. Motorway service areas.
2. Garages with full repair facilities and car sales franchises or agencies, as well as petrol forecourts.
3. Petrol service stations that as well as selling petrol, service vehicles and carry out minor repairs.
4. Petrol filling stations where the sale of petrol is the main or only part of the business.
5. Stations in categories 2, 3 and 4 with fast food restaurants as adjuncts and stations which are themselves adjuncts of hypermarkets.

From an oil company's point of view good filling stations are of most interest and value—they call for an investment wholly related to petrol sales. A good filling station will sell 1,000,000 gallons of fuel per annum whereas dual motorway service area stations will sell four or five times this volume, but the latter represent a very small part of total petrol sales in the U.K. although Derv sales are higher than normal at motorway stations.

Prices and agreements

Suppliers' scheduled prices vary to a limited extent according to supplier, to grade and to distribution zone. Scheduled (i.e. wholesale) prices are derived from bulk sale prices, but retailers usually buy at lower base prices or by arrangements under which they receive fairly standard discounts or rebates. The basic solus agreement provides that the retailer shall sell a particular brand of petrol exclusively in consideration of a rebate, and he buys at the scheduled price, less discounts and rebates. Supply agreements are now normally for periods of three to five years and advances of one sort or another might well be made free of interest, or at low rates of interest, in return for the tie.

It was in the early 1950's that the oil companies began to purchase petrol stations themselves from dealers, usually leasing them back to the dealers. Prices were high and lease back rents were comparatively low, and it was normal in those days for the valuer to arrive at a basic dealer value and then add to it the measure of special value element arising from the oil company's bid. Then the petrol companies only conditioned the market whereas now they virtually control it, so the modern method of valuation involves a direct approach to the value of the premises to a petrol company and the tied rent—the rent the dealer-tenant pays—is largely artificial in the sense that it is only one of several profit conditioning factors.

Policy

The oil companies entered the market to secure outlets for the sale of petrol and they were not particularly interested in premises with large workshops and car sales showrooms: because such stations meant an increased investment per gallon they would discount the value of these outlets. By 1965 it became clear that the major companies were not particularly interested in stations where the potential throughput was less than about 100,000 gallons per annum and now they tend to look for stations with a potential of at least 800,000 to 1,000,000 gallons per annum, although the smaller oil companies and various other retailers remain interested in stations selling upwards of about 500,000 gallons per annum. Below that level stations tend to be dealer owned and the brand of petrol retailed to be bought under solus supply arrangements of one sort or another.

It is worth noting in relation to tied rents that twenty years ago oil company yields on capital investment in terms of tied rents varied over a large range from as little as 4% to something approaching 8%, and that tied rent proportions varied between one quarter and one third of dealers' net profit after allowing for operating costs. The position remains much the same today, although volumes and prices are higher of course.

Highways and traffic volume

It is a commonplace to say that garages and petrol stations are on adjunct of the highway and petrol sales are obviously conditioned by traffic volume. Between 1959 and 1984 the number of vehicles in use increased from 8·7 million to 20·7 million and traffic mileage increased in a slightly greater proportion, but private car ownership multiplied fourfold to 16 million over the period. The forecast for 1990 is between 18 and 20 million cars. It is relevant to point out that there was only an increase of about 10% in the overall mileage of roads over the same period, although within this figure there was an absolute increase in motorway mileage. By 1978 50% of households owned a car, regional figures varying from 67% in the south to 50% in the north, the greater London figure being 52%. Today every other household has a car and one in ten has two cars.

Petrol sales have risen almost in proportion to the increase in traffic and the number of stations has now fallen to about half what it was in the 1950's so that, on average, the remaining stations have to accommodate eight times as many private cars. Then a prime station would have sold something in the region of 100,000 gallons per annum but today a prime station will sell something approaching 1,000,000 gallons per annum, so it has to be a good deal larger in terms of forecourt layout. It must be added that petrol sales have increased very little in the last three or four years but there are now signs of an improvement.

At the end of the 1940's the actual average distance between stations on trunk roads and Class 1 roads was only 1·66 miles and 2·18 miles respectively and since the number of stations has fallen to about half the new average is probably about 4 miles, but with much shorter distances on busy roads. In modern conditions only good, large throughput stations survive; unless, that is, they are supported by such ancillary operations as car sales and servicing, or supported artificially, for example by lack of competition so that prices can be increased.

Obviously the valuer must have regard to factors which might affect traffic volume, and therefore trade, such as road alterations and the possible development of new stations or the improvement of existing stations. When judging potential sales from records of past sales he should try to relate prices charged at the subject station in the past to prices charged at competitive stations on the same route or in the same vicinity. He should study the other stations in terms of their distance from the subject station, their size and their design. Visibility and easy access are important but the factors conditioning sales as between one station and another are manifold and any situation deserves the closest study. The normal speed of passing traffic conditions sales in the sense that very fast roads tend to show lower petrol sales, unless visibility in terms of stopping distance or advance warning signs is especially good; the motorist has to have time to think, decide and then slow down. The near side for departing traffic on the outskirts of a town is still the best position for a station, particularly if it also collects bypass traffic. Heavy traffic on dual or triple carriageways reduces sales.

Throughput estimating

In valuing petrol stations the valuer may be assisted by information about past sales and given the necessary information he may be able to make useful direct comparisons with other stations in the vicinity, but he will need to form his own estimate of future sales. He will bear in mind that price adjustments have a disproportionate effect on throughput and this needs to be borne in mind when examining records of past sales. Estimates of future sales have to be based on traffic flow volumes and the density of local population. Petrol purchases average four gallons per customer, although the 20% or so of customers using credit cards tend to purchase double this amount which brings the average up to something in the region of 5 gallons and motorists probably travel about 120 miles on average between fills. On motorways average cash sales are up to about six gallons and some 40% of customers use credit cards. Motorway service areas apart, the station likely to sell the largest volume of petrol will be found on a main route with high traffic flow and a large local population where there is good visibility, easy access and adequate space. The ideal site will have a frontage of 150 ft or more probably 200 ft and will be 100 ft to 150 ft deep.

For the sake of illustration, in the case of a dual carriageway with a traffic flow of 17,500 vehicles a day on each side and stations on both sides at three mile intervals, the indications would be that over 120 miles each motorist would have a choice of 40 stations without crossing, so one in forty would use a particular station, all things being equal, therefore:

$$\frac{17,500 \text{ vehicles}}{40} = 437 \cdot 5 \text{ vehicles} \times 4 \cdot 8 \text{ gallons}$$

= 2,100 gallons a day per station (or about 650,000 gallons p.a.).

The calculation given above applies to rural station, but in an urban position with a good deal of local trade the factor of 40 used above might well be adjusted to a figure of between 30 and 20, this to allow for a higher call-in rate. The following is an illustration of an appropriate calculation:

$$\frac{20,000 \text{ vehicles}}{30} = 666 \text{ vehicles} \times 4 \cdot 8 \text{ gallons}$$

= 3,196 gallons a day (or about 1,000,000 gallons p.a. or more for a 7 days a week operation).

On a road on which traffic is able to cross to buy petrol the optimum traffic figure used for calculating the call-in rate has to be increased by a proportion chosen to allow for crossing traffic; thus on a road carrying a volume of 10,000 in each direction the optimum figure would be 10,000 vehicles for the nearside traffic plus say 20%, or 2,000 vehicles, from the offside, a total of 12,000 vehicles subject to division by the appropriate factor.

Of course because of the likely variation in sales for all sorts of reasons this might mean that one station (perhaps a good modern station in competition with poor stations) would sell twice as much as another. A valuer making throughput estimates has many factors to balance. In the case of a two way flow road the matter is somewhat more complicated because of the greater or lesser tendency of traffic on the opposite side to cross for petrol and only observation can determine the likely percentage of crossing traffic. It depends to some extent on the nature and position of stations on its own side. If current traffic flow figures cannot be obtained then the valuer must necessarily carry out his own traffic count for estimating purposes and a specialized technique of observations at short intervals during different parts of opening hours is employed. These methods of estimating gallonage are very much rule of thumb and have to be used with discretion.

If the valuer is concerned with sales at motorway service areas he should bear in mind that the traffic capacity of a three lane motorway is likely to be in the region of 75,000 to 80,000 vehicles a day in both directions. Sales from such outlets probably range from 2·5 million gallons a year to over 5 million gallons a year, petrol purchases averaging 6 gallons per sale. It has been observed that the call-in rate at motorway service areas has fallen but that individual purchases have risen to compensate for this.

Forecourt rents and prices

Tied rents (and licence fees) and dealer rents are not the same thing, since tied rents are artificial rents paid to suppliers rather than market rents and are conditioned by rebate policies, whereas open market dealer rents are fixed for longer periods and can be regarded as rents paid to landlords rather than to suppliers as such. This is using the two terms in distinct senses, of course.

Open market forecourt rents, that is to say free rents or the rents an oil company might be expected to pay, are related to the cost of producing petrol, Derv and lubricants and the profits of marketing them, whereas tied rents are related to the profits derived from retailing these products, Dealer rents, in the sense of rents paid to private landlords—non oil company landlords—for low throughput stations of insufficient interest to attract oil companies, are directly derived from likely trading profits.

Oil company interest is clear at about 800,000 gallons per annum or above but there is an area upwards to it from about 500,000 gallons per annum where the interest of oil companies is variable and uncertain and depends on a variety of marketing and even extraneous factors. It can be taken for granted that at the present time even a minor oil company would probably not be interested in the acquisition of a station selling 400,000 gallons per annum or less. This does not mean that there is no demand for small throughput stations but it is a demand from dealers, retail chains or speculators.

Looking first at open market rents, a pattern of rates per gallon related to throughput and area can be discerned or at least deduced. An area differential is clear: maximum rents and prices are achieved in the southern part of the country, whereas in the Midlands rents are somewhat lower and in the north a good deal lower. In the south at the time of writing the median rent level appears to be equivalent to between 5p and 6p per gallon, or even somewhat more for exceptional stations, which can perhaps be defined as those selling over 1,000,000 gallons per annum, falling gradually down to something in the region of 3p per gallon at 500,000 or 600,000 gallons per annum. In the Midlands the median rate seems to be between 4p and 5p per gallon or slightly more for high volume stations, with the same range over a throughput scale, whereas in the north and in other remote parts of the U.K. the median rate is not usually found to be much higher than 3p per gallon, reflecting increased distribution costs, lower throughputs and narrower margins generally. There is a greater price cutting tendency in the Midlands and the north with consequently higher trading risks, and there appears to be a comparative excess of stations as well.

The following table is intended to give an approximate indication of the range of free of tie rent rates per gallon likely to be found at the time of writing, but the actual circumstances of each case will cause variations. For example overheads are not constant and will affect the tied rent element of the free rent, particularly at the lower end of the scale. In general terms the maximum rates are those that might be achieved in the London vicinity, the minimum rates those that might be found in the North and the remoter parts of the country and the mean rates those likely to apply in the Midlands and the South, but for a variety of reasons there are variations within regions as well.

Gallons p.a.	Rates per gallon free of tie		
	Maximum (p.)	Mean (p.)	Minimum (p.)
3,000,000	7·5	7·0	6·0
1,500,000	6·5	6·0	5·0
1,000,000	6·0	5·5	4·5
900,000	5·5	5·0	4·0
800,000	5·0	4·5	3·5
700,000	4·0	3·5	2·5
600,000	3·0	2·5	1·5
500,000	2·5	2·0	1·0
400,000	2·0	1·5	0·5
300,000	1·5	1·0	—

It must be appreciated that the free rent comprehends the tied rent for the simple reason that the latter is part of the oil company's gross returns. If in a given case the oil company pays a rent of 4p per gallon and receives a tied rent of 1·5p per gallon then the net cost per gallon to the oil company is 2·5p per gallon, an amount which it has to find out of its profits as a producer, or importer, and wholesaler or distributor.

Turning now to tied rents, it will be clear that they are derived from retailing profits and in some cases enhanced by the beneficial effect petrol sales can be said to have on other parts of the business. This is why petrol station shops are sometimes valued in with the forecourt since their turnover is usually closely related to petrol sales.

At a given station 4 star petrol and Derv sales might account for 70% of sales, 2 star for 20% and 3 star for the balance. Assuming that this represents an average retail price per gallon of 175·5p per gallon including duty and VAT and that the dealer tank wagon or delivery price is 144·38p, then the dealer is left with a gross profit calculated as follows:

	p. per gallon
Retail pump price	175·50
Less 15% VAT	(22·89)
Net of VAT	152·61
Scheduled price	144·38
Profit	8·23
Add rebate, say	2·27
Dealer's margin	10·50

This calculation relates to four star petrol and the schedule price includes duty at 88p per gallon. Rebate is normally paid quarterly in arrears and at the time of writing ranges from 2·5p to 3p per gallon for small volume stations, rising to about 3·5p per gallon for 1,000,000 gallon stations and perhaps 5p per gallon for stations with double that throughput. It might be found that in the case of motorway stations the rebate would be as high as 12p per gallon. Dealer support costs are normally borne by suppliers, so that retailers' margins are maintained despite competitive price cutting.

It will be noted that there is a loss on the basis of the scheduled price but that this loss is more than cancelled by the dealer's support contribution and the rebate paid by the oil company.

If a minimum and adjusted overhead cost of forecourt operation is taken as £15,000 per annum after allowing for support from other elements of the business, it follows that at these margins a station selling only 200,000 gallons per annum would produce a net profit before rent of £6,000 per annum, and the station selling only 300,000 gallons per annum would produce a net profit before rent of £16,500 per annum. A simple filling station selling these volumes would probably trade at a loss but such stations have not often survived. There are economies of scale to be taken into account and a station selling 700,000 gallons per annum might be subject to true overhead costs of about £40,000 per annum leaving a net where a dealer might operate a number of stations and achieve a very high total gallonage. In such cases oil companies have been known to agree rebates of between 6p and 8p a gallon bringing gross profits up to something in the region of 14p a gallon.

The reader will realise that the figures quoted above are to some extent hypothetical and are therefore to be applied with caution, but they do indicate the necessary analytical approach to the subject. As a final note, a dealer operating a station selling one million gallons per annum will need working capital of between £30,000 and £40,000 since one load delivery will usually cost in the region of £10,000.

As has already been remarked, the tied rent is often artificial in valuation terms because of other adjustments made between the supplier and the dealer. The free rent in a market dominated by oil companies is the rent with which the valuer will be concerned when dealing with forecourts with a potential of about 500,000 gallons per annum upwards and the disparity between the dealer rent and the free rent will become very apparent at 1,000,000 gallons per annum. The case valuations that follow illustrate this.

Motorway service areas

Motorway service areas generally occupy sites of up to 20 acres on each side of motorways and comprise petrol forecourts and restaurant facilities together with car and lorry parking. Usually the main profit arises from the restaurant and shop. The ideal situation is about two hours drive from main population centres when a call-in rate of 12% or thereabouts is often achieved. As a generality motorway traffic volume averages between 50,000 and 80,000 vehicles a day but in the case of M25 the volume has risen to about 115,000 vehicles a day which is in excess of safe capacity. With very heavy traffic the call-in rate is reduced.

The present practice is for the Department of Transport to offer to lease sites for development as motorway service areas by tender, and bids are commonly made by specialist operators as well as by oil companies. Originally turnover rents were paid but for the last few years the practice has been for the Department of Transport to grant 50 year leases at a premium with nominal ground rents. There have been great variations in the premiums paid and it is difficult to give general valuation guidance. No example is given in the studies which follow of the valuation of a motorway service area because it is a particularly complex subject and would require a chapter of its own. The principles of valuation are the same but the scale is different and it is necessary to value the ancillary parts such as restaurants and shops.

call-in rate of 12% or thereabouts is often achieved. As a generality motorway traffic volume averages between 50,000 and 80,000 vehicles a day but in the case of M25 the volume has risen to about 115,000 vehicles a day which is in excess of safe capacity. With very heavy traffic the call-in rate is reduced.

The present practice is for the Department of Transport to offer to lease sites for development as motorway service areas by tender, and bids are commonly made by specialist operators as well as by oil companies. Originally turnover rents were paid but for the last few years the practice has been for the Department of Transport to grant 50 year leases at a premium with nominal ground rents. There have been great variations in the premiums paid and it is difficult to give general valuation guidance. No example is given in the studies which follow of the valuation of a motorway service area because it is a particularly complex subject and would require a chapter of its own. The principles of valuation are the same but the scale is different and it is necessary to value the ancillary parts such as restaurants and shops.

Cost of construction and site values

At present the cost of constructing a typical fully equipped petrol service station or petrol filling station stands between £200,000 and £300,000. A good modern station will be found to have a forecourt with a frontage with at least 150 ft and a depth of about 150 ft as well, and will be equipped with three or perhaps four dual-pump islands under a canopy. The storage tank capacity of a station selling upwards of 1,000,000 gallons per annum usually consists of two or often three 12,000 gallon tanks. Deliveries are nowadays made by 6,000 gallon tankers and if three deliveries a week are assumed it will be seen that it is possible to calculate the required tank capacity when peak sales are taken into account.

The residual method of valuation is commonly used to determine site values, but speaking in very general terms the ground rent for a prime dual station site with a potential of about 1,500,000 gallons per annum might be as high as £30,000 per annum or even £40,000 per annum and good sites with smaller potential would probably command ground rents in the region of £20,000 to £30,000 per annum.

It does appear to be the case that certain oil companies which follow U.S.A. accounting principles prefer short term building leases, for example leases for 20 years, and are prepared to pay rents equivalent to those normally paid under long term leases. This follows from the usually fallacious reasoning that rent is a liability, this conclusion ignoring the fact that a lease is usually an asset. It will sometimes be found that building leases for normal long terms contain break clauses in favour of the tenant at, for example, twenty year intervals and the valuer will perceive the reason for this in the circumstances just outlined.

Parts other than the forecourt

It is normal to value parts other than forecourts on a comparative rate per square foot basis but since on analysis it is the profits made in the various parts that justify the rent paid for those parts, the valuer must come to some conclusion as to the likely profitability of the operations carried out in those parts of the premises. While the garage trade generally is working on narrow margins at present, it should be noted particularly that a shop attached to a forecourt is often very profitable and on analysis usually shows a sales volume ratio closely related to the petrol throughput.

A car sales franchise or agency is of special value. The sale of new cars is perhaps not a particularly profitable field of operation at the present time, but the valuer is concerned with more than the immediate future and second-hand car sales are still profitable. It is found that showroom rents have some sort of adventitious relationship to shop rents district for district and that workshop rents relate to industrial rents in the same way but comparisons of this sort tend to be uncertain. Repair and servicing work is now fairly profitable but profit ratios vary greatly, probably by more than 100% from one part of the country to another and hence workshop rents will also vary greatly.

The shop on a service station will usually be found to have an area of at least 300 sq ft and the sales achieved are likely to relate to petrol sales turnover. Car wash facilities are a valuable adjunct and the equipment is usually leased, the operator paying a rent which relates to a capital cost per unit of about £20,000 and includes amortization over about five years. New car sales call for covered showroom space but used cars are better sold in the open or under a canopy.

In the course of his practice the specialised valuer will accumulate a body of information about rents and capital values and he will be able to apply this information in making valuations but, as far as petrol sales are concerned, he will usually find it necessary to value from first principles, that is to say by the use of his knowledge of what petrol companies and dealers are likely to bid for what is on offer.

In its most developed form, a garage business comprehends the sale of motor-vehicles and their subsequent servicing and repair, the sale of accessories and spare parts, the sale of petrol and oil, shop sales and perhaps car washing. The value of the land and buildings from which the parts of the business other than petrol sales are conducted has to be arrived at by comparison with other garages. To speak in general terms, obviously the volume of business is important in that it supports rents and capital values. Main car sales dealerships and agencies now normally run for terms of up to five years, attaching to the business rather than the property but nevertheless bearing on the value of the latter. It should be borne in mind that the use of the forecourt for the display of cars for sale is often to the detriment of petrol sales but may not be disadvantageous in overall trading terms.

In valuing workshop space, which should be at least 14 ft to eaves, the valuer has to take into consideration areas specifically used for repairs and servicing, including greasing bays etc., space used for storage, for specialist operations such as accident repairs and re-spraying, and land or building used for the parking of cars awaiting repair and servicing. The time taken to service cars has fallen by half over a period of years, so twice as much parking space is now needed per mechanic, or half as much workshop space. The valuer should note that many specialist workshops and fitting centres for tyres, exhausts and other items are nowadays being established away from conventional repair garages and they do represent serious competition. Whereas the ideal position for a filling station is on a busy main road, the most suitable position for garage workshops may be on an industrial estate.

Ancillary offices also have to be taken into account. It is very much a question of method whether the valuer attaches his unit rate to the workshop space as comprehending the ancillary storage space or whether he values each part separately but since very few garages have ideal use allocations, the writer inclines to the view that each part should be valued separately: this is the normal valuation option. It must always be borne in mind that garages where car sales take place need an appropriate area of open or even covered parking space in connection with this purpose, as well as the showroom space itself and other display areas; this is in addition to the hard standing needed on which to park vehicles awaiting repairs and servicing. Open parking space will command rents of between £20,000 and £40,000 per acre or about £100 to £200 per annum per car on an average space occupation ratio. £50,000 per acre probably approaches the maximum figure likely to be paid at the present time for space in urban areas used by car dealers and lower rents are found depending on the availability of suitable land and the degree of demand.

The tie and the law

The simple early method of obtaining a tie was to impose a short term solus agreement under which the dealer agreed to sell the company's petrol to the exclusion of other petrols, usually in return for special wholesale price rebates on petrol sold and sometimes in return for loans also. Loans were sometimes secured by a mortgage transaction but the type of arrangement that developed very considerably was a purchase and lease-back transaction, because in that way the dealer-owner could obtain the highest price for his freehold and then lease back for a tied rent which was low in relation to value, the lower because a rebate on petrol purchases was usually arranged as well and on the other hand because the oil company could obtain a secure tie. On top of these transactions the petrol companies themselves acquired stations by outright purchase or purchased sites and built new stations. From a legal point of view all these arrangements seemed at the time to be suitable ways of securing a tied outlet but the position has been conditioned by case law and if the valuer has to deal with a tied station he is well advised to consider the precise nature of the tie and the question of whether it is binding or not.

The security of tenure provisions of the Landlord and Tenant Acts apply, and a tenant is able to claim a new lease at a rent suitably adjusted to allow for the continued imposition of a tie, although of course petrol companies are able to oppose claims for new leases on the grounds specified in the Acts. As between the 1927 Act and the 1954 Act there is no great alteration in the provisions relating to the terms of a new tenancy and while the court has a wide discretion, it is difficult to imagine a case where the petrol company would be required to grant a new lease without the tie since the tie was the company's only object in acquiring the property in the first place. On the other hand and having regard to one aspect of the reasoning in the restraint of trade cases discussed below, it is just conceivable that the courts might choose not to reimpose a tie on renewal, but in such circumstances it would seem to follow that the new rent would have to be at the free rental value level and would thus be beyond the reach on a non-oil company tenant. Rent review clauses in tied tenancy agreements would normally make the tied basis of valuation clear.

Covenants on the part of a tenant to deal with his landlord alone and to take his goods have been accepted for many years, subject only to the implied term that the landlord will supply the goods at a fair and reasonable price. Such covenants have been held to be legal and binding in equity on an assignee.

The practice of arranging for the operation of oil company stations by licensees or by wholly owned operating companies, is now fairly common. In the case of licensee operations, an extra-statutory code is applied which does give the dealer some protection and security. The normal practice is to grant a licence for a three year period, renewable on terms and with provision for compensation in the alternative. For obvious reasons the valuer will not be greatly concerned with this type of arrangement.

Contracts contrary to public policy are unlawful and agreements in restraint of trade had been held to be contrary to public policy as being against the public interest; in the past the term had been taken to include arrangements restricting business activity and limiting competition. Over a period of seven years or so starting in the mid-1960's four important petrol tie cases were decided: *Petrofina (G.B.) v. Martin* [1966] Ch 146; *Esso Petroleum Co. v. Harper's Garage* [1968] A.C. 269; *Cleveland Petroleum Co. v. Dartstone* [1969] I.W.L.R. 116; and *Total Oil G.B. v. Thompson Garages* [1972] 1 Q.B. 318. The valuer should study these cases. *Petrofina v. Martin* more or less destroyed the simple solus agreement method of obtaining a tie and *Esso v. Harper's Garage* largely destroyed the mortgage coupled with a sales agreement method but the *Dartstone* case tended to validate lease-and-leaseback or purchase-and-purchaseback type of tie arrangements and the position was strengthened by the *Total v. Thompson* case.

In a normal rent review situation the valuer will find that he is required to arrive at the open market rent on the assumption that the premises are offered to let with vacant possession and he therefore values on a "free of tie" basis. From the point of view of the tenant this may produce unfortunate results because, as will be appreciated, the free rent could be as much as double the tied rent, although in such circumstances the tenant's subsequent remedy would probably be to sub-lease the premises to an oil company at the free rent that he would otherwise have to pay himself, arranging to lease the premises back at a tied rent.

Plant and machinery valuation and goodwill valuations

It is not intended in this chapter to deal with the valuation of plant and machinery, which is a specialisation within a specialisation, but general guidance can be obtained by referring to the standard catalogues.

Again it is not proposed to deal with the valuation of goodwill in any detail but the normal principles apply. Goodwill is a balancing figure after all other assets have been evaluated; in other words it is the capital equivalent or market value of the true net, or super-profit, of a business. Complete analysis is necessary to isolate the super-profit element and it is necessary to start by calculating the value or measure of elements which are not included in goodwill so called, such as the following:

1. The value of the property itself.
2. Staff and management costs, and directors' share.
3. Rates and other outgoings of a like nature.
4. Repairs, calculated on an average basis.
5. Any loan interest.
6. Allowances for depreciation.
7. Stock in trade.
8. Work in progress.
9. Discounts received.
10. Credit facilities and the cost of giving such facilities.
11. Exceptional losses, or profits, on a non-recurring basis.

This list is not comprehensive but simply indicates the type of approach required. To produce the information it is usually necessary to examine trading accounts over a number of years, usually at least three, and to equate profits to make a future projection. It is also necessary to decide on the proper return on capital employed and, in the case of garages, to consider the nature and value of such arrangements as car franchises.

High premiums are sometimes paid on the assignment of garage leases (as is, for example, the case with shop leases) which bear little relationship to normal goodwill or profit rent valuations. Second-hand car sales potential sometimes explains such payments.

Study 1

Major service station on dual carriageway trunk road in an outer London area. Traffic volume on route 35,000 vehicles a day. Estimated petrol sales: 1,000,000 gals p.a. Frontage 200 ft.

Estimated rental value

	Area (m^2)	Rate £ per m^2	£ p.a.	£ p.a.
Forecourt 1,000,000 gals. p.a. at 6p per gal.				60,000
Remainder				
Shop	60	60	3,600	
Lubricating bays	76	30	2,280	
Oil store	10	12	120	
Workshop	75	30	2,250	
Store	20	15	300	say 8,500

Open market rental value, say £68,500

Tied rental calculation

Forecourt 1,000,000 gals. p.a. at 1·6p per gal.		16,000
Remainder—as above—		8,500
Tied rent, say		£24,500

Capital value (freehold with vacant possession)

ERV of forecourt	£60,000 p.a.	£
Y.P. at 9% in perpetuity	11·111	
		say 666,000
ERV of remainder	£8,500 p.a.	
Y.P. at 12% in perpetuity	8·333	
		say 70,000
	Capital value	£736,000

Analysis

Rental yield on value $\dfrac{£68,500 \text{ p.a.}}{£736,000} = 9\cdot3\%$

Tied rent yield $\dfrac{£24,500 \text{ p.a.}}{£736,000} = 3\cdot3\%$

Notes on Study 1

By way of comment on the above, it can be assumed that the information available to the valuer clearly points to sales of 1 million gallons per annum at normally competitive prices for the area and that an analysis on the basis of traffic volume in relation to available facilities and likely future developments supports this information. The road is a dual carriageway and the traffic flow on each side has been taken as 17,500 vehicles a day. The valuer has established to his satisfaction by inspecting other stations on the route that this good modern station in competition with poor stations can produce 1 million gallons per annum even though average sales for the route point to a somewhat lower throughput.

The forecourt has been valued at the rate of 6p per gallon because in current conditions and on available evidence this appears to be about the best rate a petrol company would pay to secure such throughput in the London area, but depending on actual circumstances the rate could be slightly higher or somewhat lower. The shop rent will be noted and it can be said that shop rents are closely related to petrol throughput because the number of customers entering the shop to pay for petrol at the cash desk is related to petrol sales volume. This shop is known to achieve a high volume of sales of a wide variety of goods. Of course the forecourt cash desk or console must be situated in the shop and then serves a dual purpose.

The two lubrication bays have been valued as one and a specific rate has been applied to the oil store even though it is a necessary adjunct of the lubrication bays, because there is an ideal size and it is necessary to be able to make allowances by adjusting the rate if the storage space is too large or too small in a given case. The workshop has been valued at an appropriate rate with an addition for the necessary storage space. The fact that the ancillary space has been taken at half the rate used for the main area is a convention that seems to be proven and is useful in analysis.

The tied rental calculation is artificial because although it can be assumed to result from a bargain between the petrol company and the tied tenant, its measure does depend on various adjustments. Probably 1·0p to 1·6p per gallon for the forecourt would be a fairly typical tied rent for a station of this sort, but an independent dealer able to come to terms with an oil company for the supply of petrol would probably offer or agree to pay a rent in the region of 3p per gallon or £30,000 per annum, half the free rate, on an arms length sale and lease-back basis. This implies an overbid of 3p per gallon on the part of an oil company as the measure of special value. The remainder of the premises has been valued at the same rates as for the open-market rental value for the simple reason that it is worth as much to the tenant as to the oil company: an oil company would not be inclined to pay more rent (for parts other than the forecourt) than it could recover and will often sever the non-petrol selling part by sale as a separate operation.

The capital valuation shows a method weighing the special value of the station, or, more accurately, the special value of the forecourt and fuel throughput, to an oil company in that the forecourt has been valued on a 9% basis and the remainder on a 12% basis. It will be seen that this means that whereas the petrol company could be expected to buy at a price to show an overall equated yield of 9.3% on estimated free rental value, and yield on the tied rent actually obtained would be no more than 3·3%.

As has already been pointed out, twenty years or thirty years ago when petrol companies first entered the market for stations, it was possible to value by first determining the price the property would command on the market then existing, a market comprised largely of dealers, and finally adding an element of special value. As the nature of the market has changed to the extent that the only real bidder for a filling or service station with a large throughput is an oil company, it is now appropriate to go directly to a figure of market value incorporating special value. Since it is realised that the oil company can recover a market return in rent on the value or cost of parts other than the forecourt, the modern method of capitalization indicated is more accurate than the old formula once employed by the author and others, which in modern terms would give too much weight to the adverse effect on forecourt value of valuable other parts such as workshops and showrooms. [See Ch. 4 p. 37 "The Valuation and Development of Petrol Filling Stations" by the author of this chapter and R. W. Westbrook (2nd. edition) (Pub. Estates Gazette Ltd—1960).]

Study 2

Major petrol service station on trunk road in Midlands. Traffic volume on route 25,000 vehicles a day. Estimated petrol sales 800,000 gals. p.a. Frontage 180 ft.

Estimated rental value

	Area (m^2)	Rate £ per m^2	£ p.a.	£ p.a.
Forecourt 800,000 gals. p.a. at 5p				say 40,000
Remainder				
Shop	60	25	1,500	
Lubricating bays	75	25	1,875	
Oil store	10	10	100	
Workshop	150	25	3,750	
Store	20	12·50	250	
				say 7,500

Open market rental value, say £47,500

Tied rental calculation

Forecourt 800,000 gals. p.a. at 1·5p per gal, say	12,000
Remainder—as above—	7,500
Tied rent, say	£19,500

Capital value (freehold with vacant possession)   £
ERV of forecourt   £40,000 p.a.
Y.P. at 9% in perpetuity   11·111
                                          ————————   say 444,000

ERV of remainder   £7,500 p.a.
Y.P. at 12% in perpetuity   8·333
                                          ————————   say 62,500

                            Capital value   £506,500

Analysis
Rental yield on value   £47,500 p.a.
                                          ———————— = 9.4%
                                          £506,500

Tied rent yield   £19,500 p.a.
                                          ———————— = 3·8%
                                          £506,500

Notes on Study 2

This study relates to a station in the Midlands similar to the one considered in Study 1. Estimated petrol sales appear to relate to a traffic volume of 12,500 vehicles on each side of the road plus some crossing traffic, but competition appears to be slightly less effective. In these cases the percentage of crossing traffic chiefly depends on the adequacy of facilities on the near side of the road. With adequate facilities on each side and with heavy traffic, the crossing tendency almost disappears. So-called "brand loyalty" is hardly effective these days; price coupled with sales promotion is the important factor.

The rate applied to the estimated gallonage is lower. In the first place rates tend to be lower in the Midlands than in the south and in the second place the gallonage itself is lower. The remaining parts have been valued with an appropriate adjustment for the different location but it will be seen that the shop bears a lower relationship to the throughput. The tied rental calculation is again artificial in the sense already mentioned but the rate per gallon is almost as for the previous study, illustrating the fact that tied rents are really policy matters and depend on other factors.

The capital value has been calculated in the same way as before to arrive at the special value element, but in this case it will be seen that whilst the rent yield on value is much the same, the tied rent yield is somewhat higher. This latter for the simple reason that there has been little adjustment downwards in the tied rent rate applied to the forecourt but, as has been said, between one petrol company and another this type of inconsistency can be anticipated.

Study 3

Major petrol filling station on trunk road in the south east of England. Traffic volume on route 55,000 vehicles a day. Established petrol sales of 1,400,000 gals. p.a. with prospect of further growth. Frontage 60 metres.

Estimated rental value £ p.a.

Forecourt 1,400,000 gals. p.a. at 6·5p per gal.   91,000
Shop 80 square metres at £40   3,200

Open market rental value, say £94,000

Tied rental calculation
Forecourt 1,400,000 gals. p.a. at 1·75p per gal.   24,500
Shop—as above—   3,200

Tied rent, say £27,500

Capital value (freehold with vacant possession)

		£
ERV of whole	£94,000 p.a.	
Y.P. at 9% in perpetuity	11·111	1,044,434

Capital value, say £1,044,000

Notes on Study 3

This is an example of a valuation of the prime type of station most attractive to oil companies; a petrol filling station and shop without servicing or other facilities. Traffic volume is high and the valuer has satisfied himself that the petrol sales figure is accurate but that there is a distinct possibility of more than normal further growth.

The rate applied to the forecourt is higher and results from the fact that great interest would be shown by oil companies in such a station. It is the case that some petrol companies apply a rate to the forecourt of this type of station which includes the value of the shop, and they are able to do this because the value of the shop does relate closely to forecourt value. In this case the overall rate is about 6·7p per gallon. The tied rental calculation is again hypothetical but it can be assumed that a somewhat higher tied rent would be charged for a station of this type.

The capital value has not been arrived at on the basis used in the previous studies as there is no particular reason with this type of station why the total rent should not be capitalized at one rate.

The value arrived at can perhaps be regarded as a maximum and can probably be taken to indicate expected further growth of throughput in the near future to about 1,600,000 gallons per annum.

Study 3A

This is an illustration of a residual site value calculation and relates to Study 3. The valuer has projected the construction of a petrol filling station with the same potential throughput at a total cost of £310,000 including fees and bridging finance.

Estimated rental value of completed station	£94,000
Y.P. at 9% in perpetuity	11·111
	£1,044,434
Defer for 2½ years at 10% to allow for construction and averaged sales growth period	0·79
	£825,102
Deduct cost (as above)	£310,000
Site value and bridging finance on site cost at 10% for 1 year, divided	say £515,000
	1·1
Site value	£468,000

Site value	£468,000	
	—————	= say £37,000
Y.P. at 8% in perpetuity	12·5	

Analysis

Ground rent	£37,000 p.a.	
	—————	= 2·6p per gallon
Gallonage	1,400,000 gals. p.a.	

Notes on Study 3A

This study illustrates in simplified form an appropriate and normal method of arriving at site value; in short the use of the residual method of valuation. The valuer has taken the cost of constructing the station together with fees and bridging finance as £310,000, but he has made no addition for developer's profit for the simple reason that the best price would be paid by an oil company, not by a developer as such, and an oil company does not in practice require a developer's profit or at least does not take one.

The estimated rental value is taken at the same figure as in Study 3 and capitalized at the same rate. The capital value of the hypothetical station has been adjusted by an element of deferment to allow for a construction period of one year and an overall sales growth period (from nil to the estimated throughput) of about three years, half this period having been added as an averaged figure but in practice an oil company might overlook this necessary mathematical adjustment.

To arrive at an equivalent ground rent, the site value has been decapitalized on an 8% basis. This is a slightly reduced rate but the theory that a ground rent can be assumed to show a substantially lower yield because of its greater security can hardly apply in this market or perhaps even with this type of valuation.

Study 4

Major petrol filling station on trunk road in the Midlands. Traffic volume on route 30,000 vehicles a day. Established petrol sales of 1,100,000 gals p.a. Frontage 60 metres.

Estimated rental value

	£ p.a.
Forecourt 1,100,000 gals. p.a. at 5·5p per gal.	60,500
Shop 80 square metres at £25	2,000
Open market rental value,	£62,500

Tied rental calculation

Forecourt 1,100,000 gals. p.a. at 1·5p per gal.	16,500
Shop—as above—	2,000
Tied rent, say	£18,500

Capital value (freehold with vacant possession)

		£
ERV of forecourt	£60,500 p.a.	
Y.P. at 9% in perp.	11·111	
	—————	say 672,000
ERV of shop (say)	£2,000 p.a.	
Y.P. at 12% in perp.	8·333	
	—————	say 17,000
	Capital value, say	£689,000

Notes on Study 4

This study compares with Study 3 but relates to a filling station in the Midlands. The ratio of sales to traffic volume is comparatively high because of lack of competition, and the valuer has assumed that competition is unlikely to be increased because this station, whilst within an easy distance of a large town, is on a road running through an area of high landscape value, so there is a clear presumption against the grant of further permission for the enlargement of existing stations or the establishment of new ones.

The forecourt rate is slightly lower than would be the case in the south but again the shop rent bears a fairly fixed relationship to throughput. The rate employed in the tied rental calculation has been adjusted if for no other reason than to emphasize the variations in practice.

The normal method of finding capital value has been applied but in this study as in the previous study there would be a good case for capitalising the combined rents at one rate. It will be appreciated that in the case of premises where the forecourt rent and the rent of the remainder are equal, the yield will be the average of the two rates employed, that is to say, on the hypothesis employed, $10\frac{1}{2}$%, but on the investment market as such, tenanted filling stations of this sort let to oil companies would probably be expected to show a yield of 12% or more, particularly where there was no indication of any possible alternative use or development prospect.

Study 5

Petrol service station on main road in rural area in south west of England. Traffic volume on route 10,000 vehicles a day. Petrol sales established at 400,000 gals. p.a. Frontage 120 ft. Some second-hand car sales.

Estimated rental value

			£ p.a.	£ p.a.
Forecourt 400,000 gals. p.a. at 2p per gal.				8,000
	Areas	Rate £		
Remainder	(m²)	per m²		
Shop	60	20	1,200	
Lubrication bay	35	20	700	
Workshop	60	20	1,200	
Store	10	10	100	
			———	3,200

Open market value, say £11,000

Capital value (freehold with vacant possession)

		£
ERV	£11,000 p.a.	
Y.P. at 12% in perpetuity	8·333	
	———	
		say £90,000

Notes on Study 5

This is an illustration of a valuation of a station unlikely to be of interest to an oil company in terms of purchase, although the dealer would be able to enter into a solus supply agreement. Sales are low and economies of scale would therefore not be achieved. The dealer's gross profits on petrol sales would probably not exceed £40,000 per annum at best with the benefit of whatever rebates he was able to obtain and his net profit after deducting a proportion of overhead charges other than rent might be in the region of £14,000 per annum leaving a true net profit of £6,000 per annum in respect of petrol sales after deducting the rent indicated. To some extent of course the petrol sales operation would be supported by repair work and second-hand car sales and there would be a reasonable contribution from shop profits even with this type of station. A simple petrol station with no other business and with such a low throughput would hardly survive.

Regarding capital value, since an oil company would not be interested in a purchase, a higher yield is called for and the total rent has been capitalised at 12% with this in mind. It is at about 500,000 gallons per annum, not less, that oil company or petrol distributor interest now normally begins to arise and there is then a disproportionate increase in value.

Study 6

Large garage and petrol station in an excellent position in a north-western London suburb with a major car sales franchise. Petrol sales ascertained to be 800,000 gals. p.a. Frontage 140 ft.

Estimated rental value

			£ p.a.	£ p.a.
Forecourt 800,000 gals. p.a. at 5·5p per gal.				44,000
Remainder	Areas (m²)	Rate £ per m²		
Shop	60	50	3,000	
Car sales showroom	195	75	14,625	
Open car sales space	200	30	6,000	
Admin. offices	120	50	6,000	
Reception office	10	35	350	
Workshop	360	50	18,000	
Parts store	90	25	2,250	
Paint shop	60	40	2,400	
Lubrication bays	90	50	4,500	
Oil store	10	15	150	
Car wash facilities	—	—	2,000	
Open parking area	2,000	5	10,000	
			say 69,000	

Open market rental value £113,000

Tied rental calculation

	£ p.a.
Forecourt 800,000 gals. p.a. at 1·6p per gal.	12,800
Remainder—as above—	69,000

Tied rent £81,800

Capital value (freehold with vacant possession)

		£
ERV of forecourt	£44,000 p.a.	
Y.P. at 9% in perp.	11·111	
		say £488,000
ERV of remainder	£69,000 p.a.	
Y.P. at 11% in perp.	9·091	
		say £627,000

Capital value, say £1,115,000

Analysis

Rental yield on value	£113,000 p.a.	
	$\dfrac{£113,000 \text{ p.a.}}{£1,115,000} = 10\%$	
Tied rent yield	£81,800 p.a.	
	$\dfrac{£81,800 \text{ p.a.}}{£1,115,000} = 7\cdot3\%$	

Notes on Study 6

This example relates to a fully developed garage and petrol station business with reasonably high petrol sales, or at least with petrol sales high enough to interest an oil company, and a good car sales franchise. It might be that in a competitive situation an oil company would attach a somewhat higher rate than 5·5p per gallon to a station of this sort, particularly if leasing the forecourt alone, but a mean figure has been assumed. The estimating of petrol sales in a suburban position requires a different technique: traffic volume figures are less relevant and it is necessary to make an estimate of car population in relation to the total number of stations in the area and their attractiveness to the motorist. Motorists tend to buy petrol in their own locality, if for no other reason than that many of them do not travel far from it. It has been assumed in the present case that sales of the volume indicated have been established.

The premises the subject of the valuation comprise extensive buildings as well as the forecourt and rates per square foot have been applied part by part on the basis of the valuer's general knowledge of transactions relating to similar premises, and allowing for the influence of general commercial, industrial and office rent levels in the area, with an allocation of rates to some extent related to the probable comparative profitability of the various parts of the garage operation. Of course the intricate nature of an analysis of the value of the respective parts of such premises as this does increase the risk of an unbalanced synthesis and technical conventions have to be applied in allocating relative values to the various parts.

It is not possible to value car wash facilities at a rate related to area and the profitability of the operation varies considerably from garage to garage. Total installation costs are in the region of £20,000 per bay, but given high volume use, overhead costs per car can be as low as 10p per wash. A large local population is required to produce such a degree of use and there is a correlation with petrol sales. A station selling much less than the subject of this valuation would hardly support a mechanical car wash and it has been postulated that a local population of 15,000 is required to support each car wash installation.

An open parking area is necessary in a station of this type because cars awaiting sale and repair and servicing have to be accommodated. Rents paid vary greatly but in this sort of position perhaps £100 per annum per car would be a reasonable average. The area of 2,000 m² given in the study would accommodate about 100 cars.

The tied rent has been calculated at a fixed rate as before and the capital value has been ascertained in the usual way but the rate applied to buildings has been put at 11% to allow for greater security of investment. In this case the market yield is 10% and the tied rent yield 7·3%, a higher figure than in the case of a petrol service station or a petrol filling station.

Study 7

Garage and petrol station in west Yorkshire town with a population of 200,000. Petrol sales established at 700,000 gals. p.a. Frontage 40 metres.

Estimated rental value

			£ p.a.	£ p.a.
Forecourt 700,000 gals. p.a. at 4p per gal.				28,000
	Areas	Rate £		
Remainder	(m²)	per m²		
Shop	50	25	1,250	
Car showroom	100	30	3,000	
Offices	80	20	1,600	
Workshop	240	25	6,000	
Parts store	40	10	400	
Lubrication bays	90	25	2,250	
Oil store	10	10	100	
Open parking area	400	2·5	1,000	
				15,600

Open market rental value, say £43,000

Tied rental calculation	£
Forecourt 700,000 gals. p.a. at 1·3p per gal.	9,100
Remainder—as above—	15,600

Tied rent, say £24,700

Capital value (freehold with vacant possession)   £

ERV of forecourt	£28,000 p.a.	
Y.P. at 9½% in perp.	10·526	
		say 295,000
ERV of remainder	£15,600 p.a.	
Y.P. at 12½% in perp.	8	
		say 124,000

Capital value, say £419,000

Analysis

Rental yield on value

$$\frac{£43,000 \text{ p.a.}}{£419,000} = 10·2\%$$

Tied rent yield

$$\frac{£24,700 \text{ p.a.}}{£419,000} = 5·7\%$$

Notes on Study 7

This study is of a similar property to the one considered in Study 6 but the location is in west Yorkshire. Petrol sales are somewhat lower than in the other case and for this reason and because rates are generally lower in the north Midlands the rate per gallon has been taken at 4p instead of at 5·5p in the previous study. The rates per square metre applied to the other parts of the premises are lower and experience indicates that this regional variation is justified. The tied rental calculation has been taken at a lower rate than in the other case to illustrate the possible variation resulting from the differing practices of the various companies: in some cases the tied rent appears to be fixed at about half the open market rate.

In this case the estimated rental values of the two parts have been capitalised at a somewhat lower years' purchase to allow for variations in approach as between the south and the north Midlands. The analysis shows the comparative yields.

Study 8

Small garage and petrol station with car sales business in a north of England town with a population of 15,000 and petrol sales of 300,000 gals. p.a. Frontage 35 metres.

Estimated rental value

			£ p.a.	£ p.a.
Forecourt 300,000 gals. p.a. at 1p per gal.				3,000
	Areas	Rate £		
Remainder	(m²)	per m²		
Shop	40	10	400	
Car showroom	66	20	1,320	
Office	12	15	180	
Workshop	160	15	2,400	
Store	30	7·5	225	
Open parking area			500	
			———	5,025

Open market rental value, say £8,000

Capital value (freehold with vacant possession)

		£
ERV of forecourt	£8,000 p.a.	
Y.P. at 13% in perp.	7·692	61,536

Capital value, say £61,000

Notes on Study 8

This study illustrates the type of case where the valuer is dealing with a property likely to be of no interest to an oil company, except from the supply point of view, and furthermore one in the north of England. The forecourt rent derives from possible gross profits of say £25,000 per annum against allocated operating expenses of an estimated £19,000 per annum and even so would be high except when regarded as an ancillary part of the business: the proprietor of such a station would probably look at the profits from the whole on the basis that each part supports other parts. A station of this type is less likely to show high profits from the sale of accessories but there is assumed to be a reasonable second hand car sales business backed up by repair facilities. The estimated rental value has been capitalised on a 13% basis to allow for the risk element.

Study 9—a special situation

In this case a lease of a major filling station selling 900,000 gals p.a. has 5 years to run at a rent of £7,250 p.a. and the tenant is assumed to have a right to renew for 21 years, with reviews, at a rack rent. Estimated rack rental value (free) £35,000 p.a. The tenant is to surrender his interest and the landlord is then to sell his freehold to an oil company. The parties agree to share the "marriage value" equally.

1. *Value of dealer tenant's interest in free station*

Rack rental value	£35,000 p.a.	
Rent reserved	£7,250 p.a.	
Profit rent	£27,750 p.a.	
Y.P. for 5 yrs. at 8%	3·993	
		say £110,000

2. *Investment value of landlord's interest*

Rent receivable	£7,250 p.a.	
Y.P. in perp. at 12%	8·333	
		£60,414
Rack rental value	£35,000 p.a.	
Rent reserved	£7,250 p.a.	
Increase on renewal of lease in 5 year's time	£27,750 p.a.	
Y.P. in perp. at 12% deferred 5 years	4·728	
		£131,202
		say £190,000

3. Open market value of premises with vacant possession to an oil company

Forecourt ERV	£25,000 p.a.	
Y.P. in perp. at 8%	12·5	
		£312,500
Remainder ERV	£10,000 p.a.	
Y.P. in perp. at 12%	8·333	
		£83,330
		say £400,000

Notes on Study 9

This study is included as an example of a special situation and reflects the effect of the full release of the special value element. The dealer tenant could sell his leasehold interest free of a tie to an oil company for £110,000 and the landlord has an investment which would sell for £190,000; but since the vacant possession value is £400,000, there is a potential £100,000 profit element available to the landlord and the tenant if they combine. In such circumstances the tenant might well be persuaded to surrender his lease to his landlord for £110,000 plus, one can assume, a further £50,000 (half the total profit element) and the landlord would then be able to sell the freehold to an oil company for £400,000. Since the cost of the surrender to the landlord would have been £160,000 and since the investment value of his own interest was £190,000—a total of £350,000—he also would have made a profit of £50,000. For simplicity, costs have been ignored in this example but would have to be taken into account in such a series of actual transactions.

Study 10

This is an example of a large modern petrol service station in the south west 100 miles from London on a major trunk road carrying a large volume of traffic. Petrol sales have been established at 1,300,000 gals. p.a. and the station includes a fast food restaurant run by a major catering chain. The restaurant produces a fixed rent of £20,000 p.a. plus 3% of gross turnover under a lease with 50 years to run, the current turnover being £300,000 p.a.

Estimated rental value

	Area (m²)	Rate £ (per m²)	£	£ p.a.
Forecourt 1,300,000 gals. p.a. 6·4p per gal.				83,200
Remainder				
Shop	150	30	4,500	
Workshop	200	25	5,000	
Car wash facilities			1,000	
			——	10,500
				93,700
Restaurant			20,000	
Plus 6% of gross turnover			18,000	
			——	38,000
Open market rental value				£131,700

£

Capital value (freehold, subject to restaurant lease)

ERV of forecourt	£83,200 p.a.	
Y.P. at 9% in perp.	11·111	
	————	say 924,000
ERV of remainder		
(excluding restaurant)	£10,500 p.a.	
Y. P. at 11% in perp.	9·091	
	————	say 95,000
Restaurant		
Fixed rent	£20,000 p.a.	
Y.P. at 12% in perp.	8·333	
	————	say 166,000
Turnover rent	£18,000 p.a.	
Y.P. at 18% in perp.	5·555	
	————	say 100,000
	Capital value	£1,285,000

Notes on Study 10

In this example the restaurant part has been valued on a split basis, the fixed rent being valued as such and the turnover rent, so called, being capitalised something between the rate applicable to a true rent and to business goodwill. Turnover rents, unlike true rents, being secured not by property but only by the expectation of continued and possibly fluctuating trading profits, probably have to be regarded as less secure but sometimes show greater growth.

(The author of this chapter wishes to thank the Institute of Petroleum, the Motor Agents Association, the British Road Federation and many others for the help he has received in compiling material for this chapter. He also wishes to give his particular thanks for the assistance given to him in his revision work for the present chapter by his old friend and one-time colleague, E. M. Broughton, ARICS, of Investors in Industry, London, SW1, and to his fellow-practitioners P. W. Squire, FRICS of Messrs. Herring Son & Daw, London W1 and M. R. Corbett, FRICS of Messrs. Grimley & Son of Birmingham as well as to others to all of whom he is grateful but to none of whom can be attributed any of the author's shortcomings or errors of omission or commission.)

Chapter 15

LEASE RENEWALS AND RENT REVIEWS OF COMMERCIAL PROPERTY

A combination of the recession, inflation and, in some cases, falling rents is leading to an increase in a breakdown of negotiations between landlords and tenants of commercial premises. If a lease has expired, then the final arbiter is the County Court or the High Court. The costs clearly are high and there is therefore an added inducement for the matter to be settled.

However, where the parties have fallen out over the terms of a rent review, then the matter will fall to be settled either by an independent surveyor or by an arbitrator, according to the lease. He tends to be a Chartered Surveyor and is normally appointed by the President of the Royal Institution of Chartered Surveyors, rather than by agreement between the parties. The settlement of the dispute by one of these methods should normally be quicker and cheaper than any court proceedings.

A significant number of references arise because the tenant is either reluctant or cannot afford to pay the increased rent and the reference itself may give some temporary relief to cash flow problems.

Increasing volume of work

The increasing volume of work dictates that the private practitioner has now to keep fully abreast of any reported Landlord and Tenant Act cases. He needs to be able to give evidence, to prepare proofs of evidence and, if the matter is going to be dealt with by a written representation, to be able to draft and write them on behalf of his client. If he is an arbitrator, then he has got to have or acquire the ability to write an award which, by the time he has set out the various arguments and recorded his conclusions in writing, may well be a document of at least twenty pages.

Significance of rent

The great significance of rent in terms of a tenant's outgoing is not generally realised. Commerce and industry in general terms pay as much in corporation tax as they do in rates; rent clearly can be more significant than both rolled together. The open market is a place where rents are settled by supply and demand. Invariably the arbitrator or expert is trying to determine what the open market is but in 1987 the evidence can very often conflict. An expanding chain of shops such as fast food shops may well pay more than the market in order to expand business. Other trades may be artificially depressed due to recession. Finding a balance is never easy and the landlord and tenant are entitled to expect a high level of professional competence. An arbitration award is usually more satisfactory to all parties because the professionals see their arguments advanced and any legal points disposed of, hopefully for all time; the client may well have an award of one page which of itself gives no indication whatsoever of the considerable work that has gone into presentation of his case. The losing client would not be human if he did not take the jaundiced view.

Lease renewals

Previously, in Chapter 4, the statutory rights to a business tenant to a new lease have been set out in summary. There is a considerable body of case law as to who or what amounts to a business tenant. The definition is far wider than plain English would indicate, and a tennis club has been held to be a business tenant as defined under the Act. There has also been a considerable amount of case law which a landlord has successfully or unsuccessfully opposed the application by his tenant for the grant of a new lease. There are seven grounds specified under Section 30 of the Landlord and Tenant Act 1954 Part II (see Chapter 4). Clearly a valuer has to have some knowledge of these, and even if the grant of a new tenancy is opposed the question of an interim rent, and therefore values, may well arise if the matter proceeds to court and the hearing is after the lease has expired. It is possible today for a business lease to be outside the terms of the Landlord and Tenant Act 1954 Part II. In the 1960's it became apparent that landlords were unwilling to grant short leases of property which they intended to redevelop, or perhaps needed for their own occupation, either because tenants could successfully apply for new leases or could delay the landlord's plans by lodging an application for a new lease. Under the Law of Property Act 1969 a business lease can now be registered in court as being outside the terms of the Landlord and Tenant Act 1954 Part II.

The valuer normally first gets involved with a lease renewal with the necessary service of statutory notices. The valuer should point out to his client that a lease is coming to an end and that certain necessary statutory notices and counter notices should be served. As the final arbiter of the new lease and its rent will be either the

County Court or in the case of more valuable property, the High Court, the services of notices of a statutory nature are best left to solicitors. A valuer concerned with a case going to the County Court or to the High Court will not only be concerned with the appropriate value that the court will be invited to determine under Section 34, but must also enquire whether either the landlord or the tenant are seeking to vary any of the terms of the original lease. Very often the original lease may either be old or expressed in an out of date language that may not reflect current market conditions or current legal thinking, particularly relating to clarification or extension of the law in reported cases. Section 35 of the Act gives the court the right to impose such terms and conditions as it thinks fit, having had regard to the current tenancy and all relevant circumstances. The valuer giving evidence must therefore be prepared to give evidence in chief or to be cross-examined upon any changes that might be made by the court and to express an expert view as to what extent such changes should be reflected in the rent determined under Section 34.

In February 1982 the House of Lords, in *O'May and Others v. City of London Real Property Company Limited* (1982) 261 E.G. 1185, gave a judgement that is some indication as to how far the courts should go in varying the terms of the lease. The facts of the case were that the landlords had sought to impose a full repairing lease upon the tenants, the High Court had thought this to be a reasonable variation. The High Court had been overturned by the Court of Appeal and the House of Lords upheld the judgement of the Court of Appeal. It was an agreed fact between the valuers that the transfer of the burden could be adequately compensated by a reduction in rent from £10·50 per square foot per annum to £10·00 a square foot per annum. The High Court set out some tests and these do not appear to have been materially dissented from in the Court of Appeal or the House of Lords. There appear to be three main tests:

1. Has the party seeking for a variation of the terms of the lease shown any reason for doing so?
2. If such a change in term is granted can it be adequately adjusted by a reduced rent determined under Section 34?
3. Will the proposed change materially impair the tenant's security in carrying out his business or profession?

Considering all three questions the court should consider whether each one is fair and reasonable between parties.

In his judgement Lord Hailsham said:

"Obviously it is to the advantage of the landlord to transfer the financial risk of fluctuation to the tenant and there can be no possible reason why, if the tenant agrees (and the evidence was that many do) he should not do so. But the crucial question is, if the current lease does not so provide and the tenant does not agree, by what possible reasoning the court should impose the burden on the tenant against his will as a condition of his receiving a new tenancy under Part II of the Landlord and Tenant Act 1954. It may be granted that the transfer of the risk from the landlord to the tenant is a perfectly legitimate negotiating aim for the landlord to entertain. But the argument is two-edged. It is equally legitimate negotiating aim of the tenant to resist the change. Granted that a reduction in rent of 50p from £10·50 per foot to £10·00 per foot is, in the limited sense described, an adequate estimate of the compensation which a landlord will offer if the risk is to be transferred. But the argument is again two-edged. It may equally be argued that an additional 50p is the adequate estimate of the rent payable to the landlord if the risk is to be kept where it is under the current lease. But neither of the two statements assists to answer the question where, in the new lease, is the risk of fluctuation to lie. If I am correct that the inference from the authorities is that the language of Section 35 requires that the party (whether landlord or tenant) requiring a change must justify as reasonable a departure from the current lease in case of dispute about its terms, the answer must be that 'prima facia' it must lie where the current lease provides and that a mere agreement about figures based on either or both of two rival hypotheses does not shift the burden in any way."

It has been suggested that the court's reluctance to vary the lease was because the lease being renewed was itself a short lease. I do not consider this is necessarily the case as the maximum length of lease the court can award is fourteen years. The acid point of the case was the transfer of a risk. While it was agreed that the market would reflect the risk in financial terms, this did not mean that the transfer of the risk itself was fair or reasonable to the tenant.

Rent reviews

The valuer will either be acting for the landlord or the tenant. Whether he be negotiating or whether he be preparing proof of evidence he first of all has to determine the basis of the valuation. The basis of his approach should be contained within the civil contract, that is the lease between the two parties. It is a basic rule of construction and interpretation of leases that they must be read strictly. The court will usually only add words missing if they are necessary to make commercial sense of the document.

In 1985 and 1986 there was considerable litigation over rent review clauses which in some instances were held, when read strictly, to require future rent reviews to be ignored on a rent review. The result in some of those cases was that what had to be valued was the unexpired period of the lease ignoring (and therefore increasing the hypothetical tenants bid) future reviews.

These results were almost certainly never intended by those drafting the leases. As each lease is often different as to the actual wording used it is not helpful to comment in general terms on such a series of cases. Recent judgements indicate that commercial sense should be supplied in construing such clauses. No doubt there will be further cases before it is possible to give general as opposed to particular guidance.

The rent review clause will normally require the value to be determined by reference to such expressions as "the full rental value of the property" or "the open market value of the property". Rarely are two clauses similar, though the Royal Institution of Chartered Surveyors and the Law Society have suggested standard appropriate wording. The whole basis of the valuation must reflect not only the rent review clause but the lease as a whole. There may be points to be disregarded, there may be points to take into account, questions of improvements, inflation and the user clause may all be relevant. There are three basic methods of approach:

A. RENTAL VALUES

With such a standard business premises as a shop, office or factory there is normally evidence of rent. The amount that a hypothetical tenant might pay, or a hypothetical landlord might accept, must, in the long run, reflect whether the tenant expects to make a profit out of his occupation. It must also reflect the fact that such a landlord would fall short of asking a rent so high that the tenant would be unwilling to pay as he could not continue trading with sufficient profit.

B. PROFITS TEST

There are a number of properties where reference to the profitability of the tenant may be the correct approach. Examples are public houses, cinemas, theatres, clubs, nightclubs and football clubs. The valuer, preferably by reference to certified accounts, should be able to devalue those accounts and calculate the total profits of the operation, then apportion those profits between the landlord and the tenant.

The certification of accounts as a true and correct record by a chartered accountant is only the point at which the valuer begins. Rarely will a valuer be told, as I was on one occasion by another chartered surveyor to his external credit, to ignore the certified accounts that had put in as his client was "well known to the Inland Revenue".

C. CAPITAL VALUES

Finally there is a small category of rent reviews where the valuer can obtain no assistance by way of market rental and the property is not an appropriate one to be valued by reference to profits. In this last resort the valuer has to consider capital values. The type of property where this arises is normally buildings built but not necessarily used for a particular purpose, such as a church or a school, and where the tenant is tied to a very restrictive user clause that otherwise makes the property, if not unmarketable, only marketable to a very limited extent. The valuer would only use this approach as a last resort and among many other matters would have regard to the age of the building, the cost of maintaining it and the cost of running it.

Evidence of value

A major part of preparing a client's case, whether it be to negotiate with another valuer, to present the case in the High Court, the County Court, to an arbitrator or to an independent surveyor, is the quality of the evidence you put forward as opposed to the quantity. There is at the moment no authoritative text book on the question of evidence as applied in arbitrations. For evidence generally and the rules of evidence, there are several excellent books currently in print but none of these cover the points relevant on a rent review. All other things being equal, which they rarely are, the valuer producing and proving the best evidence serves his client well.

The best evidence

The following is a suggested order of preference:

(a) Market evidence within the same building.
(b) Market evidence in the immediate vicinity.
(c) Rent reviews in the same property.
(d) Rent reviews in the immediate vicinity.
(e) Arbitrator's or independent surveyor's awards (quantum of award or determination).

Under the rules of evidence an arbitrator's award is probably not admissible in court as evidence. This may in due course be reconsidered as an arbitrator now can be required to give a reasoned award and the reasoned award may itself contain evidence. However, an arbitrator's award can only be as good as the evidence given to that arbitrator and upon which he made his award. An independent surveyor's award should also for very practical reasons be treated with considerable reservation. An independent surveyor can be sued for negligence and therefore the determination is rarely more than a page long and will contain no reasoning. Thus the determination may not even indicate whether the parties to the dispute were able or were invited to put forward evidence, what their evidence was, or whether the independent surveyor relied entirely upon his own practical experience.

Proof of evidence

A surveyor putting forward the rent payable on another property as evidence must be in a position to prove the transaction. In the High Court and before an arbitrator the proof required is production of the actual documentation or certified copies. As a practical point in an arbitration the arbitrator is normally perfectly happy to accept comparable evidence as being proved and fully admissible if both the parties agree this as a fact. Until recently it had been thought that post review evidence could only be admissible as evidence of trend in values and not as evidence of values as such.

In *Melwood Units PTY Limited* v. *Commissioner of Main Roads* [1979] A.C. 426, P.C., an Australian case, the Privy Council held the Land Appeal Court wrong to reject evidence of a June 1966 sale in relation to a compulsory purchase order of September 1965.

Some later cases, such as *Duvan Estates Limited* v. *Rossette Sunshine Savouries Limited* (1981) 261 E.G. 364, appear in conflict with the Privy Council case.

In *Segama NV* v. *Penny Le Roy Ltd* (1984) 269 E.G. 322, it was held, following *Melwood*, that an arbitrator was entitled to admit evidence as to rents agreed after the relevant date. However, Slaughton J. said that other judges might take a different view.

The weight that an arbitrator or independent surveyor attaches to evidence, be it pre review or post review date, is a matter of both judgement and experience. Post review evidence is therefore probably fully admissible not just of trend in values but of actual values.

Any evidence of a lower standard, such as where terms are agreed but the legal formalities are not settled, letters from other agents or correspondence marked subject to contract, should not be submitted. This will certainly be rejected by the courts or an arbitrator and therefore unless proved or agreed as being admissible should not be taken into consideration by an independent surveyor. However tempting the evidence is, if it is inadmissible it should not be put forward on your client's behalf as rather than enhancing your client's case it could positively spoil it.

Understanding the meaning of evidence, and knowing whether it is properly admissible or not is fundamental to a surveyor in preparing his case, whether he be an expert, an independent surveyor or an arbitrator. The independent surveyor may well be wise to invite the parties to the matter before him to state their views orally, or in writing, and indeed he may be actually required to receive them under the lease under which he has been appointed. It is therefore important that he is able to distinguish between evidence that should properly be admitted, and that which he should properly disregard, even if he is only exercising his own judgement. For an arbitrator it is absolutely crucial that he understands the difference. An arbitrator can now be called upon to give a reasoned award and in his consideration in a reasoned award of the evidence he must clearly indicate not only the evidence he has taken into account but must be positive in listing the evidence that he has either rejected immediately or has upon reflection decided should not be admitted.

Until 1972 the law was definitely uncertain as there had been no direct modern authority that had considered the question, however, in 1972 in *English Exporters (London) Limited* v. *Eldonwall Limited* [1973] Ch. 415, Megarry, J. considered this matter in detail, and his judgement in plain language clearly sets out what a valuer may or may not give evidence about, and also contains a clear statement as to what he can rely on when he is giving evidence of opinion as opposed to evidence of fact. Megarry, J. said:

> "... two of the heads under which the valuers' evidence may be ranged are opinion evidence and factual evidence. As an expert witness, the valuer is entitled to express his opinion about matters within his field of competence. In building up his opinions about values, he will no doubt have learned much from transactions in which he has himself been engaged, and of which he could give first hand evidence. But he will also have learned much from many other sources, including much of which he could give no first hand evidence. Textbooks, journals, reports of auctions and other dealings, and information obtained from his professional brethren and others, some related to particular transactions and some more general and indefinite, will all have contributed their

share. Doubtless much, or most, of this will be accurate, though some will not; and even what is accurate so far as it goes may be incomplete, in that nothing may have been said of some special element which affects values. Nevertheless, the opinion that the expert expresses is none the worse because it is in part derived from the matters of which he could give no direct evidence. Even in some of the extraneous information which he acquires in this way is inaccurate or incomplete, the errors and omissions will often tend to cancel each other out; and the valuer, after all, is an expert in this field, so that the less reliable the knowledge that he has about the details of some reported transaction, the more his experience will tell him that he should be ready to make some discount from the weight that he gives it in contributing to his overall sense of values. Some aberrant transactions may stand so far out of line that he will give them little or no weight. No question of giving hearsay evidence arises in such cases; the witness states his opinion from his general experience...."

"... In my judgement a valuer giving expert evidence in chief (or in re-examination):
a) may express the opinions that he has formed as to values even though substantial contributions to the formation of those opinions have been made by matters of which he has no first hand knowledge;
b) may give evidence as to the details of any transactions within his personal knowledge, in order to establish them as matters of fact; and
c) may express his opinion as to the significance of any transactions which are or will be proved by admissible evidence (whether or not given by him) in relation to the valuation with which he is concerned; but
d) may not give hearsay evidence stating the details of any transactions not within his personal knowledge in order to re-establish them as matters of fact.

To those propositions I would add that for counsel to put in a list of comparables ought to amount to a warranty by him of his intention to tender admissible evidence of all that is shown on the list.

I have spent some little time on dealing with this matter of evidence as it appears to be the subject of no direct modern authority and experience suggests that it is a matter on which there is considerable misunderstanding. When a list of comparables is being prepared for the trial, as is usual and convenient, it is all too common to include in the list transactions on which there will be no admissible evidence but only hearsay of a greater or lesser degree of reliability. If the parties exchange lists of comparables at an early date, often much time and money can be saved by the experts on each side agreeing such of the transactions in each list as, after any necessary inquiry, they feel they can accept as being reliably summarised; and in this way the additional expense of proving a favourable comparable not within an expert's own knowledge can be avoided. But if the other side will not accept the facts, then either the transaction must be proved by admissible evidence or it must be omitted as a comparable."

This is a particularly refreshing judgement, and is a very strong indication that when two surveyors are involved they should save everybody's time and expense by endeavouring to agree the facts and admissibility of comparable evidence.

Improvements

The problem of what are improvements and what are not, whether they should be taken into account and how they should be treated arises frequently. There are two main statutes that deal with this point. The provisions of the Landlord and Tenant Act 1927 are rarely met with in practice and these provisions have been summarised previously (see Chapter 4).

The Landlord and Tenant Act 1954, Part II, Section 34 states as follows:

"The rent payable under a tenancy granted by order of the Court under this Part of this Act shall be such as may be agreed between the Landlord and the Tenant or as, in default of such agreement, may be determined by the Court to be that at which, having regard to the terms of the tenancy (other than those relating to rent), the holding might reasonably be expected to be let in the open market by a willing Lessor, there being disregarded—any effect on rent of any improvement carried out by the Tenant or a predecessor in title of his otherwise than in pursuance of an obligation to his immediate Landlord."

Most problems do not arise under statute but under rent reviews. The first document the valuer must consider is the lease, and the lease will normally state that in assessing the rent the value of any improvements carried out by the tenant other than in pursuance of the lease are to be disregarded.

How to treat improvements has recently been a fruitful field of litigation, as a result of which there is now some guidance available to valuers as how they should proceed. A problem can occur where the tenant makes a "silk purse out of a sow's ear". In *Estates Projects* v. *Greenwich London Borough* (1979), 251 E.G. 851, the upper floors of four houses in Greenwich had been converted into offices. Their improved value as at the date of review was agreed between the parties as being £12,000 per annum. For Greenwich Council it was argued that the value before they were improved was nil or nominal as they could not be used as offices because the premises would not comply with the Offices Shops and Railway Premises Act 1963. (The exact figure of valuation put forward was £690·00 per annum.) The landlord's valuer put forward a value of £3,200 per annum and put forward three alternative methods to arrive at that figure. The arbitrator chose the method whereby the cost of doing the work at the date of the rent review was calculated and from that capital figure a rental figure was derived. The arbitrator awarded the rent of £1,100 per annum. The judge held this to be a wrong method. The method that commended itself to the judge was the method he had indicated earlier in the year in *GREA Real Property Investments* v. *Williams* (1979), 250 E.G. 651. In that case the tenant took a lease of uncompleted office building, where the contractor had gone bankrupt and carried out the necessary final construction works. Those construction works were the disputed improvements. The judge said that the method that commended itself to him was to determine at the date of the grant of the lease, the rental value of the finished offices, to determine their rental value as unfinished and then, probably, to apply the percentage differential at that date to any subsequent rent review, i.e. if the rental difference was say 50% and at the review, if the rental value in the open market was £10·00 per square foot the rent payable to reflect the improvements would be £5·00 per square foot. There is also some indication from these cases as to how more minor improvements should be treated. A tenant, for instance, taking a floor of an office block may be required to install his own toilets. If he took a twenty year lease with five years rent reviews, then it appears he is not entitled at each review to calculate the cost in capital terms of those toilets and to write them off over the next five years before the next review. The judgements indicate that the courts would regard that as being unfair to the landlord as such, as method would "allow the tenant to have his cake and eat it".

Frequently a tenant makes "improvements" under licence subject to a requirement to reinstate that may improve the property for the purpose of the tenants particular use but make the property less valuable in the open market. In *Pleasurama Properties Ltd* v. *Leisure Investments (West End) Ltd* (1985) 273 E.G. 67, C.A., it was held that the tenants' obligation to reinstate (which would depress the rent) should be disregarded.

In that case the licence to make the "improvements" had been given without any consideration passing and Lloyd, L.J. held that it could not have been intended that the tenant for whose sole benefit the licence was given should reap an additional benefit in the form of a reduction in rent which otherwise would have been payable on review.

Additionally a clause in a review requiring the effect of improvements to be disregarded ipso facto requires a convenant to reinstate those improvements to be also disregarded for rent review purposes.

User clause

One of the important clauses in a lease that may well be reflected in the rent is the user clause. The actual wording of the restriction is clearly important, as must be the commercial use that is rectricted, the type of property and the location, and the state of the market. User clauses could, however, be said to fall into five categories:

1. Where the use is restricted to the named tenant only.
2. Where the lease is restricted to a limited class of users.
3. Where certain otherwise acceptable users are not expressly prohibited, this type of restriction being found normally in a parade of shops where the landlord seeks not to have two tenants competing in the same line of business.
4. Where the use cannot be changed without the landlord's consent.
5. The clause restricting the user but permitting a change of user with the landlord's consent, that consent not to be unreasonably withheld.

Generally, the last type of user clause should not affect the rental value.

There are, however, a series of cases that assist with the other definitions.

1. *A use restricted to a named tenant.* In the case of the *Law Land Co.* v. *Consumers Association* (1980), 255 E.G. 617, C.A., the rent review clause was on the facts construed whereby the user clause was overridden by the requirement to find the open market value. It is clear from the judgement that, if it had not been overridden, there would have been a very significant drop in

rent. Templeman, L.J. said, "The surveyor is to determine that rent the landlords and tenants would agree after negotiations between them and them alone. I do not understand how the surveyor could arrive at a market rent, or any other rent, in these circumstances" and later, "No landlord in his right mind would be prepared to enter into such a lease", i.e. one restricting use to a name tenant.

2. *A restriction to a limited user, where the landlord's consent could be withheld unreasonably, if necessary* was considered in the case of *Clements (Charles) (London)* v. *Rank City Wall* (1978) 246 Estates Gazette 739. In this case, the user was restrictive, and whilst not conclusive, the indications are that, had the user been widened the tenant would have been required to pay an increase of 11·66% on his rent. The user clause was in fact not widened but it is fair to presume that the tenant received a rent less than market rent by approximately the figure of 11·66%. A broadly similar case was that of *UDS Tailoring Limited* v. *B.L. Holdings Limited* (1982) 261 Estates Gazette 49. This case held in the Chancery Division concerned shops premises in the Edgware Road. The user covenant restricted the use to a high class mens and womens bespoke and ready to wear tailored out-fitters. In his judgement, Mr Vivien Price, Q.C., said "The exact nature of the restrictions is of course a matter of law. I am bound to say I am not satisfied that these restrictions are no more than co-terminus with the provisions of the general law; I think that the restrictive conditions do impose a burden upon the tenant over and above that imposed by the general law, and I think therefore, it appropriate to make a substantial reduction. I think, however, that 15% is far too high a figure for that, and again in my assessment (which I must emphasise cannot be a matter of calculation), the correct figure for deduction should be 10%."

3. *Plinth Property Investments* v. *Mott Hay and Anderson* (1979), 38 P. & C.R. 361, CA. In this case the High Court was considering a case stated, referred to it by an arbitrator. The user clause was "Not to use the demised premises or any part thereof, or suffer the same to be used, otherwise than as offices ... in connection with the lessee's business of consulting civil engineers". The arbitrator was held to be correct on the terms of the lease to value having regard to the restricted user clause. The premises were in Croydon and the arbitrator determined that the value should be discounted by 31·63%.

The importance of any restrictions in the user clause are illustrated by the above cases.

The arbitrator's award

If a rent review is being determined, either by an independent expert or an arbitrator, that surveyor has to come to a decision by a logical process of thought. An independent surveyor may use his own expertise, but an arbitrator is bound in general terms by the evidence he has, whether it be evidence of comparable properties or evidence of opinion. In either event he is much assisted by the logical presentation to him of each side's case. An arbitrator can now be required to issue his award in the form of a reasoned award. On p. 467 is an example of an award that might be made by an arbitrator. This is not put forward as definitive as to how an award should be written; it does, however, show how the arbitrator might martial the facts and evidence and deal with certain of the subjects covered in this chapter, such as improvements, inflation and evidence.

Appeals

It has been a matter of grievance that appeals against arbitrators' awards have been difficult to make since the Arbitration Act 1979, unless a decision was "obviously wrong" or there was a strong prima facie "case that it was wrong." These guidelines were laid down by the House of Lords in "The Nema" [1982] A.C. 724.

In *Lucas Industries plc* v. *The Welsh Development Agency* [1986] 3 W.L.R. 80, it was held that in rent review cases the strict guidelines laid down in "The Nema" should be relaxed or varied as no two leases were identical and that a judge should allow an appeal if he was in real doubt whether the arbitrator was right in law.

The 1986 case is to be appealed but if upheld leave to appeal should be granted in more cases which previously would have been refused.

Appendix to Chapter 15

The arbitrator's award

There is no standard or approved format. The award may have to be a lengthy document depending on the arguments advanced and the complexity of the case. The true test of the quality of the award is that not only should the parties to the arbitration understand it but also that it should contain sufficient information for a judge to follow the arguments advanced and the reasons for arbitrator's conclusions.

In *Gleniffer Finance Corporation* v. *Guardian Royal Exchange Assurance Ltd*, the Hon. Mr Justice Goff (High Court, 14th April 1981) concluded his judgement with the following words:

"The Arbitrator's Award was a full and accurate one in which he reviewed all the evidence and on the basis of that exercised his judgement based on his skill and experience. The exercise of an Arbitrator's judgement on this basis is not an appropriate case for review under the Arbitration Act 1979.

I therefore dismiss this application with costs."

Whilst there is no approved method it is suggested that the award should start with four main preliminaries.

1. A recital of the appointment of the arbitrator, his meetings, directions, inspections and other factual events leading to the hearing or written representations.
2. A list of what matters have been agreed between the parties prior to or during the arbitration.
3. A brief summary of the main differences between the parties.
4. Reproduction of the rent review clause and other clauses referred to by the parties.

As an award is a privileged document between the parties it is not possible to reproduce an actual award.

The award that follows is an attempt to show how an arbitrator in a fictitious reference might summarise arguments put to him and come to reasoned conclusions when presented with difficult problems.

AWARD

in the matter of Rental Valuation

of

736 High Street, Balham

as at

December 25th 1986

Daniel Parr, FRICS   27th May 1987
Arbitrator

Graham Kimber, ARICS for the Claimant

Philip Forwood, FRVA for the Respondent

Award in the matter of
the rental value of
736 High Street, Balham.

1. WHEREAS   The President of the Royal Institution of Chartered Surveyors appointed me Daniel Parr,
FRICS, as Arbitrator on the 16 January 1987 following a dispute arising under the lease between
Balham Refurbishments Ltd. and The Agile Trading Company Ltd. My appointment was made
under clause 6 of the lease date 7th January 1977.

I directed that a preliminary meeting be held. At
that meeting on February 2nd the landlords, Balham Refurbishments Ltd. were represented by
Mr. Kimber and the tenants, The Agile Trading
Company, were represented by Mr. Forwood.

I designated the landlords as claimants and the
tenants as respondents. Both parties requested an
oral hearing and I issued directions for such a
hearing to commence on March 25, 1987 and
confirmed these directions in writing the same
day.

The hearing took place on March 25, 26 and 27,
1987; I took evidence on oath. On April 2nd,
I inspected 736 High Street, Balham and various
other comparable properties put forward by the
parties accompanied by Mr. Kimber and Mr. Forwood.

2.   Prior to the hearing the parties had at my request
agreed certain factual information as to the areas
and other facts concerning 736 High Street, Balham and certain of the comparables. Those matters of agreement were, as directed, handed to
me as an agreed bundle of documents at the commencement of the hearing.

I DO NOW HEREBY MAKE AND PUBLISH THIS MY FINAL
REASONED AWARD.

3.   *The main differences between the parties*

The major differences between the parties can be summarised as follows:

A.   Should there be a reasoned award or not.
B.   Was certain evidence admissible or not.
C.   How were certain improvements to be valued.
D.   What was the effect of the restrictive user clause in the lease.
E.   What was the rental value of 736 Balham High Street.

4.   I set out the relevant clauses in the lease relating to the rent review, the restrictive user clause and improvements.
(These would be set out at this point)

5.   I now deal in detail with the differences as listed above.

A.   *Should there be a reasoned Award?*

The claimants argued that there should be a reasoned award, the respondents argued there was no such necessity.

As a matter of fact, a reasoned award must clearly to some extent increase the costs of that award. Although I must in any event set out my own thinking in a logical manner, to record this in writing and edit together with the necessary typing is going to increase the time spent and therefore costs, and will also cause some delay in the issue of an award. As an Arbitrator, I must be mindful of the costs and I am also required to act with expedition. The tenant in his application relied to some extent on the guidelines of the Royal Institution of Chartered Surveyors which states in the third edition published in November 1985 on page 25 as follows:

"It is suggested that the Arbitrator approach the question whether or not to give reasons in the following way:
(1)   If neither party asks him to give reasons he should not do so;

(2) If both parties request an Award supported by reasons the Arbitrator should comply;

(3) If one party asks him to give reasons and the other party is either silent or under the Arbitration Act 1979 the Courts would be likely to require a reasoned Award because a question of law is likely to rise out of his Award; whether the party asking for this is acting bona fide or is merely seeking to delay matters; and whether there are other circumstances making it desirable to give an Award supported by reasons (for example, because a point of principle not amounting to a point of law is involved which is likely to recur in future dealings between the parties). Unless he is satisfied that there is no justification for making an Award containing reasons he should normally accede to the request that he should give reasons.

(4) If the dispute concerns value only, with no legal issues or issues of principle arising, then a reasoned award is not justified."

This is clearly a case where a point of principle arises and could arise again in the future. I do not however consider that this alone would justify my action in incurring the additional expense of a reasoned award. In my view, I should be guided by the Arbitration Act 1979. Under the Act the High Court has a discretionary power to order an Arbitrator to:

> "state the reasons for his Award in sufficient detail to enable the Court, should an appeal be brought under the section, to consider any question of law arising out of the award."

In my view, I would only be justified in giving a reasoned award if there were questions of law arising that have been raised by the parties.

In my directions of 2nd February, I recorded in writing that "I record that the parties stated that so far as they were aware there were no legal matters outstanding."

Both Mr. Kimber and Mr. Forwood made reference to legal cases and stated how I, in their opinion, should interpret those cases when applied to the clauses of the lease I am considering.

Mr. Kimber, although he argued that no points of law as such arose, he made two points in his representations as follows:

1. He referred to the case of *Evans (F.R.) (Leeds) v. English Electric Co.* (1972) 36 P & CR 185, Mr. Kimber said: "We feel that the word 'demanded' implies a higher level of rent than 'agreed', 'obtainable' or indeed 'expected'."
2. He contended that the "actual" as well as the "hypothetical" tenant can readily be considered to be in the market.

Mr. Forwood raised the following points:

1. That I, as Arbitrator, must assume that the obligations imposed by sub-clauses 2(vi) and 2(xiii) would be enforced in relation to a hypothetical letting. He quoted the case of *Plinth Property Investments v. Mott, Hay and Anderson* (1979) 38 P & CR 361.
2. He alleged that where there was a covenant that the tenant must comply with planning legislation, the Arbitrator must exclude from consideration the possibility of any future use of the premises in breach of planning control. he quoted the case *Compton Group Ltd. v. Estates Gazette Ltd.* (1978) 36 P & CR 148, C.A.

Mr. Kimber argued that a Reasoned Award was an unnecessary expense. Mr. Forwood argued that the points raised were not only points of law but would arise again in future rent reviews.

Before considering the merits of the arguments I have to decide first whether any do amount to a points of law, and secondly, whether they fall to be determined by me under clause 7(b) or by the Legal Arbitrator under Clause 7(a).

I reluctantly conclude that the points raised are points of law. In coming to this conclusion I particularly rely upon the Court of Appeal decision in *Compton Group Ltd.* v. *Estates Gazette Ltd.* (above). At p. 152 Sir John Pennycuick said:

> "The summons came on for hearing before Goulding J in April 1976 and he gave his judgment by April 13th. Goulding J in his judgment made the procedural objection that the summons was wholly concerned with giving directions to the surveyors, whose function was to value the rent as experts, and that it was not appropriate for the Court to give any direction at all. He considered that the justification of the Court was somewhat strained when the Court was asked to make any declaration as asked by the summons. I am to a considerable extent in agreement with what Goulding J said there but I think that the construction of the rent review provision is a question of law which must be determined by the Court in order that the surveyors may know what is the subject matter which they are required to value. Goulding J, most properly, did hear and decide the question.
>
> I should mention at this stage that I wholly agree with Goulding J, that it is not the function of the Court to give the surveyors directions as to how they shall make their valuation, that is to say, what factors to take into account and what weight to give them."

I do not accept the contention of Mr. Forwood for the respondent, that the point raised by Mr. Kimber over the meaning of the word "demand" is any different to the points raised by Mr. Forwood. I consider these points can be determined by me but should, in all the circumstances, form part of a reasoned award.

I THEREFORE, AS A PRELIMINARY POINT, DETERMINE THAT THIS BE A REASONED AWARD

B.   *Was certain evidence admissible or not*

During his evidence Mr. Forwood put forward a letter from Mr. Kimber dated 17 November 1985. This two page letter was marked "Without Prejudice". I advised Mr. Forwood that I regarded this letter as being inadmissible and that I would record this determination in my award but I would have no regard whatsoever to the contents of that letter.

Mr. Kimber submitted a schedule of shops available to let in South London. Whilst admissible these "comparables" are only evidence that certain shops are on the market. They are worthless and inadmissible if put forward (as they were) as evidence of market rents.

C.   *How were certain improvements to be valued*
I heard evidence at length on the cost to the tenant of putting in a new shop front and improving the toilet facilities.

The fact that these improvements had been made was not disputed.

In my opinion the lease dated the 7th January 1977 is a full repairing lease. I therefore dismiss Mr. Forwood's lengthy contention that I must value and take into account the condition of the property as at January 1977.

With regard to the shop front I accept the argument of Mr. Kimber that this does not increase the rental value of 736 High Street, Balham as most, if not all, tenants of comparable property install their own shop fronts normally in a "house style".

The improvements to the toilets are in my view "tenant's improvements" that I am required to exclude under the terms of the lease, I therefore accept Mr. Forwood's argument and reject that of Mr. Kimber.

The cost in 1977 of providing internal male and female WCs, to replace a single external WC in the yard was £2,000. Mr. Forward argued that this sum should be adjusted upwards for inflation to 1986 costs and written off over the 5 year review and justified a reduction in rental value of £850 p.a. In my view Mr. Forwood's approach is wholly wrong.

The correct method is either to write the expenditure off over the total period of the lease or to assess the increased rental value of the shop resulting from these improvements.

I have no evidence of fact or opinion and I therefore have to adopt a robust view which is that the effect of the improvements is to increase the rental value by 5%. This must therefore be deducted from the rental value.

D. *The Restrictive User Clause*
Under the lease the shop may only be used for the retail sale of sports equipment.

It is, I believe, a fair summary of the opinions of the two experts that Mr. Kimber's expert opinion is that no discount should apply, whereas Mr. Forwood for the tenant has put forward a figure of not less than 25 per cent and has suggested that this is a sensible figure relative to the reductions of 31·62 per cent in the Plinth case and the 10 per cent and 11·66 per cent which can be found or deduced from the decisions in *UDS Tailoring* v. *B.L. Holdings* (1982) 261 E.G. 49 and *Clements (Charles) (London)* v. *Rank City Wall* (1978) 246 E.G. 739.

In my view one fundamental factor has been overlooked in the cases presented to me. In the Plinth case the Arbitrator had stated a case in alternative figures. He had already determined that a reduction 31·62 per cent might apply, but he was uncertain as to whether a restrictive user clause applied to a rent review or not.

The restricted user clause was held to apply, and it therefore followed that the rent was discounted by 31·62 per cent. As a matter of law an Arbitrator's award, as such, is inadmissible in relation to a third party. In my view there must be in practical terms a more commonsense approach as to how I regard the decision in Plinth in relation to 736 High Street, Balham. The expert who determined the 31·62 per cent was not an independent surveyor but was an Arbitrator. The figure that he arrived at in the absence of any reasoned award I must presume to be only as good as the evidence, be it evidence of fact or evidence of opinion, that was submitted to him. Mr. Forwood suggested to me his figure of 25 per cent is in line with the Plinth case (and with two cases in London—the UDS Tailoring case and the Charles Clements case). I think I would be wrong to place any reliance at all on the 31·62 per cent for the reasons I have already given, and it must therefore follow that I would be wrong to have any regard to whether it was or was not "in line" with the Plinth case.

I must also say that the Plinth case, whilst most certainly one concerning a restrictive user, was of an office block in Croydon, which in valuation terms must be considered remote when compared with a shop in Balham.

The other two cases cited do assist me to a greater extent. I do not consider the Charles Clements case to be particularly relevant because, although a reduction of 11·66 per cent can be inferred, Mr. Justice Goulding said in his judgment that this had been referred to in argument but there was no agreement on the point. The UDS Tailoring case concerned a restriction to a shop in the Edgware Road where under that restriction the tenant was only to use the demised premises as a mens and womens bespoke and ready to wear tailors and outfitters. This restriction was to some extent less strict in that the tenant could apply to the landlord for a change of use but the landlord, at his sole option, determined whether or not that change would conflict with any other trade or business within a block of property formed by 204 to 256 Edgware Road. In UDS Tailoring at p. 49, Mr. Vivian Price, Q.C. said:

"I think that the restrictive conditions do impose a burden upon the tenant over and above that imposed by the general law, and I therefore think it appropriate to make a substantial reduction. I think, however, that 15 per cent is far too high a figure for that and, again in my assessment (which again I must emphasise cannot be a matter of calculation) the correct figure for deduction should be 10 per cent."

I recognise that both these cases relate to shops which are totally different from a shop in Balham. I accept that the UDS case is more in point than the Charles Clements case, and that the restriction was of a very different nature to the restriction that I have to presume in the hypothetical lease.

I feel however that both cases together with Plinth and my own experience are sufficient for me to reject Mr. Kimber's contention that there should be no reduction because of the restricted use clause in the hypothetical lease.

Mr. Forwood's opinion that a reduction of 25% should apply is not substantiated and I determine that the reduction shall be 10%.

E.   *The Rental Value of 736 High Street, Balham*
The parties were in basic agreement that the rental value of the shop was £5,000 but differed as to the effect of improvements and the restrictive user clause.

Mr. Kimber additionally argued the wording of rent review clause requiring determination of the rental value "as might be reasonably demanded" required me to determine a higher figure than that obtainable on the open market. Both Mr. Kimber and Mr. Forwood advanced legal arguments (referred to earlier). I do not consider those legal arguments are in any way relevant nor do the cases cited assist me. In particular, I do not accept Mr. Kimber's argument that "reasonably demanded" justifies an overbid to open market value. The expert's valuations were as follows:

	Claimant £ p.a.	Respondent £ p.a.
Open market value	5,000	5,000
Add 10% for "demanded"	500	—
	5,500	5,000
Deduction for restricted user clause	—	1,250
	5,500	3,750
Deduction for improvements	—	850
	£5,500 p.a.	£2,950 p.a.

My determination arising from this Award is:

£ p.a.

Open market value	5,000
Deduction for Restrictive User 10%	500
	4,500
Deduction for Improvements 5%	225
	£4,275 p.a.

I THEREFORE MAKE AND PUBLISH THIS MY AWARD AND DETERMINE THAT THE RENT AS DEFINED UNDER THE LEASE DATED THE 7TH JANUARY 1977 SHALL BE £4,275 P.A. (FOUR THOUSAND TWO HUNDRED AND SEVENTY FIVE POUNDS) AS AT THE REVIEW DATE DECEMBER 25, 1986.

It is open to me to determine the question of costs. Neither party addressed me on the question.

Although Mr. Forwood succeeded to some extent in his arguments and Mr. Kimber failed in all his submissions, I have been put to, in my view, the unnecessary cost of a reasoned Award as urged by Mr. Forwood.

IN MY VIEW THEREFORE NEITHER SIDE SHOULD OBTAIN COSTS AND I SO ORDER. BOTH PARTIES SHALL EQUALLY BEAR THE COSTS OF THE REFERENCE AND THE COSTS OF THIS AWARD.

Daniel Parr, F.R.I.C.S.
London
27th May 1987.

Witnessed:

© C. W. Goodwyn 1988

Chapter 16

ASSET VALUATION

Asset valuation is a term which is confusing, as all valuations involve the valuation of assets. So what is really meant by Asset Valuation which over the past decade or so has become a specialised subject and requires a different and special treatment in valuation terms? Asset valuations are those valuations which concern fixed assets that are shown in financial statements. The term financial statement covers a wide spectrum from company accounts to city securities requirements of the Stock Exchange and Take Over Panel; from standards laid down by the Institute of Chartered Accountants to government requirements under the Insurance Company Regulations.

The valuation of fixed assets encompasses land and buildings and also plant and machinery. The importance of asset valuations was recognised by the Royal Institution of Chartered Surveyors (RICS) in 1973 with the formation of the Assets Valuation Standards Committee (AVSC) which has been responsible for the publication of Guidance Notes and Standards on Asset Valuation matters.

Financial statements

(a) *Company Accounts*

Company financial accounts are published in the form of a balance sheet, a profit and loss account, together with a directors' report and a chairman's statement. In valuer's terms the balance sheet will show the capital value of the fixed assets and the profit and loss account will show items of depreciation charges, while the directors' report or chairman's statement may make reference to the valuation. All of these parts of a company's accounts are important to the asset valuer. The importance of a valuer's contribution towards the formation of company accounts has grown with the developing sophistication in preparing them. This has been marked through changing conventions due to the introduction of current cost accounting firstly as the main basis and later as a permitted alternative to historic cost. All this has led to requirements for regular valuations of fixed assets.

(b) *Stock Exchange and Take-Over Panel*

In the late 1960s and early 1970s much concern was expressed over the activities of "the asset stripper". The RICS, through the AVSC, collaborated with the Stock Exchange in preparation of detailed requirements for property companies seeking a quotation on the London Stock Exchange through their listing requirements entitled "Admission of Securities for Listing" colloquially known as the "Yellow Book". These requirements, laid down in Chapter 6 of that book, follow very closely the Guidance Notes of the AVSC and, whilst they relate to property companies, the rules apply in general to non-property companies, where a listing on the Stock Exchange is sought or where classes of transactions are undertaken that need to be reported to shareholders.

The City Panel on Take-Overs and Mergers in its book, "The City Code", lays down rules of conduct and procedure in contested and agreed take-overs. These rules and procedures incorporate the relevant guidance notes of the AVSC and need to be followed by valuers.

(c) *Accountancy Standards*

The RICS and the accountancy profession have the closest liaison and cooperation. Accountancy standards produced by the Accounting Standards Committee which incorporate matters affecting fixed assets have in the main been compiled after consultation with the AVSC and advice has been given to accountants over the appropriate valuation methods and procedure that should be adopted in company accounts.

Any valuer undertaking a valuation for company account purposes should at the outset arrange to meet the directors, their accountants and auditors to ensure that procedures, basis of valuation and presentation of the valuation are understood by all.

(d) *Insurance Companies*

Under the Insurance Companies Act 1981, various regulations under statutory instruments have been published concerning the assets of insurance companies. Throughout there has been consultation with the AVSC and guidance notes (GN) have been published by the AVSC covering the basis of valuation, its presentation and the qualification and experience requirements of the valuer.

Asset valuer

The asset valuer needs to be professionally qualified and have the appropriate experience. Professionally qualified has been defined as a corporate member of the RICS or of the Incorporated Society of Valuers and Auctioneers or of the Rating and Valuation Association, together with the necessary post-qualification experience and knowledge of valuing land in the location and of the category of the asset being valued.

Basis of valuation

As valuers are well aware, there is not just a single basis of valuation. Dependent upon the purpose of a valuation will be the basis of valuation, though normally the valuation of land and buildings will be on the basis of open market value (OMV) and will have regard to open market transactions in similar property.

The accepted definition of open market value (although not having legal standing) is set out by the AVSC on behalf of the RICS in its Guidance Note 22 as follows:

"Open Market Value"

1.1 "Open Market Value" is intended to mean the best price at which an interest in a property might reasonably be expected to be sold by private treaty at the date of valuation assuming:

(a) a willing seller;
(b) a reasonable period within which to negotiate the sale taking into account the nature of the property and the state of the market;
(c) values will remain static throughout the period;
(d) the property will be freely exposed to the market;
(e) no account is to be taken of an additional bid by a special purchaser.

1.2 The Institution stresses that if a valuer considers it appropriate to apply any qualifying words to "Open Market Value", the meaning of those words should be discussed and agreed with the client before instructions are finally accepted. The valuer should incorporate in his report the agreed meaning of the qualifying words.

1.3 It is emphasised that this definition can in no way override any statutory definition of market value which may have to be adopted for the purpose of valuations for Capital Gains Tax, compensation cases, etc."

Examples of valuations using this definition are carried in the relevant "functional" chapters in the book. They do not differ from the normal approach to valuations as they are of types of buildings which are commonly bought and sold and leased in the market place and where there is no difficulty in obtaining evidence of market price.

Problems however do arise when a valuer is faced with valuing for open market value those types of properties where there is little market evidence. These have been classified as specialised properties and are those kind of properties which are rarely (if ever) sold except by way of a sale of the business in occupation due to the specialised nature of the buildings, their construction, size, location or otherwise.

Valuations for incorporation into Company Accounts

Land and buildings are generally held as fixed assets in one of the following categories:

(a) for occupation by the business
(b) as investment properties
(c) as surplus to the requirements of the business

The basis of valuation to apply will fall within the following possible ranges:

	Open Market Value for Existing Use (OMVEU)	Depreciated Replacement Cost (DRC)	Open Market Value allowing for an Alternative Use
Owner occupation	*	**	
Investments	*		***
Surplus property	*		***

In respect of properties for occupation by the business it is necessary to bear in mind the concept of company accounts in that they reflect that the business will continue and will be profitable for the foreseeable future. The assets are therefore stated in the accounts at their value to the business as it continues to occupy them and carry on business using those assets. The concept does not envisage the assets being sold off from the business, or the business ceasing to trade and thus the assets being sold. The value of those assets is therefore to the owner occupier and is a similar amount that it would cost to replace the asset in its existing state. It is not the cost of buying another piece of land and erecting a similar property or even buying a similar property, it is the value to the business, if deprived of that asset by its identical replacement. This "deprival value" is an accountancy concept which can, in valuers terms, be defined as net replacement cost. So, for those non-specialised properties that are for occupation by the business, the valuation to be incorporated into the company accounts will be on the basis of open market value for its existing use.

For those properties held as investments, that is being owned for the purpose of letting to produce a rental income, there is not the same concept of the property being required for the continuance of the business and so the basis of valuation to be incorporated into company accounts will be to open market value. For those properties that are surplus to the requirements of the business or are held for disposal the basis of valuation for incorporation into Company Accounts is open market value. It is important for valuers to show these categories of properties separately in the valuation report and certificate. All these categories of property values will appear in the balance sheet.

A chart categorising properties into these three basic groupings is set out on p. 485. The chart also indicates the basis of valuation to be adopted and in addition indicates the approach to development properties within each category.

In the sections which follow, the appropriate methods of valuation are considered in greater detail.

Balance sheet

(a) *Open Market Value for Existing Use—Non-Specialised Properties*

The definition of open market value is adopted but with the additional assumption that the property will continue in its existing use and thus ignores any possible form of alternative use, any element of hope value, any value attributable to goodwill and any possible increase in value due to special investment or financial transaction such as sale and leasebacks which would leave the owners with a different interest from the one to be valued.

There will however be need to take into account the possibilities of extensions on undeveloped land or even redevelopment of existing buildings providing that such construction can be undertaken without major interruption to the continuing business. Existing use should not however be interpreted too narrowly. It does not carry the same meaning as in planning law. It does not necessarily mean the particular trade being carried on. Many industrial buildings for instance would have the same value irrespective of the trade that is carried on. A factory is valued as a factory, not as a particular factory and a shop as a shop, not as a particular type of shop (unless the market differentiates between the two). Where there have been special adaptations to suit the particular requirements for a factory then any value attributable to those adaptations should be reflected in the value for the existing use.

It is not unusual for a property to have a restrictive covenant in a lease, or the benefit of a personal planning permission. Both these restrictions should be ignored as the valuation is for its existing use and thus its continued occupation. Where however such a restriction produces a valuation where the alternative use value of the property is less than the existing use then the valuer must report such an occurrence to the owners, who, if the matter is material, disclose it in the directors' report, or as a note to the accounts.

There may well be included in a company's portfolio of property a non-specialised property which is in the course of development. The valuation that should be adopted is the lower of:

> (a) The open market value of the land for the proposed use plus the current cost of the development at the date of the valuation

or

> (b) The appropriate current market valuation assuming the work has been completed (with the benefit of any contracted lettings) less the estimated expenditure at current cost to complete the development.

(b) *Open Market for existing use—Specialised Properties*

For those properties which are rarely if ever sold or leased in the market place, and are classified as specialised properties, a different valuation approach is required. In the majority of cases these properties have been erected to give an adequate return on capital to the owners and thus are worthwhile to the business as long as profits can be generated. The basis of valuation of such properties is DRC. Such a valuation is an estimate of the gross replacement cost of the buildings, which is the estimated cost at the date of the valuation of erecting a modern substitute building having the same gross internal floor area but taking advantage of current building techniques. This figure is then reduced to take into account such factors as physical and functional obsolescence and environmental factors. To this is added the open market value of the land for its existing use. Any valuation prepared on a DRC basis must be made subject to the adequate potential profitability of the business. It is however the directors' responsibility to decide whether or not the business is sufficiently profitable to carry the property in the balance sheet at the full DRC or whether a lower figure should be adopted. In the case of specialised properties which are in the course of development they should be valued having regard to their existing state costs current at the date of valuation on the depreciated cost basis subject to adequate potential profitability on completion.

OWNER OCCUPIED

- **Non Specialised**
  - Existing → OMVEU (GN11)
  - Being Developed → Lower of OMV for proposed use of land plus current cost of development expended to date; or OMV of whole as complete less costs to complete (GN11).
- **Specialised**
  - Existing → DRC – subject to potential profitability (GN11)
  - Being Developed → DRC – subject to potential profitability (GN11)
- **Trading potential**
  - Existing → Trading Potential value BP7[1]
  - Being Developed → Trading potential value less costs to complete BP7

INVESTMENTS
  - Existing → OMV (GN11)
  - Being Developed → Lower of OMV for proposed use of land plus current cost of development expended to date; or OMV of whole as complete less costs to complete (GN11)

SURPLUS
  - Existing → OMV (GN11)
  - Being Developed → Lower of OMV for proposed use of land plus current cost of development expended to date; or OMV of whole as complete less costs to complete (GN11)

[1] Background paper No. 7 contained in the Guidance Notes (Second Edition) on the Valuation of Assets prepared by the Assets Valuation Standards Committee: it is entitled "Open Market Valuations Having Regard to Trading Potential"

(c) *Open market valuations having regard to trading potential*
In its GN1, the AVSC have stated that

> "because the value of a business in accountancy terms must take
> account of intangibles (particularly goodwill) and reflect overall
> earning capacity, such value cannot normally be apportioned to
> any particular property assets of the entity. It follows therefore
> that the expression 'going concern valuation' in relation to com-
> pany property should not be used."

It is however recognised by valuers that there are certain types
of property which do change hands in the open market at prices
which are based directly upon their trading potential for a particular
limited use. Such properties would include hotels, cinemas, theatres,
bingo clubs, petrol filling stations and specialised leisure and sporting facilities. These transactions are often sold to reflect and include
the goodwill, the fixtures and fittings and the trading potential.
In analysing prices paid for similar properties and valuing the particular property the valuer would have regard to trading accounts for
previous years and thus form an opinion as to the future trading potential and level of turnover achieved. Where such businesses are carried
on subject to a statutory licence it is essential that any valuation
be based on the assumption that the licence will be continued.

Categorisation of properties

The problem of deciding which category of property, specialised
or non-specialised, is the directors' responsibility but the valuer
should discuss this category division with the directors if he considers the category of class is not appropriate. Such a choice or
advice to that choice and the valuation basis to adopt can be confusing but an adapted diagram from "Property Valuation and Accounts" by C. A. Westwick BSc FCA, published by the Institute
of Chartered Accountants of England and Wales shows the line
of approach. See p. 487.

Profit and Loss Account

With the exception of property investment companies all companies,
as a result of the EEC's 4th Directive on Harmonisation of Company
Law incorporated into the Companies Act 1982, are required to
depreciate all those fixed assets which have a limited economic useful
life over the estimated life expectancy of those assets. Property
investment companies are in the main exempt but are required to
value their fixed assets on an annual basis as laid down in SSAP

A ROUTE MAP FOR ARRIVING AT A BALANCE SHEET VALUE

```
                    Is there market evidence
                    of transactions in
                    similar properties?
                         │
              YES ───────┤──────── NO
               │                    │
               ▼                    ▼
                           Calculate DRC of
                           Building plus OMV for
                           existing use of land
                                    │
                                    ▼
    Is the property          Does depreciation on
    "non-specialised"?       this leave adequate
         │                   profitability?
   YES ──┤── NO                  │
    │        │              NO ──┤── YES
    │        │               │        │
    │        ▼               ▼        ▼
    │                  Reduced so that      Use DRC of
    │                  depreciation on      Buildings plus
    │                  residue does leave   OMV for existing
    │                  adequate             use of land
    │                  profitability
    │                       │
    │                       ▼
    │                  Use DRC of Building plus
    │                  OMV for existing use of land
    │                  reduced for inadequate
    │                  profitability
    ▼
    Is the property one that
    is often sold only with the
    business (eg hotel)?
         │
    NO ──┤── YES
    │        │
    │        ▼
    │    Add the value of these to      Use Potential
    │    the existing use OMV           Profit Method
    │        │
    ▼        │
    Has the property special
    features of value only to a
    limited class of occupiers?
         │
    YES ─┤── NO
    │        │
    │        ▼
    │    Use "existing use
    │    open market value"
    │        │
    ▼        ▼
    Has a permanent diminution in the value
    of the asset been recognised?
         │
    YES ─┤── NO
    │        │
    ▼        ▼
    Amount        Existing
    receivable    use OMV
    from
    selling it
    to Current OMV
    │
    ▲
    │
    Material
    difference to
    be reported
    │
    ▲
    Is alternative
    use value
    different?
    YES
```

488   *Valuation: Principles into Practice*

19.* In accountancy concepts (both historic and current cost) it is necessary to estimate the amount of depreciation which an asset has suffered over the accounting period and to charge that amount to the profit and loss accounts.

Depreciation is defined as the measure of the wearing out, consumption or other loss of value of a fixed asset whether arising from use, effluxion of time or obsolescence through market technology and market changes. Freehold land is not normally liable to depreciation with the exception of such land that has a limited life due to depletion by mineral extraction, or which is subject to a limited planning permission. Leasehold land does however have a limited life determined by the life of the lease. The figure to be allocated to the profit and loss account is known as the depreciable amount and its assessment is the responsibility of the directors but it can be expected that valuers may be consulted over such matters, or on particular factors such as degree of obsolescence, life expectancy of buildings, etc.

As valuations incorporate into them elements of both land and buildings, there is need to apportion the valuation so that the depreciable amount can be calculated in respect of the wasting element.

The depreciable amount is calculated by either

(a) Deducting from the cost or valuation of the asset the value of the land for its existing use
   or
(b) By making an assessment of the net replacement cost of the buildings.

In (a) it is necessary to arrive at the value of the land, which is valued as in its existing use. In (b) the net replacement cost is arrived at by deducting from the gross replacement cost factors for physical function obsolescence and environmental factors. Gross replacement cost is defined as the estimated cost of erecting the building or a modern substitute building having the same gross internal area as that existing. It is important for the valuer to consult with the directors over functional obsolescence, as they will be aware of how long the buildings would be needed for their own particular business purposes. In those properties which have been categorised as specialised properties and valued on a DRC basis this figure will provide the depreciable amount. In calculating depreciation, the depreciable amount arrived at is divided by the years of future

---

* Statement of Standard Accounting Practice is issued by the Institute of Chartered Accountants. No. 19, entitled "Accounting For Investment Properties."

economic useful life, thereby providing the figure of consumption or waste during the accounting period in question. It is difficult if not impossible to put a precise life on a building or group of buildings and it is usual to adopt a system of banding so that buildings or groups of buildings are identified as having say a life of, for instance, 10 to 30 years, or 30 to 50 years. It is important for valuers to understand that the depreciation charged in the profit and loss account is not the formation of a sinking fund for the replacement of the asset but is a charge to the profit and loss account of an amount of the measure of wearing out, consumption or loss of value during the period of the account.

Directors' report or notes to the accounts

The concept of the ongoing business in the accounts of a company entails the valuation of the asset to be at its open market value for its existing use. However land and buildings may possess a value different from their existing use where there is a possible use of the property for some other purpose. Normally such values are realised on liquidation, or closure and as such are not suitable for inclusion into the accounts. Often however, the alternative use value may have relevance to the company's overall situation, for instance in possible defence situations for take-over, or in certain cases for security purposes. Where there is a materially different value as an alternative use from the existing use, it is the duty of the valuer to report the alternative use value to the client. Such an alternative value would be included in the directors' report or notes to the accounts. Should a property in a company be declared surplus to trading requirements then it will be assessed at its open market value which takes into account any possible alternative use. Such a value of surplus land would be shown in the balance sheet. It is important to remember that land and buildings held for investment or development purposes will also be valued on an open market basis, which would take into account any alternative use if appropriate.

Valuations for other purposes

Stock Exchange and Take-Over Panel

Valuations that are required for these purposes should be carried out in accordance with the rules, regulations and codes of conduct laid down by those bodies, which follow the Guidance Notes of the AVSC. In general terms they follow the broad principles outlined in valuations for incorporation into company accounts.

Insurance companies

Valuations that are required under the Insurance Companies (Valuation of Assets) Regulations have been classified under those regulations as "proper valuations". A proper valuation is one which has been made not more than three years before the relevant date and by a qualified valuer. The definition of a qualified valuer is similar to the definition of an asset valuer. Valuers concerned with the requirements of the Insurance Company Regulations are advised to consult the AVSC Guidance Notes. The valuation basis will follow the definition of open market value.

Working studies

Set out below are six study valuations as follows:

1. Non-specialised property with surplus land
2. Non-specialised property with adaptations
3. Non-specialised development property
4. Specialised property
5. Property valued by reference to trading potential
6. Investment property.

The first two studies contain depreciable amount calculations in addition to balance sheet valuations.

Study 1

In this example the property is a small printing works on a site developed piecemeal over the past 60 years. The accommodation comprises a two storey stone built mill, plus a newer single storey brick built warehouse and factory units on a 1 ha site with 0·4 ha of surplus land adjoining the warehouse. The property is located 2 miles outside the centre of a small market town in Gloucestershire, 10 miles north of Bristol and 2 miles from the M5 motorway.

Gross Floor Areas:	Square metres
Factory	1,716
Warehouse	695
Ancillary store	150
Mill first floor offices	165
Mill upper storage	570

Rental Value:	£
Factory 1,716 at £12 per sq m	20,592
Warehouse 695 at £12 per sq m	8,340
Ancillary 150 at £5 per sq m	750

Mill first floor 165 at £8 per sq m	1,320
Mill storage 570 at £3 per sq m	1,710
	£32,712

Rental value, say £32,750

Valuation:

Rental value	£32,750
Y.P. perp. 17%	5·882
	£192,635

Add surplus land, 0·4 ha at £60,000 = £216,635, say, £216,500

The property is valued by comparison with similar non-specialised properties, adopting the concepts of ongoing business, open market value and existing use.

Depreciable amount

So far as the profit and loss account is concerned, the balance sheet figure of £216,500 has to be apportioned into wasting and non-wasting elements. In this example £87,916 is wasting; the buildings are banded into those having 10 years future life and those having 15, and depreciation for the accounting period in question can be calculated by dividing depreciable amount by future economic useful life.

Method (a)

Land Value	Depreciable Amount
£84,000	£132,500

Method (b)

Description	G.R.C.*	Future	Age	Factor	N.R.C.†
1. Factory	£275,000	15	35	15/50	£82,500
2. Warehouse	£12,000	15	40	15/55	£3,273
3. Offices/stores	£15,000	10	60	10/70	£2,143
				Depreciable Amount =	£87,916

* Gross replacement cost.
† Net replacement cost—see B.P.3.

Total Depreciable Amount	Depreciable Amount	Future Life
Method (b) applicable	£82,500	15·00 years
	£3,273	15·00 years
	£2,143	10·00 years

Study 2

This example consists of a purpose built freehold EEC licensed abattoir complex on 4 ha comprising slaughter hall, lairage, pet foods and meat preparation departments, together with ancillary cold storage and offices. It was built over a period covering the last 5 to 15 years. It is situated about half a mile north of Sevenoaks town centre in a predominately residential area.

Gross floor areas:	Square metres
Lairage	675
Slaughter hall, pet foods and ancillary cold stores	4,175
Cannery/Meat factory	11,220
Ancillary accommodation	590
Total	16,660 square metres

Rental Value
The premises have had considerable adaptations carried out comprising special finishes and drainage to slaughter hall, cold storage and food processing areas. The rental value of the non-specialised portion is approximately £100,000 per annum. The net replacement cost of the adaptations is £705,000 with a future economic life remaining of approximately 54 years.

Valuation
The valuation of the property on the basis of open market value for existing use at £1,470,000 comprises the following elements:

(a) Value of the standard elements of accommodation for existing use: £765,000
(b) Depreciated replacement cost of buildings including special finishes, drainage to slaughter hall, food processing areas and permanent cold storage: £705,000

The total valuation of the property on the above basis would be subject to adequate potential profitability.

The valuation further assumes that the property continues to be occupied by the trading company concerned in connection with the business. Should the property cease to be operational, it should be valued by reference to its current open market value which, in this case, would be at or about £765,000 (in other words, disregarding the adaptations).

There are instances on the other hand where in the case of surplus properties, open market value can exceed value in use, for instance a milk depot in a central office area.

Depreciable amount

The depreciation calculation for the profit and loss account in this abbatoir study, assuming continuation in operation and adequate potential profitability, would be £770,000, calculated as follows:

Method (a)
Land Value   *Depreciable Amount*
£700,000   £770,000

Method (b)

Description	G.R.C.	Future	Age	Factor	N.R.C.
1. Main building	£2,588,916	54	6	54/60	£2,330,024
2. Coldstore, ancillary	£528,732	48	12	48/60	£422,985

Depreciable Amount = £2,753,009

Total Depreciable Amount	*Depreciable Amount*	*Future Life*
Method (a) applicable	£651,694	54·00 years
	£118,306	48·00 years

Study 3

This study consists of a 23,000 square metre warehouse property development at the half way stage of construction on an industrial estate near the M4 about 10 miles from London airport. It has been assumed that from commencement to final letting will take a period of two years.

1. *Valuation of Completed Development*

Rent received	£1,000,000	
Y.P. in perp. at 9%	11·11111	£11,111,111
Stamp duty at 2·0%	£214,239	
Agent's fee incl. VAT	£123,247	
Legal fees incl. VAT	£61,655	£399,141

£10,711,970

2. *Cost of Construction of Completed Development*
23,000 square metres gross at £195 per square metre, say

			£	
			4,500,000	
Contingencies and extra costs			50,000	
Architects, Q.S. & Eng. fees				
+ VAT at 12%	=		546,000	
Finance: 1 years interest at				
average 13%	=		331,240	
Void period of 1 years interest 13%	=		705,541	
Letting, publicity and legal costs			70,000	(£6,202,781)
Developer's profit at 25% of gross				
building cost or 14·5% of				
completed development value	=	£1,550,695		
Total cost including profit				£7,753,476

3. *Site Value*	£	£
Gross site value when complete	2,958,494	
Deferred 2 years at 13·00%	·783146	2,316,933
Stamp duty at 2·0%	44,671	
Agents fee incl. VAT	25,772	
Legal fees incl. VAT	12,907	83,350
Net value of site at commencement		£2,233,583

It will be recalled that the site is only half completed. Valuation of non-specialised development property for balance sheet purposes is the lower of OMV for the proposed use of the land plus current cost of development; or OMV of whole less outstanding costs to complete. In this example, the value is £5,334,973, illustrated as follows:

	£
Net site value for proposed use	2,233,583
Current cost of development (half built)	3,101,390
	£5,334,973

	£	
Completed value	£10,711,970	
Deferred 1 year at 13%	·884956	9,479,622
Less outstanding expenditure		3,101,390
		£6,378,232

Study 4

The property used in this example is a purpose built foundry, held freehold, which comprises interlinking industrial buildings of mainly trussed roof or portal frame construction, clad in corrugated asbestos, housing specialised plant and machinery together with ancillary and temporary office accommodation.

The property has been developed over a number of years on a site of approximately 1·86 ha. Market evidence shows that current land values are approximately £250,000 ha.

A depreciated replacement cost valuation has been defined as the "current cost of acquiring the site and erecting the premises, less an appropriate deduction for their present condition". This is again based on existing use but it is a very subjective judgement involving the valuer in a significant knowledge of buildings and industrial processes, cost, physical depreciation and functional obsolescence.

The DRC of a building is the gross replacement cost (GRC) reduced by a depreciation factor (DF), plus the open market value of the land for existing use purposes.

The GRC is the cost of erecting a modern equivalent building. The DF is used to reflect the physical and functional obsolescence and environmental factors so as to arrive at the value of a building to the business at the date of valuation. It is calculated by dividing the future economic life of a building by its total life expectancy.

SCHEDULE OF ACCOMMODATION

Building No.	Description	Date Built	Life Expectancy (Yrs)	Rebuild Period (Yrs)	GRC £
1.	Main foundry	1962	60	1·5	1,108,500
2.	Laboratory & ablutions	1967	60	1·0	81,900
3.	Canteen & offices	1971	30	1·0	59,650
4.	Preparations & storage	1977	60	1·5	31,550

VALUATION

	£	£
Building 1		
GRC	1,108,500	
DF = 40/60	0·667	
		739,370
Building 2		
GRC	81,900	
DF = 45/60	0·75	
		61,425
Building 3		
GRC	59,650	
DF = 19/30	0·634	
		37,818
Building 4		
GRC	31,550	
DF = 55/60	0·917	
		28,931
	Depreciated Replacement Cost	867,544
Plus Land Value		
1·86 ha at £250,000/ha		465,000
	TOTAL VALUE	£1,332,544

DRC valuations are not so much "valuations" as "costs" and this point should be borne in mind. Cost and value are not the same thing and any valuation of a specialised property by DRC methods must always be subject to the caveat of adequate potential profitability. The directors have the option thereby of reducing the DRC to an acceptable level prior to incorporating the figure into the balance sheet.

Study 5

In this study, the property is a hotel located close to a northern airport and comprises a modern low-rise complex of concrete frame construction with brick cavity infill panels under a flat asphalt roof. The bedroom accommodation is in two wings on ground and first floors with a third wing housing the public areas. Facilities include restaurant/coffee bar, cocktail bar, swimming pool and discotheque. The hotel has 66 single and 85 double rooms, 4 meeting rooms plus staff accommodation.

The accounts for the previous years (see p. 498 and 499) should provide the valuer with the following information:

    the number of rooms available per annum,
    the number of rooms occupied over the year,
    the average price per room.

The accounts also give details of revenue generated from other activities in the hotel, e.g. food and drink, income from conference rooms, telephones etc.

When analysing the accounts it is common for revenue and costs to be expressed as a percentage of total revenue and in this example, it can be seen that the total revenue is split roughly 50/50, between the rooms and other sources.

The accounts also give the cost of providing the various services and are broken down to show the profitability of the various activities (administration, rates and drinks etc.) and general overheads (administration, rates etc.). Again, they are expressed as a percentage of the total revenue.

Having studied the accounts and established how the trends in costs and income are moving and also bearing in mind the general situation of the hotel, the valuer then assesses the levels of future costs and revenue, on the assumptions that the hotel is managed by an efficient operator. From the resulting calculations it is possible to estimate the net operating profit. This figure is then reduced to allow for the tenant's capital employed in the hotel to leave a sum which represents the return on the land and buildings and also an element of goodwill. The valuer then uses judgement to divide the figure into the two elements which can then be capitalised at appropriate rates to give a capital value.

Efficient Operator Assessment

Room occupancy %	67½%	
	£000s	%
Sales and income		
Rooms	940	51
Food	565	30
Beverage	310	17
Telephone	33	2
Other	12	—
Total sales and income	£1,860	100
Cost of sales		
Rooms	225	12
Food	457	24
Beverage	183	10
Telephone	33	2
Total cost of sales	898	48

(continued on p. 500)

3 Year Accounts

	Yr to 30.4.78		Yr to 30.4.79		Yr to 30.4.80		5 mos to 30.9.80		5 mos to 30.9.79	
Room occupancy %	65%		72%		69%		67%		73%	
Average room rate			£16·70		£19·74		£23·42		£19·05	
	£000s	%	£000s	%	£000s	%	£000s	%	£000s	%
Sales and income										
Rooms	503·2	46	683·6	49	784·0	49	376·5	52	329·3	49
Food	363·6	33	443·8	32	491·5	31	215·9	30	207·0	31
Beverage	190·1	18	222·7	16	274·1	17	118·7	16	111·4	17
Telephone	23·7	2	26·0	2	34·2	2	11·6	1	15·6	2
Other	4·4	1	8·5	1	11·8	1	5·3	1	6·1	1
Total Sales & income	1,085·0	100	1,384·6	100	1,595·6	100	728·3	100	669·4	100
Cost of sales										
Rooms	118·2		142·1		174·1		74·5		65·1	
Food	299·7		364·8		419·2		170·5		165·8	
Beverage	105·8		132·7		169·2		60·5		66·5	
Telephone	24·8		25·9		32·0		14·2		13·3	
Total cost of sales	548·5	51	665·5	48	794·5	50	319·7	44	310·7	46
Gross operating income	536·5	49	719·1	52	801·1	50	408·6	56	358·7	54
General expenses										
Admin. & general	95·9	9	113·2	8	142·4	9	64·8	9	56·7	8
Management fee	54·2	5	69·3	5	79·8	5	36·4	5	33·4	5
Travel agency	1·8	—	2·3	—	3·1	—	1·0	—	1·3	—
Advertising	36·7	3	56·6	4	67·0	4	28·8	4	27·9	4
Heat, light, power	52·4	5	61·1	4	75·9	5	32·7	4	25·1	4
Repairs & maint.	44·3	4	56·5	4	71·3	5	33·8	5	25·9	4
Total general expenses	285·3	26	358·9	26	439·5	28	197·5	27	170·3	25

3 Year Accounts

House profit	251·2	23	360·2	25	361·6	22	211·1	29	188·4	29
Rent revenue	0·6	—	0·9	—	0·8	—	0·3	—	0·3	—
Gross operating profit	251·8	23	361·1	25	362·4	22	211·4	29	188·7	29
Fixed charges										
Rent	—	—	—	—	—	—	—	—	—	—
Insurance and taxes	32·2	3	39·0	3	48·9	3	22·4	3	18·7	3
Total rent, insurance, taxes	32·2	3	39·0	3	48·9	3	22·4	3	18·7	3
Profit before depreciation Leasing, interest, deferred Charges	219·6	20	322·1	23	313·5	19	189·0	26	170·0	26
Depreciation	41·7	4	41·0	3	48·8	3	21·5	3	20·7	3
Leasing	38·5	4	33·8	2	30·1	2	11·7	2	12·2	2
Interest	106·1	10	83·7	6	59·4	3	18·8	2	27·1	4
Deferred charges	17·3	1	10·0	1	1·2	—	0·5	—	0·5	—
Profit before taxes	16·0	1	153·6	11	174·0	11	136·5	19	109·5	17

(continued from p. 497)

Gross operating income	962	52
General expenses		
Admin. & general	232	13
Management fee	—	—
Travel agency	9	—
Advertising	65	3
Heat, light & power	102	6
Repairs & maintenance	93	5
Rates & insurance	55	3
Total general expenses	556	30
House Profit	406	22
Gross operating profit	406	22
Less interest on tenants capital £400,000 at 10%	40	2
Sinking fund to replace contents	30	1·5
Total	70	3·5
Net profit	336	18

VALUATION

	£000s	£000s
Sales and income		
Rooms	940	
Other	920	
	——	
Total estimated gross takings	1,860	
Deduct cost of sales	898	
	——	
Estimated gross trading profit	962	962
Less hotel expenditure		
General	501	
Rates & insurance	55	
	——	556
		——
		406

Less
Interest on tenants capital
  £400,000 at 10%   40
Sinking fund to replace con-
  tents   30
                                                       ____   70
                                                                  _____
Net Profit   £336,000
                                                                  ======

Take 60% approx. for rent   £
£200,000 × Y.P. 12% (8·33)   = 1,666,666
Leaves goodwill
£136,000 × Y.P. 3   =   408,000
                                  _____
                                   2,074,666
                                  _____
                          say £2,075,000
                                  ======

Study 6

In investment valuations, the axis of information revolves around cash flow. Consequently the valuations tend to differ from those of operational properties where the emphasis lies on use and floor areas.

The following freehold study sets out financial information on a typical investment property comprising a central London building in multi-occupation, with a shop on the ground floor, three office tenants above and the top floor vacant. The valuation date is January 1983.

1. Tenant: D. VINE
   Next review date 25/03/1986; Lease expiring 24/03/2001
   Rent receivable £6,250;

Show room	£	£
Zone A	27 m² at 275 =	7,425
Zone B	7 m² at 165 =	1,155
Basement	45 m² at 45 =	2,025
Total		10,605
Rental value, say,		£10,605

2. Tenant: WRIGHT
   Next review date 25/03/1985; Lease expiring 24/03/2001
   Rent receivable £3,500;

		£
West Room	90 m² at £70 =	6,300
Total		6,300
Rental value, say		6,300

3. Tenant: O. F. KINGS
   Next review date 25/12/1987; Lease expiring 25/12/1994
   Rent receivable £6,400;

		£
South room	95 m² at £75 =	7,125
Total		7,125
Rental value, say		7,125

4. Tenant: CREATIVE DESIGN
   Next review date 25/03/1986; Lease expiring 24/03/2001
   Rent receivable £5,700;

		£
Studio	90 m² at £65 =	5,850
Total		5,850
Rental value, say		£5,850

5. Tenant: VACANT
   Void Period until 24/06/1983

		£
South West Room	110 m² at £55 =	6,050
Total		6,050
Rental value, say		6,050
Total rental value, say		£35,930

Valuation

		£	£
Rent received		21,850	
Y.P. in perp. at 8%	12·5000		273,125
Rent increase		6,050	
Y.P. in perp. at 8%	12·5000		
P.V. for ·41 yrs @ 8%	·96844 12·10552		73,238
Rent increase		2,800	
Y.P. in perp. at 8%	12·5000		
P.V. for 2·16 yrs at 8%	·84641 10·58015		29,624
Rent increase		4,505	
Y.P. in perp. at 8%	12·5000		
P.V. for 3·16 yrs at 8%	·78371 9·79644		44,133
Rent increase		725	
Y.P. in perp. at 8%	12·5000		
P.V. for 4·91 yrs at 8%	·68496 8·56203		6,207
Gross capital value			£426,329
Stamp duty at 2·0%		8,217	
Agents fee incl. VAT at 15%		4,817	
Legal fees incl. VAT at 15%		2,428	15,462
NET VALUE			£410,867

say £411,000

Equated yield	8·0000%	
Initial yield	5·1192%	
Reversionary yield	6·5367%	Date 6.1983
Reversionary yield	7·1927%	Date 3.1985
Reversionary yield	8·2599%	Date 3.1986
Reversionary yield	8·4298%	Date 12.1987

Chapter 17

PUBLIC HOUSES

Capital valuations

If a public house is to be offered for sale or to let, one of the first questions that will be asked by prospective takers is: what is the trade? The trade is an influential factor in valuing licensed premises. It does not form the basis of a separate goodwill valuation as in shops and other businesses but is integral to the valuation of the property. The premises have the benefit of a justices' full on-licence and the trade is regarded, in most cases, as being an inherent attribute of the licence. Hence, goodwill, if any, is normally considered to be included in the price.

Trade

In what form can information about trade be obtained? The brewers keep records of the beers, wines and spirits delivered to each house and issue a statement annually showing the barrelage and gallonage. The beer, including the bottled beer, is shown in barrels (36 gallons) and the wines and spirits in gallons (8 pints or 6 bottles). In a "free" house selling different brews, an alternative source of information is the accounts or the receipts and purchases. If a publican employs a stocktaker periodically, say, monthly or quarterly, the stocktaker's statements can be referred to for the receipts and purchases.

Audited and certified accounts are the most reliable form of information but they are not readily available.

Methods of valuation

The two chief methods of valuation were in collision recently in a Development Land Tax case, *Commissioners of Inland Revenue* v. *Allied Breweries (UK) Ltd* (1982) 262 E.G. 153, concerning a back street pub in Birmingham. The Regional Licensed Property Valuer based his valuation on an updated brewer's profit basis, called the Kennedy Method after the judgement of Kennedy J in an earlier case (Ashby's Cobham Brewery Co. Ltd, re The Crown, Cobham and Ashby's Staines Brewery Co. Ltd re The Hand and Spear, Woking (1906) 2 K.B. 754) on redundancy compensation.

The valuation was amended by the Lands Tribunal so that at the end of the day it looked like this:

Study 1

Malt Shovel P.H., Birmingham
Current Use Value at 14.12.1976

Wholesale Profits		£
356 barrels draught beer at £3·90		1,388
36 barrels bottled beer at £6·50		234
270 gallons wines and spirits at 90p		122
		1,744
Add 25% to allow for increase over "tone" of the 1973 Valuation List		436
Wholesale profits in 1976 estimated at		2,180
Tied Rent (1974)	£1,560	
Add 15% to update	234	1,794
	Gross income	3,974
Deduct for repairs and insurance		374
	Net income	3,600
Year's purchase		10
	Current use value	£36,000

The brewers' wholesale profits in the valuation were those which formed the basis of rating assessments in 1973—the Lands Tribunal uplifted them by 25% to reflect the position in 1976, the relevant date in this case.

The reasoning behind the Kennedy Method is that it goes direct to what the brewery is making from the public house: firstly, the brewery makes wholesale profit from supplying goods and, secondly, it charges its tenants a tied rent. In the managed houses, which represent about 28% of the brewer's tied estates, the brewer makes a net retail profit instead of a tied rent.

In the Development Land Tax case under discussion, the brewers' valuer depended on a valuation per converted or equivalent barrel,* the price per barrel being derived from a scrutiny and analysis of comparable sales over a wide area. The Lands Tribunal looked selectively at the comparables and reinforced its decision by a check valuation at per converted barrel. It is interesting to note that it expressed no preference for either method. As it has done in other cases where methods of valuation have come into conflict, it rationalised the evidence and shewed how the answers on both methods could confirm each other.

The Tribunal said that the capital value of £36,000 represented £4,285 per weekly converted barrel on the Regional Licensed Property Valuer's estimate of trade (8·4 weekly converted barrels) and £4,500 on the taxpayer's surveyor's estimate (8 weekly converted barrels). "This" said the member, "seems to be in line with the view I had provisionally formed looking at the evidence of the comparables...."

It is necessary to understand that in the Midlands and North, capital values are reached by applying a price to a weekly barrel; in the South, a price is applied to a yearly barrel. The argument in favour of a weekly barrel as the measuring stick is that trade is a variable and unsteady element and capable only of an approximate, not an exact, definition.

As already mentioned, the Tribunal did not express a preference for either the Kennedy basis or the price per converted barrel method. If the participants regarded this as a contest between the two methods with the award of a prize judgement for correctness of approach, this was not apparent or forthcoming. The Tribunal executed a detailed exercise of amendment on the Kennedy valuation and then checked it against the price per converted barrel. It might seem that the more traditional Kennedy method was favoured as the chief method but the Tribunal does not state this to be so. Both methods may be regarded as having equal weight, although, in practice, the Kennedy method would generally be used where a public house could attract a brewer as a buyer, and the price per converted barrel method would be more common as the primary method for a "free" house.

There are other methods of finding capital value besides the two methods in the Birmingham case. If an open market rent is being paid and has been recently fixed, a years' purchase can be applied.

---

* Converted or equivalent barrelage is the draught and bottled beer expressed in barrels (36 gallons) plus the gallons of wines and spirits divided by three.

Study 2

Example

	£
Rent paid under lease	5,000 p.a.
Years' purchase, say	15
	£75,000

Care must be taken to establish that the rent is not a "tied rent" as, normally, this is not regarded as having been fixed under open market conditions. The tieing clause to buy goods only from the landlord-brewer is an imposition, without which a "free" tenant might pay more. There is no doubt that in recent years the brewers have tried to charge economic rents and it may well be that in many cases the tied rent is equivalent or nearly equivalent to a free rent. The security of the rent and the periods of reviews affect the years' purchase to be used.

As can be seen in the Kennedy method valuation (Study 1), when looking at a public house from the point of view of a brewer, the wholesale profits are a factor. National and regional brewers are mainly interested in houses with large, sound, all-round trades (e.g. new public houses on residential estates) and may show little or no interest in buying small or medium trade houses in out-of-the-way villages or in inferior situations in towns. Indeed, many brewers have been improving the quality of their tied estate by selling off poor houses such as these. The valuation approach is influenced by who is likely to be the purchaser: a "free" retailer or a brewer.

Despite the modern practice of take-overs and mergers among brewers, there are still a number of small brewers who are trying to add to their tied estates by purchasing good rural small to medium trade public houses provided they fit into the routes and districts covered by weekly drays.

A new prospective purchaser of modern public houses is the independent brewer who has started up to meet the demand for "real" ale from free trade outlets. Another new purchaser or lessee who has recently entered the market is the micro-brewer who can produce enough beer in a converted outbuilding to serve two or three other public houses at the same time. These independent brewers may be a weak force at present but their bids will become stronger if brewing "real" ale for free trade outlets continues to be profitable. It is certainly worthwhile circulating them with particulars of public houses for sale or to lease.

In the past it has been considered that the rental values of public houses bore no uniform relationship to the capital values. Possibly, this may still be the position. Certainly, if a lease is terminating within a few years, then it is often the practice to consider a reversion to capital value (if circumstances permit) instead of a revised lease rent.

Study 3

Example
Estimate the capital value of a public house let on a lease at £5,000 per annum, the lease expiring in 6 years' time. Its present capital value with vacant possession is estimated to be £125,000.

First 6 years	£	£
Rent under lease (well secured)	5,000	
Y.P. 6 years at 6%	4·92	24,600
After 6 years		
Reversion to capital value at the end		
of the lease	125,000	
Defer 6 years at 7½%	0·648	
		81,000
		£105,600

Compare this on the assumption that a revised rent after 6 years would be £7,500.

	£	£
First 6 years as before		24,600
After 6 years		
Revised rent	7,500	
Y.P. of reversion to a perpetuity at, say 7%	9·52	
		71,400
		£96,000

12   It is preferable to consider a reversion to capital value in this situation. If the property were a shop or an office, it might not be possible to adopt this approach because of the application of the Landlord and Tenant Acts, which provide a degree of protection to lessees upon the renewal of leases. On-licensed premises, such as public houses and wine bars, are exempted these Acts unless their business in non-alcoholic transactions is "substantial" (see Section 43 (1)(d) of the Landlord and Tenant Act 1954, as amended).

There is no provision, unless it is specified in the lease itself, that forces an owner of a normal public house to offer a renewal of tenancy to a lessee if he does not wish to do so.

Nor is there any provision for the payment of statutory goodwill compensation, although brewers and their tied tenants observe a "code of practice" which enables tenants to claim compensation in certain circumstances where the tenancy is determined prematurely.

A further method of valuation is the accounts or receipts method. If the accounts are available, a valuer should be able to adjust these to provide a medium for valuation. A typical set of "free" public house accounts may be adjusted by adding back to, or deducting from, the net profit.

Study 4

Example	£	£
Receipts		406,600
Net profit as shown in accounts		103,600
Add back interest paid on loans		2,700
		106,300
Deduct interest on tenant's capital:		
Trade inventory of furniture, fixtures and fittings valued at ingoing 3 years ago at £6,200. Allow for depreciation and additions since, say	8,500	
Stock in hand of consumable goods (actual)	12,600	
Cash required to run business, allow one month's purchases of consumable goods, say	20,000	
	41,100	
Interest at 12%, say		4,930
Adjusted net profit		101,370
Years' purchase		6
Capital value		£608,220
= receipts £406,600 × 1·495 Y.P.		

The object of adding back loan interest is to exclude the personal circumstances of the publican. A prospective buyer may be financially independent and require no loans. The deduction of interest on tenant's capital is made so that the "adjusted" net profit represents the profit emanating solely from the licensed premises.

The trade inventory and stock are purchased separately, so that the end figure will be:

	£
Licensed premises—freehold with benefit of	
licence, say	608,000
Inventory	8,500
Stock	12,600
	£629,100

The payment for stock and glassware is always adjusted at the "change" on the day of ingoing.

Many surveyors are hesitant about valuing bricks and mortar on a profits basis. It is traditional to try to reach a rent and then multiply the rent by a years' purchase. Thus, the adjusted net profit might be treated as follows.

Study 5

	£
Adjusted net profit (per Study 4)	101,370
Tenant's share 60% = £60,822, say	60,800
Rent	40,537
Year's purchase	15
Capital value	£608,055

Valuations on net profit can often be misleading and it is advisable always to check the answer on other methods.

In Study 4 it will be seen that the capital value has been devalued as a Y.P. (1·495) on the receipts. It is a method that valuers are often forced to use in a primary way because the only available evidence of trade is the receipts, the accounts for the previous year not being prepared and certified at the date the property is advertised for sale. Valuations such as this (which take one line) are attractive as time-saving exercises but they can be used reliably only by valuers with sales experience on this type of property.

Rental valuations

Apart from Study 5, this chapter has not considered rental calculations.

These have been influenced by rating practice and reference may be made usefully to Chapter 12 for advice on methods and approach, bearing in mind that the rating of licensed premises in the current (1973) list is to gross annual value, whereas, for the purpose of a normal lease, a net annual value is required. In the next (1990) valuation list, the rating assessments of licensed properties, in common with other commerical properties, will be to net annual values.

© R. W. Westbrook 1988

(Mr Westbrook is a former Regional Licensed Property Valuer in the Inland Revenue Valuation Office and now in private practice.

Chapter 18

HOTELS

Introduction

Hotels may be valued in a variety of ways depending on the evidence available. As much information as possible should be assembled and, where possible, the proprietor should be interviewed to ascertain the operating functions of the hotel.

As in the case when valuing any property whether for sale, purchase or renting it is vital to be aware of the legal constraints involved, and to have a good understanding of the physical attributes of the property, which can be obtained only by inspection. In the case of hotels the details that need to be taken into account differ from other kinds of property, in that floor area is not the essential ingredient that determines the quantum of either rental value or capital value. The information required relates to the trading potential of the property, because (normally by reason of its construction) it can only be used as an hotel and cannot easily be converted to alternative commercial uses such as offices, even where planning considerations would allow such a change of use.

Preliminaries

Thus, for a valuation of an hotel to be undertaken the following steps need to be followed.

Legal requirements

The case of *Corisand Investments Ltd* v. *Druce & Co.* (1978) 248 E.G. 315 is the leading case on the valuation of hotels and is worthy of study. It concerned the valuation of the Raglan Hall Hotel, Muswell Hill, London N10 for mortgage purposes. Mr Justice Gibson set out in his judgement the matters of principle and fact that an ordinarily competent valuer must have regard to in order to discharge his duty of care in valuing a property such as the subject hotel. These matters are enumerated in the judgement as follows:

" (i) He must by inspection of the property, and by inquiry, learn enough of the property to be able to start upon the basic method of valuation which he will apply, and thereafter to apply that method effectively by obtaining any further information he needs.

513

(ii) The purpose of the valuer's work is to determine the price which the property would fetch if offered for sale at the relevant time and in the relevant circumstances: the concept of relevant time and relevant circumstances will require further definition.

(iii) When he has sufficiently informed himself as to the size, nature and condition of the property he can select the various methods of valuation by which he will guide and check his opinion. For example, he may be able to value by the comparison method—with or without any other method— if he has sufficient knowledge of the recent sale prices of other sufficiently comparable properties. It was agreed that the direct comparison method was rarely applicable to hotels, except in some special cases, for example in parts of London where there are a number of hotels which are sufficiently similar for a comparison method to be applied by determining a room price from other sales.

(iv) Hotels are bought and owned to make money by operating them. Accordingly, in estimating what purchasers in the market would pay for a particular hotel, the principal, or at least a well-known and respected, method is to value the hotel as it is as a going concern, including goodwill and contents. The purchaser would calculate what he could expect to earn in the hotel as it stands, or as he could make it operate, and what price it is sensible to pay for the right and opportunity to earn that income. The valuer tries to make the same calculation.

(v) In a valuation for mortgage purposes it is again common ground that the valuer cannot take the open market going concern valuation. The valuer cannot, in short, include in his valuation for this purpose any valuable part of the going concern valuation which would not or might well not be there when the mortgagee attempts to realise his security. It was not in dispute that from the going concern valuation the valuer must at least exclude any sum, where appropriate, for 'goodwill' and the movable contents. The going concern valuation, less goodwill and contents, was referred to as a 'brick and mortar' valuation.

(vi) In addition to making appropriate allowances for the going concern valuation in respect of such matters as goodwill and contents, upon the theory that such assets would not be or might well not be there to be sold by the mortgagee, the valuer must—and this was common ground—make allowance for any significant defect or problem in respect of which the purchasers in the market would calculate that they would have to spend money before being able to oper- ate the hotel to make the estimated net income. This is, of course, no more than a particular elaboration of the two general principles that the concern of a valuer is to inform himself sufficiently about the property, and then to estimate what a sensible and informed buyer in the market would pay for the property. Although there was no dispute about this principle as formulated there was much dispute as to the application of it to the facts of this case with particular reference to the Fire Precautions Act 1971.

(vii) An experienced valuer, after inspecting a property, will very frequently if not always readily form an approximate esti- mate of the probable market price of an hotel. He may test that approximate estimate against the views of people who have immediate knowledge of sale prices in the market. His opportunity to do that will be improved if his own firm has a substantial sale business of hotels. Mr. Cawte was asked to accept that process as "having an instinctive figure in mind," and he accepted it thus. Mr. Gurrin called this process "knowing the value from his expertise." It was never in issue that valuers do in fact go through that process of forming and testing what was so called their "instinctive" or "expertise" estimate, or that they were acting sensibly and properly in so doing.

There was a dispute, or perhaps a difference in emphasis, between the parties as to the relative weight to be given by the valuer or by the court to the values revealed by the accounts analysis method of calculating the going concern, or 'brick and mortar' valuation, on the one hand, and to the value produced by the so-called 'instinctive' or 'exper- tise' process of the experienced valuer, whether in a large firm or not, on the other hand.

(viii) Lastly, the valuer must, as I have said, in determining and advising upon the price which the property would fetch, have regard to the relevant time and to the relevant circum- stances of the contemplated sale: upon this matter also there was dispute in the course of the trial. To what time, or times, must the valuer have regard, and to what circum- stances?"

The valuation was made on the basis of the value of the hotel for mortgage purposes with the benefit of complete vacant possession as at 28th September 1973. This was of course at the end of the

property boom and at a time when the property market was described as "high" or "booming". The problems of valuing in such
a market were considered. Dealing with the matter of principle as
to whether in a valuation for mortgage an allowance should be
made for the "forced sale" of the asset, the appropriate allowance
mentioned in this case was 20%. Gibson J said:

> "I come then to my conclusion on this matter of principle as
> to the duty of a valuer in making a valuation for mortgage pur-
> poses. There can, in my judgment, be no answer of general princi-
> ple upon this point as to the need or obligation of a valuer to
> make any specific deduction from his open market valuation,
> in any particular amount or proportion, in order properly to deter-
> mine a valuation for mortgage purposes. The answer must depend
> upon what circumstances, on the facts of any particular case,
> are shown to be relevant.
> ... The valuer must, in valuing for mortgage purposes, exclude
> from his valuation any apparent asset or valuable content of the
> hotel as a saleable property, which will not be, or may well not
> be, available for sale by the mortgagee when he attempts to realise
> the security. That sale price which the valuer must try to estimate
> for the guidance of the intending lender is that sale price which
> the property is likely to fetch—as the valuer can judge it—at
> the time relevant to the possible realisation of the security and
> in the circumstances then relevant.
> It follows that, if the current open market price which the valuer
> judges would be realised at auction at the time of valuation is
> based upon a market which the valuer knows to be 'high', and
> supported by speculative buyers apparently willing to pay prices
> not justified by ordinary principles of investment return, then
> such content of the market price so estimated as depends upon
> the market being in that state (which I shall call the 'speculative
> content') should either not be included in a valuation for mortgage
> purposes, or should be identified as such, and as so included,
> for the guidance of the lender, if at the time of valuation there
> is substantial ground for the valuer to know that the speculative
> content of his estimated market price will not or may well not
> be maintained in future, or may well not be readily realisable
> on the forced sale of the property.
> ... a mortgage valuation must look for a certain period into
> the future. The valuer cannot be expected to peer very far ahead,
> or to anticipate trends or future changes of which no indication
> has been or could then be given to an ordinarily competent valuer.
> The valuer, however, can reasonably be required to be aware

of the fact that the market is 'high', or unusually buoyant, when such are the circumstances, and to guard against over-confidence in such market conditions. He can reasonably be required to consider what the position of the property may well be in circumstances of forced sale within six to 12 months of his valuation. I was referred to the judgment of Watkins J in the case of *Singer & Friedlander Ltd* v. *John D Wood & Company*, June 3 1977 [reported at (1977) 243 E.G. 212, 295] and, respectfully, have found support for the conclusion which I have reached on this point in what the learned judge there said. . . ."

"The way in which a valuer should conduct himself so as to fulfil his duty to a merchant bank, or any other body or person, varies according to the complexity or otherwise of the task which confronts him. In some instances the necessary inquiries and other investigations preceding a valuation need only be on a modest scale. In others a study of the problem needs to be in greater depth, involving much detailed and painstaking inquiries at many sources of information. In every case the valuer, having gathered all the vital information, is expected to be sufficiently skilful so as to enable himself to interpret the facts, to make indispensable assumptions and to employ a well-practised professional method of reaching a conclusion; and it may be to check that conclusion with another reached as the result of the use of a second well-practised method. In every case the valuer must not only be versed in the value of land throughout the country in a general way, but he must inform himself adequately of the market trends and be very sensitive to them with particular regard for the locality in which the land he values lies. Whatever conclusion is reached, it must be without consideration for the purpose for which it is required. By this I mean that a valuation must reflect the honest opinion of the valuer of the true market value of the land at the relevant time, no matter why or by whom it is required, be it by merchant bank, land developer or prospective builder. So the expression, for example, 'for loan purposes' used in a letter setting out a valuation should be descriptive only of the reason why the valuation is required and not as an indication that were the valuation required for some other purpose a different value would be provided by the valuer to he who seeks the valuation. It might, however, be an indication that the valuer, knowing the borrowing of money was behind the request for valuation, acted with even more care than usual to try to be as accurate as possible. If a valuation is sought at times when the property market is plainly showing signs of deep depression or of unusual buoyancy or volatility, the valuer's task is made more difficult than usual. But it is not in such unusual circumstances an impossible one. As Mr. Ross said, valuation is an art, not a science. Pinpoint accuracy in the result is not, therefore, to be expected by he who requests the valuation. There is, as I have said, a permissible margin of error, the 'bracket' as I have called it. What can properly be expected from a competent valuer using reasonable skill and care is that his valuation falls within this bracket. The unusual circumstances of his task impose upon him a greater test of his skill and bid him to exercise stricter disciplines in the making of assumptions without which he is unable to perform his task; and I think he must beware of lapsing into carelessness or over-confidence when the market is riding high. The more unusual be the nature of the problem, for no matter what reason, the greater the need for circumspection."

Although these remarks apply to valuations for mortgage, nevertheless the duty of care inherent in the valuer's task is clear.

Another aspect of valuation also dealt with in Gibson J's judgement was the matter of any speculative content in the market. On this matter he said:

"The plaintiffs, however, have wholly satisfied me that in September 1973 an ordinarily competent valuer had substantial ground for knowing that any speculative content in his estimated open market price, estimated in that boom market, might well not be maintained in future or be readily realisable on the forced sale of the property. A valuer in fixing in September 1973 a valuation figure for mortgage purposes was not entitled to be optimistic in the sense that he could not treat as a proper basis for a mortgage valuation an open market price containing a substantial speculative content.

A valuer in September 1973 knew that any speculative content in the open market price, attributed by him to a property, might well disappear within a short period of time. There was no rational basis for supposing that such speculation in hotels as had been seen to occur must continue for any particular length of time—it could cease as it had begun. The concept of a speculator's price, as I understand it, is to pay more for a property than other buyers are then willing to pay on ordinary principles of investment return in the belief that the market will rise to and overtake the price so paid. The capacity of speculators in the market to bid for hotels must have been affected by the cost of borrowing money; and the increase in Bank Rate in the summer of 1973, and the letter of the Governor of the Bank of England to which reference has been made, were entirely sufficient to remind any valuer that a boom market may not continue and may not be there when a mortgagee comes to sell his security."

Finally, reference is made in the judgement to the need for valuers to have regard to the statutory provisions affecting the operation of an hotel. In this case it was the effect of the operation of the Fire Precautions Act 1971. On this Gibson J said:

"For reasons which I have already given, it was in my judgment the duty of a valuer preparing a valuation for mortgage purposes to make appropriate allowance for any significant defect or problem in respect of which the purchasers in the market would calculate that they would have to spend money before being able to operate the hotel to make the estimated net income.

I have no doubt whatever that ordinary inquiry in September 1973 would have produced readily information in general outline as to the nature and extent of works which would soon be necessary to comply with the requirements of the fire authority. That information would have enabled the defendants to make an estimate of the approximate cost of such works....

The burden of having to spend such a sum of money (£8,000) within a short period of time—such as 12 months or thereabouts—was plainly, in my judgment, a significant defect or problem."

Inspection

Having appreciated the significance of the legal requirements, the valuer must undertake a detailed inspection of the property. A full note of all accommodation available is required. Hotels will vary as to their main sources of income. Some will rely heavily on letting bedrooms, others will rely more on the restaurant and bar trade, others again may have extensive banqueting and conference facilities available. Whatever accommodation is available for use by the public this needs to be carefully noted down and recorded. It is unnecessary to measure all the bedrooms, but it is important to take notes of typical bedroom accommodation so that the class and style can be carefully weighed at the valuation stage. The standard of facilities provided are important. In top class hotels bedrooms should have bathrooms en suite with a toilet and adequate showering arrangements. Otherwise private bathrooms are significant. The rooms should be regular in shape, not too cramped and easily cleaned and maintained. As to furniture and fittings, in the bedroom there needs to be television, radio and good telephone service. The furniture should be strong and comfortable. A note needs to be made of the availability of room service and bar dispensers. Some of the equipment and furniture may be rented and this should be checked.

Another important aspect is the general layout of the bedroom accommodation and the signposting of bedrooms and emergency exits. These need to be clear and easily followed. An adequate passenger lift service in multi-storey buildings is essential as is the provision of goods lifts where appropriate. The bedrooms should be categorised into the numbers available in the various sizes, viz. single, twin, double, suites, etc. They should be totalled floor by floor and, where appropriate, categorised into those with good aspects, usually at the front and those at the rear, which overlook internal lift wells in the building. It will be found that higher charges are sometimes made for certain bedrooms with particular advantages. For example, hotels with seaviews on the coast or overlooking parks in a city will normally command higher room rates than those at the rear, although care must be taken to check that outside traffic or other external factors do not detract from what otherwise would appear to be an advantage.

With regard to the public rooms such as restaurants, reception/ meeting rooms, ballrooms and conference facilities, net internal floor areas should be taken. In addition the capacities of the rooms need to be noted, e.g. number of places in a restaurant, number of persons either seated or standing in reception/meeting rooms etc. Hotels with conference rooms will normally have this information readily available in a conference pack. As far as licensed bars are concerned, measurements may be necessary although the liquor trade done at the bar is its main indicator of value. However sometimes it may be of assistance to take overall measurements to give an indication of size. Where restaurant facilities adjoin a bar area and there is no physical demarcation of the two areas, it is wise to ascertain the restaurant area.

Having noted the accommodation available for the public areas, it is necessary to inspect all the non-public areas such as management offices, staff living accommodation, kitchens, boiler rooms and air-conditioning plant rooms. The location of room service pantries and food lifts are important if room service is provided.

Next, the general state of repair of an hotel is important especially when dealing with older properties. Often there are problems with the roof, which, on inspection, may turn out to comprise many different types of roof construction with large valley gutters and small downpipes that tend to get blocked and cause damp penetration. This kind of situation often occurs where several buildings have been joined together to form one hotel or where extensions have been made at different times. Flat roofs tend to leak as a result of ponding unless properly constructed in the first instance. An inspection will alert the valuer to likely annual costs of maintenance and repair and particular likely sources of expenditure should be checked when studying the trading accounts or making expenditure estimates. Another source of expenditure which will occur is the upkeep of gardens and any land forming the curtilage of the buildings.

It is thus necessary to inspect the property from the outside, having regard both to the buildings and their curtilage, which together comprise the hotel, and to check the general state of repair and condition both inside and outside before preparing any valuation.

Trading potential

In order to make a valuation of an hotel it is important to inspect the balance sheet and trading accounts for the immediately preceding three years. Sometimes these are not available, for example where a valuation for purchase is being made and the vendor will not make them available and they may not be found from published sources. Another instance is where a new hotel is required to be valued and there are no trading figures available. Nevertheless, estimates have to be made of the future maintainable income and expenditure and in this connection the following matters require attention:

(i) *Income*—Gross turnover split between the various sources, e.g. rooms, food and beverage, bar takings, conferences/banqueting and sundry income from telephones, cleaning, rents for shops/kiosks etc.

(ii) *Expenditure*—This should be categorised as far as possible between cost of sales, payroll, administrative, advertising, rent, rates, repairs and a proportion of head office expenditure in the case of group hotels.

(iii) *Tenant's capital* (from the balance sheets), i.e. original costs where available, recently incurred in equipping the hotel. The main items are normally furniture and kitchen equipment but should also include all soft furnishings, curtains, carpets and floor coverings, crockery, cutlery and linen where these are capitalised in the accounts. In addition there are items such as computer installations and cash in hand and at bank which must be remembered.

Where possible the proprietor should be interviewed and questioned on such matters as sources of business done, e.g. whether mainly private individuals, groups, holiday or business trade, differences between week-end and week-day customers, and so on. There is usually a mixture and it is important to ascertain the proportions of trade from various sources. Also it is necessary to find out whether any reductions are given for group bookings and the extent of credit card charging. Bed occupancy and room occupancy need to be ascertained as well as the achieved room rate where possible. Bed occupancy and room occupancy will normally be expressed as a percentage of the total bed or room availability over a period. These measures will vary daily and are usually available either on a weekly, monthly or yearly basis or a combination. The achieved room rate is the average amount of room income obtained per room night from bedrooms which are let and is usually expressed in the same terms as the bedroom tariff for the hotel. The achieved room rate thus needs to be compared with the daily room rate shown in the published tariff rates of an hotel and may differ substantially therefrom. In order to arrive at the estimated maintainable income for an hotel it is necessary to have regard both to occupancy and achieved room rates throughout the year.

Very important is the proprietor's view on the future trading prospects of the hotel having regard both to the economic situation generally and the effect on the business of any changes or trends in the locality. Any advantages or disadvantages in operating the hotel should be discussed with him wherever possible.

Where no trading figures are available then estimates need to be made. For this purpose, and for checking the trading accounts when available, it is necessary to ascertain the current tariffs being charged in the hotel. Those of previous years should also be examined to check the performance of the hotel by comparison with general trends in the industry. There are many sources of such information available including statistics provided by the English Tourist Board, which provide occupancy surveys annually and monthly divided into regions as well as by lower and higher tariff rates. Private sources such as Pannell Kerr Foster Associates and Horwath and Horwath (UK) Ltd also produce statistical information on the hotel industry in more detail. These provide much useful information regarding income and expenditure for hotels, occupancy rates and average room rates etc.

Investigation of market sector and competition

Having completed all the on-site enquiries, it is then necessary to examine the market sector and competition for the hotel. As a start it is important to be quite clear as to the kind of hotel that one is dealing with: whether it is upmarket, 4 or 5 star; a 3 star standard

hotel, 2 star, or a commercial hotel. Hotels can also conveniently
be divided into:

(i) Large city centre and airport hotels, grading from 5 star down
to 3 star (A.A. and R.A.C. ratings), ranging from 200 to 1,000
bedrooms in size and situated in or very close to the main
shopping and business centres. These hotels provide all amenities. All bedrooms and suites will have their own bathrooms
and radio/TV and telephone. Public rooms include large
lounges, one or more restaurants, bars, conference rooms, and
shops. The service will be 24 hour and of high quality.

(ii) The smaller provincial town or suburban hotel, usually 3 star
rating, where all the more modern hotels will have rooms with
internal bathrooms, radio or TV but in the older hotels some
rooms will only have wash-basins with separate bathrooms.
Public rooms will be smaller and of a more modest nature
and will cater mainly for a mixture of commercial and local
demand. Often hotels in this category have large grounds and
can provide facilities for golf, tennis, swimming etc.

(iii) The modern hotel near a motorway or main trunk road such
as a Post House. These hotels are built very much to a standard
design and are geared to the requirements of the travelling public.

(iv) The "holiday" hotel situated at the seaside or at inland resorts,
which cater primarily for holiday visitors. In these hotels business is seasonal and with the general exception of the larger
hotels in some resorts, many close for the winter season. Here
again many of these hotels provide additional attractions for
holiday-makers, e.g. swimming pools and sports facilities and
also indoor facilities such as ballrooms.

If an hotel is trying to compete in a class of hotel business to
which it is not really suited then the valuer will find that the accounts
will not really support an open market valuation. This may be due
to either the hotel not being properly managed or to the proprietor
aiming at the wrong sector of the market. When this kind of situation
is discovered it is very important to have regard to management
other than the management the valuer happens to find in the hotel.

Competition is another vital factor. There may or may not be
competition in the particular class of the subject hotel with which
one is dealing in the immediate locality. However any competition,
whether in being or proposed, must be carefully investigated and
the possibility of an effect on the trade of the subject hotel taken
into account.

Locational factors

The location of an hotel, like any other property, will provide either its most important advantage or disadvantage as the case may be. "It is not what it is but where it is" is an old adage which cannot be emphasised too much. Airports are prime locations and high occupancy can be expected, provided there is not an over-supply. Proximity to motorway junctions at critical journey points, within easy sight of a motorway, is another type of good location. City centres, of course, are always in need of an appropriate supply of hotel bedrooms. Certainly easy road access or closeness to public transport facilities, such as underground or bus stations, make a substantial difference to hotel profitability. This however will in turn depend on the class of hotel which is under consideration. Means of access and traffic giration are important considerations, as well as ample car parking facilities.

Evidence of sales or lettings

Most hotels are held freehold with the owner-occupier proprietor or company running the business. There is a reasonable turnover in the market of the smaller provincial hotel but unfortunately the large or city centre hotels do not often change hands singly, but rather as a group. Hotels are always bought and sold on the basis of their anticipated profitability and usually the sale includes all trade fixtures and fittings and the contents, although the latter are sometimes valued as at the day of sale. This does not necessarily mean that staff will be inherited with the purchase of an hotel, although that is usually the case with larger concerns. It does mean, however, that it is the hotel business which is sold, although the main asset in any such transaction will be the property which is generating the income. Figures are from time to time reported in the press and elsewhere but they do need very careful checking out and analysing. It is always important to ascertain the precise details of any transaction before it is used as a comparable.

Where large modern hotels are leased, often ground leases will be found. The rents are normally geared to a percentage of the takings, subject to a minimum. In the case of either ground or rack rent leases percentage rents can be related either to the gross takings of the whole hotel, or to the gross takings for the bedrooms or, sometimes, to a combination related to gross takings from bedrooms with different percentages applied to gross takings from the restaurant and conference facilities. Depending on where the hotels are situated these percentages can vary widely. The percentage taken for rent related to bedroom income will be substantially higher than the percentage for other income. Alternatively bands of income may be used and percentages varied with the income range. Whether these bands are achieved will depend on the estimated profitability and occupancy of the hotel. It is always dangerous to have any percentage for rack rent related to the total gross takings of an hotel as this will always be a burden on the hotelier. It is better to have relatively higher percentages but related to the net profit of the hotel closely defined in the lease. This provides a more accurate method of measuring performance, although the conflict between landlord and tenant must be watched. Such a basis will always reflect good, bad or indifferent management of an hotel so that minimum and maximum amounts need to be incorporated in any formula devised to ensure that good and profitable management is not discouraged. Ground rents however may be related to gross takings provided suitable percentages are adopted.

Apart from percentage rents, which should be treated with caution, evidence of open market rental values may be available, either as rack rents for land and buildings or as ground rents. These need to be analysed on a per bedroom basis with allowances made for public rooms and other amenities.

The valuation

The purpose of any valuation is, as always, a paramount consideration. In any valuation of an hotel, however, unless for fire insurance or any other purpose unrelated to the trading activities carried on therein, it is necessary first to arrive at annual or rental value, either from the profits method of valuation or by comparison or by a combination of both. Thereafter, if necessary, arrive at the capital value whether it be for sale, purchase, balance sheet or taxation purposes.

For the purposes of a case study, therefore, consideration will be given to an open market valuation of a typical 3 star hotel, which incorporates the steps necessary to arrive at rental value in the first instance. In the example The George Hotel is taken as a hypothetical case and the following is a summary of the property.

The George Hotel

Tenture:	Freehold—no unusual burdens or restrictions.
Site area:	12 acres—reasonably level.
Description:	1930 four-storey country house with 1970 addition.
Amenities:	9-hole pitch and putt course, 2 hard tennis courts, ornamental garden.

Accommodation: 150 letting bedrooms with staff annexe divided
                as follows:

	1930 House	1970 Addition	Total rooms
40 twins or doubles		90 twins	130
14 singles		6 family	20
(6 twins and 4 singles with		(all with bathrooms)	
no bathrooms)		Staff annexe	—
		Letting bedrooms	150

Other facilities:
Restaurant, bar/lounge, 2 kiosks.
5 conference rooms—3 inter-connecting.
Maximum catering capacity. 200 persons at one sitting.
Car parking for 120 cars.
Railway station close by.

From a study of the balance sheet and trading accounts for the
last three years, the following information has been extracted:

The George Hotel

Summary balance sheet at end of year 3

Assets employed
Fixed

	Freehold property £'000	Furniture plant equipment £'000	Vehicles £'000	Totals £'000
Cost	600	200	8	808
Additions	40	20	2	62
	640	220	10	870
Depreciation	—	164	6	170
Totals	640	56	4	700

	Current assets		*Current liabilities*	
	£'000			£'000
Stocks	40	Bank overdraft		110
Debtors	50	Creditors		90
Cash in hand	10	Taxation		40
Total	100	Total		240

Net current liabilities	£140,000
Net assets	£560,000
Represented by:	
Share capital	£200,000
General reserves	£360,000

Trading account year 3

Gross takings	£'000	£'000
Rooms and banqueting	780	780
Bar	148	
Tobacco	2	
		150
Telephone	16	
Kiosks (rent)	1	
Golf course	1	
Sundry	2	20
		950
Deduct cost of sales	230	230
Gross trading profit		720

Hotel expenses	
Payroll (includ. N.I.)	265
Light and heating	38
Laundry and cleaning	34
Garden	4
Telephone	20
Rates and insurance	28
Printing/stationary	15
Advertising	21
TV rental	6
General expenses	5

Repairs and renewals (building and
  plant)   81
Legal and professional   6
                                                 ———
                                                 523
Interest   17   540
                                                 ———   ———
                                                                        180
Trading profit for year   £180,000
Deduct
  Directors' emoluments   30
  Depreciation   27   57
                                                 ———   ———
                                                                        123
Balance
  Net profit before taxation   £123,000

The table on page 529 shows the analysis of the Trading Accounts
for years 1–3.

Having studied the trading accounts for years 1, 2 and 3 and
discussed the likely maintainable level of trade with the proprietor,
a view can be formed of the likely level of trade for the purpose
of the valuation. The basis for the valuation in this case is derived
from a study of all three years of accounts but having particular
regard to year 3 which shows the latest achieved trade. The right-
hand column shows the basis adopted for the valuation.

Freehold Property with 150 Letting Rooms
Valuation on the Profits Method

Assume maintainable future income   £950,000 p.a.
(Take year 3 figure)   ————————

	£'000	% Gross receipts	£'000
Take 50/50 split			
Estimated maintainable room income			
(68% occ)	475	50	
Estimated maintainable other income	475	50	
	———	———	
Total estimated gross takings	950	100	
Deduct: Cost of sales at 44% other			
income	209	22	
	———		
Estimated gross trading profit	741		741
Less: Hotel expenditure (actual and			
estimated)			
Payroll	265	28	
Light and heat	38	4	
Laundry and cleaning	34	4	

(continued on page 530)

Analysis of Trading Accounts for Years 1—3

	Year 1		Year 2		Year 3		Basis for valuation
	£'000	%	£'000	%	£'000	%	%
Gross receipts							
Rooms (incl. tel. and sundries)	243	42	408	55	475	50	50
Food and beverage	212	37	223	30	400	42 }	50
Functions	125	21	111	15	75	8 }	
Total gross receipts	580	100	742	100	950	100	100
Deduct: Cost of sales	120	20	161	21	230	25	22
Gross trading profit	460		581		720		
Hotel expenses							
Payroll (incl. N.I.)	136	23	204	27	265	28	28
Light and heat	17	3	35	5	38	4	4
Laundry and cleaning	18	3	28	4	34	4	4
Rates	13	2	15	2	16	2	2
Insurance	10	2	10	1	12	1	1
Garden telephone / Advertising general / Office printing / Legal and Professional	40	7	64	9	77	8	8
Repairs and renewals:							
(i) Premises and heavy plant	44	8	120	16	45	5	5
		48		64		52	52
(ii) Furniture, soft furnishing, equipment, china, glass, cutlery	20	3	25	3	36	4	
Total expenditure	298	51	501	67	523	56	
Room occupancy	60%		66%		68%		68%

All figures in % columns are percentages of total gross receipts

Rates	18⎤		
Insurance	13⎥		
Other expenses (excluding	⎥	16	
repairs and renewals)	80⎥		
Repairs and renewals: premises	⎥		
and heavy plant	45⎦	52	493

Estimated net profit		26	248
Less: Interest on tenants capital			
£300,000 at 12%	36		
(ii) Sinking fund for renewal of			
contents	20	6	56
		20	192

Net operating profit		£192,000 p.a.		
Take rent at say 50%	96,000 × Y.P. at 9%		=	1,056,000
Leaves goodwill	96,000 × 3 Y.P.		=	288,000
				£1,344,000

Checks

(i) Rent of £96,000 = 10·1% of   Open market value of
    gross takings.   hotel,   say £1,350,000
(ii) Capital value of £1·3m is   (including all normal items
     equivalent to: of trade fixtures and fittings
     (a) £9,000 per room   but *excluding* contents)
     (b) 1·42 Y.P. gross income.

The above is an illustration of the valuation of an hotel valued on the profits method. It will be noted that some items differ in detail from the year 3 actual accounts. For example cost of sales have been varied to have more regard to the performance in years 1 and 2. Other expenses, rates and insurance have also been fine tuned resulting from more detailed information on likely expenditure. The treatment of expenditure on repairs and renewals of furniture etc. has also been varied to take into account expenditure in years 1 and 2 and dealt with by allowing for a sinking fund for renewal of contents. All these matters of detail require careful consideration to ensure an appropriate net operating profit results. In this case £192,000 per annum has been arrived at compared with a trading profit from the accounts for year 3 of £180,000 per annum.

In the final stages of the valuation it is particularly important to note the checks that are made. These enable comparison with other similar hotels within the same class and locality.

Finally reference should be made to the R.I.C.S. Guidance Notes on the Valuation of Assets (2nd edition, background paper BP7) which relates to open market valuation having regard to trading potential.

Particular attention should be paid to paragraph 3 of that paper, which indicates that in analysing the prices paid for comparable properties in preparing a valuation, the valuer would normally have regard to the trading accounts of previous years and form an opinion as to the future trading potential and the level of turnover likely to be achieved. The background paper then goes on to expand on the kind of principles involved and is well worth close study. It will be noted that the term "bricks and mortar" valuation is not used. This phrase is intended to represent the land and buildings element of a property but an open market valuation of a fully operational business unit will generally include land and buildings, trade fixtures and fittings, furniture, furnishings, licences and goodwill which will pass with the property, on the assumption that the business continues. An apportionment of value to the land and buildings element in isolation is really a hypothetical exercise. It is more appropriate, where a valuation of an hotel is required in connection with security for a loan, that the appropriate basis should be its open market value as a fully operational hotel. The lender can then make a judgement on the amount he is prepared to lend against the open market value of the hotel arrived at on this basis.

SSAP 12 and SSAP 16 are two statements of standard account practice which relate to depreciation and current cost accounting. Reference is also made to these in Guidance Note J.1 where particular regard should be had to the future economic life of buildings and this of course is particularly important when dealing with hotel valuations. A view needs to be taken on the anticipated life of an hotel, that is to say, estimating the approximate future point in time when the hotel will need substantial refurbishment or modernisation. This will be governed by the degree of functional obsolescence inherent in the building—poor layout, bedroom size and shape, access etc. Also the question of energy conservation is important. These are often difficult questions to answer but all need careful thought. Certainly accountants will require guidance on the life that should be given to the building element of the hotel where an apportionment between land and buildings is needed for balance sheet purposes.

SSAP 16 gives the definition of terms where assets have to be included in the balance sheet and are of value to the business. Value is defined as the net current replacement cost. Paragraph 33 of the Guidance Notes on Current Cost Accounting issued by the Accounting Standards Committee refers to buildings which are specialised but with trading potential such as hotels, etc. This must be contrasted with "specialised buildings" for the purposes of paragraph 32 of the Guidance Notes, e.g. oil refineries and the like. The word "specialised" relates to specialised buildings in the context of whether or not a valuation should be on a depreciated replacement

cost basis (paragraph 32), or on a normal open market basis, i.e.
with trading potential (paragraph 33). Hotels fall into this latter
category of specialised buildings and are required to be valued on
a normal open market basis and not on a depreciated replacement
cost basis. This is because they are commonly bought and sold and
the sales include the inherent trading potential.

Conclusion

Hotels should thus always be valued to open market value as specialised buildings with trading potential. They should not be valued
on a depreciated replacement cost basis. A study of the trading
accounts must be undertaken whenever possible as hotels are bought
and owned to make money by operating them. It is of particular
importance to be aware of all the statutory provisions which affect
their operation and be knowledgeable of the hotel trade.

Further Reading

Jonathan Bodlender. Going Concern Valuations for the Hotel
    Industry. *Journal of Valuation* 3: 134–144 (1985).
Royal Institution of Chartered Surveyors. *Guidance Notes on the
    Valuation of Assets* (2nd edition).
Strand Hotels Ltd v. *Hampsher* (Valuation Officer) (1977) 20.
    R.R.C. 371.
Corisand Investments Ltd v. *Druce & Co.* (1978) 248 E.G. 315

Chapter 19

LEISURE PROPERTIES

Introduction

A brief glance at the list below, which is by no means exhaustive, will give an indication of the range of leisure properties frequently valued for rental or capital purposes.

Amusement Arcades	Golf Courses
Amusement and Theme Parks	Hotels and Motels
Bingo Clubs	Ice Rinks and Roller Rinks
Bowling Alleys	Marinas and Moorings
Caravan and Chalet Parks	Public Houses
Casinos	Snooker Clubs
Cinemas	Squash and Tennis Clubs
Discotheques	Theatres

Such properties if not entirely purpose-built for their specific use have limited potential for conversion to alternative uses, should the original use become obsolete or uneconomic.

The number of open market transactions, either sales or lettings, at any one time tends to be limited. Small changes in the level of demand can often result in a disproportionate change in the level of price which makes the valuer's job difficult in assessing the strength of the market, and underlines the necessity for a detailed knowledge of the particular aspect of the leisure industry with which he is concerned.

Virtually all leisure properties change hands in the open market at prices based directly on their trading potential for a strictly limited use and therefore the whole principle of valuation is based upon potential turnover, net profit and return on capital that a prospective purchaser or lessee would expect.

Properties are bought and sold as fully operational business units and, in most cases, include the following elements: land, buildings, trade fixtures and fittings, furnishings, together with the value of licences and "goodwill" which will pass with the property, on the assumption that the business continues.

The valuation of hotels and public houses, which are the largest categories, have been considered in detail in other chapters. The principles of the accounts method of valuation as applied to hotels

533

apply equally to other leisure properties, although the proportion of net operating profit adopted to arrive at annual rental value and the capitalisers employed will vary.

It is not proposed to repeat a detailed study of this method of valuation nor look individually at the other property types, but consider aspects of the valuation process which are common to all leisure properties.

Inspections

In addition to the usual locational and physical details, the valuer must gather all the relevant information which will influence the level of income and running costs of the leisure property.

Ease of access whether by public transport or car, with complementary parking facilities, is vitally important, so is the attractiveness and overall image of the facility.

It is the capacity of the property, and the extent to which it is realised, which is relevant rather than its size; floor areas are secondary and in many cases will not be required. Detailed information on the design and layout, type and standard of accommodation should be noted and whether or not this could be enhanced by extensive refurbishment or adaptation.

Irrespective of the availability of trading accounts, where possible the valuer should ascertain by inspection admission numbers and charges, the price structure of licensed bars, restaurants, other major and ancilliary sources of income. The valuer should make his own assessment of spend per admission from the various revenue sources either as a check against the trading information he is given or to enable him to make an assessment of total income.

It is necessary to be aware of all similar leisure properties in the locality, whether existing or planned, to consider the effect of future competition on the subject premises. This information should be linked to an appreciation of the type of trade currently being enjoyed, to assess whether or not income will be maintained.

Likewise, the inspection will provide the valuer with an opportunity to assess the factors influencing running costs, in particular staff, repairs and energy, for comparison with similar trading units. Experience will show that the cost of sales, viz food and liquor, does not vary greatly between properties of a similar type but, for example, there can be enormous differences in staff costs due to an operator's particular style of management or the design and layout of the premises. Either may materially affect the level of net profit achieved.

Tenure and licensing details

The valuer must be aware of any restrictive covenants contained in the title deeds or lease of the property which may affect its trading potential, such as the sale of alcohol being prohibited on the whole or part of the premises or a limitation on trading hours. If the property to be valued is subject to a lease the implications of the user clause must be fully taken into account.

In addition to Liquor Licences and Public Entertainment Licenses, there are many other licences and permits which may be required for the particular leisure enterprise, and are mostly renewed on an annual basis. The valuer should satisfy himself that the appropriate licences and permits have been obtained and be aware of any restrictions which may be imposed. Particularly where a Late Night Licence has been granted it is necessary to consider the prospect of its continuance, having regard to the trading history and any known objections. As will be appreciated, if a Public Entertainment Licence allowed Music and Dancing until 2 a.m., but on renewal was restrictied until 1 a.m. due to objections by the police or local inhabitants, this could seriously affect the trade achieved.

It is, of course, essential to verify that an appropriate Fire Certificate has been granted for the property.

Assessment of trading potential

Understandably, every operating company is sensitive about their trading accounts for individual enterprises. The trading details are confidential and it can be difficult to obtain full knowledge of how successfully or otherwise a certain property is trading. Landlords in particular can be at a considerable disadvantage, but whether a valuer is acting for a landlord or a tenant, it is necessary to assess and consider the trading potential in relation to comparable properties.

The general tendency for non-specialist properties is to look at comparable evidence drawn from an area close to the subject property. With many leisure properties, there are often few or no similar properties in the locality and thus it is necessary to seek evidence on a country-wide basis. Having established the physical and legal constraints of the subject and comparable properties, including their capacity, user and licensing details, the main difficulties arise from identifying similar trading conditions which will affect income, both number of admissions and spend per head, and total running costs.

The multiplex cinema, with perhaps six to ten screens, and beach resort clubs are examples of relatively new leisure concepts in this country. In such instances, it is often beneficial to look at experience abroad as well as country-wide.

The valuer's task when assessing future trading potential is to exclude any turnover which would only be available to the present owner or management, but he should reflect any trading potential that might be realised in the hands of a more efficient operator.

In the case of bingo halls, for example, the level of trade achieved can vary enormously between the various major circuit operators as well as the independent operators. Consequently, the valuer must have an awareness of operators' strengths and weaknesses and be in a position to judge whether or not the style of management is right for the particular property which he is valuing.

As far as possible, he must also be aware of changes in trading techniques and sources of income which may influence profitability on a short or long term basis. A detailed knowledge of the industry is essential in assessing the true trading potential.

Assessment of rental value

Ideally, the valuer will have been able to obtain detailed trading accounts for the last three years. If these are not available, he will make his own assessment of income and expenditure, having regard to the factors mentioned above, and thereby build up estimated accounts for the property he is valuing. He should always seek to consult with the trade and operational managers to obtain their views on trading matters.

Past history is a good guide, but the valuer's task is to assess future turnover and profit commencing with the date of valuation.

If he is using actual accounts, he must look critically at the expenses having regard to what he would expect in both actual and percentage terms. A valuer specialising in this type of work will be aware of the normal level of gross and net profits expected at certain levels of turnover for particular enterprises.

It is necessary to judge whether or not the figures shown are realistic, taking one year with another, and adjust accordingly. In the case of repairs, annual costs can vary considerably and an average figure appropriate to future repairing liabilities should be adopted.

Interest payments on mortgages and loans, depreciation and directors' remuneration should be added back but the valuer should allow a reasonable return on tenant's capital.

Major circuit operators, or independents with a number of properties, will usually show an item of expenditure in the accounts for head office or central costs. If this is shown, one should establish what is included and whether or not the figure is justified.

Frequently, the initial reaction is that the head office charge is excessive, but on fuller investigation it may be shown to be reasonable. Bulk purchasing agreements, central reservations, stock-taking, accountancy and other services provided by the head office may be cheaper than the individual operator providing the services for himself. If head office charges are not shown in the accounts, one must consider whether or not they should be included or other adjustments made to reflect the benefits provided by the head office.

Any abnormal expenditure, or an expense not necessarily incurred in running the business, must be added back.

Having formed an opinion as to future trading potential and level of turnover likely to be achieved, together with expenses properly incurred in running the business, the valuer will establish the level of adjusted net profit prior to any deduction for rent. These steps are common to the valuation of all leisure properties before assessing the proportion of net profit which the operator, on the hypothesis he is a tenant, will bid as a rental payment for the benefit of occupying and trading from the property.

The percentage bid will vary considerably between different leisure properties and will have regard to the level of net profit achieved, the sources of profit within the particular enterprise, and an assessment of whether or not the profit will be maintained or improved in the future.

The higher the level of risk in achieving the net profit, the lower will be the percentage which the operator or tenant would be prepared to pay as rent. Thus it is usual for the percentage bid to increase as the level of net profit increases. It is impossible to generalise on appropriate percentage bids to cover all the various property types and circumstances, but the proportion of net profit normally taken for rent will fall within the range of 25% to 50%.

From time to time valuers will assess rental value by reference to a percentage of gross turnover excluding VAT, particularly in the drafting of rent review clauses. It is as well to be aware of the advantages and disadvantages of this practice:–

Advantages
(a) Readily understood by both landlords and tenants and less likely to be contentious.
(b) Being the top line of trading accounts it can be checked against V.A.T. returns and eliminates any massaging of running costs.
(c) It can readily form the basis of annual reviews, subject to a fixed fall-back rent or say 70% of the previous years' payment.
(d) Turnover should be a general guide as to profitability and hence the establishment of the rental value of the property.

Disadvantages
(a) Inflation increases turnover and the amount of rent paid, but not necessarily profit.
(b) With the concept of fixed and marginal costs, net profit does not vary in proportion to gross turnover—the pattern is very difficult to predict.
(c) A rental related to turnover cannot disregard the effect on rent of goodwill or improvements.

Whenever possible, rental value should be derived from adjusted net profit in preference to gross turnover, as this is the true indicator of value to the operator or tenant and hence his ability to pay an open market rent for a property.

Capitalising rental value and residual profit

The example below is a summary of the anticipated trading results for a leisure property over the year following the date of valuation. The figures have been based on a study of the detailed trading accounts for the last three years. It is not envisaged there will be a significant departure from these results in the foreseeable future in real terms.

	£ per annum
Gross turnover (excl. VAT)	400,000
Less:	
Allowable expenditure excluding rent	300,000
Adjusted net profit	100,000
Annual rental value at say 40%	40,000
Residual profit	60,000

Any personal goodwill has been eliminated in arriving at the estimated gross turnover and is therefore not reflected in the adjusted net profit (see R.I.C.S. Guidance Notes on the Valuation of Assets Background Papers No. 7 and 11). The annual rental value is therefore assessed from a level of profit in the hands of an average efficient operator.

The figure of £60,000 shown above is often referred to, rather misleadingly, as goodwill attaching to the land and/or buildings which will pass with the property on a disposal. It is preferable to regard this as "Residual Profit", "Trade" or "Business" as it is part of the open market value of any property valued on trading potential and not a separate element in the saleable value of the business. Assuming the valuer is assessing the freehold interest in possession, the method of capitalising the adjusted net profit can vary. Operators buying a property or a group of properties as trading concerns tend to bid on the basis of the return on capital which they require and therefore are likely to employ a single capitaliser. In the above example, an operator seeking a return of 16% would adopt a Years Purchase of 6·25 to the whole of the adjusted net profit giving a capital value of £625,000.

The valuer can either follow this method or alternatively analyse transactions by considering the rental value of the property and the residual profit separately. Using the latter method, the valuer will capitalise the rental value at the appropriate remunerative rate for the property and apply a multiplier to the residual profit normally between 1 and 7, depending upon the type of business and its future prospects. Thus his valuation of the freehold interest in possession of the above property may be as follows:—

	£	£
Rental value	40,000	
Y.P. in perp. at 9%	11·1	
	———	444,000
Residual profit	60,000	
Multiplier	3	
	———	180,000
		624,000
	say	625,000

It is recommended that wherever possible the adjusted net profit is divided into two slices namely secure income (rent) and less secure income (residual profit) which are capitalised separately. This approach will enable closer examination and comparison of a business with other similar properties, and the valuer will be better able to take account of the quality of the profit generated and its likely continuance. However, the principle of valuing as you have devalued comparable properties must not be overlooked.

Such an open market valuation of the freehold interest in possession will thus be on the basis of a fully operational business unit and include land, buildings, trade fixtures and fittings, furniture, furnishings, licenses and the value of residual profit (trade or business) which will pass with the property on the assumption that its existing use continues. The basis of valuation must be clearly stated in the Valuation Certificate.

A particular point of interest emerges which should be borne in mind. Other property types, such as offices or shops, valued on the investment approach generally show no distinction between the value of the freehold interest in possession and the freehold interest as an investment, provided it is let on a modern lease at full rental value subject to regular review. In the case of leisure properties valued on trading potential, we have seen that an element of their value—the residual profit—is only available to the operator or tenant and thus the value of the freehold interest held as an investment albeit on a modern lease at full rental value, will be significantly less than the value of the freehold interest in possession.

Earlier in this section, we touched upon the valuation of goodwill which is referred to in detail in the R.I.C.S. Guidance Notes on the Valuation of Assets. Background Paper 11 adopts the shorter Oxford Dictionary definition of goodwill as follows:–

> "The privilege granted by the seller of a business to a purchaser of trading as his recognised successor; the possession of a ready-formed connection with customers considered as a separate element in the saleable value of a business."

It is recognised in Background Paper 7 that in addition to such value as is reflected in the trading potential which runs with the property, there may be cases where there is goodwill which has been created in the business by the present owner. This goodwill may have an identifiable market value if it is capable of transfer to other properties and as such should be considered separately from the valuation of a particular leisure property.

Difficulty may arise with the valuation of new leisure properties which are nearing completion and fitting out. The trading projections for a new leisure complex may show an estimated adjusted net profit before rent as follows:–

	£
Year 1	120,000
Year 2	300,000
Year 3	450,000

The day before the complex opens there should be much enthusiasm in the market but no proof as to whether or not the projections will be achieved. Therefore the risk is higher and consequently the overall return on capital required by the operator is higher, thus producing a lower capital value.

At the end of the first year, on the assumption the projected profit has been achieved and business is continuing to improve as expected, the market would pay a price which would have regard to the projections for the second and third years.

At the end of the third year, on the assumption the net profit projections have been achieved, there will be three years' trading record and thus the risk is that much lower which should reflect in a higher price being paid. Typical open market valuations of the freehold interest in possession at the various stages may be as follows:—

	£	
Day before opening	3,250,000	
End of first year	3,750,000	
End of third year	5,000,000	(the profit for year 3 represents 9 per cent return on capital).

Thus with new ventures, it is advisable to revalue annually as the trading pattern becomes established.

Valuation checks

There is a danger for those not familiar with the valuation of leisure properties to adopt valuation checks as methods of valuation. In the previous section it was suggested that the adjusted net profit should be broken down into rental value and residual profit and capitalised separately, rather than apply a single multiplier based on an overall return on capital. This latter approach should really be considered as an important valuation check, as is the freehold value represented as a multiplier of gross annual turnover excluding VAT.

These checks can be made on all leisure properties whereas others such as unit prices sper seat, per court, per table, per bedroom or per converted barrel are appropriate to specific property types. Such checks are only valuable if they are used to compare properties operating under similar trading conditions and must be interpreted with care.

Valuations for loan purposes

Where a valuation of this type of property is required in connection with security for a loan, the appropriate basis is its open market value as a fully operational business unit as previously defined. The valuer should provide an opinion as to the suitability of the property as security for the loan and the risks inherent in the business. It is recommended that he includes in his report a clause to the effect that in the event of a decline in trading potential of the subject premises, the open market value will in all probability decline as well.

It should be the role of the lender and not the valuer to reflect the degree of risk in fixing the terms of the loan, including the percentage of open market value to be advanced, the rate of interest to be charged and the terms for capital repayment.

Where the proposed lender also requires a "worst case" valuation, i.e. what will the underlying security be worth if the existing business fails, it is suggested that an alternative use valuation may be appropriate in certain circumstances. In such cases, assumptions need to be made as to planning policy and development potential, the lessors' consent to change of use (in respect of leaseholds) and the costs of achieving such change of use. These should be discussed and agreed with the client at the time of acceptance of instructions, and all assumptions clearly stated in the valuation report.

It is recommended that with leisure properties valued on their trading potential a lender should be made aware of the inappropriate and misleading use of the terms "Forced Sale" value and "Bricks and Mortar" value and advised that these terms should not be used. A "Forced Sale" valuation requires the valuer to assume the imposition of an unreasonably short time in which to complete a sale. In addition, for this type of property the valuer has to make assumptions as to the future level of trading profit (or loss) which are likely to be purely hypothetical due to changes in trading and/or market conditions. A "Bricks and Mortar" valuation supposedly represents the open market value of the land and buildings element of a property. An open market valuation of a fully operational business unit will generally include land and buildings, trade fixtures and fittings, furniture, furnishings, licences and residual profit which will pass with the property, on the assumption that the business continues. It is considered that an apportionment of value to the land and buildings element in isolation is a hypothetical exercise.

If the loan is secured on the land and buildings only, then in the absence of alternative methods of valuation, it is advisable to value the land and buildings based on the value of the whole less the value of the trade fixtures and fittings, furniture and furnishings at their appropriate replacement cost. In these circumstances the method of informal apportionment must be agreed with the lender and clearly stated in the valuation report.

© D. E. Butters, 1988

Chapter 20

EASEMENTS AND WAYLEAVES FOR SEWERS, PIPELINES AND ELECTRICITY

Introduction

Each of the various undertakings have their own different approaches to the question of easement or wayleaves. It is intended in this chapter to give a broad outline so that the reader can at least have some idea of the line of approach to the particular requirement whether it be a pipeline or an electricity cable, so translating the principles of valuation into practice.

The appendix to this chapter sets out the various principal statutes encompassed by this subject together with other references which the reader may find useful.

For convenience only and ease of reference the word "pipe" in this chapter is to be taken in the widest sense and includes any installation which is laid in, on or over the ground including water pipes, sewers, oil pipes and cables. A further abbreviation again for convenience is the word "easement" which is not entirely a correct connotation but within this context is to be taken as the permanent width within which a "pipe" is laid.

Consideration and compensation

From the outset it should be appreciated that payments made by Acquiring Authorities and Undertakings should be broken into two distinct headings, if for no other reason than taxation, in particular capital gains tax:—

1. Consideration for acquiring the easement.
2. Compensation for damage caused in laying the pipe.

Consideration for acquiring easement
There are no Statutory Specifications either for the width of an easement or for the basis of consideration. The Lands Tribunal have for upwards of 40 years provided the bases for both of these items.

In days gone by, half a chain (33 feet) used to be taken as a "norm" for an easement width and when land was worth £150 or less per acre the consideration taken at half of the full value worked out at three shillings and sixpence (about 17p) per yard run although rather better amounts were often negotiated by the Country Landowner Association (C.L.A.) and the National Farmers' Union (N.F.U.). With the escalation of land values this increased to £1.14 and £2.27 per yard run for land worth £1,000 and £2,000 per acre respectively. Consequently acquiring authorities sought to reduce this cost by reducing the width of the easement to as low as 4 metres wide.

Narrow easement widths should not be countenanced and a general rule to adopt is "can the Authority reasonably enter upon their easement to carry out repairs without going outside the easement", if it cannot, then the easement width should be negotiated to allow for this, there seems to be a general unwritten rule, now being propounded, that the easement width should be not less than 10 feet either side of the "pipe", i.e. pipe size plus 20 feet.

Authorities plead that they will never need to carry out a repair and that if they do go outside the easement then they will pay compensation for damage. Such a claim is usually minimal and causes a lot of aggravation. Why should an Authority acquire an easement right without paying the proper rate of Consideration? It must be said however that some Authorities, especially Nationalised Undertakings are generally very realistic to the extent of sometimes being generous and full consultations usually take place when the project is being planned.

Local, Water Authorities and Government Oil pipelines are not required to negotiate easements, they have a *right of entry* upon giving reasonable written notice. It is however, becoming the practice to have talks with landowners and occupiers.

Nor are these Bodies required to document the acquisition of an easement, although again this is becoming more so. In any case, letters and notices should be lodged with the Title Deeds for future reference.

Electricity, Gas and Commercial Oil pipelines have to obtain consent to enter and lay a pipe, if necessary they can apply to the Secretary of State for Compulsory Powers. They do not have power of entry by right.

Easement Consideration is calculated upon a proportion of the freehold land value relative to the interest to be vested in the Acquiring Authority.

Local Government and Water Authorities generally adhere to the rule of 50% of the freehold value. Nationalised bodies (Gas and

Electricity) and oil companies are generally more generous (up to 75%) in order to obtain easements since their Compulsory Powers are not quite so over-riding, Local Government and Water Authorities can make entry simply by giving written reasonable notice.

In agreeing an easement width it should always be confirmed and stipulated that it is for the proposed purpose and that purpose only of laying the pipe or cable. Any additional pipes or cables should be subject to additional consideration.

For the purpose of calculation "consideration" is usually paid on the "as laid" length at a price per metre or yard and the following formulae are useful short cuts to calculate these amounts:

Imperial measure
50% of land value: £/acre × width feet ÷ 290·4 = p. per yard
75% of land value: £/acre × width feet ÷ 193·6 = p. per yard

Imperial metric
50% of land value: £/acre × width metres ÷ 80·9372 = p. per metre
75% of land value: £/acre × width metres ÷ 53·9581 = p. per metre

Metric
50% of land value: £/hectare × width metres ÷ 200 = p. per metre
75% of land value: £/hectare × width metres ÷ 133·33 = p. per metre

Example
Authority—Area Water Authority
Work—sewer
Land value £2,000 per acre—vacant possession
Easement width—10 metres
Consideration—50% of freehold value
Value per metre run: £2,000 × 10 ÷ 80·9372 = £2·47 per metre

It is seldom invoked but authorities are entitled to claim betterment when the land value is enhanced by the presence of a pipe.

There are no statutory rules for consideration to a tenant, his recourse is to a reduction in his rent. However some undertakings do recognise their dependence upon the co-operation of the tenant or occupier and accordingly make payments to encourage this co-operation.

In addition to the payment for the easement line, payments for ancillary equipment such as inspection chambers, valve chambers, marker posts and in fact any item other than the pipe should be claimed. The value of these of necessity must vary and is dependent upon the "nuisance" value which they cause. A manhole in the middle of a field will cause infinite nuisance to farming operations, whereas a manhole in a hedge-row will be of minimal nuisance.

There are various calculations which can be made to arrive at the consideration for these ancillary items, including the area of land which will be missed in each crop, the value of such lost crops capitalised at current interest rates in perpetuity plus an indefinable sum for inconvenience.

Also to be taken into consideration in calculating the consideration is whether the pipe is laid below, at or above ground level and it will readily be appreciated that there are widely varying values for the easement acquisition from the complete sterilisation of an area of land to virtually no interference whatsoever.

Electricity Area Boards and Central Electricity Generating Board have their own system of calculation for wayleave consideration in that annual rentals for the various types of equipment are agreed with N.F.U. and C.L.A. and in most cases these rentals can be capitalised. Where underground cables are laid the same rules as for other pipes apply.

The calculation of the consideration is the relatively simple part of a pipe-laying operation, especially when authorities and undertakings make substantial offers well above the rule of thumb established by the Lands Tribunal of 50% of the freehold value, which is also often enhanced.

Compensation

This next part of the chapter is far more complex and requires very careful consideration. It may appear that a lot of detail is included but reflection will show that these points are necessary in order to arrive at a satisfactory calculation of "compensation":

It is intended to follow the basic procedures of laying a pipeline (including electricity lines and equipment) so incorporating the various items which must be considered.

Wherever possible it is advisable for a meeting to be held at the inception of the pipeline between the owner, the occupier and their land agents together with the authority's officer in charge and any technical advisers. Amongst the matters that should be discussed are:

1. The route of the proposed pipeline.
2. The easement and working widths.
3. Temporary fencing requirements. If it is through pasture land then stockproof fencing may be required.

4. Crossing points over the working widths for both livestock and farming machinery.
5. Continuity of water supplies and other services.
6. Land drainage.
7. Sporting rights—including interference with shooting during the season.
8. Possible noise and other physical annoyances (dust etc.) and what proposals there are to control these.
9. A further meeting with the authority's site agent and the contractors when the contract has been let.

When the contract has been let the meeting (under No. 9 above) should be held to go through the various matters already agreed so that the contractors are fully aware of any arrangements which have been made and this should be followed by further matters directly affecting the contractors including:

1. The authority's site agent, where he can be contacted including a 24 hour telephone number.
2. Any variations to the Standard Codes of Practice.
3. The start date.

Referring to land drainage it should always be ensured that "pipes" are laid at a sufficient depth below the level of any existing or possible future land drainage systems. Never assume that a field will not be drained since the modern farming methods this is always a possibility if not a probability. British Standards Institute recommend a minimum depth to the top of a pipe of one metre.

"Ditches"—pipes should be laid well below the true bottom of a ditch and should be protected by a cover of at least 12″ of concrete.

"Proximity to Buildings"—While the pipeline designers may set out the line so as to avoid buildings it is well to think ahead to any buildings which may be required in the future. It is always easier to get a pipe laid along a different line than to get it moved at a later date.

Compensation takes in everything that is not covered by "consideration" and requires careful overseeing to ensure that a proper claim is made and paid and the following Heads are given as a lead to various matters which need attention:

(a) Diary. From the moment that a pipeline is intimated, owners, occupiers, tenants and their agents should each in their own way keep a detailed diary of *everything* that happens even down to the initial knock on the door enquiring into the land-ownership, an event may appear insignificant at the time but in 6 or 12 months it can have become an important item of claim, therefore "record everything" and it is sometimes helpful to photograph a particular problem.

(b) Record of Condition: It is imperative that a careful and full Record is made together with photographs before the works commence. It is the acquiring authority's duty to prepare this record and supply a copy to the owner/occupier and/or their land agents, together with photographs before work commences so that it can be checked as a "true record of state and condition". This document is most important since from this will stem all claims for damage. The record should also include items outside the working width, such as a gate which may be convenient for the contractor although it is outside his area of authority.

(c) Working Width: This is usually wider than the easement width to allow sufficient room to lay the pipe.

Claim—losses arising on this width.

(d) Conditions of Working:

(i) Soil separation—always ensure that the top soil and the sub-soil are kept separate, preferably on opposite sides of the working width.

(ii) Land drains—these must be marked as they are found so that it is ensured that they are reinstated. If land drainage plans are available then they should be produced so that at least the contractor is aware that he should find something.

(iii) Excessively wet weather—it is not always easy to get a "stop work clause" because of the penalties involved under contracts. It is however recommended that wherever possible such a clause should be made so that work can be stopped in very bad weather, this is particularly important where work has not started, since in very wet conditions it is difficult to separate the top and sub-soils without causing considerable damage to the soil structure.

(iv) Inspections—it should be confirmed at the outset that the occupier will be compensated for any reasonable inspections he may make, this is particularly important where livestock are concerned. A prudent farmer will always wish to check that gates have been shut and fences left in order when the contractor has finished at night and particularly at week-ends. This can come under the heading of "Mitigating Claims"

It has been known for contractors to fracture water mains and leave them running, the water lost being registered through a meter at the cost of the Occupier.

Reinstatement

Land Drains: arrangements must be made for land drains to be inspected as they are reconnected/reinstated. It pays to have close co-operation between the claimant/valuer and the authority so that an inspection can be readily made since the contractors are usually working to a tight schedule and are likely to be more co-operative in getting the job done properly if they know that their work will be inspected within say 24 hours of notification. This is perhaps the one occasion where direct liaison between the contractor and the claimants or valuer can be countenanced.

There are several acknowledged methods of reinstatement of the land drains, the method to be used in any instance should be agreed "without prejudice" before the work starts. If the pipe trench is wide then header drains should be considered since as the reinstated trench settles it can distort any cross connections. In any case all connections made across the trench whether wide or narrow should be well supported by substantial timber with good bearing at least one foot on either side of the trench.

Soils

Following the previous requirement for top and sub-soils to be stacked separately, after the sub-soil has been back-filled a necessary requirement is that the whole of the working width is ripped to a depth of at least 18 inches *before* the top soil is replaced. Arrangements must be made for this to be inspected and approved before any top soil is replaced.

Claims for compensation

There are two basic principles to which Valuers should adhere:

1. *The claimant is entitled to be left in no worse a position than he would have been had the event not taken place and where there is no other means of restitution then Compensation by money shall be made.*

   This very definition places upon the valuer an onerous task, since while the claimant will undoubtedly provide considerable detail of various items of claim, it is the valuer's duty to look to full depth for items of claim not always readily apparent. Some of these items are referred to, but by experience the list is always subject to new additions.

2. *It is the claimant's duty to mitigate wherever possible any claim that may arise.*

If there is any doubt then consultation with his Valuer should be held to ensure that anything that is done will be taken in as mitigation in a true endeavour to reduce a claim and not as a means to enhance a claim. Sometimes there is a very fine dividing line and consultation with the pipelaying authority's valuer can often determine that an act of mitigation will be accepted as such in the final claim, whether or not it has succeeded.

The following are some heads of claim to which other items should be added in particular circumstances:

Loss of crop or crops

This should be calculated on the actual loss sustained and where possible the crop harvested from the remainder of the field should be recorded. It is not always satisfactory to take the average crop over the farm, this can be two-edged in that if the particular field bears a bumper crop then the Compensation should reflect this, conversely if it is a bad crop or even unharvested the claim should reflect the actual loss, if any.

Actual crop losses can extend into second or third crops if the reinstatement has prevented the planting of a crop, including further delays by weather immediately after reinstatement.

Where no crop has been planted and consequently no crop has been lost there will be a claim for "loss of profit" on the crop which should have been grown.

Future loss of crops

This is a heading of claim which is just as important as the actual loss of crops.

Provided that the land has been properly reinstated and has not been unduly damaged during the course of the works the rule of thumb for future losses can be 50% in the first year after the pipelaying, 25% in the second year and 10% in the third year.

In the case of grassland this can generally be reduced to two years' reduced crop.

If, however, considerable damage has been caused to the land during the laying for any reason whatsoever, not least very wet weather, then it is possible to establish losses of crop for up to 8 or even 10 years. In these circumstances it is often advisable to arrange that the claim can be kept open for future claims.

Damage to soil structure

This is a very difficult matter to assess and dependent to a great degree on the weather at the time of the work. The two extremes are very dry conditions with light equipment, this should produce the minimum damage to the structure of the soil. The converse extreme is a very wet season with heavy rutting equipment with the consequential damage to the soil structure in particular the natural drainage attributes.

Land fertility

It is advisable to have the land tested when the work has been completed, since it is inevitable that the fertility has been affected especially in very wet weather. Generally speaking the fertility can be reinstated by the use of manures especially with good dressings of farmyard manure, but this can be expensive but nevertheless a claim should be pursued.

Severed land

This can arise when a small area is cut off from the remainder of the farm, by the pipeline. A decision as to what to do in these circumstances is not easy. If the severed land is reasonably accessible and is of a reasonable size and shape then every effort should be made to continue cropping or grazing. If however it is too small, say less than one acre, or inaccessible, then the attention of the authority should be drawn to the fact that a claim for loss of crop will arise thereon. In any case there will inevitably be extra costs involved on such severed land even if it is continued to be worked there will be a claim for "short working" in other words having to combine an awkward piece rather than as part of a bigger field, or getting the cows in from the far side across the pipeline and if it is wet the pipeline will inevitably be muddy which means that the cows have got to have extra cleaning when they get back to the parlour, the extra costs of getting the stock in and the extra costs of getting tractors and equipment across the pipeline.

Surplus and deficiency of soil

It is recommended that surplus soil is never allowed to be removed from the site, even with the largest pipelines when the soil has settled there seldom appears to be any substantial surplus. It is always better to leave a trenchline proud and after settlement any surplus can be worked in with the remainder.

Deficiency of soil is more difficult to remedy. It is better to incorporate heavy dressings of farmyard manure thus reproducing the top soil humus albeit that there may be a greater loss of crop for a year or two. To bring in top soil can be disadvantageous since unless it is compatible with the adjoining soil it can be like a heart transplant and be rejected.

Fences and hedges
This is a comparatively simple matter of restoration but so far as hedges are concerned due allowance for proper double protective fencing especially against pasture fields where stock can lean over and nibble the tops of new plants out and an allowance for at least up to three years and maybe five years for re-establishment of hedges should be made. Fencing is a simple reinstatement matter, notwithstanding that something better will be put back than was there in the first instance.

Noise and proximity of working to confined animals
This item arises where pipeline work is carried out close to a milking parlour or a poultry farm or even a cattle yard. The stress placed upon animals by unusual noises can be very substantial and careful records must be kept of reduced milk yield, egg production and even of fatting cattle losing weight rather than making weight.

The occupier's personal inconvenience
This is something that should be treated fairly carefully and includes the previously referred to headings of claims for inspections. Whilst there is no obligation on the occupier to check up on the contractor at the end of a day's work, it is no consolation to him to be called out in the middle of the night to a herd of cows which have broken out and are wandering the countryside. It is better to be safe than sorry.

Injurious affection
This can include any item whereby the property through which the pipeline passes is reduced in value by the presence of the pipe, including loss of privacy.

Sporting rights
The laying of pipelines can quite easily upset Sporting Rights and when it is possible for the works to be carried out other than during the breeding or shooting seasons, this should be negotiated. Very careful records should be made of the sporting rights which are lost including the number of birds shot as against previous years.

Disturbance
This is the heading under which many items of an extraordinary nature can be listed including dust and noise from the workings,

interference with privacy during the working time and anything which can be defined as having a "disturbing" nature.

Negotiation and settlement of claims

1. Negotiation is only relevant where there are genuine differences of opinion, which are matters of discussion and reaching mutual agreement between the valuers. Negotiation is not a proper term where claims are deliberately inflated or falsified and these will undoubtedly be rejected with a counterclaim.

   It is for the claimant's valuer to make the claim and provided that the claim is proper and reasonable it should be settled quickly. There may be variations up and down between the individual items, these can be discussed, by all means, just to show that the valuers are on the same wavelength but the sooner the overall claim is agreed and settled the happier everyone can be after what has probably been quite a traumatic experience.

   The settlement of claims for *Consideration and Compensation* comes within the terms of the Land Compensation Act 1973 and it is reasonable to request 90% advance of final settlements.

   Interest is payable on the "Consideration" for the easement or wayleave from the date of entry, at the statutory rates as periodically prescribed by Statutory Instrument.

   Interest on compensation can arise if there is a long delay between the physical loss and settlement, in some cases it may be a year before a claim can be formulated and settlement made in which case it is not unreasonable that the claimant should be entitled to interest on his money which he would otherwise have had in the bank, otherwise it is reasonable to anticipate settlement claims within four to six weeks of receipt by the acquiring authority and if the settlement of the claim goes over this period through no fault of the claimant or his valuer then it is not unreasonable to expect interest to be paid.

2. Where possible compensation claims should be claimed from year to year where a project takes more than one year, thus spreading the tax load.

3. Whilst claims can reach a final state, they should not be closed, especially in regard to land drainage whether man-made or natural, defects can take as much as three or four years to reveal themselves.

Fees

The general rule in regard to all reasonable fees and costs is that they will be borne by the acquiring authority and where legal documentation is required the cost of having this work done is payable.

whilst Ryde's Scale has been considerably improved there are still nevertheless instances where this is insufficient especially where the land agent has had to carry out extra work due to the short-comings of the contractor and here the basic rules of compensation must be reiterated, that is that "the claimant should be left in no worse a position than he would have been had the event not taken place". For a claimant to have to contribute to a valuer's fees must be considered iniquitous unless the valuer has not done his job properly and consequently brought upon himself extra work or if the valuer has done things under the instructions of the claimant which had no grounds, in those cases it is right that the additional fees should be made against the claimant. Valuers should take strenous steps at the outset to ensure that all their reasonable and proper fees will be recoverable from the acquiring body including the event that the proposed project does not proceed after talks and negotiations are opened.

Contractors and contracts

Whilst not directly concerned with the practice of valuation, the relationship between the authority (the principal to the contract), the contractor (the employee to the contract) and the owner/occupier of land is very much concerned with the principles of valuation.

Strictly speaking there is no relationship between the contractor and the owner/occupier and wherever possible this non-relationship should be maintained, thus making the principal (the authority) responsible for the shortcomings of the contractor and liable for any compensation.

However, there are occasions when the contractor transgresses and the principal is not available, viz. leaving gates open at night and cattle escaping. On these occasions the owner/occupier must take action in his own intersts. It is imperative that the principal is contacted at the very earliest opportunity so that acknowledgement of any claim is made, otherwise the principal could disclaim any liability, which would leave the owner/occupier to make and fight a claim with the contractor. Contractors' site agents do not like their efficiency being questioned and consequently will defend themselves with vehemence and this will undoubtedly be followed by an insurance assessor who may be involved; after all it is the latter's job to reduce claims to a minimum.

If a contractor makes a private or direct arrangements with an owner/occupier, this will fall outside the principal contract and the authority will not be liable for nor will countenance any claims arising from such private arrangements.

It is absolutely essential that the owner/occupier is fully and properly protected and such arrangements should include:

(1) A form of agreement, setting out precisely the agreed term to be signed by the contractor's company secretary or at least a director, before work commences.
(2) Payment of all monies due, including agent's fees, before entry is permitted.
(3) A deposit or bond held by a stakeholder, preferably the owner/occupier's agent, against any unforeseen claims.

The following publications are recommended for further study and consideration:

"Statutes"
Public Health Act 1936
Land Compensation Acts 1961 and 1973
Gas Acts 1948 (Sect. 11) and 1965
Water Act 1945
Local Authorities (Miscellaneous) Provisions Order 1977
Pipe Lines Act 1962
Acquisition of Land Act 1981

References:
Standard Code of practice for Pipelines (British Standard Institute 8010 Pipelines on Land: General)
M.A.F.F. leaflets on Land Drainage
Chartered Surveyor, March 1963 "Water Mains, Sewers and other pipelines"
C.L.A. Advisory Memorandum NO1/84—"Pipelines in Agricultural Land"
C.L.A. Publication A5/86—"Sewers and Water Mains"
"Modern Methods of Valuation"—Published by Estates Gazette.

Case Law (inter alia):
Markland & Felthouse v. *Cannock R.D.C.* [1973] E.G.D., 646
Wathall v. *Uttoxeter R.D.C.*—[1968] R.V.R., 362
Ward v. *Secretary of State for War* [1954] E.G.D., 100
Quartons (Gardens) v. *Scarborough R.D.C.* (1955) 5 P & C.R. 190
Frost v. *Taunton Corporation* (1957) 9 P & C.R. 123
Lucey's Personal Representatives & Wood v. *Harrogate Corporation* (1963) 14 P & C.R. 376
Radnor Trust v. *C.E.G.B.* (1960) 12 P & C.R. 111.

© W. R. Betts 1988

Chapter 21

VALUATIONS FOR INSURANCE PURPOSES

Insurance is essentially a device by which the losses of the few are made to fall as lightly as possible upon the many. It is a social arrangement which provides financial compensation for the effects of misfortune, the payments being made from the accumulated contributions of all parties participating in the scheme.

While valuation for insurance purposes is primarily concerned with cost and value, the surveyor's advice to his client cannot be restricted solely to this area. He must be clearly aware of what is to be insured, what risks or perils can be covered, what provisions the policy contains and what the basis of insurance should be. The question of insurance valuations has been taken lightly by surveyors in the past but it is a complex subject, requiring careful consideration before advice is given to a client.

What is to be insured?

There is no doubt that the principal assets of any company will be the buildings which it occupies to carry on its business, the machinery which it utilises to manufacture its goods for sale and its stock and work in progress. Such assets will be protected in terms of material security by walls, gates, roofs and alarms but they should also be protected in terms of financial security by insurance. A prudent businessman will insure by separate policies a potential loss of profit, legal liability to the public or to his employees and such other risks as are thought appropriate.

A prudent householder will ensure that his major investment, the fabric of his house, is protected by insurance and will in the same way protect the house contents, his personal liability and money.

What risks or perils can be covered?

The standard fire policy

The standard fire policy for a commercial concern would cover the following perils:

557

(a) FIRE, subject to certain exclusions and provisions regarding origin and ignition.
(b) LIGHTNING, whether fire results or not.
(c) EXPLOSION,
  (1) of boilers used for domestic purposes
  (2) in a building not forming part of a gas works of gas used for domestic purposes or for lighting or heating the building.

The exclusions referred to under section (a) above are where fire is occasioned by or happens through

(a) its own spontaneous fermentation or heating or its undergoing any process involving the application of heat;
(b) earthquake and subterranean fire;
(c) riot and civil commotion, and
(d) insurrection, rebellion, war, invasion and other acts of foreign enemy.

Special perils extension

In these recessionary times there are many businesses which, for reasons of cost, have restricted their insurance cover to that provided by the standard fire policy and there are numerous other businesses, principally in high risk inner city areas, which have had their insurance cancelled by insurers or which have been refused renewal terms, amounting to the same thing. There are others, however, which regard the cover of the standard fire policy to be inadequate since it provides only partial protection and the need for "special perils" insurance has arisen. The special perils for which insurance cover is normally provided can be separated into four main groups:

(a) Perils of a chemical type:
    Explosion
    Spontaneous combustion, heating or fermentation.
(b) Social perils:
    Riot, civil commotion, strikers, locked-out workers, or persons taking part in labour disturbances, or malicious persons, and theft.
(c) Perils of nature:
    Storm and tempest
    Flood
    Hail and thunderbolt
    Earthquake
    Subterranean fire
    Subsidence and landslip

(d) Miscellaneous perils:
Bursting or overflowing of water tanks, apparatus or pipes.
Aircraft.
Impact by vehicles, horses or cattle.

Cover against special perils, which is not necessarily evidenced by a separate policy but by an endorsement to the fire policy, usually follows the fire policy and has the same sums insured.

Insurable interest

Little need be said to surveyors about this aspect except that all property whether material or represented as a right is insurable provided that the party seeking insurance has an insurable interest in the property or right for which insurance is sought. The insured need not, however, have an insurable interest at the time insurance is effected but he must have such an interest at the time of the loss. For example a freeholder has an insurable interest in the property which he owns because if it is destroyed he stands to sustain a loss. However, he will not have an insurable interest in an adjoining property which he does not own or lease even though its destruction could cause him loss in terms of, say, loss of support for his own building.

Calculation of rebuilding costs

Method of measurement

The method to be adopted in valuing buildings for insurance purposes requires that industrial and commercial properties be measured to obtain the total gross internal floor area. This is attained by taking measurements from inside external walls, including all areas within the envelope of the building, and multiplying the result by the number of floors in the building. It is not unusual to obtain the cube measurements of the property by taking heights of individual floors.

Property type

The unit cost of a building will depend on many factors but the surveyor will need to establish the basic description of the property, whether it is single or multi-storey, a factory, warehouse or office building and in the case of a house, detached, semi-detached, terraced or a bungalow.

Construction type

As complex foundations can add considerably to the cost of re-construction, it will be necessary to ascertain details of the site and any particular problems which it might present. Principle construction details will be required such as whether the building to be valued is of traditional brick and slate construction, or a light steel framed metal clad or reinforced concrete framed brick building.

Quality of construction

The survey will encompass details on thicknesses of walls, quality of floor and roof finishes, types of windows and doors, quality of internal and external finishes and the extent of internal and external services.

Method of valuation

The calculation of rebuilding costs is generally by applying unit cost rates to superficial or cube measurements of a building, adjusting the rates to particular types of building. In certain cases it will be preferable to produce priced full or elemental bills of quantities.

Sources of cost information

Surveying practices involved with building projects will be able to analyse details of costs and record them for future valuation use. Other sources of building costs are the Building Cost Information Service of the RICS, the Property Services Agency and technical books such as Spons and Laxtons.

Additions to the basic valuation

So far we have reached the stage of establishing the cost of rebuilding a particular property but there are several additions required to complete a valuation suitable for fire insurance purposes.

As specific allowances need to be made in the valuation and in the policy to insure the requirements of public authorities, debris removal costs, professional fees, building regulations and planning fees, special comment is given below.

Public authorities clause

This clause, which must be specifically included in the policy for the insured to gain its benefits, covers the additional cost incurred in reinstatement of damage to comply with building or other regulations made in pursuance of any Act of Parliament or bye-laws. The costs to be incurred under this item are not separately insured but are to be included in the overall sum insured on the buildings.

Debris removal clause

As with the public authorities clause it is necessary to extend the policy to include for debris removal. By removal of debris it is usually meant to refer to the cost of removing debris, demolishing, shoring up or propping necessarily incurred by the insured with the consent of the insurer. As far as buildings and machinery are concerned the cost of removal of debris is included within the relevant sum insured. However, stock debris removal is insured as a separate item with a separate sum insured.

Architects', surveyors' and consulting engineers' fees clause

Here too professional fees are not automatically insured and special provision by means of a relevant clause in the policy must be made for them. They will normally form part of the overall sum insured on buildings and relate to fees necessarily incurred in reinstating or repairing the damage not for preparing a claim.

Fees for building regulations and planning applications

As the cost of fees for building regulations approval and for planning applications can amount to several thousand pounds in the case of industrial and commercial building projects, allowance should be made for them in the valuation at the appropriate levels.

Value Added Tax

Value Added Tax does not need to be added to a valuation covering the cost of reinstating a building destroyed by fire because the rebuilding would be considered new work and therefore zero rated. VAT would be payable on most cases of partial reinstatement but in fixing the sum insured no regard need be taken of this. Moreover, any business with an annual turnover of £21,300 or more would probably be VAT registered and able to recover any Vat paid. However, certain types of organisations including certain property companies, charities and churches etc. are unable to recover Value Added Tax on purchases in which case any valuation of the contents including machinery, plant and office equipment should be increased by the standard rate of VAT.

Insurance of buildings

Valuers will be aware of the two main bases of cover available under which buildings can be insured, namely indemnity and reinstatement, and perhaps be familiar also with two special types of cover for buildings, namely "first loss" and "obsolete buildings". As, however, there seems to be a fundamental misunderstanding of the scope and application of these bases of insurance it could be a worthwhile exercise to describe each basis and to illustrate them with valuation examples.

Indemnity

The Standard Fire policy allows the insurer to:

> "pay to the insured the value of the property at the time of the happening of its destruction or the amount of such damage or at its option reinstate or replace such property or any part thereof."

Insurers rarely ever take the option to reinstate or repair an insured's property but it is a device available to them if they are dealing with a difficult or intransigent insured. It is an option, however, which is of doubtful advantage to the insurer for reasons which it is beyond the scope of this chapter to comment upon.

The insurers have agreed by the above wording to pay "the value of the property" but the policy does not define "value". It is reasonable to assume, however, that its normal tort definition would apply whereby value would be the amount which would place the insured by payment or otherwise in the same position as he was immediately before the fire, neither better nor worse. In these circumstances indemnity value would probably be the cost of reinstatement or repair less a deduction for betterment because the replacement of the fire damaged roof or walls has provided something better because they are newer rather than superior or more extensive. If the reinstated building were to be more extensive or superior than the original then the additional costs involved would not be recoverable from the insurers.

Study 1

The insured owns an old four storey factory in Birmingham with a gross internal floor area of 4,000 square metres. The construction is standard with brick walls, timber floors and a slated roof on timber trusses. The building, which is in reasonable condition, is heated by warm air blowers and is protected by a sprinkler installation. Because of the recession the insured's business is failing and occupies only the lower two floors of the premises. He has been advised to insure the building on an indemnity basis. What sum insured should he select?

Gross internal area	4,000 sq m
Reinstatement cost per square metre	£300
	£1,200,000
Add	
Professional fees and debris removal costs, say 15%	180,000
Reinstatement cost	£1,380,000
Deduct	
Betterment, age, wear and tear, say 25%	345,000
Indemnity value (bricks and mortar basis)	£1,035,000

There are at least two important points to be raised in connection with Study 1. Firstly, there can be no set rule or guide as to the calculation of the deduction for betterment and each case must be dealt with on its merits. If the building in question had been erected only one year ago it would be clearly incorrect in normal circum stances to calculate the indemnity value by reducing the reinstatement cost by as much as 25% since the level of depreciation would be small. Secondly, it is important to realise that the reinstatement cost of the building which is used to arrive at the indemnity value should be that prevailing at the time of reinstatement not that which would be appropriate at the time of the loss.

In deciding what should be the correct indemnity value for insurance purposes the surveyor might need to consider the merits of a sum insured based on a market value. There are many cases where the cost of reinstating a building which has been badly damaged or destroyed will be far greater than the market value of the rein stated building and the insured might decide that it would be point less to reinstate. In the case of *Reynolds and Anderson* v. *Phoenix Assurance Co. Ltd* (1978) 247 E.G. 995, the judge believed the evidence of the insured that they intended to reinstate and awarded them £343,320 which was the estimated cost of reinstatement duly adjusted for betterment. The insurers initial calculation of the loss was on a diminution in market value basis at £5,000 against a total sum insured of £550,000. They later increased this offer to £55,000 arguing that this would be a fair settlement repre senting as it did the cost of a modern equivalent building since no commercial man in his senses would think of spending so much on an obsolete building if he could buy a modern structure for so much less.

However, settlement of a claim in the case of *Leppard* v. *Excess Insurance Co. Ltd* [1979] 2 All E.R. 668, was found to be correct on a market value basis where the insured had placed his house on the market for sale shortly before it was destroyed by fire. The insured argued that an indemnity was £8,694, the cost of reinstatement less an allowance for betterment, despite the fact that he expected to receive £4,500 from the proceeds of sale.

If the calculation in Study 1 is revised so that the indemnity value is on a market value basis the sum insured would be radically different.

Study 2

The insured owning a four storey factory in Birmingham has indicated that in the event of serious damage to the building he would not intend to repair or rebuild the damaged premises. In such a case what are the insurers likely to offer in settlement of a claim for total destruction?

Gross internal area		4,000 sq m
Capital value per square metre		£55
		£220,000
Add		
The cost of demolishing and removing the building debris		10,000
		£230,000
Deduct		
Market value of the site which will remain in the insured's ownership		7,000
Indemnity value		
(Diminution in market value basis)		£223,000

It will be apparent that there is a considerable difference between the indemnity value of £1,035,000, calculated by reference to depreciated rebuilding costs, and the indemnity value of £223,000, calculated on the basis of diminution in market value. The criteria to be adopted to decide which is the correct sum insured must be this. If there is an intention to rebuild, the basis of insurance must be depreciated replacement cost at £1,035,000 but it does not follow that if the insured expresses an intention not to rebuild, in the event of a serious loss he can insure the building on a market value basis. What if the property is only partially damaged to the extent of repair costs of £10,000? He will most certainly wish to repair it and he will expect the insurers to pay in full. As the basis of the payment of £10,000 will be depreciated replacement cost, the sum insured must also be on this basis at £1,035,000 otherwise the insured's claim will be reduced substantially by average.

In short the indemnity value of a building for insurance purposes should be based on reinstatement cost less an allowance for betterment. But if the building is destroyed or badly damaged and the insured does not reinstate he can expect his claim to be settled on the basis of diminution in market value which could be at a much lower figure than the sum insured.

Insurers have devised other methods of insuring buildings which allow the insured to select a lower sum insured than that provided by reducing the reinstatement cost for betterment, without suffering the penalties of average for under insurance. These will be considered later.

Reinstatement

Under statute

It will be recalled that under the standard fire policy the insurers have an option to reinstate a building if they so wish but we know that the option is seldom used. However, insurers can be required by statute to reinstate or replace any property. The Fires Prevention (Metropolis) Act 1774 contains provisions which relate to the reinstatement of houses and other buildings and which require insurers "to cause the insurance money to be laid out and expended, as far as the same will go, towards rebuilding, reinstating or repairing ..." unless within a specific period the insured gives an assurance that he will himself expend the money or unless the insurance money is laid out within the same period to the satisfaction of all parties. The most usual circumstances where the provisions of the Act are invoked is where a tenant gives notice under the Act to the insurer of buildings so that the tenant can be sure that the landlord will be required to expend monies in the reinstatement of the building.

Reinstatement Memorandum

Insurance arranged on a reinstatement basis provides the optimum level of cover but to be effective the policy must contain the Reinstatement Memorandum. The Memorandum provides that the amount payable in respect of any destroyed item shall be the reinstatement of the item destroyed or damaged subject to certain special conditions.

Reinstatement is defined in the Memorandum as

"The carrying out of the aftermentioned work, namely:

(a) Where property is destroyed the rebuilding of the property, if a building, or, in the case of other property, its replacement by similar property, in either case in a condition equal to but not better or more extensive than its condition when new.

(b) Where property is damaged, the repair of the damage and the restoration of the damage portion of the property to a condition substantially the same as but not better or more extensive than its condition when new."

It will be apparent that the reinstatement policy goes further than an indemnity policy, which places the insured in the same position as he was before the fire, since it allows him to rebuild, replace or repair a property to a condition equal to or the same as "its condition when new".

It is often overlooked at the time of a valuation that the Reinstatement Memorandum does not allow an insured to obtain settlement of a claim for replacement or repair on a reinstatement basis if the act of replacement or repair is not carried out. This and other controls on the insured are exercised by the "Special Provisions" which form part of the Reinstatement Memorandum and which, because of their importance, deserve some mention.

The work of reinstatement may be carried out on another site provided the liability of the insurers is not increased. This means that the insurers would not object to the insured's decision to relocate to London a factory destroyed in Glasgow provided that the cost to insurers would not be greater. To take an even more extreme view it would be possible for the factory to be relocated to, say, Italy and for the insured to obtain the insurer's agreement to this.

The Special Provisions provide that the work of reinstatement must be carried out with reasonable despatch which is taken to mean that there must be no unreasonable delays in the rebuilding or repair of a property which would result in the insurers being asked to pay a higher amount.

Special Provision 3 is of vital importance and knowledge of it should prevent a surveyor from blindly valuing a building on a reinstatement basis which he knows his client will not intend to rebuild or repair. It states

"3. No payment beyond the amount which would have been payable under the policy if this memorandum had not been incorporated therein shall be made until the cost of reinstatement shall have been actually incurred."

If the cost of reinstatement is not incurred, the insured will only be able to recover settlement of the claim on an indemnity basis.

If the insured does intend to reinstate but it will be a long time before completion of the reinstatement or replacement he can apply for a payment on account equal to an indemnity settlement (on a diminution of market value basis) pending completion of the reinstatement and payment therefor.

At this point it would be useful to consider a basic reinstatement valuation and to extend its calculation later to show the effect of the average clause.

Study 3

The gross internal floor area of 6 small modern factories in one building on an open site in Edinburgh is 1,079 square metres. The construction consists of a steel portal frame, brick facings and shallow pitched roof with TAC "Double Six" asbestos cement roof sheeting. The services provided are basis, each unit having toilet facilities, nominal power and lighting installations but no heating. Define the reinstatement value for insurance purposes including professional fees and rebuilding costs. Make allowance for inflation bearing in mind that it would take 6 months to rebuild the property.

Total gross internal floor area	1,079 sq m
Reinstatement cost per square metre	£192
	£207,168
Architects', surveyors and engineers' fees 12·5%	26,000
	£233,168
Debris removal costs	6,000
	£239,168
Reinstatement value (base value) 1.1.87 say	£240,000
Inflation provision	
Insurance year plus 7·5%	18,000
	£258,000

Inflation provision
Building period 6 months plus 4%   10,320

Reinstatement value for insurance purposes   £268,320

A note about inflation

Study 3 shows not only a base reinstatement value as at 1st January 1987 (£240,000) but also increases to this value to cover inflation. The dangers of fixing the sum insured at £240,000 without any inflation provision are easily explained. On 1st January 1987 the sum insured at £240,000 would represent the cost of reinstating the six small factories in Edinburgh but already 1 month later with inflation running at 7·5% per annum the cost of reinstatement would have increased to £241,500. By 30th June 1987 the sum insured at £240,000 would be 3·75% out of date and the cost of reinstatement would have increased to £249,000.

By 30th November 1987 the reinstatement value of the buildings in question will have increased by 6·875% since January to £256,500. If the buildings were destroyed by fire on 30th November the insured would receive insufficient funds to reinstate them. Consider the following facts:

Sum insured   £240,000

Cost of reinstatement on 1st January 1987   240,000
Inflation 1st January to 30th November, plus 6·875%   16,500

Cost of reinstatement on 30th November   £256,500
Inflation during the rebuilding period,
   6 months, plus 4%   10,260

Cost of reinstatement on 31st May 1988   £266,760

Provided that the insured reinstates the factory units in question and incurs £266,760 he will receive £240,000 from the insurers, being his own insurer for £26,760. The practice of building inflation provision into a sum insured is one method of dealing with the problem of under insurance. Insurers have devised other similar methods to assist the insured and these will be considered later.

Average conditions

Ordinary pro rata average

Most valuation surveyors will be aware of the punitive effect of the average clause which is now incorporated into most classes of fire and special perils insurance. The pro rata condition of average operates where there is under insurance and provides that the insurer will be required to pay only that proportion of the loss that the sum insured bears to the value of the property insured at the time of the fire. The pro rata condition of average affects valuations calculated on an indemnity basis and it is an attempt to ensure that the indemnity value is correct, at the time of the fire, not at the time of reinstatement

In Study 1 the indemnity value of the factory in Birmingham was calculated to be £1,035,000. Let us assume that the insured decided not to insure the property to its full value but fixed the sum insured at £500,000. Shortly after the valuation the property was damaged by fire and the cost of reinstatement was estimated to be £12,000. The repairs would provide some betterment so that an equitable assessment of the loss on an indemnity basis would be £10,000. It is clear that there is under insurance and that average will apply on the following basis:

Pro rata condition of average formula

$$\frac{\text{Sum Insured}}{\text{Value at the time of the fire}} \times \text{Loss}$$

$$\frac{£500,000}{£1,035,000} \times £10,000$$

Insurer's liability   £4,831

Reinstatement average

Policies containing the Reinstatement Memorandum are also subject to average but its application is slightly different from that of the pro rata average. As we have seen pro rata average requires that the sum insured should be equal to the value of the property at the time of the fire. Reinstatement average determines that the sum insured should be equal to the value of the property at the time of reinstatement which, in a large rebuilding contract, could be two or three years after the fire.

Combatting inflation

There are several schemes available which have been devised to combat the effects of inflation and an awareness of each is necessary since the valuer might be required to make adjustments to his valuations.

Escalator clause

This clause can be incorporated into the policy at extra cost and it provides that the sum insured at the renewal date will be increased each day automatically by 1/365th of the specified percentage increase. The specified percentage increase is the insured's estimate of the annual increase in inflation. Its disadvantage is that the addition stops at the time of the loss and because of this there will be no insurance cover for any cost increases which take place after the fire before rebuilding is completed.

85% Reinstatement Memorandum

As a temporary amendment to the Reinstatement Memorandum insurers decided to restrict the operation of the average clause to those cases where, at the time of reinstatement, the sum insured is less than 85% of the full reinstatement value. For example if the sum insured represents 90% of the reinstatement value the average clause will not be applied to reduce the amount of the claim (unless of course the property is totally destroyed in which case the insured will have to stand 10% of the loss himself). Where however the sum insured at the time of reinstatement represents 80% of the full reinstatement cost, any claim will be subject to average as if the 85% concession did not exist.

Notional Reinstatement Value Scheme

This scheme is available to industrial and commercial concerns with sums insured in excess of £5m. The insured is allowed to select a declared value to represent the cost of reinstatement of the property at the time of renewal and this is loaded by the insured's estimate of inflation increases during the year of insurance and the period of reinstatement. Each year the insured should review the declared value and the percentage increases to ensure that they are accurate. There is no requirement for any of the figures to be supported by a professional valuation.

Valuation-Linked Scheme

In this scheme the base or declared value must be calculated by a qualified valuer (RICS, ISVA or RVA) and reassessed at least every four years. The base value is increased to cover inflation in the insurance year and in the period of reinstatement. There are certain premium benefits but the sum insured cannot be subject to the 85% concession and normal 100% average applies.

Day One Reinstatement Scheme

With the Day One Scheme the insured declares the total rebuilding cost at prices ruling at renewal each year. Cover for inflation is provided by reason of the fact that the sum insured is deemed to be 50% more than the declared value at the beginning of the insurance year. However, the declared value must be accurate because it will be used as the basis for the average calculation at the time of a loss.

Inflation indices

Buildings

Every valuer needs to have access to inflation indices and there are several good sources of information.

The Building Cost Information Service of the RICS calculates the Tender Price Index which indicates the movement of tender prices for new building work in the United Kingdom. Because the data is derived from actual tenders, the indices reflect the conditions prevailing at the time of pricing. The indices measure not only changes in building costs such as labour rates and materials prices but also influences of economic conditions operating at the time in the competitive market.

The index gives details of actual changes in tender prices and also forecasts likely changes in the immediate future, the latter being of assistance to valuers in giving recommendations on escalator clauses and inflation projections.

Machinery

The Corporate Intelligence Unit provides indices covering changes in annual average prices for a wide range of plant and machinery. There is a composite index covering chemical and allied plant, food manufacturing machinery, machine tools and office equipment.

There are separate indices covering other industries including textile machinery, printing machinery, clothing manufacturing machinery.
The information is available on a quarterly or on an annual basis.

The Business Statistical Office, part of the Department of Trade and Industry, calculates "Price Index Numbers for Current Cost Accounting" which appears monthly and which includes indices for plant and machinery, building and works, retail prices and stocks etc.

Alternative methods of insuring buildings

Obsolete buildings insurance

Several years ago the Fire Offices' Committee devised a special basis of valuation for obsolete industrial and commercial buildings. The scheme is still available and applies to buildings which conform to the following conditions:

(a) The design and construction of the building is such that it would be impracticable for the insured to rebuild in like manner.
(b) The building is not subject to any statutory or other obligation to reinstate damage in the existing style and materials in whole or in part.

Where a building qualifies for this scheme the basis of valuation for the purpose of average will be

 (i) the cost of purchasing a similar building to the insured building plus, if required, an allowance for removal of debris costs, or
(ii) the cost of erecting a modern building providing comparable facilities to the insured building including, if required, an allowance for professional fees, debris removal costs and additional costs to comply with local authorities requirements.

The obsolete buildings scheme is attractive to owners of large industrial properties like traditional multistorey mills where there would be no intention to rebuild in the event of serious damage. The sum insured chosen by the property owner would be sufficient either to build a modern building on the same site or elsewhere or to buy a similar building to that destroyed in the open market. The difficulty with the scheme is that the sum insured chosen must be sufficient to provide funds to repair partial damage and in the case of a sum insured on an open market basis this might not be the case.

Whereas the selection of a sum insured on a market value basis would probably be subject to only a modest premium, a sum insured to provide adequate funds for the erection of a modern alternative building would probably be so high as to not offer any premium advantage and the insured might be better advised to insure under a conventional indemnity policy.

Partial losses will be paid on a reinstatement basis subject to a deduction for betterment and subject to any limitations imposed by the level of the sum insured.

First loss insurance

A policy of this type is one in which the sum insured is deliberately restricted to a figure which is less than the full value of the property. In a case where the building is destroyed the insurers will pay losses up to the sum insured without the application of average. There is no technical expertise required in the fixing of the sum insured and it is an area of advice in which the surveyor should not become involved, for obvious reasons.

Insurance of machinery and chattels

The methods of insuring machinery and chattells are almost identical to those used for insuring buildings in that a decision is required as to whether a reinstatement or indemnity sum insured would be appropriate. Where there is no intention to reinstate or repair damaged machinery, insurers will wish to pay no more than a market value and a plant and machinery valuer will need to bear this in mind in fixing the appropriate values.

In many instances a valuer will be asked by his client to produce not only a report giving a recommendation as to the correct sum insured on plant and machinery but to prepare also a detailed inventory of the contents of the factory. The inventory will describe individual machines, give type and serial numbers and individual reinstatement or indemnity values. The benefits of an inventory are at least two-fold as it provides the insured with a detailed record of his plant, machinery fixtures and fittings, which he can revise regularly, and it is an invaluable record of these should the premises be destroyed.

Study 4

Your client has taken delivery of a second-hand tool grinder and is unsure whether to insure it on a reinstatement or indemnity basis. Calculate the appropriate values allowing for delivery and installation costs.

Machine Description: A "Samand" Model TGO precision twin wheel tool grinding and lapping machine, serial no. TGO/79 669

Reinstatement Valuation:

New Replacement Cost of the basic machine		1,825
Add for attachments		
Tool rest		60
Diamond holding slide		60
Low volt light		127
2 grinding wheels		46
Diamond wheel		180
		£2,298
Delivery costs	£30	
Installation costs	£45	75
Cost of reinstatement with new		£2,273
	say	£2,300

Indemnity Valuation:

Either reinstatement cost	£2,300
Deduct	
Betterment, age, wear and tear say 25%	575
Indemnity value (depreciated reinstatement cost)	£1,725

OR

Cost of purchasing a similar second- hand tool grinder with all attachments		£600
Delivery costs	£30	
Installation costs	£45	75
Indemnity value (market value basis)		£675

A sum insured calculated on a reinstatement basis provides the optimum level of cover and, should the tool grinder be destroyed, the insured would be able to replace it and recover the full cost from the insurers.

There seems to be some disagreement as to whether an indemnity calculated by reference to a depreciated replacement cost or by reference to market value provides the second best level of insurance. If the insured is advised to insure his machinery on a market value plus delivery and installation costs basis, he can expect to be paid on this basis in the event of total destruction. If the insured's machinery is seriously damaged and no second hand replacements are readily available, he might be forced to repair the damaged machines and the cost of so doing could be considerably greater than the market value. In the circumstances it would seem prudent to insure the machines on a depreciated replacement cost basis.

Installation costs

Care needs to be taken in fixing the cost of installing machinery because such costs can vary substantially from industry to industry (e.g. engineering machines might cost 10% of their replacement cost to install whereas with flour mills the addition could be as high as 40%).

Debris removal costs

Whatever value is chosen for the insurance of machinery it will need to be increased to cover the cost of removing machinery debris from the premises after the fire.

Engineers' fees

If it is a complex plant which is to be insured it is almost certain that the services of a qualified engineer will be required in the event of its replacement. In the circumstances the value needs to be increased to allow for such fees.

Inflation provision

As in the case of buildings insurance some provision needs to be made in the valuation for inflation.

Sources of cost information

Details of machinery replacement costs can be obtained from manufacturers or their agents or from the valuer's own records. Market values can be obtained by discussion with machinery dealers and careful consideration of information contained in various publications and of auction records.

Other forms of insurance

Loss of rent

A landlord who has let his property will probably wish to insure the potential loss of rent which he would incur if the property were damaged or destroyed. He can do this under a fire policy by means of a separate item specifying the period and the amount of the rent to be covered. The rent clause, which will be added to the policy, defines that loss of rent will be paid during the period the property is unfit for occupation, not during the period it remains unoccupied after repairs have been completed when new tenants might be sought.

Consequential Loss Policy

To avoid the loss of rent which might be incurred in any subsequent period while new tenants are found, a property owner could decide not to extend his fire policy by the addition of an item on loss of rent but to take out a separate Consequential Loss Policy. This type of policy covers all losses incurred during a specific period including expenditure incurred to minimise a loss of rent such as additional travelling expenses to alternative accommodation.

In a more conventional role a Consequential Loss or Loss of Profits Policy as it used to be known, provides the support to a fire policy which covers material losses. Here a Consequential Loss Policy contains two sections, a Gross Profit Section and an Increase in Cost of Working Section. The Gross Profit Section covers the gross profit lost on sales as a result of an insured loss during a specific period, say one year, when the company has been unable to trade at all or only partially. The Increase in Cost of Working Section provides cover for the insured to incur expenditure on measures which will minimise a loss of sales. Such measures might include the setting up of a temporary production plant or the increased cost of having goods made elsewhere, the total cost of the measures being limited by the policy to economic levels.

Employers' liability policy

Employers' liability insurance, which become compulsory in 1969, covers the employer's liability to his employees for injuries or death arising out of the negligence of the employer or persons for whose negligence he is responsible arising out of and in the course of the employees employment. In certain circumstanaces an employee need not establish negligence.

Public liability policy

A public liability policy covers the liability of an individual or firm to pay damages to a third party, members of the public, for accidents caused by the negligence of the insured or his or their employees or defects in the insured's premises, machinery or plant. It is not compulsory.

TABLE OF CASES

(In some instances, cases carry Lands Tribunal's own references, e.g. LT REF/47/1977 or LT LVC/754/1976. In others the references in the text differ from those in the index)

INDEX

A

589

K

"Kennedy" method 505-508

L